EXCEL 2000
IN A NUTSHELL

A Power User's Quick Reference

EXCEL 2000
IN A NUTSHELL

A Power User's Quick Reference

Jinjer Simon

O'REILLY®

Beijing • Cambridge • Farnham • Köln • Paris • Sebastopol • Taipei • Tokyo

Excel 2000 in a Nutshell

by Jinjer Simon

Copyright © 2000 O'Reilly & Associates, Inc. All rights reserved.
Printed in the United States of America.

Published by O'Reilly & Associates, Inc., 101 Morris Street, Sebastopol, CA 95472.

Editor: Troy Mott

Production Editor: Maureen Dempsey

Cover Designer: Hanna Dyer

Printing History:

> August 2000:   First Edition.

CIP data can be found at *http://www.oreilly.com/catalog/excel2000ian/*.

ISBN: 1-56592-714-1
[VH]

Table of Contents

■ Part 3: Function Reference

■ Part 4: Appendices

Preface

On the surface Excel appears to be a very straightforward program. But it doesn't take long to figure out that there is really more to it than you initially realized. Although I had used Excel extensively prior to taking on this project, I never realized its full complexity until I had to write about it. Excel is a large, powerful program that provides a lot of features, which are covered extensively in this book.

When I decided to write this book, I wanted to create something different than what was already available on the market. After all, every other publisher has at least a couple of Excel books on the market. So my efforts turned to filling the void of what was missing.

The first thing that was missing was a good reference to the hundreds of functions available in Excel. Yes, some books had provided a description of each function, but I wanted to get in and really describe when and how to use each function. As a result, the third section of this book has been devoted entirely to the functions within Excel, containing good examples, tips, notes, and other details.

The other major effort in writing this book was to provide an in-depth reference for the menu commands available within Excel. Each of the Excel menus is covered, and I try to avoid telling you the obvious, but attempt to get in and tell you what you really need to know.

This book fits the title of the "In a Nutshell" series. It provides a great reference for finding the stuff you need to know without weighing you down with a bunch of unimportant drivel. Hopefully with this book you will not only realize what is sitting under the hood of Excel, but also how to use it when you need it.

Organization of This Book

Excel 2000 in a Nutshell is structured in four parts:

Part 1, *Excel 2000 Overview*

Excel 2000 Overview covers the basic features and functionality of Excel.

Chapter 1, *Excel Basics*, provides a quick reference to the basics of Excel. The chapter is designed around a Task List that provides a function list of the capabilities of Excel.

Chapter 2, *Excel Anatomy*, provides an in-depth look at the Excel environment and how to customize menus and toolbars to meet your own needs.

Part 2, *Menu Reference*

Menu Reference provides an in-depth look at each Excel menu. The chapters are organized by menu commands. The chapters not only tell you what each command does, but they provide a reason for why you might want to use them.

Chapter 3, *File*, describes the menu commands available for creating, saving, printing, and sending workbooks.

Chapter 4, *Edit*, describes the menu commands available for moving, locating, and modifying the contents of your worksheet.

Chapter 5, *View*, describes the menu commands available for changing the way your worksheet looks on the screen and when it prints.

Chapter 6, *Insert*, describes the menu commands available for adding things to you worksheet such as functions, charts, and objects. This menu also provides commands for adding additional cells to the worksheet.

Chapter 7, *Format*, describes the menu commands available for formatting the contents of the worksheet.

Chapter 8, *Tools*, describes the menu commands available for checking spelling, correcting errors, merging workbooks, creating macros, and customizing your environment.

Chapter 9, *Data*, describes the menu commands available for analyzing data within your worksheet.

Chapter 10, *Chart*, describes the menu commands available for modifying a selected chart.

Part 3, *Function Reference*

This part goes beyond the typical list of Excel functions by providing detailed descriptions of the functions available within Excel, along with examples of how to use them. The chapters are organized alphabetically by function, and cover not only the functions that come installed with Excel, but also the functions that are added when loading the Analysis ToolPak add-in.

Chapter 11, *Working with Functions*, provides a stepping stone for the remaining function chapters by describing how functions are used to create formulas.

Chapter 12, *Financial Functions*, describes the functions provided for working with financial data.

Chapter 13, *Date and Time Functions*, describes the functions provided for creating and manipulating dates and times.

Chapter 14, *Mathematics and Trigonometry Functions*, describes the functions provided for performing mathematical and trigonometrical functions.

Chapter 15, *Statistical Functions*, describes the functions provided for summarizing data and performing basic statistical tasks.

Chapter 16, *Lookup and Reference Functions*, describes the functions available for looking up and referencing specific values within your workbook.

Chapter 17, *Database Functions*, describes the functions provided for working with database tables (lists).

Chapter 18, *Text Functions*, describes the functions available for converting and manipulating text values within your worksheet.

Chapter 19, *Logical Functions*, describes the six different functions that allow you to return a logical value based upon the results of a condition.

Chapter 20, *Information Functions*, describes the functions provided to gather specific information about your worksheet and the computer system you are working on.

Part 4, *Appendices*

This section includes quick-reference lists.

Appendix A, *Keyboard Shortcuts*, is a comprehensive reference to Excel's keyboard shortcuts.

Appendix B, *Tip Reference*, is a complete list of all the tips included in the book.

Conventions Used in This Book

The following typographical conventions are used in this book:

`Constant width`
> Used to indicate command-line computer output, code examples, and registry keys.

`Constant width italic`
> Used to indicate variables in examples and in registry keys. It is also used to indicate variables or user-defined elements within italic text (such as path names or filenames). For instance, in the path *Windows**username*, replace *username* with your name.

Constant width bold

Used to indicate user input in examples.

Constant width bold italic

Used to indicate replaceable user input in examples.

Italic

Used to introduce new terms and to indicate URLs, variables in text, user-defined files and directories, commands, file extensions, filenames, directory or folder names, and UNC pathnames.

TIP # 1

Tip Title

This is an example of a tip, which gives specific instructions on how to use a given Excel element that the author feels is important and beneficial to the user.

 This is an example of a note, which signifies valuable and timesaving information.

WARNING

This is an example of a warning, which alerts to a potential pitfall in the program. Warnings can also refer to a procedure that might be dangerous if not carried out in a specific way.

Path Notation

We use a shorthand path notation to show you how to reach a given Outlook or Windows user interface element or option. The path notation is relative to a well-known location. For example, the following path:

Tools → Options → Edit

means "Open the Tools menu (in Excel), then choose Options, then choose the Edit tab."

Keyboard Shortcuts

When keyboard shortcuts are shown (such as Ctrl-Alt-Del), a hyphen means that the keys must be held down simultaneously, while a plus sign means that the keys should be pressed sequentially.

How to Contact Us

We have tested and verified the information in this book to the best of our ability, but you may find that features have changed (or even that we have made mistakes!).

Please let us know about any errors you find, as well as your suggestions for future editions, by writing to:

O'Reilly & Associates, Inc.
101 Morris Street
Sebastopol, CA 95472
(800) 998-9938 (in the U.S. or Canada)
(707) 829-0515 (international/local)
(707) 829-0104 (fax)

You can also send us messages electronically. To be put on the mailing list or request a catalog, send email to:

info@oreilly.com

To ask technical questions or comment on the book, send email to:

bookquestions@oreilly.com

We have a web site for the book, where we'll list examples, errata, and any plans for future editions. You can access this page at:

http://www.oreilly.com/catalog/excel/

For more information about this book and others, see the O'Reilly web site:

http://www.oreilly.com

Microsoft Office 2000 Service Releases

Prior to the release of this book, Microsoft released two service releases for Microsoft Office 2000, SR-1 and SR-1A. These service releases were meant to fix some of the documented bugs within the Office 2000 programs; however, these fixes do not impact the information in this book. The SR-1A update includes all of the bug fixes that were fixed with SR-1 along with the Office 2000/Windows 2000 Registry Repair Utility.

More detailed information about these service releases can be found at: *http://officeupdate.microsoft.com/2000/downloadDetails/O2kSR1DDL.htm.*

You can also find additional information about what is included in these updates at: *http://www.microsoft.com/office/ork/2000/appndx/toolbox.htm* along with additional administrative tools and utilities.

Acknowledgments

Probably one of the most difficult tasks for me on a book is writing the acknowledgments. Not necessarily because it is a hard task to perform, but I am always afraid I might overlook someone who was involved in the process of producing this book.

Because as authors, we typically never see the other people involved in this enormous process, it is easy to miss everyone who deserves a thank you.

I would like to acknowledge the efforts of the O'Reilly team. This has really been an impressive group to work with. There are so many people whose efforts were necessary in getting this book to market. Troy Mott, the editor on the book, was fantastic. It has really been impressive to work with an editor who understands the product you are writing about. Troy has been great at finding those little things that I may have overlooked, and making sure they were covered. He did a great job making sure this book came together. Also, Tara McGoldrick did a great job making sure everything was submitted on time, working through all the edits, and figuring out when I changed a figure without notifying her. I would also like to thank Richard McClung and Tamera Frediani for taking time to review portions of the book. To everyone else involved with this book at O'Reilly, thank you for all your hard work.

I would like to acknowledge the efforts of my two technical reviewers. It is always difficult to find people willing to take the time to review a book and make sure the information is correct. Brian Jersky and Dennis Wallentin did a fantastic job of reviewing everything. I especially want to acknowledge Brian Jersky's efforts with the Statistical Functions chapter. He was able to pick up where I was lacking and help make that chapter very powerful.

Finally, I need to thank my own family, my husband, Richard, and two children, Alex and Ashley, for their patience and support during this project, especially during the last few weeks as we worked to pull everything together and get it to production.

—Jinjer Simon
May 2000

Part 1

Excel 2000 Overview

Chapter 1

Excel Basics

Excel is one of a series of computer programs commonly referred to as "spreadsheet software." Spreadsheet programs have become quite popular, because they provide the ability to work with data, typically numeric data, by placing it in a series of rows and columns. The location where a specific row or column intersects is referred to as a cell. Each cell typically holds a specific value that could be text, numeric, logical, or a formula, as shown in Figure 1-1. Calculations can be performed on the values in specific cells. If the values used in a calculation change, Excel automatically recalculates.

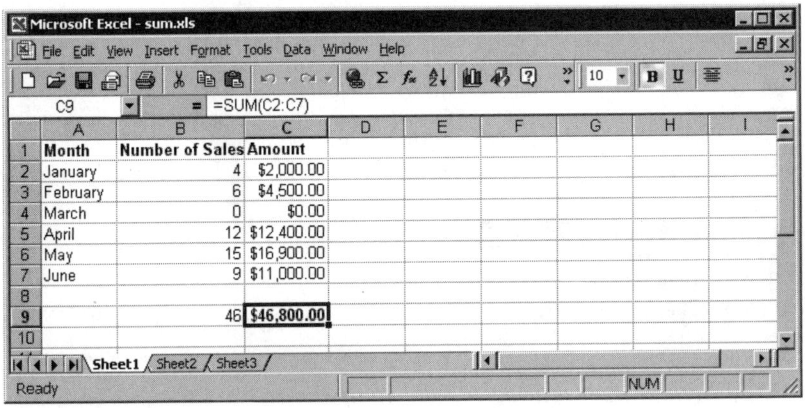

	A	B	C	D	E	F	G	H	I
1	**Month**	**Number of Sales**	**Amount**						
2	January	4	$2,000.00						
3	February	6	$4,500.00						
4	March	0	$0.00						
5	April	12	$12,400.00						
6	May	15	$16,900.00						
7	June	9	$11,000.00						
8									
9		46	$46,800.00						
10									

C9 = =SUM(C2:C7)

Figure 1-1: Spreadsheet programs provide convenient methods for performing calculations and organizing related data

Excel provides a multitude of unique features, which are covered in detail in this book. Some of the most prominent features include:

Extensive File Compatibility
Although Excel workbooks have the file extension of XLS, Excel has the ability to open files from several different sources including all Microsoft Office products, HTML, and other major spreadsheet programs. Excel can also save workbooks in several different formats so that they can be opened by other programs. (See Chapter 3, *File*.)

Workbooks for Organizing Common Files

Excel uses workbooks to store multiple related worksheets (commonly referred to as spreadsheets by other programs) and charts. You can switch between different sheets in the workbook by clicking on the corresponding tab, as shown in Figure 1-2. By default, each workbook is created with three worksheets. Additional worksheets can be added using Insert → Worksheet and new charts are added using Insert → Chart. Refer to Chapter 6, *Insert*, for more information. The default worksheet names are Sheet1, Sheet2, and Sheet3.

	A	B	C	D	E	F	G	H
1		**Automobile Loan Worksheet**						
2								
3		$505.65	360	480	240	180		
4		6.50%	505.65	468.37	596.46	696.89		
5		7.00%	532.24	497.15	620.24	719.06		
6	I	7.25%	545.74	511.74	632.30	730.29		
7	n	7.50%	559.37	526.46	644.47	741.61		
8	t	8.00%	587.01	556.25	669.15	764.52		
9	.	8.25%	601.01	571.31	681.65	776.11		
10		8.50%	615.13	586.48	694.26	787.79		
11	R	8.75%	629.36	601.74	706.97	799.56		
12	a	9.00%	643.70	617.09	719.78	811.41		
13	t	9.25%	658.14	632.53	732.69	823.35		
14	e	9.50%	672.68	648.05	745.70	835.38		
15	s	10.00%	702.06	679.32	772.02	859.68		
16								
17								
18		Loan Amount	$80,000.00					
19		Interest Rate	6.50%					
20		Loan Term	360					

Figure 1-2: Workbooks are designed to hold multiple sheets

SDI (Single Document Interface)

Excel 2000 uses a Microsoft Windows feature called Single Document Interface. This feature allows you to have multiple workbooks open simultaneously but only one version of Excel is actually running. On the View tab on the Options window (Tools → Options) you can specify whether each open workbook should be listed on the toolbar. By default, Excel displays an icon for each workbook so that you can switch between the open workbooks by clicking on the corresponding icon on the toolbar.

Extensive List of Built-In Functions

Excel comes with a multitude of built-in functions that can be used to add more complex calculations and data manipulations to your workbook. These functions can be selected using the Insert → Function command. Additional functions are available by loading the Analysis ToolPak that comes with Excel. This book provides detailed descriptions of the Excel functions. For more information, refer to Part 2 of this book.

Extensive Text Formatting

Excel allows you to perform extensive text formatting. Not only can you apply different formatting to each cell in the worksheet, but Excel allows you to format each character within the cell differently. For example, you may want the first character in the word to be bold and the remaining characters to be in italics. You can also change the orientation of the text within the cell, as shown in Figure 1-2, where the text "Int. Rates" displays vertically within the cell.

Useful Charts

Excel comes with several different default chart types that can be used to chart the data within a worksheet. These charts can be selected using the Insert → Chart option. You can also create custom chart types. For more information, refer to Chapter 10, *Chart*.

Installing Excel 2000

You will be installing Excel 2000 from either the Office 2000 or the Excel 2000 CD-ROM. When you insert either one of these CDs the installation process should begin automatically. The installation program will prompt you for your name and company name, request the CD key listed on the back of the CD case, and then prompt you for the components to load.

Office 2000 products provide a different approach to the installation process. Figure 1-3 shows the Excl installation options. The Selecting Features option presents a Windows Explorer tree where you select the method for installing each of the components. You can expand the component list by clicking on the + next to each list.

 Figure 1-3 is from the installation of the Office 2000 Professional CD. If you purchased Excel as a separate product, you will not have the option of selecting the other Office products.

You can choose to install each Excel component in a number of ways:

Run from My Computer

This installs the selected component on your hard drive.

Run all from My Computer

Taking things one step further, this option installs the software and all of its components on your hard drive. This eliminates the need to keep the CD handy because everything is installed on your machine, but it does require more hard disk space.

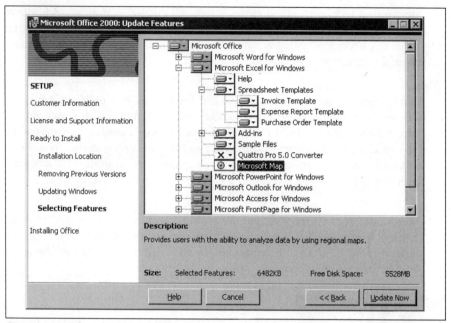

Figure 1-3: Select the Excel 2000 components to install

Run from Network

You won't see this if you're installing on a stand-alone PC. This option lets you run Excel from a network server, and not from the local drive. You don't want to choose this unless you have continuous access to the network server, or you risk not being able to run the software later.

Run all from Network

Again, you will not see this option if you do not have access to a network. This option installs every component of Excel on the network, not just the main program.

Run from CD

This type of installation sets your computer up to initiate the program and then demand the Office or Excel CD whenever you attempt to run that component of the program.

Run all from CD

This option puts a shortcut to the program on your computer. When you double-click the shortcut (or select it from the Start menu), you're prompted to insert the CD, and then the program runs. When you choose this option, the main program and all of its parts are run from the CD, and none of it is loaded on your computer.

Installed on First Use

This is a good option if you're not sure which components you will need. Components are installed only when they are first used and the Office installation files are required. Again, make sure you keep the CD handy so that you can insert it if requested.

Not Available

Choose this option to make a component completely unavailable within Excel. For example, in Figure 1-3 I marked the Quattro 5.0 Converter component as not available because I do not anticipate needing that feature. If you choose to make a component unavailable and then later decide you want it, you have to rerun Setup to get it.

When you select the installation method the icon next to the selected component changes to reflect the type of installation selected for the component.

NOTE *If you insert the Office 2000 CD into a computer on which Office 2000 is already installed, the installation options change to allow you to add or remove components from your installation, repair your existing installation, or remove the installation from your computer altogether. You will want to select the Repair option if you need to reinstall your Office 2000 programs based upon the original settings.*

Opening Excel

When you open Excel using the icon or the Start Menu option, the program opens and presents a "blank" workbook. The word blank is emphasized because the workbook is opened based upon the default settings. If you want to overwrite those settings you can create a template called *book.xlt*. You can find more information about creating templates in Chapter 3.

If you select an existing workbook to open either using the Windows Explorer or My Computer the selected workbook is opened up within Excel. In order to do this, locate the folder that contains the workbook you want to open and double-click on the desired workbook. Again, keep in mind that if Excel is already open the selected workbook is opened although there is really only one instance of Excel running. The program remains open until you close all Excel workbooks.

Excel Menus and Shortcuts

Excel provides a multitude of commands that can be used to design your worksheet. These commands are available from the ten different menus covered extensively in the corresponding chapters within this book. This section provides an overview of these menus and provides some important shortcuts and tasks.

File

The File menu provides the means for dealing with the actual workbook file. This menu contains options for opening, closing, saving, and printing the workbook. Basically, this menu contains all of the options needed to deal with the actual workbook file—whereas, the other menus provide the commands for manipulating the contents of the workbook.

The first six icons on the Standard toolbar are the most frequently used File menu commands. Although the commands are the same, the Print command on the toolbar and File → Print produce slightly different results. The File → Print option opens the Print dialog where you are able to verify the print settings. The Print command prints the selected print area to the default printer. Another difference exists between the New command on the Standard toolbar and the File → New option. File → New opens a dialog where you can select a template to apply to the new workbook and the New command on the toolbar opens a blank workbook based upon the default workbook settings. For more information about these menu options, refer to Chapter 3.

File Task List

Create a new workbook based upon a template: Chapter 3, page 46
Open an existing file: Chapter 3, page 48.
Open a recently used file: Chapter 3, page 70
Save a workbook: Chapter 3, page 53
Specify the portion of the worksheet to print: Chapter 3, page 61
Print the selected portion of a worksheet: Chapter 3, page 63
View file properties: Chapter 3, page 68
Exit the current workbook and close Excel if no other workbooks are open: Chapter 3, page 70

Keyboard Shortcuts

Create a new workbook: Ctrl+N
Open an existing file: Ctrl+O
Save a workbook: Ctrl+S
Save a workbook with a new name, location, or format: F12
Print the selected area: Ctrl+P
Exit Excel: Alt+F4

Edit

The Edit menu provides the commands you need for moving, locating, and modifying the contents of your worksheets. The five most commonly used Edit menu commands, Cut, Copy, Paste, Undo, and Redo, can also be found on the Standard toolbar.

Besides the commonly used commands, the Edit menu also provides the ability to create a list of related values using Edit → Fill → Series. For example, this command can be used to insert a series of dates that are 15 days apart. For more information about these menu options refer to Chapter 4, *Edit.*

Edit Task List

Undo the most recent changes to a workbook: Chapter 4, page 73
Remove specific information from selected cells: Chapter 4, page 74
Insert the most recent cut or copied information: Chapter 4, page 75
Fill selected cells with a value in a specified series : Chapter 4, page 78
Remove the specified type of values from the selected cells: Chapter 4, page 85
Remove the selected worksheet from the workbook: Chapter 4, page 86
Search for specific values and change them: Chapter 4, page 88
Modify the links between a workbook and other files: Chapter 4, page 92

Keyboard Shortcuts

Undo last action: Ctrl+Z
Redo last undone action: Ctrl+Y
Cut content: Ctrl+X
Copy content: Ctrl+C
Paste cut or copied content: Ctrl+V
Fill down the selected range of cells: Ctrl+D
Fill the selected range of cells to the right: Ctrl+R
Delete the contents of the selected cells: Del
Find specified text or formatting codes: Ctrl+F
Replace found content with new content: Ctrl+H
Go to a particular page or section: Ctrl+G (or F5)

View

You can use the commands on the View menu to change the way your worksheet looks on the screen and when it prints. You can either view the worksheet in a regular window or you can use the Full Screen command to remove the toolbars and display the worksheet so that it fills the entire screen.

You can use the View Comments command to show all of the comments that have been placed in the worksheet. If you want to remove them from the display, you simply need to select the View Comments command again.

Depending upon the size of your worksheet, you may want to change the display size using the Zoom command so that you can see more cells on the screen at one time. For example, if you Zoom at 50% you will be able to see twice as much of the worksheet, but everything will be the size of 100% view.

You can use the Custom Views command to save the current view of the document so that it can be selected in the future. This is very useful for creating views of the workbook with specific print settings or hidden cells.

Probably one of the most important features on the View menu is the ability to view and set the page breaks for your worksheet using the Page Break Preview command. When you select this command the view indicates the location of the existing page breaks. You can adjust those page breaks by clicking on them with the mouse and dragging them or you can insert new page breaks. For more information about these menu options, refer to Chapter 5, *View*.

View Task List

Specify page breaks when printing a worksheet: Chapter 5, page 96
Toggle the display of comments off and on: Chapter 5, page 102
Select the specific toolbars that display: Chapter 5, page 96
Turn the display of the Formula and Status bars off and on: Chapter 5, page 98 and Chapter 5, page 99
Create custom workbook views: Chapter 5, page 102
Create and modify the header and footer for the workbook: Chapter 5, page 99
Switch to Full Screen view: Chapter 5, page 106
Choose a Zoom percentage for your workbook: Chapter 5, page 106

Insert

The Insert menu provides the ability to add several different things to your workbook. If you need additional space in your worksheet you can use one of the first three commands to insert a specific number of cells, rows, or columns into your worksheet. Keep in mind that each worksheet can only have a maximum of 256 columns and 65,536 rows. Therefore, when you insert a row or column in the middle of a worksheet one is removed from the end.

One command you are likely to use frequently is Insert → Function. This command allows you to add various functions to your worksheet for calculating and manipulating data. For example, if you have a series of numbers that you want to total you can insert the SUM function.

If you want to be able to provide a graphical representation of your data, you can insert a chart either directly into a worksheet or as a separate sheet in the workbook. For more information about these menu options refer to Chapter 6.

Insert Task List

Add additional cells, rows, or columns to a worksheet: Chapter 6, page 107; Chapter 6, page 108; Chapter 6, page 109
Insert additional worksheets into your workbook: Chapter 6, page 110
Add charts to your workbook: Chapter 6, page 111
Insert page breaks at specific locations in a worksheet: Chapter 6, page 114

Add functions to your worksheet: Chapter 6, page 116
Create names for groups of cells within your worksheet: Chapter 6, page 119
Add comments to specific cells: Chapter 6, page 123
Insert pictures directly into your worksheet: Chapter 6, page 125
Insert an object from another application: Chapter 6, page 130
Add hyperlinks to web sites or other documents: Chapter 6, page 131

Keyboard Shortcuts

Repeat the last action: Ctrl+Y (or F4)
Edit the comment in a cell: Shift+F2
Create names for rows or columns: Ctrl+Shift+F3
Fill the selected range of cells with the initial entry: Ctrl+Enter
Fill down: Ctrl+D
Fill to the right: Ctrl+R
Define a name for range of cells: Ctrl+F3
Insert a Hyperlink: Ctrl+K

Format

There are various levels of formatting available within Excel. You can format specific cells by specifying number format, alignment of text within each cell, borders and patterns for the cell, and the font types, colors, and sizes. You can format rows and columns by changing the height or width, and by hiding specific rows and columns. Finally, you can format the worksheet by renaming it, hiding it, or selecting a background image to display on it.

You can also use the AutoFormat command to select a predefined format for the worksheet. If you want to apply a specify format to a cell based upon its contents, you can use the Conditional Formatting command. Finally, you can create predefined styles that you can select from for formatting cells. For more information about these menu options refer to Chapter 7, *Format.*

FormatTask List

Format the text in a cell: Chapter 7, page 135
Hide specific rows or columns: Chapter 7, page 139 and Chapter 7, page 140
Modify the width of a row or the height of a column: Chapter 7, page 139 and Chapter 7, page 140
Hide a specific worksheet in the workbook: Chapter 7, page 141
Rename a worksheet: Chapter 7, page 141
Insert a background image on a worksheet: Chapter 7, page 141
Select a predefined format for your worksheet: Chapter 7, page 143
Format cells based upon specific criteria: Chapter 7, page 144
Create styles: Chapter 7, page 145

Keyboard Shortcuts

Display the Style dialog box: Alt+'
Display the Format Cells dialog box: Ctrl+1
Apply the General number format to selected cells: Ctrl+Shift +~
Apply the Currency format with two decimal places: Ctrl+Shift+$
Apply the Percentage format with no decimal places: Ctrl+Shift+%
Apply the Exponential format with two decimal places: Ctrl+Shift+^
Apply the Date format in the format mm/dd/yy: Ctrl+Shift+#
Apply the Time format with specified number of hours and minutes and indicating A.M. or P.M.: Ctrl+Shift+@
Apply the Number format with two decimal places, thousands separator, and minus sign (-) for negative values: Ctrl+Shift+!
Apply or remove bold formatting: Ctrl+B
Apply or remove italic formatting: Ctrl+I
Apply or remove underline: Ctrl+U
Apply or remove strikethrough formatting: Ctrl+5
Hide specified rows: Ctrl+9
Unhide rows: Ctrl+Shift+(
Hide specified columns: Ctrl+0 (zero)
Unhide columns: Ctrl+Shift+)

Tools

The commands available on the Tools menu provide the ability to run and customize the features available within Excel. The menu provides the ability to spell check the text within your worksheet and set up automatic spell checking with the AutoCorrect feature. The Add-Ins feature available by selecting Tools → Add-Ins provides the ability to add additional features to Excel such as the Analysis ToolPak, discussed frequently in this book, which provides several additional functions that can be used within your worksheet.

You set the options for how Excel looks and acts using the Options dialog that displays when you select Tools → Options. This dialog contains eight tabs for controlling options such as the appearance of the Excel window, the default file location, and the default file format. You can also customize the look of the toolbars using Tools → Customize. For more information about these menu options refer to Chapter 8, *Tools*.

Tools Task List

Check the spelling and grammar of the text within your worksheet: Chapter 8, page 147
Specify the desired automatic correction options: Chapter 8, page 149
Protect the worksheet and workbook to eliminate unwanted changes: Chapter 8, page 157

Use the collaboration tools Track Changes and Online Collaboration: Chapter 8, page 153 and Chapter 8, page 160

Merge together two copies of the same workbook: Chapter 8, page 156

Determine the value needed in a cell to provide the desired end result for a graph or formula using Goal Seek: Chapter 8, page 163

Create "what-if" scenarios for values in a chart: Chapter 8, page 163

Determine the precedents and dependents for a cell: Chapter 8, page 167

Record or run a macro: Chapter 8, page 173

Load additional Excel features (Add-Ins): Chapter 8, page 179

Customize your toolbars and menus: Chapter 8, page 180

Set options for the Excel and the active workbook: Chapter 8, page 181

Keyboard Shortcuts

Spelling and Grammar: F7

Open the Visual Basic Editor window: Alt+F11

Open the Microsoft Script Editor window: Alt+Shift+F11

Data

The Data menu provides a series of commands for analyzing data within your worksheet. The Sort command provides the ability to sort a series of cells in ascending or descending order based upon the value in the indicated columns or rows. The Filter command allows you to hide the rows that do not meet the criteria you specify.

You can use the Forms command to quickly enter data into a list of columns. If you want to limit the values that can be specified in a cell, you can use Data → Validation to specify the acceptable values. For more information about these menu options, refer to Chapter 9, *Data*.

Data Task List

Sort the selected portion of a worksheet based upon the specified criteria: Chapter 9, page 188

Filter out rows that do not meet the specified criteria: Chapter 9, page 191

Specify data for a form: Chapter 9, page 196

Add subtotals to your list: Chapter 9, page 197

Restrict the values that can be specified in a cell: Chapter 9, page 200

Use "what-if" comparisons with a table of values to determine the results of a formula with different values: Chapter 9, page 203

Convert text pasted from another source into columns: Chapter 9, page 206

Create custom templates: Chapter 9, page 208

Merge data from multiple workbooks: Chapter 9, page 212

Outline your workbook: Chapter 9, page 214

Create PivotTables and PivotChart Reports: Chapter 9, page 219

Add data from an external data source: Chapter 9, page 224

Keyboard Shortcuts

Select an Entire PivotTable report: Ctrl+Shift+*

Chart

The Chart menu provides commands for modifying the selected chart. This menu only displays when a chart is selected; otherwise, the Data menu displays in that location. The Chart menu provides options for changing basically all features of the chart including modifying the chart type and the data used to create it. For more information about these menu options, refer to Chapter 10, *Chart*.

Chart Task List

Select a different type or sub-type of chart: Chapter 10, page 251
Alter the range of data used by the selected chart: Chapter 10, page 254
Customize the look of the chart: Chapter 10, page 256
Specify the name and location for the chart: Chapter 10, page 260
Add data to a chart: Chapter 10, page 260
Alter the display for 3-D charts: Chapter 10, page 262
Add a trendline to a chart: Chapter 10, page 263

Window

The Window menu allows you to switch between open Excel workbooks or view multiple workbooks simultaneously. If you have a large worksheet you can use the Split command to split it, and scroll individual portions of the workbook. Since Excel 2000 uses SDI (single document interface) you can also switch between open workbooks simply by clicking on the icon for the desired workbook on the Taskbar.

Window Task List

Arrange the open worksheets within one Excel window: Chapter 2, page 21
Hide the current workbook: Chapter 2, page 22
Split the active workbook window into four panes: Chapter 2, page 22
Freeze panes within a worksheet: Chapter 2, page 22
Switch between open workbooks: Chapter 2, page 21

Keyboard Shortcuts

Switch between open workbooks: Alt+Esc or Alt+Tab
Move to previous pane: Shirt+F6
Minimize workbook window to icon: Ctrl+F9
Maximize workbook window: Ctrl+F10

Help

Like the other Office 2000 products, Excel's online help comes through an animated Office Assistant that lets you type a question and choose a help article from those offered. If you get tired of this little guy sitting on your screen, you can turn the assistant off and use a more traditional help window. If none of the articles offered seem to meet your needs, you can choose to search for help on the Web, and if you're online at the time, choosing to do so will take you to the tech support section of the Microsoft web site.

Other help features include special tools, such as a *What's This* feature that allows you to click on an item to get a pop-up description, and the Detect and Repair command that searches for problems in Excel's application files and attempts to fix them.

Help Task List

Activate the Office Assistant: Chapter 2, page 23
Use What's This?: Chapter 2, page 24
Run Detect and Repair: Chapter 2, page 24
Go to Office support on the Microsoft web site for help: Chapter 2, page 24
View Excel version and system information: Chapter 2, page 24

Keyboard Shortcuts

Open Word Help: F1
Activate What's This? Help: Shift+F1

Chapter 2

Excel Anatomy

Before you start using Excel it is important to understand some of its basic terminology. Although many of the elements used in Excel are found in other Microsoft Windows programs, Excel does introduce a few new ones. For example, if you have used other Windows programs, the concepts of windows and the status bar are probably nothing new. But, if you are not familiar with spreadsheet programs, then formulas, functions, cells, and rows may present a degree of unfamiliarity.

This chapter provides an under-the-hood look at Excel by describing some of the basic features you will encounter. In this chapter, we explore the following main topics:

The Excel Window
Basically everything that happens within Excel occurs within this window.

The External Side of Excel
Use templates to create a default look for you workbooks.

Using Styles
Change the appearance of the data in your worksheet consistently using styles.

Customizing in Excel
Design your menus and toolbars to contain the commands you frequently use.

The Excel Window

Just like every other Microsoft Windows program, everything that happens in Excel occurs within the Excel window. The Excel window is made up of all the standards windows features, as shown in Figure 2-1.

1. *Title Bar.* The title bar displays across the top of the Excel window. It indicates the name of the current workbook. On the right side of the windows there are icons that minimize, maximize, or close the Excel window. When you minimize the window, the window is closed but it remains active and can be opened by selecting the corresponding icon on the taskbar. When you maximize the window the window is expanded to cover your entire monitor screen. When you select the close button the current workbook is closed; if there are no other workbooks open Excel is also closed.

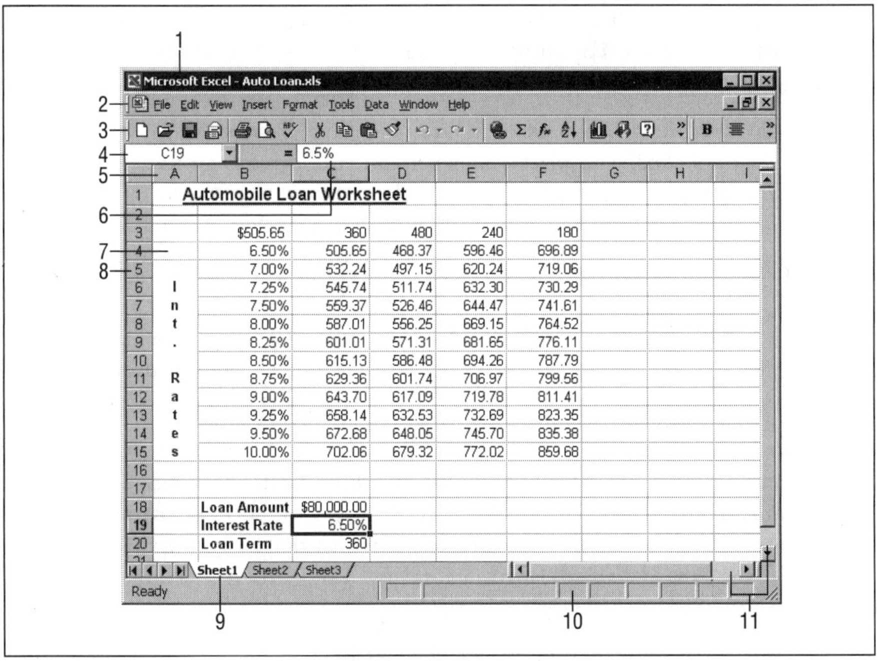

Figure 2-1: The Excel window resembles all other Microsoft programs

2. *Menu Bar.* Contains a list of eight different menus. When you click on one of the words on the menu a list of additional menu items display. If you have a chart selected the Data menu is replaced with a Chart menu. Chapters 3 through 10 discuss the various options available on the menu bar.

Just like other toolbars available within Excel, the Menu bar can be moved by simply clicking on it and dragging it to the desired location.

TIP # 1

Dealing with Adaptive Menus

Excel 2000 comes with new adaptive menus designed to provide access to commonly used commands and suppress those used less frequently. You can tell a menu is suppressed when the last item in the list is an arrow. You can expand the menu by clicking on the arrow. These adaptive menus are designed to make the menus less confusing by suppressing the less commonly used menu options. You can eliminate the adaptive menus, which we recommend, by selecting Tools → Customize → Options and removing the checkmark from the "Menus show recently used commands first" checkbox. This will change all of your Office 2000 program menus.

3. *Toolbars.* Toolbars contain different icons (little pictures) that can be selected to perform different options within Excel. For example, to save a workbook you can select the icon that resembles a floppy disk. Excel provides several default

toolbars, some of which display by default at the top of the Excel window. The toolbars can be moved within the window simply by clicking on them and dragging them to the desired location.

Toolbars are normally "docked" to the top of the Excel window, but they can also be "undocked" and placed anywhere on your screen. To undock a toolbar you simply click on it and drag it to the desired location. When you close Excel it remembers not only which toolbars were last open but also where they were located. The next time you open Excel the toolbars will be placed in the same locations.

You can select the toolbars that display by selecting View → Toolbars (refer to Chapter 5, *View*). You can also create and customize toolbars using Tools → Customize and selecting the Toolbars tab (refer to Chapter 8, *Tools*).

4. *Name Box*. Displays the name of the selected cell, object, or range of cells. If you have created named ranges within the worksheet, those names display in the box. You can select from the named ranges by clicking the down arrow button next to the box. When you select a named range Excel jumps to the first cell in the range. Named ranges are created using Insert → Name. For more information refer to Chapter 6, *Insert*.

5. *Column*. Everything within an Excel worksheet is organized into rows and columns. Columns run vertically within the window and are identified by the letter across the top. You can select an entire column by clicking on the column identifier.

Each Excel worksheet has 256 columns. If you use the options on the Insert menu (refer to Chapter 6, *Insert*) to add a column, Excel actually removes a column from the end of the worksheet. Excel will only allow you to add columns as long as the last column (IV) does not contain a value.

TIP # 2

Hiding Rows and Columns

If you don't want a row or column visible you can hide it by using Format → Column → Hide or Format → Row → Hide. When you select either one of these options, Excel is actually just changing the column width or the row height to zero. When the row or column is hidden the contents can still be accessed by formulas.

6. *Formula Bar*. If a selected cell contains a formula, it displays in the Formula Bar. Whenever you make changes to the contents of a cell you need to press the Enter key or select the Enter icon to update the value within the cell. If you select the Cancel icon the value of the cell remains the same.

You can remove the Formula Bar and do all of the cell editing directly in the cell by selecting Tools → Options → View and unselecting the Formula Bar checkbox (refer to Chapter 8).

7. *Cell.* One of the first things you notice when opening Excel is that the window is covered with a bunch of empty boxes. These boxes are commonly referred to as "cells." Each cell typically contains one value or string of text. Since each cell is within one row and one column the cells are typically referenced using the unique row and column names. For example, in Figure 2-1, the cell that contains the value $80,000 is in column C and row 18, therefore it would be referenced as cell C18. That reference is unique because there is only one location where column C and row 18 intercept. Instead of using the letters to reference columns you can also use the R1C1 reference style where the location of the cell is indicated by providing both a row and a column number. Using this method cell C18 would be R18C3, indicating the cell is located in the eighteenth row and the third column.

Cells on each worksheet have a default size. The height of the cell is measured using points with 72 points in an inch. The default height of a cell is 12.75 points. The width is based upon the default font, which is Arial for Excel. The default width of the cell is 8.43 characters. Since the characters in most fonts, especially Arial, vary in size this measurement may seem a little meaningless. But the measurement is based on the number of zeros that can be placed in the cell which is 8.43. You can use the formatting options available in Excel to change the size of the cell. Refer to the "Formatting in Excel" section later in this chapter.

Although the cells are evenly spaced out on the worksheet, a corresponding cell for each row and column, you can combine cells using the merge option. When you merge cells using Format → Cells → Alignment → Merge Cells the selected cells are joined together forming one cell. When you merge cells the contents of the upper left cell are retained and anything in the other cells is deleted.

If you are entering a range of values in a series of cells (such as the months of the year, or evenly spaced numbers) you can use the Edit → Fill options to speed up the process. When you use these options you can fill the cells with the same value or a series of values. For more information refer to Chapter 4, *Edit.*

TIP # 3

Changing the AutoEntry Direction

If you press the Enter key after typing something in the cell, the active cell becomes the one below the current cell. This feature allows you to quickly enter a series of values into a worksheet. If you want the active cell to move in a different direction you can use Tools → Options → Edit and change the direction specified for the "Move selection after Enter" checkbox. For more information about the Options dialog refer to Chapter 6.

8. *Row.* Everything within an Excel worksheet is organized into rows and columns. Rows run horizontally within the window and are identified by the

---

Absolute vs. Relative Cell References

When you reference a cell in a formula there are two different types of references you can create: relative and absolute. A relative reference is created by simply specifying the row and column name, such as B3 (R3C2 in the R1C1 reference style). When you specify a relative reference Excel automatically updates the reference when you paste the formula in a new cell. For example, if you have the formula =SUM(A1,A2) in cell A3 when you copy it to cell B3 Excel changes the formula to =SUM(B1,B2).

If you want to maintain the entire cell reference, or a portion (row or column) of it, you need to create an absolute reference. When you paste a reference, if any portion of the reference is absolute it is not changed. An absolute reference is specified by placing a dollar sign ($) in front of the portion that you want to be absolute. For example, if you have the reference B3, that reference remains the same each time it is pasted, but with the reference B$3 the column is adjusted based upon where it is pasted.

---

number down the left side of the window. You can select an entire row by clicking on the row identifier.

Each Excel worksheet has 65,536 rows. If you use the options on the Insert menu (refer to Chapter 6) to add a row, Excel actually removes a row from the end of the worksheet each time you insert a row. Excel will only allow you to add additional row, as long as the last row does not contain a value.

9. *Sheet Tabs.* Each tab represents a different worksheet or chart sheet within the current workbook. You can switch between the different sheets by clicking on the corresponding tab.

Excel provides the ability to rename, add, and delete sheets using the commands available on the menu that displays when you click the right mouse button on the selected sheet tab. By selecting the tabs for all of the worksheets you can apply formatting options to all of the selected worksheets simultaneously.

10. *Status Bar.* The status bar displays at the very bottom of the Excel window and provides various messages when working in Excel. Typically you are going to see the message "Ready" indicating that Excel is ready to perform another calculation. On the right side of the bar Excel indicates when certain keys, such as Caps Lock, Num Lock, and ScrlLk, have been pressed on the keyboard.

If you do not want the status bar displayed on the window, you can remove using the options on the Option dialog that displays when you select Tools → Options. For more information refer to Chapter 8.

11. *Scrollbars.* Since it is virtually impossible to see all 256 columns and 65,536 rows in of a worksheet simultaneously, Excel provides two different scrollbars that can be used to move around within a worksheet. The horizontal scrollbar displays at the bottom of the window allowing you to scroll the worksheet from left to right. The vertical scrollbar display on the right side of the window and allows you to scroll up and down within the worksheet.

Excel Anatomy

TIP # 4

Getting Around with the Keyboard

The scrollbars are not the only way to navigate around the worksheet; you can also use the Ctrl and Arrow Keys. If you want to move to the last cell that contains a value in a row press Ctrl+Right Arrow. If the row is empty, when you press the keys the active cell moves to the last column in the worksheet. For more tips about moving around your worksheet, refer to Appendix A.

Working with Multiple Workbooks

As discussed in Chapter 1, *Excel Basics*, Excel uses single document interface (SDI), meaning that each workbook is placed in its own unique window. Each time you open a new workbook, a separate Excel button appears on the taskbar for that workbook. You can switch between the various workbooks by clicking on the corresponding taskbar buttons.

Even though Excel has multiple workbooks open, it only runs the program once. If you close a workbook, the program remains running until you close the last workbook.

TIP # 5

Switch between documents using Alt+Tab

Because SDI behaves as if each open workbook is a different application, you can also use the Alt+Tab or Alt+Esc keyboard shortcuts that are normally only good for switching between applications.

Arranging multiple workbooks

Instead of having each open workbook display a separate Excel window, you can arrange them to display within one window by selecting Windows → Arrange. This opens the Arrange Windows dialog display, allowing you to specify one of four ways to arrange the open workbooks in the current window:

Tiled
 The open workbooks are sized so that each one fits within the space of the window.

Horizontal

The open workbooks are placed in the window, taking up the entire space vertically, and they are placed vertically across the window.

Vertical

The open workbooks are placed in window and fit the height of the window, and are placed vertically across it.

Cascade

The open workbooks are stacked like playing cards in the window, allowing you to select a given workbook.

TIP # 6

Freezing Panes

If you have a worksheet split into multiple panes, you can freeze different panes so they can't be scrolled. To freeze a pane, select a cell within the desired pane and then select Window → Freeze Panes. If you want to freeze multiple panes, select a range of cells that includes the frames to want to freeze. You can unfreeze panes by selcting Window → Unfreeze Panes.

Hiding the current workbook

You can hide the current workbook by selecting Window → Hide. The workbook then remains open in Excel, but is not listed on the toolbar for selection or in the list of open windows on the Window menu.

You can unhide a workbook by selecting Window → Unhide and then selecting the desired workbook from the Unhide dialog.

TIP # 7

Hiding Workbooks

The selected workbook is only hidden during the current session. The next time you open the workbook, it will not be hidden. Keep in mind that any hidden workbooks will not be listed on the Window menu or Taskbar. If you want to view a hidden workbook, you need to unhide it using Window → Unhide.

Splitting the active workbook

If you have a large worksheet, you may want to split it into mulitiple panes to view different sections simultaneously. Before you split the worksheet, place your cursor at the location on the worksheet where you want to make the split, and select Window → Split. Once you split the worksheet, you can scroll each section independently using the corresponding scrollbars. You can change the location of the split by clicking on the split bar and dragging it to the desired location.

Getting Help with Excel

Microsoft Excel comes with a fairly robust online help file that can be used when you need to find a quick answer to a problem. Navigating the help system, however, can be difficult, and is almost like another program in itself. The online help features are available on the Help menu. There are several different options on the menu. So the question becomes, which option should I use?

TIP # 8

Hiding the Office Assistant

When you first install Excel you will have a cute little icon (Office Assistant) sitting on your screen waiting to answer all your questions. Or he might just get on your nerves. You can hide the Office Assistant by selecting the Options button on the Office Assistant's dialog box and unchecking the Use Office Assistant option.

Help → Microsoft Excel Help

If the Office Assistant option is enabled, this option opens a dialog in which you type the information you are looking for. If the Office Assistant is disabled, this option opens the Microsoft Excel Help dialog shown in Figure 2-2.

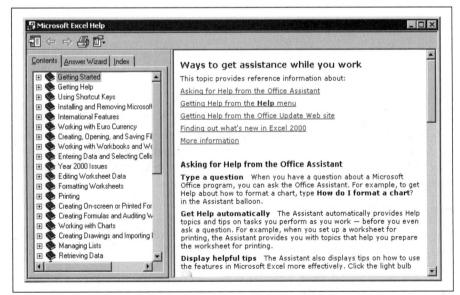

Figure 2-2: The Microsoft Excel Help dialog allows you to search the Contents, index, or use the Answer Wizard to locate the desired topic

The help dialog is divided into two sections. The left side contains three tabs: Contents (a tree-like display of the contents), Answer Wizard (find topics for the specified word or phrase) and Index (type a keyword or select from one of the keywords in the list to see topics) When you select a topic, the contents of the topic display on the right side of the dialog.

Help → Hide the Office Assistant

This command only hides the Office Assistant temporarily, until you request help again. If you want to get rid of the Office Assistant, you need to use the Options button on the Office Assistant's dialog box and uncheck the Use Office Assistant checkbox.

Help → What's This

This option changes your mouse cursor to a question mark. When this option is enabled, you can click on a menu command, area of the screen, or field, and a text pop-up will display a description of the selected item. Selecting this option is the same as pressing Shift+F1.

Help → Office on the Web

This option opens your Internet browser and displays the Microsoft Office Update site. This is a great place to check for updates to Excel, download add-ons, and look for new tricks you can try. Of course, if you don't have access to the Internet this option will not work.

Help → Lotus 1-2-3 Help

This is useful for former Lotus 1-2-3 users. It provides them with the equivalent commands in Excel.

Help → Detect and Repair

This option looks at the time/date/version stamps on the files that Excel requires to run properly. If there is anything that is not correct, you will be prompted to insert the Office CD-ROM so the problem files can be restored. Keep in mind that if you have installed other patches or updates you will probably have to reinstall those after running this utility.

Help → About Microsoft Excel

This option provides technical information and the Product ID for your version of Excel on the dialog that pops up. You may be asked to access this dialog if you contact Microsoft for support.

The External Side of Excel

Besides the menus and toolbars there are some external elements that affect the way Excel works. In order to effectively use Excel, you need to have a firm grasp on the concepts of worksheets, workbooks, and templates.

Even if you have used other spreadsheet software packages, if you are new to Excel the concept of workbooks and worksheets may be a little foreign. Excel uses the concept of a book that contains multiple related pages and creates workbooks that contain related sheets or worksheets. Each workbook contains different chart sheets.

 You can change the way Excel opens by using switches. For example, if you always look at the Sales workbook, you may want to create a shortcut that opens up the workbook when you run Excel (C:\Program Files\Microsoft Office\Office\EXCEL.EXE or C:\AnnualSales\Sales.xls). You can find more information about using switches in Chapter 3.

By default a workbook is created with three worksheets. Workbooks have an extension of *.xls*. By default, Excel names workbooks Book1, Book2, etc. and worksheets are name Sheet1, Sheet2, etc. You can rename a workbook when you save it and you can rename a worksheet by right-clicking on the sheet tab and selecting the Rename option. You can switch between the worksheets by clicking on the corresponding sheet tab at the bottom of the window. Additional worksheets can be added using Insert → Worksheet (refer to Chapter 6). Chart sheets are created when you create a new chart using Insert → Chart and indicate that you want it placed on a separate sheet (refer to Chapter 6).

TIP # 9

Avoid Altering File Extensions When Saving

Although you can give a worksheet any unique name, you should avoid trying to alter the file extension (characters that appear after the period). Microsoft Windows recognizes all files with an extension of .xls as Excel workbooks and files with extensions of .xlt as Excel templates. If you click on a file with either one of these extensions it will be opened up within Excel.

Understanding Templates

If you ask someone to tell you what a template is, probably one of the first statements they will say is that a template is just a workbook that has been saved in a template format. So, why would you want to do that?

Templates in Excel function just like the plastic templates we all used in math class to draw consistently uniform circles. A template allows you to create a worksheet with the same layout as a previous worksheet.

Templates are created by designing a worksheet with the desired layout (borders, headers, footers, etc.) and then saving it in a template format. When you save a workbook as a template Excel gives it an extension of *.xlt*. Once the template is saved, you can apply it to a new workbook by selecting the corresponding icon on the New dialog box that displays when you select File → New. (Refer to Figure 2-3.) When you create a new workbook using a template, all settings in the selected template are copied into the new workbook.

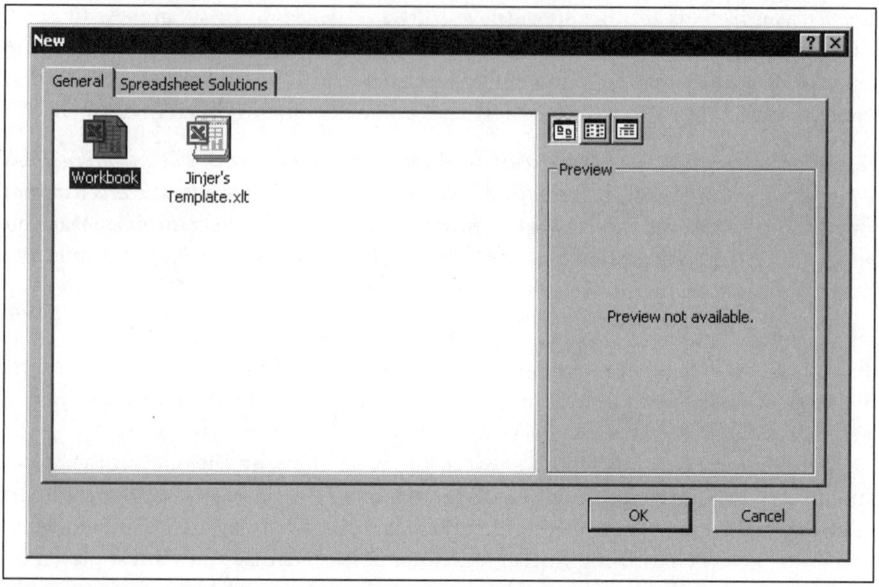

Figure 2-3: The General tab indicates any custom templates that have been created

You will notice that there are two tabs on the New dialog. The Spreadsheet Solutions tab contains four different templates that have been provided by Microsoft. The General tab contains the default workbook template (*book.xlt*) and any custom templates that have been created and placed in one of the three template locations:

- *C:\windows\Profiles\user_name\Application Data\Microsoft\Templates* (keep in mind that the drive letter may be different on your machine).

- The *XLStart* folder is where Excel looks for the *book.xlt* template used to create workbooks. This folder is typically located in *C:\windows\Profiles\user_name\ Application Data\Microsoft\Excel\XLStart*.

- The location you specified in the Tools → Options → General tab. Refer to Chapter 8 for more information.

> **NOTE** *The templates will only be listed on the General tab of File → New if they are placed in one of these three template locations. If you know you have created a template, but do not see it listed, make sure it is in the correct folder location.*

Changing default workbook and worksheet templates

When you select the Workbook template icon on the New dialog Excel creates a new workbook using the default system settings. For example, by default each workbook has exactly three worksheets. If you consistently make specific changes to each workbook when you create it, such as adding a company logo and changing the default font to Times Roman, you may want to consider creating a default template to do that automatically.

Excel allows you to create a custom template that overrides the system settings. In order to do this, you must create a custom template called *book.xlt* and place it in the *\XLStart* folder (usually *C:\Windows\Profiles\Username\ApplicationData\ Microsoft\Excel\XLStart*). If Excel finds the *book.xlt* template, it uses those settings as the defaults whenever the New button is selected on the toolbar, or whenever you select the Workbook option on the General tab of the New dialog. To reset the settings to use the system default, simply remove the template from the folder. By creating the *book.xlt* template you can specify fonts, formatting, borders, macros, and so on to use for any new workbooks.

There are also default worksheet template settings. These default settings are used to indicate how a worksheet should look when it is added to a workbook using Insert → Worksheet. Just like the workbook defaults, you can override these default settings by creating a template called *sheet.xlt* and placing it in the *XLStart* folder. If this template exists, it will be used whenever Insert → Worksheet is selected. Since this template is for creating new sheets, it does not display on the New dialog; the only way to see it is to use Windows Explorer. To reset the settings so that a blank worksheet is added, simply remove the template from the folder.

The *sheet.xlt* template can contain multiple pages. Each time you select Insert → Worksheet, the entire contents of the template are inserted into the current workbook. In other words, if *sheet.xlt* contains four pages, then four pages are added to your workbook. If you want to have your logo on each worksheet, you could place it on the *sheet.xlt* template and then each time you add a sheet you would get a worksheet with your logo.

> **NOTE** *Excel allows you to format at the cell, column, and row level. You can resize rows and columns by clicking on the right edge of the column or the bottom edge of the row with the mouse and dragging them so that they are larger or smaller. You can also use the options on the Format menu to format the cells, rows, and columns as discussed in Chapter 7.*

Using Styles

There are essentially three methods that can be used to select a style for a cell:

- Formatting Toolbar icons
- Style Tool
- Format → Style

TIP # 10
Use of Fonts in Workbooks You Want to Distribute

If you give the workbook to someone who doesn't have the fonts you used, Excel will attempt to open the workbook using a similar font. Unfortunately, you do not always get the desired results. Therefore, on workbooks you are going to distribute electronically use the standard Windows fonts: Arial, Courier New, Symbol, Times New Roman, and Wingdings.

There are three style icons that are placed on the Formatting Toolbar as a default: Comma Style, Currency Style, and Percent Style. To apply one of these styles, simply select the range you want to apply the style to and then select the appropriate icon.

 If you have used styles in Word you probably remember that there is a Style Tool that always indicates the style of the current selection. Although it is initially hidden, that feature also exists within Excel. If you have any intention of working with styles in your workbooks I would highly recommend that you add the Style Tool to your toolbars, as illustrated in Figure 2-4.

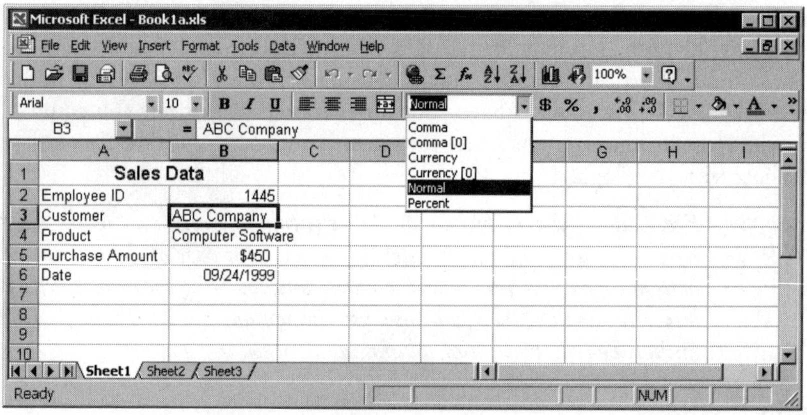

![Microsoft Excel - Book1a.xls screenshot showing the Style Tool dropdown with Comma, Comma [0], Currency, Currency [0], Normal, and Percent options]

Figure 2-4: You can use the Style Tool to select the desired style

You need to use the Customize dialog (Tools → Customize) to add the Style Tool to one of the toolbars, as outlined in the following steps:

1. Display the Customize dialog by selecting Tools → Customize.

2. Select the Commands tab.

3. Click on the Format category in the Categories list.

4. Click on the command labeled Style and drag it to the desired toolbar. I would recommend placing it on the Formatting toolbar, but you can place it anywhere.

5. Close the Customize dialog.

Once you have added the Style Tool, you simply need to select the desired range and then select the Down Arrow button next to the Style Tool and highlight the desired style for the selected range.

Finally, you can also select a style for a range using Format → Style on the Style dialog detailed in Chapter 7.

If you are constantly changing the font style, size, color, etc. within various cells you should definitely look into creating styles to perform that task. For example, you can create a style called "Bold Arial" with the characteristics of Arial as the font and bold as the style. You can select the Bold Arial style each time you wanted those font characteristics.

The really cool thing is that if you modify the style, such as adding italics, all of the places where you applied the style are updated to the new settings, eliminating the need to manually go through and add the italics to the appropriate cells.

Styles can be created to specify any combination of the following attributes:

- Number format
- Font (type, size, and color)
- Alignment (vertical or horizontal)
- Borders
- Pattern
- Protection (locked or hidden cells)

Default Excel Styles

Excel comes with six standard built-in styles that can be applied to your worksheets. Although these styles can be useful, they are only a small dent in the types of styles that can be created. By default, all cells in the worksheet have the Normal style applied. With the exception of the Normal style, the default styles all apply to how numeric values are displayed in a cell, as outlined in the following list:

Normal
Excel's default style. Numbers display aligned with the right side of the cell.

Comma
Inserts a comma as a thousands separator and each number has two decimal places. This is the style applied if you select the Comma Style icon on the Formatting toolbar.

Comma(0)

Inserts a comma as the thousands separator but there are no decimal places.

Currency

Left-aligns the numeric value with a dollar sign in front and two decimal places. This is the style applied if you select the Currency Style icon on the Formatting toolbar.

Currency(0)

Left-aligns the numeric value with a dollar sign and no decimal places.

Percent

Converts the numeric value to a percentage and places the percent sign after it. There are no decimal places with this style. This is the style applied if you select the Percent Style icon on the Formatting toolbar.

Creating a New Style

Excel allows you to create an unlimited number of custom styles using the Style dialog. The best method for creating a new style is to first specify the desired formatting for a cell (or range of cells) and then select Format → Style to display the Style dialog shown in Figure 2-4.

You need to indicate which cell formatting options you want to be included in the style. For example, if you do not want the alignment to be changed when you apply the style to other cells, you would remove the check mark from that option. Type the name that you want to use for the style in the Style name field and click the OK button.

> **NOTE** *Be aware that the styles you create are stored in the current workbook. If you want to use the custom styles in other workbooks, you need to use the Merge option discussed later in this chapter. If you have styles that you use frequently, you should consider creating a template that contains all of those styles.*

If you have added the Style Tool to your toolbars you can also create a new style by typing a style name in that box. If you do this, though, all of the six formatting attributes listed on the Style dialog will be assigned to the Style.

Using Styles from Other Workbooks

When you create new styles Excel stores them in the workbook where you created them. To alleviate the need to recreate the styles each time, the Style dialog provides a Merge option.

In order to merge styles from one workbook to another, you need to open both workbooks. From the workbook where you want to place the styles, select Format → Style → Merge to display the Merge Styles dialog shown in Figure 2-5. One downside to merging styles is that Excel merges all of the styles from the selected workbook; you cannot specify the styles you want.

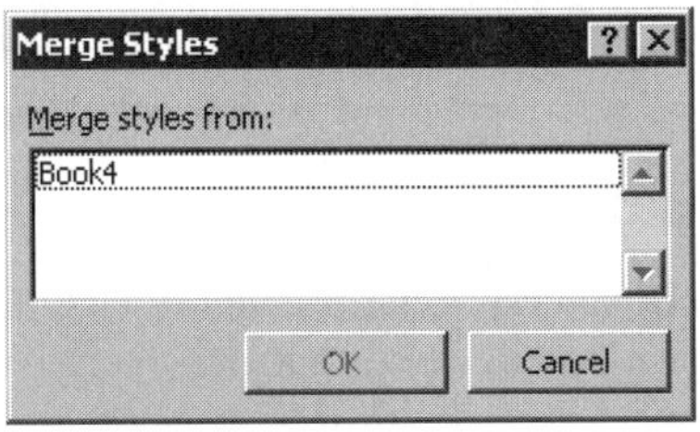

Figure 2-5: Select the workbook from which you want to merge styles

NOTE *You can eliminate any unwanted styles by selecting Format → Style to display the Style dialog. Select the style you no longer want and then select the Delete button. If you have the style in multiple workbooks it is only deleted from the current workbook.*

Customizing in Excel

Although adaptive menus provide some customization of your environment by automatically suppressing the options you don't use, they are not the only type of customization available within Excel. By using the Tools → Customize command you can customize your Excel environment even more. Keep in mind that as you make some of these customizations some of the options selected affect all Office programs; others—such as toolbar and menu customizations—remain local to the program they are used in.

NOTE *Make sure you check out the context menus that are available throughout Excel. These menus display when you right-click on a particular location. They contain options that are relevant to your current location. For example, if you right-click on a cell you see options for cutting, copying, pasting, adding a comment, formatting the cell, etc.*

Use the Tools → Customize command to perform three different types of customizations to your Excel environment:

Tools → Customize → Options
> Set general customization options that govern how Excel's personalized (adaptive) menus work and how icons appear on menus and toolbars.

Tools → Customize → Toolbars
> Use this tab to create new toolbars, rename and delete existing toolbars, and reset default toolbars.

Tools → Customize → Commands
> This tab lets you add, remove, and modify commands in Excel's menus and toolbars. It's also used to create new menus.

```
                              TIP # 11
```

Quick Access to the Customize Dialog

Access the Customize dialog quickly by right-clicking on any toolbar and choosing Customize from the context menu or by selecting View → Toolbars → Customize.

Setting Customization Options

Select Tools → Customize → Options, shown in Figure 2-6, to adjust adaptive menus or eliminate them. Keep in mind that the changes you make to your adaptive menus affect all of your Microsoft Office 2000 programs. This tab also provides other options for customizing the menu bar.

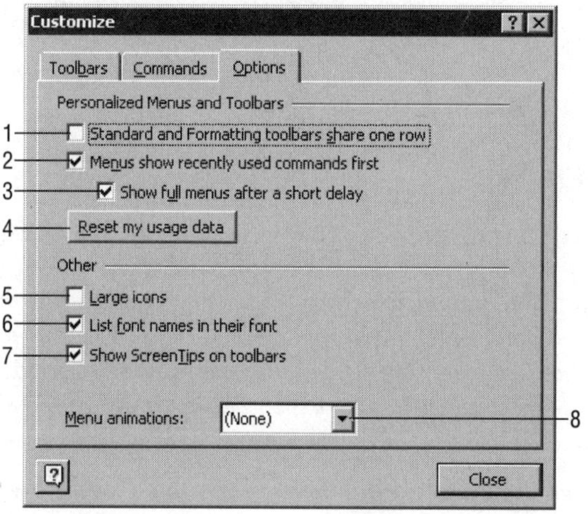

Figure 2-6: Make changes to the menu bar options with Tools → Customize → Options

1. *Standard and Formatting toolbars share one row.* By default, Word displays the Standard and Formatting toolbars on a single row. Turn this option off to display each on its own row. An even faster method is to simply drag one of the toolbars to a new row; which implicitly turns off this option. If you have turned off one or both of the toolbars using View → Toolbars this option will be dimmed on the tab. Keep in mind that selecting this option in Excel does not affect the other Office 2000 programs.

2. *Menus show recently used commands first.* Turn this option off to disable adaptive menus so that Excel shows all menu commands when you select a menu. If this option is disabled in one Office application, it is disabled in all Office applications.

3. *Show full menus after a short delay.* This option is only available if adaptive menus are turned on. With this option on, Excel displays the full menu

automatically if no command is chosen for about five seconds after opening a menu. If this option is turned off, you must select the arrow graphic at the bottom of a menu to display the full menu.

4. *Reset my usage data.* This button deletes the adaptive menu history stored in Excel. After resetting your data, Excel relearns your style and adapts the menus again. Selecting this button only affects the menu settings within Excel. It does not affect the other Office 2000 programs.

5. *Large icons.* This option displays large icons on Excel's toolbars and even displays toolbars on two or more rows to fit all the buttons in. Though most users won't find much use for it, it is handy for those who can't see small objects so well or those who work on particularly large monitors in high resolution.

6. *List font names in their font.* This option displays fonts from the font list on the formatting toolbar in their actual typefaces. If you don't use that many fonts or find it a bit slow to generate the displays, turn this option off.

7. *Show ScreenTips on toolbars.* Select this option to display ScreenTips as you drag your mouse over a toolbar option. ScreenTips are little pop-up windows that display the name of the selected button.

8. *Menu animations.* By default, no menu animations are used in Excel. There are three types of menu animations that can be selected (Random, Unfold, and Slide). The Unfold option makes the menu look as though it is unfolding from its top-left corner. The Slide option displays the menu as if it were sliding down from its top edge. The Random option randomly switches between Slide and Unfold each time a menu opens.

Creating and Removing Toolbars

You have probably already noticed that the toolbars in Excel provide access to a lot of different features, although they may not be all the features you use. Excel's toolbars can all be customized and additional ones can be created using the Customize dialog that displays when you select Tools → Customize.

 Remember that all customizations applied to toolbars and menus are specific to Excel. For example, if you eliminate the Paste icon from the Standard toolbar in Excel it will still remain on the Standard toolbar within Word and any other Office application.

The Toolbars tab, shown in Figure 2-7, allows you to create and delete custom toolbars. If you want to customize a toolbar that is not currently displayed, you can display it by selecting the corresponding checkbox. Once the toolbar is displayed, you can use the Customize tab to add options to it.

The Toolbars tab lists all of the toolbars that exist within Excel, including the Menu bar, which is also another toolbar that you can customize. Any custom toolbars that you create will also be listed on this tab. You can only delete and rename new custom toolbars that you create; you cannot delete any of the toolbars that come installed with Excel.

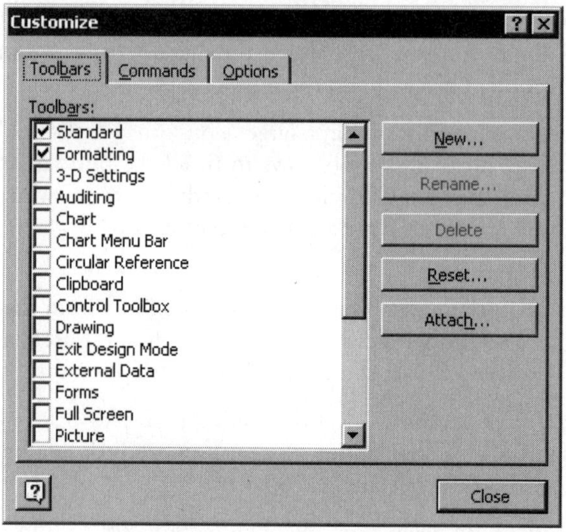

Figure 2-7: Use Tools → Customize → Toolbars to create and remove custom toolbars

If you ever want to undo the customizations of one of the standard Excel toolbars, you can simply select the toolbar and then select the Reset button. Keep in mind that the toolbar will be set back to the installed settings. This option even works with the Menu bar, if you need to restore it to the original settings.

TIP # 12

Turning Toolbars On and Off

Toolbars can be turned off and on by selecting the corresponding checkbox on Tools → Customize → Toolbars or by selecting View → Toolbars.

Customizing Toolbar and Menu Commands

You can add and remove options from Excel toolbars and menus by selecting Tools → Customize → Commands. This tab, shown in Figure 2-8, lists all of the commands that are available within Excel, including any macros that have been created.

When you have the Commands tab displayed you can make modifications to any menu or displayed toolbar by dragging commands onto or off the toolbar or menu.

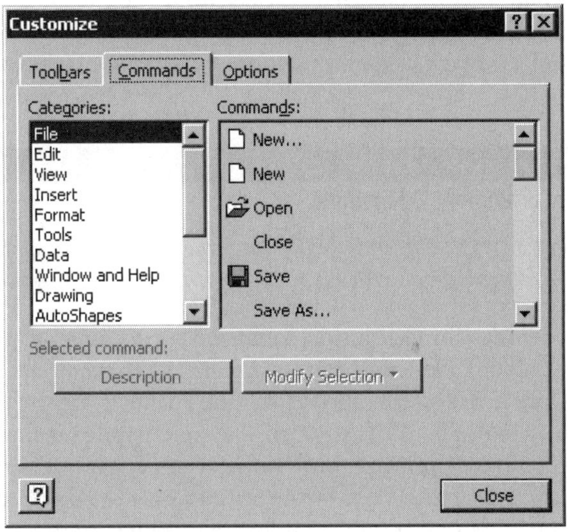

Excel Anatomy

Figure 2-8: Use Tools → Customize → Commands to add commands to menus and toolbars

 NOTE *The commands on the Commands tab are grouped together according to function. For example, all commands that deal with files (opening, saving, etc.) are listed under the File category. The groupings on the tab make locating the desired command convenient; you can add these groupings to any toolbar or menu, as desired.*

When the Commands tab is displayed there are a number of actions that can be performed:

- Place a command on a menu or toolbar simply by clicking on it and dragging it to the desired location. When you release the mouse it will be added to the new location. Besides selecting commands on the Command tab you can also move commands to a different place on the same menu or toolbar, or to a different menu or toolbar.

TIP # 13

How to Copy Commands Without Moving Them

By default, if you click on a command in a toolbar or menu and drag, the command is moved from the original location to the new location. If you want to keep the command in the original location and place a copy of it on a different menu or toolbar you need to hold down the Ctrl key while dragging the command. Keep in mind that this is not necessary when dragging commands from the Tools → Customize → Commands dialog. The commands remain on the Commands dialog even though they have been placed on a menu or toolbar.

- Remove a command by dragging it away from the menus and toolbars altogether. Remember, if you remove a built-in button from a toolbar you can always restore the original toolbar settings by selecting Customize → Toolbars → Reset.

TIP # 14

Quickly Move or Remove Commands

You can move or remove a command from a toolbar that is displayed on the Excel window by holding down the Alt key and dragging the desired command.

- Modify the settings for an existing command by clicking on it once and then clicking the Modify Selection button on the Commands tab to display the menu in Figure 2-9. You can also display this menu by right-clicking any command (on a menu or toolbar) to open the same pop-up menu. Note that the right-clicking on the command only works if the Tools → Customize → Commands option is selected. Most of the settings on the pop-up menu deal with how the command displays on the toolbar.

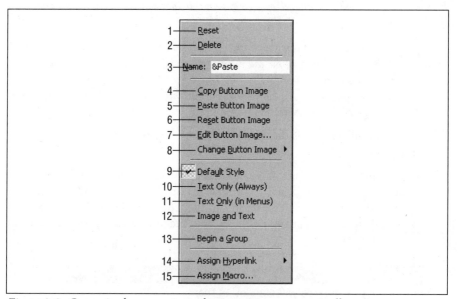

Figure 2-9: Customize how a command appears on a menu or toolbar

1. *Reset.* This resets the command, button, or entire menu to the built-in default setting.

2. *Delete.* This removes the selected command. This produces the same results as dragging the command away.

3. *Name.* For a menu or menu command, the name is what appears on the menu. For a button, the name is what appears in the ScreenTip. The ampersand (&)

sets the keyboard accelerator for the menu. For example, in Figure 2-9 the Modify Selection button was selected for the Paste button. The default name for the command is &Paste because you can press Alt+E to access the Edit menu and then press P to issue the Paste command. An underscore under the appropriate letter of a command visually denotes it as an accelerator.

4. *Copy Button Image.* This command is only available on buttons and menu commands. It places a picture of the button in the clipboard and can be pasted onto another button within Excel or another Office application using the Paste Button Image command.

5. *Paste Button Image.* This command is only available on buttons and menu commands. It replaces the selected button's image with the one in the clipboard. The button image can even be pasted onto a button in another Office application or right into a document.

6. *Reset Button Image.* This command resets the button image to its default state. Be aware that if you created your own button image with the Button Editor, it will be lost when you select this command. If you want to save the image you need to copy and paste it to another location before performing the reset command. This option is not available for menus themselves, only for commands on the menus and on toolbars.

7. *Edit Button Image.* This command opens the Button Editor shown in Figure 2-10. When you select this command on a button with an image, the image is loaded into the Button Editor, where it can be modified or replaced. If you select this command for a button that does not have an image the Button Editor starts with a blank canvas. This option is not available for menus themselves, only for commands on the menus and on toolbars. The canvas indicates the maximum size for the button image. You can use any of the 16 colors to create your image by simply clicking on the desired color and then clicking on the appropriate pixel (box) on the canvas. When you have completed your button, select the OK button to save it.

8. *Change Button Image.* Instead of redesigning your button image you can use this command to select from a number of built-in button images, as shown in Figure 2-11. This option is not available for menus themselves, only for commands on the menus and on toolbars.

9. *Default Style.* This option sets the command to its default display. Each command has a specific default for how it displays on menus and toolbars. Some commands, such as the Paste command, display as an image on a toolbar and both the image and text on a menu. Other commands may only have a text option. You can change the way the command displays by selecting one of the following three styles: Text Only (Always), Text Only (Menus), or Image and Text.

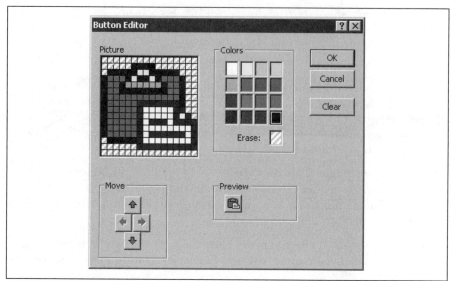

Figure 2-10: The Button Editor

Figure 2-11: Selecting a built-in button image from the Change Button palette

10. *Text Only (Always).* This option makes commands display only as text in both menus and toolbars.

11. *Text Only (in Menus)* This option displays menu commands as text only. This means the picture of the icon is not displayed in the menu, but remains unchanged on the toolbar.

12. *Image and Text.* This option displays both the text and the associated image for menu and toolbar commands. Menu commands with an associated image use this by default.

13. *Begin a Group.* When this option is activated for an item, a divider is inserted *above* the selected item on a menu, helping to group like commands. For top-level menus and toolbars, the divider is usually placed to the left of the corresponding command.

14. *Assign Hyperlink.* This option opens the Assign Hyperlink dialog, shown in Figure 2-12, allowing you to assign a hyperlink to a command on a menu or toolbar. This is the same hyperlink dialog opened by Insert → Hyperlink.

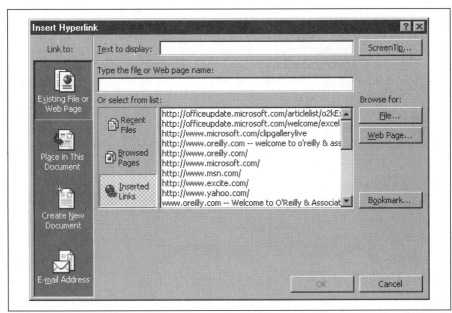

Figure 2-12: Use Assign Hyperlinks dialog to assign a specific hyperlink to a command

The Link to icon bar on the left presents four different choices related to the type of hyperlink to assign:

Existing File or Web Page

Use this option to enter the name of a file or Internet address in the form of a URL. You can select from one of the lists displayed: Recent Files indicates a list of the most recently accessed files stored by the operating system; Browsed Pages are the most recently accessed pages by Internet Explorer; Inserted Links are a list of recent links that have been cut, pasted, or otherwise inserted into the document recently. If you don't find the desired hyperlinks in those lists you can either browse for the file or web page by selecting the corresponding buttons or you can type the appropriate address in the Type the file or web page name field.

Place in this Document

Normally, this option creates a hyperlink to a bookmark in the current document. However, this option is not available to commands.

Create New Document

This option creates a new document. Choose whether to edit the document now or later. Notice that choosing the "later" option places a hyperlink on a menu or toolbar. Issuing the command later actually creates that new document.

E-mail Address

This option creates a command that opens a new email message with the address and even subject line filled in as specified.

15. *Assign Macro.* This option opens the Assign Macro dialog, shown in Figure 2-13, allowing you to assign a macro to a command on a menu or toolbar. This is the same dialog opened by Tools → Macro → Macro. When you select this option from the menu the Edit and Record buttons will be grayed out. You can only select a macro to assign to the selected button or menu command. You cannot create or modify a macro from this location. If you want to create a macro you need to select Tools → Macro → Record New Macro, as discussed in Chapter 8.

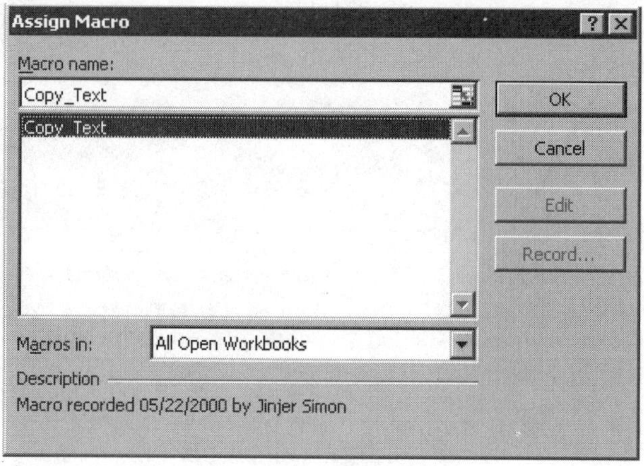

Figure 2-13: You can insert a macro as a command with the Assign Macro dialog

Part 2

Menu Reference

Chapter 3

File

The File menu provides various options for dealing with workbook files. One of the most useful features available on this menu is the ability to print the contents of a specific worksheet. Unfortunately, printing within Excel 2000 is not as intuitive as it may appear. Before you select the File → Print option you need to make sure you specify the portion of your worksheet that you want to print using the File → Print Area option. You can verify the desired page layout by selecting File → Print Preview. If you don't like the margins or page breaks, you can make modifications directly on the Print Preview dialog.

If you have access to email, instead of printing a hardcopy of your workbook to give to another individual, you can use the File → Send To options to send a copy of the workbook to others. If you have access to Microsoft NetMeeting you can even send it to the participants in an online discussion, as long as you are the host of the discussion.

Excel 2000 works well with many different applications by providing the ability to both open files from these applications and save Excel workbooks in a compatible format. The File menu also provides options for dealing with various file types. Although Excel is typically used to work with workbooks, the ability to open and save a variety of different types of files allows you to share important information with various applications and earlier versions of Excel as well.

This chapter frequently mentions workbooks and worksheets. For more information about these terms, refer to Chapter 2, *Excel Anatomy.*

Microsoft Excel Files

With each version of Excel, there have been modifications made to the format that workbooks are saved in. Each version of Excel has been backwards compatible, meaning that it could always open and save in the format of a previous version. Because of this, Excel 2000 can open files from all previous versions of Excel, but, with the exception of Excel 97, earlier versions of Excel will not be able to open Excel 2000 formatted workbooks. Excel 2000 uses the same file format as Excel 97, which is why the two versions are compatible. Excel can also open and save to several other formats, as described later in this section. Unless otherwise stated,

Excel has the ability to both open and save in the following specified formats using the File → Save As or the File → Open options:

Microsoft Excel Files
Saves in a format that can be used by users of both Excel 2000 and Excel 97.

Microsoft Excel 5.0/95 Workbook
Saves the selected workbook in the appropriate format for Excel 5.0/95. Any features that are specific to Excel 97 or Excel 2000 are removed from the workbook when it is saved.

Microsoft Excel 97–2000 & 5.0/95 Workbook
Saves the workbook in a file that can be used by Excel 97–2000 and Excel 5.0/95 users, although, Excel 97–2000 features that exist in the workbook are not available for the Excel 5.0/95 user.

Microsoft Excel 4.0/3.0/2.1 Worksheet
Saves only the first worksheet of the workbook in a format that can be opened by Microsoft Excel 4.0/3.0/2.1 and removes all Excel 97–2000-specific features from the worksheet.

Microsoft Excel 4.0 Workbook
Saves only the worksheets, chart sheets, and macro sheets in the workbook in a format that can be opened by Microsoft Excel 4.0 and removes any Excel 97–2000 specific features.

Microsoft Excel 4.0 Macros
Opens an Excel 4.0 macro sheet.

Microsoft Excel 4.0 Charts
Opens an Excel 4.0 chart sheet.

Templates
Saves the selected workbook in a template format that can be used to create a future workbook.

Microsoft Excel Add-in
Saves the selected workbook so that it can be attached to another workbook as an add-in. When a workbook is saved as an add-in, only the macros in the workbook are accessible.

Web Page

You can both open and save HTML files within Excel, the file format typically used to create web pages. However, Excel does not provide a good environment for creating web pages and the HTML code that it produces is rather messy. I would only use it if you want to save a worksheet with interactive spreadsheet functionality.

When you add the interactive spreadsheet functionality, the data can be manipulated within the cells directly on your web site, similar to working in Excel. When the user views the web page, an ActiveX object is used to add the interactive functionality to the worksheet. This gives the web page a similar look and feel to a worksheet within Excel.

 ActiveX is a technology developed by Microsoft that provides more sophisticated capabilities than are available on a standard HTML page. The ActiveX control is an interactive component that allows users to modify the worksheet data within their browser. In order for another user to use the interactive functionality they must have either Office 2000 installed on their system or the Office Client Pak, which provides the interactive ActiveX controls.

Text File

Excel will both open and save text files. Keep in mind that when dealing with text files you lose all formatting and graphical images.

When you select to open a text file, the Text Import Wizard allows you to specify how the text is separated into rows and columns. You can indicate whether the text should be evenly divided into columns or if a space or character separates each item by selecting the appropriate radio button on the wizard.

There are different types of text files that can be created, depending upon the way you want your text file to be formatted:

Tab delimited
　　The values from each cell are separated in the text file by a tab.

CSV (Comma delimited)
　　The values from each cell are separated in the text file by commas.

Formatted Text
　　The values from each cell are separated by a space.

Lotus 1-2-3 Files

When you open up a Lotus 1-2-3 file, Excel uses the associated formatting file (*.fmt*, *.fm3*, or *.all*) to determine how to format the file within Excel. You need to make sure the format file is stored in the same folder as the Lotus 1-2-3 file, so that Excel can locate it. Otherwise Excel will not apply the correct formatting to the Lotus 1-2-3 file.

Quattro-Pro Files

Excel 2000 can open files from Quattro Pro for Windows 8.0 and all earlier versions of Quattro Pro. If you are running a newer version of Quattro Pro for

Windows you will need to save the file in the 8.0 format, or an earlier format before attempting to open it in Excel.

Excel does not import Quattro Pro graphs when it opens a Quattro Pro file. Therefore, you will need to recreate the desired graph within Excel.

Excel does not run Quattro Pro macros. You can rewrite the macros in Excel using Visual Basic for Applications (VBA), which Excel 2000 uses to create all macros.

Microsoft Works Files

Excel can open Microsoft Works files that were created in version 2.0 or earlier. If you are using Microsoft Works Version 3.0 or later you need to save the file in one of the following formats before attempting to open it in Excel:

- Works for Windows 2.0/Works for DOS

- Excel SS

- Lotus 1-2-3

dBase Files

When saving a workbook to one of the dBase formats, Excel only saves the text and the values within the cells. Any formatting, page layout settings, graphics, objects, or other Excel 2000 features within the workbook are not saved. Also, all rows in the selected range of cells are saved, but the DBF 2 format only saves 32 columns, the DBF 3 format saves 128 columns, and the DBF 4 format saves 256 columns.

If the first row contains text values, they are truncated to 10 characters and used as dBase field names. The data values in the first row determine the data type for each column in dBase.

File → New

When you select File → New, the New dialog displays, providing the option of selecting a template to design your workbook, (see Figure 3-1). To create a new Excel workbook from the New dialog either click on the Workbook icon on the General tab, or one of the custom workbook templates listed on one of the tabs.

When you apply a template to a worksheet, all of the formatting, styles, macros, formulas, etc., that exist in the template file are copied into the new workbook. If you select Ctrl+N or the New button on the toolbar, Excel bypasses the open window and opens up a new workbook using the workbook template from the General tab. For more information about templates, refer to Chapter 2.

You can typically preview a template on the New dialog by clicking once on the corresponding icon. If the preview does not display in the preview pane, the template is blank or the template was not saved with the Save preview picture

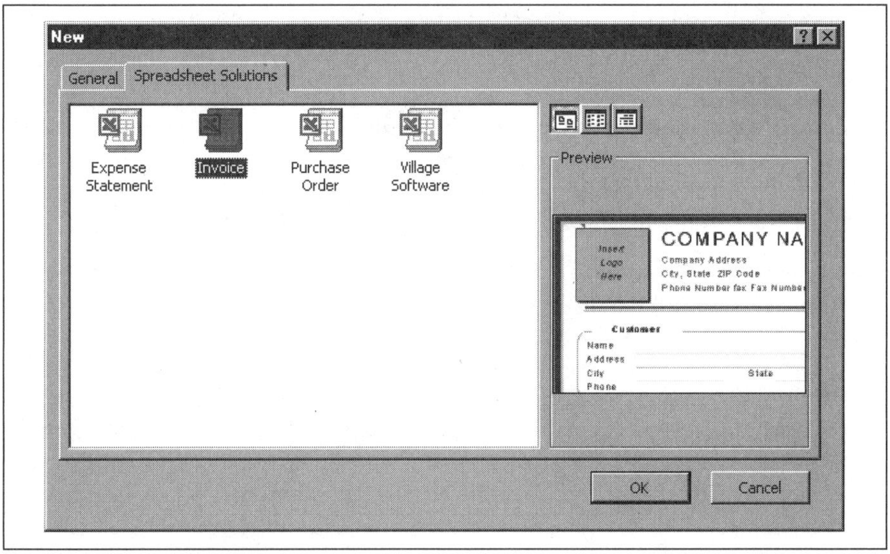

Figure 3-1: The New dialog

option. This option can be selected on the Summary tab of the Properties dialog before saving the template (see "File → Properties").

TIP # 15

Preview Selection for a Template

You can remove the preview for a template from the New dialog by selecting the Properties option for the template and removing the checkmark from the Save Preview Picture checkbox on the Summary tab. If you want to display the preview again you need to open the template file and select the Save Preview Picture checkbox on the Summary tab of File → Properties.

There are three types of templates that exist in Excel: custom workbook templates, default workbook templates, and default worksheet templates.

Custom workbook templates are any workbooks that have been saved as templates (*.xlt*) and contain custom formatting and formulas. Excel provides some custom templates that you can use such as the Invoice template, which helps you create a generic invoice. These templates are available on the Spreadsheet Solutions tab.

Excel uses default system settings to create the Workbook template option that displays on the General tab. By default that template file does not exist. You can override the default setting by creating a custom template called *book.xlt* and placing it in the *XLStart* folder. If the *book.xlt* template exists, it is used whenever the New button is selected on the toolbar, or whenever you select the Workbook option on the General tab of the New dialog. To reset the settings to use the system default, simply remove the template from the folder. By creating the *book.xlt* template you can specify fonts, formatting, borders, macros, and so on to use for any new workbooks. For example, if you want all your workbooks to contain four worksheets and to have Times Roman as the default font, create a template with those settings.

To create a workbook using the *book.xlt* template, select the New button on the Standard toolbar. This toolbar option creates a workbook based only on the settings for the *book.xlt* template. If you want to create a workbook using a custom template, select the New option in the File menu or create your own custom new button for a template as described in Chapter 8, *Tools*.

The default worksheet template is used whenever you select Insert → Worksheet. It specifies the look of the worksheet that is added to the workbook. Just like the default workbook template, the default worksheet template does not exist by default on your system. Excel uses default settings to create a blank worksheet. You can design a template called *sheet.xlt* and place it in the *XLStart* folder. If this template exists, it will be used whenever Insert → Worksheet is selected. This template does not display on the New dialog; the only way to see it is to use Windows Explorer. To reset the settings so that a blank worksheet is added, simply remove the template from the folder.

The *sheet.xlt* template can contain multiple pages. Each time you select Insert → Worksheet, the entire contents of the template are inserted into the current workbook. In other words, if *sheet.xlt* contains four pages, then four pages are added to your workbook.

Excel looks for templates in the following locations:

- *C:\windows\Profiles\user_name\Application Data\Microsoft\Templates*

- The *XLStart* folder, typically located in *C:\windows\Profiles\user_name\ Application Data\Microsoft\Excel\XLStart*

- The location you specified at Tools → Options → General tab

TIP # 16

Locating a Saved Template

If you don't find a previously saved template listed on the New dialog box, it was not saved in the appropriate location. Refer to the list of template locations above.

File → Open

This option is typically used to open a workbook, although there are several types of files that can be opened within Excel. When you select File → Open, the Open button, or Ctrl+O, the Open dialog (shown in Figure 3-2) displays the workbooks in your default Office folder (found at Tools → Options → File Locations) or the last folder you opened a workbook from during this session.

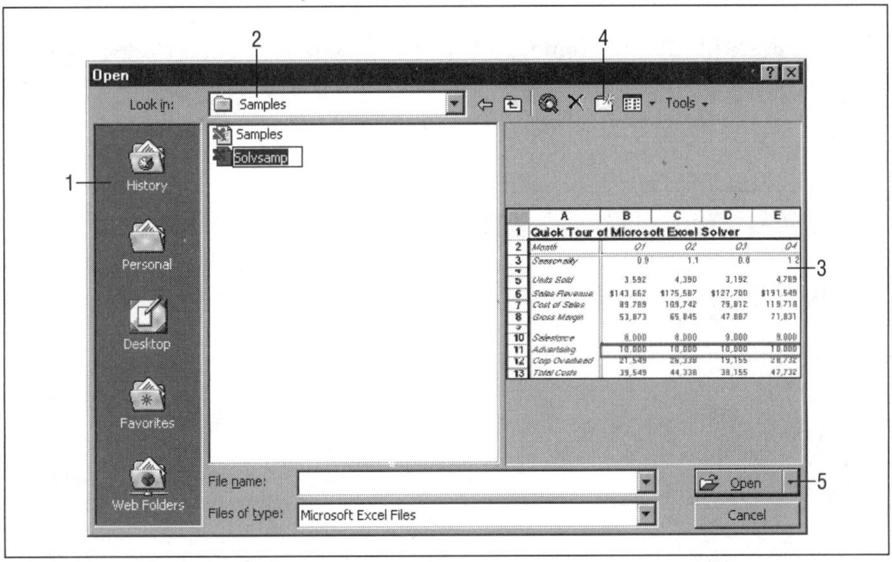

Figure 3-2: The Open dialog

1. *Places Bar.* One new feature added by Microsoft to Office 2000 is the addition of the Places Bar on the left side of the Open dialog. This bar contains short-cuts to the following locations: History, My Documents (renamed in Figure 3-2 as Personal), Desktop, Favorites, and Web Folders.

> **NOTE** *Excel does not provide an option for modifying the contents of the Places Bar. However, Microsoft has released a utility called WOPR 2000 PlaceBar Customizer that provides the ability to customize the contents of the PlaceBar for all of your Microsoft Office applications. The easiest way to find this application is to select Help → Office on the Web and then select Downloads on the web site that opens. Of course, you need to be connected to the Internet before selecting this option. At the time this book was written, the URL for the control was http://officeupdate.microsoft.com/2000/downloadDetails/PlaceBar.htm.*

2. *Look In field.* This field indicates the folder location where you want to look for the workbook, or other file type you want to open. To see a list of the available folders, select the Down Arrow button; the contents display in the file list.

3. *Preview of Selected File.* This section displays a preview of the highlighted file, if available. The preview will not display under the following circumstances:

   – The file is blank.

   – The file is not an Excel workbook, template, or chart.

   – The file was saved with a format of Excel that does not support previews.

   – The file was saved without selecting the Save Preview Picture checkbox on the Summary tab of File → Properties.

4. *Tools.* The Tools menu provides useful commands for printing, deleting, and renaming a file directly from the Open dialog. Also, if you don't know the location of the file you want to open, you can select the Find option and search for it based on certain criteria. When you select Tools → Find, the Find dialog displays, as shown in Figure 3-3.

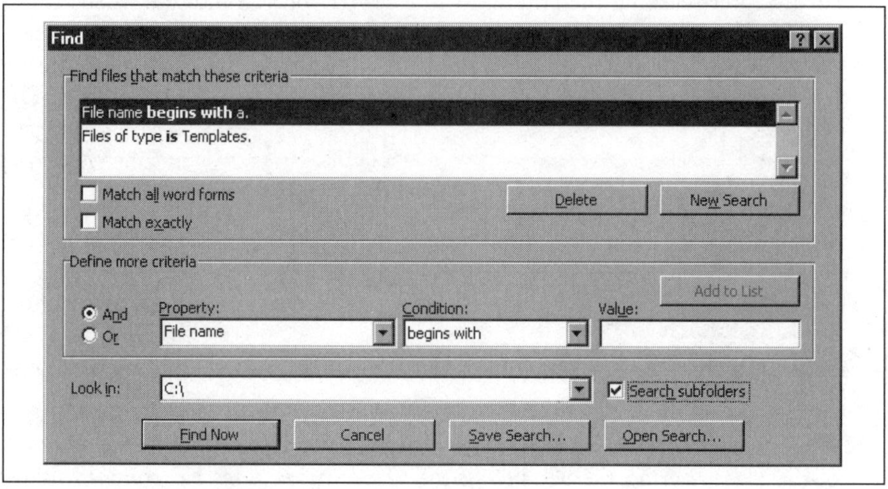

Figure 3-3: The Find dialog

The Find dialog is divided into three different sections. The top window contains the specific criteria that should be used to search for the file you want to locate. The criteria for the search are specified in the "Define more criteria" section. In Figure 3-3, Excel will locate all template files on the *C:* drive that start with *a*.

Specifying the criteria for the search can seem a little confusing at first, but once you create the criteria statement, you select the "Add to List" button to add it to the window at the top of the dialog. There are only four things you need to keep in mind:

– Select the property that you want to use for the search. Typically this is the file name or type, but you can even search based upon the number of characters in the file.

– Select the condition that you want to use for the search. The conditions that are available in the list vary based upon the property selected. For example, if you select Files of Type for the property, the Condition field lists various file types to select from.

– Depending upon the values selected for the Property and Conditions fields, you may need to specify a value. For example, if you want to find all workbooks that start with A, you would place an A in the Value field.

– Specify whether the new criteria should be combined with the existing search criteria (the And radio button), meaning that the file must meet this criterion along with the existing criteria. If you select the Or radio button, the criteria will be used independent of the current criteria, meaning that Excel will locate all files that meet this criterion or the existing criteria.

Finally, after selecting the criteria for the search you can indicate where Excel looks for the files. The Find option allows you to look for files on any of the drives on your computer. If you want to search multiple drives simultaneously, you can type the drives separated by semicolons in the "Find In" field, for example: *C:\;D:\.* Unfortunately you cannot select a network drive to search with the Find dialog. If you need to search on the network, use the Windows Find option available on the Start menu.

 Once you have created your search criterion, you can save it for future use by selecting the Save Search button. The next time you select the Find option, simply select the Open Search button and select the desired search option from the list.

5. *Open.* There are four different ways you can open a file in Excel, depending upon the actual file type. To select a method, other than opening the original, select the down arrow button next to the Open button.

Open Original
Opens the existing copy of the workbook for modifications.

Open Read-Only
Opens the file as read-only to eliminate modifications to the original. It can still be modified and saved under a different name using the Save As option.

 If you attempt to open a file that is being used by another user on a LAN you will get a "Network File in Use" message box. You have the option of opening the file as Read-Only or waiting for the other user to finish using the file. If you open the document as read-only you will not be able to save changes in the original document; but you can save changes to the worksheet under a different name by selecting the Save As option.

Open as Copy
Opening a file as a copy creates a new copy of the selected file in the same folder where the original file resides. This option ensures that modifications are not made to the original file by naming the copied file *Copy of filename.*

Open in Browser
This option is available when you have selected an HTML (*.htm*) file in the list. This opens the file up in your default browser.

Switch the Way Excel Opens

If you find that you have a workbook or template that you always use in Excel, you can set up a shortcut that always opens up that specific file whenever you open Excel. To do this, you need to create an Excel shortcut that uses a switch. A switch is just a code that is added to the end of the file path in a shortcut that gives Excel specific instructions on how to open.

First you need to create a shortcut for Excel. The easiest way to do this is to locate the *excel.exe* program with the Windows Explorer and select the Create Shortcut option. Once you create your shortcut you need to select File → Properties for the shortcut icon and modify the Target field on the Shortcut tab to include one of the following switches. The switch should be placed after the path by inserting a space and then the desired switch. For example, to open Excel without a default workbook, the Target field would read: "C:\Program Files\Microsoft Office\Office\EXCEL.EXE" /e.

- /e opens Excel without displaying the startup screen and without loading a default workbook.

- /r *path\file name* opens the specified workbook as read-only.

- /p *path\folder name* specifies the working folder. This is the folder that is opened first when you attempt to open or save workbooks.

- *path\file name* opens a specific folder or template up within Excel. If you have a couple of different templates that you frequently use you can create a separate shortcut that calls each template.

Microsoft Office 2000 does not allow you to modify the properties of the shortcuts that are created on your system when you install Office. But you can create as many custom shortcuts as desired.

TIP # 17
Opening Several Files in a Folder at Once

There are two ways to do this: To select a group of files, hold down the Shift key while you click on the first file and then click on the last file in the group. Or to select multiple files (at different locations within the list), hold down the Ctrl key and click on each file you want to open.

File → Close

This option closes the currently open workbook. If any modifications have been made, a message box displays asking if you want to save the workbook before closing. If you have multiple workbooks open, the Close command only closes the active workbook (the one open in the window).

A quick method for closing a workbook is to select the Close Window icon on the menu bar. When you select this icon Excel will make sure all the changes have been saved before closing. Be careful about selecting the correct Close Window icon. There is also one on the Title bar, but if you select this one the program is closed along with any other open workbooks.

As discussed in Chapter 1, Excel 2000 uses the Single Document Interface (SDI), so each time you open up a file in Excel it is opened in a new window. By the same token, when closing a workbook, that window closes, but Excel remains running until all Excel workbooks are closed.

File Menu

TIP # 18

Closing Several Workbooks at Once

To close all Excel workbooks simultaneously, hold down the Shift key before selecting the File menu and select the Close All option. The Close All option only displays on the File menu if you hold down the Shift key before selecting the menu.

File → Save

The File → Save option saves the currently selected workbook. If the workbook has not been previously saved, you will be prompted to specify a name and location for the workbook when you select File → Save, the Save button, or Ctrl+S.

Remember, someone running Excel 5.0/95 or earlier will not be able to open any workbooks saved in the Excel 97–2000 format. If you want to give a copy of the workbook to another user, first verify the format that the workbook is saved in by selecting the File → Save As option.

TIP # 19

Save Often

To eliminate the aggravation of lost data, remember to save often. There is nothing more frustrating than spending two hours entering data into a worksheet only to have the power go out. To ensure that your workbook gets saved automatically you can also set the Tools → AutoSave option. The AutoSave option is an Add-in that comes along with Excel. It can be loaded by selecting the AutoSave Add-In on Tools → Add-Ins. (Refer to Chapter 8).

File → Save As

This option saves the currently selected workbook in the specified format, name, and location. When you select it, the Save As dialog displays your default Office folder or the last folder in which you saved or opened a workbook. To save the workbook for use with another program, or to give it to a user running an earlier version of Excel, make sure you select the appropriate file format.

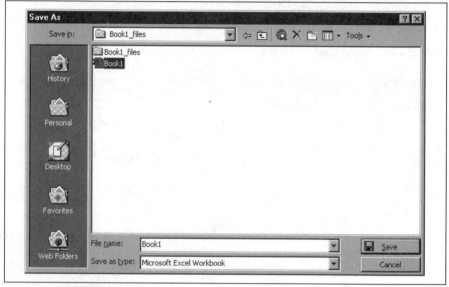

Figure 3-4: The Save As dialog

The only way to ensure all the formatting of the document is saved is to select the Microsoft Excel Workbook option. Otherwise you will lose any Excel 97–2000 features that have been added to the workbook.

When you select *.xlt* from the drop-down list on the Save As dialog to save a workbook as a template, Excel takes you to the Templates folder. This folder is located at *C:\windows\Profiles\user_name\Application Data\Microsoft\Templates*. (See File → New for more information about template locations.) Make sure you save the template in this folder so Excel will display it as an option on the New dialog when you select File → New to create a new workbook.

NOTE *Depending on the file type selected, you may only be able to save the first worksheet in a workbook. If this is the case, Excel displays a message box indicating that only the first worksheet in your workbook will be saved in the selected format.*

If you have created a workbook with sensitive data, you should consider password protecting it. Select the Tools option on the Save As Window and then select

General Options. You can select one password for opening the file and another for making modifications. Make sure you use a password that is easy to remember, such as the name of your first pet. Microsoft does not provide an easy way to recover your password. If you forget your password, there are several different utilities available on the Internet that claim to be able to recover a lost password. A couple of common sites are *http://www.accessdata.com* and *http://www.lostpassword.com*.

TIP # 20

Making Frequently Used Options Available

If you have options you want to use globally, you can save them in the global template book.xlt. For example, you can create a template containing the options you want to use regularly, such as the options on the Edit tab of Tools → Options.

File Menu

File → Save As Web Page

The File → Save As Web Page option saves the current workbook as a web page. This option is the same as selecting the Save As option and then selecting Web Page as the type.

To save a worksheet as a web page make sure you select the Web Page option in the Save as Type field. This changes the options on the Save As dialog box. Select the Publish button to display the Publish as Web Page dialog, as shown in Figure 3-5. This dialog provides more capability for customizing the web page than the options found on the Save As dialog.

1. *Items to publish.* The currently selected range of cells is indicated in this section. Typically you select the range of cells you want to publish prior to selecting the Save as Web Page option. If you selected a range of cells, the Choose field will contain the value "Range of cells" and the cell range will be specified in the format =sheetname!range, as shown in Figure 3-6. To quickly specify or change the range click on the Collapse Dialog button next to this field to temporarily close the Publish as Web Page dialog and select the desired range of cells. Keep in mind you cannot publish portions of worksheets that contain an interactive chart. If you want to save the chart for a web site, it must be selected and saved separately.

   You can also choose to publish the contents of a worksheet within the current workbook by selecting the worksheet name from the menu that displays when you select the down arrow next to the Collapse field.

TIP # 21

Publishing Selected Areas of a Worksheet

If you select a worksheet, Excel will only publish the print area of the selected worksheet. If a print area is not defined, all cells that contain values will be published.

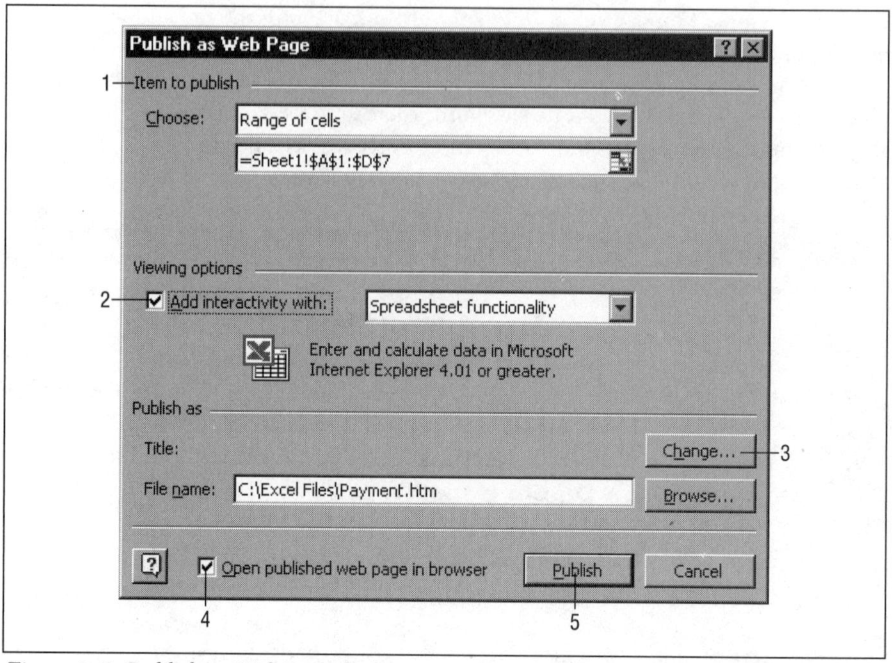

Figure 3-5: Publish as Web Page dialog

2. *Add interactivity with.* Selecting this option gives users the ability to select the way they view the data on the web page. After selecting this option, you need to select the type of interactivity you want to add from the drop-down list. If you want the data to be static, make sure the checkbox is not selected.

3. *Change.* Select this button to specify the title for your web page. This name also appears at the top of the web browser when you view the web page.

4. *Open published web page in browser.* Select this checkbox if you want to immediately view the new web page in your default browser after selecting the Publish button.

5. *Publish.* Once you have specified the desired options, select this button to create the web page using the options specified on the dialog.

WARNING

Although the option is available, Excel is not the best program to use for modifying an HTML file. Since Excel is a spreadsheet program, it does not provide the tools for manipulating HTML code found in web site packages, such as Microsoft FrontPage. Also, when you open an HTML file within Excel all information in the file is placed in the first column. And Excel will not open an HTML file that contains frames.

HTML File Ins and Outs

When you save a workbook as a web page, it is saved in a format that can be viewed by any web browser. Creating a web page allows you to give your workbook to basically anyone with Internet access, because they will have some type of web browser. The downside comes in the limitations of the web page compared to an Excel workbook file.

When you save the workbook as a web page, the text in each column is saved out exactly as it appears in the Excel window. In other words, if the text in a cell is cut off because the column is not wide enough, the text will display cut off on the web page; in fact, the web page will not even know about the remaining contents of the cell. Since the HTML page is just one large page, you do not see the gridlines that normally separate cell values within Excel. To compensate for the lack of gridlines, Excel makes sure there is space between each cell value.

If your workbook contains macros, charts, and/or pivot tables Excel actually creates supporting files to handle those elements. The supporting files are stored in a subdirectory within the directory where you store the HTML file. The subdirectory is named to correspond with the HTML file. For example, if you named the HTML file "Sales Figures" the subdirectory would be named "Sales Figures Files." Make sure that if you give the HTML file to another user, you remember to send the subdirectory.

If you decide to save your workbook as an interactive HTML file, the HTML file does begin to resemble the Excel environment by allowing data to be modified. You will want to add the interactivity to your HTML page if your workbook contains PivotTables and charts that you want to have modified.

File → Save Workspace

The File → Save Workspace option allows you to save the necessary information about all the currently opened workbooks. This lets you open workbooks all at once in the future by simply opening the desired workspace. The workspace files have the extension of *.xlw.* When Excel saves the workspace it is only saving information about the specific workbooks, such as the file name and locations; it does not save the actual workbooks. Make sure you save any changes to the workbooks in the specific workbooks.

Be careful not to move a workspace or the corresponding workbook files. Excel looks for the workbooks in the same locations where the workspace was created. If Excel is unable to locate the workbook files, you will get an error message when you attempt to open the workspace.

TIP # 22

Benefits of the XLStart Folder

To set the same workbooks to always open when you launch Excel, save your work-space file in the XLStart folder. This folder is located in your Office folder. See Chapter 2, for details about using the XLStart folder.

File → Web Page Preview

The File → Web Page Preview option displays the contents of the currently selected worksheet in your default web browser. The worksheet contents are displayed as static text on the browser. This is useful for previewing the information.

File → Page Setup

The File → Page Setup option sets the various options related to how the worksheet is printed and viewed from Excel. The Page Setup dialog contains four different tabs for specifying the print options, as shown in Figure 3-6. The Print and Print Preview buttons on the Page Setup dialog, for example, perform the same results as selecting File → Print or File → Print Preview. Options allows you to customize settings for your specific printer, such as whether to print in duplex mode.

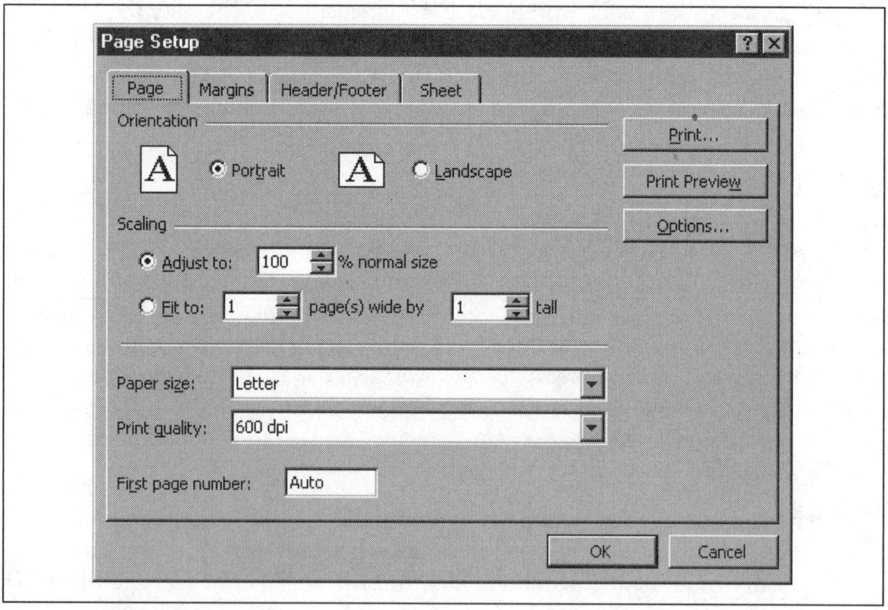

Figure 3-6: Page Setup dialog

Page Tab

The Page tab, shown in Figure 3-6 indicates the orientation, scaling, paper size, print quality, and first page number for printing the workbook. By scaling the worksheet you can resize (enlarge or shrink) it proportionally to change the amount that prints on each sheet of paper. Scaling can range from 10% to 400% of the normal size of the worksheet.

Make sure the appropriate paper size and print quality are selected for your document. The selections available for each option are based on the specific capabilities of the currently selected printer.

TIP # 23

Making the Worksheet Fit the Paper

If you want to make sure your worksheet is only one page wide, but are not concerned about the length, you can specify 1 for the "page(s) wide" of the "Fit to" option and leave the "tall" field blank. Do this for any width you want; Excel will automatically scale the printout so that it uses the appropriate number of pages.

Margins Tab

This tab specifies the size of all margins on the page. Keep in mind that each printer has its own minimum margin size and even though you may specify a smaller margin, the printer will maintain the minimums. For example, if you want a 1/4" margin but the minimum is 1/2" for you printer, you will get a 1/2" margin. Check the printer documentation to find out what the minimum size is for margins. As a general rule, printers with ink cartridges allow wider margins than laser printers.

Header/Footer Tab

The Header/Footer tab allows you to select headers and footers for your document. You can select one of the default headers or footers from the list by clicking on the down arrow button next to the field. Excel creates the default headers based on the information gathered during the install (user name, company name, etc.) and the name of the document. You can also select the Custom Header and Custom Footer buttons and design a custom header and/or footer. For more information refer to View → Header/Footer in Chapter 5, *View*.

Sheet Tab

The Sheet tab, shown in Figure 3-7, allows you to specify the actual portions of the sheet that are printed. You can also specify a row and a column that appear on each page of the printout. For example, if the first row contained the headings, those headings would be printed on each of the pages, even if the page did not include page one.

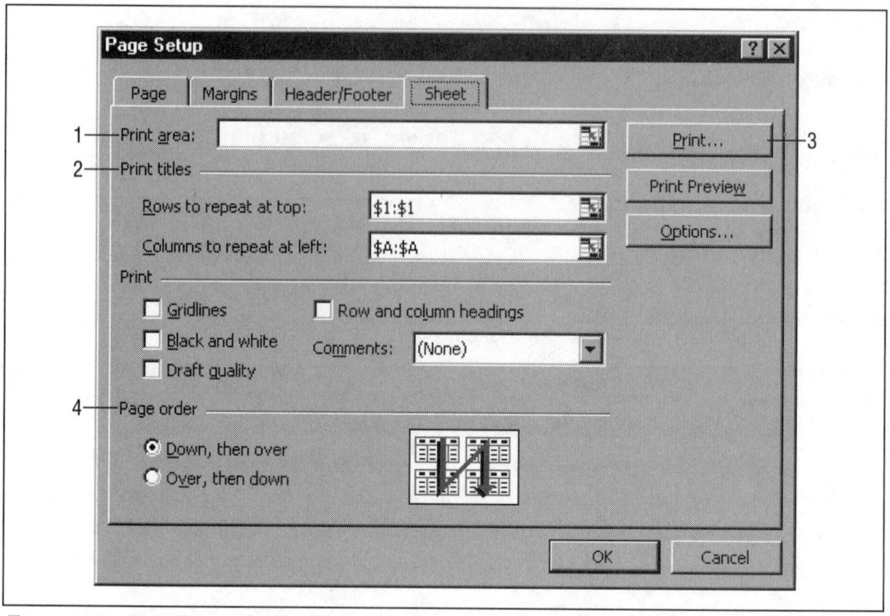

Figure 3-7: Page Setup dialog sheet tab

1. *Print area.* The Print area field indicates the portion of the worksheet that was set as the print area using File → Print Area prior to selecting the Page Setup option. (If blank, a print area has not been specified). To change the print area, either type the changes in the field or click on the Collapse Dialog button to minimize the Page Setup dialog and then drag the cursor across the range of cells in the worksheet that you want to print. When you have selected the desired cells, click on the button again to redisplay the dialog.

2. *Print titles.* Typically when a worksheet is created, the first row and first column contain descriptive information about the contents of the worksheet. If your worksheet prints out on more than one page, it can be confusing to interpret the data without these titles. By using the fields in the Print Titles section, you can select these title areas so they print on all pages. To select the column or row to be repeated, click on the Collapse Dialog button to minimize the Page Setup dialog and then drag the cursor to select the columns or rows in the worksheet that you want to print. When you have selected the desired cells, click on the button again to redisplay the dialog.

TIP # 24

Specifying the Print Title Cells on the Page Setup Dialog

The rows you select for the titles must start at the top of the worksheet, and the columns need to start at the left (Column A). You cannot select columns or rows in the middle of the worksheet.

---

3. *Print.* These options allow you to customize the way the workbook prints by selecting gridlines, black and white, draft quality printout, display of row and column headings, and printing of comments. If you choose to print a draft quality version of your document, Excel does not print embedded charts, drawing objects, cell gridlines, or borders on the worksheet.

 Printing row and column headings is different than printing print titles. The row and column headings are the letters that appear across the top of the worksheet in the window, and the numbers that appear down the left side. These can be very useful for referencing the location of the information within the worksheet.

4. *Page order.* As Excel prints a worksheet only a certain number of rows and columns will fit on each sheet of paper. This is all determined by printer settings and the settings you have indicated on the Page Setup dialog. You can indicate the order you want Excel to follow when printing the worksheet information by selecting one of the radio buttons. For example, if you select the "Over then down" radio button Excel will print all of the information horizontally across the worksheet and then down to the next section.

File → Print Area

The File → Print Area option sets and clears the portion of the worksheet that should be printed when you select the Print option. As a default, Excel defines a print area to fit on one sheet of paper based on the currently selected printer. If you do not define a custom print area, Excel will print the entire contents of the worksheet based on the setting defined on the tabs at File → Page Setup.

Set Print Area

Marks the selected area of the worksheet as the only portion that should print when you select the File → Print option. Whatever portion of the worksheet that is highlighted when you select the File → Print Area → Set Print Area option becomes the new print area. If you mark a print area that is too large for one sheet of paper, Excel will print the remaining selection on additional sheets of paper as needed. Excel prints the selection using the print order specified on the Sheet tab of File → Page Setup. To modify the size of the print area, select the View → Page Break Preview option.

Clear Print Area

Eliminates the currently selected print area. Excel uses the current page size as the print area if you print the worksheet without marking the print area.

File → Print Preview

The File → Print Preview option can save you a lot of frustration during the print process. Since Excel allows you to create extremely large worksheets, you can end up using an excessive amount of paper when you decide to print. This option provides the ability to preview the selected printer output prior to printing, as shown in Figure 3-8. The Print Preview dialog also displays when you select the Print Preview button from the Standard toolbar. To modify the print area, select the Page Break Preview button. It provides the same capability as the View → Page Break Preview.

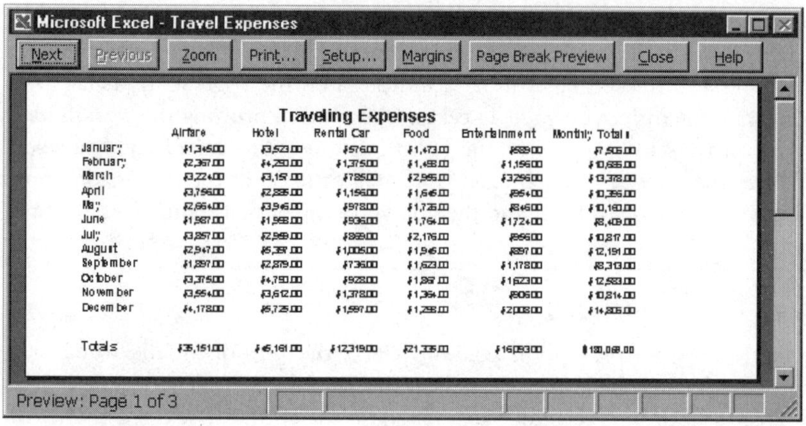

Figure 3-8: Print Preview

Using the Print Preview option gives you access to the various options you need to modify the way your printout looks directly from the preview by selecting the corresponding buttons. You can determine the number of pages that will be printed by looking at the Status Bar at the bottom of the window. It also indicates the currently displayed page number. You can scroll through the pages by selecting the Next and Previous buttons or using the Page Up and Page Down buttons. The Margins button provides the ability to adjust the margin and column sizes for the printout. Any changes made on a page will affect all pages of the print selection. In other words, if you make column A wider on page 1, all of the pages that contain that same column A will print at the specified width. To adjust margins, click on the line and drag it to the desired location. To modify column or row width, click on the corresponding column or row marker and drag it to the desired width. The Print button provides the same capability as selecting File → Print. The Setup button displays the Print Setup dialog; this option is also available by selecting File → Print Setup.

TIP # 25

Customizing Margins in Print Preview

The Margins button is a great way to visually adjust the margins. When you select it, Excel draws dotted lines indicating the location of the current print margins. You can adjust them by clicking on one and dragging it. Keep in mind there is not an undo command during Print Preview, so you cannot undo any changes you make. It is probably a good idea to check the actual margins settings by selecting the Setup button and looking at the Margins tab. That way if you want to return to the original margin settings, you can manually specify them on that tab.

File → Print

The File → Print option prints the selected portion of the workbook, based on your selection in the Print Range section of the Print dialog. Just like Page Setup, the Print dialog, shown in Figure 3-9, provides additional selections that can be made to customize your output. Keep in mind, if you select the Print button on the Standard toolbar, the worksheet is sent to the printer without displaying the Print dialog.

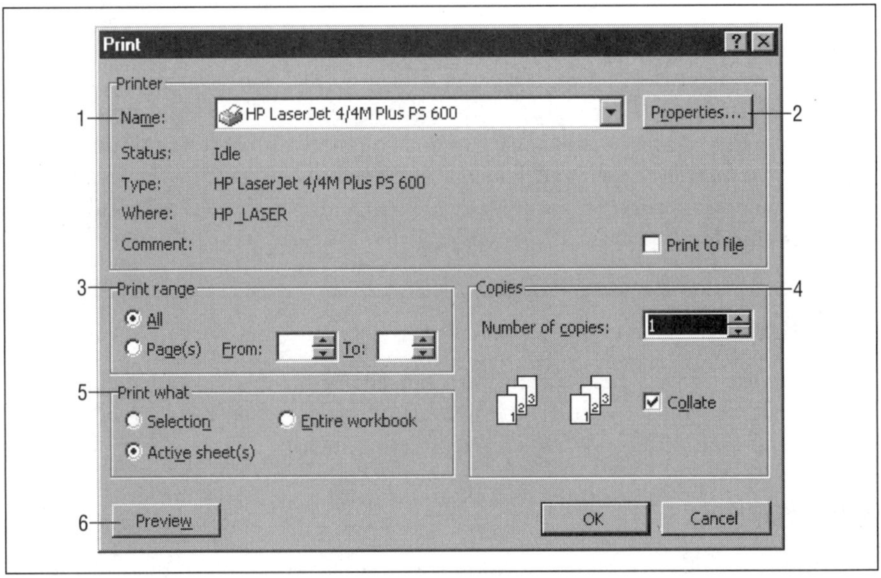

Figure 3-9: Print dialog

1. *Name.* This field indicates the name of the currently selected printer. If you have the ability to print to multiple printers from you computer, you can select the Down Arrow button and highlight the desired printer. Keep in mind that each printer has its own settings when it comes to margins; therefore, selecting

a different printer could change the location of the page breaks if your page is larger than the selected printer can print. It is recommended that you select the Preview button before printing to ensure that the page layout is still acceptable.

2. *Properties.* The Properties button displays a custom properties page for the selected printer. This is where you select options like duplexing, if your printer provides that option.

3. *Print range.* These fields allow you to indicate whether the entire print area should print, or only specific pages. Since you typically indicate a print area prior to selecting the Print option, you will normally just select the All radio button. If you need to reprint specific pages, select the Pages radio button and indicate the page numbers in the From and To fields.

4. *Copies.* The "Number of Copies" field indicates the number of copies that should be printed. By default, Excel only prints one copy of your selection. To print multiple copies, select the Collate checkbox so the copies will be printed out in the correct order (pages 1–4, etc.)

5. *Print what.* Select a radio button to indicate whether you want to print your selected print area on the active worksheet, all worksheets that contain print areas, or all worksheets in the workbook that contain data. Each time a new worksheet is printed it is printed on a new page. If you have a chart selected, you will see Active Chart listed as one of the radio buttons.

6. *Preview.* Select the Preview button to display a preview of the printout with the appropriate page breaks. This is the same as selecting File → Print Preview. You can use this option to adjust margins and column widths before printing. If you have not previously selected File → Print Preview, I would highly recommend selecting this button to ensure you are going to get the desired results when your selection is printed.

File → Send To

The following options are available with the File → Send To command: you can either email the worksheet, transfer it to a shared folder, route it to a list of users, or provide it to users during a Microsoft NetMeeting session.

Mail Recipient

This option provides the ability to either send a copy of the worksheet as an HTML formatted message, or as an attachment to the message. When you select this option, a dialog appears allowing you to select the radio button that indicates how you want the message sent. Sending the a copy of the worksheet as part of the message is a useful method for transferring information to users who do not have Excel installed on their machine, as long as the recipient's email software can handle HTML. When you select this option the selected worksheet, or portion of a worksheet, will take up the body of the message. Note that the recipient must be using an email program that allows him to view HTML formatted messages. This feature is available with the current version of Microsoft Outlook

Once you select the "Send the current sheet as the message body" option, select Mail Recipient again during the session, Excel assumes you want to send the attachment in the message body again. It does not show the email dialog again during the session. If you decide you want to send it as an attachment, select the Mail Recipient (as Attachment) option. Do not select the Mail Recipient option if you want to send the workbook as an attachment in an email message. It is much faster to select the Mail Recipient (as Attachment) option.

TIP # 26

Deciding How to Send a Worksheet

If you send the worksheet as the body of a message, the recipient can only view the information. Any formulas that were created in the workbook are not available in the HTML copy. Also, the recipient will not be able to manipulate the information in any form, such as filtering, sorting, etc.

Mail Recipient (as Attachment)

This option sends the selected workbook as an email attachment. When you select this option, your default email program is loaded and a new message is created with the desired workbook inserted as an attachment.

The steps for sending the message vary depending upon which email package you are using. Typically, you simply need to specify the recipient(s), add any desired text, and select the appropriate option for sending the message.

WARNING

If the recipient of the message is using Office 5.0/95, or an earlier version, any formatting within the workbook will be lost (unless saved in this format). You may want to consider sending the message as part of the body of the email using the Mail Recipient option. If you are using a web-based email package, such as Hotmail, this option will not work properly. To send a workbook as an attachment, save the workbook, then open your email browser, and include the file as an attachment.

Routing Recipient

Select this option if you want the workbook to be reviewed by multiple recipients. Selecting this option as opposed to the Mail Recipient option allows you to have the workbook routed to one person at a time with each able to make her desired comments and to have the comments passed on to the next recipient (along with the workbook attachment). This option functions much like the routing envelopes still used in many corporations to pass information from one person to the next.

To route the message to different individuals, one after another, you need to make sure the email addresses are listed in the appropriate order in the To field found on the Routing Slip dialog shown in Figure 3-10. If you select the "One after another" radio button, Outlook will route the message containing the workbook to the first person on your list. Once that person completes her review, the workbook along with any comment from the first person is forwarded onto the next person. This process continues until everyone on your list has reviewed the workbook.

If you select the "All at once" radio button, the message will be sent to all recipients simultaneously. This is basically the same as sending an email message to multiple recipients.

You can also have the message returned to you with everyone's comments by selecting the "Return when done" checkbox. If you sent the message to all recipients simultaneously you will receive a return message from each recipient on your list. Otherwise, you will receive the message after all other recipients review it.

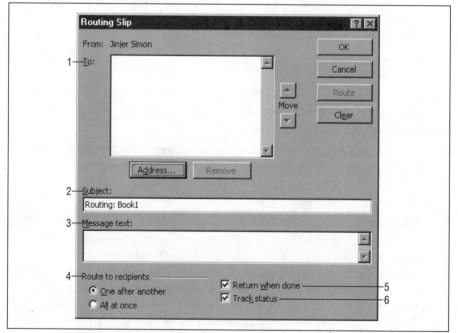

Figure 3-10: The Routing Slip dialog

1. *To.* This field indicates the list of recipients for the workbook. To add a recipient, select the Address button and highlight the desired addresses. You can use the Move arrows to indicate the appropriate order for receiving the workbook. In other words, the first person on the list is going to be the first one to receive the message, if you have indicated you want the message routed to each person one after another (see #4).

2. *Subject.* Excel creates a default subject that specifies the workbook name, but you can change this easily to something more specific.

3. *Message text.* Indicate any type of message or instructions that you want placed in the body of the message.

4. *Route to recipients.* Select the "One after another" radio button if you want the message to be sent to the first recipient on your list and then forward on to the next recipient when that person finishes. This process continues until all recipients have received the message.

   If you select the "All at once" radio button it is sent to everyone in the list simultaneously. This is essentially the same thing as using the Mail Recipient options and sending it to several different people. The only difference is that you can track the message with this option and can also have the message returned when each recipient has finished reading it.

5. *Return when done.* This option returns the message to you after the recipients on the list have read it. This is especially useful if you are expecting changes to be made to your workbook by the recipients.

6. *Track status.* This option keeps track of the workbooks status. Each time the message is routed to the next recipient you receive an email message indicating its status. This allows you to quickly determine the location of the message.

Exchange Folder

If you are working with Microsoft Exchange, you have the option of placing the selected workbook in a shared folder that other people can access. When you select this option you need to select the folder where the workbook should be placed. Keep in mind you must have write access for the folder in order to copy into it.

TIP # 27

Sharing a Workbook When Using Exchange

Before copying a workbook to the folder make sure those people you want to access the workbook also have access to the selected Exchange folder. Keep in mind, everyone with access to that folder will be able to access your workbook. However, if you place a shared workbook into an Exchange folder the workbook will no longer be shared.

Online Meeting Participant

You can select the Online Meeting Participant option to send a copy of the workbook to all participants in a current NetMeeting discussion. Remember, everyone participating will receive a copy. Only the host of the NetMeeting can send workbooks to the other participants. If you are a participant in the meeting, you need to use the options within NetMeeting for sending files to send the workbook to the other participants.

File → Properties

The File → Properties option keeps track of the file size and location information, who created the file, when the file was last modified, etc. This information is available on five different tabs as shown in Figure 3-11.

General Tab

The General tab provides information about the file, such as filename, location, size, when the file was created, when it was last accessed, and attributes such as being read-only. The information that displays on this tab is read-only and cannot be modified.

 If you want to change one of the attributes listed for the file, run Windows Explorer, locate the desired file and select the File → Properties option. You will be able to change the attributes for the file (Read-only, Archive, Compressed, and Hidden) by clicking on the desired checkboxes. You can select any of the checkboxes, with the exception of the System checkbox; which is used to indicate files required by your operating system. The Read-only attribute makes the file read-only so it cannot be modified or deleted. If you select the Hidden attribute, you must know the exact name of the file in order to open it; the file will not be listed when you view the contents of the folder.

Summary Tab

This tab provides descriptive information about the file, as shown in Figure 3-11. By filling out this information you provide more information about the file. This is useful when trying to determine which file you want to open on the Open dialog; it can also be used as search criteria when you are trying to locate the desired file.

There are two fields on the Summary tab that are quite useful: "Hyperlink base" and "Save preview picture." If you intend to link to other documents either on your machine, a network machine, or web server, you can specify the base address for the files in the Hyperlink base field. For example, if the files located in *C:\Excel Files\ Budget* specify that base address in the Hyperlink base field, then when you link to each document in your workbook you only need to specify the document name. If the filename is *Jan99* your link would be to *Jan99.xls* instead of *C:\Excel Files\ Budget\Jan99.xls*. See Chapter 6, *Insert*.

In order to see a preview of the workbook from the Open or New dialogs, you need to select the "Save preview picture" checkbox. This creates a snapshot of the first

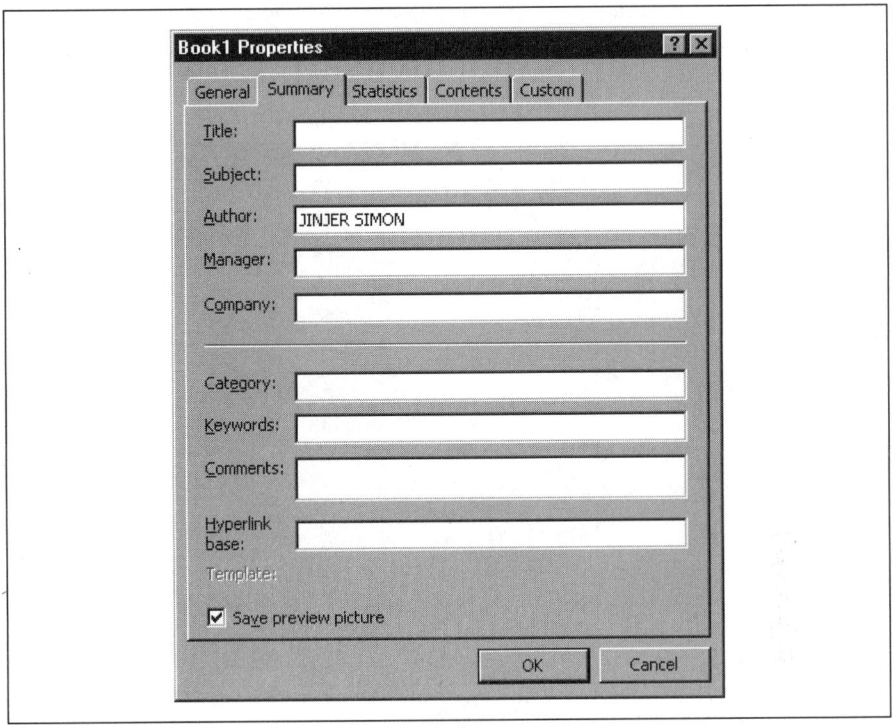

Figure 3-11: Summary tab on Properties dialog

page of the workbook. If you select this option it will slightly increase the size of the file to allow for storage of the snapshot.

Statistics Tab

The Statistics tab provides useful statistics about the file such as when it was last modified or accessed, who saved it last, the number of revisions made to the file, and the amount of time that has been spent working on the document.

Contents Tab

The Contents tab describes the contents of the file. If the file contains worksheets, the name of each worksheet is listed.

Custom Tab

The Custom tab provides the ability to add custom properties for the file. You can either use the list of predefined variables or type your own variable name in the Name field. The most useful option is the ability to show a link to a named field in your workbook. For example, if your worksheet contains several totals, you can create custom links to those fields so that the values can be viewed by looking at the File

Properties without opening the document, as shown in Figure 3-12. Name the field using Insert → Name, then on the Custom tab create a name for the property, select the Link to Content checkbox, and select the name of the field in the Source field.

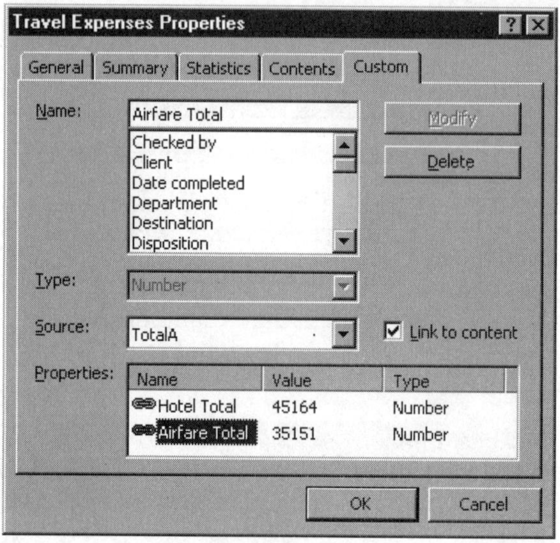

Figure 3-12: Custom Tab of Properties dialog

File → 1–4

By default Excel remembers the last four files you opened and lists them on the File menu between the Properties and Exit options, numbered 1 to 4. However, Excel only keeps track of the file location when you opened the file. If you have moved or deleted the file since you last opened it, Excel will not be able to locate it from this list. You will need to use the File → Open option to locate the file.

> **NOTE** *You can have Excel keep track of a maximum of nine recently opened files. To change the number of recently opened files that Excel remembers click on the General Tab of Tools → Options → General and then change the value in the "Recently used file" list field.*

File → Exit

The File → Exit option closes Excel and any open workbooks. If there are changes to a workbook that have not been saved, a message box prompts you to save the files before closing. You can also select the Close Window icon in the upper-right corner of the Excel window. This option works the same as selecting File → Exit.

Chapter 4

Edit

The Edit menu provides several different options for moving, locating, and modifying the contents of your worksheets. Each of these options is covered in detail within this chapter.

You can use the Edit → Links and Edit → Object options to work with OLE objects (Object Linking and Embedding) that have been inserted or linked to within your worksheet. If you need to insert a bunch of related data values into a row or column within your worksheet, such as a list of dates, you can select the Edit → Series option to have Excel quickly create the list of values.

Many of the options available on the Edit menu use the clipboard to store copied or cut information until it is pasted into another location.

To go along with the standard Windows Clipboard that is used by almost every Windows application, Office 2000 has added a new clipboard commonly referred to as the Office Clipboard. Both clipboards can store anything that you copy from Excel, namely text, graphics, and objects.

Windows Clipboard Versus Office Clipboard

The Windows Clipboard is a temporary storage space available to all Windows programs. Text and graphics that are cut or copied in a Windows application are temporarily stored in the clipboard. Remember, temporary means that it is only there until you copy or cut in another location or shut down your computer. Once the information has been stored in the clipboard it can be pasted into any Windows application that accepts that type of data. For example, you can copy data from an Excel worksheet and paste it into a Word document.

You view the contents of the Windows Clipboard using the Clipboard Viewer program. This is a standard Windows program that can typically be found by selecting Start → Programs → Accessories. For more information, refer to *Windows 98 in a Nutshell* (O'Reilly & Associates).

The Office Clipboard, on the other hand, is only available for Office programs: Excel, Word, Access, Outlook, and PowerPoint. The Office Clipboard lets you copy up to 12 different items to the clipboard, and is only activated when you do one of the following:

- Copy and/or cut two different items consecutively in the same Office program.

- Copy one item, paste the item, and then copy another item in the same Office program.

- Copy the same item twice in succession.

When the Office Clipboard is activated, it displays as shown in Figure 4-1. You can quickly see the contents of each item in the clipboard by dragging the mouse across the icon. If the clipboard contains 12 items and you try to cut or copy another item, the clipboard prompts you to overwrite the first item in the clipboard or to not make the selected cut or copy.

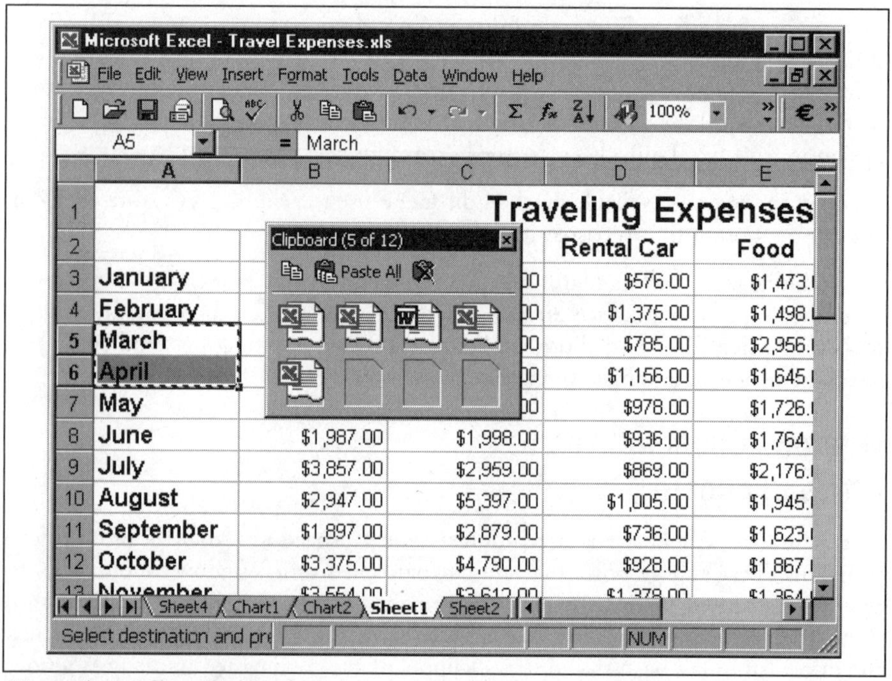

Figure 4-1: Office Clipboard

Each time something is added to the activated Office Clipboard, the item is also copied to the Windows Clipboard. That way, if you open a non-Microsoft Office program you will be able to paste the last thing you cut or copied.

Edit → Undo

The Edit → Undo command undoes or reverses the changes you have made to the document during a session. In other words, when you select Edit → Undo or Ctrl+z the most recent change is undone first, followed by the change made prior to that, and so on. If you undo more commands than you intended, you can use Edit → Redo to redo a command.

The Undo option takes the name of the most recent action. For example, if the last thing you did was bold the text in a cell, the menu option is Undo Bold. If an action cannot be undone, the menu option says Can't Undo and is grayed out. This is the case when you open a worksheet or if you save a worksheet. (Once you save the worksheet, all stored Undo actions are erased.)

You can also select the Undo icon on the toolbar. It performs the same action as Edit → Undo. If you need to undo several actions you can select the Down Arrow button next to the Undo icon and highlight the actions that you want to undo.

TIP # 28

The Benefits of Using AutoSave

If you have the AutoSave option turned on (Tools → AutoSave) the Undo list is reset each time an autosave is performed. You may want to set the AutoSave option at five- to ten-minute intervals. The AutoSave option is an Add-in that comes along with Excel. It can be loaded by selecting the AutoSave Add-In on Tools → Add-Ins (refer to Chapter 8).

Edit → Redo

The Edit → Redo command reapplies a change that has been undone in the worksheet. For example, if you type "12.45" in cell A1 and then select the Undo option to remove it, Edit → Redo or Ctrl+Y will place the value back in the cell. Just like the Undo option, Redo restores changes in reverse order by starting with the most recent change, then the prior reversed change, and so on.

The Redo command is only available immediately after you undo something. As soon as you make additional edits, the Undo command grays out. If there are no actions that can be redone, the menu option will say Can't Repeat and also will be grayed out. This will be the case anytime the last action performed was not an undo. If you redo more commands than you intended, you can use Edit → Undo to reverse the Redo command.

As with the Undo command, you can select the Redo icon on the toolbar. It performs the same action as Edit → Redo. If you need to redo several recent undo actions you can select the Down Arrow button next to the Redo icon and highlight the actions that you want to redo, just like the Undo command.

Edit → Cut

This command removes the selected information from the worksheet and stores the selection in the Windows clipboard. This clipboard information can be pasted into another location using the Edit → Paste option. You can also cut information by selecting Ctrl+X or the Cut icon on the toolbar.

If you decide you do not want to cut the selected section, you can press the Esc key on your keyboard to cancel. Excel also automatically cancels one cut action if another range of cells is selected to be cut or copied.

Excel does not allow you to cut multiple cell ranges simultaneously. For example, if you want to cut cells A1–A5 and cells C3–C6 and then paste them into cells F1–F8, you will need to cut the first range (A1–A5) and paste them in the appropriate location, and then cut the second range of cells.

When you select a range and cells to be cut, the contents of those cells will remain the same until the Paste option is selected. Excel will remind you that the cells have been selected by placing dotted lines around the contents as shown in Figure 4-2.

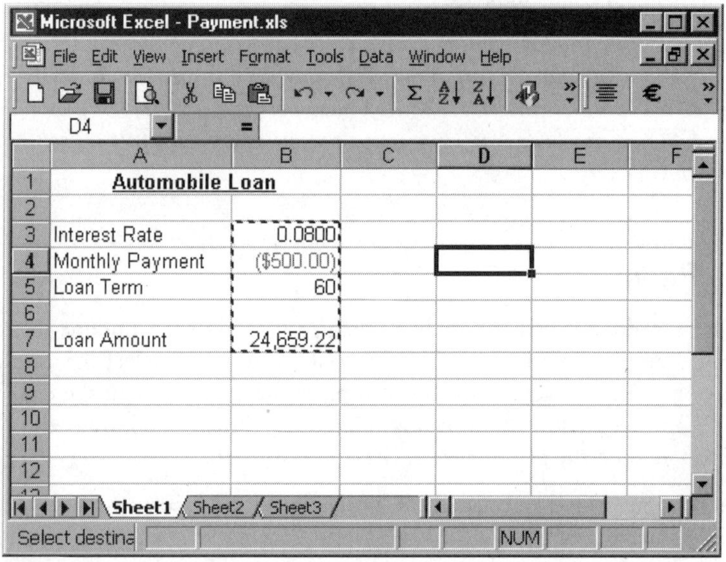

Figure 4-2: Excel marks the cut or copied range of cells

Edit → Copy

This option copies the information selected and stores it in the clipboard. This information can be pasted into another location using the Edit → Paste option. You can also copy information by selecting Ctrl+C or the Copy toolbar icon.

As with the Edit → Cut command, Excel does not allow you to copy multiple cell ranges simultaneously. If you attempt to do this by selecting multiple ranges of cells before selecting Edit → Copy, an error message displays indicating the copy will not occur.

When you select a range and cells to be copied, Excel also will mark the selected cells within your worksheet with dotted lines as shown in Figure 4-2. The cells remain marked until you select another range of cells to be cut or copied.

Edit → Paste

The Edit → Paste option pastes the current clipboard contents at the selected location on the worksheet. If the clipboard is empty, the Edit → Paste option is not available and the command is grayed out. Information is added to the clipboard using the Edit → Cut or Edit → Copy option within Excel or another Windows program. You can also paste information by selecting Ctrl+V or the Paste icon on the toolbar.

If the Office Clipboard is active, you can paste a copied item by clicking on the corresponding icon on the clipboard. You can also paste the entire contents of the clipboard by selecting the Paste All button (see Figure 4-1).

If you want to customize the way the clipboard contents are pasted into a worksheet you can use the Edit → Paste Special option. Refer to the Edit → Paste Special section, next, for more information.

TIP # 29

Pasting the Contents of the Clipboard into the Worksheet

Be careful when pasting the contents of the clipboard into your worksheet. I recommend simply selecting the first cell location where you want to paste the information and then selecting Edit → Paste. Otherwise, if you don't select the exact number of cut or copied cells in the paste range, you will get an error message. In other words, if you copy four cells, and then try to paste those cells into a range of five cells, you get an error message. You must either select the same number of cells for pasting, or you can simply specify the location for the paste and let Excel place the values in the appropriate number of cells.

Edit → Paste Special

The Edit → Paste Special command also pastes the selected contents of the clipboard in a specified worksheet location. Use this option for copying formats from one location to another or for switching the contents of a row to a column. Keep in mind that if the Windows Clipboard is active, the Paste Special option only pastes the last item copied to the clipboard. The paste selections are specified on the Paste Special dialog shown in Figure 4-3.

Figure 4-3: Paste Special dialog

Select the option in the Paste section that indicates how you want to paste the selected information into the worksheet. If you select the All radio button, the entire contents of the selected cells will be pasted into the new location, just like selecting Edit → Paste. This includes not only the value of the cell, but also any formatting, comments, or data validation that have been applied to the cells.

If you indicate that you want to paste only the comments, data validation, or formats, the existing values in the cells where you are pasting will not be modified. If you paste the formulas, the values will only change if a formula is pasted in the cell. For example, if you copy cells A1 through A4 and cell A4 contains a formula, when you paste into cells B1 through B4 only the value in B4 will change.

If you select the Values radio button, only the values of the selected cells are pasted into the new cells. Any formulas, comments, etc., will not be copied. For example, if you copied cells A1–A5 and A5 contains a formula that calculates the sum of A1–A4 only the value, not the formula, in A5 will be pasted.

The Column Widths radio button does not affect any values in the cells. It changes the column widths of the selected cells to match the widths of the copied cells.

If desired, you can perform a mathematical operation on the pasted information by selecting one of the radio buttons in the Operation section, as outlined in Table 4-1.

Table 4-1: Edit → Paste Special Operation Options

Option	Description
Multiply	Multiplies the pasted data by the existing data.
Add	Adds the pasted data to the existing data.
Divide	Divides the existing data by the pasted data.
Subtract	Subtracts the existing data by the pasted data.

Figure 4-4 provides an example of each of the Operation options on the Paste Special dialog. Column A shows the values that are being pasted. Column B indicates the contents of columns C–F prior to the selection of the corresponding operation on the Paste Special dialog. For example, if cells A1–A9 are pasted into Column C and the Multiply operator is selected, cell A1 is multiplied by C1 and the result is placed in C1; this is repeated for all cells in the selected range.

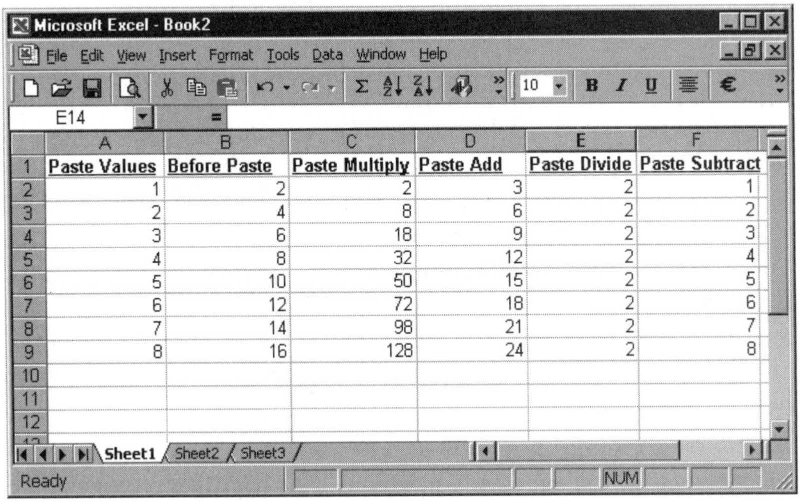

	A	B	C	D	E	F
1	Paste Values	Before Paste	Paste Multiply	Paste Add	Paste Divide	Paste Subtract
2	1	2	2	3	2	1
3	2	4	8	6	2	2
4	3	6	18	9	2	3
5	4	8	32	12	2	4
6	5	10	50	15	2	5
7	6	12	72	18	2	6
8	7	14	98	21	2	7
9	8	16	128	24	2	8
10						
11						
12						

Figure 4-4: Paste Special Operation options

You can transpose the pasted data from row to column, or vice versa, by selecting the Transpose checkbox. For example, if you copy cells A1–A4 and select to paste in cell B1, the values will be pasted in B1, C1, D1, and E1.

If you don't want to paste blank values into the pasting range, select the Skip Blanks option. When Skip Blanks is selected, Excel does not paste a blank value into another cell; the cell maintains its original value. For example, in Figure 4-4, if cell A4 had been blank and the Skip Blanks option was selected, when A4 was pasted into cell B4 the cell would have retained its original value of 6.

TIP # 30

Using the Paste Link Button

Select the Paste Link button if you want to paste the data as a link to the original location. The values of the original cells are pasted in the location with links back to the previous cells. If the values of the previous cell change, the corrections are reflected in the pasted cells. This is similar to the Edit → Paste as Hyperlink command. The only difference is that the values display with this command and the links display with the Edit → Paste as Hyperlink command.

Edit → Paste as Hyperlink

The Edit → Paste as Hyperlink option places a link to the previously selected location within your worksheet. When you click on the link, the specified location is displayed. You can create links within the current worksheet, to another worksheet, or even to another workbook.

Figure 4-5 shows how you can link to another worksheet to provide more detailed information. For example, cell A2 provides a hyperlink back to Sheet1, which contains detailed information about the annual travel expenses. When you paste a hyperlink into a cell, if the cell already contains a value, such as A2, which contained the text Travel, Excel maintains the cell value and creates a hyperlink. Changing the color of the cell contents to blue and underlining the text indicates the hyperlink. If the cell is blank when you paste into it, the actual hyperlink address is placed in the cell.

This command is similar to the Paste Link button on the Paste Special dialog that displays when you select Paste → Special. The main difference is that the command places a link in the selected cell, and the Paste Link button places a copy of the text with a link to the original location so that if the value of the original cell changes the pasted cell changes.

If you want to modify the display contents of a cell that contains a hyperlink, you can simply select the cell and type a new value. The hyperlink remains in the cell until you cut, clear, or delete the cell using the appropriate options on the Edit menu (Edit → Cut, Edit → Clear, and Edit → Delete). Deleting the contents of the cell with the Delete key on the keyboard does clear the hyperlink from the cell.

If you link to another workbook the workbook path is placed in the hyperlink. Be careful when moving workbooks; if the workbook is not found in the specified location, the link will not work.

TIP # 31
Save your Worksheets Before Using the Paste as Hyperlink Option

You cannot link to a worksheet that has not been previously saved. The "Paste as Hyperlink" option will remain grayed out until the workbook has been saved.

Edit → Fill

The Edit → Fill options fill the selected range of cells with the appropriate values based upon the value in the first cell in the range. With most of the fill options, Excel is basically just copying the value in the first cell (either the farthest right or top) and pasting it into the other cells in the selected range. These options work great if you want to use the same formula in each cell of a row or column, you can

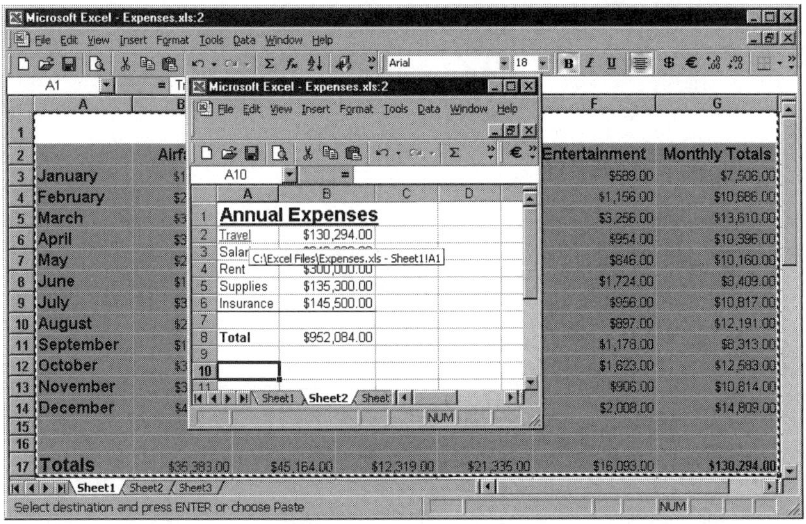

Figure 4-5: You can paste a hyperlink to another cell or range of cells

simply create the formula in the first cell and then use Edit → Fill to copy it into each of the remaining cells in the range.

If you select the Series option, Excel fills the cells in your selected range with values that create the type of series you specify. For example, you can create a series of dates that are exactly 15 days apart.

Edit → Fill → Down

Fills the cells in the selected range with the value of the top cell in the range. You can also select Ctrl+D. For example, in Figure 4-6, you can use the same formula in cell G3 to calculate the monthly totals by highlighting the range of cells and selecting Edit → Fill → Down. As Excel pastes the formula in each cell in column G, the formula is adjusted to sum the appropriate cells. For example, the formula pasted in cell G4 is =SUM(B4:F4).

Edit → Fill → Right

Fills the cells in the selected range with the value of the first cell on the left. You can also select Ctrl+R. This is similar to the example shown in Figure 4-6, but the formula would be copied from left to right instead of down. For example, in row 15 you could sum the totals of each column by creating a formula =SUM(B3:B14) in cell B15 and then use Edit → Fill → Right to copy that formula into cells C15 through G15.

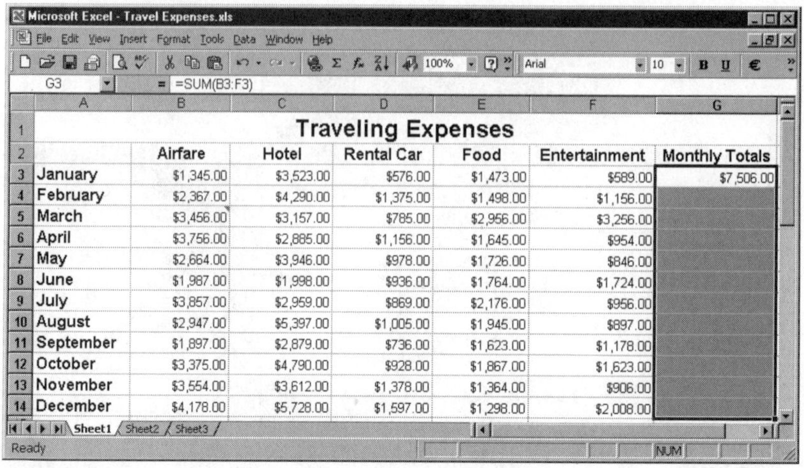

	A	B	C	D	E	F	G
1	Traveling Expenses						
2		Airfare	Hotel	Rental Car	Food	Entertainment	Monthly Totals
3	January	$1,345.00	$3,523.00	$576.00	$1,473.00	$589.00	$7,506.00
4	February	$2,367.00	$4,290.00	$1,375.00	$1,498.00	$1,156.00	
5	March	$3,456.00	$3,157.00	$785.00	$2,956.00	$3,256.00	
6	April	$3,756.00	$2,885.00	$1,156.00	$1,645.00	$954.00	
7	May	$2,664.00	$3,946.00	$978.00	$1,726.00	$846.00	
8	June	$1,987.00	$1,998.00	$936.00	$1,764.00	$1,724.00	
9	July	$3,857.00	$2,959.00	$869.00	$2,176.00	$956.00	
10	August	$2,947.00	$5,397.00	$1,005.00	$1,945.00	$897.00	
11	September	$1,897.00	$2,879.00	$736.00	$1,623.00	$1,178.00	
12	October	$3,375.00	$4,790.00	$928.00	$1,867.00	$1,623.00	
13	November	$3,554.00	$3,612.00	$1,378.00	$1,364.00	$906.00	
14	December	$4,178.00	$5,728.00	$1,597.00	$1,298.00	$2,008.00	

Figure 4-6: Filling Cells with a Formula

Edit → Fill → Up

Fills the cells in the selected range with the value in the cell on the bottom. For example, you could have placed the formula in cell G14 of Figure 4-6 and then used Edit → Fill → Up to copy the formula to cells G3 through G13.

Edit → Fill → Left

Fills the cells in the selected range with the value of the furthest right cell in the selection. This is basically the reverse of the Edit → Fill → Right. If Cell G15 contains the desired formula, use the option to copy it to cells B15 through F15.

Edit → Fill → Across Worksheets

Copies the selected range of cells across all of the currently selected worksheets. The values are copied to the same cells on all worksheets. When you select this option a dialog provides you the option of copying everything in the cell (including formatting), the contents, or just the formatting. This option is useful if you are trying to set up several different worksheets with the same format.

TIP # 32

Selecting More than One Worksheet

You can only fill across multiple worksheets if you have more than one worksheet selected. To select multiple worksheets, hold down the Ctrl key and click on each worksheet tab.

Edit → Fill → Series

If you need to fill a range of cells with numeric values or dates that follow a specific pattern, you can have Excel create the values for you by selecting the Edit → Fill → Series option. The Series dialog, shown in Figure 4-7, provides the options to create a series of related values based upon the starting value and the step value. This option allows you to create a series of dates or numbers based upon a specific pattern. For example, if your cell contains the date 6/15/2000 you could fill the cells with dates that increase by one month by selecting the Month as the Date Unit and specifying 1 as the Step value.

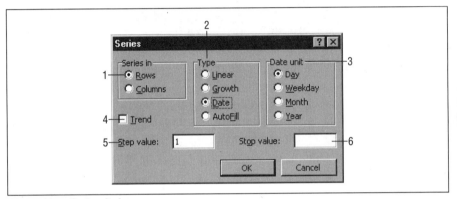

Figure 4-7: Series dialog

1. *Series in.* Indicates whether you want to create the series by filling across the selected row, or down the selected columns. If you select Columns the values in the first row are used as the starting values for the series; otherwise, the values in the first column are used to fill across rows.

2. *Type.* Indicates the type of fill you want to use for the selected series of cells. There are four different types of fill available:

   a. *Linear.* Fills the selected cells with a linear series based on the values in the first cells of the selected range. The way the series is created depends on whether or not the Trend checkbox is selected. If you do not select the Trend checkbox the series is created by adding the value in the Step field to the value in the previous cell. For example, if the first cell contains the value 2, and the step value is 1.5, the series becomes: 2, 3.5, 5, 6.5, etc.

   If you select the Trend checkbox a linear trend is determined based on the values in the selected range of cells. Typically, all values in the range will be replaced with the appropriate trend values. For example, if the first cell contains a value of 2 Excel calculates the trend (or best-fit line) to fill the cells in the range with values that are evenly spaced so that they would create a line if placed on a graph. When you select the Trend checkbox, the values in both the "Step value field" and the "Stop value field" are ignored, and Excel calculates the trend based on the values that are currently in the range of cells. The values will be calculated so that they are evenly spaced and form a straight line if placed on a graph, where m is the slope of the least-squares regression line using the formula y=mx+b, as shown in Figure 4-8.

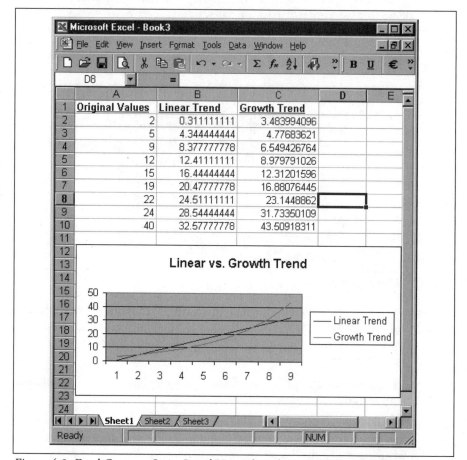

Figure 4-8: Excel Creates a Series Based Upon the Selections on the Series Dialog

    b. *Growth.* Fills the selected cells with a growth series based on the values in the first cells of the selected range. The way the series is created depends upon whether or not the Trend checkbox is selected. If you do not select the Trend checkbox, the series is created by multiplying the value in the Step field by the value in the previous cell. For example, if the first cell contains 2 and the step value is 2 the series becomes 2, 4, 8, 16, etc.

If you select the Trend checkbox, a geometric growth trend is determined based on values in the selected range of cells. Typically all values in the range of cells will be replaced with the appropriate growth trend values. When you select the Trend checkbox, any value that exists in the Step field is ignored and Excel calculates the trend values based on the values that are currently in the range of cells, as shown in Figure 4-8.

   c. *Date.* Fills the selected range of cells with dates. The way the dates increase in each cell is determined by the options selected in the Date Unit section. The date values are incremented based on the value specified in the Step field. You will want to format the cells as dates using the Format → Cells option prior to selecting Edit → Fill so that the dates display properly.

   d. *Autofill.* Fills the blank cells in the selected range of cells with the same data that exists in the selection. In other words, if the first cell contains the value 13.5 and the remaining cells are blank, that value is copied into all cells within the range; whereas, if the cells contained a series of data such as 2, 4, 6, that series is continued with the value of 8, 10, 12, etc. Any values in the Step field are ignored with the Autofill selection.

3. *Date unit.* Indicates how the series of dates will be incremented within the cells; by days, weekdays, months or years. This selection is only available when the Date option is selected in the Type section.

For example, if you wanted to, you could create a column that started at 1/15/2000 and increments one month at a time. You would type the date in the first cell of the range and then select the Month radio button for the Date Unit, specifying 1 as the increment value in the Step value field.

4. *Trend.* Select the Trend checkbox to create a trend of data within the selected series of cells based on the existing values in the cells. The type of trend is based on whether the Linear or Growth option is selected in the Type section. When the Trend checkbox is selected, the Step Value field is ignored.

When you indicate that you want to create a trend, Excel determines the appropriate values needed to create the type of trend selected. For example, if you specify the linear trend with a start value of 15 and a Stop value of 63, Excel will determine the step value needed to evenly space the numeric values out so that the cells are evenly incremented between the start and stop value.

5. *Step value.* Indicates the value that should be used to step, or increase, the value in each cell within the selected range.

For example, if you have a value of 12 in the first cell and you want to increment the cell values by 2.5, you would place 2.5 in the Step value field.

6. *Stop value.* Indicates the value where you want the series to end. This can be either a positive or negative number, depending upon the type of series you are creating. If the selection of cells is filled before reaching the value specified in the Stop Value field, the series ends. If the series reaches the Stop Value prior to filling the selecting cells, the remaining cells in the selection are left blank. It is

not necessary to specify a value in the Stop Value field; if it is blank the selected range of cells is filled with the specified series.

Using the Fill Handle

Excel provides the option to quickly fill a series of cells without selecting the Edit → Fill menu option. This is accomplished by using the fill handle. The fill handle is the black square that appears in the bottom right corner of a selected range of cells, as shown in Figure 4-9. If you drag the cursor across that location, the cursor changes to a + sign. If you drag the + with the left mouse button, the series is continued when you release the mouse button, similar to selecting the Autofill option on the Edit → Series command. If you drag the + with the right mouse button, when you release the button a menu displays allowing you to select the type of fill you want to use for the selected range of cells.

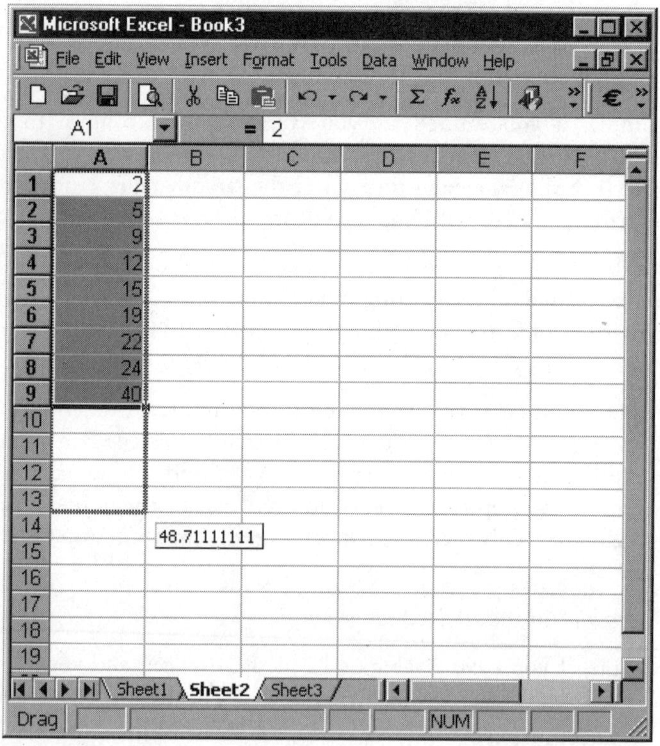

Figure 4-9: Using the fill handle option

Edit → Fill → Justify

Used only with text, it justifies the contents of the selected range of cells within the cells. In other words, the contents of the cells are merged together, if they fit within the width of the selected cells.

TIP # 33

Merging Cells with Edit → Fill → Justify

If you select Edit → Fill → Justify and cells are merged together, the characters will be merged with no spacing between. For example, if the first cell contains the word "the" and the second cell contains the word "dog" the justification would join the two cells if the column is wide enough and the results would be "thedog."

Edit → Clear

The Edit → Clear option allows you to clear information from the selected range of cells. You can clear the formats, comments, contents, or everything in the cells by selecting the appropriate option on the sub-menu. If you clear a cell, the value of the cell becomes zero. Any formulas that refer to the cell will receive a value of zero.

Unlike Edit → Delete, the cell contents are removed when using Edit → Clear, but all adjoining cell values remain in their original location. When you select Edit → Delete the contents of the cells are removed and the surrounding cells are adjusted to compensate for the removed cells.

TIP # 34

When Not to Use the Edit → Clear Option

If you want to be sure you do not remove the cell formatting or attached comments for the cell, use the Backspace or Delete keys. These commands only remove the contents of the cell.

Edit → Delete

The Edit → Delete option deletes the contents of the selected cells and adjusts the surrounding cell values as specified on the Delete dialog shown in Figure 4-10. Keep in mind that formatting and comments of the selected cells are also removed when using Edit → Delete. If you want to delete the contents of the cells without moving any of the adjoining cells, you need to use the Edit → Clear option.

1. *Shift cells left.* Deletes the selected cells and moves the contents of all cells on the right side of the selection to the left to fill the gap left by the deleted cells. For example, in Figure 4-10, if you delete cells D2 through D17 and select this

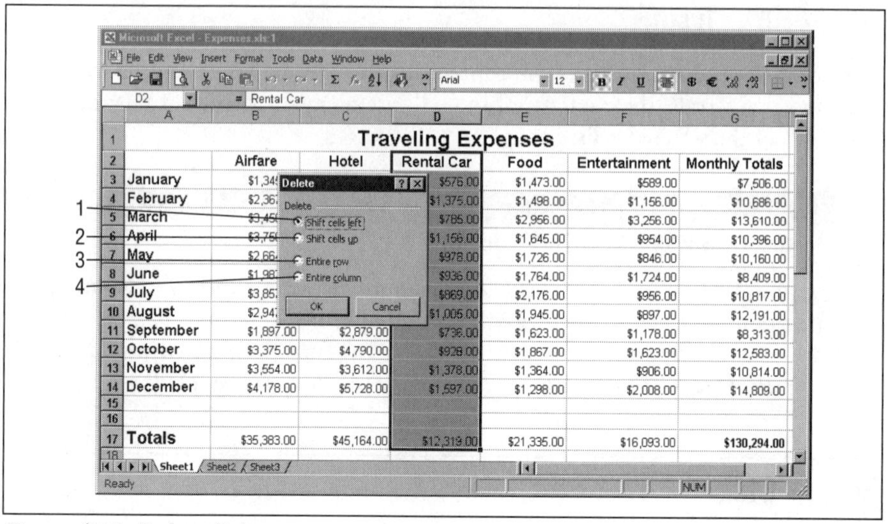

Figure 4-10: Delete dialog

option, the value of cell E2 is moved to cell D2 and cell F2 becomes E2, etc., for all remaining values on each row within the selected range of cells.

2. *Shift cells up.* Deletes the selected cells and move the contents of the cells below up into the deleted cells. All cell contents below are shifted up to match the deleted space. For example, in Figure 4-10, the value of cell D18 would be shifted up to cell D2, the value of D19 would be moved to cell D3, etc.

WARNING

Be careful when selecting either "Shift cells left" or "Shift cells up." These options move the values in the worksheet to the specified direction to cover up the hole left by the cells you have deleted. This can mess up your totals if you are not careful.

3. *Entire row.* Deletes the contents of all rows within the selection and moves the contents of the rows below the selected rows up.

4. *Entire column.* Removes the contents of all columns within the selection and moves the contents of the remaining columns to the left to fill the void.

Edit → Delete Sheet

Removes the selected sheet from the workbook. To remove multiple sheets, hold down the Ctrl key and click on the sheet tabs that you want to select. Once a sheet is deleted, the delete action cannot be undone; you can close the file without saving, however. Make sure you have selected the appropriate sheets before selecting this option.

Edit → Move or Copy Sheet

Moves or copies the selected sheets within the selected workbook to another open workbook or to a new workbook. You specify how you want to copy or move the worksheets on the Move or Copy dialog, as shown in Figure 4-11.

You can only copy or move worksheets between currently open workbooks, or to a new workbook. Make sure you open the workbook where you want to move or copy the worksheet prior to selecting this option.

Select the "Create a copy" checkbox if you want to place a copy of the worksheet in another workbook without changing the location of the original.

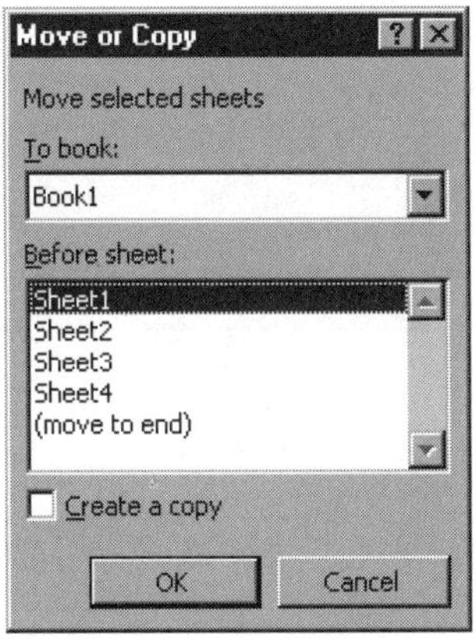

Figure 4-11: Move or Copy dialog

Select the workbook location to move or copy the worksheet to. By default, the currently selected workbook is listed in the "To book" field. To select another open workbook, select the down arrow button and highlight the name of the workbook to move or copy the worksheet to. If you select (new book), a new workbook is opened and the selected worksheet is copied or moved into the new workbook. If you select the (new book) option in the To book field, the "Before sheet" list will be empty because the worksheet is placed in the new workbook as the only worksheet. You can also drag a worksheet to a new location by clicking on the sheet tab and dragging it to another location in the workbook or to another open workbook. This method can be more tedious if your workbook has several worksheets.

If you move the worksheet to another workbook that contains a worksheet with the same name, Excel modifies the name of the copied worksheet, since you cannot have two worksheets with the same name within the same workbook. For example, if the copied worksheet is named *Sheet 1* it becomes *Sheet1 (2)*.

NOTE *When you copy or move a worksheet, all custom formatting and defined names are copied into the new workbook.*

Edit → Find

Edit → Find, or Ctrl+F, locates the specified text or function within your worksheet. Depending upon what you specify in the Find dialog, shown in Figure 4-12, Excel looks for the text in the cell value, formula, or in comments.

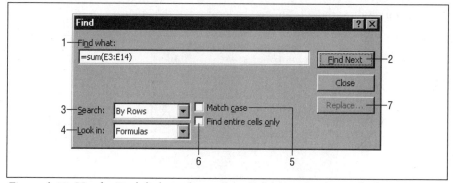

Figure 4-12: Use the Find dialog to locate the cell that contains a specific formula

1. *Find what.* Indicates the value to locate on the worksheet. You can search for the value within the contents, formula, or comments for a cell.

2. *Find Next.* Select this button initially to start the search, and again to look for the next occurrence of the text within your worksheet. You can cancel a search by selecting the Close button.

3. *Search.* Indicates whether you want to search the worksheet by rows or by columns to locate the text. If you select By Rows, Excel starts searching at the currently selected cell and searches across each row until it locates the specified text. If you select By Columns it searches down each column.

4. *Look in.* Indicates whether you can look at the values, comments, or formulas to find the text specified in the "Find what" field.

5. *Match case.* If checked, only finds the locations of the text where the case matches. For example, if the text is in all uppercase, Excel will only stop on all uppercase occurrences.

6. *Find entire cells only.* If checked, only finds locations where the text is an exact match to the text specified in the "Find what" field.

7. *Replace.* Displays the Replace dialog, which is detailed in the "Edit → Replace" section.

Edit → Replace

The Edit → Replace option finds the specified text, number, formula, or cell reference within the worksheet and replaces it as indicated. Selecting either this option or Ctrl+H displays the Replace dialog, shown in Figure 4-13. The Replace dialog resembles the Edit dialog that displays when you select Edit → Find, but it can only be used to replace text within the cell value; it does not find and replace text within the formula or comments.

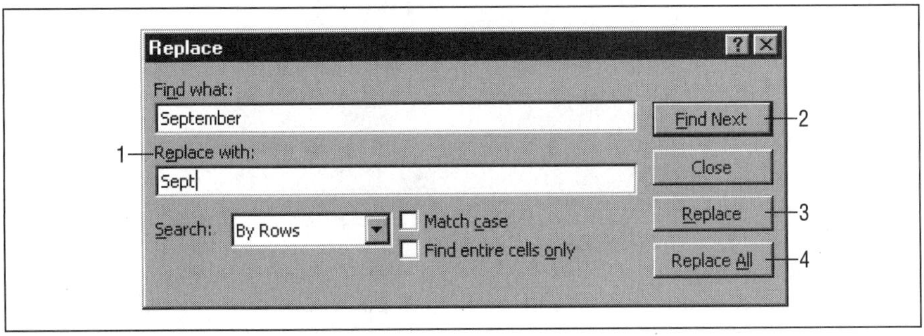

Figure 4-13: Replace dialog

1. *Replace with.* Indicates the text that you want to use as a replacement when the text specified in the "Find what" field is located. This replacement will not occur until the Replace or Replace All buttons are selected.

   Keep in mind that Excel will only replace the value of the cell, it will not replace a formula or a comment. Therefore, if the value you want to replace is actually the result of a formula, Excel will not find or replace that value.

2. *Find Next.* Select this button to find the next occurrence of the text without making a replacement.

3. *Replace.* Replaces the currently located text within your worksheet.

4. *Replace All.* Replaces all occurrences of the text within the worksheet, from the current cursor location, to the end of the worksheet.

Edit → Go To

The Edit → Go To command locates a specific location within your worksheet. With this command, or Ctrl+G you look for a named range of cells by selecting it from the Go To dialog. Named ranges are created using the Insert → Name → Define option. Refer to Chapter 6, *Insert*, for more information. If you want to find a specific type of information, such as comments or formulas, select the Special button to display the Go To Special dialog, shown in Figure 4-14.

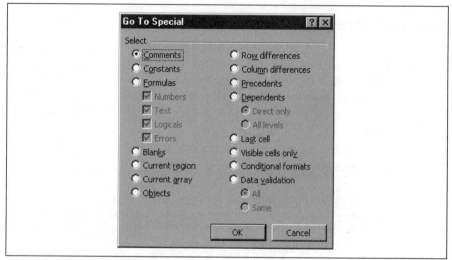

Figure 4-14: Go To Special dialog

The following selections are available on the Go To Special dialog:

Comments
    Selects all of the cells on the worksheet that have attached comments.

Constants
    Selects all cells that contain constants. Typically the constants are the cells whose values do not start with an equal size or do not contain a formula. They can be a date, numeric value, or text. You can specify the type of constants that you want to select by selecting one of the checkboxes under the Formula option.

Formulas
    Selects all cells that contain formulas. Select the appropriate checkboxes to indicate the type of formulas that you want to select. For example, if you want to find all formulas that return numeric values, select the Number checkbox.

Blanks
    Selects all blank cells on the worksheet up to the last cell that contains a value. Blank cells with comments or formatting are also selected.

Current region
    Selects a rectangular region of cells around the active cell. Typically the range is determined by bordering rows and columns of blank cells. If you select a cell that is surrounded by blank cells, no region will be selected.

Current array
    If the active cell is contained within an array, the entire array is selected; otherwise, nothing is selected.

Using Arrays

If you have ever attempted any form of computer programming, you are probably very familiar with the term array. An array is simply a rectangular collection of items, e.g., rows and columns of data. Excel uses arrays in a similar fashion. The array is simply a collection of cells or constants that are treated as a group. The array values can either be stored in individual cells, or they can be added as constants in the array formula.

Array formulas allow you to use multiple arrays of values to generate one sum, or apply the same formula to multiple arrays. An array formula is created like a regular formula, with one exception. When you are finished specifying the values for the array, you need to press Ctrl+Shift+Enter to specify it as an array formula. When you do this, Excel places brackets ({}) around the formula.

An array formula allows you to perform multiple calculations within one cell. For example, if you want to determine the total sales for the year, you could either add up each salesperson's sales amounts for each month and then total the amounts, or you could create an array formula that sums all of the rows simultaneously and comes up with the annual total, such as {=SUM(C3:H3+C4:H4+C5:H5+C6:H6+C7:H7+C8:H8)}

Objects

Selects all of the graphic objects or images on the worksheet including charts and buttons.

Row Differences

Selects the cells within the selected range where the contents of the cell are different from the comparison cell in the row. The comparison cells are in the same column as the active cell (the first cell selected when the range was highlighted).

This option is very useful for comparing large amounts of data. You can select a range of cells and have Excel show you the first cell where the values in the rows are not the same.

Column Differences

Selects the cells within the selected range where the contents of the cell are different from the comparison cell in the column. The comparison cells are in the same row as the active cell (the first cell selected when the range was highlighted).

Precedents

Selects all of the cells that are referenced by the formula in the active cell (the currently selected cell). You also need to select one of the radio buttons listed under the Dependants option to indicate whether you want to select only direct references where the cell reference is located within the actual formula, or all references where the cell reference may be located in another cell that is referenced by the active cell.

Dependants

Selects all of the cells that contain formulas that refer to the active cell. You also need to select one of the radio buttons to indicate if you want only direct references to the active cell, or all references. For example, if Cell A1 is the active cell and cell E5 contains the formula =SUM(A1:A5), E5 is a direct reference to the active cell. But if cell G5 contains the formula =SUM(E5:F5), G5 refers to cell A1 indirectly because cell E5 contains the sum of cells A1 through A5.

Last Cell

Selects the last cell on the worksheet that contains any type of data or formatting.

Visible cells only

Selects only the visible cells within the worksheet. This allows you to quickly make changes to the visible cells without affecting any hidden cells.

Conditional Formats

Selects all of the cells that have conditional formats applied. You also need to select one of the radio buttons under the Data Validation option to indicate that you either want all conditional formatted cells or only the ones with the same conditional formatting as the active cell.

Data Validation

Selects all of the cells that have data validation rules applied. You also need to select one of the radio buttons to indicate that you either want all cells with data validation, or only the ones with the same data validation as the active cell.

TIP # 35

Edit → Go To Command

Aside from named ranges, Excel remembers the last four locations where you performed the Edit → Go To command and lists those in the Go To list. These are only the last four occurrences during an edit session.

Edit → Links

This option displays a dialog that contains a list of all external links within the workbook. These are links to other files such as Excel workbooks, graphic files, Word documents, etc. These links are typically created using the Insert → Object option and selecting the "Link to file" option.

The external links within the workbook display on the Links dialog, as shown in Figure 4-15. You can update the worksheet to contain the current contents of the linked file by selecting the Update Now button. This is recommended if you know the file has been modified since you opened your Excel workbook, or if the Manual update option is selected for this link.

Edit → Links only shows external files that have been linked to the document. It does not show links to other sheets or locations within the workbook or hyperlinks to web sites or other file locations.

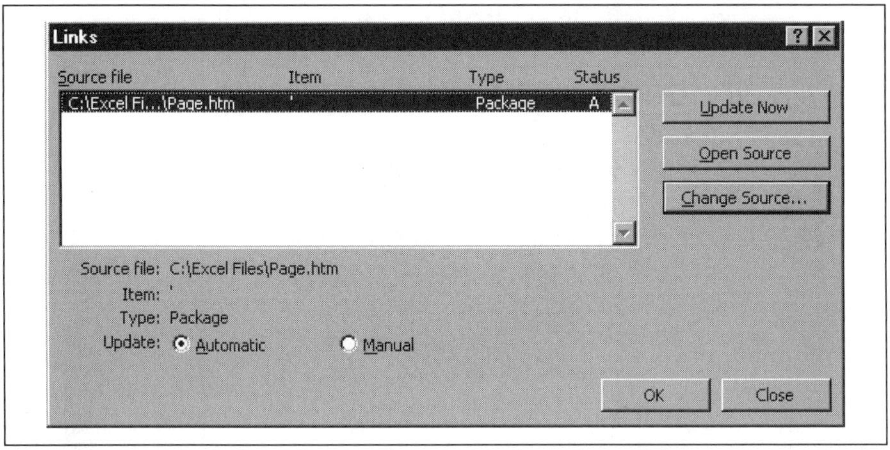

Figure 4-15: Links dialog indicates all external links in the worksheet

---

WARNING

When you save your workbook containing an external link, the most current version of the linked file is saved in your workbook. When you open that workbook again, Excel prompts you to update the links. Be careful not to link to documents that may be moved or deleted in the near future. Excel remembers the full path of the linked file; if the file is moved, the link will be broken.

Edit → Object

Excel provides the ability to add an OLE (Object Linking and Embedding) object directly into your worksheet. This means that you are placing an object from another Windows program into your worksheet that, when selected, provides you with the ability to use the other program's editing tools to modify it. Objects are added to your worksheet using Insert → Object.

When you have a worksheet option that contains an object you can use Edit → Object to make modifications to the object that has been selected within the worksheet. The submenu options that display vary depending upon the type of object selected. With most objects you have the option of editing the object within the application that created it, by selecting the Edit → Object → Edit command. For example, if you have added a Microsoft Map to your worksheet, you can select Edit → Microsoft Map Object → Edit to make modifications to the selected map, as shown in Figure 4-16.

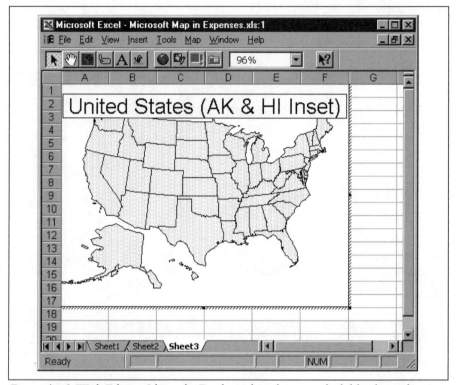

Figure 4-16: With Edit → Object the Excel window changes to look like the application that created the selected object

---

TIP # 36

Object Command Name

When you select an object, the Object command name changes to reflect the type of image you have selected. For example, if you select a bitmap image, the Object command appears as Bitmap Image Object on the menu, with submenu options that allow you to Edit, Open, or Convert the image.

Chapter 5

View

Excel allows you to select how a workbook is viewed or printed. This type of setting is called a view. Excel provides some basic view modes that are available on the View menu for all workbooks that you open. For example, the Normal option displays the entire contents of the workbook, with the exception of any cells that may be hidden. If you select the Page Break Preview option you are able to see exactly where the page breaks will occur in your worksheet if you print it, and make any desired modifications.

Excel also allows you to create custom view modes for each workbook that you open. These view modes are custom created for each workbook using the View → Custom Views option. For example, you might want to set a custom view that hides the individual sales figures for each employee and only displays the totals.

With each custom view you create, Excel stores the following information:

- Active cell

- Active worksheet

- Widths of all columns within each worksheet in the workbook

- Display options that are specified when you select Tools → Options

- Size and position of the Excel window

- Selected cells within the active worksheet

- Hidden rows, hidden columns, and filter settings for a workbook, if you select the "Hidden rows, columns and filter settings" checkbox on the Add View dialog that displays when you create a new custom view (see View → Custom Views)

- Print settings, if you select the Print settings checkbox on the Add View dialog that displays when you create a new custom view

View → Normal

Display the worksheet in standard mode so that modifications can be made. Typically you will use this option to switch back from the View → Page Break Preview option.

You can use the options on the Window menu to customize the way the worksheet displays, or even view multiple worksheets within the active workbook simultaneously with the Window → Arrange option.

View → Page Break Preview

System-defined page breaks are indicated with a dotted line and user-defined page breaks are indicated with solid lines, as shown in Figure 5-1. You can modify a page break location by clicking on it and dragging it to the desired location. You can also insert a new page break at the location of the active cell by selecting Insert → Page Break.

This option is also available while doing a print preview by selecting the Page Break Preview button. If you preview your worksheets before printing, which is highly recommended, you will probably use the button on the print preview window more frequently than the option on the View menu.

Keep in mind that each printer has predefined limits to the amount of information that fits on one page. Therefore, as you modify the page breaks the size of the information on the page is rescaled so it will fit the page. For example, if you adjust the page break so that two pages fit on one page, Excel reduces the text size of everything on each page proportionally so it all fits. Before setting your page breaks, make sure you have the correct printer selected using File → Print.

TIP # 37
Returning to System-Defined Page Breaks

If you want to return to the original, system-defined page breaks so that the text prints at the originally intended size, remove all the page breaks you have added and then select File → Page Setup. Adjust the Scaling section of the Page tab to 100%.

View → Toolbars

When you select View → Toolbars, a submenu displays listing all of the toolbars that are available for use in Excel. A toolbar is selected if a checkmark displays next to it in the menu. All existing toolbars display in the menu; this includes both default toolbars that come standard with Excel and any custom toolbars you have created. Find more information about customizing toolbars in Chapter 8, *Tools*.

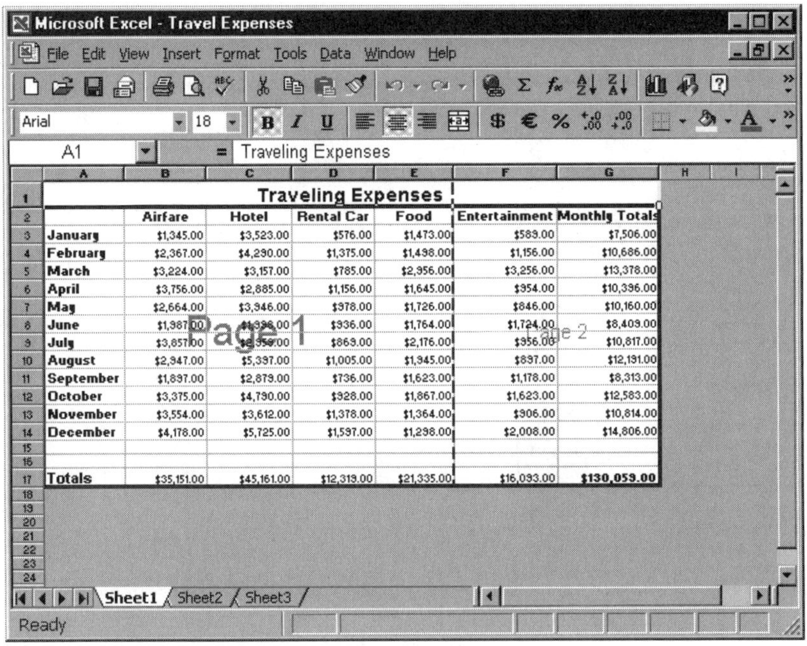

Figure 5-1: Page Break Preview indicates the locations of the page breaks within the worksheet

Toolbars either sit "docked" attached to the edge of the window, usually the top, or "floating" on the screen. You can move a toolbar simply by dragging it to the desired location. Any changes you make to the toolbars are saved in the customized toolbars file (*Excel.xlb*) so that the changes will be available the next time you run Excel. This file is typically located in *C:\windows\Profiles\user_name\Application Data\Microsoft\Excel*.

You can quickly modify the buttons that display on a toolbar by selecting the arrow button next to the toolbar title on a floating toolbar, or at the end of a docked toolbar. The Add or Remove Buttons button displays when you select the arrow button for the selected toolbar. Click the button to display a list of menu options, as shown in Figure 5-2. Click on the desired options to add or remove them from the toolbar. Keep in mind that only the buttons that are system defined for that toolbar or that you have added to the toolbar display on the menu.

To add buttons you need to use the Customize option. By launching the Customize dialog you can specify how toolbars display by creating new toolbars, modifying the buttons on existing toolbars, and even resetting a system toolbar back to its original settings. Refer to Chapter 2, *Excel Anatomy*.

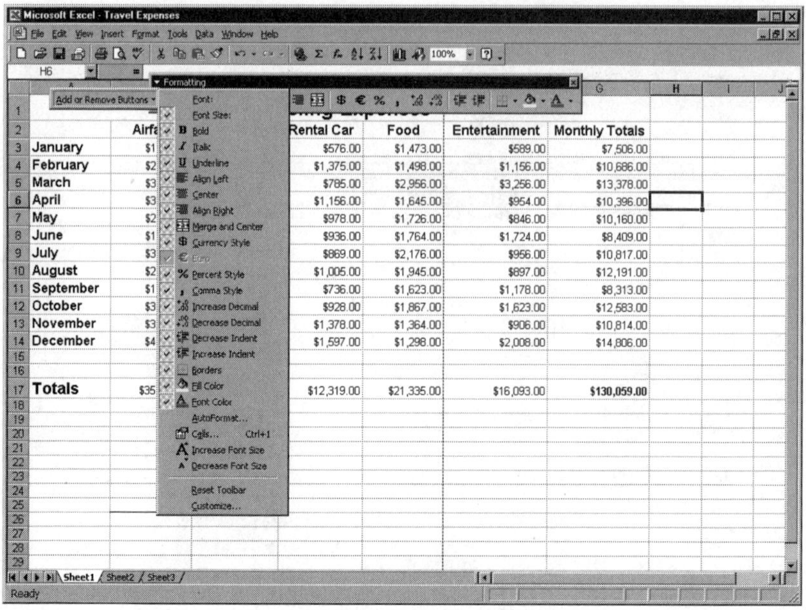

Figure 5-2: Selecting Icons for a Floating Toolbar

View → Formula Bar

The Formula Bar displays under all docked toolbars, as shown in Figure 5-3. The Formula Bar actually consists of the Name field on the left, where you can select a named section, and the Formula Bar where you add and modify the contents of a cell. Although the Formula Bar, provides a nice location for working with the contents of the cell, as discussed in Chapter 2, you do not have to use it. In fact, Excel allows you to edit directly in the particular cell.

You can remove the Formula Bar from the Excel window by selecting View → Formula Bar. A checkmark displayed next to the Formula Bar option on the View menu indicates that it is selected. Keep in mind that when you remove the Formula Bar, you are also removing the Name field. For more information, refer to "Insert → Name" in Chapter 6, *Insert*.

1. *Name field.* Indicates the name of the selected cells. You can display a particular name range by clicking on the name in this field. Names are created using Insert → Name. Naming fields eliminates the need to remember the cell location for the important calculations on your worksheet

2. *Formula bar.* Provides a location for modifying the contents of a cell. When you modify the cell contents in the Formula Bar you can select the X button to cancel modifications and keep the original value. The = (equal sign) button inserts an equal sign so you can create a new formula.

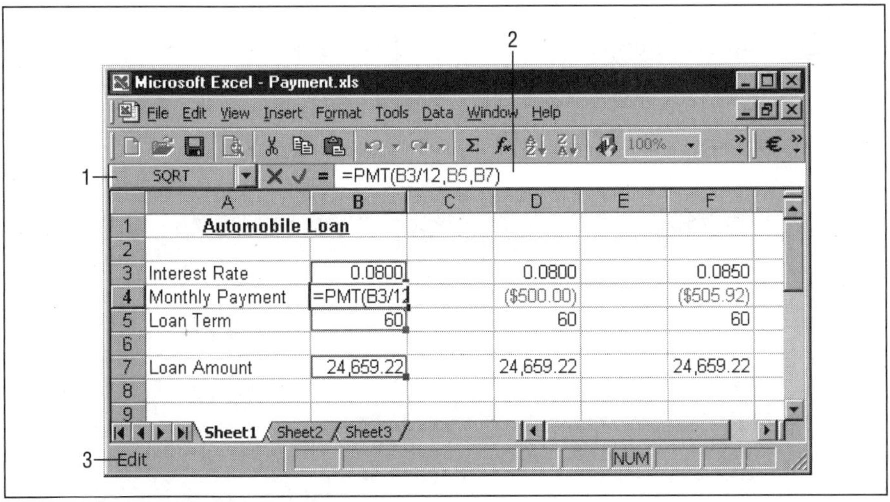

Figure 5-3: Formula and Status bars

3. *Status bar.* Displays various messages about your worksheet. It also indicates whether the Num Lock, Caps Lock, and Scroll Lock keys are selected on your keyboard.

If you decide to remove the Formula Bar, you need to make sure the "Edit directly in cell" checkbox is selected on the Edit tab of Tools → Options. This option indicates that you want to edit directly in a cell whether or not the Formula Bar is displayed. If you do not select this option, when you remove the Formula Bar you will not be able to place the cursor within a cell.

Removing the Formula Bar from one instance of Excel removes it from all other Excel windows that are open, because Excel stores all modifications to toolbars in a central location, *Excel.xlb*. This file is referred to for all workbooks that are opened.

View → Status Bar

As indicated in Figure 5-3, the status bar displays at the bottom of the Excel window. It provides status information for Excel. You can display or remove the Status Bar from the Excel window by selecting View → Status Bar. Removing the Status Bar from one instance of Excel removes it from all other Excel windows that are open and any future uses of Excel.

View → Header and Footer

Headers print at the top of each page and footers print at the bottom of the page. Headers and footers are typically used to print reference information, such as page numbers and dates, on each page or odd or even pages of a document when it prints.

When you select the View → Header and Footer option the Header/Footer tab of the Page Setup dialog displays. Excel creates default header and footer options that can be selected by clicking on the down arrow button next to the Header or Footer field as shown in Figure 5-4. When you select an option from the list a preview of the selection displays in the appropriate preview section.

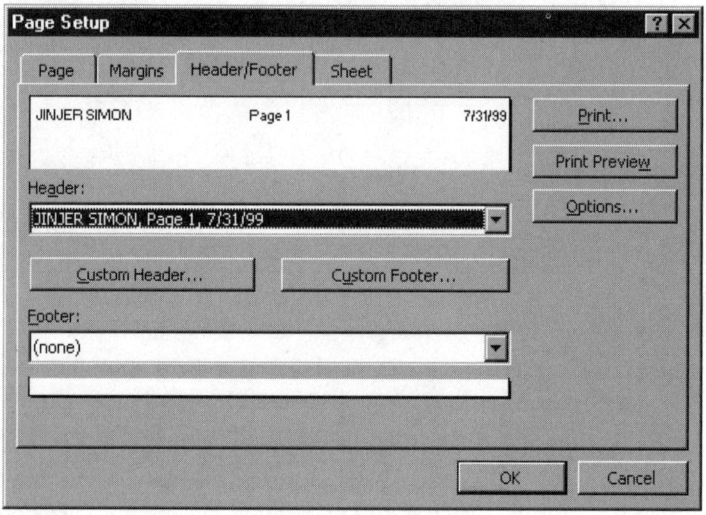

Figure 5-4: Header/Footer dialog

If you don't like the headers or footers in the list, you can create custom headers and footers by selecting the appropriate Custom button to display the dialog shown in Figure 5-5. This dialog divides the header or footer into three sections: left, center, and right. You can type text in each section and use the buttons above the sections to select additional information that you want to add, such as page numbers, date, time, etc.

When you select one of the buttons, Excel inserts a field code using the format of &[code] that identifies the type of information you want placed in the header or footer. For example, if you want to place the page number in the left section of the header, Excel places the code &[Page]. The ampersand (&) at the beginning of each code indicates that Excel needs to gather the appropriate information and replace the code.

TIP # 38
Putting an Ampersand in a Header or Footer

If you type text in a header or footer that contains an ampersand (&) such as Smith & Jones, you need to use double ampersands (Smith && Jones). Excel uses the single ampersand to indicate a code such as &[Page] for adding the page number.

You can specify as many lines as you want in the header and footer. To force a line break, use Alt+Enter. You need to make sure you do not create a header or footer larger than the header and footer specified for the worksheet at File → Page Setup. There are approximate five lines available in the default header and footer margins of 0.5".

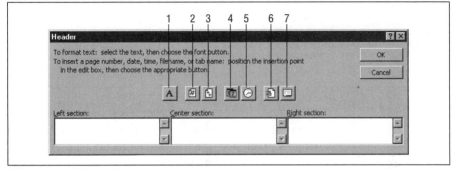

Figure 5-5: Header Dialog

The options available in the Header dialog are:

1. *Font button.* Displays the Font dialog so you can select the font type, size, and style for the text. For more details about the Font dialog refer to Chapter 7, *Format.* The font attributes can be set for both the text and the codes added by the other buttons.

2. *Page number button.* Inserts the code &[Page] indicating that the current page number should be printed. To begin numbering of the worksheet on a page other than 1 use + or - after the &[Page] code. For example, to start numbering the document on page 5 the code should read &[Page}+4. Essentially the plus sign (+) increases the current page number by the indicated number and the minus sign (-) decreases it.

3. *Total pages button.* Inserts the code to print the total number of pages in the worksheet. For example, instead of saying Page 1, you could have it say Page 1 of 7.

4. *Date button.* Inserts the code to print the current date. Use the date on worksheets that you plan to make modifications to so you can quickly see if you have the latest copy of the worksheet.

5. *Time button.* Inserts the code to print the current time. The time is like the date: it allows you to see when a worksheet was printed and if that printout is the most recent.

6. *File name button.* Inserts the code to print the file name of the workbook. This is only the name of the file, not the complete path. Printing the name of the workbook gives the reader a reference as to the actual file that was printed.

View Menu

Since Excel does not provide the ability to select the entire path of the document, if you want the path to print you will need to manually type the path in the header or footer of the document.

7. *Sheet name button.* Inserts the code to print the name of the worksheet. I would only use this option if you were also printing the workbook name. Otherwise, you do not know which workbook the sheet was printed from.

> *If you want to repeat a series of cells at the top of each page, set the Print Titles option on the Sheet tab of File → Page Setup.*

View → Comments

This option allows you to view all the comments that have been placed in the worksheet. When View → Comments is selected, the Reviewing toolbar displays options for ease in scrolling through comments and modifying as needed, as shown in Figure 5-6. The review toolbar displays undocked on the worksheet; in Figure 5-6, sitting on the center of the worksheet.

Comments are added to a cell using Insert → Comment. To eliminate having comments overlap, as shown in Figure 5-6, you can click on a comment and drag it above, below, or to the left side of the corresponding cell.

TIP # 39

Turn Off Red Triangle in Cells with Comments

If you don't want to see the red triangle displayed in the corner of cells with comments, you can remove them from the display by selecting the None radio button in the Comments section on the View tab of Tools → Options. Nevertheless, as soon as you select View → Comments again, the triangle displays in each cell with a comment, even after turning off comments.

TIP # 40

Delete a Comment

To delete a comment select the Delete icon on the Review toolbar or select Edit → Clear → Comments after selecting the comment.

View → Custom View

Excel allows you to create custom views for each workbook. When you create a custom view you set it up to display only pertinent information. For example, while upper management may only need to see the regional sales figures, each sales person would need to see specific sales within her region. By creating a view that displays

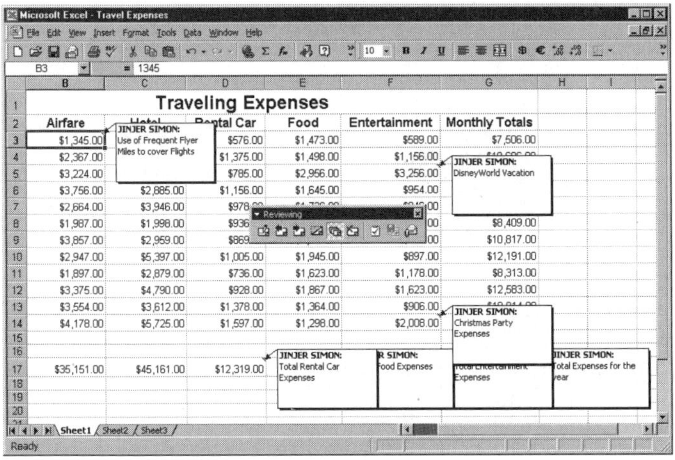

Figure 5-6: View Comments with Review Toolbar

that entire worksheet, and another that only displays the totals, you could use the same data to meet each requirement. You create, select, and delete custom views on the Custom Views dialog shown in Figure 5-7.

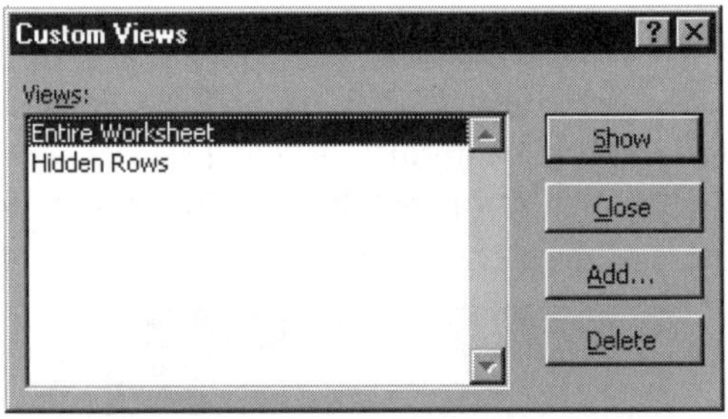

Figure 5-7: Custom View dialog

When you decide to add a view, you need to determine if you want to save the current print settings and hidden rows, columns, and filter settings, as shown in Figure 5-8. If you do not save the settings, Excel will use the settings that are currently active for the workbook when you select the view. In other words, if you open the workbook and switch to a view that does not have the print settings saved, Excel will print the view using the print settings for the original view. I would recommend selecting both checkboxes to ensure that you always get the current results when you select the view.

Custom views keep track of the settings for the entire workbook. If a sheet, row, or column is hidden when the view is saved, it will be hidden each time you select the view, as long as you have selected the "Hidden rows, columns and filter settings"

Figure 5-8: Add View Dialog

checkbox on the Add View dialog. The defined print area is saved in the view if you select the Print settings checkbox on the Add View dialog.

One of the most useful things you can do with custom views is to create custom reports for you worksheet. A custom view can be selected as the report area with View → Report Manager.

View → Report Manager

You may not always want to print the entire contents of a workbook. Excel provides the ability to create reports that specify the information that should print. Reports are created by selecting different custom views, scenarios, and worksheets. For example, you may have one workbook that contains the office expenses for all departments within the company. With View → Report Manager you can create one report the summarizes the information and provides totals for each department, or one that shows only the expenses for the Human Resource department.

Figure 5-9: Report Manager dialog lists custom reports created for the current workbook

You create and select reports using the Report Manager dialog shown in Figure 5-9. This option displays when you select View → Report Manager. This option is very similar to View → Custom View. The main difference is that this option is only designed for creating a custom report by combining different views and scenarios within a workbook. This option does not affect the worksheet information that is displayed on your screen. This option may not be currently loaded on your system. The Report Manager dialog is an add-in option that can be added at any time using Tools → Add-Ins. If you want to design custom reports based on the data within a specific workbook, this is definitely a good option to load. For more information about add-ins, refer to Chapter 8.

1. *Print*. Select this button to print the specified number of reports based on the current print settings. Make sure your printer settings are correct before selecting this option. When you select the OK button on the Print dialog the report is immediately sent to the printer. Unlike File → Print, you do not have the ability to preview the report or modify the print settings. The only option you have is to specify the number of copies you want to print.

2. *Add*. Create a new report for the workbook by creating combinations of sheets, views, and scenarios, as shown in Figure 5-10. For example, you may select the summary views from each worksheet to create a report that summarizes the expenses for the year.

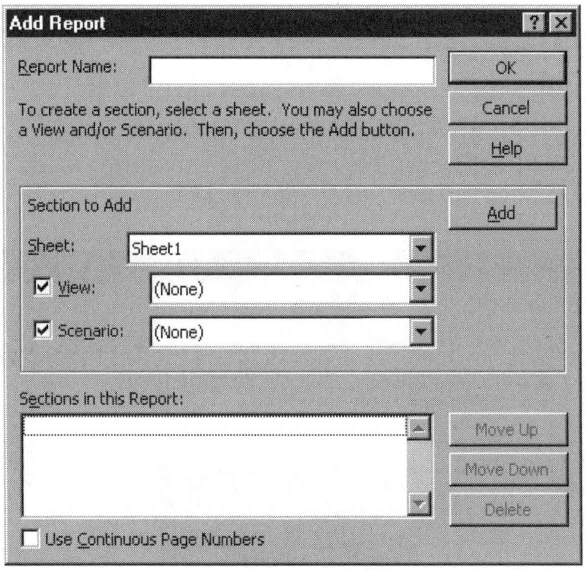

Figure 5-10: Add Report Dialog

To create the report, select at least one report section. The section can be any combination of worksheets, views, and scenarios. For each report, select a worksheet; the views and scenarios are optional. Views are created using View → Custom View and scenarios using Tools → Scenarios. To select one, make sure it is displayed in the corresponding field and select View or Scenario. The section is selected and added to the "Sections in this Report" field with the Add button.

The "Sections in this Report" field lists the sections that have been selected. Reorder the sections by highlighting the section and choose Move Up or Move Down.

TIP # 41

Create a Report That Prints All Worksheets Within a Workbook

View → Report Manager can also be used to create a report that prints all worksheets within a workbook. To do this, simply select each worksheet on the Add Report dialog and place them in the desired print order.

View → Full Screen

View the worksheet so that it fills the entire screen of your monitor. The title bar, toolbars, status bar, and Windows task bar do not display when this option is selected, allowing you to see more of the worksheet without scrolling. You can return to the original view mode by selecting View → Full Screen again or selecting the "Close Full Screen" option on the Full Screen toolbar that displays when you select View → Full Screen.

View → Zoom

Resize the display of the worksheet within the window using the Zoom dialog as shown in Figure 5-11. The settings only affect the current worksheet. Note that page breaks are inserted between each section of the report.

TIP # 42

Modifying the Scaling of the Worksheet

The sizing done with View → Zoom does not affect the way the worksheet prints. It only changes how things display within the Excel window.

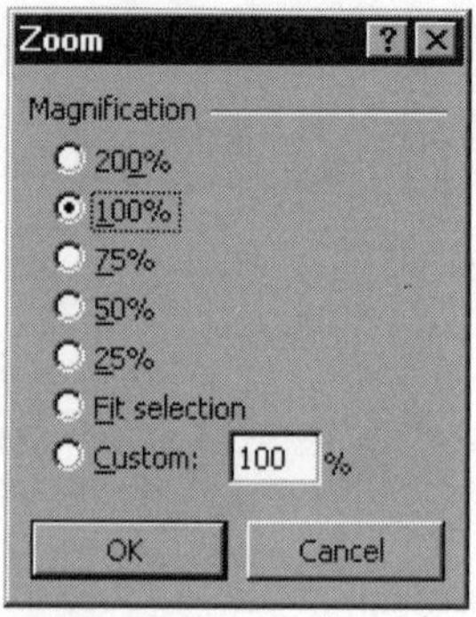

Figure 5-11: Zoom dialog

Chapter 6

Insert

The real power of an Excel worksheet lies in the many things you can add to it. The most powerful functionality that can be added to a worksheet is a formula. If you didn't use formulas in your worksheet all you'd have is just a big sheet of numbers. Formulas use a combination of the various functions available in Excel, including cell references, numeric and text values, and operators (such as +, -, etc). Although this chapter discusses the dialog that displays when you select Insert → Function, there is extensive information about functions covered in Part 3 of this book.

In addition to manipulating values, Excel provides the ability to create a graphical representation of data using charts. Not only can you select from one of the built-in chart types, you even create custom charts. Remember that after the chart is created, it needs to be modified using the options on the Chart menu covered in Chapter 10, *Chart*.

Insert → Cells

This option allows you to quickly add additional cells, rows, or columns at the location of the active cell, (the currently selected cell within your worksheet) using the Insert dialog shown in Figure 6-1. The number of cells, rows, or columns inserted is based on the number selected. For example, to insert three cells above the selected cell, highlight that cell and the two below it and select the shift cells down option.

Select one of the radio buttons to indicate how the blank cells should be inserted in the worksheet. Keep in mind that if you select to shift the cells right or down, the same movement will continue for the cells that follow. For example, if you shift cells right, the cells will be shifted right all the way across the worksheet. For example, in Figure 6-1, the contents of cells A7-A9 would be moved to cells B7-B9. The B column cell contents move to the corresponding cells in column C. This cell contents of all cells in the corresponding rows are moved right. Selecting the "Entire row" radio button inserts the row above the selection, just like selecting Insert → Rows. Selecting the "Entire column" radio button inserts the column to the left of the selection, just like selecting Insert → Columns.

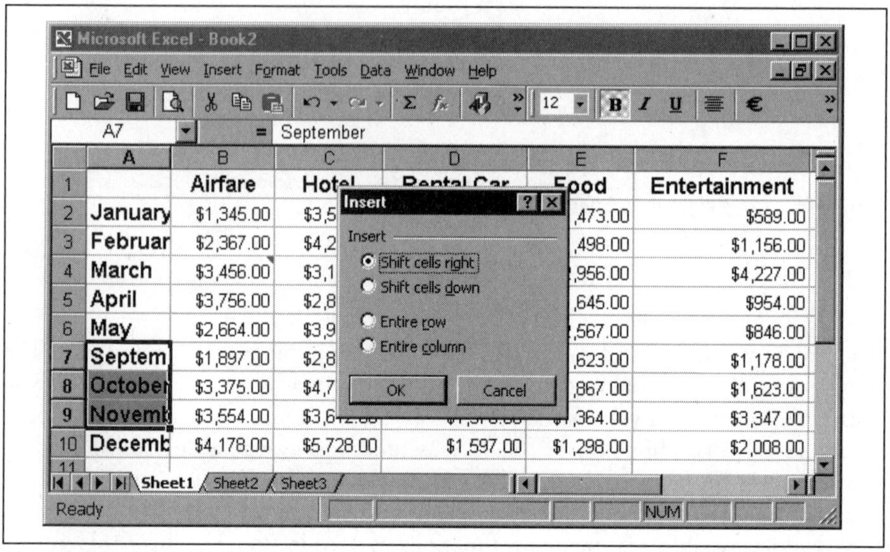

Figure 6-1: Insert Dialog

NOTE *The actual size of each worksheet in Excel is fixed. A worksheet always contains 256 columns and 65,536 rows. Therefore, when you insert a new row or column a row or column is removed from the end of the worksheet. If the last row or column of the worksheet contains a value, you cannot insert a row or column. This can come in handy if you want to ensure that no one adds a column to your worksheet, simply place a value in column 256 (or row 65,536 to keep rows from being inserted.) You can move to the last row or column quickly by using Edit → Goto. By the way, the last column is column IV.*

Insert → Rows

This is a quick method for inserting new rows in your worksheet. Make sure you have selected a cell in the row below where you want the new row inserted before selecting Insert → Rows. As the new rows are inserted, the rows below are moved down. To insert multiple rows simultaneously, simply select the desired number of rows before selecting Insert → Rows. As shown in Figure 6-2, where cells B4-B7 are highlighted you only need to highlight one cell in each row to indicate the number of rows you want to add. When Insert → Row is selected, four blank rows will be inserted above row 4. The new rows are always added above the active cell. The active cell is the first cell that was selected, in Figure 6-2, this cell is the one in the selection that is not highlighted (cell B4).

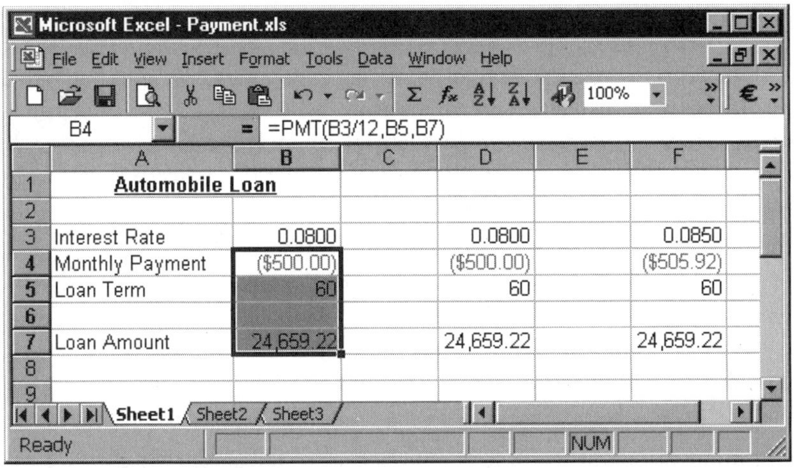

Figure 6-2: Highlight the number of rows you want to insert. Excel will add four new rows about between the Interest Rate and Monthly Payment rows

Insert → Columns

This is a quick method for adding new columns to your worksheet. Select a cell in the column to the right of where you want to insert the new column before selecting Insert → Columns. To insert multiple columns simultaneously, simply select cells from the desired number of columns, as shown in Figure 6-3, to the right of where you want the new columns before selecting the option. For example, in Figure 6-3, three columns will be inserted between columns A and column B.

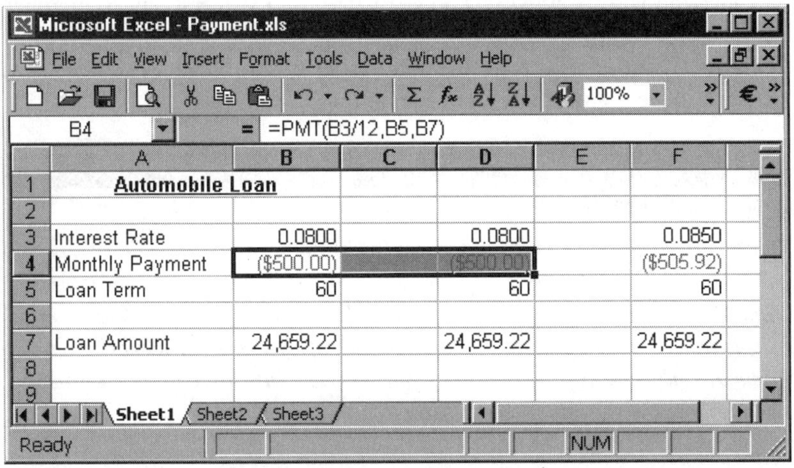

Figure 6-3: Highlight cells from the number of columns you want to insert

Insert → Worksheet

When Excel creates a new workbook there are three worksheets that are added by default, unless you change the default setting by selecting Tools → Options and specifying a different number on the General tab (refer to Chapter 8, *Tools*). You can add additional worksheets to your workbook at anytime using Insert → Worksheet. If you want to add more than one, simply hold down the Ctrl key and click on the desired number of worksheet tabs before selecting this option.

When you add new worksheets to a workbook, Excel simply adds each new worksheet in front of the currently selected sheet. You can rearrange the order of the worksheets with Edit → Move or Copy. When you use the Edit → Move or Copy option, you are able to specify the exact order for the sheets currently available in the workbook.

Keep in mind you can customize the properties of the sheet that is added to your workbook by creating a worksheet template called *sheet.xlt* and placing it in the *XLStart* folder. To create a worksheet template, take a workbook and delete all but one worksheet. Make the desired modifications to the worksheet such as name of worksheet, column widths, named styles, etc. You can even place text on the worksheet template. Once you create you worksheet template, place it in one of the default template locations:

- *C:\windows\Profiles\user_name\Application Data\Microsoft\Templates.*

- The *XLStart* folder where Excel looks for the *book.xlt* template used to create workbooks when you select the New icon on the toolbar or the Workbook icon on the New dialog. This folder is typically located in *C:\windows\Profiles\user_name\Application Data\Microsoft\Excel\XLStart.*

- The location you specified at Tools → Options → General tab. Remember, this template does not display on the New dialog; the only way to see it is to use the Windows Explorer. To reset the settings so that a blank worksheet is added, simply remove the template from the folder.

TIP # 43

Customizing Sheet Names

When sheets are added to a workbook they are named Sheet1, Sheet2, etc. You can customize the sheet names using Format → Sheet → Rename. If you have created a custom worksheet template with a custom sheet name, Excel still adds a number to distinguish between each sheet. For example, if you inserted a worksheet with the name Accounting, the second time you inserted into that same workbook, Excel would name the worksheet Accounting(2).

Insert → Chart

Provides the showiest option within Excel, by helping you create a graphic representation of the data within your worksheet, workbook or multiple workbooks. By creating charts you are able to give others the ability to quickly compare values within your workbook.

Your worksheet should contain the data you want to place on the chart, before selecting Insert → Chart. You can modify the data as needed once the chart is created and the changes will be reflected in the chart. Also, before selecting Insert → Chart, you can highlight the data in your worksheet that you want to appear on the chart. This allows you to quickly see how the data will look as you are determining which chart type you want to select during the first step of the Chart Wizard. Just remember, the data should come before the chart. That way you don't have to retrofit you data into a chart that is not designed to hold it all.

When you select Insert → Chart, the Chart Wizard displays as shown in Figure 6-4. The Chart Wizard leads you through four different steps to create your new chart. Each step is a different dialog with multiple tab options. You can scroll between each of the steps using the Forward and Back buttons.

 With all of the different selections available with the Chart Wizard, it can seem a little overwhelming. Don't be too concerned about the process because once the chart is created you can modify each of the selections as needed using the options on the Chart menu.

The first step in the Chart Wizard process is the selection of the type of chart you want to create from one of the two tabs. Each of the chart types listed on the Standard Types tab has multiple sub-types that can be selected. If you selected the chart data before selecting Insert → Chart you can quickly see what your data will look like on a particular chart type by selecting the type and then clicking the "Press and Hold to View Sample" button. If you select one of the Custom Type tab charts a sample of the chart with your selected data displays in the preview pane.

The next step of the Chart Wizard, shown in Figure 6-5, deals with verifying the data ranges for the chart and specifying the orientation of the data (indicating whether you want to place the data on the chart based on the values in rows or columns). The data range that displays is the cells that you selected prior to selecting Insert → Chart. If you did not select a range, you need to either use the Collapse dialog button and highlight the range of data you want on the chart or manually type the desired range.

 Excel allows you to have a maximum of 255 data series in most charts; with the exception of the pie chart that can only display one data series. Within each series, Excel allows you to have a maximum of 32,000 data points for standard charts, and 4,000 data points for 3D charts.

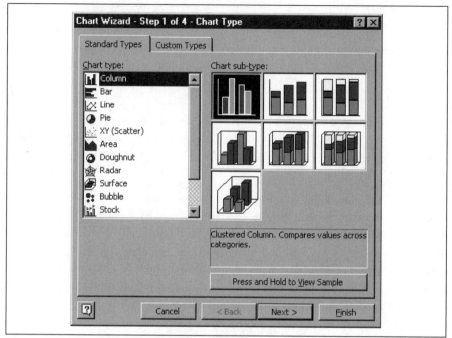

Figure 6-4: Chart Type Dialog - Chart Wizard

The orientation (Series in radio buttons) that you select determines the values selected on the Series tab. For example, if you select the Rows radio button, by default Excel uses the first cell in each row as the series name for the chart. The series name is the information that appears in the legend.

You can customize the series names on the Series tab. To change a series name, highlight the name in the series list and type the desired name in the Name field. You can also click on the Collapse Dialog button and select another field that contains the desired series name. Keep in mind, any modifications made to the series names do not affect the values in the worksheet.

The third step of the Chart Wizard, displays the Chart Options dialog shown in Figure 6-6. This is where you customize the look of the chart. The actual customization options (tabs) that are available vary depending upon the type of chart selected. To customize the chart you need to select each tab and designate the appropriate values for each field. As you make modifications to the chart options, you will be able to see the results in the chart view section that appears on the right side of the dialog. For example, if you are creating a Pie Chart, only the Titles, Legend, and Data Labels tabs display on the Chart Options dialog.

The final step of the Chart Wizard, shown in Figure 6-7, is where you indicate the location for the new chart. You can either place the chart directly in any worksheet in the workbook or add it to the workbook as a new sheet.

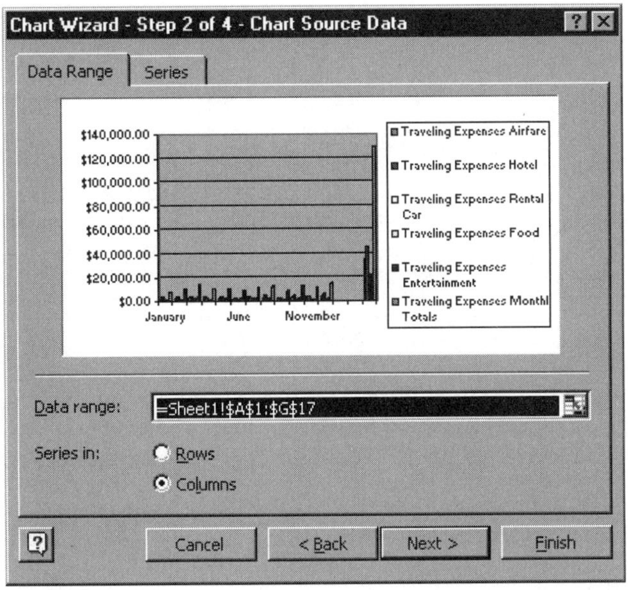

Figure 6-5: Chart Source Data Dialog - Chart Wizard

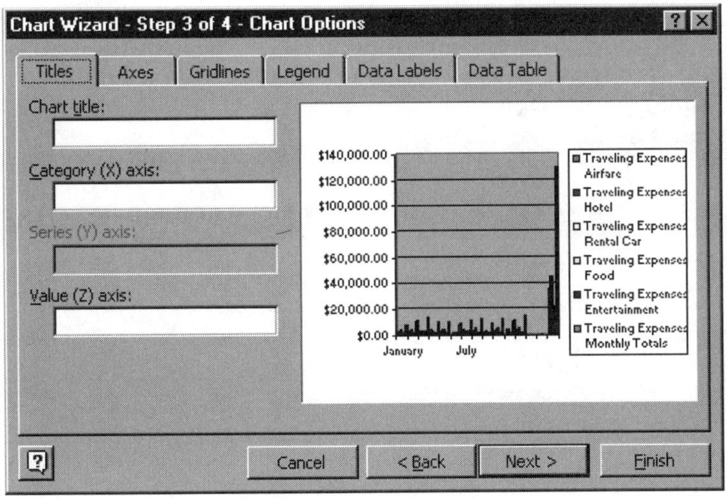

Figure 6-6: Chart Options - Chart Wizard

When you place a chart on a new sheet it is placed on a chart sheet. This is the best option to select if you only want to print the chart, without the actual data of the worksheet. The chart sheet displays the chart as it will be printed on a sheet of paper (WYSIWYG). If you want to place the chart directly on a worksheet, you can select the "As object in" radio button and then indicate the worksheet where you want to

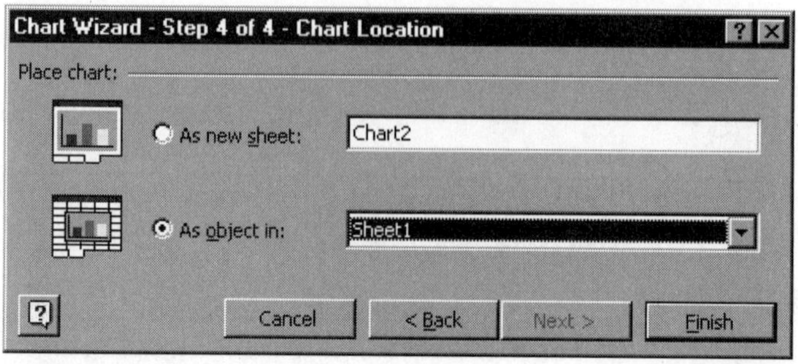

Figure 6-7: Chart Location Dialog - Chart Wizard

insert the chart in by selecting the down arrow button next to the field. If you have created a fairly small graph, I would suggest placing it directly on the worksheet so that you can easily reference the data that was used to create the chart.

Keep in mind that in order to see the Chart menu, detailed in Chapter 10, you must either select a chart that is embedded on a worksheet, or display a chart sheet. The Chart menu replaces the Data menu whenever it displayed. Since you typically are working with different data within Excel, you will rarely see this menu.

TIP # 44

Creating More Chart Types

You can create custom chart types that display on the Custom Types tab with Chart → Chart Type. Before you can add a custom chart, you must first create the chart and then select it.

TIP # 45

Default Chart Shortcut

You can quickly create a chart using the default chart type by selecting the desired data in the chart and then pressing F11. The default chart type is selected using Chart → Chart Type.

Insert → Page Break

Inserts page breaks in the worksheet at the specified location. Depending upon the location of the active cell, Excel either inserts a horizontal page break (between columns) or a vertical page break (between rows).

To insert a horizontal page break, select the cell in the first row of the worksheet that is to the right of where you want to insert the page break. To insert a vertical page break, select the cell in the first column of the worksheet below where you want the page break. You can remove a page break by selecting the correct cell, just like adding the page break and selecting Insert → Remove Page Break. To remove a vertical page break, you need to select a cell below the page break. Select a cell to the right of a page break for a horizontal page break, as shown in Figure 6-8 since B10 is selected the vertical page break between columns A and B will be removed. The Remove Page Break option only appears on the Insert menu when the active cell is either below or to the right of a page break. In other words, this option is only there if it is possible to remove a page break, such as shown in Figure 6-8.

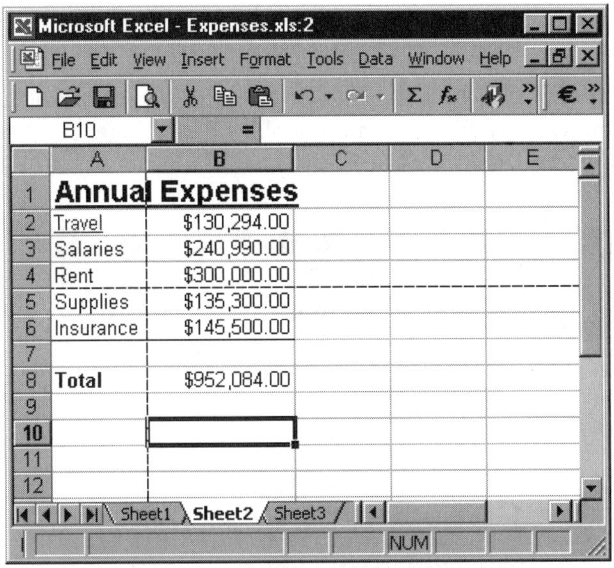

Figure 6-8: Select Cell to Right of a Vertical Page Break to Remove it

The easiest way to see the page breaks for the worksheet is to select View → Page Break Preview. You can also move and remove page breaks in this mode.

If the active cell is not in the first row or column of the worksheet, Excel creates both a horizontal and vertical page break at that location. If you did not want both page breaks, the easiest way to remove one is with View → Page Break Preview.

If you select a cell that is both directly below a page break and to the right of another page break, both page breaks will be remove when you select Insert → Remove Page Break.

TIP # 46

Eliminating Page Breaks

To quickly remove all of the page breaks that you have manually placed in the worksheet, select CTRL+A and Insert → Reset All Page Breaks.

Insert → Function

One of the most powerful options available within Excel is the ability to quickly perform a complex calculation by using one of the built-in functions that are available. Functions provide the ability to quickly perform complex calculations. For example, you can select a function to determine what you payment will be on a loan; you simply tell Excel what the interest rate, number of payments, and loan amount is and Excel uses the function to calculate your payment. The values that you supply to the function are commonly referred to as the function's arguments. For more information about functions and formulas, refer to Chapter 11, *Working with Functions*.

The Insert → Function option adds a built-in function into the active cell to create a formula. When you select Insert → Function or Shift+F3 the Paste Function dialog, shown in Figure 6-9, displays a list of currently installed functions.

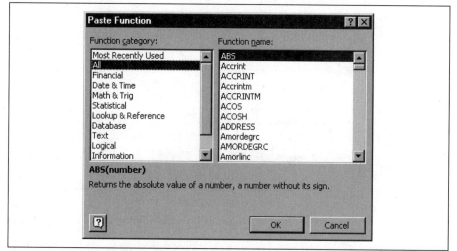

Figure 6-9: Paste Function Dialog

The functions listed on the Paste Function dialog are sorted into different categories to make it easier to locate the type of function you are looking for. Excel remembers the functions you have used most recently and lists them under the Most Recently Used category.

Excel provides a multitude of different functions that can be added to your formulas. You can add even more functions by selecting Tools → Add-Ins and then selecting the add-ins you want. (For example, Excel comes with an add-in called Analysis ToolPak that provides additional functions that can be added to Excel. All of the functions provided with Excel are covered in detail in Part 3. Additional functions can be added by purchasing third-party packages, or even created using VBA (refer to Appendix A).

When you select a function from the Paste Function dialog the Formula Palette appears, as shown in Figure 6-10. The Formula Palette provides the ability to quickly select the arguments for the function. You can use the values from cells in your worksheet as the arguments for the function. To do this either type the range of the cells or select the Collapse Dialog button next to the argument field and select the desired cells. You can also manually type a value in each argument field.

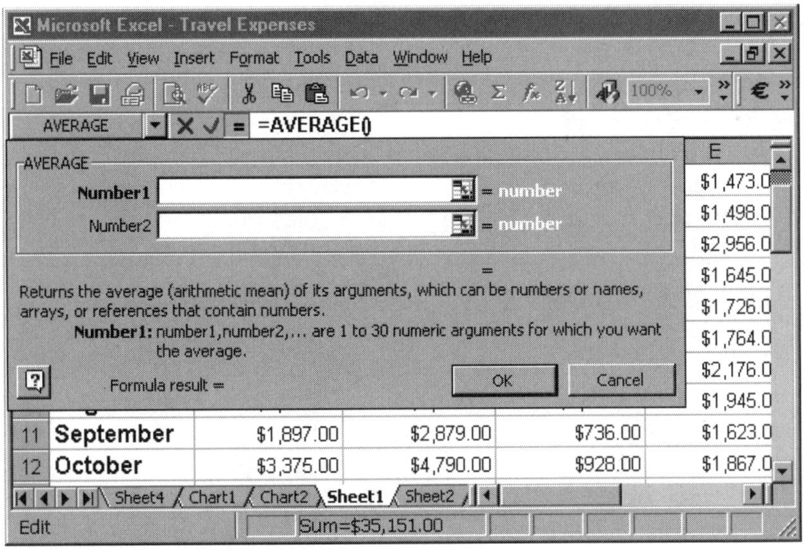

Figure 6-10: The Formula Palette

When the Formula Palette dialog displays the Name box changes to the Function List box. You can quickly change the function on the Formula Palette by selecting one from the Function List box.

The number of arguments that display on the Formula Palette dialog varies based upon the function selected. For many functions as you add values to each of the argument fields additional fields will be added, allowing you to add as many arguments as desired. For example, the Average function, shown in Figure 6-10 can have multiple values; when you type a value in the Number2 argument field, a new argument field will be added. As you specify the values for each argument for the function, the value of each argument displays on the right side of the field.

You can quickly select one of the functions in the Most Recently Used category by clicking on the Edit Formula button in the formula bar (the equal sign button) and then selecting the desired function from the drop-down list in the spot where you normally find the Name box.

If you are familiar with the name of the desired function and the type of arguments it takes, you can manually type it in the cell. Make sure you type an equal sign at the beginning of the function. If you forget to type an ending parenthesis for the arguments, Excel will automatically add it. When you add a function manually, Excel converts the name of the function to uppercase. This is a great way to make sure you typed the function properly because if Excel does not recognize the name of the function, it will not convert it to uppercase.

TIP # 47

Don't Remember the Arguments Needed for a Function?

Type the name of the function and press Ctrl+Shift+A. Excel will insert place-holders for the arguments you need to add.

To add a function to an existing formula, select the cell that contains the formula and then select the Edit Formula button to display the Formula Palette, as shown in Figure 6-11. Select the desired function to add to the formula.

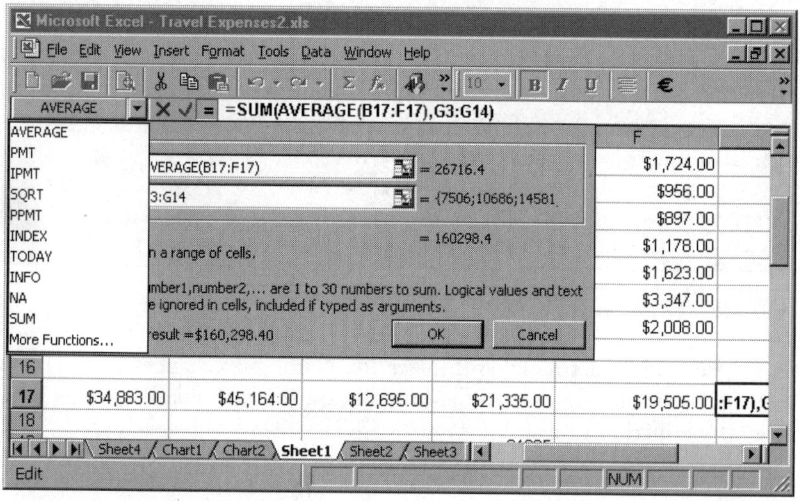

Figure 6-11: Add Additional Functions to a Formula by Selecting the Edit Formula Button

If you want to perform a function on a column or row of data, such as summing, and the selected row or column has a label, you can use the label in your function to represent the range of cells. Before you can do this, you must first select the Accept labels in formulas option on the Calculation tab of the Tools → Options. Once that checkbox is selected, you can simply type the name of the column label as the argument for your function.

Insert → Name

The Insert → Name option provides options for creating and working with named ranges of cells. By naming cells you don't have to remember the exact cell location where the information you want exists; you simply remember the name of the cell. For example, if cell C56 contains the total salaries for 1999, you could name that cell Salary to make it easier to reference. Once you name a cell, you can use the cell name in a function instead of the cell reference. For example, to determine the total costs, you could sum the columns name Salary, Rent, Utilities, and Supplies.

Define Option

The Define option allows you to assign a name to a specific cell or range of cells. Select the cells you want to name and then select Insert → Name → Define or Shift+F3 to display the Define Name dialog shown in Figure 6-12. By defining names for cells, you can select the name for use in a Formula, you can also quickly jump to a named location by selecting it from the Name box.

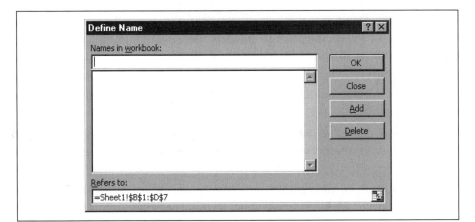

Figure 6-12: Define Name Dialog

Type the name for the selected cell or range of cells in the field under Names in workbook and select the Add button. Excel uses the specified name to refer to the range indicated in the "Refers to" field. For example, in Figure 6-12, you could type Costs for the range name in the "Names in workbook" field. If you want to add additional names, you can select the Collapse Dialog button next to the "Refers to" field and highlight a new range, or you can manually type the new range in the field. If you type the range in the field, start the range with the equal sign.

You can also create a name that represents a formula or a constant value. To do this type the desired name in the "Names in workbook" field and type the contents of the formula or constant value in the "Refers to" field. This can be a handy feature if you need to use the same formula at multiple locations within the worksheet.

A faster way to name cells is to use the Name box, on the Formula Bar at the top of the Excel window. Simply highlight the cell or range of cells you want to name and click on the Name box. Type the desired name for the cells and then press the Enter key. Make sure you press the Enter key, or Excel will not remember the new name.

TIP # 48

Renaming a Range

Excel will allow you to assign more than one name to a range of cells. Although you probably want to avoid doing this to eliminate confusion, you use this method to rename a range by selecting a name on the Define Name dialog and modifying the name as needed. After you save the new name by selecting the Add button, simply highlight the old name and select the Delete button to remove it from the list.

The names you create must follow these rules:

* The name cannot contain spaces. If you want to use more than one word as a name you can use other characters, such as a period or underscore to combine the words. For example, Total_Cost, or Total.Cost.

* You can use any combination of numbers and letters but the name must begin with a letter or an underscore. Also, you cannot assign a name that resembles a cell reference such as C3.

* The only symbols that can be used are underscore (_), period, question mark, and backslash (\).

* The name cannot exceed 255 characters, although if the name is larger than 253 characters, you cannot select it from the Name box.

* Excel is not case-sensitive when dealing with names. The name can be in any case, for example, all uppercase, or initial uppercase, but names with the same spelling are considered to be the same. In fact, Excel only accepts the name the first time, if you use that name again it just ignores it and assumes you want to use the name with the first definition. Unfortunately, it does not tell you that you have already used that name and need to select another one. Therefore, it is a good idea to check the list of names on the Define Name dialog to make sure you are using a unique name.

* Be careful when deleting names. If you delete a name that is used in a formula, the formula will return the value #NAME?.

Paste Option

The Paste option allows you to assign the value of a named cell or range of cells to another location in your worksheet. This is a great method for adding a name to a formula. You can either select Insert → Name → Paste or F3 to display the Paste Name dialog shown in Figure 6-13.

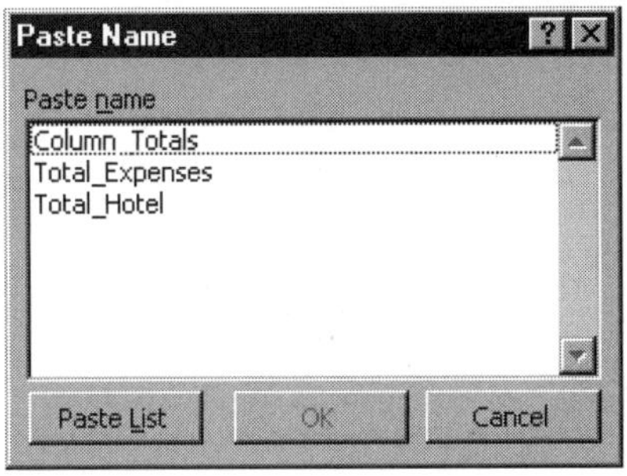

Figure 6-13: Paste Name dialog

If you want to quickly see a list of the names in your worksheet and what they refer to, as shown in Figure 6-14, you can select the Paste List button, on the Paste Name dialog. Make sure you place your cursor on a blank cell with enough room (blank cells below) for the contents of the list. Excel will paste the information into two columns. The first column will contain the names, and the second will contain the corresponding references.

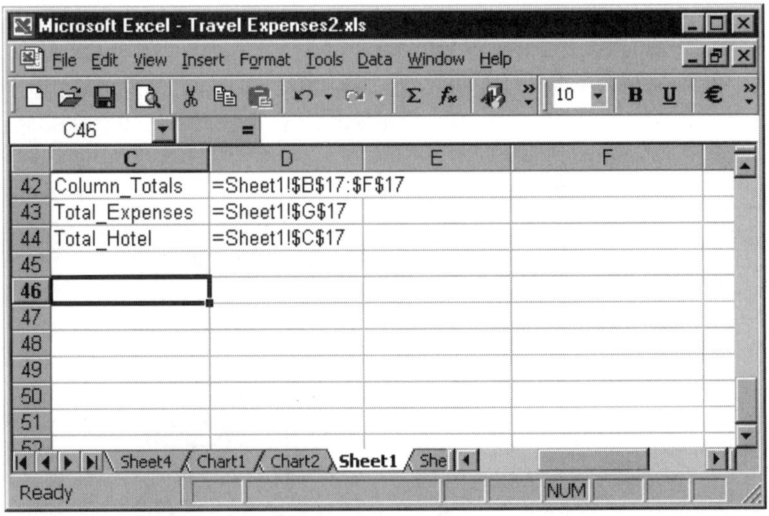

Figure 6-14: You can view a list of the defined names and the cells they reference

Create Option

The Create option allows you to use your row and column headings as names for the adjacent cells. Select the cells containing the name text and the corresponding cells you want to name and then select the Insert → Name → Create option to display the Create Names dialog as shown in Figure 6-15.

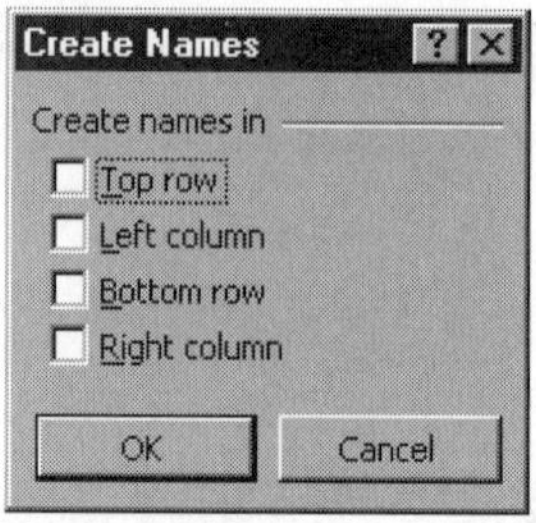

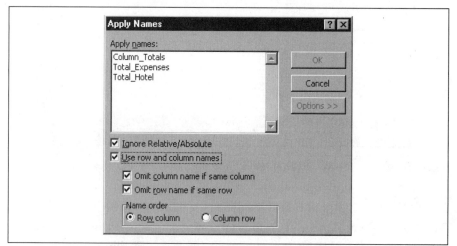

Figure 6-15: Create Names dialog

Excel creates the names based upon the name requirements outlined in the Define Option section. For example, if the text contains multiple words such as Total Expenses, Excel joins the words with an underscore to read Total_Expenses. If one of the text fields contains a formula, a name is not assigned to the corresponding cells. Also, if one of the name cells is larger than the other name cells in the selection, a name is not assigned to the corresponding cells.

Apply Option

This option allows you to change the cell references within formulas in your worksheet to the names you have created for the corresponding references. When you select this option the Apply Names dialog displays as shown in Figure 6-16. If you select the first cell in the worksheet before selecting this option, all formulas within the worksheet are based on your selections; otherwise, only the formulas within the range of cells you have selected are updated.

Figure 6-16: Apply Names dialog with the Options button selected

If the "Ignore Relative/Absolute" checkbox is selected, Excel replaces the cell references with the corresponding name regardless of whether or not the name and cell references are relative or absolute. For more information about relative and absolute cell references, refer to Chapter 2, *Excel Anatomy*.

Select the "Use row and columns name" checkbox to indicate that you want Excel to use the row and column names as references for cells in each formula if the cell does not have a name. For example, if row 2 is named January and column B is named Airfare then cell B2 will be referenced as January Airfare in a formula. You can indicate whether you want the row or column name to appear first in the reference by selecting the appropriate radio button in the Name Order box.

Label Option

It is normally easier to refer to a cell on your worksheet based upon its row and column headings. Unfortunately Excel only recognizes headings if they exist in the first row and column of the worksheet, as needed for the Create option. If your labels exist in another location, you can use Insert → Name → Label to remedy the situation.

When you select this option the Label Ranges displays as shown dialog shown in Figure 6-17. Once you have specified the labels, you can use the row and column labels to indicate a cell reference in a formula. Although, unlike the Create and Define options, the labels specified do not display in the Names box.

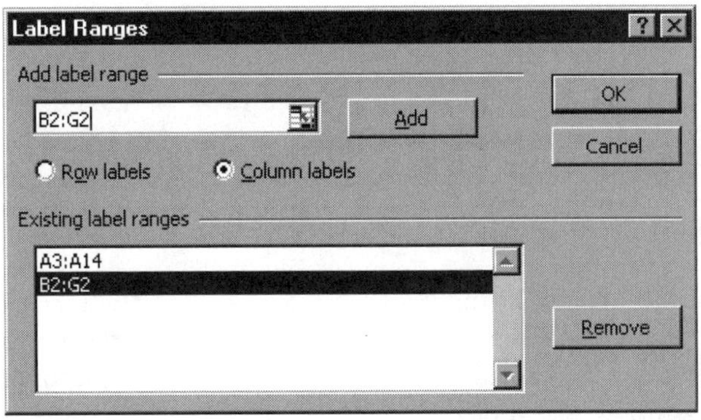

Figure 6-17: Label Ranges dialog

Insert → Comment

Select the cell where you want to place the comment and then select either Insert → Comment or Shift+F2 to insert a comment box for the cell. When the comment is created it contains your name, or the name that was used when Excel was installed on your system, and space for you to enter the a comment, as shown in Figure 6-18. You can modify the entire comment, including modifying or removing the name.

When you insert a comment in a cell a red triangle displays in the upper-left corner of the cell, as shown in Figure 6-18. When you drag the mouse cursor across a cell that contains a comment, it displays on the worksheet as long as you have not hidden the comments. If you do not want to see the comment indicators you can hide them on the View tab of Tools → Options.

TIP # 49

Determining Owner of a Comment

If you are sharing workbooks with other users, it is a good idea to have a name assigned for each user's comments.

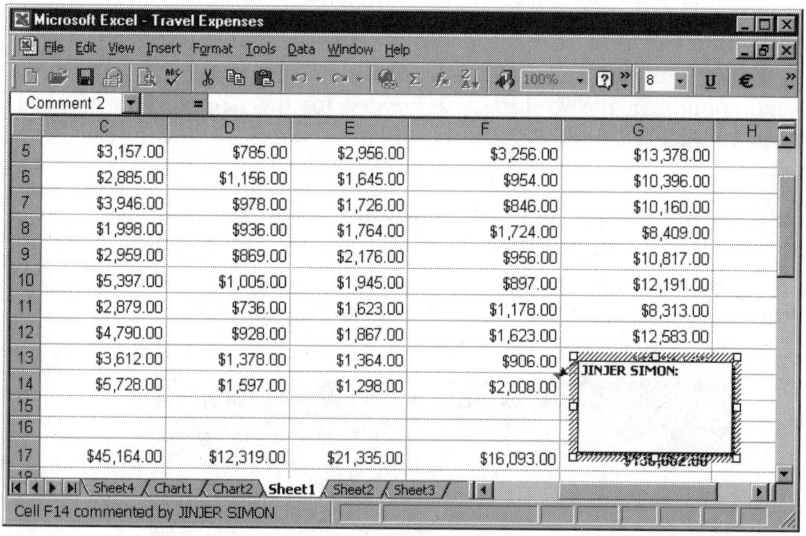

Figure 6-18: Comment Box Displays on the Worksheet

You can see all the comments in the worksheet by selecting View → Comments. Keep in mind that if you eliminated the comment indicators on the worksheet with Tools → Options, as soon as you select View → Comments again the comment indicators will display again on the worksheet.

TIP # 50

Removing Comments in a Cell

To remove a comment in a cell, right-click on the desired cell with the mouse and select the Delete Comment option. Of course, if you are using the Tools → Track Changes option to keep track of revisions to your worksheet, the comment will not be removed until the modifications are accepted.

Insert → Picture

If you want to add graphics to your worksheet, such as the company logo, or a picture, you need to use Insert → Picture. Excel provides a variety of different types of graphics that can be added to your worksheet using the various options available on the Picture menu. Most of these features are available for all Microsoft Office products.

Clip Art

Insert → Picture → Clip Art allows you to select a picture, sound file, or motion image from the Clip Gallery application that is available to other Microsoft Office applications. When you select this option, the Insert ClipArt dialog displays, as shown in Figure 6-19.

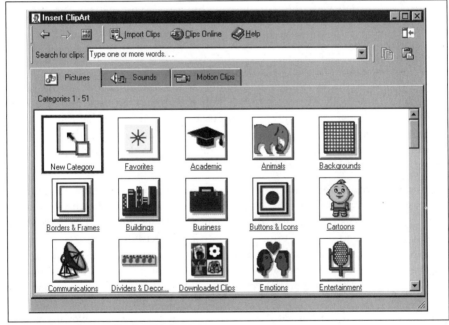

Figure 6-19: Insert ClipArt Dialog

The various clips available are sorted into categories to make it easier to locate what you are looking for. If you cannot find the clip you are looking for you can search Microsoft's web site for more clips by selecting the Clips Online option. Keep in mind that if you insert a motion clip it will only appear animated if you save your workbook as a web page and view it through your web browser.

NOTE *You can add more clips to the Clip Gallery by selecting the Import Clips option. This is a handy feature to use if you want to make your images available to other Microsoft Office Applications.*

From File

Excel also allows you to add standard graphic files to your worksheet, by selecting the From File option. When you select this option the Insert Picture dialog opens so you can select the desired graphic file. The Insert Picture dialog resembles the Open dialog that displays when you select File → Open, the only difference is that Excel only lists the files that match the graphic types it can import on the Insert Picture dialog. In other words, Excel does not list .xls (workbook files) on the dialog because they are not graphics files.

If you insert an animated GIF file in your worksheet the image will only appear animated if you save the workbook as a web page and then view it in your web browser. When you view the worksheet within Excel, you will just see the first frame of the animated GIF.

AutoShapes

Displays the AutoShapes toolbar, shown in Figure 6-20 so you can select one of the shapes that come with Microsoft Office. When you click on each button on the toolbar a drop-down menu shows the various shapes available in that category. For example, the first button on the toolbar is for lines. When you select that button six different lines types display. To insert one, simply click on the desired type and then drag it on the worksheet to create the line.

Once you insert a shape in the worksheet, you can move or resize the shape using the mouse. You can modify the properties for the shape by selecting Format → AutoShape or Ctrl+1 to display the Format AutoShape dialog. The AutoShape option only displays on the Format menu when you have a shape selected on the worksheet. The Format AutoShape dialog provides options for customizing how Excel draws the shape such as color of lines, whether or not the shape is filled, etc. The actual tabs that display on the Format AutoShape dialog vary based on the type of shape selected. For example, if you select one of the Callout autoshapes, the only tab that displays on the Format Autoshape dialog is the Font tab allowing you to customize the text settings for the callout.

You can add shadows and three-dimensional effects to your shapes using the Drawing toolbar. To do this you need to make sure the Drawing toolbar is displayed by selecting the Drawing icon on the Standard toolbar or by selecting View → Toolbars and selecting the Drawing toolbar. Then select the shape you want to add the effects to and select the appropriate button on the Drawing toolbar.

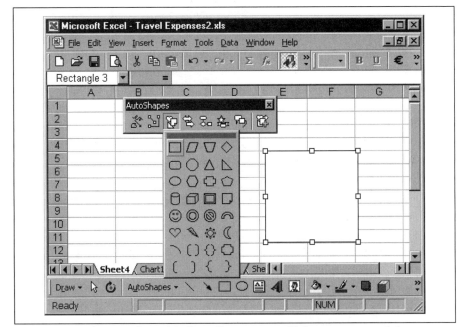

Figure 6-20: The AutoShapes Toolbar allows you to add shapes to you worksheet

Organization Chart

This option opens the Microsoft Organization Chart application so you can create an organization chart. An organization chart is similar to a flowchart, it is typically used to show the layout of the positions within a company, basically who each employee reports to. If you are familiar with genealogy, an organization chart looks just like a family tree. In fact, this feature can be used to for any purpose where you need to show a hierarchical order.

The Microsoft Organization Chart application comes with the Microsoft Office 2000 software. If it is not currently installed on your machine, Excel will give you the option to install it when you select the Organization Chart option.

Another way to create an organizational chart is to use the shapes and lines on the AutoShapes toolbar. AutoShapes provides you a little more freedom to design the look of your chart, but you have to manually draw each job box and then draw the lines to show who the job reports to. For example, if you look at Figure 6-24 you will see that the sample organization chart could have easily been created by inserting three boxes and connecting them with lines.

WordArt

This option opens the WordArt Gallery, shown in Figure 6-21, another feature included with Microsoft Office. With the WordArt Gallery you can create text with special effects.

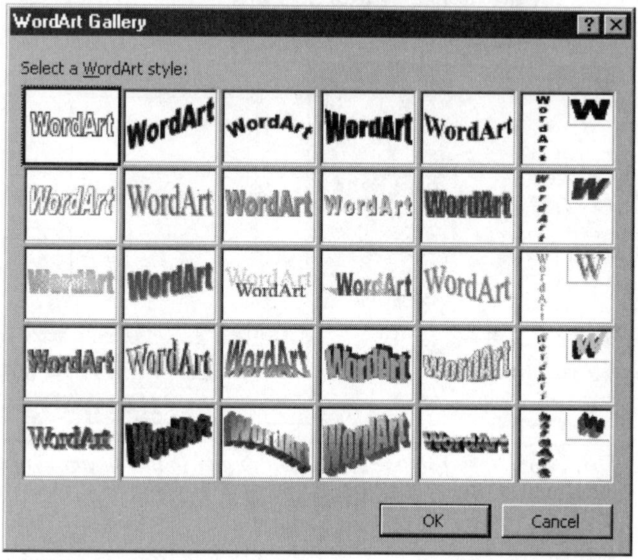

Figure 6-21: WordArt Gallery Dialog

After you select the type of special effects you want to add to your text the Edit WordArt Text dialog box displays where you indicate the specific text you want to apply the effects to. You also need to specify the font type and size on this dialog. The cool thing about adding WordArt and other graphics is that Excel converts the images to *.gif* images if you save you workbook as an HTML file. Once the WordArt text is added to your worksheet it is easy to make modifications to it. Simply click on the text and the WordArt toolbar will display. In addition to the modifications available on the WordArt toolbar, you can also select the Shadow and 3D buttons on the Drawing toolbar to add additional effects.

From Scanner or Camera

If you have a scanner or digital camera connected to your machine, you can use this option to insert a picture from the device. Your scanner or digital camera must be TWAIN compatible and you need to install the appropriate software for the device. Refer to the documentation that came with your scanner or digital camera for more information about its compatibility If you have not used this feature before, you will need to install the appropriate features from the Microsoft Office CD-ROM.

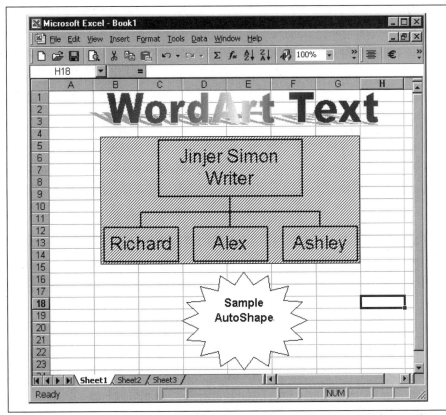

Figure 6-22: Samples of WordArt, Organization charts, and AutoShapes that can be added to your worksheets

NOTE *TWAIN is an interface that is used to get images from scanners and cameras. TWAIN support allows you to scan the pictures directly into Excel instead of bringing it into another package and then saving it in a format to import into Excel. TWAIN Version 1.7 is supported by Excel 2000.*

You will need to select the type of quality that should be used to import the image into Excel. You can select from two types of quality (Print Quality and Web Quality). If you plan to print the image you will want to select the Print Quality option to get a higher resolution image, the downfall to selecting this type is that it creates an image with a larger file size. Since images that are going to be placed on the Web need to be as small as possible so that they download quickly when people view you site, you can select the Web Quality option to have Excel create a lower resolution image.

Insert → Object

Excel allows you to insert an OLE (Object Linking and Embedding) object directly into your worksheet. This means that you are placing an object from another windows program into your worksheet. When you select the object, Excel provides you the ability to use the other programs editing tools to modify it. For example, Figure 6-23 shows a sample of a Microsoft Map object that has been embedded in a worksheet. When the object is added, the Microsoft Map toolbars display providing the ability to modify the object directly within Excel.

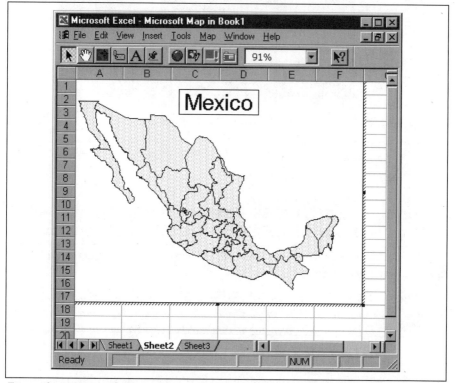

Figure 6-23: Microsoft Map Object with Editing Tools displayed within Excel

When you select Insert → Object, the Object dialog displays as shown in Figure 6-24. There are two different tabs that allow you to either create a new OLE object by selecting one of the object types listed on the Create New tab, or insert an existing object by locating the desired object on the Create from File tab.

Only the programs on your machine that support OLE objects will be listed on the Create New tab. When you select one of the programs on the Create New tab, the program environment opens within your worksheet so you can create your OLE

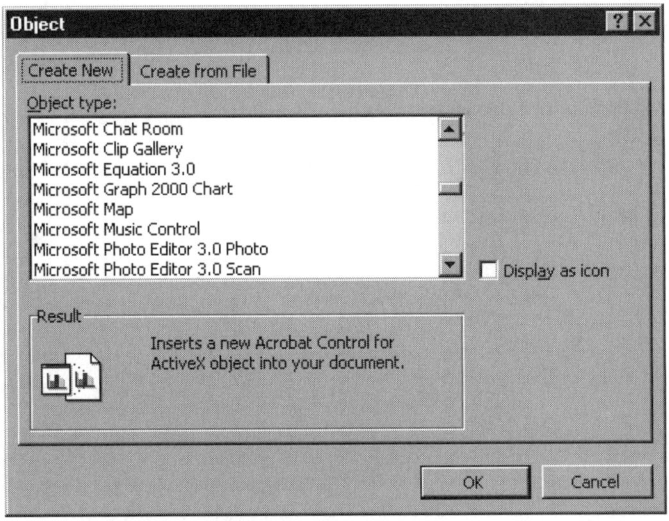

Figure 6-24: Object Dialog

image. For example, in Figure 6-23 a map of Mexico was inserted directly into the worksheet using the Microsoft Map control.

If you select the Display as Icon checkbox on either tab an icon that corresponds to the image type displays in your worksheet. You need to click on the icon to actually see the image.

Once the object has been added to you worksheet, you need to use Edit → Object to make modifications. This displays the object toolbars again as shown in Figure 6-23 so you can make the desired modifications.

Insert → Hyperlink

Excel allows you to create hyperlinks, links to other files, within your worksheet. The hyperlinks can be linked to text or an image. When you select Insert → Hyperlink, or Ctrl+K the Insert Hyperlink dialog displays as shown in Figure 6-25. The Insert Hyperlink dialog access the Most Recently Used (MRU) list for Windows. The MRU list keeps track of the files and web pages that you have recently viewed. You can create a link by selecting one of this files or web pages or you can type in a new link.

The Insert Hyperlink dialog allows you to create links to specific web sites, files on your machine, locations within the existing workbook, new workbooks, or email address, by selecting the appropriate icon in the Link To bar. The address used to specify the location of files you link to is based on the hyperlink base address specified on the Summary tab of File → Properties. If you want the link to exist for a specific line of text or graphic, make sure you select it prior to selecting the Insert →

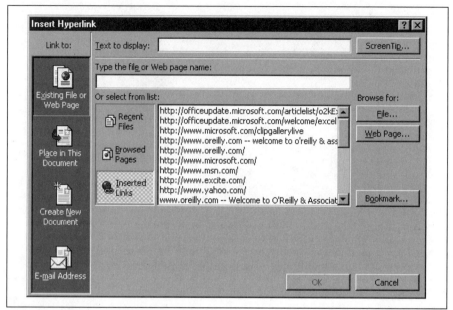

Figure 6-25: Insert Hyperlink Dialog

Hyperlink option. You need to select the text so that Excel knows where you want to place the link. Excel will create an HTML hyperlink on that text so that when someone clicks on the text the Microsoft link you select will open in your browser.

Some Hyperlink Tips

Keep the following items in mind when using hyperlinks in Excel:

- You cannot create hyperlinks for controls that were created using the Forms toolbar or from buttons and graphics that have macros assigned to them.

- You can create a hyperlink to a web site or an email address by typing the appropriate address directly in the cell.

- If you do not specify a screen tip for your hyperlink the address of the link will display as the screen tip when the cursor is dragged across the link.

- For example, if you want to create a link in your worksheet to O'Reilly and Associates, you can perform the following steps:

    a. Select the cell where you want to place the link.

    b. Select Insert → Hyperlink to display the Insert Hyperlink dialog shown in Figure 6-25.

    c. Make sure the "Existing File or Web Page" icon is selected.

d. If the active cell does not contain text or a graphical image you can indicate the text that will be placed in the cell in the "Text to display" field. In other words, instead of having the web address (URL) of *http://www.oreily.com* you could indicate that you want the text of the hyperlink to be "Check out O'Reilly and Associates."

e. If you want to display a tip message when you drag the cursor over the link, select the ScreenTip button and specify the message you want to display.

f. Type the URL, for the location. In this instance, it would be *http://www.oreilly.com*. If you have previously selected this URL either by adding it as a hyperlink or even by viewing it in your web browser, you can also select the Inserted Links button and highlight the appropriate link from the list.

g. Select the OK button to add the link to your worksheet.

Chapter 7

Format

Excel uses formatting to determine how the contents of a cell should display (i.e., bold, italics, font size, left justified, etc.). Besides specifying the look of cell contents, you can also indicate how numeric values should be handled by applying a number format to a cell. By default, all cells within a worksheet have General formatting. There are actually 12 different default number formats that can be applied to a cell and each one can be customized.

 By default Excel left justifies the contents of a cell if it contains text and right-justifies the cell if it contains a number. You can modify this justification by changing the alignment of the cell using Format → Cells → Alignment or by selecting the corresponding icon on the toolbar.

General

This is the default format applied to all cells. A number displays basically the way it is entered in the cell. If the cell is not wide enough to fit the entire number, scientific notation is used.

Number

Provides the ability to specify the actual number format by indicating the number of decimal places, if a comma should separate the thousands, and the method used to display negative numbers (a minus sign, in red, in parentheses, or in red and in parentheses).

Currency

Typically this format is selected because you want the number to have a currency symbol (a dollar sign in the United States), which you can select for your location. Just like the Number format, you can indicate the number of decimal places, if a comma should separate the thousands, and the method used to display negative numbers (a minus sign, in red, in parentheses, or in red and in parentheses).

Accounting

The only difference between this format and the Currency format is that the currency symbols line up vertically within a column.

Date

> Provides 15 different date formats that you can select. For example, you need to indicate if the date should be 5/27/2000 or May 27, 2000.

Time

> Provides eight different time formats you can select. For example, you can select whether you want to see 1:30 PM or 13:30:23.

Percentage

> Converts the numeric value to a percentage and allows you to specify the number of decimal places. There is always a percentage sign at the end of the number.

Fraction

> Provides nine different fractions you can select. Only decimal values will be converted to fractions.

Scientific

> Converts numbers to exponential notation (with an E). For example, the number 123 would display as 1.23E+02. You need to indicate the number of decimal places that display on the left side of the E.

Text

> Select this format to have numbers treated like text. The number will be left-aligned in the cell just like text. This format would be selected for something like a model number or a flight number; values you don't want to use in calculations.

Special

> Provides formats for Zip Codes, Zip Codes + 4, phone numbers, and Social Security Numbers.

Custom

> Provides the ability to create custom number formats if you cannot find the format you need in one of the other 11 formats. The process of creating a custom format is described later in this chapter.

If you only want to specify formatting applied to the cell under specific conditions, you can use Format → Conditional Formatting. With this option you can set up specific criteria that must be meet before a cell receives the indicated formatting. The nice thing about Conditional Formatting is that you can apply one format to the cell and have the formatting change based on the contents of the cell.

Format → Cells

Displays the Format Cells dialog, shown in Figure 7-1, where you can customize the way data displays in the selected cells. Although there are six different tabs that

Format Menu

provide several different options for customizing the cell format, many of the options on these tabs can also be set using the Formatting toolbar.

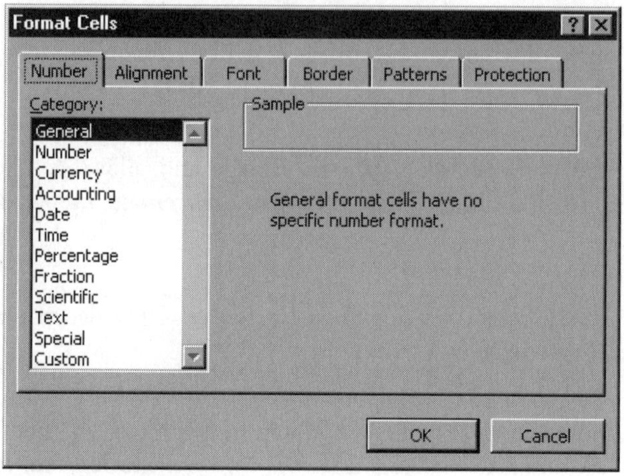

Figure 7-1: Format Cells dialog

Number

The Number tab provides the ability to specify the type of data that is stored in the selected cells in the worksheet. When you select the data type, you also indicate how Excel should format the contents of the cell. For example, if you select a number, you need to select the number of decimal places, whether you want a separator for amounts over 1000, and how negative numbers should display. The options available for each data type vary.

Besides selecting from the 11 pre-set types, you can also define custom number formats by selecting the Custom category. The Custom category allows you to create formats that are not included in any of the other format categories. This category allows you to specify the format for positive numbers, negative numbers, zero values, and text all at once.

The easiest way to create a custom format is to select one of the formats in the Type list and then make the desired modifications. As indicated, you can specify up to four sections of format codes, in the following order, with each section separated by a semicolon:

```
Positive Number Format; Negative Number Format; Zero Value Format; Text
Format
```

You do not have to specify all four sections; in fact, if you only specify one code, that code is used for all numbers. If you specify two codes, the first is used for positive numbers and zero values and the second is used for negative numbers. If you want to hide the values in the selected cells, you can specify a format of ; ; ;.

When you make the modifications to a custom format you can use the codes as outlined in Table 7-1.

Table 7-1: Custom Formatting Codes

Code	Description
#	Displays only the significant zeros in the value. For example, 80.05 would display all zeros but 8.500 would display as 8.5.
0	Displays insignificant zeros if the number has fewer digits than specified in the format. For example, if the format is 0.000, then 8.5000 displays as 8.500.
?	Adds zeros to the number on either side of the decimal point so that the numeric values line up when a fixed-width font is applied.
.	Indicates the decimal point location within the format.
,	Indicates the location of the thousand separator, or scales the number down by multiples of 1000. For example, 14000 would display as 14 if the definition was 0.
[Black], [Blue], [Cyan], [Green], [Magenta], [Red], [White], [Yellow]	Indicates the color that should be applied to the values that meet the format.
"	Places text you want displayed within a set of double quotation marks.
$ - + / ( ) : space	Displays the specified character in the text.
*	Indicates that you want to use whatever character follows the asterisk to fill the remaining contents of the cell.
@	Indicates the location in the format where you want to display the text that is entered into the cell.

You can also create custom date and time formats for your cells using the Custom format category. The date and time formats can be created using any combination of the codes in Table 7-2.

Table 7-2: Date and Time Format Codes

Code	Description
M	When dealing with dates, a single M displays the month number without leading zeros for 01-09. Mm displays the month number with leading zeros. Mmm displays the month as an abbreviation (Jan - Dec). Mmmm displays the month as its full name. When dealing with times, M displays the minutes without leading zeros, and MM displays the minutes with leading zeros.

Table 7-2: Date and Time Format Codes (continued)

Code	Description
D	A single D displays the day of the week without leading zeros, Dd displays the day of the week with leading zeros, Ddd displays the three-digit abbreviation for the day of the week, and Dddd displays the full name of the day of the week.
Y	YY displays the year as a two-digit number, YYYY displays the year as a four-digit number.
H	H displays the hour without leading zeros, HH displays the hour with leading zeros.
S	S displays the seconds without leading zeros, SS displays the seconds with leading zeros.
AM/PM, A/P	Indicates whether a 12-hour clock or a 24-hour clock should be used.

Alignment

The alignment tab allows you to specify how the text/numbers display within the cell. Not only can you indicate how it is justified, but you can also rotate the text in the cell. Another way to justify the text within your cells is to select Edit → Fill → Justify.

Probably the most important option on this tab is the ability to merge cells together on your worksheet. This checkbox is very useful for creating a heading over a series of cells.

Font

The Font tab is used to specify font characteristics for the selected cells. The characteristics that initially appear on the tab are those assigned to the Normal font style. If you alter the font characteristics, you can return to the settings for the Normal font style by selecting the Normal font checkbox. Check out Tools → Options for information about changing the Normal font settings.

Border

You can use the Borders tab to design custom borders around various cells on your worksheet. You can select both the line type and color. If you are using borders on your worksheet you may want to turn off the grid display on the View tab of Tools → Options to make the borders show up better.

Patterns

The Patterns tab allows you to select the color and pattern that displays on the background of the cell. If you do not select a pattern the entire cell is filled with the selected color.

If you want to use a graphic file as the background for the worksheet, select Format → Sheet → Background.

Protection

If you are using sheet protection, you can use the options on the Protection tab to lock and hide the contents of the selected cells. These options only work when the sheet is protected using Tools → Protection → Protect Sheet.

When the Hidden checkbox is selected the contents of the cell still display on the worksheet when it is protected. The only difference is that the formulas in the cell do not display on the Formula Bar when the cell is selected.

TIP # 51

Double Underline Contents of Selected Cells

A faster way to double-underline the contents of the selected cells is to hold down the Shift key while you click on the Underline button on the toolbar.

Format → Row

The Row menu options provide the ability to specify how the selected row displays on your worksheet by adjusting the row height. In Excel, each row is measured in points (a measurement commonly used to refer to font sizes, such as 12 pt). The default column height is based upon the Normal font style. As you add text with different font sizes to a row, Excel automatically adjusts the row size to accommodate the largest font.

Height

The Height option is used to specify a row height on the Row Height dialog, shown in Figure 7-2. When you manually specify the row height, Excel no longer automatically resizes the row to accommodate a larger font.

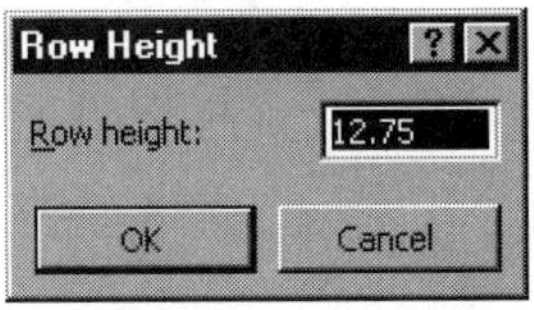

Figure 7-2: Row Height dialog

Another quick way to resize a row is to click on the row border under the row heading and drag it to the desired size.

AutoFit

The AutoFit option automatically sizes the selected row to accommodate the largest font in the row. This can also be accomplished by double-clicking on the row border under the row heading.

This option is only necessary if you have manually sized the row; otherwise, Excel will automatically resize the row when you add larger text.

Hide

Makes the selected row appear to be hidden from display. When you select the Hide option, Excel actually just sets the row height to zero so that the contents do not display. You can also quickly hide a row by selecting Ctrl+9 or by dragging the row border under the row heading until the row does not display.

Unhide

Unhides the specified row by resizing it so it is visible. Before selecting this option select cells above and below the hidden row. You can also select Ctrl+Shift+9 to unhide the row.

Format → Column

The Column menu options provide the ability to specify how the selected column displays on your worksheet by adjusting the column width. In Excel, the default width is about 8.43 characters based on the average number of zeros that can fit within the cell based upon the default font (the Normal font style). Keep in mind that this is an average number of characters; since most the fonts we use are proportional fonts, the letters are all different sizes. Therefore, you could fit more letter Is in each cell than letter Ms.

Width

The Width option is used to specify a column width on the Column Width dialog, shown in Figure 7-3. When you manually specify the column width, Excel no longer automatically resizes the column to accommodate a larger font.

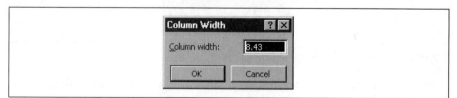

Figure 7-3: Column Width dialog

Another quick way to resize a column is to click on the column border on the right side of the row heading and drag it to the desired size.

Autofit Selection

The AutoFit Selection option sizes the selected column to accommodate the widest cell in your selection. This can also be accomplished by double-clicking on the column border to the right of the column heading.

Hide

Makes the selected column appear to be hidden from display. When you select the Hide option, Excel actually just sets the column width to zero so that the contents do not display. You can also quickly hide the column by selecting Ctrl+0 or by dragging the column border to the right of the column heading until the column does not display.

Unhide

Unhides the specified column by resizing it so it is visible. Before selecting this option, select cells from the columns on each side of the hidden column. You can also select Ctrl+Shift+0 to unhide the column.

Standard Width

Excel sets the default column width based upon the default font size. You can modify the default column width by selecting this option to display the Standard Width dialog shown in Figure 7-4.

Figure 7-4: Standard Width dialog

When you specify a new column width, all columns where the width has not been adjusted are resized to the new width.

Format → Sheet

The Sheet menu options provide the ability to customize how the selected worksheet displays by hiding it, adding a background image, or specifying an appropriate name for it.

Rename

Allows you to rename the current worksheet. By default, Excel names each worksheet based on the order in which it was added to the workbook,—Sheet1, Sheet2, etc. You can use custom names for your worksheets by selecting this option or by clicking on the worksheet name. When you select this option the worksheet name is selected; simply type the desired name.

Hide

Hides the selected worksheet within the workbook. This is a good option if you have a worksheet that contains data that is being used to calculate data in other worksheets.

Unhide

Makes a hidden worksheet visible within your workbook. When you select this option, the Unhide dialog shown in Figure 7-5 displays, allowing you to select the worksheet that you want to display.

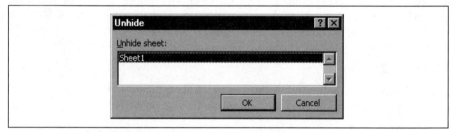

Figure 7-5: Unhide dialog

Background

Pastes an image on the background of your worksheet. When you select this option the Sheet Background dialog provides the ability to select the image you want used as the background. This dialog resembles the Open dialog that displays when you select File → Open.

Excel wallpapers the selected image on the background by repeatedly pasting it so the entire worksheet is covered. Keep in mind that the background image is for display purposes only and will not be printed. If the Background option is grayed out, there is probably more than one sheet tab selected. This option must be selected for each sheet that you want to apply it to.

Background images do not save when you publish the individual worksheet as a web page; but it will save if you publish the entire workbook. To remove the background image, select Format → Sheet → Remove Background.

Format → AutoFormat

Provides the ability to apply a predefined format to a range of cells on your worksheet. Excel provides several different formats that can be selected using the AutoFormat dialog shown in Figure 7-6.

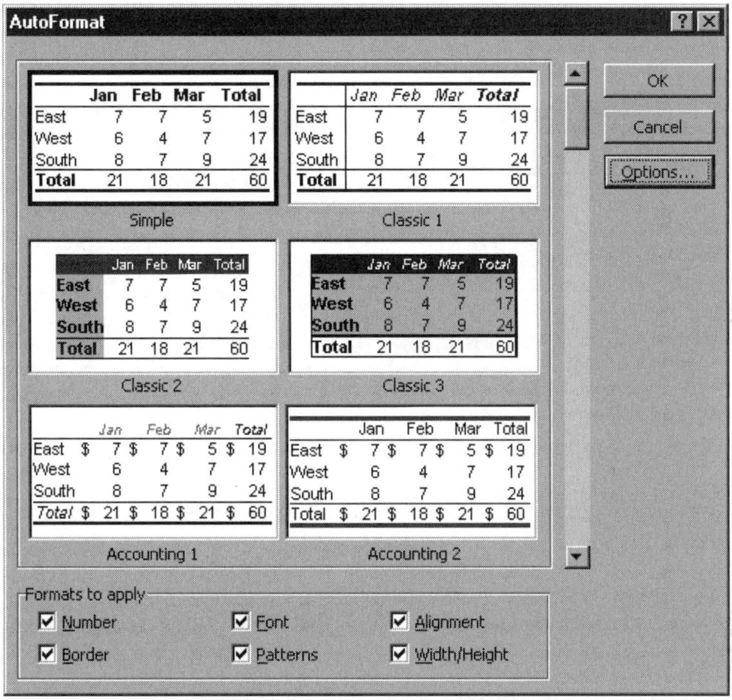

Figure 7-6: AutoFormat dialog

Excel examines the data in the cells you selected for the autoformatting and then applies the formatting that matches the format style you selected. Excel applies the formatting in six different categories that you can see by selecting the Options button. You can specify which formatting categories you want to use by removing the checkmark from the appropriate checkboxes. For example, if you want to maintain the existing fonts on your worksheet, remove the checkmark from the Font checkbox.

TIP # 52

Create Custom Styles

You cannot create your own autoformats, but you can use Format → Style to create custom styles that you can apply to your worksheet.

Format Menu

Format → Conditional Formatting

Specifies conditional formatting to apply to the selected range of cells. The conditional formatting is specified on the Conditional Formatting dialog shown in Figure 7-7. The formatting can be specified for either the value of a cell or the cell's formula if it is a logical formula (returns a value of either True of False). For example, you may want the cells whose values exceed $5000.00 to be bold so that they stand out on the worksheet.

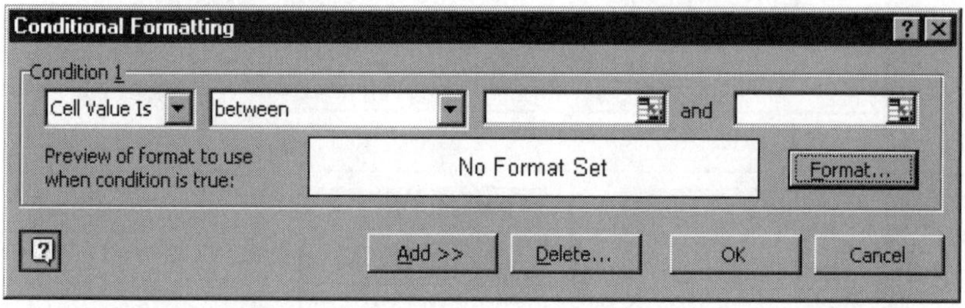

Figure 7-7: Conditional Formatting dialog

You can specify up to three different conditions for the selected cells by selecting the Add button to add each new condition. If you decide to eliminate one of the conditions, select the Delete button to display the Delete Conditional Format dialog and select the condition that you want to eliminate.

Depending upon the condition specified, Excel displays the appropriate number of reference boxes. For example, in Figure 7-7 "between" is selected as the condition, so you need to specify two different references.

Once you specify the condition you need to indicate the format that should be applied when the condition is met by selecting the Format button. This option displays the Format Cells.

To locate cells within your worksheet with conditional formatting select Edit → GoTo and then select the Special button and the Conditional Formatting option. You can either locate the cells with the same conditional formatting as the current cell or cells with any type of conditional formatting.

WARNING

If you paste data into a cell, the conditional formatting in the cell will also be replaced.

Format → Style

The use of styles is probably one of the most useful features for customizing the look and feel of a worksheet. A style basically indicates how a certain type of data should display. For example, you may want to have all totals displayed in a large, bold font; if you create a style called Totals, each time you create a total you can apply that style to the cell and all totals within the worksheet will be consistently formatted. If for some reason you decide to modify the style and you now want the totals to be bold and italic you simply need to modify the style and it will be changed throughout the worksheet.

You create, select, and modify styles using the Style dialog shown in Figure 7-8. Excel provides seven different default styles that can be modified as needed, or additional styles can be created to meet your needs. The Normal style is the default style assigned to all cells in a worksheet.

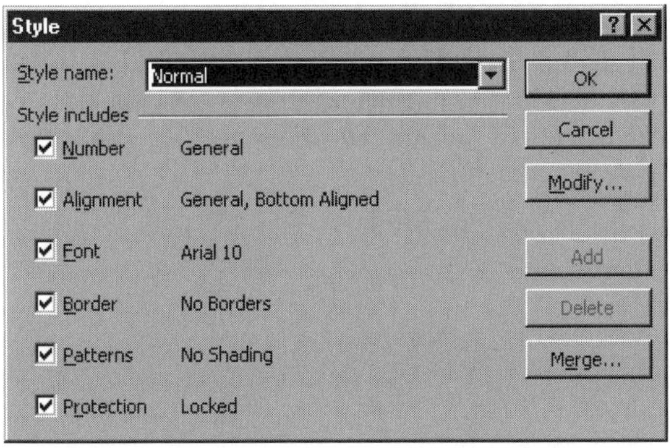

Figure 7-8: Style dialog

 NOTE *Once you have styles set up, you can save them in a template so that they can be applied to other documents using the File → Save As option.*

To make modifications to a style, make sure the desired style is selected and select the Modify button to display the Format Cells dialog shown in Figure 7-1. There are seven different attributes that can be specified about a style, as listed on the Style dialog. If you want to eliminate an attribute of the style, select the appropriate checkbox. Keep in mind that if you remove the checkbox from an attribute and then reselect an option for the attribute on the Format Cells dialog, the attribute will be reselected on the Style dialog. You can create new styles by typing a unique name in the Style name field and then making the appropriate modifications for the style using the Modify button.

To apply a style, select the desired cells for the style, select Format → Style and then select the style you want to apply. There are also buttons on the Formatting toolbar for the Currency, Percent, and Comma styles. If you have loaded the Euro Currency Tools with Tools → Add-ins there is also a Euro style button on the toolbar. Any modifications you make to these styles on the Style dialog will be reflected when you select one of the buttons.

 You can add a Style Tool to a toolbar or menu through Tools → Customize as detailed in Chapter 2. This is a more efficient tool for using styles.

If you want to copy styles you have created in one workbook into another workbook you can use the Merge option. In order to do this, both workbooks must be open. When you select the Merge option the Merge Styles dialog displays so you can select the workbook that you want to merge the styles from. If you only want to merge the styles you have created that do not exist in the other workbook, make sure you select the No button on the message box.

If you want to modify an existing style based on the formatting of the active cell, type the name of the existing style in the Style name field in the Style dialog and then select the OK button. Do not select the style from the drop-down list or the formatting in the active cell will be replaced with the existing formatting of the selected style.

Chapter 8

Tools

The Tools menu provides several different tools for working with your workbook. If you have worked with other Microsoft Office products, many of these menu options will look familiar. For example, if you have ever used Microsoft Word you are probably very familiar with the Spelling option, which allows you to check the spelling for a worksheet within Excel.

The Customize option works great for customizing your menus and toolbars so that those features of Excel that you use frequently are readily available. You can also use Options to make additional selections about the functionality of Excel. For example, you can indicate whether you want the Formula Bar and Status Bar to display on the window.

Part of what makes the Microsoft Office products so powerful is the ability to easily share information with others. By using the Online Collaboration options you are able to view and discuss a workbook with others online using NetMeeting.

 In this book you have seen mention of the Add-ins that come with Excel. Because there are so many different types of Excel users, it would be somewhat daunting to provide coverage of all this specialized functionality. To eliminate some of this confusion, and still provide specialized options for various users such as engineers and statisticians, Excel allows you to add that functionality as needed through the Add-ins option. I have attempted to cover each of these Add-in options that come with Excel in this book in the corresponding chapters.

Tools → Spelling

Checks the spelling for all text within the selected worksheet. If you have a section of the worksheet highlighted, Excel only checks the spelling in that section. You can check spelling by selecting this option, clicking the Spelling button on the Standard toolbar, or by pressing F7.

When Excel checks the spelling it uses the default dictionary that is loaded for the selected language and any custom dictionaries you have created. When a word is encountered that does not exist in either location the Spelling dialog displays as shown in Figure 8-1.

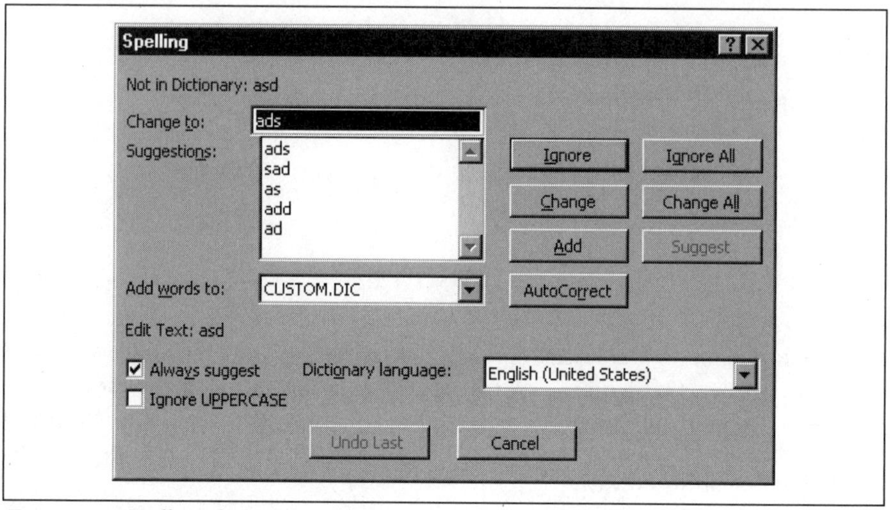

Figure 8-1: Spelling dialog

Excel tries to locate words in the dictionary that resemble the word that was found in the worksheet. You can either select one of the words in the list, type the correct spelling, add the word to the custom dictionary, or keep the word as is, by selecting the Ignore button. If you don't want Excel to suggest replacements for words that are not located in one of the dictionaries, remove the checkmark from the "Always suggest" field.

If the word selected is one that you use frequently, you can add it to a custom dictionary by making sure the custom dictionary is selected in the "Add words to" field and then selecting the Add button.

If you typically mistype a word in the pattern selected, you can add that word to the AutoCorrect list so that Excel replaces the word each time you mistype it. This the same list that displays when you select Tools → AutoCorrect. Before selecting this option, make sure the correct spelling is specified in the "Change to" field. Excel will replace the text with the correct spelling and add the occurrence to the list that displays on the AutoCorrect dialog.

WARNING

Be careful about selecting another dictionary. If you do not have the selected dictionary installed on your machine, you will be given the option of installing it after you close and reopen the Spell Check dialog. You cannot open the Spell Check dialog if Excel cannot locate the selected dictionary. To fix this minor problem, insert your installation CD and allow Excel to add the new dictionary to your machine.

Selecting the AutoCorrect button adds the entry to the AutoCorrect list that displays when you select Tools → AutoCorrect.

Creating a Custom Dictionary

If you have different words or terms that you use frequently you will probably want to add them to a custom dictionary so that Excel will not stop on them each time you select Tools → Spelling. You can either do this by adding each one to the custom dictionary as Excel finds them in your dictionary, or you can create a custom dictionary that contains all the terms you frequently use.

Excel provides a custom dictionary that you can use called *custom.dic*. You can also create additional custom dictionaries if you want to keep your terms sorted based on when you use them. Keep in mind that Excel only uses one custom dictionary at a time. The dictionary used is the one that appears in the "Add words to" field.

The easiest way to create a new custom dictionary, or to modify an existing one, is to use the Notepad program that is available from the Start menu. You can either open and modify the *custom.dic* dictionary or create a new one. The dictionary you create must have the *.dic* file extension and must reside in the same location as the main dictionary. Excel places the dictionary in the following location:

Root*OS*\\Profiles*User_name*\\Application Data\\Microsoft\\Proof

Each entry in the dictionary must be separated by a hard page break. This is inserted by pressing the Enter key between each entry.

Tools → AutoCorrect

Provides the ability to modify the list of typing mistakes that Excel automatically corrects in your document. You can also select the other type of corrections that Excel makes to your worksheets, such as whether it should allow the first two letters of a word to be capitalized. When you select this option the AutoCorrect dialog displays as shown in Figure 8-2.

Select the AutoCorrect options that you want to be used as you work on your workbooks in Excel. These settings affect all workbooks that you edit. If you select the "Replace text as you type" checkbox you can specify the corrections that you want Excel to make as you type. For example, if you tend to type the word "the" as "teh" you can add that to the list.

If you select the first two options, "Correct TWo INitial CApitals" and "Capitalize first letter of sentence" you can specify exceptions to those settings by selecting the Exceptions button. For example, if you were to add the abbreviation "approx." to a sentence on your worksheet, you would not want the next word to be capitalized, so it is listed as one of the exceptions on the AutoCorrect Exceptions dialog. You can

Tools Menu

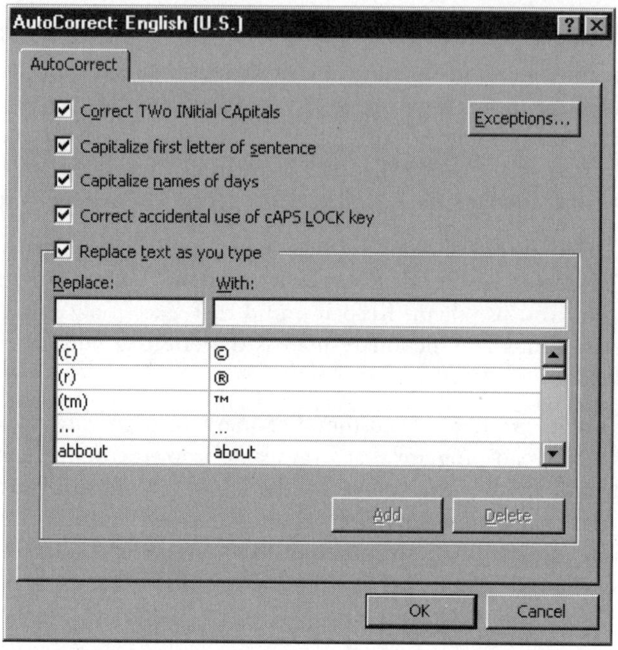

Figure 8-2: AutoCorrect dialog

add options to the list that displays on both tabs by typing the desired text and selecting the Add button.

TIP # 53

Shortcuts Using AutoCorrect and AutoComplete

The AutoCorrect feature can be used to create shortcuts for different words or phrases that are frequently used. For instance, instead of typing "Microsoft Excel 2000" you could create or add a definition where each time you type "exc" it is replaced with the correct phrase.

Another method for eliminating the need to retype long words is to use the Auto-Complete feature located on the Edit tab when you select Tools → Options. When you have this option selected, Excel will automatically complete an entry when the same entry already exists in the column.

Tools → AutoSave

Automatically saves the workbook you are working on at the specified interval of time. If you do not have the AutoSave option available on the Tools menu, you will need to load the AutoSave Add-in using Tools → Add-Ins.

When you select Tools → AutoSave, the AutoSave dialog displays as shown in Figure 8-3. Specify the amount of time you want to have elapse between each save.

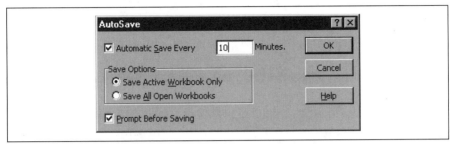

Figure 8-3: AutoSave dialog

If you want to eliminate being bothered each time your workbook is automatically saved, you remove the checkmark from the Prompt Before Saving checkbox. Keep in mind, if you are creating a new workbook, Excel will still prompt you the first time so that you can specify the name and location of the workbook.

Once you load the AutoSave feature it is started up each time you run Excel, even if you disabled it during the previous session. If you don't want to use it, simply select Tools → AutoSave and remove the Automatic Save Every checkmark.

Tools → Share Workbook

Allows you to share a workbook so that up to 256 people can make modifications to the workbook simultaneously. When you select this option the Share Workbook dialog displays, as shown in Figure 8-4, so that you can not only indicate that you want to share the workbook, but also specify how Excel should handle the changes that are made to the workbook. Users must be running at least Excel 97 (or later) in order to share a workbook.

Once you select the checkbox on the Editing tab to allow more than one person to modify the workbook, you can select the Advanced tab so that you can keep a history of the changes that are made to the workbook and also indicate how conflicts should be handled when the workbook is saved. When you select the OK button, Excel will prompt you to save the workbook so that it can be shared.

TIP # 54
Making Sure Workbooks Can Be Merged Back Together

To eliminate problems that may occur when the change history has not been kept for the appropriate length of time, it is a good idea to set the change history to the maximum length of 32,767 days. For example, if you do not have a change history that goes back to when the workbook was copied, you cannot merge workbooks back together.

Tools Menu

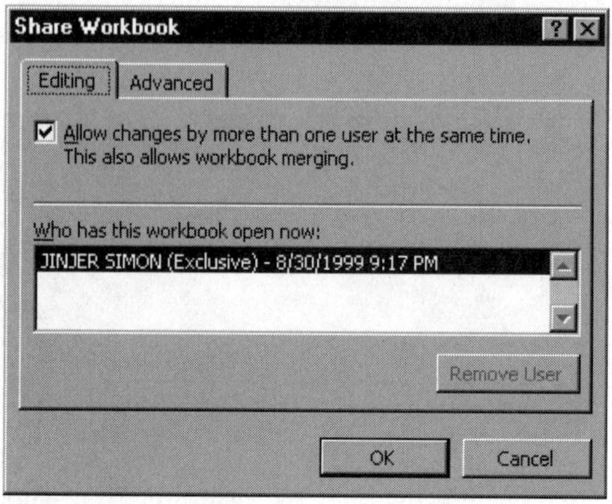

Figure 8-4: Share Workbook dialog

The ability to track changes is a great feature, especially when the workbook is being shared among multiple users. If you find something has been incorrectly modified within the workbook, you can quickly find out who was responsible for making the change by checking the change history. To view the changes that have occurred to the workbook, select Tools → Track Changes → Highlight Changes.

When you share a workbook you, or anyone else editing it, will not be able to perform the following options in the shared workbook. Therefore, if you want to perform any of the following options you need to do it prior to saving the workbook as shared:

- Merge cells

- Insert or delete blocks of cells; you can only insert and delete entire rows and columns

- Delete worksheets from the workbook

- Add or modify charts, pictures, objects or hyperlinks

- Use any of the drawing tools available when you select the Drawing icon on the toolbar

- Password protect any portion of the workbook; nonetheless, any password protection that was added to the workbook prior to sharing it remains in effect

- Create or modify scenarios, PivotTables, outlines, or data tables

- Write, modify, view, record, or assign macros to the shared workbook; however, you can create a macro and save it in a workbook that is not shared

- Modify the dialog boxes or menus

- Define or apply conditional formats

- Create or modify the data validation restrictions and messages

You can stop a user from working in the shared workbook by selecting Tools → Share Workbook on the Editing tab, highlighting the user that you want to disconnect from the workbook, and then selecting the Remove User button.

WARNING

If you want to ensure that the user cannot change the share or change history status for the workbook, you need to select Tools → Protection → Protect and Share Workbook and set a password for the workbook.

Tools → Track Changes

Provides the ability to keep track of changes that are made to the workbook by highlighting them on the screen. You can then determine whether the changes should be accepted by using the Accept and Reject Changes option.

Highlight Changes

Indicates that you want to highlight the changes that are made to the workbook. When you select this option the Highlight Changes dialog, shown in Figure 8-5, displays so you can indicate which changes you want highlighted.

 By selecting the option to highlight changes, the workbook is also saved as a shared workbook. There are certain options that are not available when a workbook is shared. For more information refer to "Tools → Share Workbook."

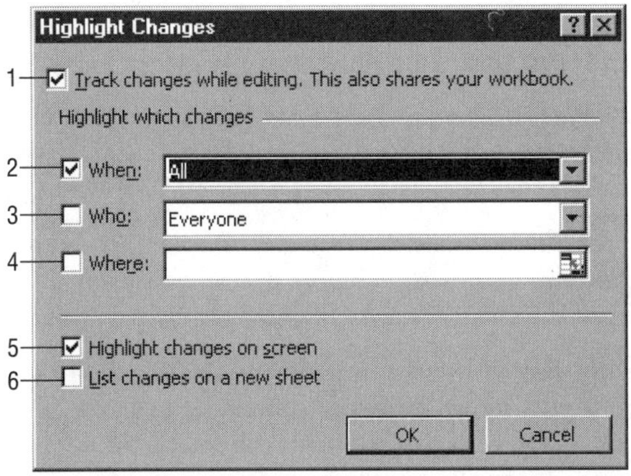

Figure 8-5: Highlight Changes dialog

1. *Track changes while editing.* Indicates that you want to keep track of the changes to the workbook while it is being edited. If you have already shared the workbook using Tools → Share Workbook and you indicated that you want to track changes, this option will already be selected when you view this dialog. This option must be selected before you can select any of the other options on the dialog.

2. *When.* Indicates the time frame for the changes you want highlighted on the screen. If you unselect this checkbox, by default all changes are selected. If you select the "Since date" option the current date will display in the When field; you can change this to reflect the date you want to use. Remember, you can only display changes back to the point when the workbook was originally shared out and the change history was created. Also, keep in mind the time frame you specified for the change history with Tools → Share Workbook. If you indicated to keep track of the changes for the last 30 days, you will not be able to see changes that happened two months ago.

3. *Who.* Indicates the person whose changes you want to highlight on the screen. You can select a specific name, changes made by all users, or changes by everyone but you.

4. *Where.* Indicates the location where you want to highlight any changes. To specify the area, select the Collapse Dialog icon next to the field and highlight the desired area. If you do not select this checkbox Excel will keep track of the changes within the entire workbook.

5. *Highlight changes on screen.* Highlights the changes made that meet the criteria specified in the When, Who, and Where fields. You can see the change history for the highlighted cell, as shown in Figure 8-7, by resting the mouse pointer over the cell.

6. *List changes on a new sheet.* Lists all the changes that have been made on a separate History sheet, as shown in Figure 8-6. This is a great way to quickly review the changes. If you have a long list of changes you can filter the list using the arrow next to a specific column heading.

 Excel does not automatically update the history list. To update it with the most recent changes select Tools → Track Changes → Highlight Changes and select the "List changes on a new sheet" checkbox again.

When you rest the mouse pointer on a cell you can see both the changes and comments for the cell, as shown in Figure 8-7. If you print a worksheet that has highlighted changes, the changes are highlighted on the printout.

If you want to keep track of the changes to your workbook, but you do not want to give others access to it, you can password protect it. That way it will still be shared so that the changes are tracked, but you will not have to worry about others accessing it as long as no one knows the password.

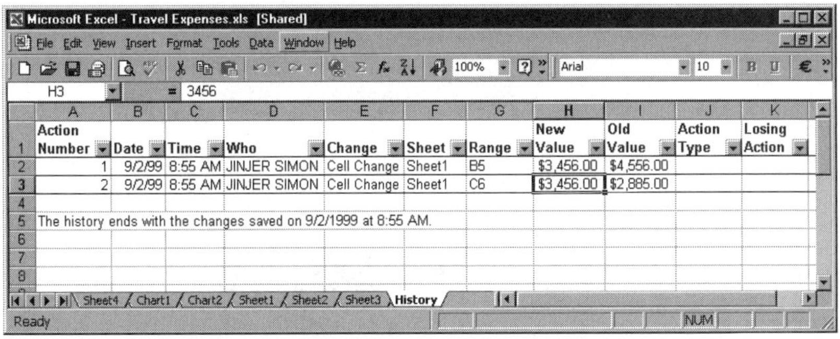

Figure 8-6: Change History page

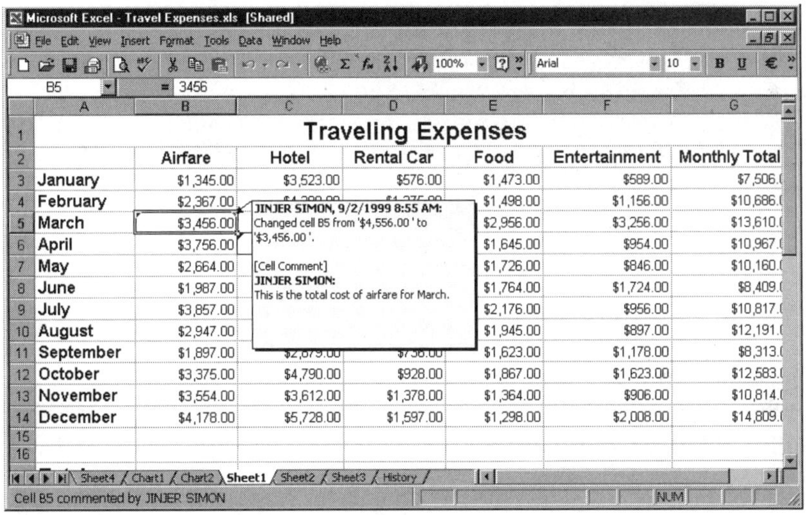

Figure 8-7: Change history and comments for the selected cell

Accept and Reject Changes

Allows you to accept and reject changes that have been made to the workbook. When you select this option the Select Changes to Accept or Reject dialog displays as shown in Figure 8-8. On this dialog you indicate the specific changes that you want to look at by making the appropriate selections for the When, Who, and Where fields. To review all changes remove the checkmarks from each of the fields.

When Excel locates a change within the currently selected worksheet the Accept or Reject Changes message box displays, as shown in Figure 8-9. If you reject any changes, the changes no longer appear highlighted on the screen and the value of the cell returns to the original value.

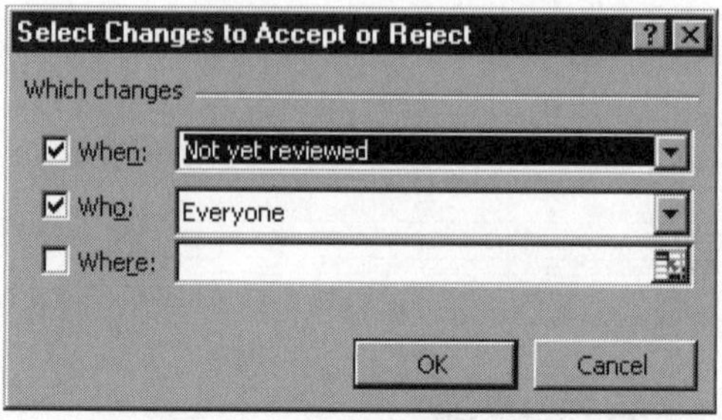

Figure 8-8: Select Changes to Accept or Reject dialog

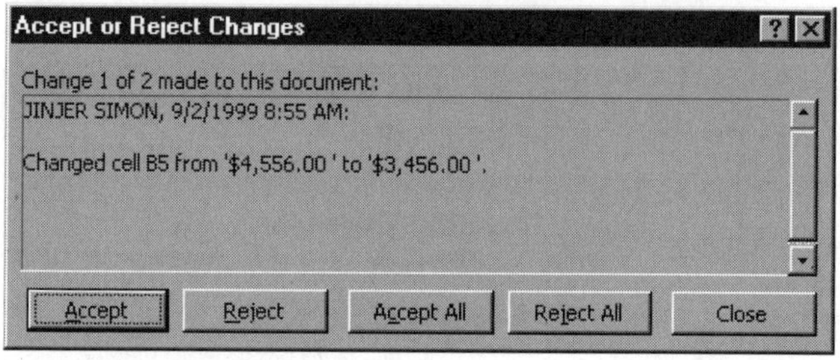

Figure 8-9: Accept or Reject Changes message box

You can see any rejected changes on the History page by selecting the "List changes on a new sheet" option on Tools → Track Changes → Highlight Changes.

Tools → Merge Workbooks

Merges together copies of the same workbook. By using this feature you can give different individuals copies of the same workbook to modify, and then merge them back together so that all changes get applied back into the original workbook. In order to use this feature the workbooks must meet the following criteria:

- They must all be copies of the same workbook, with different names.

- The original workbook must have been shared with the Change History option prior to making the copies.

- Only the workbook that you plan to merge the data into should be open.

- If the workbooks have passwords they must be the same passwords.

- When you merge the workbooks together the change history must have been maintained for the entire amount of time that has elapsed since the workbook copies were created. For example, if the workbooks were make two months ago but the change history has only been maintained for 30 days, you will not be able to merge the workbooks.

When you select Tools → Merge Workbooks the Select Files to Merge into Current Workbook dialog displays as shown in Figure 8-10. This dialog is similar to the File → Open dialog. Select the workbook copy that you want to merge into the currently open file. If you want to select multiple workbooks hold down the Ctrl key while you select each one.

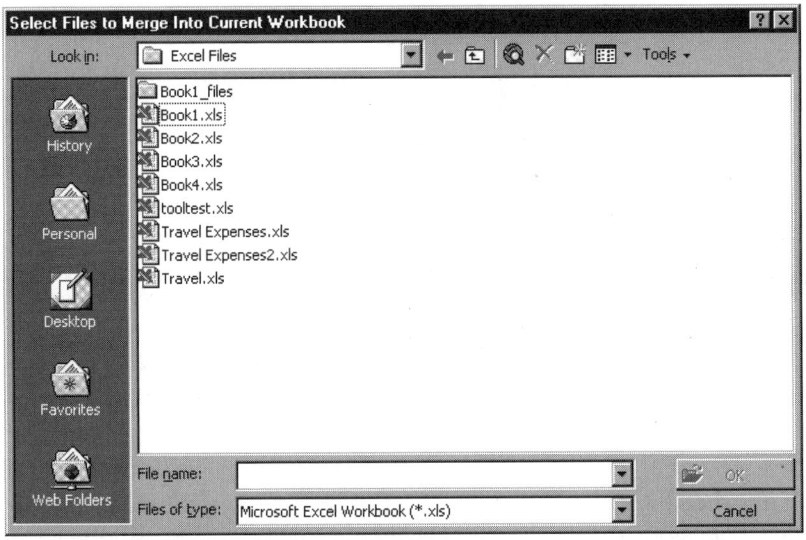

Figure 8-10: Select Files to Merge into Current Workbook dialog

Tools → Protection

Provides the ability to protect a workbook or worksheet so that the specified modifications cannot be made. You can also protect and share a workbook. There are various options that display on the Protection submenu based upon the current status of the open workbook/worksheet. For example, if you have a protected sheet selected the Unprotect Sheet option displays on the menu.

Protect Sheet

Protects the currently selected worksheet or chart sheet so that the type of modifications specified on the Protect Sheet dialog, shown in Figure 8-11, cannot be made to it. The restrictions are specified by selecting the appropriate checkboxes on the dialog. The best way to ensure that the changes cannot be made to the worksheet is to password protect it.

Contents
> Select this checkbox if you want to prevent any changes to the cells on the worksheet or to data on a chart sheet. This also prevents others from viewing the contents of hidden rows, columns, and formulas.

Figure 8-11: Protect Sheet dialog

NOTE *When you select the Contents checkbox, Excel actually only protects those cells that have the Locked property turned on, which by default is all cells. If you want to leave some cells unprotected, such as cells where you want another user to input data, you need to remove the locked property for those cells prior to selecting the Protect Sheet option. To change the locked property on a cell select Format → Cells and then remove the checkmark from the Locked checkbox on the Protection tab.*

Objects
  Select this checkbox to prevent changes to graphic objects on the selected worksheet or chart sheet.

Scenarios
  Select this checkbox to prevent changes to scenarios on the selected worksheet.

Password
  Password protects the worksheet or chart sheet so that the protection specified cannot be modified by another individual. If you do not password protect it another user can easily change the protection on the sheet simply by selecting Tools → Protection → Protect Sheet.

Protect Workbook

Protects the entire workbook with the type of protection specified on the Protect Workbook dialog shown in Figure 8-12.

Select the Structure checkbox to keep another user from adding, removing, hiding, or unhiding worksheets in the workbook. If you want the workbook to always open up in the same size window and location on the screen, select the Windows checkbox.

Remember, if you don't password protect these settings, someone can easily modify the settings simply by selecting the Tools → Protection → Protect Workbook option.

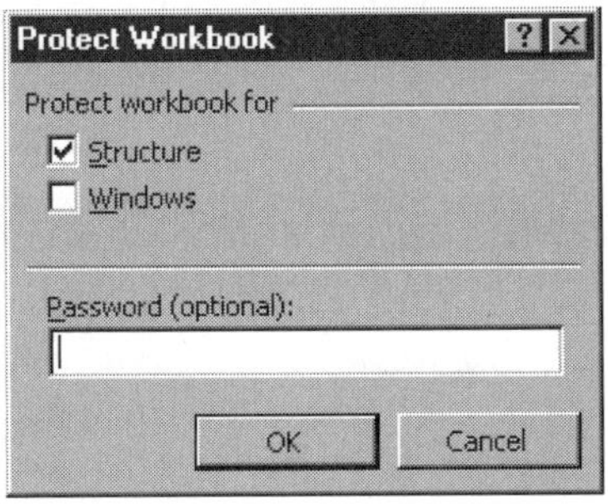

Figure 8-12: Protect Workbook dialog

 NOTE *If you add a password protected workbook to a binder the protection is removed from the workbook. You will be prompted to enter the password when you add the workbook to the binder, but once it is added the protection will no longer exist.*

Unprotect

Select this option to unprotect a worksheet, chart sheet, or workbook. If the item is protected you will be prompted for the password before it can be unprotected.

Protect and Share Workbook

Shares the workbook and keeps other users from removing the share status and modifying the change history status. If the workbook is already shared, the option is called Protect Shared Workbook. When you select Tools → Protection → Protect and Share Workbook or Tools → Protection → Protect Shared Workbook the Protect Shared Workbook dialog displays as shown in Figure 8-13.

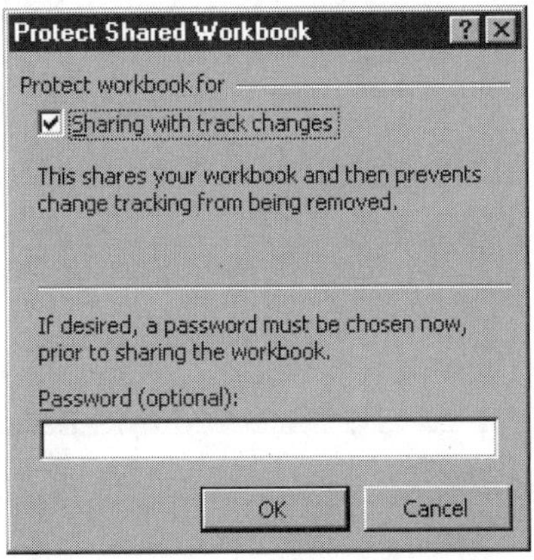

Figure 8-13: Protect Shared Workbook

If the workbook is already shared you will be able to select the "Sharing with track changes" checkbox to protect the sharing and change history for the workbook, but you cannot password protect it.

TIP # 55

Protecting a Workbook to Prevent Accidental Changes

If you want to protect the workbook just to eliminate accidental changes, you may want to do the following. On the Protect Shared Workbook dialog, leave the Password field blank. That way you don't have to remember a password. If you want to unprotect the sheet, simply select the OK button on Tools → Unprotect. This method only keeps the workbook from accidentally being modified, it does not secure it, since it really does not have a specific password.

Tools → Online Collaboration

The Online Collaboration submenu provides options for communicating about a workbook online using either Microsoft NetMeeting or Web Discussions.

Meet Now

The Meet Now option allows you to create an online meeting where you can allow others to view and modify your workbook in real time using Microsoft NetMeeting. When you select Tools → Online Collaboration → Meet Now, NetMeeting opens and displays the Place a Call dialog, shown in Figure 8-14. You need to select the Directory you want connect to and then select the users that you want to invite to your meeting. Remember, the individuals you invite must be currently running NetMeeting, or you will not be able to invite them to the meeting.

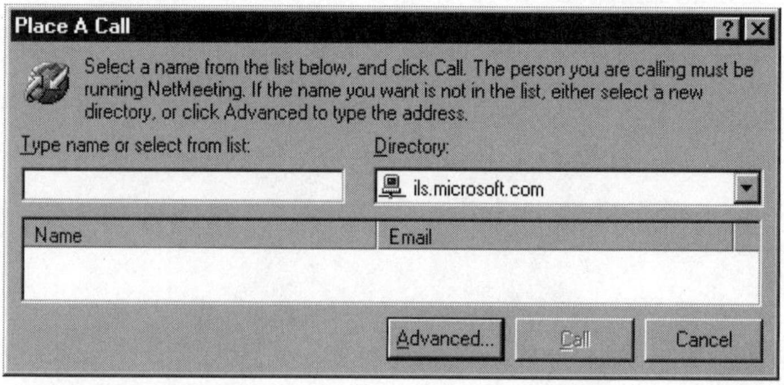

Figure 8-14: Place a Call dialog

NOTE *When you select the Directory you will notice that there are several different Microsoft directory servers that you can select from. Microsoft provides these for general use, but they are typically rather busy. If you are using an internal corporate server within your organization for NetMeetings, you can check with your System Administrator to determine the name of the directory server you can connect to internally.*

When the online meeting starts, each participant in the meeting can see your workbook on their screen, but you are the only person who has control of the workbook. If you want to allow other participants to modify the workbook, you can turn on collaboration within NetMeeting by selecting Tools → Start Collaborating. If collaboration is turned off, the other participants cannot make any changes, but they are able to watch you work. When collaboration is turned on, each person in the online meeting can take turns editing and controlling the workbook. In other words, only one person at a time can modify the workbook. When a meeting participant has control of the workbook, you will not have the use of your pointer for any other purpose. The initials of the person in control of the workbook appear next to the mouse pointer.

Microsoft NetMeeting

Microsoft NetMeeting is a free program that Microsoft has developed. It is part of the Internet Explorer installation. If you do not have it installed, you can download it from the NetMeeting web site at *http://www.microsoft.com/windows/NetMeeting/default.asp.*

For more information about using the various functions within NetMeeting, refer to the online help.

If you want to chat with the meeting participants, turn off the collaboration. It is much faster to chat if the workbook is not being modified by other users.

When you use NetMeeting to collaborate about a specific workbook, you are the only person who needs to have Excel and the workbook installed on your machine. The other members of the meeting are able to view and modify the workbook when you select the Start Collaborating option.

Schedule Meeting

This option allows you to schedule an online meeting using NetMeeting. When you select Tools → Online Collaboration → Schedule Meeting a schedule meeting dialog displays from Outlook, as shown in Figure 8-15.

If you want to schedule an online meeting using NetMeeting, make sure the "This is an online meeting using" checkbox is selected. If this checkbox is not selected Outlook assumes you are scheduling a physical meeting.

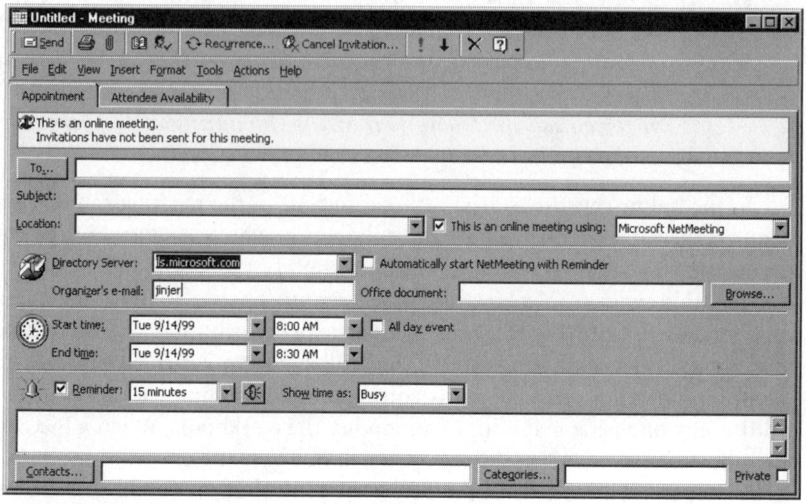

Figure 8-15: Schedule a Future NetMeeting

When your online meeting option is selected, the options display in the center, where you can specify the Directory Server, the document you want to meet about, organizer's email, and whether you want NetMeeting to start automatically when it is time for the meeting. The server that is listed in the Directory Server field is the one that you have set up as your default directory in NetMeeting. In the Office document field specify the workbook that you want to discuss during the meeting. This workbook will be opened when the meeting is started.

Web Discussions

This option allows you to create discussions about a particular workbook within Excel, as shown in Figure 8-16. When you use Web Discussions people are able to add comments to the document at anytime.

This option creates threaded discussions within the selected workbook. This means that you can create multiple discussions with the workbook, and the comments for each discussion are stored under that discussion. To create a discussion, select the "Insert Discussion about the Workbook" button or select Discussions → Insert about the workbook. This displays the Enter Discussion Text dialog where you enter the subject of the new discussion and text you want to add about it.

In order to use the Web Discussions option you must have access to a collaboration server. If you are working in a corporate environment, you can contact your Systems Administrator to get the URL for your collaboration server. The collaboration server is set up as part of the Office Server Extensions installation. This is available either on the Microsoft Office 2000 Professional Disc 1 or Office 2000 Premium Disc 3.

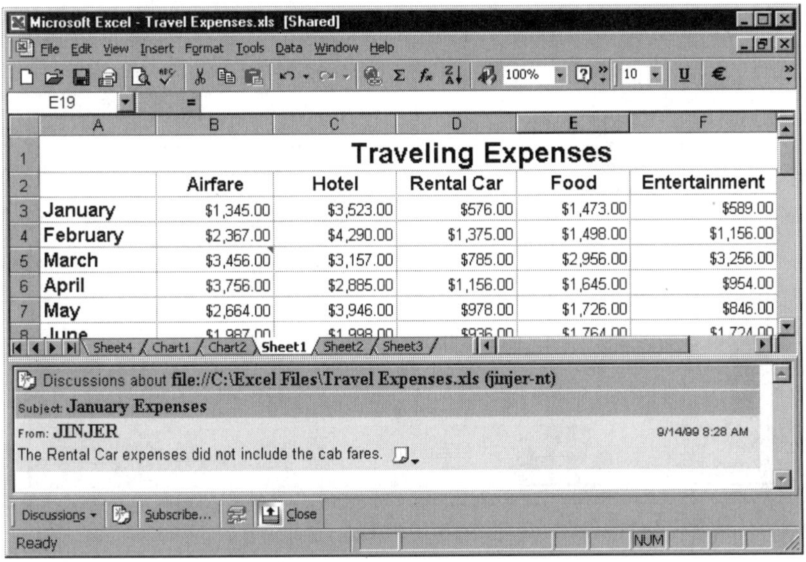

Figure 8-16: Web Discussion for an Excel workbook

 NOTE *If you only want to view comments from a specific user or during a certain time-frame, you can select Discussions → Filter Discussions to filter out any unwanted comments.*

Tools → Goal Seek

Allows you to quickly determine the value needed in a cell so that a formula or graph produces the desired result. For example, assume you are trying to determine the amount of car you can afford to buy if you can afford to pay $500 a month. If you were to use the PMT function (refer to Chapter 12, *Financial Functions*) to determine the payment amount, it would require you to know how much the total cost of the car is in order to determine the payment amount. To calculate this correctly you could use Tools → Goal Seek to determine the amount of loan you can afford, as shown in Figure 8-17.

NOTE *Tools → Goal Seek can only find the value for one cell. If you want to find the value for more than one cell at a time, you need to use Tools → Solver.*

Tools → Scenarios

Allows you to create scenarios, or "what-ifs," for values in a worksheet. For example, if you are trying to determine the payment amount based on loans with different interest rates and different number of payments, you could create scenarios to

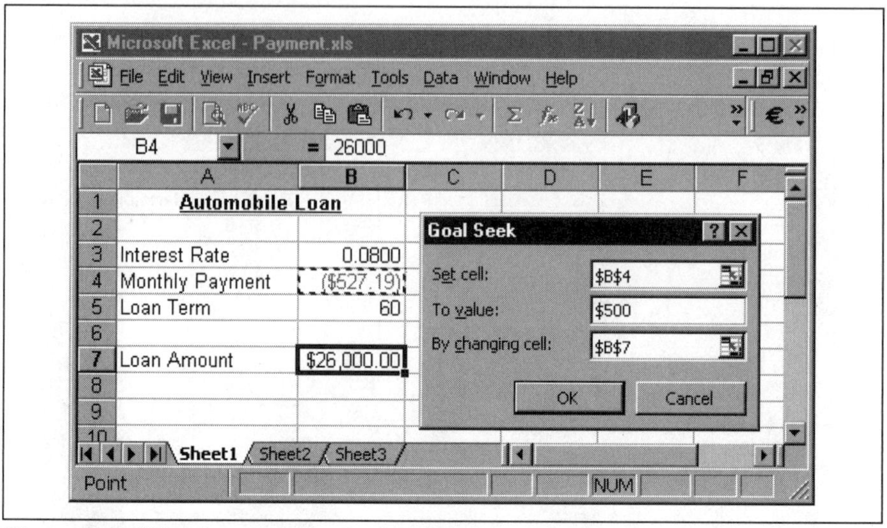

Figure 8-17: Worksheet with the Goal Seek dialog

quickly see the difference. When you select Tools → Scenarios the Scenario Manager dialog displays as shown in Figure 8-18.

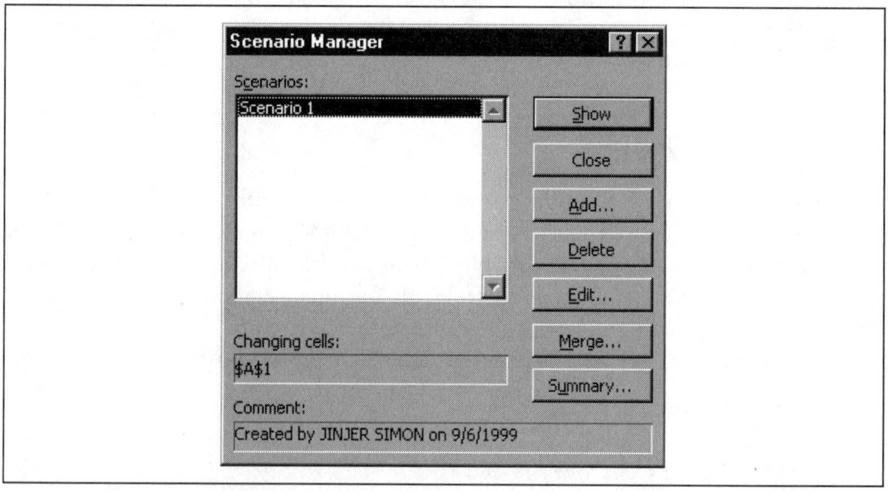

Figure 8-18: Scenario Manager dialog

Create Scenarios

The first thing that you need to do is create your scenarios. To do this, you need to select the Add button to display the Add Scenario dialog shown in Figure 8-19.

You need to specify a name for the scenario and select the cells that should change when the scenario is selected in the Changing Cells field. You can select the cells by

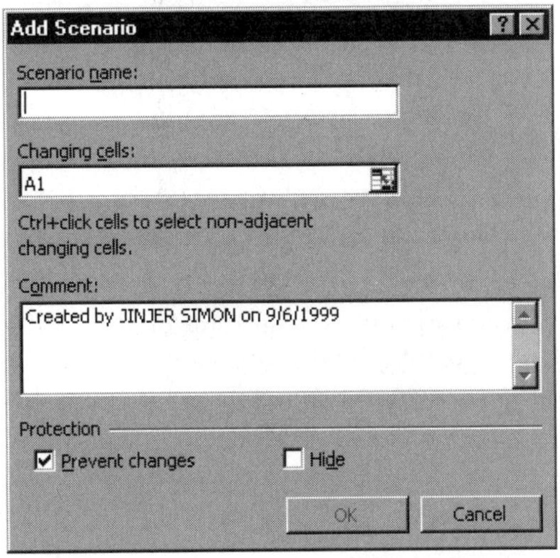

Figure 8-19: Add Scenario dialog

selecting the Collapse Dialog button and highlighting the appropriate cells, or you can type the cells in the field. If you select cells that contain formulas, the values of the cells are replaced with the constants you specify when the scenario is selected.

It is not necessary to type a comment in the Comments field, but I would definitely recommend that you indicate the purpose of the scenario so that you can remember why you created it in the future.

NOTE *If you are using the Tools → Protection → Protect Sheets option you can select the Prevent Changes and Hide checkboxes to protect you scenario. You need to select these checkboxes prior to protecting the sheet, or the options will be grayed out. If you have selected the Prevent Changes option, the scenario cannot be modified when the sheet is protected. If the Hide is selected, the scenario will not be visible when the sheet is protected.*

When you have selected the cells that should change when the scenario is selected, select the OK button to display the Scenario Values dialog, shown in Figure 8-20, where you indicate the new values for the selected cells. These are the values that will be placed in the cells each time the scenario is selected.

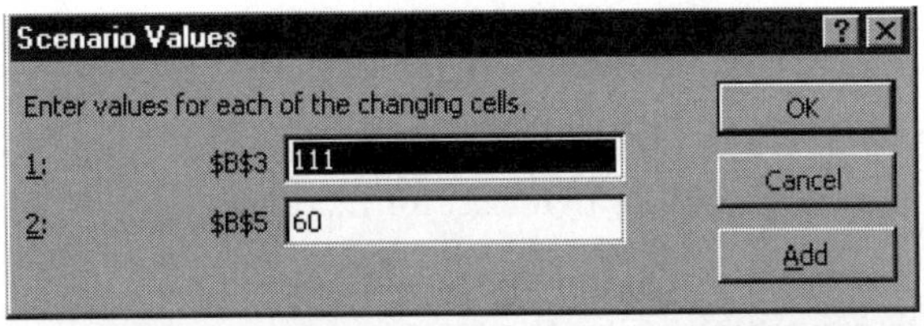

Figure 8-20: Scenario Values dialog.

To make sure you can always redisplay the original cell values, make sure you create a scenario that contains those values.

Selecting a Scenario

If you want to apply a scenario to you worksheet, you need to select the desired scenario and select the Show button. This will change the values in cells specified by the scenario.

If you did not create a scenario that contained the original cell values, you will have to use the Undo button to redisplay the original values. When you save the worksheet, Excel will save the current scenario values in the worksheet. You can change them again by selecting a different scenario.

Merging Scenarios

If you have created scenarios in another workbook or worksheet, you can merge those scenarios into the current worksheet by selecting the Merge button to display the Merge Scenarios dialog shown in Figure 8-21.

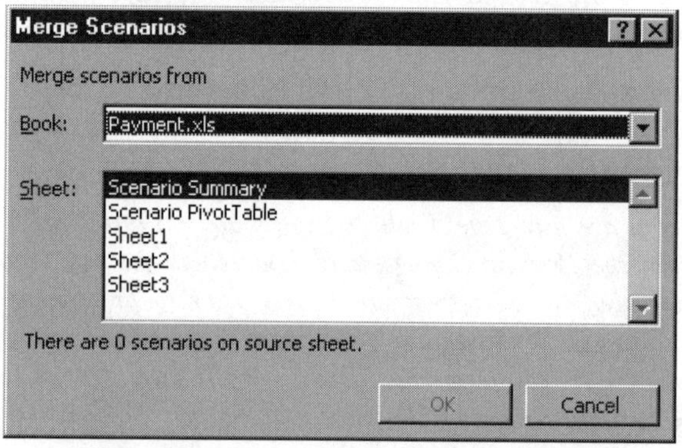

Figure 8-21: Merge Scenarios dialog

Select the workbook that contains the scenarios you want to merge in the Book field. Excel only allows you to merge scenarios from workbooks that are currently open. Therefore, you need to make sure the workbook that you want to merge from is open.

Select the actual sheet in the workbook that contains the scenarios you want to merge. Typically this is a worksheet. As you select each worksheet in the list, Excel indicates the number of scenarios that exist for that sheet.

Keep in mind that Excel is going to merge all of the scenarios from that worksheet into your existing worksheet. If you don't want one of the scenarios, you can remove it after the merge by highlighting the scenario name on the Scenario Manager dialog and selecting the Delete button.

If both worksheets contain scenarios with the same name, Excel adds the date to the end of the new scenarios when they are added to the current worksheet.

Summary Information

A rather cool feature of the Scenario Manager dialog is the ability to create a summary report that compares the results of each scenario. You can get this information by selecting the Summary button, which displays the Scenario Summary dialog, as shown in Figure 8-22.

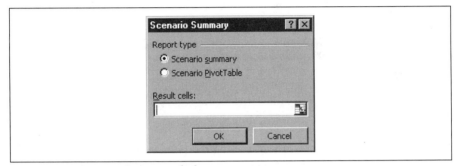

Figure 8-22: Scenario Summary dialog

Select the type of report that you want to see. Typically the scenario summary report provides sufficient information. If you have a worksheet with several different scenarios and result cells, you may decide to create the Scenario PivotTable. For more information about PivotTables, refer to "Data → PivotTable and PivotChart Report" in Chapter 9. Excel creates a new sheet in your workbook for the summary information.

 A scenario cannot have more than 32 changing cells. If you need to change more cells, you will need to define multiple scenarios that can be selected.

Tools → Auditing

Provides the ability to quickly see the cells that provide the data for a formula (precedents) or the formulas that rely on other cells (dependents). These options are very useful when you are trying to determine why a cell does not contain the anticipated value. When you select each option, Excel provides a graphical representation by drawing arrows between the cells to show the relationship, as shown in Figure 8-23.

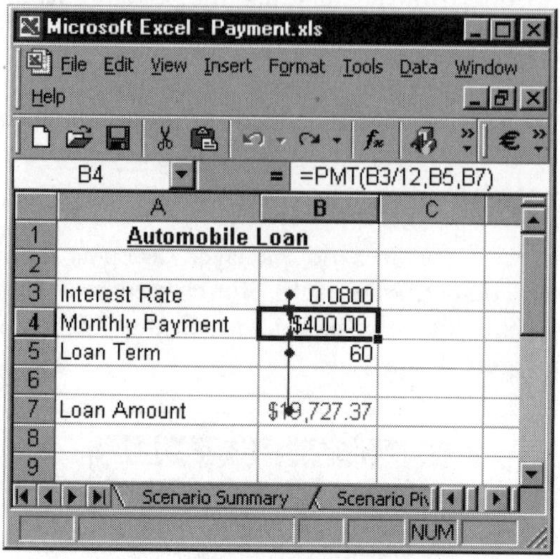

Figure 8-23: Arrows showing the Precedents for the formula

Trace Precedents

Select this option to display arrows showing the precedents for the formula in the selected cell. If the selected cell does not contain a formula, Excel will display a message box indicating that you need to select a cell containing a formula. You can also perform this option by selecting the Trace Precedents button on the Auditing toolbar.

If you want to see the precedents for multiple cells, you will need to select each cell independently. This option does not allow you to select multiple cells.

Trace Dependents

Select this option to display arrows showing the cells that are dependent upon the selected cell. This is a great way to quickly check to see if changing the value or style of a cell is going to affect the results of your worksheet. You can also perform this option by selecting the Trace Dependents button on the Auditing toolbar.

If you want to see the dependents for multiple cells, you will need to select each cell independently. This option does not allow you to select multiple cells.

Trace Error

Select this option to determine the cause of the error value in the selected cell. Excel draws arrows from the selected cell to the cell that is causing the error value to appear. You can also select the Trace Error button on the Auditing toolbar.

Remove All Arrows

Select this option to remove all of the arrows that have been placed in your work-sheet by the Auditing options.

Show Auditing Toolbar

Displays the auditing toolbar, if it is not already displayed. If the toolbar is displayed you can select the auditing options either from the toolbar or from Tools → Auditing.

There are actually three other options available on the Auditing toolbar that are not available with Tools → Auditing:

New Comment button
> Provides a quick way to add a new comment to a cell. This is the same as selecting Insert → Comment.

Circle Invalid Data
> Draws a circle around any cells that contain invalid data based upon the criteria specified with Data → Validation.

Clear Validation Circles
> Removes all of the circles that were drawn around invalid data on your worksheet.

Tools → Solver

Provides a more complex method for finding the cell values needed to produce the desired results. This option is similar to the Tools → Goal Seek but it provides the ability to change the value in multiple cells to achieve the desired result from the formula.

 If this option does not exist on the Tools menu you will need to load Solver Add-in on the Add-ins dialog by selecting Tools → Add-Ins.

When you select this option the Solver Parameter dialog displays as shown in Figure 8-24. This is where you specify the parameters you want to use to achieve the desired result.

These options are very useful when you are trying to determine why a cell does not contain the anticipated value.

1. *Set Target Cell.* Specify the cell that is the target value you want to solve for. The cell you specify must contain a formula. It can be selected by either typing the cell reference in the field or selecting the Collapse Dialog button and clicking on the cell.

   Once you specify the target cell, you need to indicate how you want to set the value of the cell. You can either set it to the maximum possible size (Max),

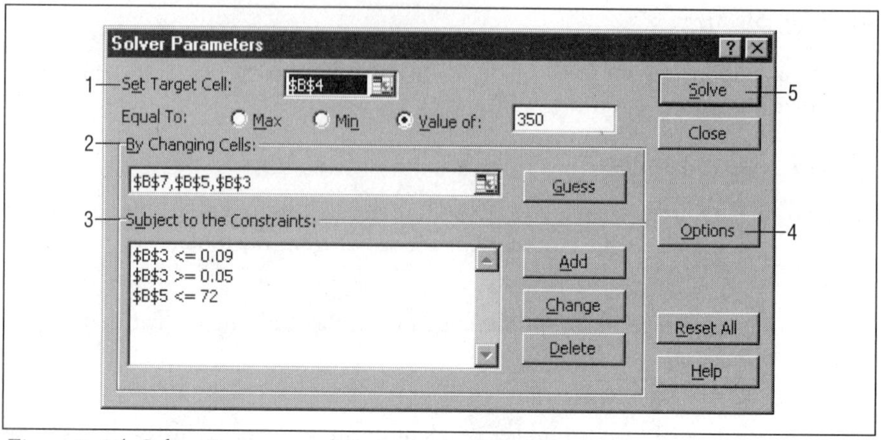

Figure 8-24: Solver Parameters dialog

minimum size (Min), or a specific value by typing the value in the "Value of" field.

2. *By Changing Cells.* Indicate the cells whose values Excel should modify in order to achieve the specified results for the target cell. You can select these cells either by typing their references in the field or by selecting the Collapse Dialog button. To select multiple cells, hold down the Ctrl key while you click with the mouse. You can specify a maximum of 200 cells.

You can also have Excel automatically select the cells based upon the cells referenced in the target cell formula, by selecting the Guess button.

3. *Subject to the Constraints.* You can indicate any limitations you want applied to the changing cells or the target cell by creating a constraint. For example, you may want to make sure the percentage rate is not more than 10% or that the total number of months for the loan does not exceed 72. To create a constraint, select the Add button to display the Add Constraint dialog shown in Figure 8-25.

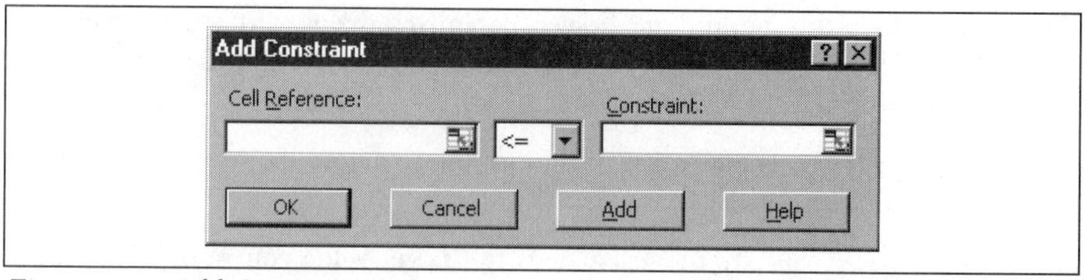

Figure 8-25: Add Constraint dialog

For each constraint you create there are five different operators that can be selected: less than or equal (<=), greater than or equal (>=), equal (=), integer value (int), and binary values (bin). The int and bin operators can only be applied to the changing cells.

4. *Options.* You can refine the process by which Excel performs a series of internal calculations to derive values for cells that produce a desired result by selecting the Options button.

Probably the most confusing part of the Solver option is the Solver Options dialog that displays when you select the Options button, as shown in Figure 8-26. This dialog provides several different options for indicating how Excel locates your results:

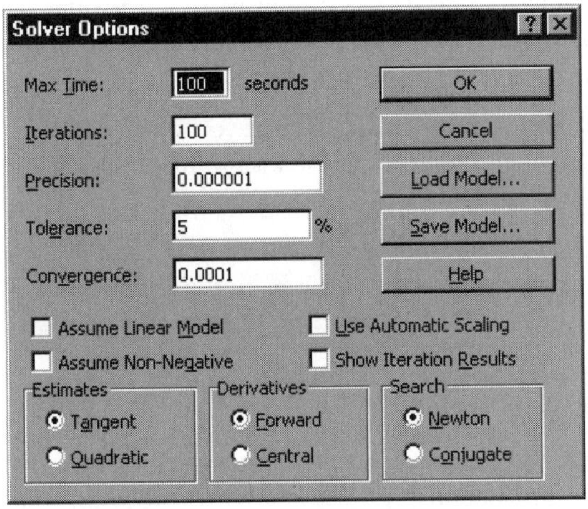

Figure 8-26: Solver Options dialog

— *Max Time.* Indicates the maximum number of seconds that Excel will spend trying to find the correct results. If you get a message indicating that the time was exceeded before finding the results, you can increase the value in this field to allow more time.

— *Iterations.* Indicates the maximum number of trial solutions that you want Excel to try in an attempt to find the solution that produces the closest results.

— *Precision.* Indicates how closely the results must meet the specified constraints. Typically Excel will find an answer more quickly when there is less precision that is required, but it may not be the best or even the right answer.

— *Tolerance.* Indicates the maximum percentage of error that is allowed for integer solutions. This field is only relevant if you have created integer constraints.

— *Convergence.* Indicates the amount of relative change allowed in the last five iterations before Excel provides the solution. The smaller the number in this field, the less relative change that is allowed.

- *Load/Save Model.* If you are using more than one set of Solver parameters for your worksheet, you need to save the parameters using the Save Model button. When you select this option the Save Model dialog displays allowing you to specify the range of cells in the worksheet where Excel should save the parameters. Since the model is only identified by the range where it is stored, you will want to remember where you stored this model so you can load it later using the Load Model button.

- *Assume Linear Model.* Indicates that Excel should assume that all relationships are linear. This option cannot be selected if the values in the adjustable cells are multiplied, divided, or use exponents. If you select this option it will speed up the process.

- *Use Automatic Scaling.* Indicates that you want to use automatic scaling to deal with large differences in the magnitude of the adjustable cells and the constraints.

- *Assume Non-Negative.* Indicates that you want Excel to assume that the values of the adjustable cells should be non-negative values (zero or greater) if you have not specified a constraint that indicates otherwise.

- *Show Iteration Results.* Indicates that you want Excel to stop and display the results of each iteration.

- *Estimates.* The selected radio button specifies the approach that Excel should use to obtain initial estimates of the basic variables in each one-dimensional search. In most circumstances the Tangent option is the best selection. If you have a nonlinear problem you can try the Quadratic option to see if it improves the results.

- *Derivatives.* The selected radio button specifies the differencing that Excel should use to estimate partial derivatives of the objective and constraint functions. For most problems the Forward option is best. If you have a problem where the constraints change rapidly, select the Central radio button.

- *Search.* The selected radio button specifies the algorithm that Excel should use at each iteration to determine the direction to search. Typically the Newton option is best because it requires fewer iterations. If you have a large problem or there are memory issues, use the Conjugate option.

5. *Solve.* Excel attempts to find the results that most closely match the target value and the specified constraints. When Excel completes the process, the Solver Results dialog displays, as shown in Figure 8-27.

Excel places the results directly in the appropriate cells in the worksheet. If you are happy with the results, select the Keep Solver Solution radio button; otherwise, select the Restore Original Values radio button to remove the results and display the original cell contents.

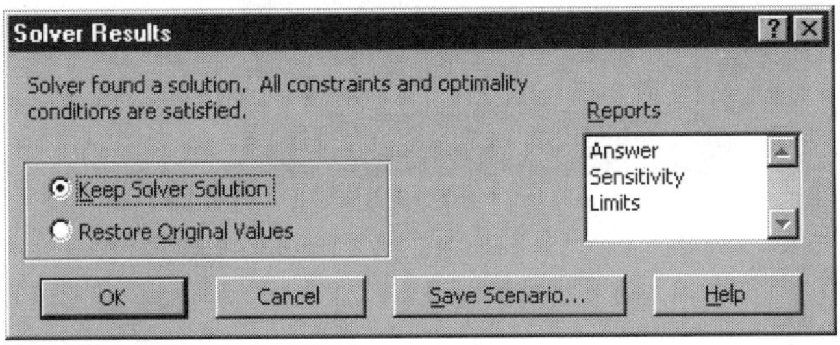

Figure 8-27: Solver Results dialog

You can select a report to see more information about the solver process by selecting one of the reports listed in the Reports list box.

If you want to save this scenario for future use, select the Save Scenario button. This displays the Save Scenario dialog where you need to specify a scenario name. The scenario is added to the list of scenarios available when you select Tools → Scenarios.

Tools → Macro

If you find that you have a series of steps that you are consistently performing within your worksheet, you should probably consider creating a macro. A macro is basically just a series of instructions used to automate a process within Excel. The macro is called with one command eliminating the potential for errors caused by forgetting a step in the process.

When you select Tools → Macros you will find a submenu that contains five other options. You will probably use the first two options, Macros and Record New Macro, most frequently. If you are a real wiz and want to create some advanced macros, you will find the Visual Basic Editor option very useful.

Macros

Select Tools → Macro → Macros or Alt+F8 to display the Macro dialog, as shown in Figure 8-28. From this dialog you can select a macro to run, modify, create, or delete a specific macro.

If the macro has a shortcut key sequence you can run the macro either by using the shortcut or by selecting it from the list box and then selecting the Run button. If you are not sure what the shortcut is for the macro or you want to change the shortcut, select the Options button to display the Macro Options dialog where you can view or change the shortcut keys.

If you type a new name in the Macro Name field and select the Create button, the Visual Basic Editor opens and creates a new macro for you to modify. This is a nice

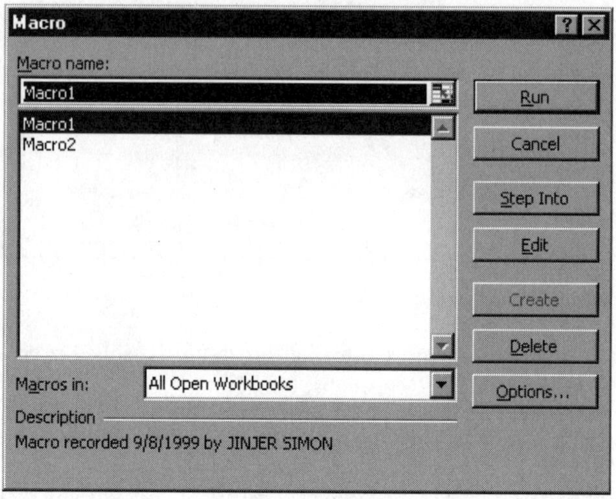

Figure 8-28: Macro dialog

way to add a macro if you want to create it from scratch using VBA (Visual Basic for Applications), This method is best used for creating complex macros that cannot be recorded using Tools → Macros → Record New Macro.

There are basically two different methods for modifying a macro. You can either select the Edit or the Step Into button. Selecting both buttons opens up the macro in the Visual Basic Editor. The Step Into button allows you to step through the macro so you can see which command is performing each step. If you are not familiar with Visual Basic for Applications, the Visual Basic Editor can be a little intimidating. See *Writing Excel Macros* (O'Reilly) for more information about VBA and macros in Excel.

Record New Macro

Provides the ability to create a new macro by recording a series of actions within your worksheet. When you select this option, the Record Macro dialog, shown in Figure 8-29, displays. This is where you indicate a name for the macro, the key sequence you want to use to select it, where it is stored, and a description.

If you are going to create a macro, the Shortcut key is definitely something that you should specify for it. By specifying the shortcut you can quickly use the macro at any time by pressing the Ctrl key and the key specified in the field. You can also create a shortcut that includes the Shift key by holding down the Shift key while you type a letter on your keyboard. This is much easier than selecting Tools → Macro → Macros and locating the desired macro.

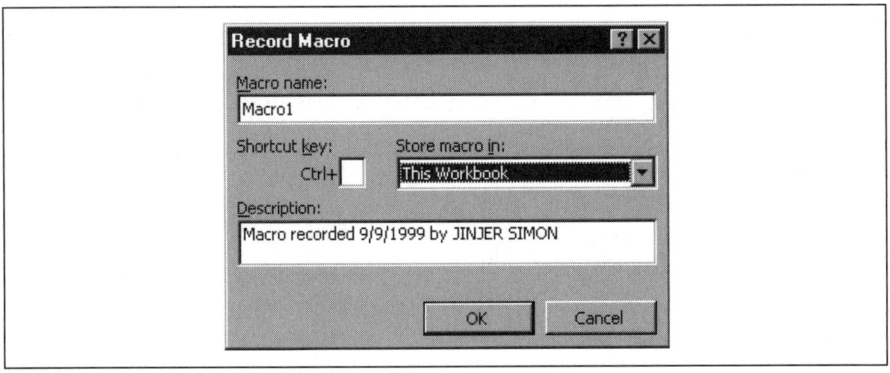

Figure 8-29: Record Macro dialog

> **NOTE** *Excel gives you three different locations where you can store you macro: in the current workbook, a new workbook, or your Personal Macro Workbook. The Personal Macro Workbook is a cool feature that allows you to store macros that you want to use in multiple documents in a central location. The file is called personal.xls, and it is only created when you store a macro in it. Any macros stored in the file are available to all Excel workbooks. Excel automatically opens this file each time you run Excel and if you add any new macros to it, you will be requested to save the workbook before closing Excel. Don't worry that you can't see it, Excel opens it up in a hidden window so that it does not get in your way.*

After you select the OK button the Record Macro dialog closes and the Stop Recording toolbar displays. Excel is now ready to record all of your actions. For example, if you copy and paste text between cells, that action is stored in the macro. Excel continues to record until you click on the Stop Recording button on the toolbar or select Tools → Macro → Stop Recording.

Besides the Stop Recording button, there is another button on the Stop Recording toolbar called Relative Reference. If you select this button Excel creates the macro using relative references instead of exact cell references. This means that instead of Excel remembering that you copied cells A1–A5 and pasted the information into cells C1–C5, it simply remembers that you copied five cells starting at the currently active cell and then moved over two columns and pasted them. It is remembering relative location, not actual.

Once your macro is created you can modify it at anytime by selecting it on the Macro dialog and then selecting the Edit button. Keep in mind you only have the option to record the steps when the macro is created. Once it is created you have to use the Visual Basic Editor to make any modifications to it.

You can assign a macro to a toolbar button by using View → Toolbars → Customize. Select the Macros category and drag the Custom Button icon to the desired toolbar. Right-click on the toolbar icon and select the Assign Macro option to display the Assign Macro dialog. Select the desired macro for the icon.

Tools Menu

Security

The Security option is definitely one you need to use if you find you are receiving a lot of different workbooks from other users. I am sure you have heard about all the different viruses that are flying around these days, and many of these are sent in the form of a macro. To help alleviate the potential of receiving a macro that could cause damage when you open a workbook, the Security dialog, shown in Figure 8-30, provides the ability to specify how you want to deal with macros in workbooks you receive from other individuals.

 Besides setting the macro security it is a good idea to run an antivirus software program on your machine that can check for macro viruses. If you use this type of software, each workbook will be checked for viruses before it is opened.

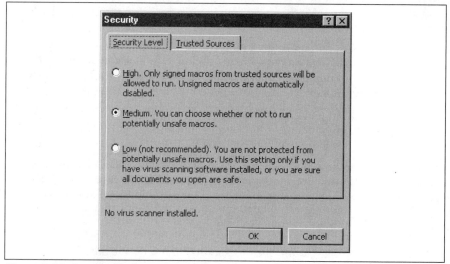

Figure 8-30: Security dialog

You can select any one of the three options on the Security Level tab. I would recommend just keeping the default setting of medium. With this option selected Excel will prompt you each time you open a workbook from another user that contains macros. You will either be able to accept them, or open the document with all macros disabled.

The Trusted Sources tab lists any sources that you have selected as reliable. If a source is listed here, Excel will automatically open workbooks with macros no matter what setting you have specified for the security level. If you want to add a source to the list, you need to open up a workbook from the source and then select Tools → Macro → Security and on the Trusted Sources tab select the "Always trust macros from this source" checkbox. To remove a source from the list, highlight the source and select the Remove button.

Visual Basic Editor

This option opens the Microsoft Visual Basic Editor, as shown in Figure 8-31. The Visual Basic Editor provides the ability to create advanced macros that cannot be created using the Record Macro option. The Editor is also opened when you select either the Edit or Step Into buttons on the Macros dialog, or by pressing Alt+F11.

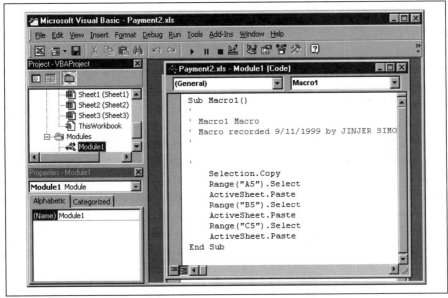

Figure 8-31: Visual Basic Editor window

Each macro is referred to as a module within the Visual Basic Editor window. When you select Tools → Macro → Visual Basic Editor there will not be a module open on the Visual Basic Editor window. To locate an existing macro within the current workbook, locate the macro name under the Module node of the tree within the Project window.

To create a new macro for your workbook, select Insert → Module. Add the appropriate code for the macro.

Microsoft Script Editor

The Microsoft Script Editor, shown in Figure 8-32, provides the ability to add web scripts to a worksheet that will be saved as a web page. By adding scripting using Visual Basic for Scripting (VBScript), JavaScript, or another scripting language you can add functionality to the web page that is not available with standard HTML.

Tools Menu

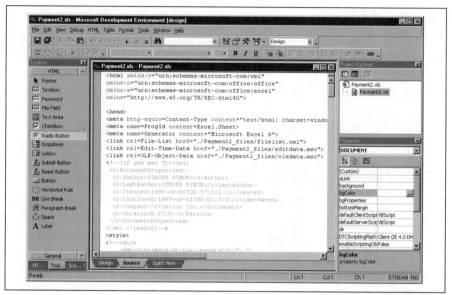

Figure 8-32: Microsoft Script Editor

> **NOTE** *If you are going to add scripts to a worksheet that you want to save as a web page, you will want to add some new menu items to Tools → Macro. Use Tools → Customize and select the Commands tab. In the Categories list box select the Tools option. Select the Insert Script option and drag it up to the Tools menu. When the Tools menu displays drag the option to the Macro submenu and release it. You will probably want to do the same thing for the Remove All Scripts and Show All Scripts options.*

If your worksheet already contains scripts, their locations will be identified on your worksheet with a script icon representing the specific scripting language. If you select one of those scripts, the Microsoft Script Editor opens up and shows the selected script for the worksheet. To view the script for the entire worksheet, select Tools → Macro → Microsoft Script Editor or Alt+Shift+F11.

If you have added the additional scripting commands to the macro menu you can insert a new macro in your worksheet by selecting the location for the script and then selecting Tools → Macro → Insert Script. If you don't have the commands available, you can select Tools → Macro → Microsoft Script Editor and insert the script in the desired location.

Keep in mind that when you open up the Microsoft Script Editor, a separate copy of the worksheet is opened. Changes you make to the worksheet will not be reflected until you save within the Script Editor and refresh the worksheet within Excel. For more information about using the Microsoft Script Editor refer to *Writing Excel Macros* (O'Reilly).

Tools → Add-Ins

This option provides the ability to add functionality to Excel by selecting an Add-in on the Add-Ins dialog shown in Figure 8-33. Add-ins are basically just Excel worksheets that have been saved as Microsoft Excel Add-Ins (*.xla*). Microsoft includes several different add-ins within the installation that can be selected at anytime.

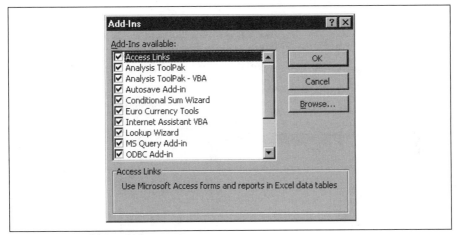

Figure 8-33: Add-Ins dialog

The Add-Ins available list box lists only the Add-ins that are available in your library folder (typically *c:\Microsoft Office\AddIns*) or your profile folder (at *c:\Windows\user name\Application Data\Microsoft\AddIns*). If you don't find the desired add-in in the Add-Ins available list box select the Browse button and locate the add-in. When you locate and select a new add-in it is added to the Add-Ins available list box. You must select the checkbox next to it in order to load it.

Creating Add-Ins

Any workbook can be saved as an Add-in, but this is only beneficial if the workbook contains macros. When a workbook is saved as an add-in only the macros are usable; all other information within the workbook becomes unusable, since the add-in is actually hidden. Creating an add-in is a good way to prevent access to VBA code that you may have created for your macro.

To create an Add-in you simply need to select File → Save As and then select the "Microsoft Excel Add-In (*.xla*)" option in the Save as Type field. When you save the add-in, Excel prompts you for descriptive information about the add-in. Be sure to specify a name for the add-in in the Title field. This is the name that will show up on the Add-Ins dialog. Once the add-in is created you will be able to add it to any worksheet by selecting Tools → Add-Ins.

Tools → Customize

Provides the ability to customize the way toolbars display within Excel by adding and removing commands. You can also create new toolbars. You can display the Customize dialog, shown in Figure 8-34, by selecting Tools → Customize, clicking on a toolbar with the right-mouse button and selecting the Customize option, or selecting View → Toolbars → Customize. See Chapter 2 for more details.

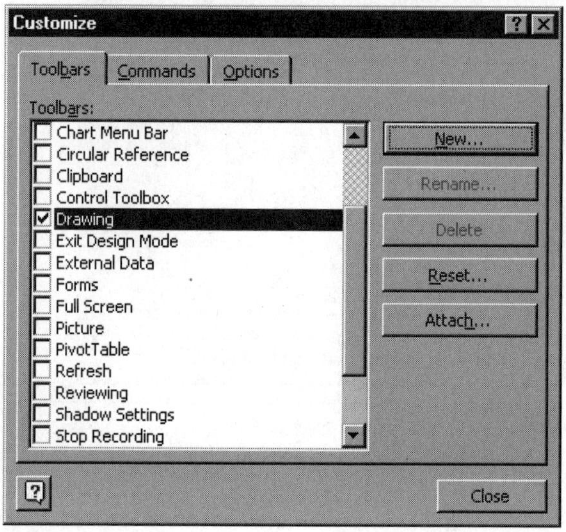

Figure 8-34: Customize dialog

Toolbars Tab

The Toolbars tab lists all of the available toolbars, including any custom toolbars that you have created. The checkboxes are selected next to each of the toolbars that are displayed. If you want to make modifications or add or remove options, you will need to make sure the toolbar is displayed.

You can create a new toolbar by selecting the New button. Excel will prompt you for a name by displaying the New Toolbar dialog. When the toolbar is created it does not contain any commands. You will need to select the toolbar and then select the Commands tab to add the desired commands to the new toolbar.

The Rename, Delete, and Attach buttons are only available when you have a custom toolbar selected. The Attach button allows you to attach the toolbar to the current workbook so that when you give the workbook to another user the toolbar goes with it.

The Reset button restores the commands on the selected toolbar back to the original settings. This command only works with built-in toolbars.

Commands Tab

The Commands tab provides a list of all the available buttons within Excel. You can add these buttons to a toolbar by clicking on the desired button and dragging it onto the desired toolbar. The buttons are grouped into categories to make them easier to locate. You can see all of the buttons available in the specific category by selecting the appropriate category.

Another way to add buttons to a toolbar is to select the down arrow button at the end of the toolbar to see a list of the available buttons, as shown in Figure 8-35. The buttons that are listed are the ones that have been predefined as button options for that toolbar. The ones that are currently displayed on the toolbar are selected. You can add buttons by selecting them. If the button you are looking for is not displayed, you can select the Customize option and search for the additional buttons.

Tools → Options

The Options dialog, shown in Figure 8-36, provides general settings for various features of Excel. For example, on the General tab you can indicate the number of worksheets that should be placed in each workbook as it is created. If you change any of these settings it affects all currently open workbooks, and any that Excel may open or create in the future.

View Tab

The View tab provides options for specifying how your Excel window displays a workbook on the screen. There are basically four different groups of options on this tab. You select options in each group by selecting the appropriate radio button or checkbox.

Calculation Tab

The Calculation tab indicates how Excel should handle calculations. By default Excel automatically recalculates data in the worksheet whenever you change a value or formula. If you have a large worksheet with several formulas you may want to select the Manual option. If you select manual the worksheet will not be recalculated until you select the Calc Now or Calc Sheet button or press F9. The worksheet will also be recalculated when you save it if the "Recalculate before save" checkbox is selected.

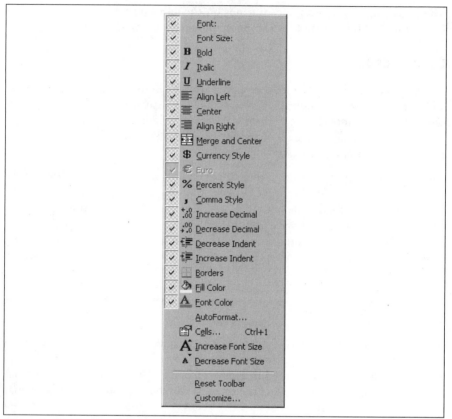

Figure 8-35: Toolbar Selection menu

The Iterations section limits the number of iterations that Excel makes for goal setting or for resolving circular references. For more information refer to "Tools → Goal Setting."

The Workbook options section provides several options for dealing with data in workbooks. Probably the most confusing is the 1904 date system option. This option was mainly put there for dealing with workbooks from Macintosh computers. By default Excel for Windows calculates dates based on the first date being January 1, 1900, whereas the Macintosh systems calculate dates with January 1, 1904 as the first date. Therefore a date value of 2000 will produce different results depending upon the date setting selected. I would only select this option if you are working with files from the Macintosh, otherwise, you are not going to get the date results you expect.

Edit Tab

The Edit tab provides different settings for how data is modified within your worksheet. Most of these options are fairly self-explanatory. Keep in mind that if you do

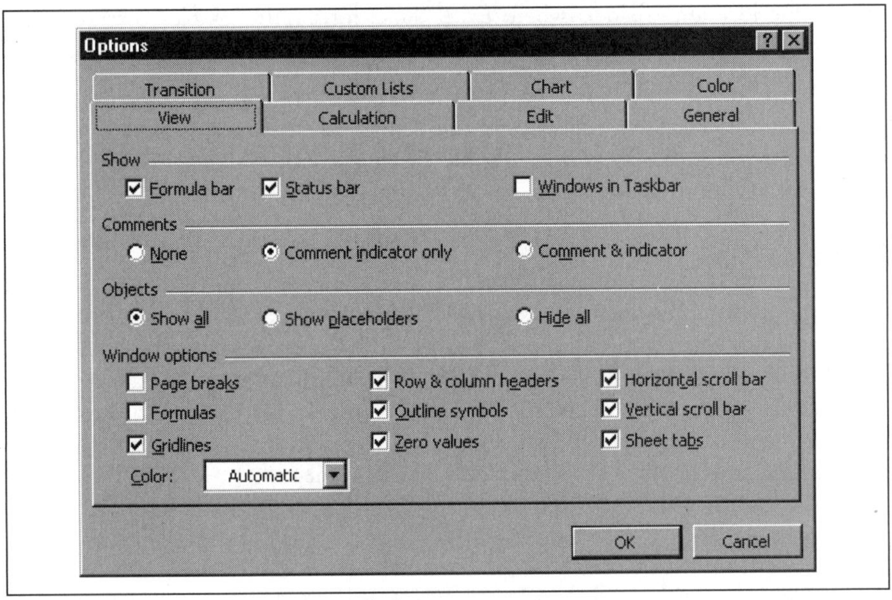

Figure 8-36: View tab on Options dialog

not select the "Edit directly in cell" option you will want to make sure the Formula Bar option is selected on the View tab so that you can add and modify the contents of a cell.

The "Move selection after Enter" checkbox indicates that you want Excel to move to the next cell when you press the Enter key. The cell that becomes active is determined by the direction you specify in the Direction drop-down list.

General Tab

The General tab provides the ability to set the general setting for Excel, such as the number of sheets that should be added to each workbook when it is created and the default font used within workbooks.

The "R1C1 reference style" checkbox allows you to change the way that Excel refers to cell locations from the default of a letter and a number, such as C14, to the R1C1 format, such as R14C3.

If you want to keep track of the recently used files by listing them on the file menu, make sure the "Recently used file list" option is selected. By default, Excel remembers the last four files, but you can increase this number to nine or decrease this number to zero.

The "Default file location" is the folder where Excel will attempt to open or save files when you select the corresponding options on the File menu. The "Alternate startup file location" field is where Excel looks for additional files that you may want to open automatically when Excel opens.

The Web Options button is used to specify how Excel data will look when it is viewed in a web browser. You can indicate settings such as how files are organized, the target monitor display type for people viewing your web data, and default fonts on the Web Options dialog.

Transition Tab

The Transition tab is where you specify the default format used to save files from Excel. It is also where you indicate the key that you can press to select the menu bar. Avoid using a key that you type frequently. By default Excel uses the slash key (/) as the key that activates the menu bar. If you press this key as the first character in a cell, the menu bar is activated and a slash is not added to the cell, but if you type another character first, the slash key places a slash in the cell.

Custom Lists Tab

The Custom Lists tab is used to create custom fill lists or sorting orders for data within your worksheet. By default Excel creates the custom lists for the days and months. You can add a new list by typing the list entries in the "List entries" box and then selecting the Add button. Make sure you press the Enter key after each item in the list.

You can also create a new list by selecting a list of data items in your worksheet and then selecting Tools → Options. On the Custom Lists tab select the Import button.

Chart Tab

The Chart tab is where you can specify how charts are created within Excel. With the "Plot empty cells as" fields you select how you want to handle any empty cells that exist in the data selected for creating the chart.

Color Tab

The Color tab is used to identify the colors that are available for use within your workbook. These include colors for chart fills and for lines.

Tools → Wizard

The options on the Wizard submenu are add-ins that must be installed using Tools → Add-ins to install the Conditional Sum Wizard and the Lookup Wizard.

Conditional Sum

The Conditional Sum Wizard, shown in Figure 8-37, helps you to create formulas that will sum up specific values in a column based upon the values of other cells within a list. For example, if you were to look at the example shown on the wizard, the sales amounts would only be added for Retail sales, not the wholesale sales.

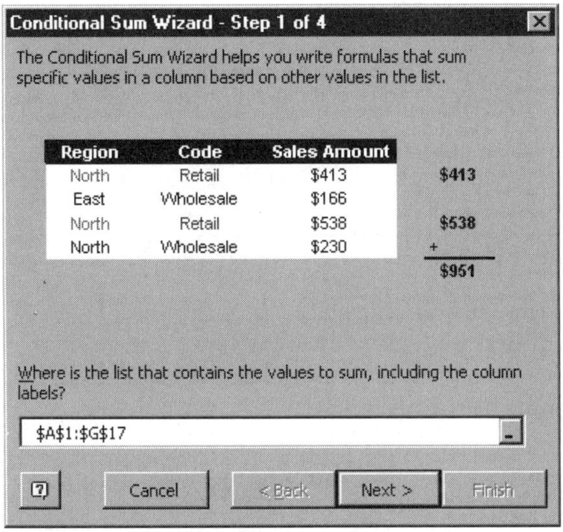

Figure 8-37: Conditional Sum Wizard

The wizard steps you through the process of creating the conditional format. You need to specify the column that you want to sum and create the conditional statement indicating the values to be summed.

Lookup

The Lookup Wizard, shown in Figure 8-38, allows you to create a formula that finds the value where a specific row and column intersect.

The Lookup Wizard steps you through the process by requesting the range of cells to search, as shown in Figure 8-38. You then indicate the specific row and column that you want to intersect. If they exist, Excel will use the column and row names specified in your worksheet to refer to the rows and columns.

Tools → Data Analysis

This option displays on the Tools menu if you have loaded the Analysis ToolPak add-in using Tools → Add-Ins. This option provides a set of analysis tools that can be used to develop complex statistical and engineering analyses. When you select

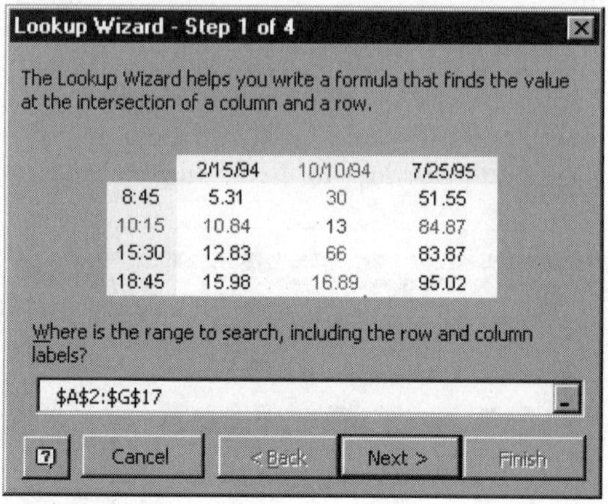

Figure 8-38: Lookup Wizard

this option the Data Analysis dialog displays, as shown in Figure 8-39, with a list of the tools you can select from. Since these tools are very technical and require prior knowledge of these concepts, this book does not cover these tools. You can find specific tips on using these tools by selecting the Help button.

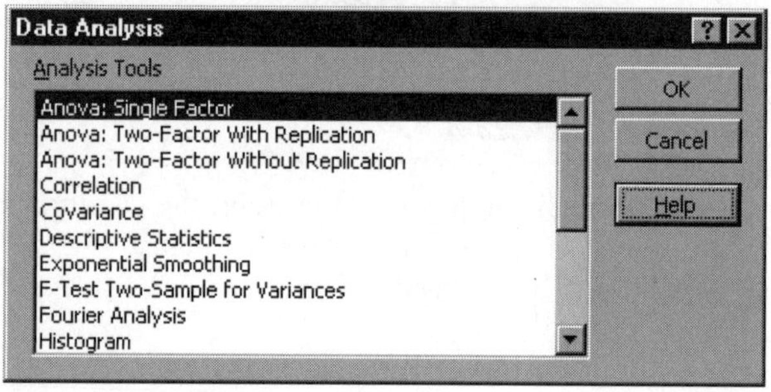

Figure 8-39: Data Analysis dialog

Tools → Update Add-In Links

This is an add-in option that is available if you load the Update Add-In Links option on Tools → Add-Ins. You will only want to load this option if you are working with workbooks from Excel 4.0. This option converts any add-ins that refer to Excel 4.0 add-ins so that they directly access the built-in functionality of Excel 2000. When you select this option the Update Add-In Links dialog displays as shown in Figure 8-40.

Indicate whether you want to update the links in the active document or all open Excel documents.

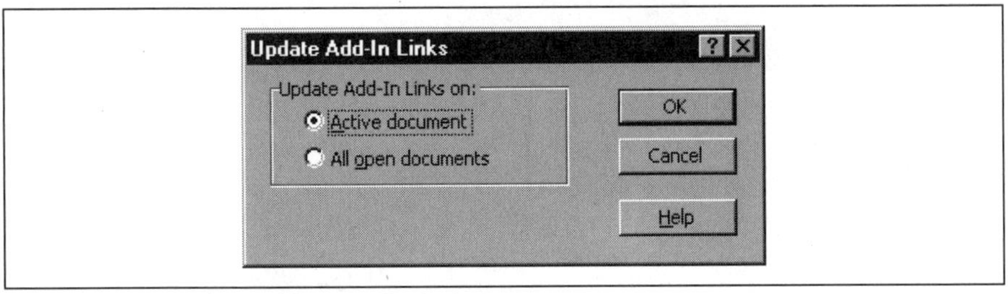

Figure 8-40: Update Add-In Links dialog

Chapter 9

Data

The Data menu provides several useful options for working with large data lists. This menu provides various methods for locating the desired data:

Sort

Sorts the data based upon the values within one or two columns. When using this option you still see all of the data, it is just reorganized based upon the way you decide to sort (Ascending or Descending, based upon the selected column).

Filter

Hides the values that do not meet the specified criteria. For example, you may only want to see the sales in Texas and Florida. The values that are hidden are still used within formulas.

Subtotals

Subtotals are added to the data list to provide a better description of the information. For example, you may want to subtotal the sales for each territory.

Group and Outline

Groups together related values so that they can be expanded and collapsed. For example, you could group the monthly sales for Texas with the annual total.

PivotTable and PivotChart Report

Creates a dynamic summary of the selected cell values. You can change the view of the PivotChart by selecting a different data value.

If you have a chart selected the Data menu will be replaced with the Chart menu. For more information refer to Chapter 10, *Chart*.

Data → Sort

Sorts the selected portion of the worksheet based upon the specified sort criteria. For example, you can select a specific column that you want to use to sort the data and then decide whether to sort it in ascending or descending order. When you select Data → Sort the Sort dialog displays, as shown in Figure 9-1. You can select up to three different columns to sort by and the order in which to sort. Excel will sort by the first column first, then by the second, and finally by the third column, if one is specified.

Figure 9-1: Sort dialog

If the first row of the selected columns contains headings, select the Header row radio button. Excel will allow you to select that column name, instead of a column reference, when you specify the sort order. Also, when the values are sorted, the values will not be altered in the header row.

If you want to sort by rows instead of columns, select the Options button to display the Sort Options dialog and then select the "Sort left to right" option. This will place the row references or names in each drop-down list.

You can create or select custom sort orders. This is useful when you want to sort the column in an order other than alphabetical. For example, Excel maintains custom sort orders for months and days of the week. If your first sort column contains the months of the year, you probably want them sorted in the order they come on the calendar, not the alphabetical order. To do this, you need to select the custom sort order for months. You can select a custom sort order on the Sort Options dialog, shown in Figure 9-2, that displays when you select the Options button on the Sort dialog.

To select a custom sort order, select the down arrow button next to the "First key sort order" field and highlight the sort order you want to use. Remember, you can only specify a custom sort order for the first column, or row, that you are sorting by. If the Normal option is selected, Excel will use the standard sort rules and sort the data alphabetically.

You can create a custom sort order on the Custom Lists tab of the Options dialog that displays when you select Tools → Options. If you have custom lists that you use internally within your organization, you can create that list in the order in which you typically sort it.

Understanding Excel's Sort Order

Whenever you sort cell values, there are certain sort rules that Excel uses to determine how to sort. These rules, outlined in the following list, determine how Excel deals with numbers, alphanumeric, and other types of values when sorting in ascending order. If you sort the values in descending order this list is reversed, with the exception of the blank values, which are always at the end of the sort no matter what order you sort in.

- Custom sort order is specified using the Sort Options dialog that displays when you select the Options button on the Sort dialog.

- Numbers are sorted from the smallest value to the largest value. For example, -23, -5, 4, 123.

- Alphanumeric values are sorted by comparing character by character in each value. The characters are compared based upon the following order: 0 1 2 3 4 5 6 7 8 9 (space) ! " # $ % & ( ) * , . / : ; ? @ [\ ] ^ _ ` { | } ~ + < = > A B C D E F G H I J K L M N O P Q R S T U V W X Y Z. For example, if you have the values ROOM103 and ROOM11, the value ROOM103 will be placed before ROOM11 in the list.

- Logical values are sorted with FALSE before TRUE.

- All error values are treated as the same. In other words, Excel will leave them in the order in which they appear.

- Blank values are always placed at the end of the list, even when you sort in descending order.

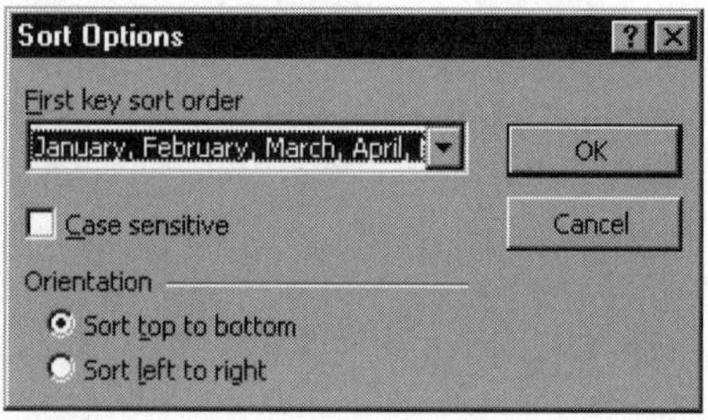

Figure 9-2: The Sort Options dialog

Sorting Columns in Ascending or Descending Order

To sort a single column in ascending order, highlight the desired column and select the Sort Ascending button on the Standard toolbar. If you want to sort in descending order, select the Sort Descending button. Keep in mind that these buttons only work for sorting columns, if you want to sort a row, select Data → Sort.

Data → Filter

Filters a list of data to hide those rows that do not meet the specified criteria. For example, you may only want to see the sales figures for Texas during January. You can perform simple filters on individual columns using the AutoFilter option, or more complex filters with the Advanced Filter option.

AutoFilter

The Data → Filter → AutoFilter option allows you to perform simple filtering upon the columns within the selected range. When you select this option, Excel looks at the data you selected and places arrow buttons in the header row. You can filter on specific values in the column by clicking on the down arrow button and selecting the desired option from the menu, as shown in Figure 9-3.

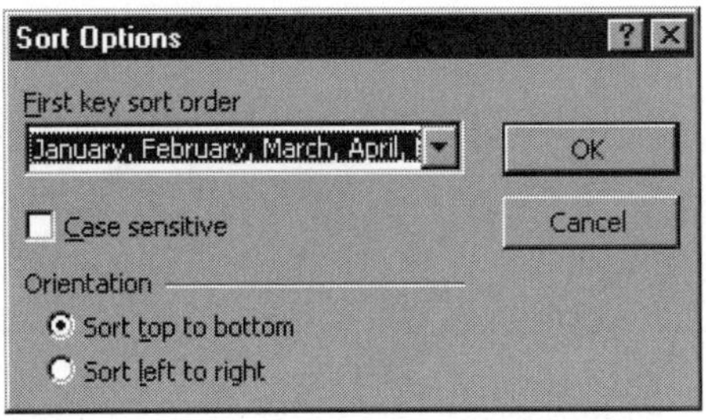

Figure 9-3: AutoFilter menu

 NOTE *If you have any formulas within your worksheet that are displayed outside the selected filter range but that use the values in the range, the formulas will continue to calculate using all of the values, both those displayed and hidden with the filter. In other words, if you look at Figure 9-3, the Total Sales amount remains the same no matter what values are currently displayed on the screen.*

The AutoFilter menu lists all of the unique values in the column for selection along with the following options:

All

Displays all items in the column. If you have previously filtered on this column you can select this option to display all values in the column. You can also select Tools → Show All to redisplay the entire contents of the worksheet.

Top 10

Used with numeric values to display either the highest or lowest number of values. You specify how many values and whether you want the top or bottom values on the Top 10 AutoFilter dialog, shown in Figure 9-4. This is a great way to see the top ten sales figures for the year.

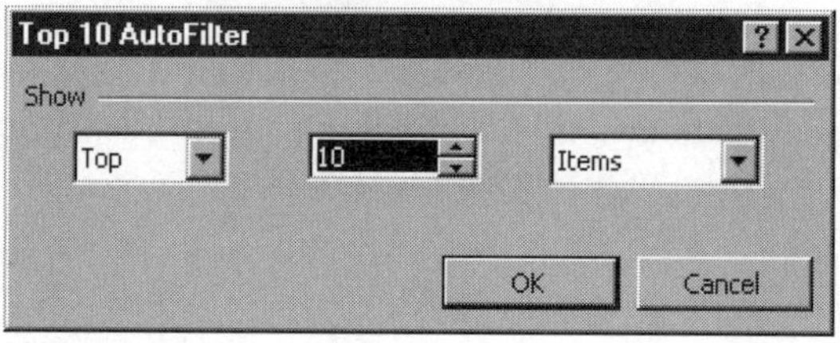

Figure 9-4: Top 10 AutoFilter dialog

Custom

Allows you to specify a little more complex filtering using multiple items to define the filtering. For example, you can indicate that you want to see all sales amounts between $20,000 and $45,000, or all sales in Texas and Florida. When you select the Custom option the Custom AutoFilter dialog displays as shown in Figure 9-5.

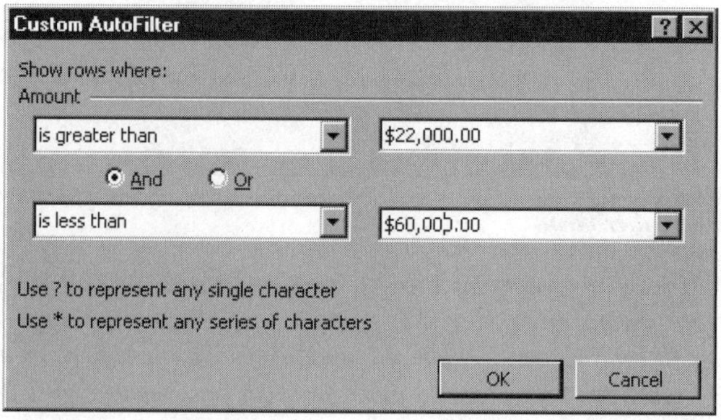

Figure 9-5: Custom AutoFilter dialog

You can create two different filter definitions, as shown in Figure 9-5. You can either find the values that meet both criteria by selecting the And radio button, or the values that meet one or the other criteria by selecting the Or button. For example, with the definitions specified in the figure it would select all sales that are greater than $22,000 and less than $60,000 By selecting the Or radio button, Excel would show you all the sales that are greater than $22,000 or the sales that are less than $60,000 (all sales figures would meet one of those criteria, so all sales figures would still display). Keep in mind the difference between selecting the And radio button versus the Or radio button; the wrong one can greatly alter the expected results.

You can also type wildcard characters in your filter definition. If you remember using wildcards in DOS to display files, this should be old hat to you. You can use a ? (question mark) to represent a single character and using an * (asterisk) replaces a series of characters.

Blanks
Selects all rows that contain a blank value in that column.

NonBlanks
Selects all rows that do not have a blank value in that column. This option only appears in the menu if there are blank cells in the selected column.

TIP # 57

Eliminating the Down Arrow Buttons

The down arrow buttons remain on your worksheet until you cancel the AutoFilter option. You can cancel this option by selecting Data → Filter → AutoFilter again.

Show All

Select this option if you want to display all values in the worksheet. If you have the AutoFilter option selected the down arrow buttons remain at the top of each column.

If there is not a filter active for you worksheet, this option will be grayed out. Therefore, if the Show All option is not available you know you are viewing the entire contents of your worksheet.

TIP # 58

Charting Only the Filtered Portion of the Worksheet

You can create a chart that shows only the visible information selected with the AutoFilter option. To do this, select the chart you want to create using the Insert → Chart option. Next, you need to make sure the "Plot visible cells only" checkbox is selected on the Chart tab of Tools → Options.

Data Menu

Advanced Filter

This option allows you to use a more complex filter definition to filter the selected columns. If you use this information, you need to create you filter definition on your worksheet before selecting Tools → Filter → Advanced Filter. Figure 9-7 shows a sample filter definition for an advanced filter. When you create the filter definition it must meet the following criteria:

- It must have at least two rows in the definition.

- The first row must contain some of the field (column) names. You only need to list the ones that you are going to be filtering on, although to eliminate confusion I would recommend listing them all so you can quickly see which rows are being filtered on.

- The remaining rows contain the filtering criteria. Your definition can appear on multiple rows, as shown in Figure 9-6. The criteria specified in a row is joined with the AND operator. Each row is joined with the OR operator.

You can specify the filter definition in any location on your worksheet. Since it is not data that you want visible, you will probably want to place it in a location that is not visible.

TIP # 59

Using Operators and Wildcards in the Filter

You can use comparison operators (=, >, >=, <, <=< <>) in the cells to create your filter definition. For example, you can specify all sales figures over $20,000 by specifying >$20,000 in the Amount column. You can also use the * and ? wildcards to specify text string values.

Once you specify your filter definition select Data → Filter → Advanced Filter to specify your advanced filter. When you select this option the Advanced Filter dialog displays, as shown in Figure 9-7.

The List range field is where you select the range of cells that you want to filter on. Make sure the cells that contain the filter definition are specified in the Criteria range field. Remember, to select the range you can select the Collapse Dialog button and highlight the appropriate cells.

You can either filter the list in the current location on the worksheet so that the rows that do not meet the criteria are hidden, or you can copy the rows that meet the criteria to another location. For example, if you were filtering out the sales figures for a particular region, you could copy that information into another worksheet so that the sheet could be printed and given to the appropriate salesperson.

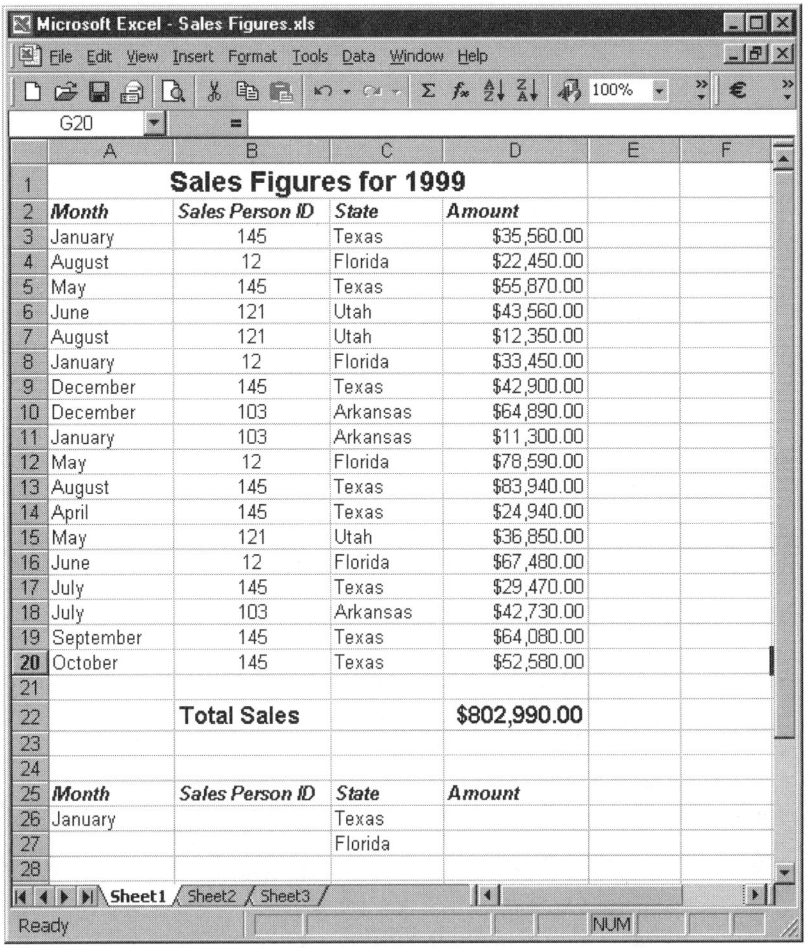

	A	B	C	D	E	F
1		Sales Figures for 1999				
2	*Month*	*Sales Person ID*	*State*	*Amount*		
3	January	145	Texas	$35,560.00		
4	August	12	Florida	$22,450.00		
5	May	145	Texas	$55,870.00		
6	June	121	Utah	$43,560.00		
7	August	121	Utah	$12,350.00		
8	January	12	Florida	$33,450.00		
9	December	145	Texas	$42,900.00		
10	December	103	Arkansas	$64,890.00		
11	January	103	Arkansas	$11,300.00		
12	May	12	Florida	$78,590.00		
13	August	145	Texas	$83,940.00		
14	April	145	Texas	$24,940.00		
15	May	121	Utah	$36,850.00		
16	June	12	Florida	$67,480.00		
17	July	145	Texas	$29,470.00		
18	July	103	Arkansas	$42,730.00		
19	September	145	Texas	$64,080.00		
20	October	145	Texas	$52,580.00		
21						
22		**Total Sales**		**$802,990.00**		
23						
24						
25	*Month*	*Sales Person ID*	*State*	*Amount*		
26	January		Texas			
27			Florida			
28						

Figure 9-6: Advanced Filter definition in rows 25–27

TIP # 60

Displaying Only the Unique Values of the Worksheet

If you only want to see the unique (nonduplicated) values in the worksheet you can select the "Unique records only" checkbox on the Advanced Filter dialog. Only the record cells that contain values that are not duplicated within the worksheet will display.

Figure 9-7: Advanced Filter dialog

Data → Form

Provides an easier method for entering data into a list. When you select this option a dialog displays, as shown in Figure 9-8, where you can add new data for your list, remove data from the list and locate a specific data record.

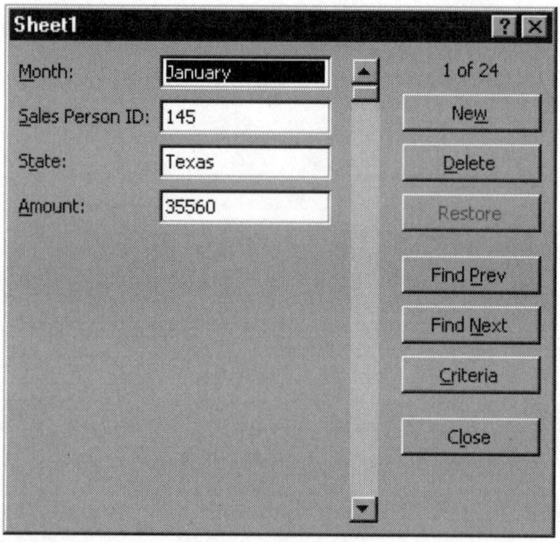

Figure 9-8: Dialog that displays when selecting Data → Form

Before selecting Data → Form, make sure you have at least one of the cells in the range selected. You will be able to add new data to your list as long as there are empty rows available between the list and other data on your worksheet. For example, if you only have one blank row between the end of your list and a row of column totals for the list, the dialog will only allow you to add one new data row.

You can scroll through the data in the list either by using the vertical scroll bar or by selecting the Find Prev and Find Next buttons. If you want to look at the records that meet a certain criteria, such as sales amounts over $30,000, you can select the Criteria button and then type the search criterion in the appropriate fields, >$30,000 in the Amount field for this example. Then select the Find Prev and Find Next buttons to scroll through the list of records that meet the specified criteria. Once you specify the search criterion, Excel continues to use that criterion to scroll through data records. To remove the search criterion and view all data, select the Criteria button and delete the criterion from the appropriate fields.

The Restore button will restore the field values in a data record back to the original values, but it must be selected before clicking on another button.

TIP # 61
Using Database as a Range Name
If you name the range for your data list Database, the range definition will be extended automatically each time you add a new record using the dialog. This only works if the range is named Database. If you have named the range something else, you will have to manually update the range using Insert → Name → Define.

Data → Subtotals

Allows you to automatically insert subtotals and totals for values in a list. In order to effectively use this option you need to first sort your data based upon the column for which you want to display subtotals. For example, if you want to see the sales totals for each month, you should sort the list based on months before selecting this option. (Refer to "Data → Sort.") You also need to have column headings defined for your data.

TIP # 62
Update Formulas After Inserting Columns
If you have formulas that perform calculations upon specific columns within the data list, such as a column total, the formula will not be updated when you add a new column using Data → Form. You will need to update your formulas manually.

When you select Data → Subtotals, the Subtotal dialog displays as shown in Figure 9-9. The dialog makes default selections based upon the data that you selected prior to selecting this option. You must have a data list selected before selecting Data → Subtotals.

Excel automatically recalculates the total and subtotals as you make modifications to the data in the list.

Data Menu

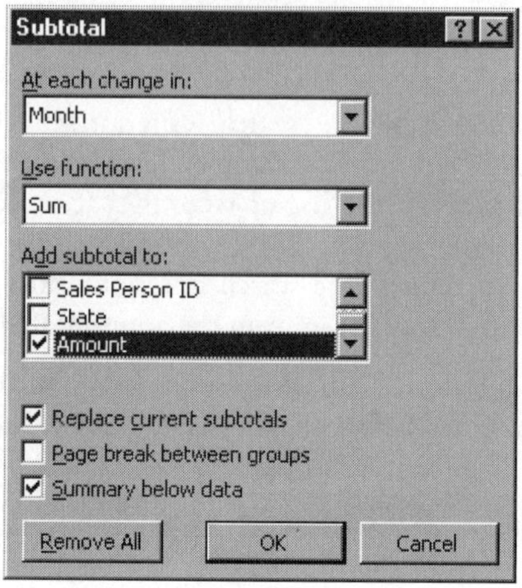

Figure 9-9: Subtotal dialog

At each change in

You need to select the column that you want to create subtotals on in the "At each change in" field. For example, since we want to see the subtotals for each sales month we have selected Month for this field.

Use function

Although this option is called Subtotals, you do not have to sum the data. For example, you may want to display the average sale for the month. You can select the type of function you want from the drop-down list in the Use function field.

Add subtotal to

Select the specific columns that you want to create subtotals for. The function that you selected in the Use function field will be used for each of these totals.

Replace current subtotals

Select this option to replace any subtotals that are currently in the worksheet with the new ones currently specified on the Subtotal dialog. If you are adding new subtotals for a different column, or using a different function, and you want to keep the original subtotals, make sure this checkbox is cleared.

For example, you may want to show both a sales sum and an average for each month. In other to do this, you would have to create each subtotal definition separately by selecting Data → Subtotal twice.

Page break between groups

Inserts a page break after each subtotaled group. This is only useful if you plan to print out your worksheet so that each group displays on a separate page.

Summary below data

Select this checkbox to insert the subtotals below each group. If this checkbox is not selected, the subtotal amounts display above the corresponding group. This checkbox also determines where the list total is placed: if the checkbox is selected it is at the end of the list; otherwise, it is at the top of the list.

After specifying the options on the Subtotal dialog, Excel inserts the subtotals specified and outlines the list so that each subtotal row is grouped with the corresponding detail rows, as shown in Figure 9-10. The grand total row is grouped with the subtotal rows.

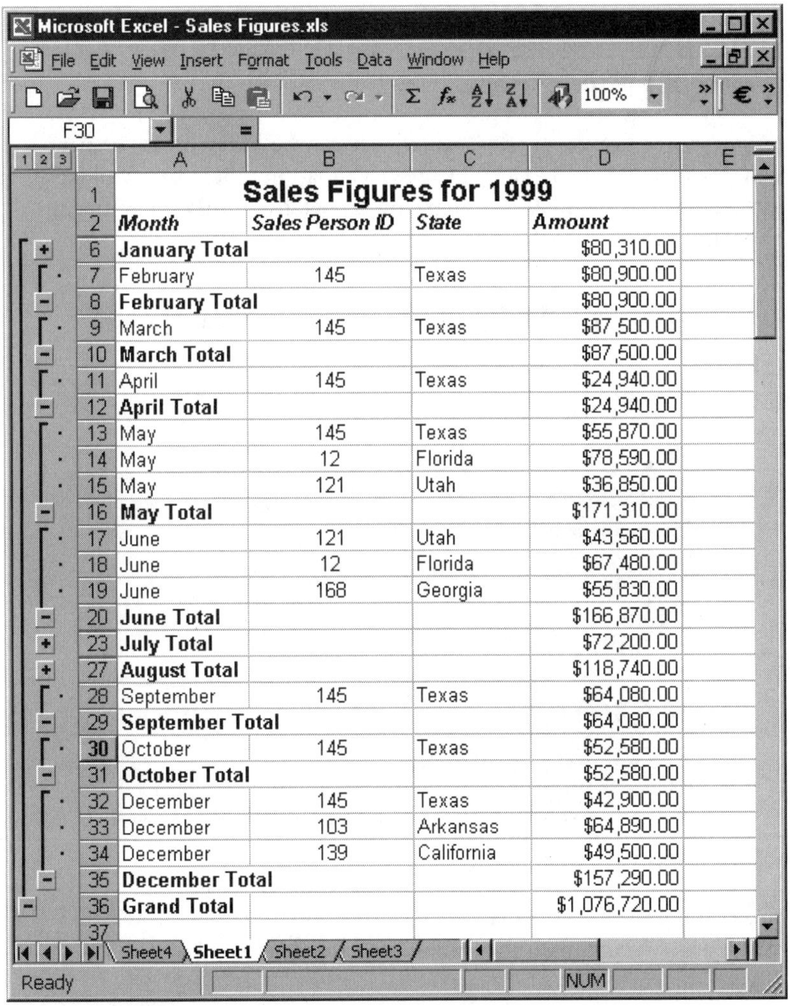

	A	B	C	D
1	**Sales Figures for 1999**			
2	***Month***	***Sales Person ID***	***State***	***Amount***
6	**January Total**			$80,310.00
7	February	145	Texas	$80,900.00
8	**February Total**			$80,900.00
9	March	145	Texas	$87,500.00
10	**March Total**			$87,500.00
11	April	145	Texas	$24,940.00
12	**April Total**			$24,940.00
13	May	145	Texas	$55,870.00
14	May	12	Florida	$78,590.00
15	May	121	Utah	$36,850.00
16	**May Total**			$171,310.00
17	June	121	Utah	$43,560.00
18	June	12	Florida	$67,480.00
19	June	168	Georgia	$55,830.00
20	**June Total**			$166,870.00
23	**July Total**			$72,200.00
27	**August Total**			$118,740.00
28	September	145	Texas	$64,080.00
29	**September Total**			$64,080.00
30	October	145	Texas	$52,580.00
31	**October Total**			$52,580.00
32	December	145	Texas	$42,900.00
33	December	103	Arkansas	$64,890.00
34	December	139	California	$49,500.00
35	**December Total**			$157,290.00
36	**Grand Total**			$1,076,720.00

Figure 9-10: Subtotals for a data list

You can expand and collapse subtotal and total groupings by clicking on the outline symbols on the left side of the window. For example, in Figure 9-10 the subtotals groups are collapsed for January, July, and August so that only the subtotal display and not the individual data rows.

TIP # 63

Understanding how Excel Determines Values of Totals and Subtotals

Excel calculates the grand total based upon the individual data in the list and not the subtotal amounts. For example, if you select the SUM function for the subtotaling, Excel will sum all of the values in the list, and not just the subtotal amounts.

Data → Validation

Allows you to restrict the type of values that can be entered into a specific cell or range of cells. When you select Data → Validation, the Data Validation dialog displays as shown in Figure 9-11. There are three tabs on this dialog that are used to create the data validation definition.

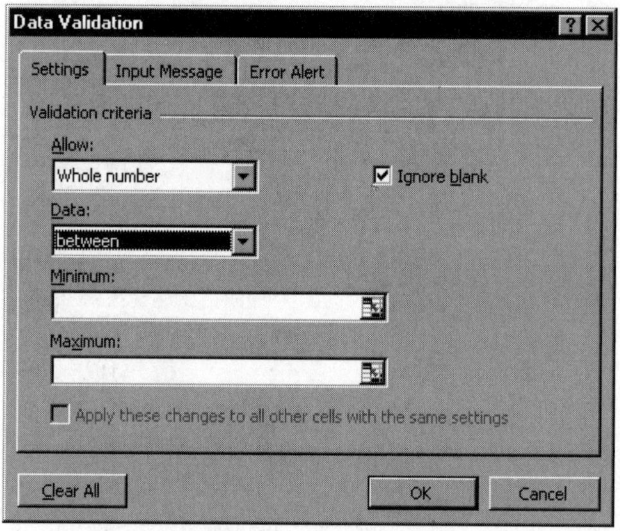

Figure 9-11: Data Validation dialog

To cancel all data validation that has been specified for the selected range of cells, select the Clear All button on the Data Validation dialog.

Settings

The Settings tab is where you indicate the type of data you want to be entered into the selected cells. By default the cells will allow any type of data; to specify a type, use the down arrow button next to the Allow field and select the type of data you want.

Once you indicate the type of data you want to be placed in the cells, you need to indicate the range for the data. Select the comparison operator you want to use in the Data field. The operators that display in the drop-down list vary based upon the type of data you selected in the Allow field. Once the comparison operator is selected you will need to indicate either an acceptable value in the Value field or a range in the Minimum and Maximum fields. The fields that display vary based upon the comparison operator selected. The given cell(s) will now only accept the type of data you have setup using the settings tab.

Input Message

The Input Message tab allows you to indicate a message that displays when you select a cell within the range of the data validation definition, as shown in Figure 9-12.

Error Alert

The Error Alert tab allows you to customize the error message that displays when the wrong type of data is entered into the cell. If you do not specify a message, Excel displays a generic message that indicates that a value was entered that does not meet the data validation set for the cell.

By customizing the message, you can indicate specific data requirements for the cell in the message, as shown in Figure 9-13.

The type of message selected indicates how Excel handles the error. For example, if you select a Stop error alert in the Style field, a message box displays as shown in Figure 9-13 requiring that they enter the appropriate value by selecting Retry or select the Cancel button to maintain the original cell value.

If you select the Warning style of error alert, the user sees the error message you indicate and then has the option of selecting a new value or keeping the current value even though it does not meet the data validation requirements.

Finally, the Information style only displays a message box containing your custom message. It does not require any modifications to the cell value. I would only use this option if a value outside the data validation definition does not have adverse effects on your worksheet.

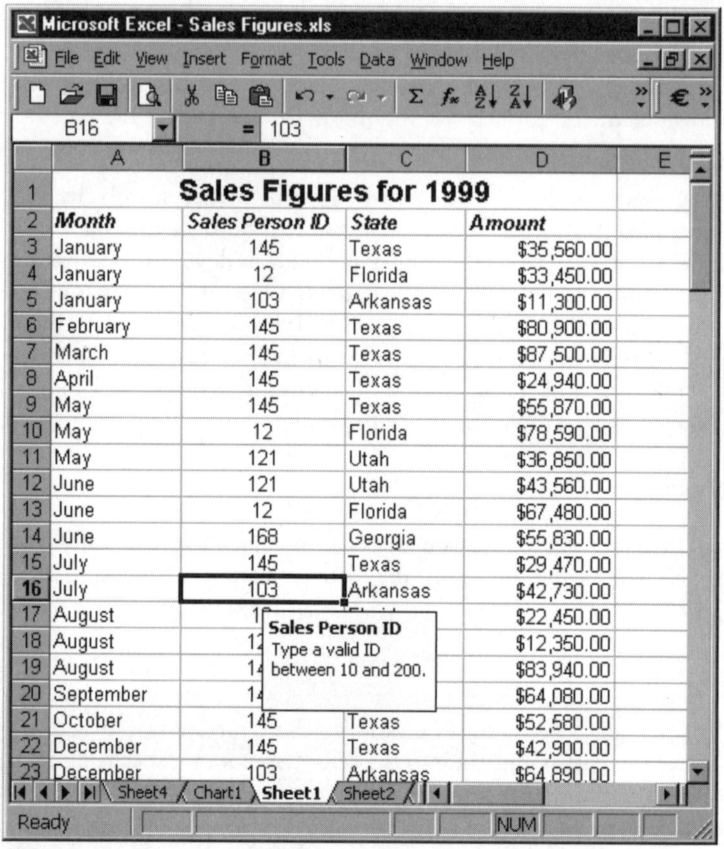

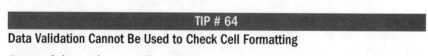

Figure 9-12: Data validation Input Message

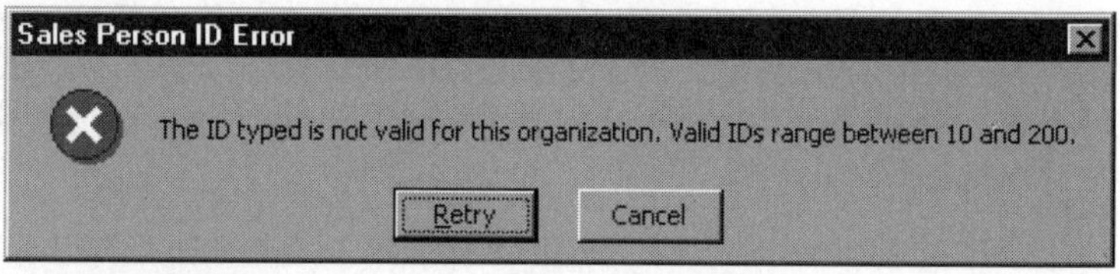

Figure 9-13: Error Alert custom message for data validation

TIP # 64

Data Validation Cannot Be Used to Check Cell Formatting

Data validation does not affect cell formatting. In other words, Excel will allow you to have the cells formatting for dates yet specify that only whole numbers between 1 and 100 can be entered into the cells.

Data → Table

If you find that you need to try different values within a formula to achieve the desired results, you should consider using Data → Table. The Data → Table option allows you to use what-if comparisons to determine the values of formulas if cells contain different values. For example, if you are trying to determine what your payment will be on a loan at various interest rates, you could either manually modify the function, or you could use the Data → Table option.

When you use the Data → Table option, you create a table that contains the values you want to compare and the results of the comparisons, as shown in Figure 9-14. In the figure, column B contains a list of the possible interest rates for the loan. When you select Data → Table, Excel will use the formula in cell C3 to calculate the payment for the loan based upon the various interest rates and place the payment amount in the cell next to the interest rate. The cells in column F are used to calculate the formula in C3, =PMT(F3/12,F4,-F5).

Before selecting the Data → Table option, you need to select the data table, as shown in Figure 9-14. The data table is essentially the column that contains the values that will be substituted in the formula and the column where the results will be placed. Keep in mind you can also use rows for this.

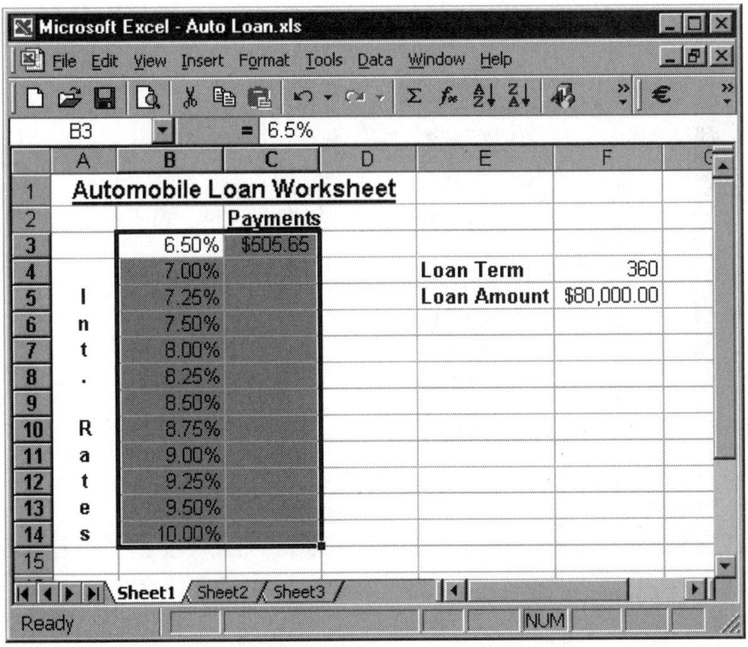

Figure 9-14: Create a data input table for your formula

After selecting the data table range, you can select Data → Table to display the Table dialog shown in Figure 9-15. This is where you indicate the location of the input cell for the formula. Since in our example we are modifying the interest rate, the input cell is B3.

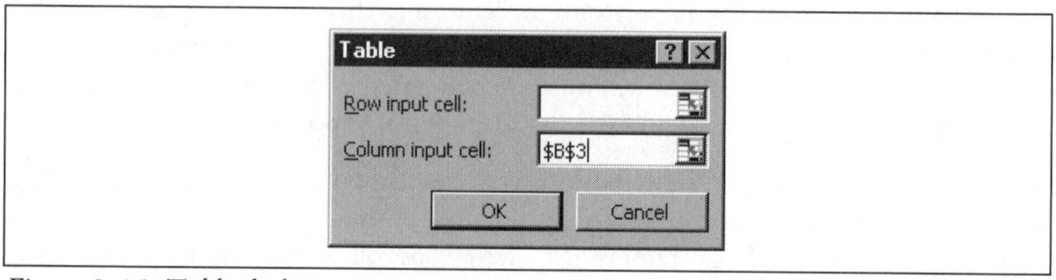

Figure 9-15: Table dialog

Once you indicate the input cell, Excel calculates a value for each of the input values in your table, as shown in Figure 9-16. The process of modifying one value in a formula using a table is referred as a one-input data table. With a one-input data table the input values can be placed in a row or a column in the table.

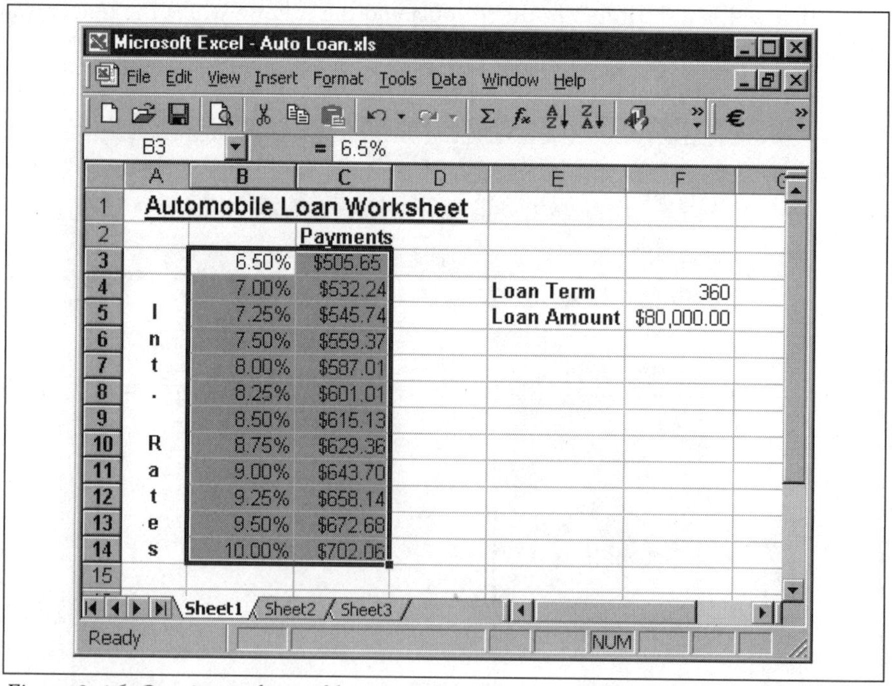

Figure 9-16: One-input data table

TIP # 65

Using Multiple Formulas in a One-Input Data Table

You can have more than one formula in a one-input data table, as long as all of the formulas use the same input cell. For example, in Figure 9-16 you could create another formula in Column D that determined the total amount paid on the loan (principal + interest) for each of the interest rates.

You can also create a two-input data table where two values in the formula are replaced. For example, we could not only replace the interest rate in our example, but also the loan term to determine the payment amount. If this was the case, the interest rate would remain Column B, but we would add the different loan terms in Row 2. On the Table dialog you would indicate both a row and column input cell. With a two-input cell, these values must be initially referenced outside of the table, as shown in Figure 9-17. Also, you will see that the formula sits in cell B2, in the corner of the table, another requirement when creating a two-input table. The formula has only been altered to reference the initial cells `=PMT(C19/12,C20,-C18)`

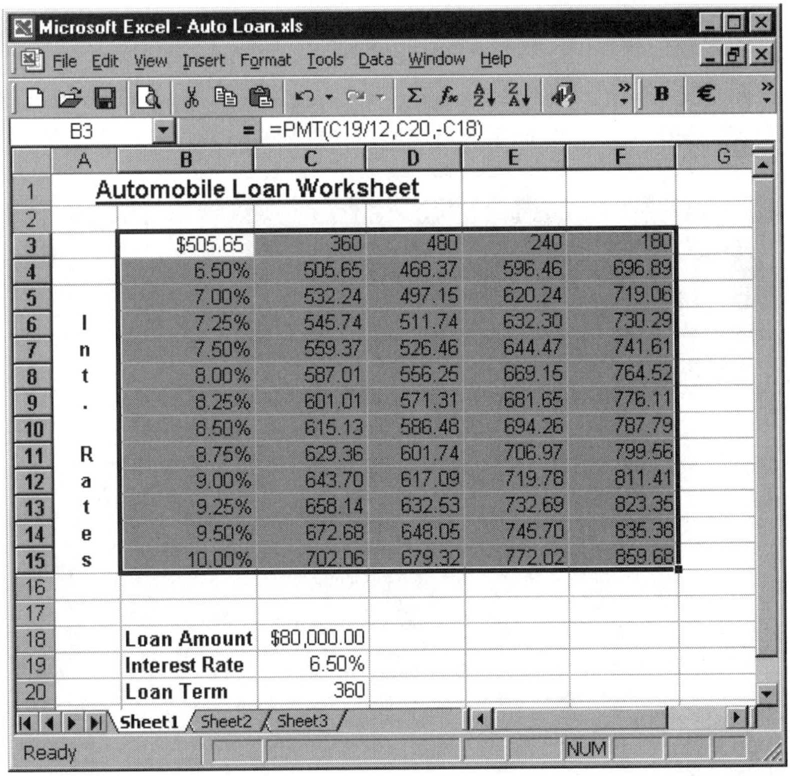

	A	B	C	D	E	F
3		$505.65	360	480	240	180
4		6.50%	505.65	468.37	596.46	696.89
5		7.00%	532.24	497.15	620.24	719.06
6	I	7.25%	545.74	511.74	632.30	730.29
7	n	7.50%	559.37	526.46	644.47	741.61
8	t	8.00%	587.01	556.25	669.15	764.52
9	.	8.25%	601.01	571.31	681.65	776.11
10		8.50%	615.13	586.48	694.26	787.79
11	R	8.75%	629.36	601.74	706.97	799.56
12	a	9.00%	643.70	617.09	719.78	811.41
13	t	9.25%	658.14	632.53	732.69	823.35
14	e	9.50%	672.68	648.05	745.70	835.38
15	s	10.00%	702.06	679.32	772.02	859.68
18		Loan Amount	$80,000.00			
19		Interest Rate	6.50%			
20		Loan Term	360			

Figure 9-17: Two-input data table

Data → Text to Columns

If you have pasted the contents of another file into your worksheet, you may find that all the text was pasted in the first column. To put it into separate columns, you can use the Data → Text to Columns option. When you select this option, the Convert Text to Columns Wizard displays, as shown in Figure 9-18.

Before selecting the option, you need to select the text that you want to covert. You can only do this a column at a time.

The wizard takes you through three steps or pages where you indicate how the text should be converted into columns. At any point during the process you can select the Finish button to complete the conversion. If you skip a page, Excel uses the default settings for the skipped page. Since the wizard only has three steps, I would recommend completing the process by going though each step to specify exactly how the text should be converted.

On the first page you need to indicate how the data is separated, for example, if there is a single space or comma between each word, you need to select the Delimited radio button. The "Fixed width" radio button is selected only if data is evenly spaced so that it appears to line up in columns.

This is the same process you go through if you open a text file up within Excel using File → Open and when you select Data → Get External Data → Import Text File.

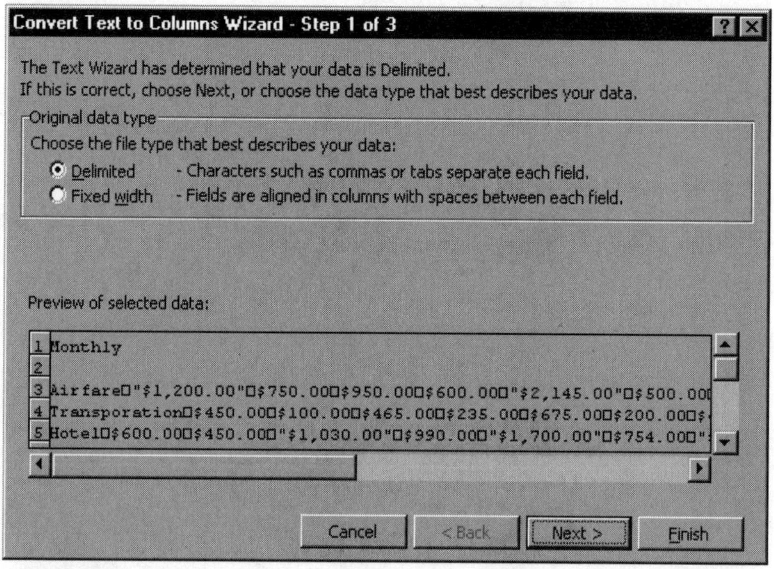

Figure 9-18: Step 1 of the Convert Text to Columns Wizard

The page that displays for the second step of the wizard differs depending on whether you selected the Delimited or Fixed Width radio buttons. Figure 9-19 indicates how Step 2 displays for delimited data. You need to select the appropriate checkboxes that indicate how the data is delimited (separated) within your column. You can specify a unique delimiter by selecting the Other checkbox and typing the delimiter in the field next to the checkbox.

Select the "Treat consecutive delimiters as one" checkbox to ensure that if Excel finds two or more of the delimiter characters between your data, they are treated as one.

As you select the different delimiter characters, you are able to see a preview of how the text will be converted in the Data preview portion of the page.

Convert Text to Columns Wizard - Step 2 of 3

This screen lets you set the delimiters your data contains. You can see how your text is affected in the preview below.

Delimiters

☑ Tab ☐ Semicolon ☐ Comma ☐ Treat consecutive delimiters as one

☐ Space ☐ Other: [ ] Text qualifier: [" ▼]

Data preview

Monthly					
Airfare	$1,200.00	$750.00	$950.00	$600.00	$2,145.00	$500.
Transporation	$450.00	$100.00	$465.00	$235.00	$675.00	$200.
Hotel	$600.00	$450.00	$1,030.00	$990.00	$1,700.00	$754.

[Cancel] [< Back] [Next >] [Finish]

Figure 9-19: Step 2 of the Convert Text to Columns Wizard

NOTE *If you select the "Fixed width" radio button on the first page of the wizard, a different page displays for Step 2. Since you indicated that the data was a fixed width, Excel allows you to specify where the delimiters are by clicking in the desired location on the Data preview portion to insert a break line.*

The final page of the Convert Text to Columns Wizard is where you can indicate the type of data that is in each column. This is done by selecting a column and then selecting the data type for the column by selecting the appropriate radio button in the "Column data format" section. Keep in mind, you can also eliminate a column by selecting the "Do not import column" radio button.

Data Menu

Convert Text to Columns Wizard - Step 3 of 3

This screen lets you select each column and set the Data Format.

'General' converts numeric values to numbers, date values to dates, and all remaining values to text.

Column data format
- ◉ General
- ○ Text
- ○ Date: MDY
- ○ Do not import column (skip)

Advanced...

Destination: A1

Data preview

General	General	General	General	General	General	Gener
Monthly						
Airfare	$1,200.00	$750.00	$950.00	$600.00	$2,145.00	$500.
Transportation	$450.00	$100.00	$465.00	$235.00	$675.00	$200.
Hotel	$600.00	$450.00	$1,030.00	$990.00	$1,700.00	$754.

Cancel | < Back | Next > | Finish

Figure 9-20: Step 3 of the Convert Text to Columns Wizard

You also can specify the location where the converted text should be placed in the worksheet in the Destination field. You can either type the cell reference, or select the Collapse Dialog button and select the reference in the worksheet.

If the data uses a different character to represent a decimal or the thousands separator than you have set up in your Regional Settings option on the Control Panel, you need to select the Advanced button and specify the character that is being used. For example, if a comma is being used for a decimal value and your Regional Settings indicate that periods indicate a decimal, you need to select this option. You can find more information about specifying your Regional Settings in Windows 98 in a Nutshell (O'Reilly).

Data → Template Wizard

Provides the ability to create a custom template that can be used to gather data and store it in a database. For example, if you want to gather the sales figures from each individual salesperson you could create a template that is linked to a central database that each salesperson could use to enter information about a sale. At any point you can access the database to determine what the current sales figures are.

> **NOTE** *This option may not be currently loaded on your system. The Template Wizard dialog is an add-in option that can be added at anytime using Tools → Add-Ins. If you want to design a method to gather information using Excel, this is definitely a good option to load. For more information on add-ins, refer to Chapter 8.*

When you use the Template Wizard option you can use one of the following types of databases as long as you have the necessary database ODBC (Open Database Connectivity) driver and components installed: a Microsoft Excel list, a Microsoft Access database, Microsoft FoxPro database, or a dBase database. The ODBC driver is the database driver that allows you to connect to that type of database. If you are going to have other people access the database and template, make sure you select a database type that they have access to. If you are not sure which types of ODBC drivers you or the other user of the template have installed, I would suggest using the Microsoft Excel list. This option just creates another workbook where the data is compiled. You can open this workbook at anytime and see the results.

Before selecting the Data → Template Wizard you need to create your template within Excel, as shown in Figure 9-21. In the figure, we have created a simple template that requests information about a recent sale.

Figure 9-21: Workbook template

When you select Data → Template Wizard, the Template Wizard displays as shown in Figure 9-22. There are five different steps or pages to this wizard that allow you to indicate the name of the workbook that contains the template you are using for the database, the name and location of the new template, the database type, the database location, and the cells that contain values to be added to the worksheet.

Data Menu

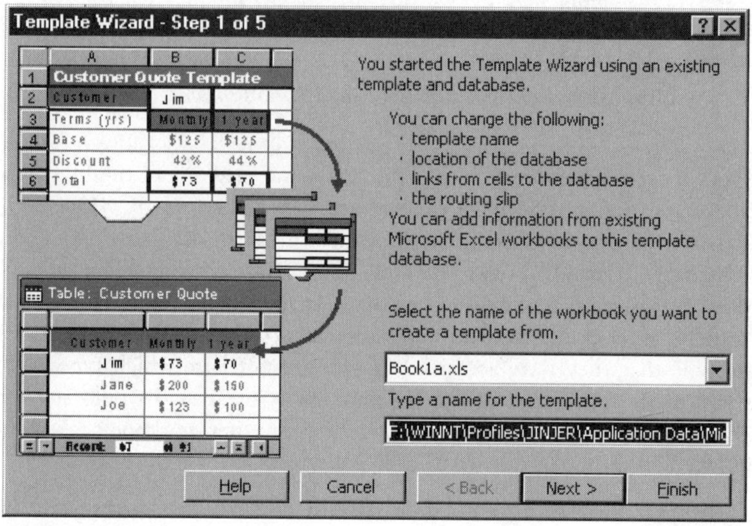

Figure 9-22: Template Wizard Step 1

On the first page of the wizard you need to indicate the workbook that you want to create the template from. You can only select from the open workbooks. You also need to indicate the location where the template should be placed. If you want the template to be listed on the New dialog when you select File → New, you need to place the template in one of the following locations:

- *C:\windows\Profiles\user_name\Application Data\Microsoft\Templates*.

- The *XLStart* folder. This folder is typically located in *C:\windows Profiles\user_ name\Application Data\Microsoft\Excel\XLStart*.

- The location you specified at Tools → Options → General tab.

TIP # 66

Making a Template Available to Multiple Users

If you want the template to be accessible to multiple users you need to place it in a network location that all users have access to.

On the second page of the wizard you need to indicate the type of database that you want to create, and where you want to store the database. You can either select an existing database for Excel to add the data to, or create a new one.

The third page of the wizard, shown in Figure 9-23, is where you indicate the fields within the template whose values should be placed within the database and the name of the database table and fields where the data should be placed.

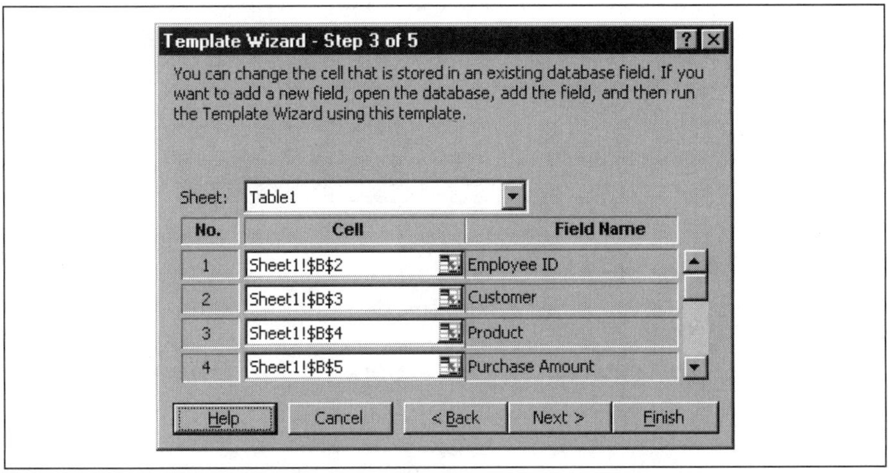

Figure 9-23: Step 3 of the Template Wizard

Sheet

> In the Sheet field you need to indicate the name of the table or sheet in the database where the data will be placed. If you are creating a new database, you can specify the table, or use the default name that is created by Excel. If you are using an existing database, you need to select one of the sheets or tables from the list that appears when you select the down arrow button.

No.

> Indicates the number of the field within the database. The fields are numbered from left to right in the database.

Cell

> Indicates the location of the cell in the worksheet that will capture the data for that database field. You can select a field from any sheet within the workbook, but you need to make sure you indicate both the sheet name and cell reference, as shown in the figure. To select a field from the workbook, select the Collapse Dialog icon and highlight the desired cell.

Field Name

> Indicates the name that will be assigned to the database field. If you are creating a new database you can specify a name in this field. Once the database is created the field names cannot be modified.

The fourth step of the Template Wizard provides the option of adding data from other workbooks to the database. If you have any other workbooks that contain the appropriate data within the same cells indicated on Step 3 of the wizard, you can use this option to add the data to the selected database. If you select the "Yes, include" radio button, another version of Step 4 displays, as shown in Figure 9-24.

When you select the Select button the "Select Files to Convert" dialog displays so you can select the specific workbooks that contain the data to add to the database,

Data Menu

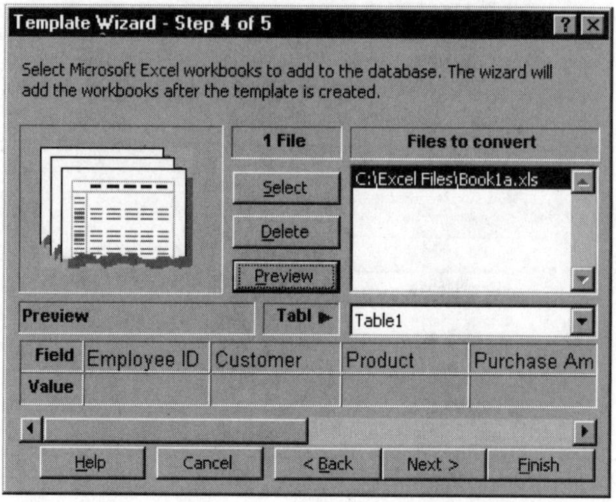

Figure 9-24: Selecting additional workbooks that contain data for the database

The Select Files to Convert dialog displays so you can select the specific workbooks that contain the data to add to the database. The Select Files to Convert dialog is basically the same as the Open dialog that displays when you select File → Open. If you want to verify that the selected workbook contains the appropriate data values you can select the Preview button to display the values from the workbook in the Value fields under each field name.

The final step of the wizard indicates that the database and template have been created. If you want to be notified each time the template is used to add data to your database, select the "Add Routing Slip" button and indicate the users that should receive a copy of the new workbooks that are created. For more information about routing workbooks, refer to "File → Send To."

Data → Consolidate

The Data → Consolidate option provides the ability to merge data from multiple workbooks. For example, if you have multiple workbooks that contain the sales figures for the year, you can consolidate those into one file.

When you select Data → Consolidate the Consolidate dialog displays as shown in Figure 9-25. Before selecting this option make sure you have selected the top-left cell on the worksheet where you want the consolidation data to be placed. On the dialog you need to specify the workbook ranges that need to be consolidated and the type of consolidation that should be done, as outlined in the descriptions that follow.

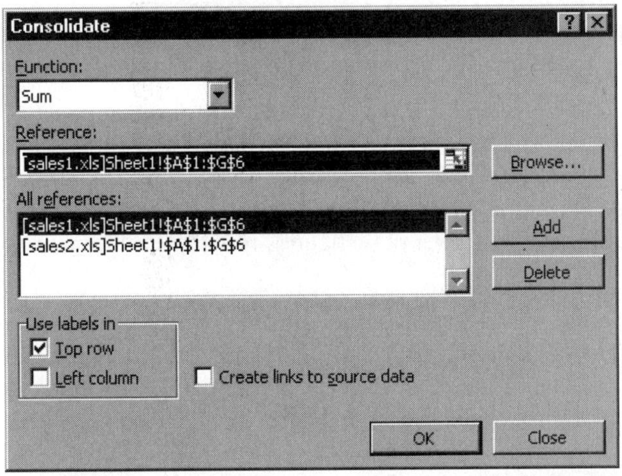

Figure 9-25: Consolidate Dialog

Function

Select the type of consolidation that you want performed. Excel provides the different types of consolidation functions that can be selected. Typically the Sum option is selected. For example, if you consolidate two different workbooks that contain sales figures for the year, if Excel finds the sales figures for the same salesperson in both workbooks, those figures will be summed.

Reference

Specify the source of the data that you want to consolidate. You can either type the range in the field, use the Collapse Dialog button and select the range from an open workbook, or select the Browse button and locate the workbook that contains the data. As shown in Figure 9-25, you must specify the entire range of the data, not just the workbook name. The data can come from the same worksheet, another worksheet in the workbook, or another workbook. You need to make sure the appropriate path information is indicated for the workbook. For example, if you reference a data range within the same worksheet, you only need to specify the cell references, whereas, if you want to consolidate data from another workbook you need to specify the workbook name and the cell reference. If the workbook is located in a different file location on your system than the consolidation workbook, you need to specify the path.

Once the reference is specified, click the Add button to place the reference in the "All references" list box.

NOTE *If your workbook has names assigned to the specific cell ranges that you want to consolidate, you can use the names instead of the cell references. For example, [sales1.xls]AnnualSales. For more information on named ranges, refer to "Insert → Name."*

Data Menu

All references

Indicates the references that will be used to consolidate the data into the current workbook. You can remove a reference using the Delete button.

"Use labels in" checkboxes

If you select either the "Top row" or the "Left column" checkboxes, or both, Excel consolidates the data by using the row and column labels to match data in the worksheets. For example, if it finds sales figures for the same salesperson in multiple worksheets, those figures are summed during the consolidation.

Create links to source data

If selected, Excel creates formulas that link back to the source workbooks that contain the consolidation data. Otherwise, the cells just contain the consolidated values. This option will allow the data to be updated dynamically if it changes in the source workbooks.

TIP # 67

Refresh a Consolidation

Excel remembers the consolidation references that you specify on the Consolidate dialog. Refresh the consolidation at anytime by selecting Data → Consolidate again.

Data → Group and Outline

If you have ever written a report you are probably very familiar with the concept of creating an outline. An outline typically lists all the headings and subheadings for a document. This is a feature that is commonly used within word processing packages, such as Microsoft Word.

Excel also provides this feature by allowing you to group common information in sections and then expanding and collapsing each section as needed. These features are accomplished using the submenu options of Data → Group and Outline.

With these features you can either manually create your outline by selecting the columns or rows in each selection and then selecting Data → Group and Outline → Group or you can let Excel automatically create the outline using Data → Group and Outline → Auto Outline.

TIP # 68

Use of a Predefined Consolidation Name

If you name the consolidation range Consolidate_Area, you don't need to select the range each time you want to update or modify the consolidation. Consolidate_Area is a predefined name within Excel used to reference a consolidated area within a workbook. Although, if you have multiple consolidations within the same workbook, you will only be able to name one of them.

Hide Detail

When you create an outline, Excel creates various outline levels that can be expanded and collapsed. The various levels are indicated with the numbers on the left side of the window (1, 2, 3, etc.). You can collapse and expand each of the levels by clicking on the number at the top of the level. The first button, number 1, is set to encompass the entire list. If you click on this button the entire list collapses and only the summary information for the list displays.

Besides using the number levels, you can also collapse a specific group by clicking on the minus sign (-) in the outline or by selecting a cell within the group and then selecting Data → Group and Outline → Hide Detail.

Show Detail

If a group within your outline has been collapsed, you can expand it by performing one of the following:

- Select the plus sign (+) in the outline that corresponds to the group you want to see.

- Select at least one cell in the group and select Data → Group and Outline → Show Detail.

- Select the number button that corresponds to the outline grouping. Keep in mind that this will expand all groups that are collapsed within that outline level.

Group

The Data → Group and Outline → Group option allows you to group data within a list manually to create an outline. Typically you will want to use this option if your worksheet is not designed in a format where Excel can perform an Auto Outline. For example, you may want to group together all the sales for the month of January.

To group either rows or columns in your list, highlight the desired selection and select either Data → Group and Outline → Outline or Alt+Shift+Right Arrow. If you only select a range of cells, and not the entire rows or columns, the Group dialog displays as shown in Figure 9-26.

Ungroup

The Data → Group and Outline → Group option provides the ability to ungroup the selected rows or columns. You can ungroup just one row or column from the entire group or remove the entire grouping. You specify the rows or columns you want to ungroup by highlighting them and then selecting either Data → Group and Outline → Group or Alt+Shift+Left Arrow.

Data Menu

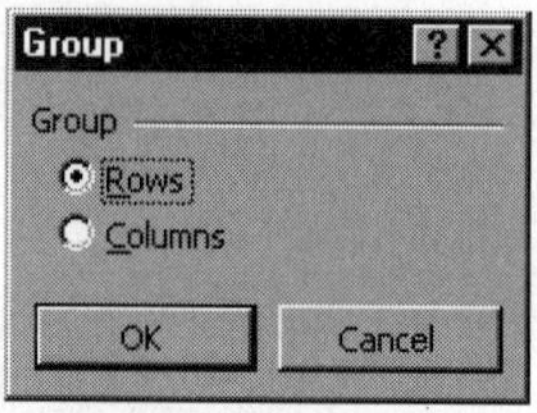

Figure 9-26: Group dialog

If you do not select the entire row or column the Group dialog box displays as shown in Figure 9-26. You need to indicate whether Excel should ungroup the rows or columns within the selected range of cells.

Auto Outline

You can have Excel automatically create an outline for you based upon the contents of the cells within a list by selecting Data → Group and Outline → Auto Outline. To accomplish this, Excel examines the contents of the list and outlines it based upon the formulas within the list. For example, if your list has subtotals and then a final total, as shown in Figure 9-27, Excel groups the cells together with each subtotal, and then creates a larger group that encompasses all cells in the total.

To have Excel create an automatic outline make sure the active cell is somewhere within the desired list, or to ensure Excel selects the right cells, select the appropriate list of cells. Excel will create a column outline, row outline, or both, depending upon the cell contents.

If the list already has an outline Excel will prompt you to make sure you want to replace that outline. If you select the Yes button on the message box, Excel replaces the entire outline with a new outline.

Clear Outline

If you want to clear an outline from your workbook, select Data → Group and Outline → Clear Outline. When you select this option, all collapsed columns and rows are expanded and the outline is removed. Make sure you really want to do this because you cannot undo this option.

Settings

When you select Data → Group and Outline → Settings, the Settings dialog displays, as shown in Figure 9-28. The Settings dialog allows you to specify settings affecting the appearance of an outline.

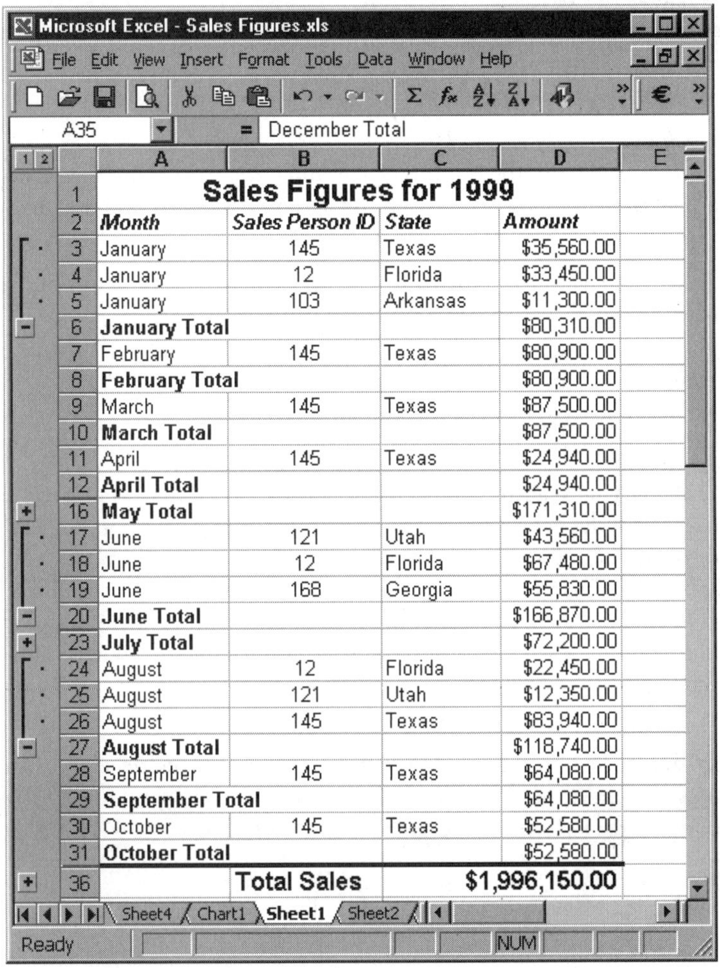

Figure 9-27: Auto outlining

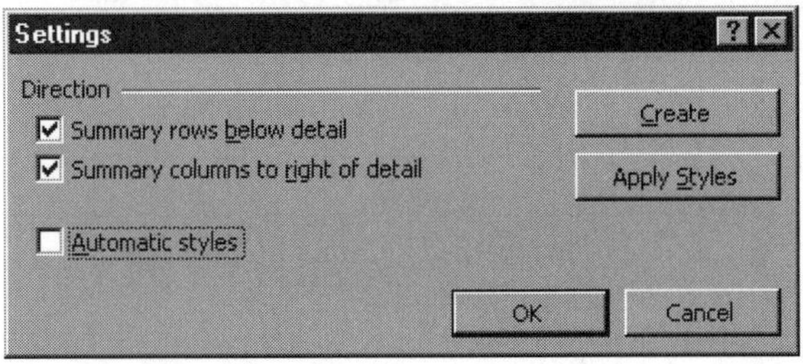

Figure 9-28: Settings dialog

Summary rows below detail

Select this option if the summary rows, typically group totals, are located below each group. If the checkbox for this option is not selected, Excel assumes that the detail rows are located above each group or rows that you select.

Summary columns to right of detail

Select this option if the summary columns are located to the right of each group. If the checkbox for this option is not selected, Excel assumes that the detail rows are located left of each group of columns that you select.

Keep in mind that these two options are really only applicable to manually created groups. When you select Data → Group and Outline → Auto Outline Excel uses the formulas within the list to determine where the summary rows are. In other words, if cell D5 sums the values in cells A5–C5, Excel automatically determines that column 5 is the summary row.

Automatic styles

Excel allows you to automatically apply styles to an outline as it is created, if the "Automatic styles" checkbox is selected. In order to have the styles applied they need to first be created using Format → Style. If you create styles you need to make sure you use the naming format that Excel looks for outlines. All row styles are named RowLevel_1, RowLevel_2, etc., where the numeric value indicates the outline level. Column styles need to be named ColLevel_1, ColLevel_2, etc.

Create

Select this button to create an automatic outline for the selected list using the settings that have been specified on the Settings dialog. This is the same as selecting Data → Group and Outline → Auto Outline.

Apply Styles

Applies styles to the currently selected outline.

Excel automatically creates an outline whenever you use Data → Subtotals to insert subtotal formulas within your list.

TIP # 69
Reduce the Need to Expand and Collapse the List

If you are consistently expanding and collapsing portions of the list to show different scenarios, you probably should consider using View → Custom Views to create the various views of the worksheet. That way you can simply select a new view when you want to see a different combination of rows and columns.

Data → PivotTable and PivotChart Report

If you are new to Excel you have probably never heard the term PivotTable or PivotChart. Actually even if you have used Excel in the past, chances are you probably never explored these useful data analysis tools. PivotTables and PivotCharts are features that were developed by Microsoft to provide a more dynamic method for examining database data.

So what exactly is a PivotTable? A PivotTable allows you to create a dynamic summary of data that is either contained in an Excel list or an External database. You can summarize large amounts of data within a dynamic table, as shown in Figure 9-29. You can dynamically select the data that displays in the chart by selecting a different value in a field. For example, sales totals are displayed for all months, and you can view figures for a specific month by selecting the Down Arrow button next to the Month field and highlighting the desired month. When this selection is made the table is updated to reflect the totals for that month.

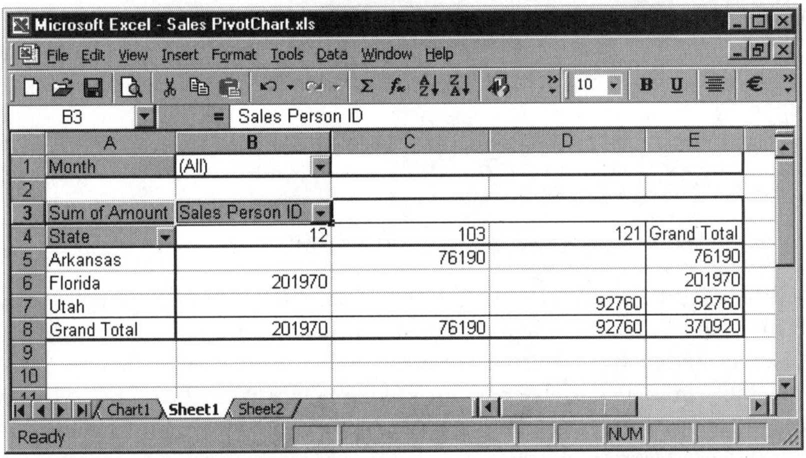

Figure 9-29: Sample PivotTable

PivotCharts have the same characteristics as PivotTables. The values displayed in the chart can be updated dynamically simply be selecting a different value for one of the fields. Figure 9-30 shows a PivotChart that represents the same data as shown in the PivotTable.

As mentioned earlier, PivotTables and PivotCharts are designed to work with large lists of data typically stored within an Excel worksheet or an external database. They are most beneficial when used with lists that contain a data value, such as the sales figures used in our examples, and some type of category (we used the state, Sales Person ID, month, and category values).

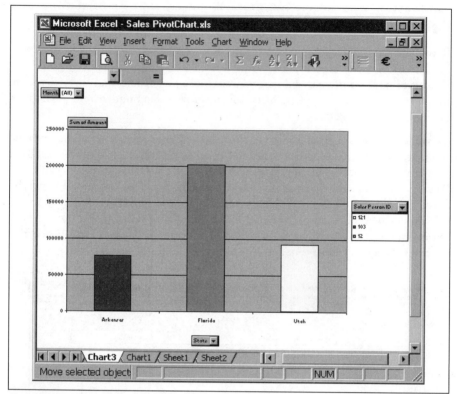

Figure 9-30: Sample PivotChart

PivotTables and PivotCharts are created by selecting Data → Group and Outline → PivotTable and PivotChart Report. When you select this option, a wizard displays as shown in Figure 9-31. This wizard is divided into three different steps or pages used to build your PivotTable and PivotChart. Once your PivotTable and Pivot-Chart are created, you can make additional modifications using the PivotTable toolbar discussed later in this section.

TIP # 70

Changing the Options of a PivotChart

PivotChart options can be modified by using the options on the Chart menu. This includes selecting another chart type. Keep in mind that the PivotTable and Pivot-Chart Wizard creates the chart based upon the chart type selected as the default chart. For more information refer to Chapter 10.

You need to indicate the source of the data that you want to analyze by selecting the appropriate radio button. The second step of the wizard displays differently based upon the type of data source selected. For example, if you select a "Microsoft Excel list or database" you are prompted for the location of the list.

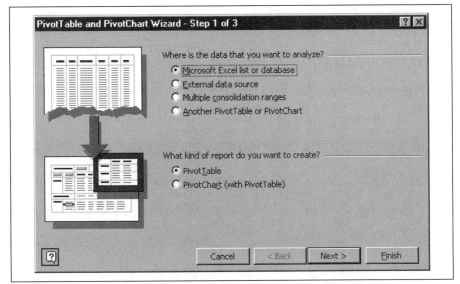

Figure 9-31: PivotTable and PivotChart Wizard

Microsoft Excel list or database

Typically this is the option that will be used most often, as it allows you to analyze data stored within an Excel worksheet, often referred to as a list. The first row in the list must contain the field names. Keep in mind that due to the size limitations of worksheets, Excel lists are limited to 256 fields (columns) and 65,535 records (rows). Be aware that you will probably have problems both in efficiency and memory if you try to create and work with a list of that size. Therefore, large lists should probably be stored in a database of some type.

External data source

If your data is stored in an external database, such as Microsoft Access or even an SQL database, you need to select this option. When you select the second step of the wizard you will need to select the data source for the data by selecting the Get Data option. This will take you to the Choose Data Source dialog where you select the ODBC data source for your data. This is a Windows option that is also available on the Control Panel. Once you select your data source you will need to create a query using Microsoft Query that selects the data that should be used in your PivotTable.

Multiple consolidation ranges

Allows you to consolidate data in multiple worksheet lists. Remember when you consolidate data each source should contain the same type of data.

Another PivotTable or PivotChart

Provides the ability to create another PivotTable that uses the same data as the original PivotTable. Of course, this option is only available when another PivotTable exists within the workbook. From the standpoint of memory usage by your machine, this feature is more efficient than reselecting the data and creating a new PivotTable.

Keep in mind that you can either create just a PivotTable or a PivotTable and PivotChart. Excel does not allow you to create only the chart.

The final step of the wizard provides the ability to customize the location and appearance of the PivotTable, as shown in Figure 9-32.

Figure 9-32: Step 3 of PivotTable and PivotChart Wizard

If you select the New worksheet option Excel inserts a new sheet for the PivotTable and another one for the PivotChart within the current workbook, if that option was selected. If you select the Existing worksheet option they are both added to the existing worksheet, but you can specify the cell location using the Collapse Dialog button next to the field or by typing the starting cell reference.

The Layout button provides the ability to design your PivotTable and PivotChart by specifying the location of the various fields from the database. Keep in mind, the PivotChart will be laid out in the same format as the PivotTable you design. When you select the Layout button, the PivotTable and PivotChart Wizard Layout dialog displays, as shown in Figure 9-33.

To design the table simply click on the desired field name and drag it to the appropriate location on the table layout in the center of the dialog. There are four different locations or sections of the table: Page, Column, Row, and Data. Remember, the Data field is the data you want summarized in the PivotTable. Typically you select a field that contains a numeric value.

The Page location can seem a little confusing, but you need to just place values here that you want to use as the page items in the PivotTable. For example, in Figure 9-29 we used the Month field as the Page item. Therefore, the values display in the other areas of the table as long as they match the value of the Month field.

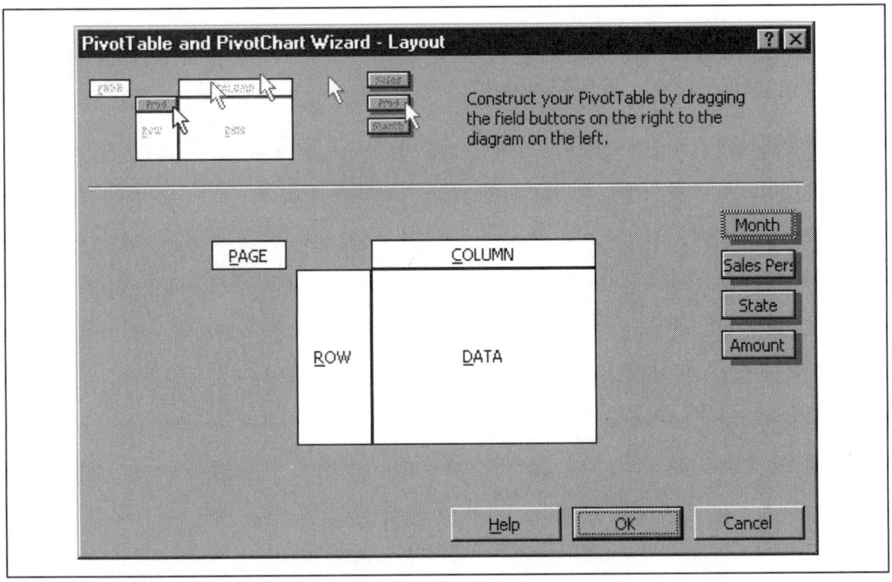

Figure 9-33: PivotTable and PivotChart Wizard Layout dialog

TIP # 71

Using Toolbar Options with a PivotChart

You can quickly make modifications to a PivotChart or PivotTable by using the options available on the PivotTable toolbar. This toolbar display automatically when you create or open a PivotChart or PivotTable. If you cannot locate it, select View → Toolbars → PivotTable.

The Options button displays the PivotTable Options dialog shown in Figure 9-34. This dialog provides the ability to specify how the PivotTable looks and functions. You can select any of the options as long as they are not grayed out. Some options, such as the ones under "External data options" are available based on the type of data source selected for the PivotTable.

If you want Excel to total the rows and columns in the PivotTable, as shown in Figure 9-29, you need to select the "Grand totals for columns" and "Grand total for rows" options on the dialog. These totals are dynamic, meaning they are recalculated whenever you change the value in one of the fields.

You can indicate how Excel deals with error values by selecting the "For error values, show" checkbox and then typing the value you want displayed on the Pivot-Table if Excel encounters an error. This same process is true for empty cells; simply select "For empty cells, show" and indicate the value that should display.

You can speed up the processing of the PivotTable by selecting the "Save data with table layout" checkbox. This causes Excel to save a copy of the database values with the workbook that contains the PivotTable. The cached data copy allows Excel to

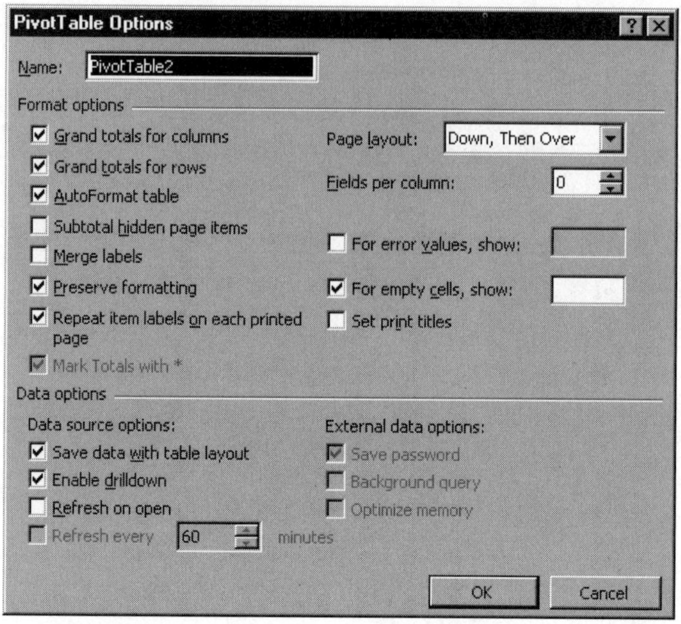

Figure 9-34: PivotTable Options dialog

recalculate the PivotTable values more quickly. If you have a memory issue on your computer, you will want to uncheck this option.

The "Enable Drilldown" option allows you to double-click on a cell in the Pivot-Table and see specific details about that value. For example, with this option selected it you double click on cell C5 in Figure 9-29, you get a table similar to the one shown in Figure 9-35 that shows more detail as to where that cell's value came from. The cell detail is normally placed on a separate worksheet within the same workbook.

TIP # 72

Applying a System Format to a PivotChart

You can select Format → AutoFormat and select one of the system-defined formats to apply to the chart.

Data → Get External Data

The Data → Get External Data submenu options provide the ability to get data from different non-Excel sources and place it in your worksheet. You can get data from different databases using queries. This option is useful for database file types

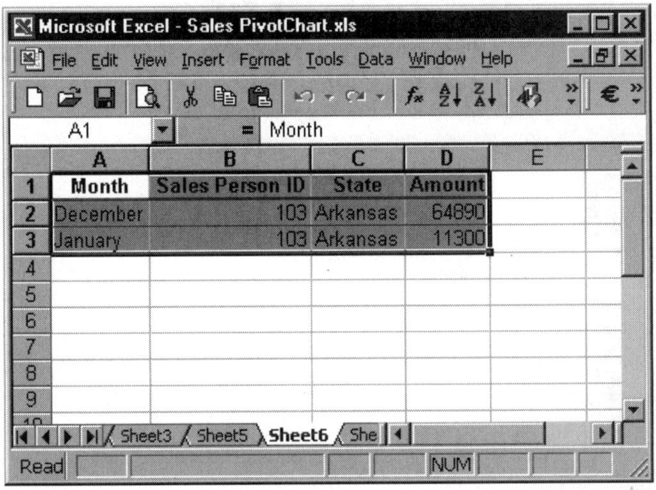

Figure 9-35: Drilldown Detail for a PivotTable cell

that Excel cannot open or ones that are too large to open. You can also create queries to gather data from a web site.

NOTE *When you create and run a database query you are actually using Microsoft Query. This is a separate program that must be installed on your system. If it is not installed, when you run Data → Get External Data → New Database Query you will be prompted to install it by rerunning the setup program for either Excel or Microsoft Office.*

Run Saved Query

This option provides the ability to run a previously saved query. When you select this option the Run Query dialog displays as shown in Figure 9-36. You can select from both web and database queries.

NOTE *The options available on this dialog are the same as the Open dialog that displays when you select File → Open.*

When you select the Get Data button Excel displays the "Returning External Data to Microsoft Excel" dialog, as shown in Figure 9-37. This dialog allows you to specify the location where you want to place the results of the query.

By default Excel assumes you want to place the queried data starting in the active cell of the currently selected worksheet. To place it in a different cell location, select the Collapse Dialog button and select the cell location. You can also place the data in a different worksheet or a PivotTable report. If you select the PivotTable report option the PivotTable and PivotChart Wizard displays (refer to "Data → Pivot-Table and PivotChart Report").

Data Menu

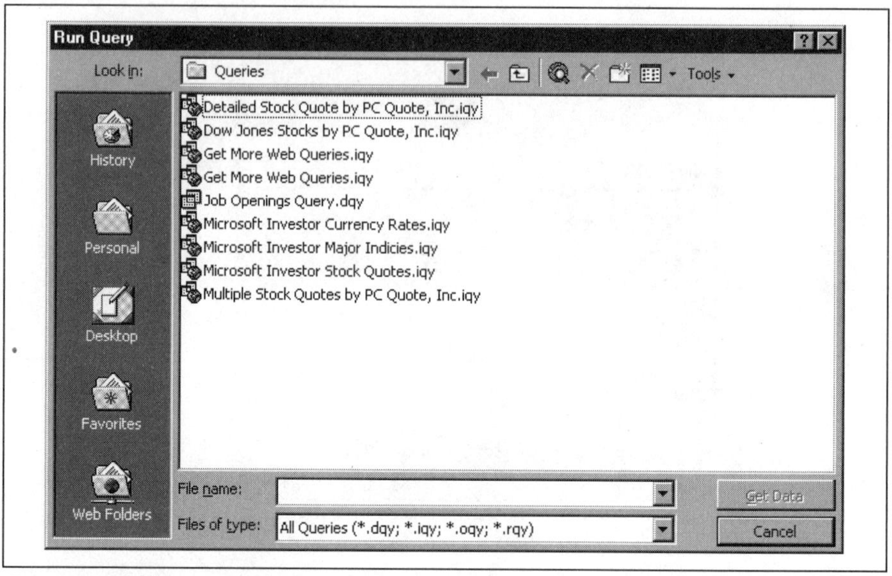

Figure 9-36: Run Query dialog

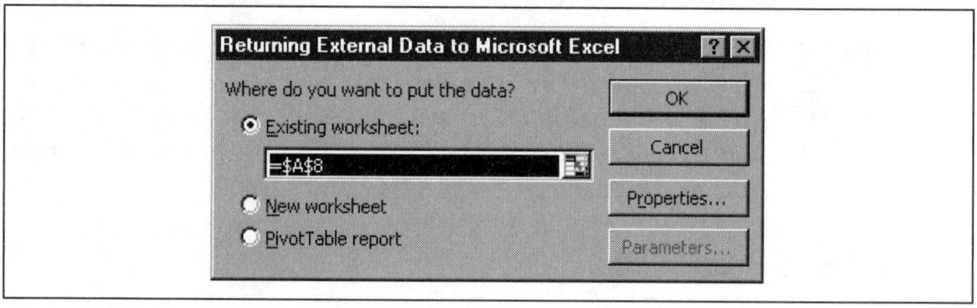

Figure 9-37: Returning External Data to Microsoft Excel dialog

You can make modifications to the external data range properties by selecting the Properties button on the dialog to display the External Data Range Properties (refer to "Data Range Properties" later in this chapter). You can also make modifications to the properties after the external range is placed in your workbook by selecting the external data range; select Data → Get External Data → Data Range Properties.

If parameter queries were created for the selected external query, you can select the Parameters button to make modifications. This button is grayed out if the parameter queries where not created (refer to "Parameters" later in this chapter).

New Web Query

Excel allows you to collect data that exists in an HTML file or an ASP (Active Server Page) page using a web query. When a web query is performed, Excel copies the data on the HTML page into your worksheet so it can be manipulated.

When you select Data → Get External Data → New Web Query, the New Web Query dialog displays, as shown in Figure 9-38.

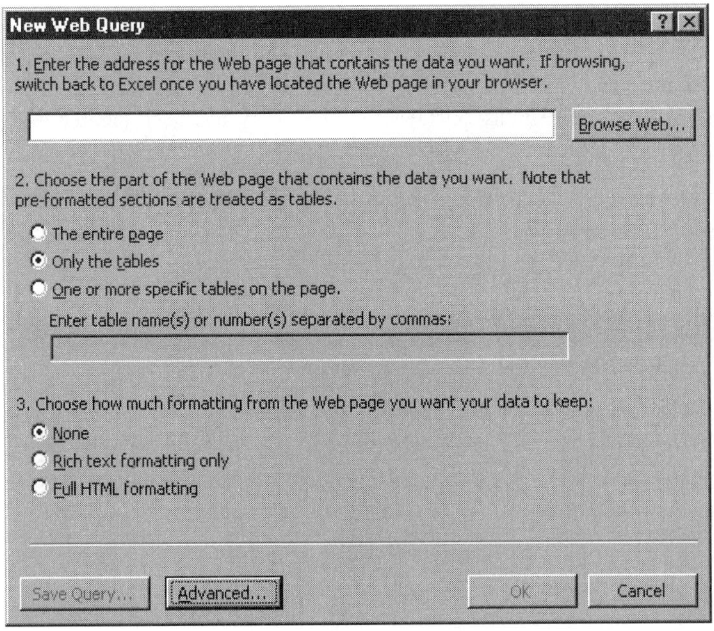

Figure 9-38: New Web Query dialog

The New Web Query dialog divides the process of creating the query into three different sections. In the first step, you need to specify the location of the HTML page that you want to query. This HTML page can be located anywhere that your current system can access—the Internet, a corporate intranet, a network, or on your local system. You can either type the URL or file location of the HTML file or select the Browse Web button to locate the appropriate HTML page. When you select the Browse Web button, your Internet browser is opened so you can locate the web site that contains the HTML page you want to query. Once you locate the desired page in the browser, select Excel again and the URL will be placed in the field for section 1.

In the second section on the New Web Query dialog you need to specify the portion of the HTML page that you want to query. Typically you only want the data that is contained in a table, but Excel provides the ability to query all of the information that is contained on the HTML page. If you select the third option, "One or more specific tables on the page" you need to indicate the tables and sections in the field. If the tables or sections are named on the HTML page, you can use those names, or you can use numbers to indicate the desired sections. When you specify the sections that you want to query, Excel places them in your worksheet in the order they appear on the HTML page, not the order you specify.

In the third section you need to indicate the type of formatting you want applied to the data from the query. If you select "Full-HTML formatting" you will see the same formatting that exists on the selected web page.

If you want to be able to use this query again in the future make sure you select the Save Query button. Otherwise, Excel does not prompt you to save the query. If you want to make sure you the query gets the desired results before saving, you can select the Data → Edit Query option once the query has been created and save the query so that if can be used elsewhere.

Once your web query is created, you can make additional modifications to how the query displays by selecting Data → Get External Data → Data Range Properties (refer to "Data Range Properties" later in this chapter).

TIP # 73
Figuring Out Why You Don't Get Query Data

The Web Query does not query pages that contain frames. If you are trying to query data from a web site and you do not get data, it is probably a frames page. If you do not know the URL for the actual portion of the frames page that contains the desired data, you can typically find it by viewing the source for the HTML page.

New Database Query

Excel allows you to query data from external databases that you have access to. In order to access these database sources, you must have the appropriate access to the database and a data source created on your machine using the ODBC Data Sources option on the Control Panel.

When you select Data → Get External Data → New Database Query, the Choose Data Source dialog displays, as shown in Figure 9-39. Select the data source you want to use for your query from the list on the Databases tab, and then select the OK button.

Make sure the "Use the Query Wizard to create/edit queries" checkbox is selected. This will allow you to use the Query Wizard, discussed in this section, instead of Microsoft Query to create the database query. The Query Wizard steps you through the process of creating your query, simplifying the process.

Depending upon the data source you selected, you will probably be required to log into the corresponding database at this point. Once you specify this information, a connection is made to the database specified by selected data source and the Query Wizard displays, as shown in Figure 9-40.

The first step of the Query Wizard is to select the columns of data from the database that you want to query. The Available tables and columns lists the names of all tables within the database. You can view the columns within the table by clicking on the + (plus sign) next to the table name. You can select all columns within a

ODBC Data Sources

ODBC (Open Database Connectivity) is a standard created by Microsoft to use various drivers to access different types of database files. The settings for these drivers are stored in a data source. Each data source not only indicates the driver that is being used to access the database, but also the location of the database, and appropriate login information for connecting to it. Once the data source is created, it can be accessed from any application that works with ODBC data sources.

Typically when an application is installed on your system, it creates the appropriate data sources. But data sources can be created and modified using the ODBC Data Source options available from the Control Panel.

You can also create a data source when creating a new database query by selecting the <New Data Source> option on the Choose Data Source dialog. You will need to select the driver that should be used with the data source and indicate the location of the database you want to connect to.

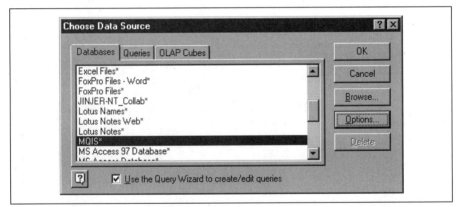

Figure 9-39: Choose Data Source dialog

table by clicking on the table name and then selecting the > button to move the column names to the "Columns in your query" list. When you select the entire table only the names of the columns within the table will be listed in the "Column in your query" list. You can also add individual columns by clicking on them.

If you want to see an example of the type of data within a particular column, select the desired column name and then click on the Preview Now button. The "Preview of data in selected column" field will display the sample.

Once you have selected the columns that you want to use for your query, select the Next button to display the second step of the Query Wizard, as shown in Figure 9-41. On this page of the wizard, you can specify the type of filtering you

Data Menu

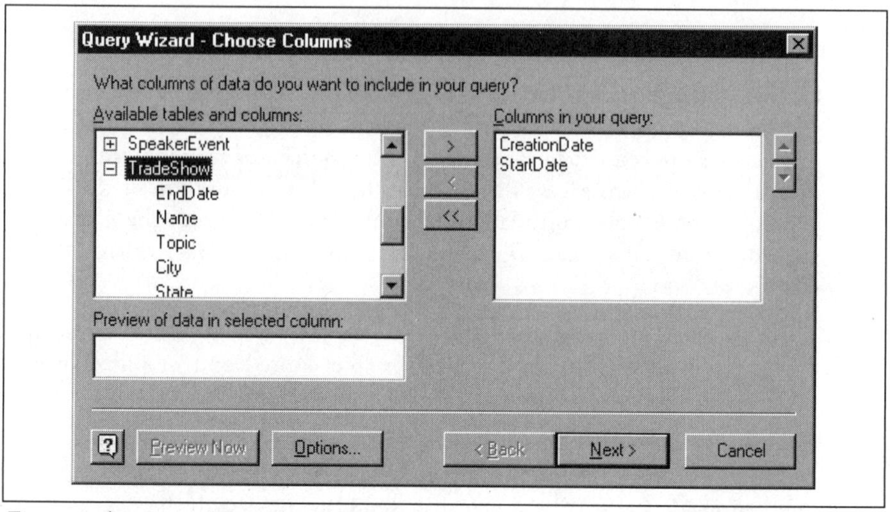

Figure 9-40: Query Wizard - Choose Columns

want to use for the data. For example, you may only want to see the items with a Start Date after 1/1/1999.

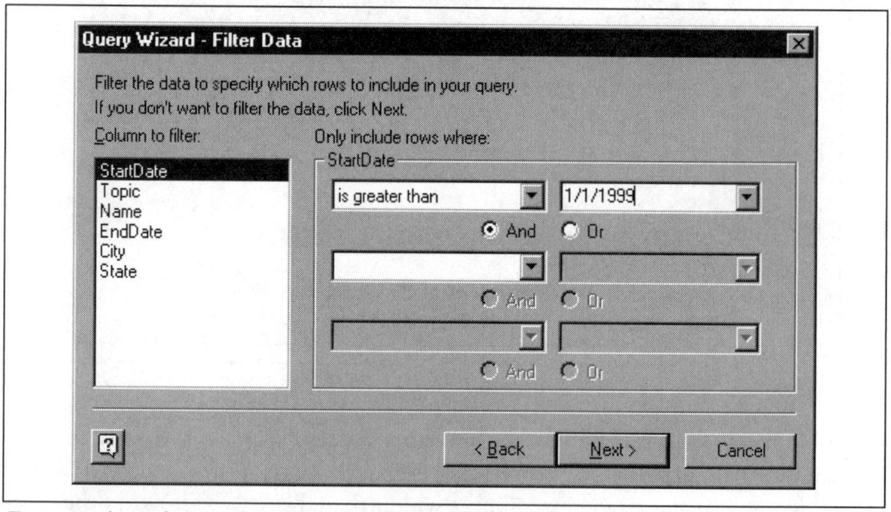

Figure 9-41: Filtering data with Query Wizard

You do not have to create any filter definitions for the query. If you do not filter the data, all of the data within the selected columns will display in your worksheet. To specify filter information, select the desired column from the "Column to filter" list. Then select the appropriate operator for the filter definition in the first list box and indicate or select the value for the definition in the second list box. You can create filter definitions for as many of the columns as desired. Keep in mind that the data from the table will need to satisfy all the filter definitions created on the page.

When you select the Next button the Query Wizard allows you to specify how the records should be sorted, as shown in Figure 9-42. You can select as many sort fields as you want, but Excel will use the top definition first.

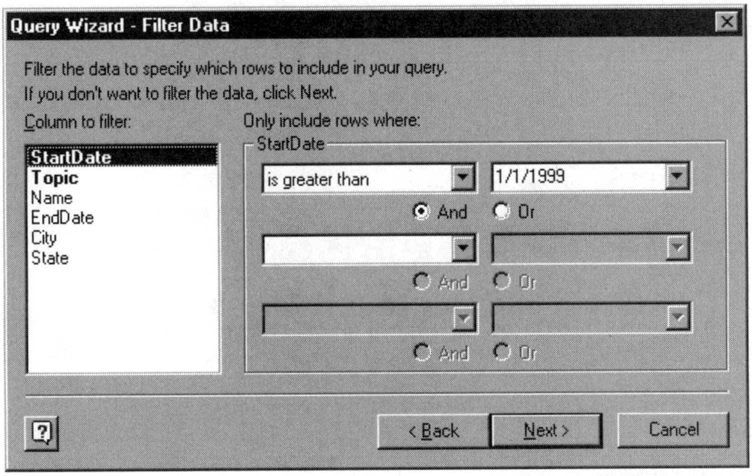

Figure 9-42: Sorting data with Query Wizard

To specify the sort order, select the column name in the Sort by field and then select the appropriate radio button to indicate whether you want to sort in ascending or descending order for the column. You can specify another sort value in the "Then by" field. You can continue to specify the sorting for each column in your query.

To complete the query process, select the Next button again to display the Finish page of the Query Wizard. Make sure the first radio button, "Return Data to Microsoft Excel" is selected. If you want to save this query for future use, select the Save Query button.

If you want to check the query before saving it, you can save the query at any time by selecting Data → Get External Data → Edit Query, and selecting the Save Query button.

Import Text File

You can also get data from a text file by selecting Data → Get External Data → Import Text File. When you select this option the Import Text File dialog displays so you can select the specific text file that you want to import into Excel. The Import Text File dialog is just like the Open dialog that displays when you select File → Open. When you find the desired file, select the Import button to display the Text Import Wizard, as shown in Figure 9-43.

Text Import Wizard - Step 1 of 3   ? ☒

The Text Wizard has determined that your data is Delimited.
If this is correct, choose Next, or choose the data type that best describes your data.

Original data type
Choose the file type that best describes your data:

⦿ Delimited   - Characters such as commas or tabs separate each field.
◯ Fixed width   - Fields are aligned in columns with spaces between each field.

Start import at row: [1 ⬍]   File origin: [Windows (ANSI) ▾]

Preview of file C:\Excel Files\Book1.txt.

```
1 Monthly Travel Expenses□□□□□□□□□□□□
2 □January□February□March□April□May□June□July□August□September□0
3 Airfare□"$1,200.00"□$750.00□$950.00□$600.00□"$2,145.00"□$500.00
4 Transporation□$450.00□$100.00□$465.00□$235.00□$675.00□$200.00□$
5 Hotel□$600.00□$450.00□"$1,030.00"□$990.00□"$1,700.00"□$754.00□"
```

[Cancel] [< Back] [Next >] [Finish]

Figure 9-43: Text Import Wizard

On the first page you need to indicate how the data is separated in the file, for example, if there is a single space or comma between each word you need to select the Delimited radio button. The "Fixed width" radio button is selected only if data is evenly spaced so that it appears to line up in columns.

You can specify the first row of data that you want to import in the "Start import at row" field. Excel will import from the indicated row to the end of the text file. You cannot, however, indicate the ending row.

 This is the same process you go through if you open a text file up within Excel using File → Open and when you select Data → Convert Text to Columns. For more specific information on the different pages that display for this wizard, refer to "Data → Convert Text to Columns."

The second page of the wizard differs depending on whether you selected the Delimited or Fixed Width radio buttons. The final page of the wizard is where you can indicate the type of data that is in each column.

Edit Query

The Data → Get External Data → Edit Query option allows you to make modifications to the settings for either a web query or an external database query. To modify a query, select at least one cell in the query and select this option. When you select this option, the query definition opens up in the appropriate dialog. For example, in Figure 9-44 the Query Wizard opens for an external database query selected within the worksheet.

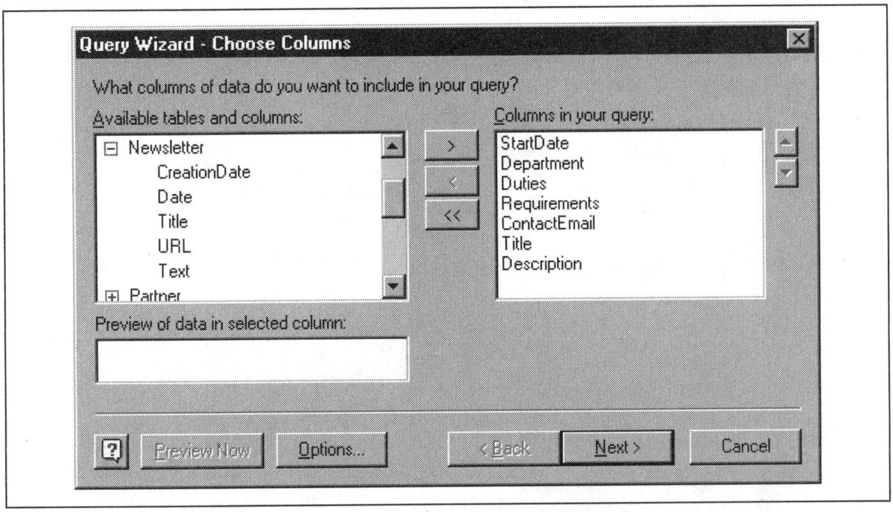

Figure 9-44: Query Wizard opens to modify an external database query

Data Range Properties

The External Data Range Properties dialog, shown in Figure 9-45, provides the ability to change the properties of the selected data range. This dialog displays when you select the Properties button on the Query Wizard or by selecting Data → Get External Data → Data Range Properties for an existing external database query.

Name
> Indicates the name of the external data range. This is the name that will be used to refer to the data range within your worksheet. Just like names created using Insert → Name, you can select the name from the Name box on the Formula bar. Remember that Excel will replace any spaces in the name with underscores (_) when the name is placed in the Name box.

Query Definition
> Allows you to indicate the portions of the query that are saved with the worksheet. If you select the "Save query definition" radio button, a copy of the query you create is saved with the worksheet. I would recommend always doing this so that you can refresh the query at anytime. Also, if your database requires a password to connect to it, you can select the "Save password" radio button to have Excel save the password information with you worksheet. If Excel has the password, you won't be required to re-enter it each time you refresh the query.

Refresh Control
> This section allows you to indicate when Excel refreshes the data in the query. When a refresh occurs, Excel performs another query on the database and replaces the current query results in the worksheet. If you do not want Excel to do this automatically, do not select any options in this section, and you can manually refresh the data by selecting Data → Refresh Data.

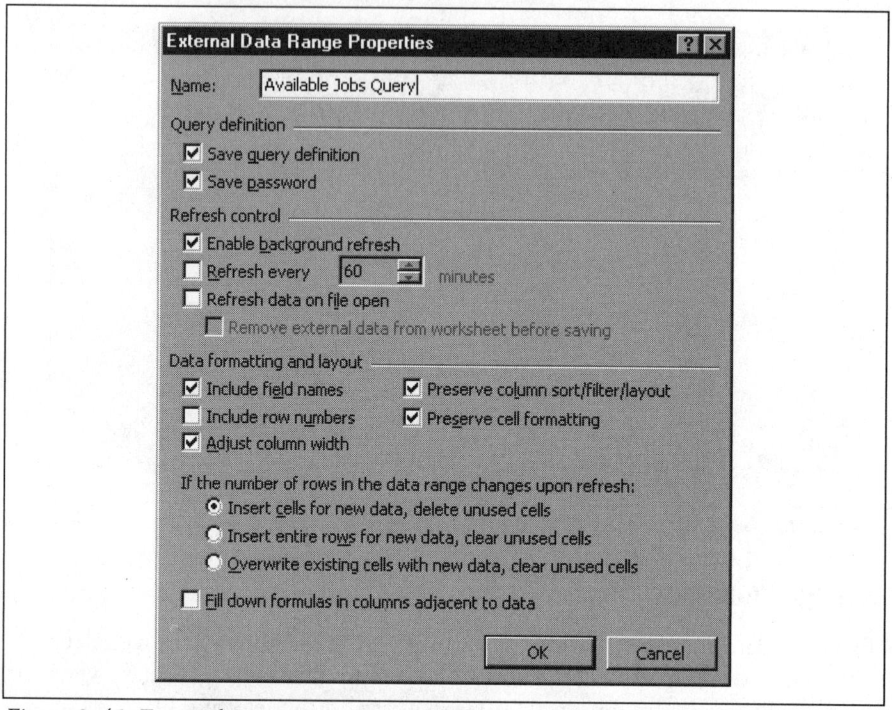

Figure 9-45: External Data Range Properties dialog

Data Formatting and Layout
> Use the options in this section to specify how the data from the query appears in your worksheet.

Parameters

The Parameters dialog allows you to modify the way Excel gets the value for a parameter query that was created using Microsoft Query. Once a parameter query has been created you can modify its settings within Excel by selecting Data → Get External Data → Parameters. When you select this option the Parameters dialog displays, as shown in Figure 9-46.

The selection you make on the Parameters dialog specifies how Excel will look for the value to the parameter query when the Data → Refresh Data option is selected. You have three different options that can be selected:

Prompt for value using the following string
> You can modify the request that is made in the Enter Parameter Value dialog by selecting this radio button and specifying the desired text.

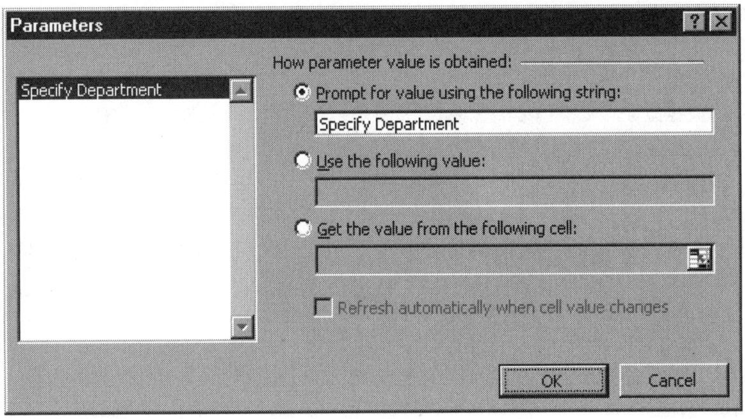

Figure 9-46: Parameters dialog

Use the following value

You can indicate a specific value that should always be used for the parameter query. If you specify a value, Excel will not prompt the user for a value when the Data → Refresh Data option is selected.

Get the value from the following cell

You can specify a cell that contains the value you want to be used for the parameter query each time the Data → Refresh Data option is selected. To select the cell from the worksheet, select the Collapse Dialog button next to the field. If you select this option, you can select the "Refresh automatically when cell value changes" checkbox. Excel will automatically refresh the data within the worksheet each time you change the value in the specified cell.

If you choose to use Microsoft Query directly to create your database query, you can create sophisticated queries that allow the worksheet user to customize the data that displays on the worksheet. For example, if you are querying a database that contains the current job openings for your corporation, you could create a query that allows the user to view the availabilities within a specific department.

Parameter queries are created in Microsoft Query by selecting the down arrow button in one of the Criteria Field fields and selecting the column from the database that you want to create the parameter query for. Then specify the query that the user will see by placing it in the Value field enclosed in square brackets [ ], as shown in Figure 9-47.

Once your parameter query is created select the Return Data icon on the toolbar to return to Excel. Before closing Microsoft Query, you will be prompted to specify the parameter value that will be initially used to display the data in the worksheet. If you want to change the parameter value, simply select Data → Refresh Data and the Enter Parameter Value dialog will display, as shown in Figure 9-48.

Data Menu

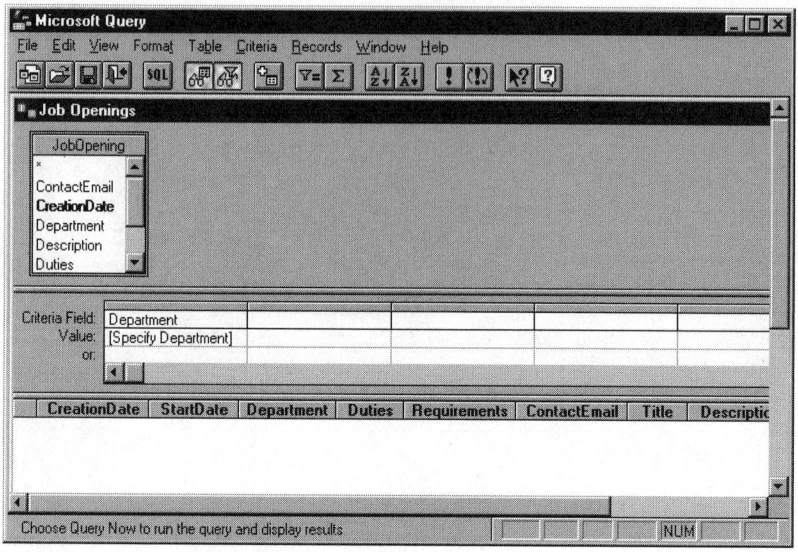

Figure 9-47: Parameter Query in Microsoft Query

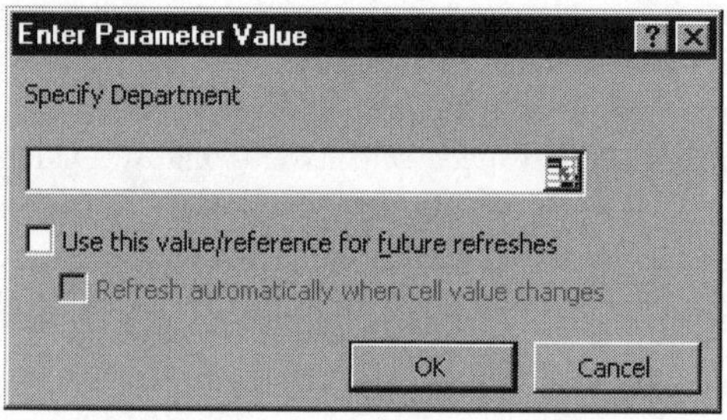

Figure 9-48: Enter Parameter Value dialog

Chapter 10

Chart

The Chart menu provides options that allow you to modify the settings for an existing chart. This menu can only be used with an existing chart; you cannot create a new chart with it. To create a new chart you must select Insert → Chart. In fact, you can only see this menu when you have a chart selected within a worksheet or on a chart sheet. When the Chart menu displays it temporarily replaces the Data menu.

If you have a chart selected, you can change the chart type, modify the source for the data used to create the chart, or just change the chart options such as whether to include axes titles. This menu also provides the ability to create custom chart types by selecting the Chart → Chart Type option.

So what type of chart should I create? It doesn't take long to become totally overwhelmed by the vast number of chart types available within Excel; you can even create your own custom chart types. Once you select the type of chart you want to create, you have the option of selecting from several sub-types. So which one should you use? Amazingly enough, with all the types of charts available, most people only use Column, Line, Pie, Scatter, and Area charts. Make sure you try some of the less commonly used chart types; it is not always what you say, but how you say it.

Excel divides the chart types into two basic but broad categories: Standard Types and Custom Types. The category names actually have very little significance. The Standard Types tab contains 14 different chart types and each of these types has at least two different sub-types or variations of the type. If you select a chart from the Standard Types tab you also need to select a subtype. The chart types listed on the Custom Types tab do not have subtypes—these are really just additional variations of chart types from the Standard Types tab. The tab is named Custom Types because this is also where Excel stores any additional custom chart types that you create.

Column Charts

You are probably very familiar with column charts. They are frequently used to show a relationship between a group of data values, and they typically show data changes that occur over time. A column chart always displays vertical columns that are oriented along a horizontal axis, such as the total sales over the past five years, shown in Figure 10-1.

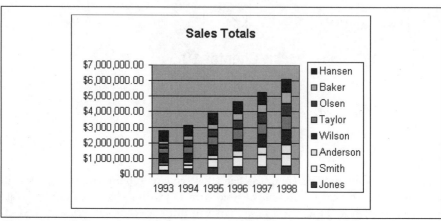

Figure 10-1: Column charts allow you to view data changes over time

The column type provides seven different subtypes that you can select from:

Clustered Column

The Clustered Column chart creates a standard column chart. This chart type creates a vertical column for each data value. If the chart is showing multiple data series, the values are grouped based upon the category value. For example, if a Clustered Column chart was selected for Figure 10-1, the sales by each salesperson would display as separate columns above the corresponding year.

Stacked Column

The Stacked Column chart, shown in Figure 10-1, shows the corresponding data series stacked. For example, the figure shows the sales figures for each year stacked, allowing you to compare the total sales between each year. If you only have one data series selected, this chart appears the same as the Clustered Column chart.

100% Stacked Column

The 100% Stacked Column chart shows the corresponding data series values stacked as a percentage of the total. Instead of comparing total amounts you are able to see what percentage of the total that value is. For example, if this subtype was selected to show the data in Figure 10-1, you would be able to see the percentage of sales that each salesperson made for each year. This chart type is similar to creating multiple Pie charts.

3-D Clustered Column

The 3-D Cluster Column chart takes the standard Clustered Column chart and adds a three-dimensional perspective look.

3-D Stacked Column

The 3-D Stacked Column chart takes the Stacked Column chart and adds a three-dimensional look.

3-D 100% Stacked Column

The 3-D 100% Stacked Column chart takes the 100% Stacked Column chart and adds a three-dimensional look.

3-D Column

The 3-D Column chart is probably the showiest of the seven column subtypes. This type of chart provides a true three-dimensional chart by creating a third axis. The third axis creates the depth that gives the chart the 3-D perspective. For example, if this chart type was selected for Figure 10-1 the foreign sales figures would display behind the domestic figures.

Bar Charts

A Bar chart is very similar to a Column chart. In fact the main difference is that a Bar chart has bars that run horizontally from the left edge. It resembles a Column chart that has been rotated 90 degrees. If you have a large number of data values that you need to show, a Bar chart is typically a better choice than a Column chart if you plan to print the chart. Figure 10-2 shows how a Bar chart can be used to see the percentage of sales that occurred in each region.

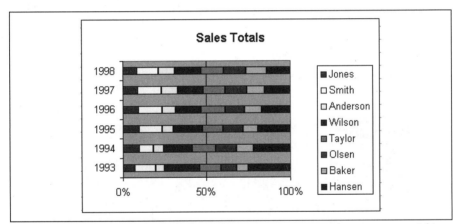

Figure 10-2: With a 100% Stacked Bar chart you can compare the percentages within different categories

The bar type chart provides six different subtypes that you can select from:

Clustered Bar

The Clustered Bar chart creates a standard Bar chart. This chart type creates a horizontal column for each data value. If the chart shows multiple data series, the values are grouped based upon the category value.

Stacked Bar

The Stacked Bar chart displays the corresponding data series stacked. If you only have one data series selected, the chart appears the same as the Clustered Bar chart.

Chart   239

100% Stacked Bar

The 100% Stacked Bar chart, shown in Figure 10-2, shows the corresponding data series values stacked as a percentage of the total. Instead of comparing total amounts, you are able to see what percentage that value was of the total. This chart type is similar to creating multiple Pie charts.

3-D Clustered Bar

The 3-D Cluster Bar chart takes the standard Clustered Bar chart and adds a three-dimensional look.

3-D Stacked Bar

The 3-D Stacked Bar chart takes the Stacked Bar chart and adds a three-dimensional look.

3-D 100% Stacked Bar

The 3-D 100% Stacked Bar chart takes the 100% Stacked Bar chart and adds a three-dimensional look.

Line Charts

A Line chart provides the ability to plot continuous data values. With this type of chart you can show trends that have occurred in your data. For example, if you wanted to show the value of your stock of the last year you could use a Line chart to plot the values, as shown in Figure 10-3.

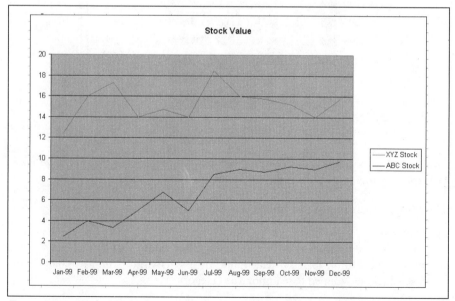

Figure 10-3: With a Line chart you can quickly illustrated any trends (ups or downs) that have occurred in your data

The Line type chart provides seven different subtypes that you can select from:

Line

> The Line chart creates a chart with a solid line that connects the various data points on the chart.

Stacked Line

> The Stacked Line chart displays the corresponding data series stacked. If you only have one data series selected, this chart appears the same as the Line chart. If you have multiple data series it charts the first data series and then charts the second data series above it. For example, in Figure 10-3 instead of charting the value of each stock, you can show the total value of the stocks where the top line shows the value of adding the first stock to the second one.

100% Stacked Line

> The 100% Stacked Line chart shows the corresponding data series values stacked as a percentage of the total. Instead of comparing total amounts you are able to see what percentage that value was of the total. This chart type is similar to creating multiple Pie charts.

Line with Data Markers

> The Line with Data Markers chart takes the standard Line chart and adds data markers to identify the individual data values.

Stacked Line with Data Markers

> The Stacked Line with Data Markers chart creates a Stacked Line chart with data markers that represent each data value.

100% Stacked Line with Data Markers

> The 100% Stacked Line with Data Markers chart creates a 100% Stacked Line chart with data markers that represent each data value.

3-D Line

> The 3-D Line chart creates a chart with a three-dimensional representation of each data series.

Pie Charts

A Pie chart allows you to easily show each value proportional to the whole. For example, Figure 10-4 uses a Pie chart to show how monthly expenses were allocated. Keep in mind that a Pie chart works best if you do not have more than six or seven different values. It also only works with one data series.

 You can make a piece of the Pie chart appear to be removed or exploded by clicking on it and dragging it away from the center of the chart.

Chart   241

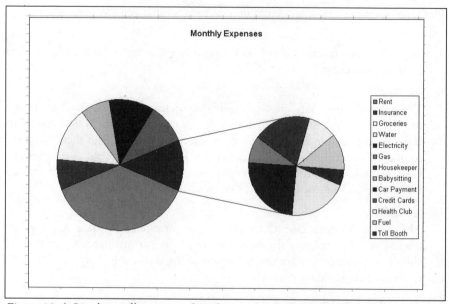

Figure 10-4: Pie charts allow you to show how individual values contribute to a whole

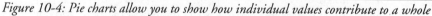

The Pie type chart provides six different subtypes that you can select from:

Pie

> This option creates a standard Pie chart.

3-D Pie

> This option creates a Pie chart with a three-dimensional perspective.

Piece of Pie

> This chart type, shown in Figure 10-4, allows you to emphasize certain elements of the chart by moving them into a smaller Pie chart that correlates to a specific section of the larger chart. For example, if you have several smaller data values you can drag them onto the smaller pie so that they are easier to see.

Exploded Pie

> This chart type explodes or removes each piece from the pie. You can adjust the location of the pieces by clicking on each pie and dragging to the desired location.

Exploded 3-D Pie

> This chart type creates an exploded Pie chart with a 3-D perspective.

Bar of Pie

> This chart type is very similar to the Piece of Pie type. The only difference is that the values removed from the pie are displayed on a bar (similar to a vertical column on a Bar chart) instead of on a pie. Adjust the values that are displayed on the bar by dragging pieces between the Pie chart and the Bar chart.

XY (Scatter) Charts

The XY or Scatter chart is commonly used to plot scientific data, but it can be used for any chart where you want to see the relationship between two different numerical variables and compare trends across uneven time periods. For example, Figure 10-5 shows the number of support calls that were received compared to the number of sales during each month over a year.

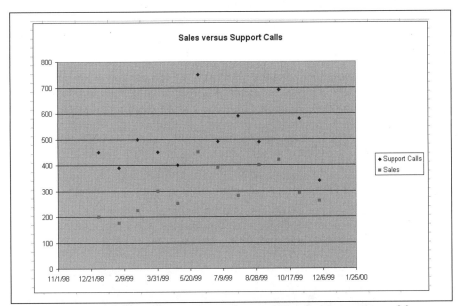

Figure 10-5: Scatter charts allow you to see the correlation between two sets of data

The XY (Scatter) type chart provides five different subtypes that you can select from:

Scatter
> The Scatter chart type creates a chart using data markers to show each value. If you are comparing two or more data series, each data series is represented with a different color and/or shape.

Scatter with Smoothed Lines
> This chart type takes a standard Scatter chart and connects the data markers in each series with smoothed lines. The lines are smoothed by removing any jagged points that may occur when you connect two data markers.

Scatter with Smoothed Lines and No Data Markers
> This chart type takes the Scatter with Smoothed Lines chart and removes the data markers. This chart type closely resembles a Line chart.

Chart   243

Scatter with Lines
> The only difference between this chart type and the Scatter with Smoothed Lines is that the lines that connect the data points are not smoothed. Therefore, the lines tend to look a little more jagged as they connect the data markers.

Scatter with Lines and No Data Markers
> This chart type uses lines to connect the data points but there are no data markers to indicate where the data values are located.

Area Charts

An Area chart is similar to a Line chart. In fact, they can be easily interchanged and show the same results. The only difference is that an area chart is colored in to emphasize each data series. In Figure 10-6 you can see the total sales and compare the retail sales versus Internet sales.

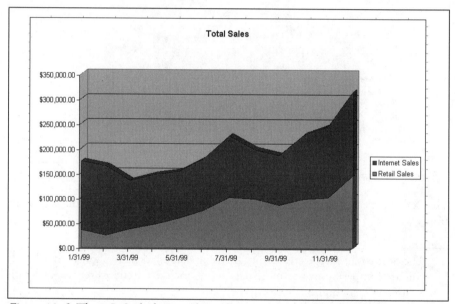

Figure 10-6: The 3-D Staked Area Chart allows you to quickly compare values from different data series

The Area type chart provides six different subtypes that you can select from:

Area
> The Area chart creates a chart with each data series colored in. Excel places the data series on the chart in the order listed on the worksheet. For example, if column A is the first column selected, it is placed on what appears to be the back of the chart so that if there is a larger data value in Column B it will appear to cover up the Column A value on the chart.

Stacked Area

The Stacked Area chart displays the corresponding data series stacked, similar to Figure 10-6. If you select this subtype, you will not get the 3-D perspective shown in the figure.

100% Stacked Area

The 100% Stacked Area chart shows the corresponding data series values stacked as a percentage of the total. Instead of comparing total amounts you are able to see what percentage that value was of the total. This chart type is similar to creating multiple Pie Charts.

3-D Area

The 3-D Area chart takes the standard Area chart and gives it a three-dimensional perspective.

3-D Stacked Area

The 3-D Stacked Area chart creates a Stacked Line chart with a three-dimensional perspective, as shown in Figure 10-6.

3-D 100% Stacked Area

The 3-D 100% Stacked Area chart creates a 100% Stacked Line chart with a three-dimensional perspective.

Doughnut Charts

At first glance a Doughnut chart appears to just be a Pie chart with a hole in the middle. This is basically true if you are plotting one data series. But unlike the Pie chart, you can use a Doughnut chart to show more than one data series.

When you create a Doughnut chart with multiple data series, as shown in Figure 10-7, the first data series is placed in the center of the doughnut. Each successive series forms a ring on the doughnut. Keep in mind that although a data item may appear larger on the outside of the ring than one on a ring toward the center of the chart, the size is proportional to the values within the series.

Although Doughnut charts provide a catchy way to illustrate the data values, they can be rather difficult to read, especially if you have multiple data series. You will probably find that a Stacked Column chart provides a more readable chart. In fact, most avid Excel users try to avoid using the doughnut chart because it can be more confusing.

There are really only two types of Doughnut charts: a standard chart and an exploded chart. Keep in mind that with either chart type you can move elements by clicking the desired element of the chart and dragging it.

Chart   245

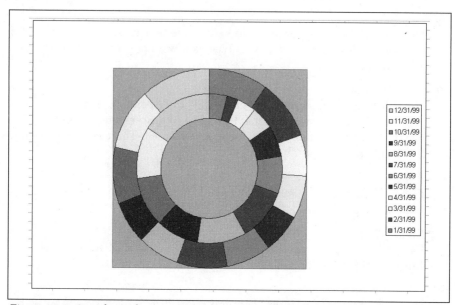

Figure 10-7: Doughnut charts provide an interesting way to compare data

Radar Charts

You don't have to look at a Radar chart long to figure where it got its name. Anyone who has watched the evening news is familiar with the weather radars that are used by meteorologists. But this type of graph can be used for any type of data.

When you create a Radar chart you have a separate axis for each category of data, as shown in Figure 10-8. It basically has the appearance of spokes on a bike tire. In fact, if all data values in a series have the same values it will look like a perfect circle on your spokes (axes).

The Radar type chart provides three different subtypes that you can select from:

Radar
> The standard Radar chart type creates a radar chart with lines showing the value of each data item within the series. Different colors are used for each series.

Radar with Data Markers
> The Radar with Data Markers chart type creates a radar chart with markers for each data value and lines used to connect the data values within each series.

Filled Radar
> The Filled Radar series, shown in Figure 10-8, takes the standard radar chart and fills in the area created by the lines.

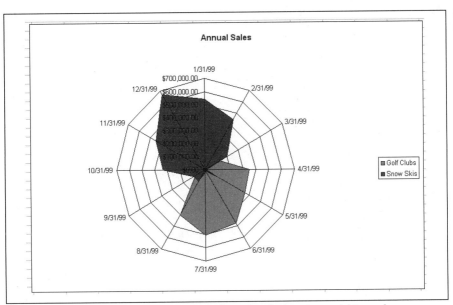

Figure 10-8: Radar charts illustrate the values of each data item within each category

Surface Charts

A Surface chart provides an interesting way to show combinations between data values. Surface charts look like topographical maps, as shown in Figure 10-9, because they use colors and patterns to indicate where data values are the same.

There are four different types of surface charts:

3-D Surface
    The 3-D Surface chart creates a topographical look at the data values, as shown in Figure 10-9.

3-D Surface (wireframe)
    The 3-D Surface (wireframe) chart creates a surface chart without filling it in with color.

Surface (top view)
    The Surface (top view) chart provides a view of the surface chart from above.

Surface (top view wireframe)
    The Surface (top view wireframe) chart provides a view of the wireframe surface chart from above.

Bubble Charts

A bubble chart is basically just an XY (scatter) chart with an additional data series. For example, Figure 10-10 illustrates the revenue earned for each training seminar. The x axis indicates the cost paid by each attendee for the seminar and the y axis

Chart   247

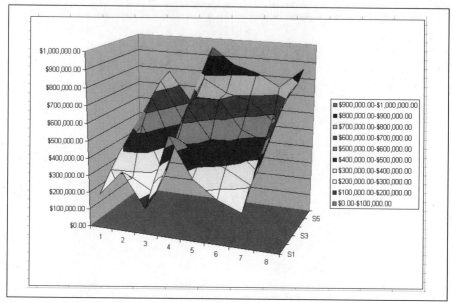

Figure 10-9: Surface Charts provides a topographical type of view of the data values

indicates the number of people that attended the seminar. The size of the bubbles represents the amount of revenue earned from each seminar. This type of chart allows you to determine when you produce the desired results.

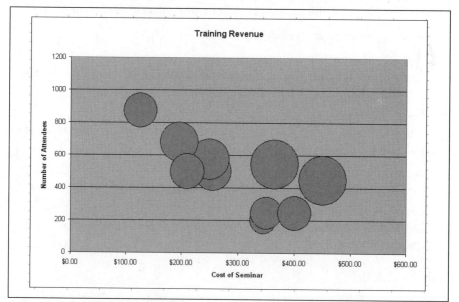

Figure 10-10: Bubble charts provide an interesting method for showing the correlation between three sets of data values

You can either create a standard bubble chart, as shown in Figure 10-10, or one with 3-D bubbles.

Stock Charts

Stock charts are typically used to illustrate results of stock market information. Each of these charts requires at least three data series, and chart data must be arranged in the appropriate order. Figure 10-11 illustrates a High-Low-Close chart that requires the high, low, and closing value for each day.

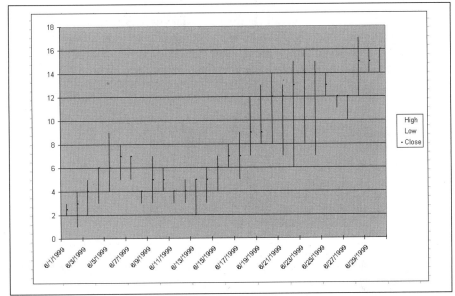

Figure 10-11: Stock charts are designed to show the results of stock market information

There are four different types of stock charts available. You need to have the corresponding stock values for the chart that you select. These chart types are more temperamental than other Excel charts. You need to have the appropriate data values selected on your sheet before selecting this chart type.

High-Low-Close

> Select this chart subtype to create a stock chart, like Figure 10-11, that shows the highest value, lowest value, and closing values. You need to make sure these values are arranged in the order highest value, lowest value, and closing value on your worksheet, or Excel will not create the chart.

Open-High-Low-Close

> Select this chart subtype if you have the opening value, highest value, lowest, value, and closing values (arranged in the same order).

Chart   249

Volume-High-Low-Close
Use this chart type to compare the stock's trading volume to the highest, lowest and closing prices. The data in your worksheet must be arranged in the order of volume: high, low, and closing.

Volume-Open-High-Low-Close
Use this chart if you have your data in the order of trading volume, opening value, highest value, lowest value, and closing value.

Cylinder, Cone, and Pyramid Charts

These three chart types are essentially the same. The only difference is the type of graphic image used on the chart. These charts types are interchangeable with column and Bar charts to show a relationship between a group of data values; typically they show data changes that occur over time, as shown in Figure 10-12.

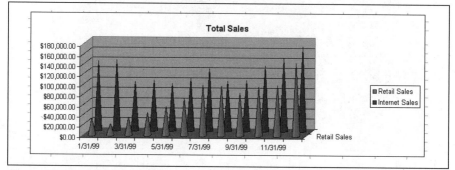

Figure 10-12: Cylinder, Cone, and Pyramid charts provide an interesting alternative to standard column and Bar charts

There are seven different subtypes that you can select from:

Clustered Column
The Clustered Column chart creates a standard column chart using the selected shape (cylinder, cone, or pyramid) in place of the column. This chart type creates a vertical column for each data value. If the chart is showing multiple data series, the values are grouped based upon the category value.

Stacked Column
The Stacked Column chart shows the corresponding data series stacked. If you only have one data series selected, this chart appears the same as the Clustered Column chart.

100% Stacked Column
The 100% Stacked Column chart shows the corresponding data series values stacked as a percentage of the total. Instead of comparing total amounts you are able to see what percentage that value was of the total. This chart type is similar to creating multiple Pie charts.

Clustered Bar

The Clustered Bar chart creates a standard Bar chart using the selected shape for the bar (cylinder, cone, or pyramid). This chart type creates a horizontal column for each data value. If the chart is showing multiple data series, the values are grouped based upon the category value.

Stacked Bar

The Stacked Bar chart displays the corresponding data series stacked. If you only have one data series selected, this chart appears the same as the Clustered Bar chart.

100% Stacked Bar

The 100% Stacked Bar chart shows the corresponding data series values stacked as a percentage of the total. Instead of comparing total amounts you are able to see what percentage that value was of the total. This chart type is similar to creating multiple Pie charts.

3-D Column

The 3-D Column chart is probably the showiest of the subtypes. This type of chart provides a true 3-D chart by creating a third axis. The third axis creates the depth that gives the chart the three-dimensional perspective.

Chart → Chart Type

The Chart → Chart Type option allows you to change the chart type for the currently selected chart. The option also provides the ability to make the currently select chart type the default chart and to create a custom chart type. When you select this option, the Chart Type dialog displays, as shown in Figure 10-13. The currently selected chart type is indicated on the Chart Type dialog. For example, if you currently have one of the standard chart types selected, that chart and its sub-type will be selected on the Standard Types tab.

Standard Types Tab

The Standard Types tab, shown in Figure 10-13, displays a list of several different chart types that can be selected in the Chart Type list box. When you select one of these types, a selection of sub-types display in the Chart sub-type section. If you want to preview how your data will look on your new chart selection, select the "Press and Hold to View Sample" button.

If you have made modifications to the formatting of the chart, you can have Excel resort back to the default formatting for the selected chart type by selecting the Default formatting option.

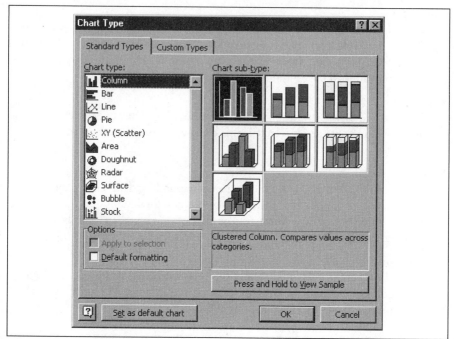

Figure 10-13: Chart Type dialog

Custom Types Tab

The Custom Types tab, shown in Figure 10-14, displays a list of custom chart types that can be selected. These chart types are either ones that were included with Excel or ones that you have customized and saved.

> *The only real difference between the built-in chart types that appear on the Custom Types tab and those on the Standard Types tab is that the ones on the Custom Types tab do not have the sub-type selections. Other than that, they are just additional chart types that can be selected.*

You can either select Built-in (Microsoft-created) charts or user-defined charts by selecting the appropriate radio button in the Select from box. If you select the User-defined radio button you have the option of saving a custom chart for future selection. A custom chart is created by modifying one of the existing chart types to meet your desired criteria. When you select the User-defined radio button, the Add and Delete buttons display on the dialog box, allowing you to create and delete custom charts. When you select the Add button, the "Add Custom Chart Type" dialog displays, as shown in Figure 10-15.

You need to specify a name for the new chart type. The description that you specify will display when you click on the chart name on the Chart Type dialog. Keep in mind that to find this chart type in the future you will need to select the Custom Types tab on the Chart Type dialog and then select the User-defined radio button.

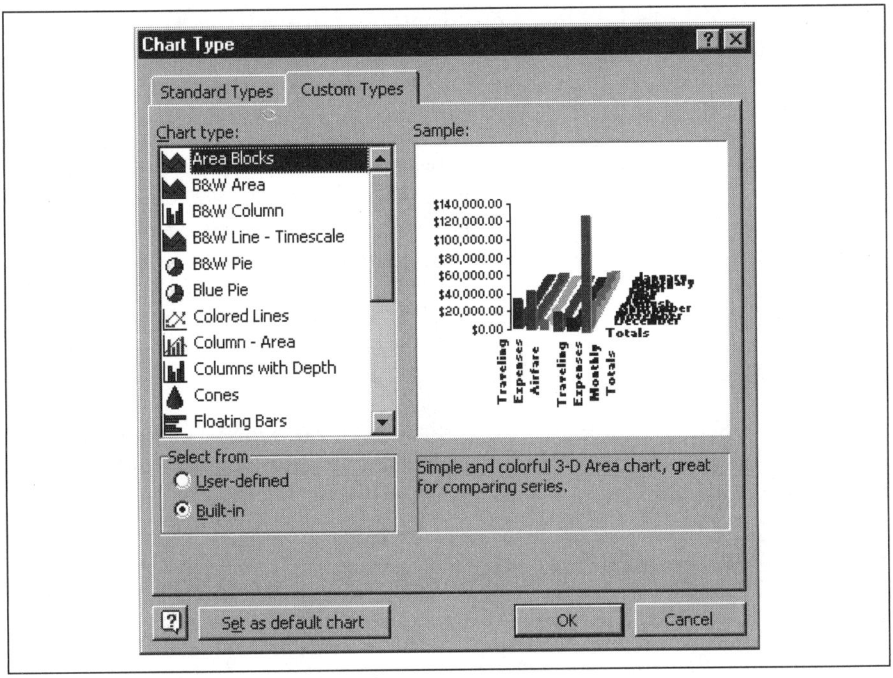

Figure 10-14: Selecting a Custom Chart

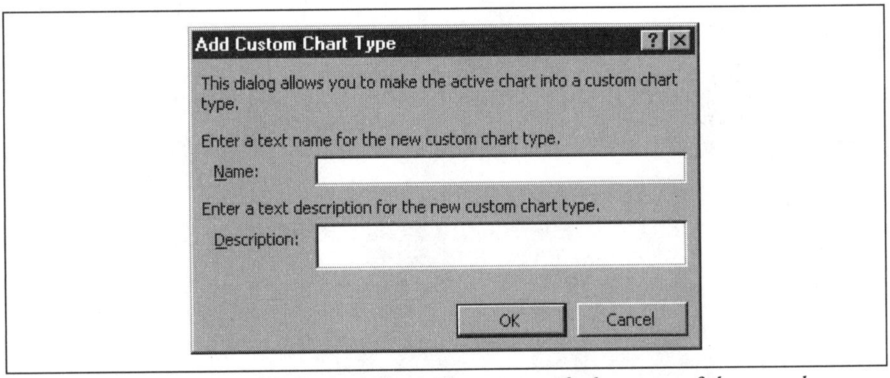

Figure 10-15: Use the Add Custom Chart Type to specify the name of the new chart

You can change the default chart that is used by Excel by locating the desired chart type on the Chart Type dialog and then selecting the "Set as Default Chart" button. You can quickly create a chart using the default chart type by selecting the desired data in the chart and then pressing F11. The default chart type is selected using Chart → Chart Type.

If you have made custom modifications to your current chart, such as changing colors of data series, those changes are typically lost if you select a different chart type. Therefore, make sure you have the desired chart type selected before you start customizing it. If you have not created any user-defined charts, Excel displays Default as the chart type option. This is the default chart type that you have selected with the "Set as Default Chart" button. If you have not changed the default chart type, Excel uses the standard Clustered Column chart as the default chart type.

You can create a chart that combines more than one chart type. For example, you may want to create a Bar chart that includes a Line chart for one series of data. To do so, you first chart and then select the data series that you want to change and select Chart → Chart Type then select the chart type you want for the selected range.

Chart → Source Data

The Chart → Source Data option allows you to make modifications to the data ranges and data orientations for the selected chart. When you select this option, the Source Data dialog displays, as shown in Figure 10-16.

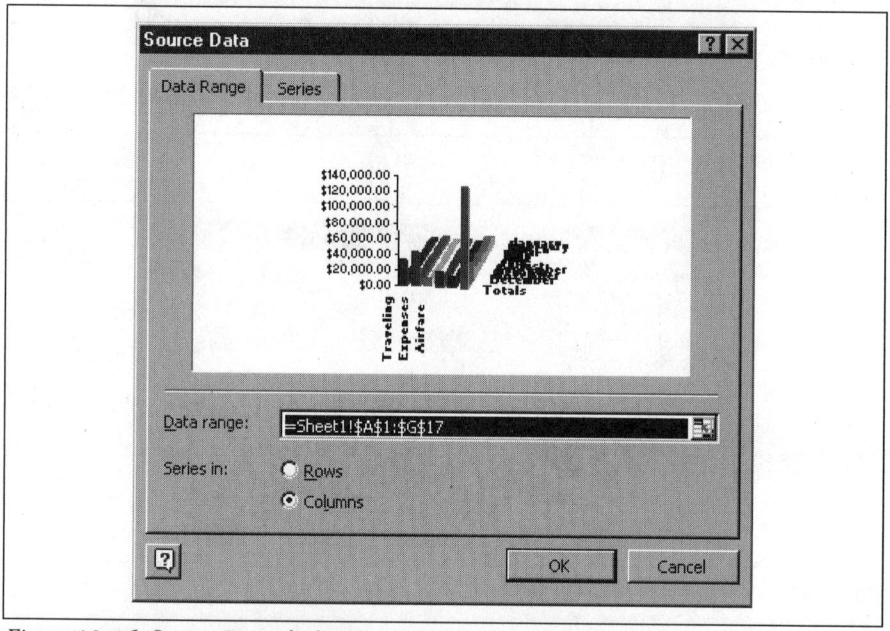

Figure 10-16: Source Data dialog

Data Range Tab

The Data Range tab is used to specify the data range that is used to create the chart and whether the data is placed on the chart based upon the values in the rows or columns of the worksheet. The orientation (Series in radio buttons) that you select determines the values selected on the Series tab. For example, if you select the Rows radio button, by default Excel uses the first cell in each row as the series name for the chart. This is the information that appears in the legend.

Series Tab

The Series tab, shown in Figure 10-17, allows you to customize the series names for your chart. To change a series name, highlight the name in the series list and type the desired name in the Name field. You can also click on the Collapse Dialog button and select another field that contains the desired series name. Keep in mind, any modifications made to the series names on this tab do not affect the values in the worksheet.

The "Category (X) axis labels" field indicates the location of the X axis labels for your chart. You can change the reference by clicking on the Collapse Dialog button.

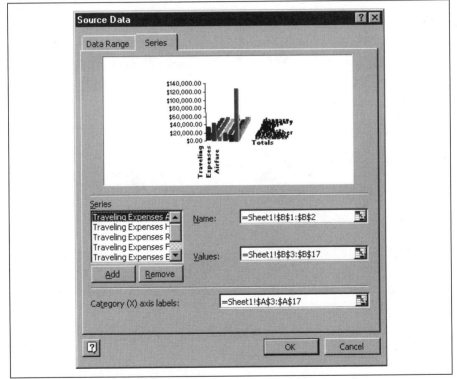

Figure 10-17: Series Tab on Data Range dialog

 Excel allows you to have a maximum of 255 data series in most charts; with the exception of the Pie chart that can only display one data series. Excel allows you to have a maximum of 32,000 data points for standard charts, 4,000 data points for 3-D charts.

Chart → Chart Options

The Chart → Chart Options option provides the ability to customize the look of the selected chart. You can indicate items such as the name of the chart, whether gridlines should display, location of the legend, etc. The actual customization options that are available vary depending upon the type of chart selected. When you select this option, the Chart Options dialog displays, as shown in Figure 10-18. The dialog provides several different tabs that can be selected to customize the chart. There are actually six different tabs available on this dialog, but they do not display for all chart types. For example, if you have a Pie chart selected, you will only see the Titles, Legend, and Data Labels tabs.

To customize the chart you need to select each tab and designate the appropriate values for each field. As you make modifications to the chart options, you will be able to see the results in the chart view section that appears on the right side of the dialog.

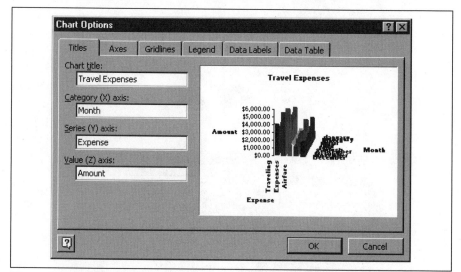

Figure 10-18: Chart Options dialog

Titles Tab

The Titles tab, shown in Figure 10-18, provides the ability to add custom labels to different parts of your chart. The label types available vary based on the chart type selected.

When you create a title Excel places it in a default location on your chart. Remember, you can drag the titles to any location on the chart.

Axes Tab

The Axes tab allows you to specify whether you want to see the values for a specific axis. The number of axes is different depending upon the chart type selected. For example, Pie and Doughnut charts have no axes; whereas, a 3-D chart has 3 axes. You select each axis by selecting the corresponding checkbox.

The Category axis represents that chart's categories. For example, in Figure 10-18, we are viewing the Travel Expenses for each month of the year, so each month is a category on the chart.

You can customize the look of a specific axis on your chart by clicking on the axis with the right mouse button and selecting the Format Axis option. On the Format Axis dialog you have the ability to change the pattern used to indicate each axis. For example, you may want to make the axis and tick marks red so that they show up better. Be careful when modifying the Scale tab, shown in Figure 10-19. Excel automatically scales your chart based upon the data values in the chart. Manually adjusting the scale of an axis can have a dramatic effect on the look of your chart. For example, if you are showing the values 10, 5, 6, and 9 on your chart and you set the range of the axis to be 0 to 100, the values will almost look like the same number on your chart. Keep in mind that the values on the Scale tab vary depending upon the chart type selected.

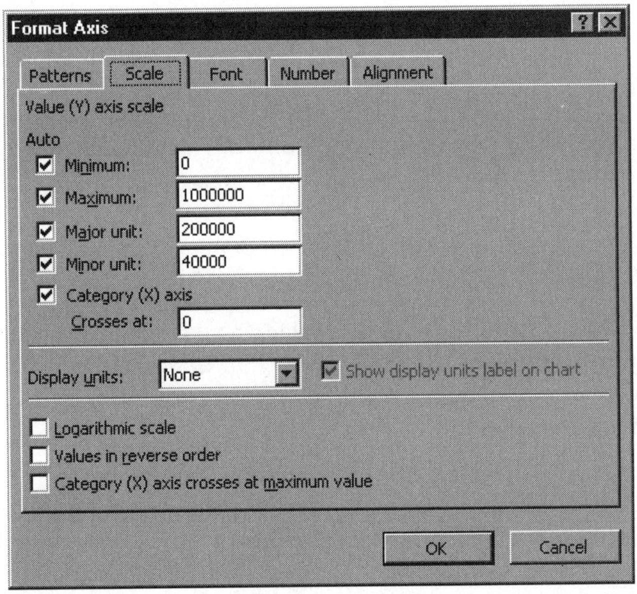

Figure 10-19: Be careful about modifying the scale of your chart

Gridlines Tab

On the Gridlines tab you can select the corresponding checkboxes to specify whether you want to have gridlines displayed for each axis. Gridlines help to show what numeric values are represented on the chart. A gridline simply extends the tick marks on the axes across the chart. Gridlines should only be used to improve the readability of your chart.

There are two different types of gridlines: major and minor. The major gridlines display at each label on the axis. For example, if your chart has the values of 10, 20, 30, 40 on the axis, a major gridline would be created for each of those labels. The minor gridlines display between the labels. Typically the major gridlines are adequate in showing your data; but use of the minor gridlines can help show a more exact representation of the data.

Legend Tab

Excel gives you the option of providing a legend for your chart. A legend is made up of text and keys. Each key is basically just a small graphic (typically a colored square) that corresponds to data series on the chart. Each key has a text value next to it that provides a description of the data series. The Legend tab provides the ability to select and/or remove the legend from the chart by selecting the Show Legend checkbox.

By default Excel always places the legend on the right side of the chart. You can change the location by selecting one of the radio buttons. You can also manually move the legend by clicking on it and dragging it with the mouse.

The actual text for the legend comes from the cells that you selected on the Series tab of the Source Data dialog. If you want to change the values, you need to select Chart → Source Data.

Data Labels Tab

If you do not have a lot of different data values in your chart, you may want to use labels to identify each value. The Data Labels tab provides the ability to apply labels to the actual chart values. The actual options that are available is based upon the type of chart you have selected.

The cool thing about using the data labels versus manually placing labels is that the labels are linked to the data in the worksheet. Therefore, if your data values change, the labels on the chart will be updated to match. You can, however, manually change a label by selecting it on the chart and then typing the desired text or cell reference for the label in the formula bar.

Data Table Tab

If you have placed your chart on a chart sheet you are aware that the data used to create the chart is not available on that sheet. You can place the data on the sheet within a data table using the options on the Data Table tab.

If you want to add a data table, select the Show data table checkbox. You can have the legend keys displayed next to each element of the table by selecting the Show legend keys checkbox.

If you decide to add the legend, my recommendation is to use the Show legend keys checkbox and then remove your legend. As you can see in Figure 10-20, it is rather redundant to have both the legend and the data table.

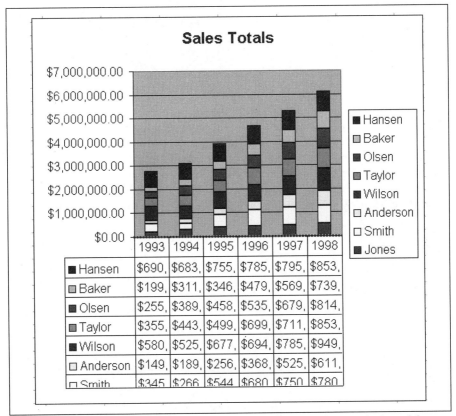

Figure 10-20: If you use a data table, add the legend keys and remove the legend from the chart

Chart → Location

When you create a new chart you indicate whether you want to place the chart directly in a worksheet or in a separate chart sheet. Once a chart has been created, you can move it to another location by selecting Chart → Chart Location to display the Chart Location dialog shown in Figure 10-21.

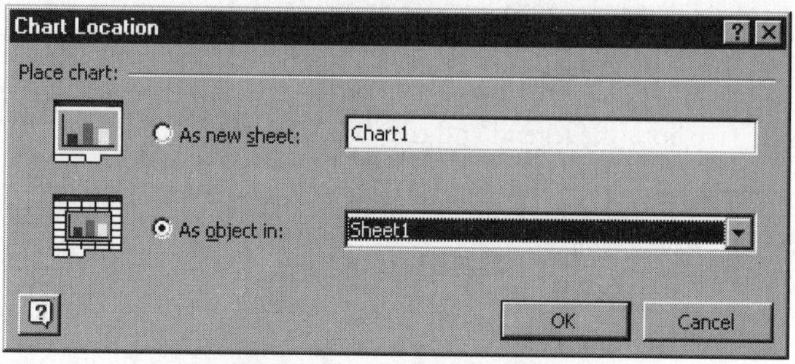

Figure 10-21: Chart Location dialog

When you place a chart on a new sheet it is placed on a chart sheet. This is the best option to select if you only want to print the chart, without the actual data of the worksheet. The chart sheet displays the chart as it will be printed on a sheet of paper (WYSIWYG). If you want to place the chart directly on a worksheet, you can select the "As object in" radio button and then indicate the worksheet where you want to insert the chart in by selecting the down arrow button next to the field.

Chart → Add Data

It is not uncommon to decide you want to add data to a chart once it has been created. The easiest method for doing this is to select the Chart → Add Data option. When you select this option the Add Data dialog displays, as shown in Figure 10-22.

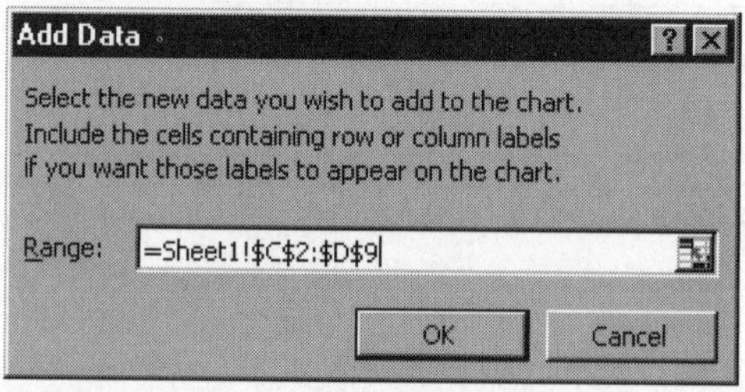

Figure 10-22: Select the range of cells that you want to add to your chart

As you can see from the figure, this is really a simple dialog. To add data to your chart you can either type the data range in the Range field, or you can select the Collapse dialog button and highlight the desired range of data.

When you select the OK button, Excel displays the Paste Special dialog, shown in Figure 10-23, so you can indicate how you want to add the new data to the chart.

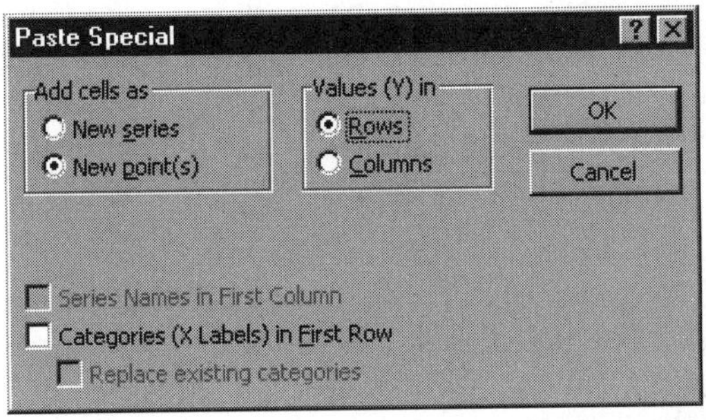

Figure 10-23: You need to specify how the new data should be added to the chart

Although the Paste Special dialog is rather small, it can also be a little confusing to use. You need to use the options on this dialog to tell Excel how the data should be added to the chart. For example, do you want to add a new data series or should the data values be added to the existing data series.

Add cells as
> In the "Add cells as" section, select the appropriate radio button to indicate how you want the new data added to the chart. If you select "New series," Excel will create a new data series on the chart that consists of the selected values. For example, if you have a Line Chart, a new line will be created for these values. If you select the "New point(s)" radio button, the selected data values will be added to the existing data series.

Values (Y) in
> Select this option to indicate whether the data series should be created based on each row or column within the selected range. For example, if you have a list of sales totals for each salesperson, you need to indicate if the totals are specified by rows or columns.

Series Names in First Column (Row)
> The name of this option changes based upon the radio button selected in the Values (Y) in section. If the first row or column contains the series names, select this checkbox.

Categories (X Labels) in First Row (Column)
> The name of this option changes based upon the radio button selected in the Values (Y) in section. If the first row or column contains the category names, select this checkbox.

Replace Existing Categories
Select this option to replace the existing category labels with the ones in the range you are pasting.

Chart → 3-D View

You have probably already found that the most appealing charts available within Excel are the 3-D ones. Although Excel has several charts that are labeled 3-D, not all of them are true 3-D charts. A 3-D chart has three different axes; some of the charts that are labeled as 3-D are really just two-dimensional charts that have a perspective added to give them 3-D appeal.

If you have a true 3-D chart selected you can modify the way it displays by rotating it using the 3-D View dialog that displays when you select Chart → 3-D View. If this option is grayed out the chart is not 3-D. The 3-D View dialog, shown in Figure 10-24, provides options for changing the elevation and rotation of your chart. You will see the effect of your selection in the center of the dialog.

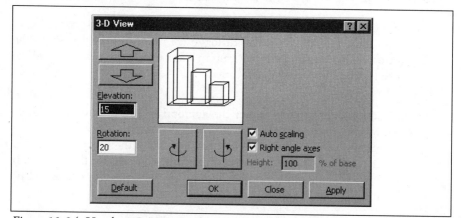

Figure 10-24: Use the 3-D View Dialog to rotate a 3-D chart so that it emphasizes the desired data

Changing the Elevation

When you change the elevation of your chart you are basically just rotating it toward the top or bottom. For example, if you want to create the perspective of looking down into your chart you could use the Up Arrow button to rotate the chart so you could see the top.

There are two different methods for changing the elevation. You can use the Up and Down Arrow button to move it or you can manually type the height you want to view the chart from in the Elevation field. For most chart types you can type a value between -90 and 90 degrees. As you click on each button the elevation value is modified in the Elevation field.

Changing the Rotation

You can modify the rotation of your chart by rotating it right or left. To rotate it you can use the Left and Right buttons or you can manually type a value in the Rotation field. A chart can be rotated between 0 and 360 degrees.

Setting the Chart at Right Angles or Using Perspective

If you want to have the axes remain at right angles as you change the rotation and elevation, you need to the select the Right angle axes checkbox. If you remove the checkmark from the box, the Perspective options display on the dialog. By changing the perspective you make the chart look like it has more depth, but it can also make the chart look a little more skewed.

TIP # 74

Quickly Rotating a 3-D Chart

A quick method of rotating a chart is to hold down the Ctrl key and then click on a corner with the mouse and drag it on the screen. As you drag the corner the chart will rotate on the screen.

If you don't like the way your chart appears after changing the rotation, perspective, or elevation you can select the Default option on the 3-D View dialog to change the chart back to the original settings.

Chart → Add Trendline

Trendlines provide the ability to show trends that exist within your data. They can also be used to forecast future data, although you should not base too much on the trendline created. You can add a trendline to your chart by selecting Chart → Add Trendline to display the Add Trendline dialog shown in Figure 10-25. Trendlines can be added for each data series. In fact, a data series can have multiple trend lines.

The Add Trendline dialog has two different tab options. The Type tab is where you select the type of trendline that you want to add to your chart. There are six different trendlines that you can select, as shown in Figure 10-25. Each of the trendlines uses a specific formula to calculate the values of the trendline based upon the selected data series. The most commonly used type of trendline is a linear trendline. It is of course only valid if there really is a linear relationship between the two variables in your chart. This option creates a straight trendline that shows the trend of the selected data series.

The Options tab allows you to indicate the text that will represent the trendline within the legend. Probably the most useful feature is the ability to forecast previous or future data values for the selected series. For example, if you want to project the

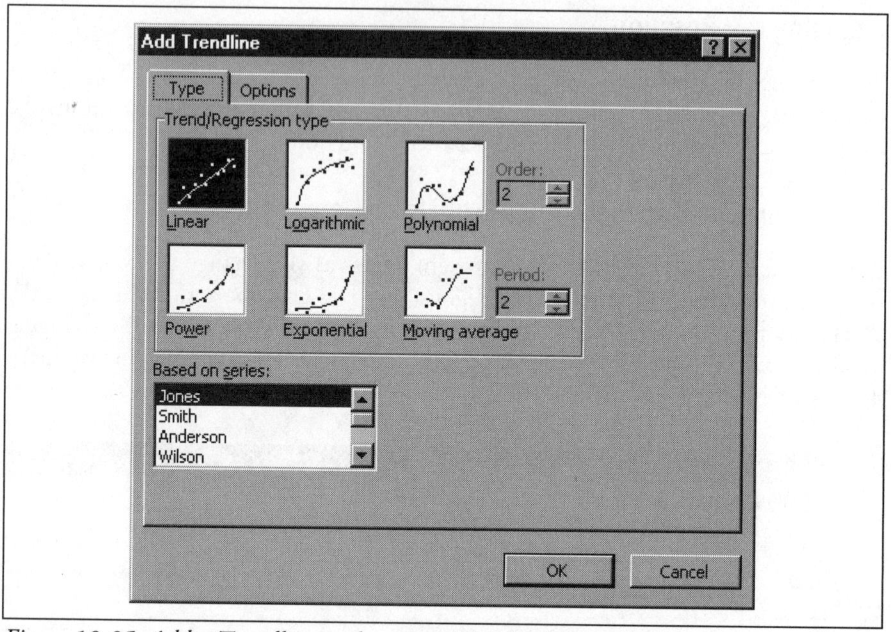

Figure 10-25: Add a Trendline to show trends in the data and to forecast future data

sales of wrenches for the next six months you can indicate that you want to forecast forward six periods.

NOTE *On some charts trendlines may appear to be just another data series, but Excel knows the difference. By default, the trendline is given a name such as "Jones Trendline 1." You can double-click on a trendline to display the Format Gridlines dialog where you can modify the name, and formatting options for the selected trendline.*

Part 3

Function Reference

Chapter 11

Working with Functions

Excel is brimming with built-in functions designed to add more complexity to your individual formulas. If, however, you have not previously used these functions, the sheer number available can seem intimidating. This second part of the book details the primary functions available in Excel 2000, from the Financial to the Information functions. Each chapter details the functions providing descriptions, examples, and tips designed to ease the learning curve.

Function or Formula?

The terms function and formula as they apply to Excel are frequently interchanged. It is confusing to differentiate between the two, but this may clarify things: functions are built-in tools for performing specific calculations, comparisons, and so on. A function in Excel performs a desired task. For example, the SUM function adds numbers together. When you use the SUM function in a cell to sum the values in two cells, such as =SUM(A1,A2), it becomes a formula.

When selecting one of the built-in functions for a formula you don't need to know exactly what calculations are required to determine the factorial of a number—you can select a function to do the calculation for you.

Excel provides many different functions that can be accessed on the Paste Function dialog by selecting Insert → Function. See Figure 11-1.

Function Categories

Detailed descriptions of each function category and the corresponding functions are covered in the remaining chapters in this book (Chapters 12–20). To make functions easier to locate on the Paste Function dialog, they are divided into the following categories:

Financial
    Provides functions designed to perform various financial calculations such as determining the accrued interest on an investment, or determining the effective annual interest rate. For more information, refer to Chapter 12, *Financial Functions*.

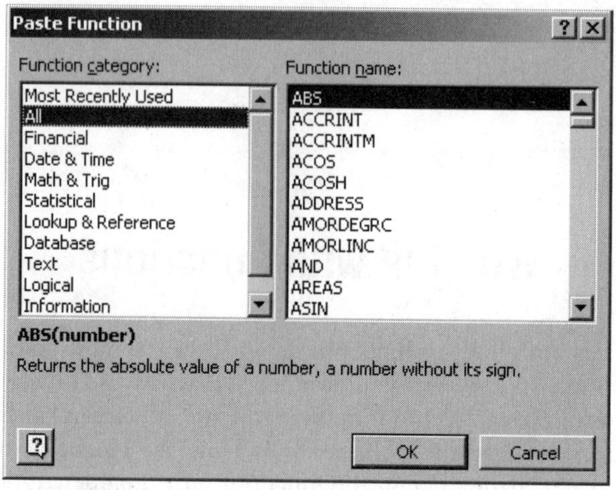

Figure 11-1: The Paste Function dialog provides access to the various functions available within Excel

Date and Time

Includes functions for working with specific date and time values within a worksheet. These functions allow you to insert the date or time based on your system clock, determine which date is the specified number of days away, or return a portion of a date or time. For more information, refer to Chapter 13, *Date and Time Functions*.

Math and Trig

Includes functions for performing mathematical and trigonometrical calculations. For example, there are functions for determining the sine, cosine, and tangent of an angle. For more information, refer to Chapter 14, *Mathematics and Trigonometry Functions*.

Statistical

Provides functions for performing statistical calculations such as finding the probability of a specified type of distribution. For more information, refer to Chapter 15, *Statistical Functions*.

Lookup and Reference

Provides functions for looking up and referencing specific values within your worksheet. For more information, refer to Chapter 16, *Lookup and Reference Functions*.

Database

Provides several functions for working with database tables. For more information, refer to Chapter 17, *Database Functions*.

Text

> Includes several functions for manipulating and converting text values within a worksheet. For more information, refer to Chapter 18, *Text Functions*.

Logical

> Provides functions that allow you to perform logical comparisons. For more information, refer to Chapter 19, *Logical Functions*.

Information

> Includes functions to return specific information about your worksheet and computer system. For more information, refer to Chapter 20, *Information Functions*.

 Although engineering functions are not covered in this book, if you load the Analysis ToolPak functions discussed in the "Analysis ToolPak Functions" section, an Engineering category is added to the Function Category list. This category contains several different functions for performing engineering calculations.

Analysis ToolPak Functions

Excel 2000 comes with a series of additional functions that are not part of the initial install. These functions make up the Analysis ToolPak, which can be loaded by selecting Tools → Add-ins and clicking on the Analysis ToolPak checkbox, as shown in Figure 11-2. A new category of functions is created called *Engineering* and additional functions are added to the Financial, Date and Time, Math and Trig, Statistical, and Information categories. Once you install the new functions they are available for selection from the Paste Function dialog.

 Chapters 12 through 20 of this book all begin with a list of functions covered in that particular chapter. The functions marked with an "AT" symbol are part of the Analysis ToolPak included with Excel. If you have not loaded the ToolPak, you will get an error message if you try to use any of these functions. If you are sent an Excel file that used these functions, you can still view the results of the given formula, but you can't edit the formula unless you load the Analysis ToolPak.

Function Arguments

Nearly all of the functions require certain values to be specified. These values are referred to as arguments. The arguments for a function are enclosed in parentheses and each argument is separated by a comma (argument1, argument2, argument3, argument4).

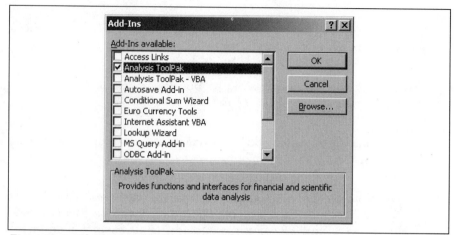

Figure 11-2: The Analysis ToolPak comes with several useful functions that can be quickly added to Excel

Each function has specific requirements for the type of arguments it expects, as outlined in Chapters 12–20. The type of argument that can be specified falls into the following categories:

Cell Reference

This is the most commonly used value for an argument. This value is simply a reference to a cell or range of cells that contain the appropriate values for the argument. For example, if you are adding the values in two cells you would specify =SUM(A1,A2) to add the values in cells A1 and A2.

If the argument accepts a cell reference it must meet the data requirements for the argument. For example, if the argument requires a numeric value, the referenced cell must contain a numeric value.

Literal Argument

A literal argument is a text string, date, time, logical, or numeric value that is specified directly as an argument for a function. For example, if you specify =SUM(3,4) in a cell, the value of the cell is always 7.

When text strings, dates, or times are specified as a literal argument they must be enclosed in double quotes. For example, =CONCATENATE("Microsoft" "Excel") joins the two text strings together. If the text strings are specified in cells that are referenced by the function, they do not need to be in quotes.

Other Functions

Finally, most Excel functions allow you to use the results of another function as an argument. For example, you could create the following formula: =SUM(SQRT(A1),A2). When you have another formula as the argument, Excel works from the inside out. In other words, Excel would first find the square root of the value in cell A1 and then add that value to the value in cell A2.

> ## TIP # 75
>
> **Maximum Formula Size**
>
> *Formulas can be created out of any combination of functions, operators, cell refer-ences, and literal arguments as long as they do not exceed 1,024 characters in length.*

Inserting a Function

There are basically two methods for adding a function to a worksheet. You can either manually type the function and the appropriate arguments in the cell or paste them into the cell using the Paste Function dialog.

If you are using a function you are familiar with, it is quicker to manually type the function in the cell. For example, as Figure 11-3 illustrates, if you type the SUM function in cell A3 it requires a comma between each argument you want to add. However, in order for Excel to recognize it as a function, it must be preceded by an equal sign.

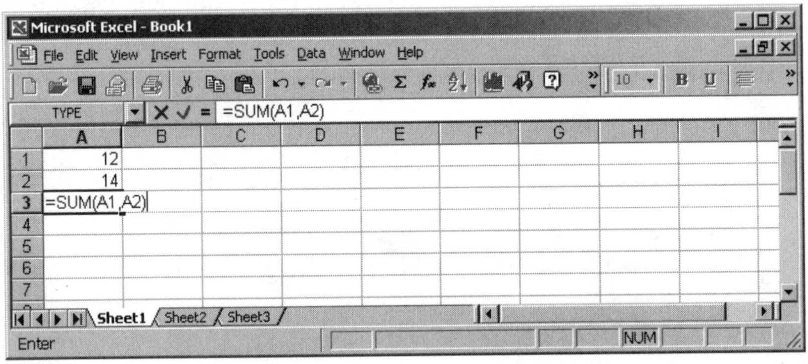

Figure 11-3: If you manually type a function into a cell, make sure you remember to put an equal sign (=) in front of the function

When you are creating formulas be sure to properly use the different symbols. For example, there must be a colon separating the beginning and ending value in a range of cells. Table 11-1 outlines the various symbols to use to create a formula and their functionality.

Table 11-1: Symbols Used in Formulas

Symbol	Purpose
Comma (,)	Used to separate arguments in a function.
Colon (:)	Used to separate the beginning and ending value in a range of cells. For example, A1:A5 would represent a range of cells including A1, A2, A3, A4, and A5.
Parentheses	Used to indicate the arguments for a function.

Table 11-1: Symbols Used in Formulas (continued)

Symbol	Purpose
Brackets {}	Used to specify an array function. For example, `{=FREQUENCY(A2:A15,C2:C16)}` places the results of the function within the specific range of cells. The brackets are also used to specify array values used as arguments for a function. For example, `=FORECAST(15, {13,15,16,19}, {21,14,19,13})` forecasts the next y value based upon the specified values from each array.
Equals Sign (=)	Always used to identify a function.

The most reliable method for adding a function to a worksheet is to select Insert → Function and use the Paste Function dialog, as shown in Figure 11-1. The dialog also displays when you select the Paste Function icon on the toolbar or Shift-F3.

The Paste Function dialog displays a list of function categories on the left. When you select one of these categories, the corresponding functions are listed on the right side of the dialog. When you select one of these functions, a dialog box displays that allows you to specify the actual arguments for the function, as shown in Figure 11-4.

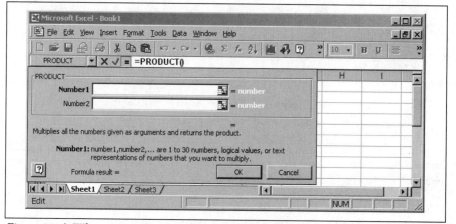

Figure 11-4: When you use Insert → Function, Excel provides a dialog that lets you quickly select the desired values for each argument

Each argument for the function displays as a separate field. You can either type the appropriate value for the argument in the field, or select the Collapse Dialog button next to the field and select the desired cells from your worksheet. After the cell is selected, the Paste Function reappears, allowing you to finish selecting all of the arguments for the function. When you have finished with the arguments select the OK button or hit Enter and the formula will be applied to the appropriate cell.

Chapter 12

Financial Functions

Microsoft Excel is most widely used to track and calculate financial information. Excel provides several different functions for making financial calculations easier. The difficulty with these functions is not in using them, but in determining which function produces the desired results. This chapter provides you with descriptions and examples of how and when to use each of the financial functions available in Excel. The "AT" represents those functions that exist only by loading the Analysis Toolpak. See Chapter 11, *Working with Functions*, for details.

The following functions are covered in detail later in this chapter:

ACCRINT *AT*	EFFECT *AT*	PRICE *AT*
ACCRINTM *AT*	FV	PRICEDISC *AT*
AMORDEGRC *AT*	FVSCHEDULE *AT*	PRICEMAT *AT*
AMORLINC *AT*	INTRATE *AT*	PV *AT*
COUPDAYBS *AT*	IPMT	RATE
COUPDAYS *AT*	IRR	SLN
COUPDAYSNC *AT*	ISPMT	SYD
COUNCD *AT*	MDURATION *AT*	TBILLEQ *AT*
COUPNUM *AT*	MIRR	TBILLPRICE *AT*
COUPPCD *AT*	NOMINAL *AT*	TBILLYIELD *AT*
CUMIPMT *AT*	NPER	VBD
CUMPRINC *AT*	NPV	XIRR *AT*
DB	ODDFPRICE *AT*	XNPV *AT*
DDB	ODDFYIELD *AT*	YIELD *AT*
DISC *AT*	ODDLPRICE *AT*	YIELDDISC *AT*
DOLLARDE *AT*	ODDLYIELA *AT*	YIELDMAT *AT*
DOLLARFR *AT*	PMT	
DURATION *AT*	PPMT	

Use these functions if you need to do the following:

- Calculate the depreciation of an asset

- Determine the amount of interest paid on an investment

- Figure out the current value of an investment

- Determine the amount of income (yield) on a security or a Treasury Bill

Understanding the Financial Jargon

If you are like me, your day-to-day activities probably don't revolve around financial transactions other than withdrawing money from the ATM and balancing your checkbook. So when you start hearing terms such as annuities, yield, or securities, it is easy to get that glazed-over look in your eyes. However, by understanding some basic financial terms, you will better understand the functions described in this chapter and how to use them to get the desired results.

Annuity

A type of investment that guarantees a specific return. The payments are either at specific times or in a single lump sum. Annuities are sold by financial institutions and insurance companies. There are two types of annuities: fixed and variable.

Fixed Annuities

Have a guaranteed rate of interest that is paid over several years.

Variable Annuities

Investments in fund-like portfolios where the return on the annuity is based on the performance of the portfolio you select. You are also typically charged annual fees with a variable annuity.

Cash Flow

Used to refer to money coming in or going out. If the money is coming in (earned) it is referred to as positive cash flow. Money that is going out (spent) is negative cash flow.

Coupon

The portion of a statement or a page from a coupon book that is sent in when a payment is due. Many of the functions in this chapter refer to the coupon date, which is basically just the date that a payment is due.

Day Count Basis

Indicates how days in a month and days in a year are counted when performing calculations. For example, although we all know that all years (except for leap years) have 365 days and each month has either 30 or 31 days (except for February); the 30/360 Day Count Basis assumes each month has exactly 30 days and a year has 360 days. By using this type of calculation, the interest paid can be calculated as the same amount each month.

There are five different Day Count Basis methods available within Excel. They can be selected for the Basis argument with several functions outlined in this chapter by specifying a value between 0-4, as outlined in Table 12-1.

Table 12-1: Day Count Basis Values

Basis Value	Description
0	This value selects the US (NASD) 30/360 day count basis that assumes that each month has 30 days and the total number of days in the year is 360 (calculated as 12 months x 30 days per month.) All the functions using the `Basis` argument compare at least two different dates. This method makes adjustments for February and months with 31 days. If the date is 2/28 or 2/29 (leap year) it is adjusted to be 2/30. For months ending with 31 days, the method is a little more confusing. If the first date has 31 days (such as 1/31/2000) the date is converted to 30 days, such as 1/30/2000. If the second date has 31 days it is changed to 30 days as long as the first date was not 2/28 or 2/29. If the first date was a February date, the second date does not change. This day count basis is typically used with mortgages and agency notes.
1	This value uses the day count basis referred to as Actual/Actual. This basis calculates the actual number of days between two dates and assumes the year has either 365 or 366 days depending on whether the year is a leap year. In other words, if the date range for the calculation includes the date February 29 (a leap day), the year is 366; otherwise it is 365. This day count basis is typically used with U.S. Treasury Notes.
2	This value uses the day count basis referred to as Actual/360. This basis method calculates the actual number of days between two dates and assumes the year has 360 days. Many money market calculations with less than a year to maturity use this day count basis. This day count basis is typically used with Certificates of Deposit (CDs), U.S. Treasury Bills, and Agency Discount Notes.
3	This value uses the day count basis referred to as Actual/365. This calculates the actual number of days between two dates and assumes the year has 365 days. Keep in mind that even leap years are assumed to have 365 days.
4	This value uses the day count basis referred to as 30/360 European. This day count basis is similar to the US 30/360 basis. The only difference is how it treats months with 31 days. All dates with a day value of 31 are converted to 30 days (for example, 1/31/2000 is treated as 1/30/2000). February dates of 2/28 or 2/29 are converted to 2/30.

Financial Functions

Depreciation

This is a method used in accounting to spread the cost of an asset over a period of time to reduce taxable income. For example, if you purchase a new computer for $2,000 that you plan to use for four years, you could depreciate it over that time by *realizing* (obtaining a profit) $500 each year. By depreciating it over that time period, the asset will have no value at the end of the depreciation.

Maturity

The maturity date is the date when an investment becomes due and payable. For example, a bond contains a date when the principal payment is due. If you purchase a $500 bond for five years the maturity date is when the $500 and any unpaid interest is paid.

Security

A security is a generic term that refers to publicly traded stocks and bonds.

Settlement

The settlement date refers to the actual date when the funds are paid for an investment from the buyer to the seller, and the appropriate sell transfer documentation is signed.

Treasury Bill

Treasury Bills are short-term government securities that are sold through the Federal Reserve Bank. Typically they sell for between $10,000 and $1,000,000.

Yield

Yield is a generic term that refers to the interest earned on a bond or the dividend paid on a stock or mutual fund.

The Financial Functions

As we stated earlier in this chapter, Excel provides several different functions used to perform financial calculations. These functions are covered in alphabetical order, but can be categorized as follows:

To determine the depreciation of an asset:

AMORDEGRC (French function for determining depreciation)
AMORLINC (French function for determining depreciation)
DB (fixed-declining depreciation)
DDB (double-declining depreciation)
SLN (straight-line depreciation)
SYD (sum-of-years depreciation)
VBD (depreciation amount over multiple periods)

To work with loans and annuities with compounded interest:

CUMPRINC (principal paid on a loan)
DISC (discount rate)
FV (future value of an investment)
FVSCHEDULE (future value of investment with variable interest)
IRR (internal rate of return)
MIRR (modified internal rate of return)
NPER (number of payments for future value)
NPV (present value of cash flows)
PMT (investment payment)
PPMT (amount applied to principal for a period)
PV (present value of investment)
RATE (interest rate for an annuity)
XIRR (rate of return for non-periodic cash flows)
XNPV (present value of non-periodic cash flows)

To figure out the number of coupon days in a period:

COUPDAYBS (days between start of period and settlement)
COUPDAYS (days in settlement date period)
COUPDAYSNC (days from settlement date until next period)
COUPNCD (coupon date after settlement)
COUPNUM (number of coupon dates between settlement and maturity)
COUPPCD (determines the coupon date before settlement)

To determine interest paid on an investment:

ACCRINT (total amount of accrued interest by settlement)
ACCRINTM (total amount of interest paid at maturity)
CUMIPMT (total interest paid on a loan)
EFFECT (effective annual interest rate)
INTRATE (interest on a security)
IPMT (interest payment for a specific period)
ISPMT (interest payment for a specific period)
NOMINAL (nominal annual interest rate)

To calculate the price of an investment:

ODDFPRICE (abnormal length of first period)
ODDLPRICE (abnormal length of last period)
PRICE (cost of security)
PRICEDISC (cost of discounted security)
PRICEMAT (cost of security that pays interest at maturity)
TBILLPRICE (cost of a Treasury Bill)

To convert between fractional and decimal dollar amounts:

DOLLARDE (fractional to decimal)
DOLLARFR (decimal to fractional)

To determine the yield on an investment:

ODDFYIELD (abnormal length of first period)
ODDLYIELD (abnormal length of last period)
TBILLEQ (bond-equivalent interest on a Treasury Bill)
TBILLYIELD (interest on a Treasury Bill)
YIELD (interest on a security)
YIELDDISC (interest on a discounted security)
YIELDMAT (interest on a security that pays at maturity)

To determine the duration of a security:

DURATION (Macauley duration)
MDURATION (modified duration)

Recurring Arguments

The following arguments are available on a recurring basis in many of the functions discussed in this chapter. If differences in the implementation exist in a particular function, they are explained in that function's section.

Basis

This argument must be an integer value between 0 and 4 that indicates the way the days in a month and year are counted. If this argument is omitted, the function uses a value of 0 for a US 30/360 NASD count. For more information about specifying the day count basis, refer to Table 12-1.

Frequency

This argument must be an integer value of 1, 2, or 4, indicating the number of times per year that interest is paid on the security. A value of 1 indicates payments made annually, 2 specifies payments made semiannually (every six months), and 4 specifies payments made quarterly.

FV Indicates the future value of the investment. If you take out a loan, the future value will be 0 when you make the last payment. For an investment such as a savings account, this is the amount you want the investment to be worth at the end of the specified number of payments (deposits). If you do not specify a value for the *FV* argument, it assumes a value of 0.

Issue

Indicates the date the security was issued. The date specified must be prior to the date specified for *Settlement*. The argument can be an actual date, a cell reference (e.g., A3), or the results of another function.

Maturity

Indicates the date when the security expires. This is the date when the initial value of the security is repaid. The argument can be an actual date, a cell reference (e.g., A3), or the results of another function.

Nper

Specifies an integer value that indicates the total number of payments. For example, if you make monthly payments over 30 years the total number of payments is 360 (12 × 30).

PR

Indicates the face value of the security. This is the value for which the security was purchased. The price must be per $100 of the face value of the security. For example, if you paid $95 for a $100 security the value of the argument is $95. If you purchased five of these securities, only specify a value of $95.

PV Indicates the present value of the investment. If you have a loan, this is the loan value without interest payments. For example, if you purchased a home for $150,000 that is the value of the loan. If you have an investment such as a savings account, this is the current value of the account.

Redemption

> Specifies the value of the security when it matures. This is the amount per $100 of face value of the security. If the security is worth $100 when it matures, that is the value of this argument.

Salvage

> Indicates the amount you could sell the asset for at the end of its useful life. For example, if you are depreciating an automobile, the salvage value is the amount you should be able to resell the car for.

Settlement

> Indicates the date when the payment was actually made to purchase the security. The argument can be an actual date, a cell reference (e.g., A3), or the results of another function.

Type

> Specifies either 0 or 1 as a value for this argument to indicate when the payment is made. If the payment is made at the beginning of the period (beginning of the month), specify a 0, otherwise specify 1 for the end of the period.

ACCRINT

If you have a security that pays interest periodically you can use ACCRINT (an Analysis ToolPak function) to determine the amount of interest accrued between the issue date and settlement date for the security. To use this function you need to know the date the security was issued, the first date you will receive interest, the settlement date, the rate used to calculate interest, and the frequency at which it pays interest.

Use ACCRINTM if you have a security that pays the interest in one lump sum at maturity.

To Calculate

    =ACCRINT(Issue, First_Interest, Settlement, Rate, Par, Frequency, Basis)

The *Par* and *Basis* arguments are optional. All other arguments require a value.

First_Interest

> Indicate the first date that interest is paid on the security. The argument can be an actual date, a cell reference (e.g., A3), or the results of another function.

Rate

> Specifies a decimal value that indicates the rate that is used to determine the amount of interest received for the security.

Par

> Optionally specifies the original value of the security. If this argument is omitted, the function uses a value of $1000.

Example

ACCRINT allows you to determine how much interest you will have received on a security between the time the security was issued and the settlement date. Figure 12-1 compares the results of ACCRINT with ACCRINTM, which shows the total amount of interest accrued on a security at maturity.

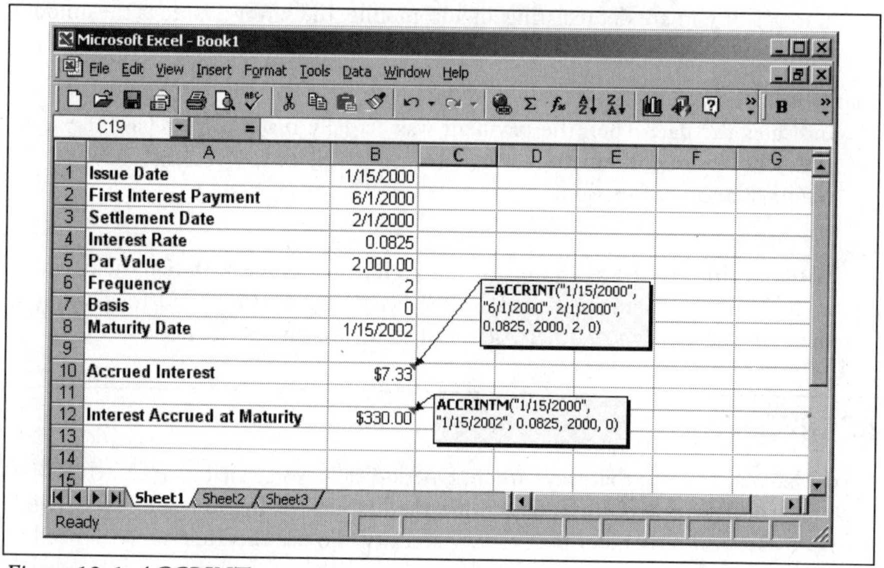

Figure 12-1: ACCRINT returns interest accrued until settlement, whereas ACCRINTM determines interest accrued until maturity

ACCRINTM

If you have a security that pays all interest when it matures, you can use ACCRINTM (an Analysis ToolPak function) to determine the amount of interest you will receive. To use this function you need to know the issue date of the security, when it matures, the rate used to calculate the interest, and the count basis used to perform the interest calculations.

To Calculate

    =ACCRINTM(Issue, Maturity, Rate, Par, Settlement, Basis)

The Par and Basis arguments are optional. All other arguments require a value.

Settlement

Although the name of the argument is Settlement, the function is expecting this argument to contain the date when the security will mature. The argument can be an actual date, a cell reference (e.g., A3), or the results of another function.

Rate

Specifies a decimal value that indicates the rate that is used to determine the amount of interest received for the security.

Par

The *Par* argument is optional. It specifies the original value of the security. If this argument is omitted, the function uses a value of $1000.

Example

Figure 12-1 illustrates how ACCRINTM can be used to determine the total amount of interest accrued on a security between the date it was issued and the maturity date.

AMORDEGRC

Use AMORDEGRC (an Analysis ToolPak function) if you are working with data from a French accounting system. This function calculates the depreciation of an asset for the specified accounting period. The depreciation amount will be pro-rated if the asset was purchased in the middle of the specified period. The only difference between this function and AMORLINC is that this function applies a depreciation coefficient based upon the life of the asset. The depreciation coefficient is 1.5 for assets that are three to four years old, 2.0 for assets that are five to six years old, and 2.5 for assets older than six years.

To Calculate

=AMORDEGRC(*Cost*, *Date_Purchased*, *First_Period*, *Salvage*, *Period*, *Rate*, *Basis*)

All arguments are required.

Cost

Indicates the actual purchase amount for the asset.

Date_Purchased

Indicates the date when the asset was purchased. The argument can be an actual date, a cell reference (e.g., A3), or the results of another function.

First_Period

Indicates the date when the first depreciation period ends. The argument can be an actual date, a cell reference (e.g., A3), or the results of another function.

Period

Indicates the number of the period for which you want to calculate the depreciation of the asset.

Rate

Indicates the rate used to determine the amount of depreciation for the asset.

Example

Figure 12-2 illustrates how AMORDEGRC can be used to determine the amount of depreciation that occurred for each period. The depreciation is calculated based on the life of the asset as opposed to AMORLINC, which calculates the depreciation amount entirely based on the *Rate* specified.

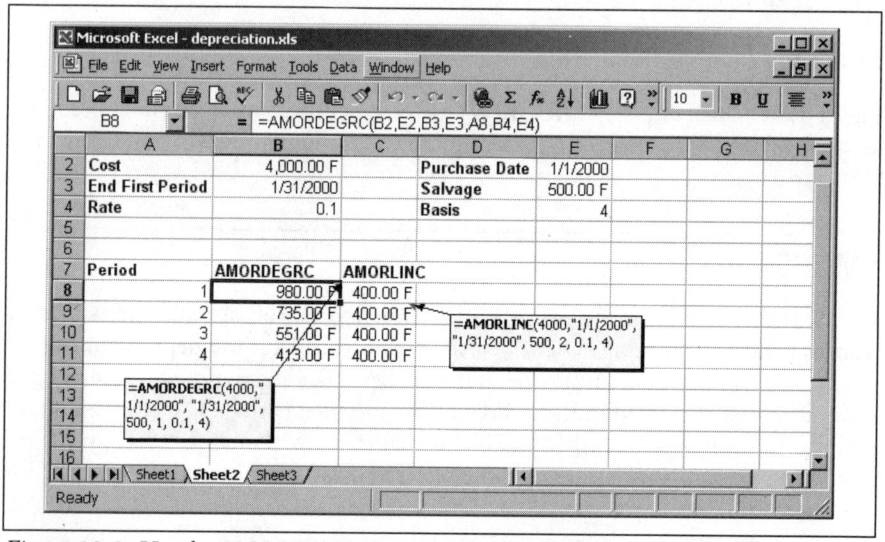

Figure 12-2: Use the AMORDEGRC or AMORLINC depreciation functions to determine the depreciation for a French asset

AMORLINC

Use AMORLINC (an Analysis ToolPak function) if you are working with data from a French accounting system. This function calculates the depreciation of an asset for the specified accounting period. The depreciation amount will be pro-rated if the asset was purchased in the middle of the specified period.

To Calculate

=AMORLINC(*Cost, Date_Purchased, First_Period, Salvage, Period, Rate, Basis*)

The following arguments are required:

Cost
Indicates the actual purchase amount for the asset.

Date_Purchased
Indicates the date when the asset was purchased. The argument can be an actual date, a cell reference (e.g., A3), or the results of another function.

First_Period

Indicates the date when the first depreciation period ends. The argument can be an actual date, a cell reference (e.g., A3), or the results of another function.

Period

Indicates the number of the period for which you want to calculate the depreciation of the asset.

Rate

Specifies a decimal value that indicates the rate that is used to determine the amount of depreciation for the asset.

Example

Figure 12-2 shows how you can use the AMORLINC function to determine the depreciation of an asset using a fixed depreciation amount for each period.

COUPDAYBS

Use COUPDAYBS (an Analysis ToolPak function) to determine the number of days between the start of the coupon period and the settlement date for a security. In order to use this function you must know the settlement date for the security, when the security matures, and the frequency of the coupon payments.

To Calculate

=COUPDAYBS(*Settlement, Maturity, Frequency, Basis*)

The *Basis* argument is the only optional argument. The other arguments must have values.

Example

Figure 12-3 illustrates how you can determine the number of days between the start of a coupon period and the settlement date. Keep in mind that in order to use this function you must know the settlement date, maturity date, and how often the payments are made each year.

COUPDAYS

Use COUPDAYS (an Analysis ToolPak function) to determine the number of days within the coupon period that contains the settlement date for a security. To use this function you must know the settlement date for the security, when the security matures, and the frequency of the coupon payments.

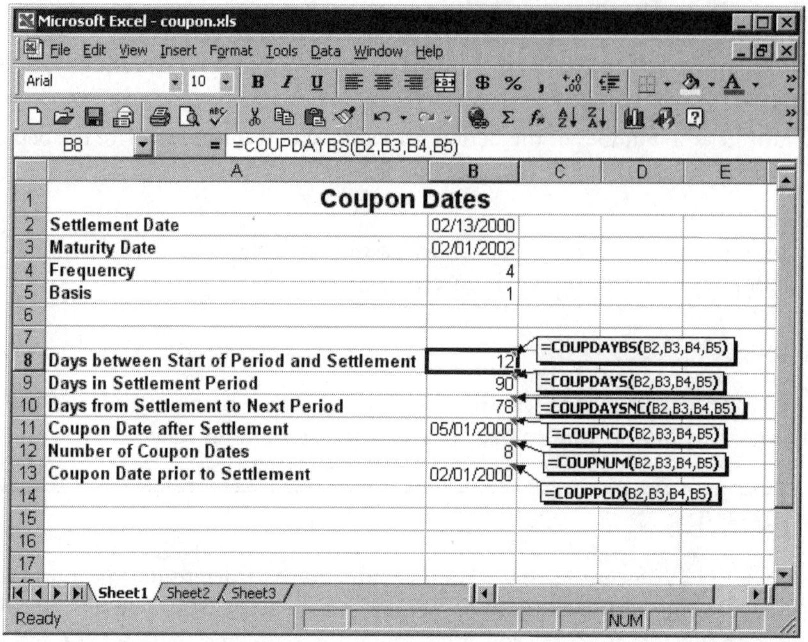

Figure 12-3: There are several different functions available for determining specific information related to coupon dates

To Calculate

=COUPDAYS(Settlement, Maturity, Frequency, Basis)

The *Basis* argument is the only optional argument. The others must have values.

Example

Figure 12-3 illustrates how you can use COUPDAYS to determine how many days are in the coupon period containing the settlement date.

COUPDAYSNC

Use COUPDAYSNC (an Analysis ToolPak function) to determine the number of days from the settlement date to the next coupon due date for a security. To use this function you must know the settlement date for the security, when the security matures, and the frequency of the coupon payments.

To Calculate

=COUPDAYSNC(Settlement, Maturity, Frequency, Basis)

The *Basis* argument is the only optional argument. The others must have values.

Example

Figure 12-3 illustrates how you can use COUPDAYSNC to determine the number of days between the settlement date and the next coupon date.

COUPNCD

Use COUPNCD (an Analysis ToolPak function) to determine the next coupon date that follows the settlement date. To use this function you must know the settlement date for the security, when the security matures, and the frequency of the coupon payments.

To Calculate

=COUPNCD(Settlement, Maturity, Frequency, Basis)

The *Basis* argument is the only optional argument. The other arguments must have values.

Example

Figure 12-3 illustrates how you can use COUPNCD to figure out the date of the next coupon payment after the settlement date.

COUPNUM

Use COUPNUM (an Analysis ToolPak function) to determine the number of coupon dates between the settlement date and the maturity date. The function returns a whole number that is rounded up, if necessary. For example, if you have monthly payments and there are 5 1/3 months between the two dates, the function returns a value of 6. To use this function you must know the settlement date for the security, when the security matures, and the frequency of the coupon payments.

To Calculate

=COUPNUM((Settlement, Maturity, Frequency, Basis)

The *Basis* argument is the only optional argument. The other arguments must have values.

Example

Figure 12-3 illustrates how you can use COUPNUM to determine the number of coupon periods between the settlement date and the maturity date.

COUPPCD

Use COUPPCD (an Analysis ToolPak function) to determine the coupon date prior to the settlement date. To use it you must know the settlement date for the security, when the security matures, and the frequency of the coupon payments.

To Calculate

=COUPPCD(*Settlement*, *Maturity*, *Frequency*, *Basis*)

The *Basis* argument is optional. The other arguments must have values.

Example

Figure 12-3 illustrates how you can use the COUPPCD function to figure out the coupon date prior to the settlement date.

CUMIPMT

CUMIPMT (an Analysis ToolPak function) is used to determine the total amount of interest that you will pay on a loan. You can determine the interest for the entire life of the loan or just for a specific time frame. For example, you may want to use this function to see how much interest you paid on your mortgage loan last year.

TIP # 76

Rate Is by Period, Not by Annual Interest

Be careful about specifying the interest rate for the Rate argument. You must specify the rate used for each period, not the annual interest rate. For example, if there is a 10% interest rate charged annually for the loan and the payments are made monthly you need to indicate the amount of interest charged each month. That is determined by dividing the annual rate by the number of periods (months) in the year. For example, in Figure 12-4 we divided the annual interest rate of 8.5%, expressed as a decimal (0.085) by 12 to get a monthly interest rate of 0. 0070833333 for each payment.

To Calculate

=CUMIPMT(*Rate*, *Nper*, *PV*, *Start_Period*, *End_Period*, *Type*)

The following arguments are required:

Rate

    Indicate the interest rate used to calculate the rate for each period. For example, if you make monthly payments and the interest rate is 12% you need to specify an interest rate of 0.01 (0.12/12) as the rate for each month.

Start_Period

Since you can calculate the interest for the entire loan or a portion of the loan, you need to indicate the first loan period in order to calculate the interest. If you want to look at the entire loan, you would specify 1 and the value for this argument.

End_Period

Indicate the integer value for the last loan period you want to calculate interest on. For example, if you are determining the amount of interest paid for the first year, you would specify 12 for this argument if you make monthly payments.

 The value specified for the End_Period must be greater than the Start_Period value.

Example

Figure 12-4 shows how you can use CUMIPMT to determine the total amount of interest paid on a loan each year. This example determines the amount of interest paid each year for a $500,000, 30-year loan. Since the payments are made monthly the interest rate is determined by taking the annual interest rate of 0.085 and dividing it by 12 to get an interest rate of 0.007 percent. This example also determines the amount of principal paid each year using CUMPRINC.

TIP # 77

How to Determine Same Period Interest

If you want to determine the amount of interest paid for each period, specify the same period number for both the Start_Period and End_Period arguments. For example, to determine the amount of interest paid in the second month, you specify a value of 2 for each argument.

CUMPRINC

To determine how much principal you have paid on a loan, use CUMPRINC (an Analysis ToolPak function). This function determines the principal amount between two periods. For example, you can find out how much principal you paid on your mortgage during the second year.

To Calculate

```
=CUMPRINC(Rate, Nper, PV, Start_Period, End_Period, Type)
```

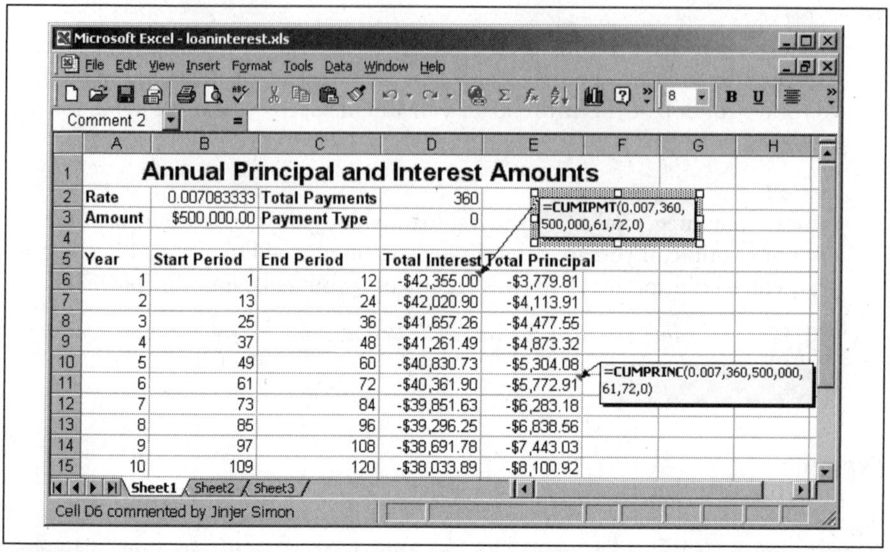

Figure 12-4: Determine the cumulative amount of principal or interest on a loan

The following arguments are required:

Rate

Indicates the interest rate used to calculate the rate for each period. For example, if you make monthly payments and the interest rate is 12% you need to specify an interest rate of 0.01 (0.12/12) as the rate for each month.

Start_Period

Because you can calculate the interest for the entire loan, or a portion of the loan, you need to indicate the first loan period you want to calculate interest for. If you want to look at the entire loan, you would specify 1 and the value for this argument.

End_Period

Indicates the integer value for the last loan period you want to calculate interest on. For example, to determine the amount of interest paid for the first year, you would specify 12 for this argument if you make monthly payments.

Example

Figure 12-4 illustrates how CUMPRINC can be used to determine the amount of principal paid annually on a $500,000 loan. The function returns a negative value indicating that it is a payment you are making and not income.

DB

Use DB to determine the amount of depreciation for an asset during the specified time frame. The depreciation is calculated using the fixed-declining balance method, which calculates the depreciation of the asset using a fixed rate.

To Calculate

=DB(*Cost, Salvage, Life, Period, Month*)

The *Month* argument is optional. All other arguments must have a value.

Cost

A numeric value that indicates the total amount paid to acquire the asset.

Life

An integer value that indicates the number of periods that the asset will be depreciated over. For example, if you purchase a computer that will have a useful life of five years you would specify a value of 5 for the Life argument.

Period

An integer value that indicates the period that you want to calculate the depreciation for, such as 2 for the second year's depreciation amount.

Month

An optional value that indicates the number of months in the first year of depreciation. If you omit this argument, the DB function will use a value of 12, meaning that the asset will be depreciated for the entire year.

Example

Figure 12-5 shows how you can use DB to determine the annual depreciation over four years for a computer that costs $4000 and has a salvage value of $500. This example also allows you to compare the results to the depreciation amounts calculated by DDB, SLN, and SYD.

DDB

Use DDB to determine the amount of depreciation for an asset during the specified time frame. The depreciation is calculated using the double-declining balance method as a default. You can specify a different method by specifying a value for the *Factor* argument.

To Calculate

=DDB(*Cost, Salvage, Life, Period, Factor*)

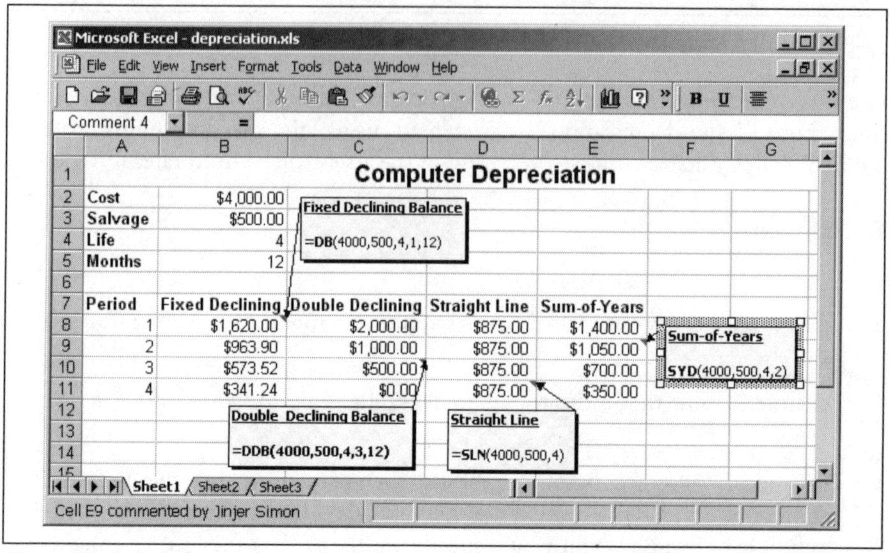

Figure 12-5: Excel provides multiple functions for determining the depreciation amount of an asset

The `Factor` argument is optional and is only required if you want to use a different factor to determine depreciation. All of the other arguments are required.

Cost

A numeric value that indicates the total amount paid to acquire the asset.

Life

An integer value that indicates the number of periods that the asset will be depreciated over. For example, if you purchase a computer that will have a useful life of five years you would specify a value of 5 for the Life argument.

Period

An integer value that indicates the period that you want to calculate the depreciation for, such as 2 for the second year's depreciation amount.

Factor

By default, the function uses a `Factor` value of 2 for double declining balance depreciation. If you want to use a different factor to calculate the depreciation for the asset you can specify the factor here.

Example

Figure 12-5 allows you to compare the depreciation amount calculated for assets using DDB to the results of DB, SYD, and SLN.

DISC

Use DISC (an Analysis ToolPak function) if you want to determine the discount rate for a security. To use this function you need to know the settlement date, the date the security matures, the face value of the security, and the redemption value.

To Calculate

=DISC(*Settlement, Maturity, PR, Redemption, Basis*)

The *Basis* argument is the only optional one. All other arguments must have values.

Example

As specified for the arguments of DISC, to determine the discount rate for a security you must know the settlement date, maturity date, cost of purchasing the security, and the amount at which the security is redeemed. Figure 12-6 illustrates how you can use this information to determine the discount rate of a security.

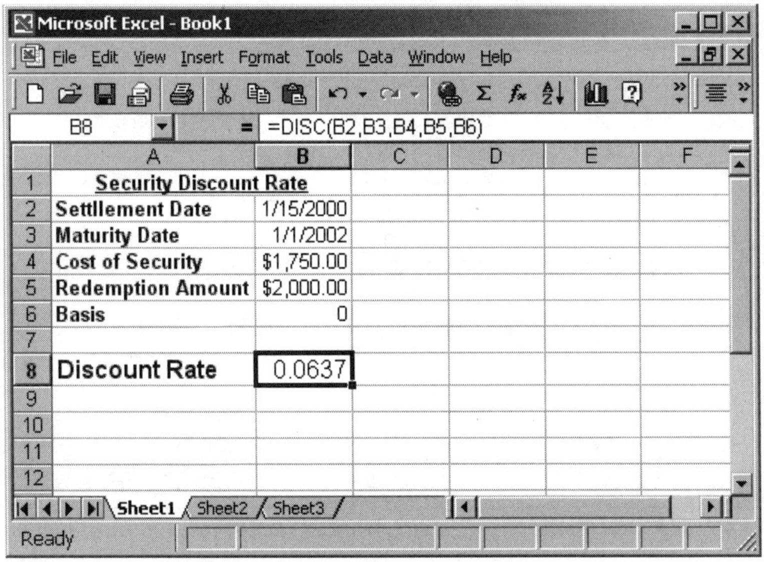

Figure 12-6: Use DISC to determine the actual discount rate on a security

DOLLARDE

DOLLARDE (an Analysis ToolPak function) allows you to convert a fractional dollar amount to a decimal amount. You can use this function to convert the price of a security, typically represented as a fractional amount, to a decimal amount that can be used for other calculations.

To Calculate

=DOLLARDE(Fractional_Dollar, Fraction)

Both of the arguments are required for this function.

Fractional_Dollar

A decimal value that indicates the whole number and numerator value (top value of the fraction). For example, if the fractional dollar amount is 1 the value of this argument will be 1.1.

Fraction

Indicates the denominator of the fraction. If the fraction is 1/2 the value of this argument is 2.

Example

As indicated earlier in this chapter, DOLLARDE works to convert a fractional amount into a decimal amount. Figure 12-7 illustrates how DOLLARDE can be used to convert a fraction into a decimal amount.

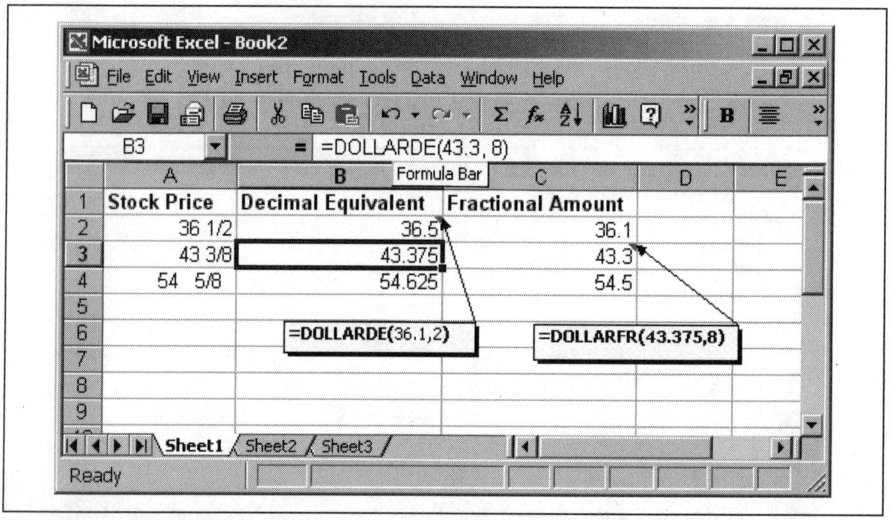

	A	B	C	D	E
	Stock Price	Decimal Equivalent	Fractional Amount		
1					
2	36 1/2	36.5	36.1		
3	43 3/8	43.375	43.3		
4	54 5/8	54.625	54.5		
5					
6		=DOLLARDE(36.1,2)	=DOLLARFR(43.375,8)		
7					
8					
9					

Microsoft Excel - Book2

File   Edit   View   Insert   Format   Tools   Data   Window   Help

B3   = =DOLLARDE(43.3, 8)

Formula Bar

Sheet1 / Sheet2 / Sheet3 /

Ready

Figure 12-7: Use DOLLARDE and DOLLARFR to convert between fractional and decimal values

NOTE *When you type a fractional amount in a cell, Excel automatically stores the value as a decimal value.*

DOLLARFR

DOLLARFR (an Analysis ToolPak function) allows you to convert a decimal dollar amount to a fractional amount.

To Calculate

```
=DOLLARFR(Fractional_Dollar, Fraction)
```

Both of the arguments are required for this function.

Decimal_Dollar
> Must be a decimal value that indicates dollar amount.

Fraction
> Indicates the denominator of the fraction. This is the value that you want to appear on the bottom of the fraction. For example, if you want the bottom of the fraction to be 8, such as 3/8 the value of the argument would be 8.

Example

Figure 12-7 shows how you can use DOLLARFR to convert a decimal value into the equivalent fractional amount.

DURATION

DURATION (an Analysis ToolPak function) allows you to determine the Macauley duration of a security. The security is assumed to have a par value of $100.

To Calculate

```
=DURATION(Settlement, Maturity, Coupon, Yld, Frequency, Basis)
```

The *Basis* argument is the only optional argument. All other arguments must have values.

Coupon
> Specifies a numeric value that represents the annual coupon rate for the security. For example, if the security has a coupon rate of 9% the value of this argument is 0.09.

Yld
> Indicates the annual yield (interest paid) of the security. The value of the argument should be a numeric value that represents the yield percentage. For example, if the security pays 5% annually, the value of this argument would be 0.05.

Example

Figure 12-8 shows how you can use DURATION to determine the duration of a security. The example allows you to see the difference between the results of this function and results returned by the other duration function, MDURATION.

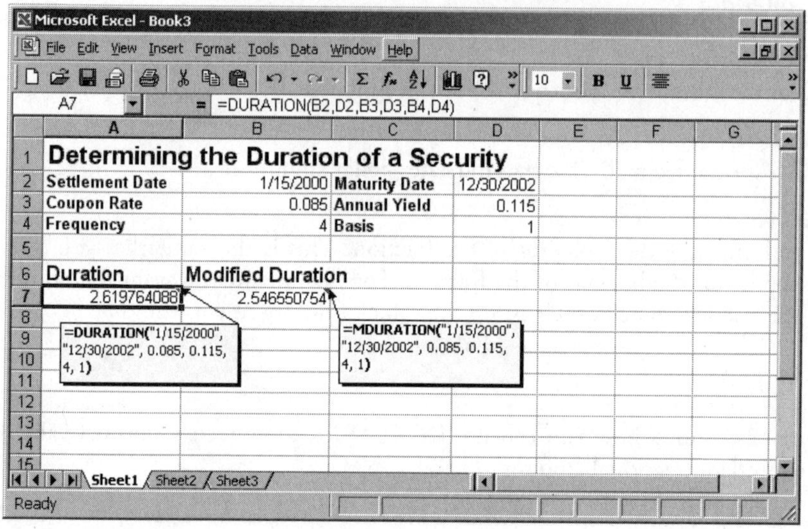

Figure 12-8: Excel provides two different functions, DURATION and MDURATION that can be used to determine the duration of a security

---

EFFECT

You can use EFFECT (an Analysis ToolPak function) to determine the effective annual interest rate for an investment. To use this function you need to know the nominal annual interest rate and the number of times that interest is compounded per year.

To Calculate

```
=EFFECT(Nominal_Rate, Npery)
```

Both arguments are required for this function.

Nominal_Rate

A numeric value that indicates the nominal interest rate for the investment. For example, if the interest rate is 10.5% the value of this argument would be 0.105.

Npery

A numeric value that indicates the number of times per year that the interest is compounded.

Example

Figure 12-9 illustrates the results of converting a 12% nominal interest rate paid monthly to the equivalent effective rate. Because the interest is compounded, it is actually a 12.68% effective rate. The example also converts a 12% effective rate to the equivalent nominal rate.

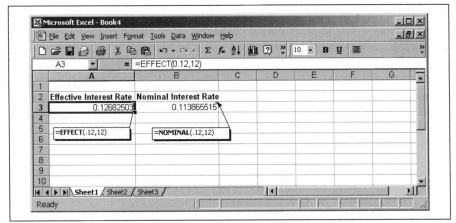

Figure 12-9: Excel provides functions for converting between the effective and nominal interest rates

FV

FV is very useful for determining the future value of an investment. This function is used with both loans and investments, such as a savings account. If you have a loan, the future value of the loan should be 0. This function is used only with investments that have both constant payments and a constant interest rate.

To Calculate

`=FV(Rate, Nper, Pmt, PV, Type)`

You must specify a value for either the *Pmt* or *PV* arguments, but you do not have to specify both. The *Type* argument is optional; the *Rate* and *Nper* arguments must have values.

Rate

Indicates the interest rate used to calculate the rate for each period. For example, if you make monthly payments and the interest rate is 12% you need to specify an interest rate of 0.01 (0.12/12) as the rate for each month.

Pmt

Indicates payment that is made for each period. For example, if you are making monthly payments of $355, that is the value of the *Pmt* argument. The value of this argument should be negative if the amounts are paid out, such as a loan or deposit in an account. If the payment is received, such as dividend checks, this argument should have a positive value. If you do not specify a value for the *Pmt* argument you must specify a value for the *PV* argument.

> **NOTE** *If you want to determine the future value of an investment with a variable or adjustable interest rate, you need to use FVSCHEDULE.*

Example

Figure 12-10 illustrates how FV can be used to determine the future value of an investment if you know the annual interest rate, number of payments, and the payment amount for each payment period. In the example, the payments were made monthly so the annual interest rate had to be converted to a monthly rate of 0.00833333 by taking the annual rate of 0.1 and dividing it by 12. This example also uses PV to determine the present value of the investment.

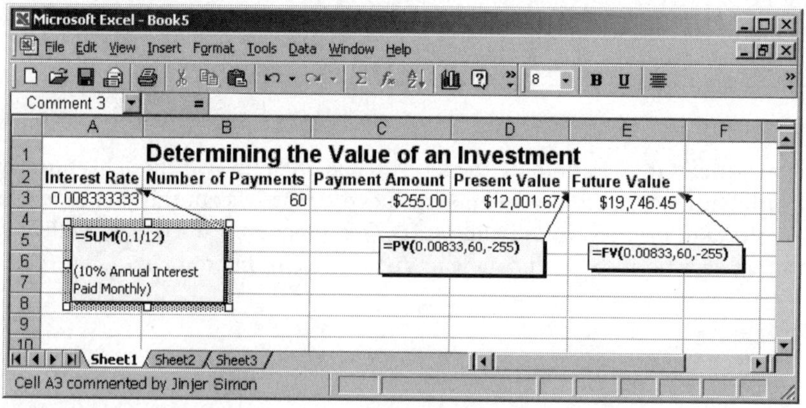

Figure 12-10: When you are determining the present or future value of an investment, the payment amount is typically negative, indicating money paid out

FVSCHEDULE

If you have an investment that has a variable rate of interest, use FVSCHEDULE (an Analysis ToolPak function) to calculate its future value. This function takes all the variable interest rates for the investment and compounds them to determine the value of the investment.

To Calculate

```
=FVSCHEDULE(Principal, Schedule)
```

You must specify values for both of the arguments.

Principal

A numeric value that specifies the current value of the investment (what it is worth today).

 The values specified for the Principal and Schedule arguments must be numeric or an error is returned. For example, if the interest rate is 10% you need to indicate that rate as a decimal value of .1.

Schedule

Specifies an array of several numeric values that indicate the different interest rates for the investment. You need to place the values inside brackets ({}) separated by commas. For example, if your investment has variable rates of 10%, 12%, 14%, and 15% you specify a *Schedule* value of {.1, .12, .14, .15}. Also, you need to specify the interest rate for each period. So if the rate is 10% for the first three years and then it changes to 12% for the final two years you need to specify a *Schedule* value of {.1, .1, .1, .12, .12}.

TIP # 78

Using Schedule with Blank Cells

The Schedule argument can reference blank cells without an error. If the cells are blank the FVSCHEDULE function assumes that the interest rate is 0 for that period.

Example

Figure 12-11 illustrates how FVSCHEDULE determines the future value of an investment that pays a variable rate of interest. Keep in mind you want to keep the interest rates specified for equal time periods. In this example, we provide an interest rate for each year.

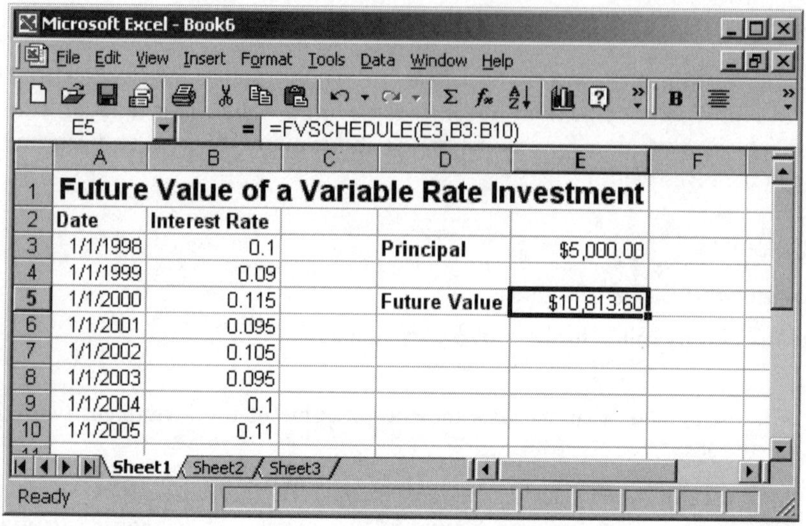

Figure 12-11: Make sure the rates are specified for equal periods of time with FVSCHEDULE

INTRATE

You can use INTRATE (an Analysis ToolPak function) to determine the interest rate on a fully invested security.

To Calculate

```
=INTRATE(Settlement, Maturity, Investment, Redemption, Basis)
```

The Basis argument is the only optional argument. All other arguments must have values.

Investment

Specifies a numeric value that indicates the total amount invested in the security.

Example

As shown in Figure 12-12, INTRATE can be used to determine the interest rate on an investment. In this example, we have a $5,000 investment that matures on 3/1/2004 and will be worth $7,500. INTRATE takes these values and determines the interest rate required to achieve a $2,500 return on that date.

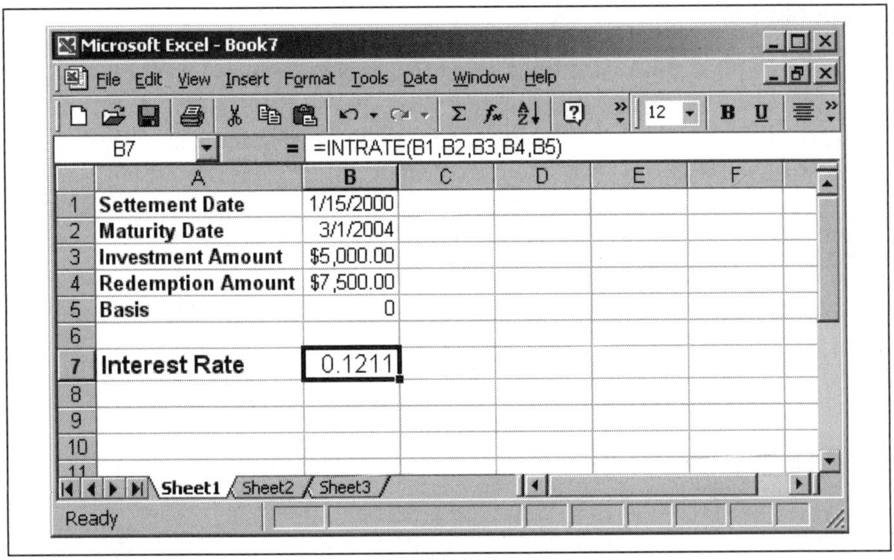

Figure 12-12: INTRATE can be used to determine the interest rate on an investment with a consistent interest rate

IPMT

Use IPMT to determine the interest payment of an investment for a specific period. This function is used with both loans and investments, such as a savings account. This function is used only with investments that have both constant payments and a constant interest rate.

To Calculate

=IPMT(*Rate*, *Per*, *Nper*, *PV*, *FV*, *Type*)

The *FV* and *Type* arguments are optional; but the *FV* argument is omitted only when calculating the interest payment for a loan. All other arguments are required for this function.

Rate

Indicates the interest rate used to calculate the rate for each period. For example, if you make monthly payments and the interest rate is 12% you need to specify an interest rate of 0.01 (0.12/12) as the rate for each month.

Per

An integer value between 1 and the value specified for the *Nper* argument indicating the period that you want to calculate the interest payment for. For example, if you want to see the amount of interest paid during the third month of a loan, the value of this argument would be 3.

Example

Figure 12-13 illustrates how IPMT is combined with PMT and ISPMT to determine the amount of each payment that is applied to principal and the interest amount. In this example, we are calculating the payments for a mortgage, so the payment amounts are negative since this is money to be paid out and not received. Also, we did not specify a future value for the functions since the future value of a loan should be 0.

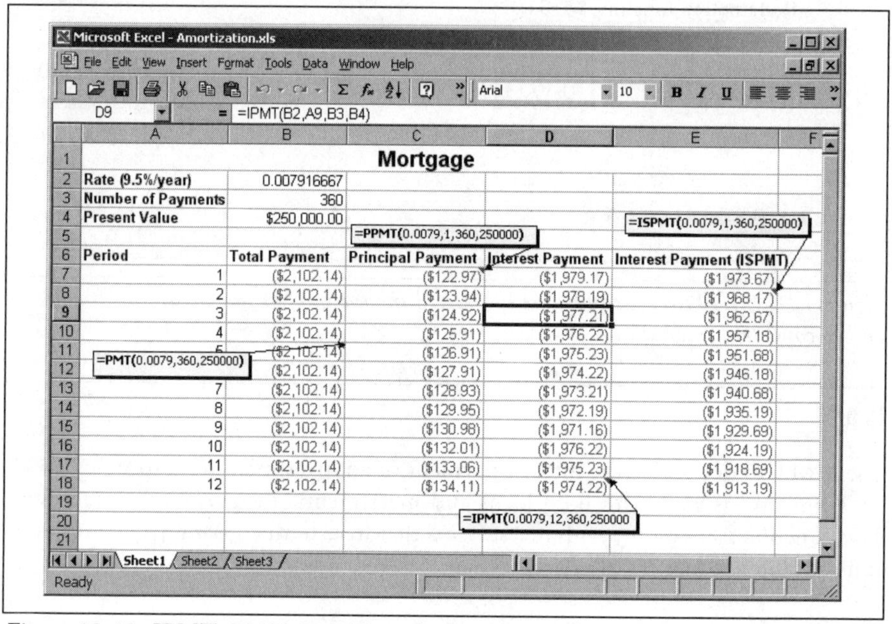

	A	B	C	D	E
1			Mortgage		
2	Rate (9.5%/year)	0.007916667			
3	Number of Payments	360			
4	Present Value	$250,000.00			
5					
6	Period	Total Payment	Principal Payment	Interest Payment	Interest Payment (ISPMT)
7	1	($2,102.14)	($122.97)	($1,979.17)	($1,973.67)
8	2	($2,102.14)	($123.94)	($1,978.19)	($1,968.17)
9	3	($2,102.14)	($124.92)	($1,977.21)	($1,962.67)
10	4	($2,102.14)	($125.91)	($1,976.22)	($1,957.18)
11	5	($2,102.14)	($126.91)	($1,975.23)	($1,951.68)
12		($2,102.14)	($127.91)	($1,974.22)	($1,946.18)
13	7	($2,102.14)	($128.93)	($1,973.21)	($1,940.68)
14	8	($2,102.14)	($129.95)	($1,972.19)	($1,935.19)
15	9	($2,102.14)	($130.98)	($1,971.16)	($1,929.69)
16	10	($2,102.14)	($132.01)	($1,976.22)	($1,924.19)
17	11	($2,102.14)	($133.06)	($1,975.23)	($1,918.69)
18	12	($2,102.14)	($134.11)	($1,974.22)	($1,913.19)

Figure 12-13: IPMT, PMT, PPMT, and ISPMT provide the ability to determine total payment and principal and interest payments for each period

IRR

You can use IRR to determine the internal rate of return for a series of cash flows. The function returns a decimal value that represents the rate of return for a payment and the income for the initial payment. To get the appropriate return value, you need to specify income amounts based on regular time intervals. For example, you can indicate the amount of income for each year.

To Calculate

```
=IRR(Values, Guess)
```

The `Guess` argument is optional.

Values

Contain a series of numbers that you want used to determine the internal rate of return. The series must contain at least one positive and one negative value. For example, to determine the rate of return for a $100 investment over five years your first value in the series would be -100 followed by five positive values indicating the interest received each year (i.e., {-100, 10, 20, 25, 40, 55}.

The series of values must be enclosed in brackets ({}) and the values must be separated with commas.

Guess

This is an optional argument that can be used to indicate your guess as to the rate of return. If this argument is omitted, Excel starts at 0.1 (10%) and tries to calculate the rate of return to be accurate within 0.00001 percent. If the IRR function cannot find an accurate result within 20 tries, an error value of #NUM! is placed in the cell.

If you get the error value, you will want to specify a value for the Guess parameter.

Example

As shown in Figure 12-14, IRR is used to determine the percentage earned on an investment. In this example, we had an initial investment of $500. This amount was entered as a negative amount since it was paid out. The amounts received during the year amounted to an 8% return on the investment.

ISPMT

ISPMT provides essentially the same results as IPMT. This function is available mainly to provide compatibility with Lotus 1-2-3. If you are exporting the worksheet to Lotus 1-2-3, consider using this function instead of IPMT.

You can use ISPMT to determine the interest payment of an investment for a specific period. This function is used with both loans and investments, such as a savings account. This function is used only with investments that have both constant payments and a constant interest rate.

To Calculate

    =ISPMT(*Rate, Per, Nper, PV*)

All arguments are required for this function.

Rate

The *Rate* argument indicates the interest rate used to calculate the rate for each period. For example, if you make monthly payments and the interest rate is 12% you need to specify an interest rate of 0.01 (0.12/12) for each month.

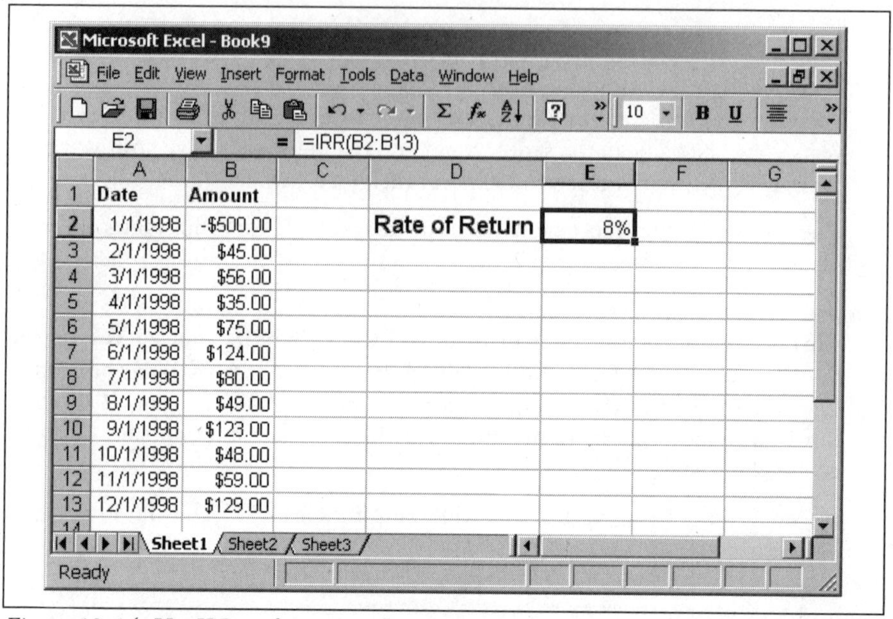

Figure 12-14: Use IRR to determine the return rate for an investment when you have a series of payments

Per

This argument needs to be a number between 1 and the value specified for the *Nper* argument indicating the period that you want to calculate the interest payment for. For example, if you want to see the amount of interest paid during the third month of a loan, the value of this argument would be 3.

Example

Figure 12-13 illustrates how ISPMT is used to determine the interest payment for an investment. ISPMT calculates a slightly different interest payment than IPMT. This is due to different time frames used to calculate interest.

MDURATION

MDURATION (an Analysis Toolpak function) allows you to determine the modified duration of a security. The security is assumed to have a par value of $100.

To Calculate

```
=MDURATION(Settlement, Maturity, Coupon, Yld, Frequency, Basis)
```

The *Basis* argument is the only optional argument. All other arguments must have values.

Coupon

Specifies a numeric value that represents the annual coupon rate for the security. For example, if the security has a coupon rate of 9% the value of this argument is 0.9.

Yld

Indicates the annual yield (interest paid) of the security. The value of the argument should be a numeric value that represents the yield percentage. For example, if the security pays 5% annually, the value of this argument would be 0.5.

Example

The DURATION function covered in this chapter has an example of using MDURATION to determine the modified duration of a security.

MIRR

MIRR provides the ability to determine the modified internal rate of return for a series of cash flows that occur on a regular schedule. This is accomplished by using not only the income amounts for the investments, but also the rate of return received when you reinvest the income. To use this function, all the income must be reinvested at the same rate.

 NOTE *If you don't intend to reinvest the returns, or they are being invested at different rates, you will need to use the IRR function to calculate the rate of return on the initial investment.*

To Calculate

=MIRR(*Values, Finance_Rate, Reinvest_Rate*)

All of the arguments are required for this function.

Values

Contains a series of numbers that you want used to determine the internal rate of return. The series must contain at least one positive and one negative value. For example, to determine the rate of return for a $100 investment over five years your first value in the series would be -100 followed by four positive values indicating the interest received each year (i.e., {-100, 10, 20, 25, 40, 55}.

The series of values must be enclosed in brackets ({}) and the values must be separated with commas.

Finance_Rate

Specifies a numeric value that represents the interest rate that is paid on the initial investment. For example, if you purchase a CD that pays 10% interest the value of the *Finance_Rate* argument is 0.1.

Reinvest_Rate
> Specifies a numeric value that represents the interest rate that is paid for reinvesting the cash flows from the initial investment.

Example

As shown in Figure 12-15, MIRR is used to determine the percentage earned on an investment. It not only considers the initially invested amount, but also assumes that you will reinvest the amounts received. In this example, we had an initial investment of $500. This amount was entered as a negative amount since it was paid out. The amounts received during the year and reinvested amounted to a 12% return on the investment.

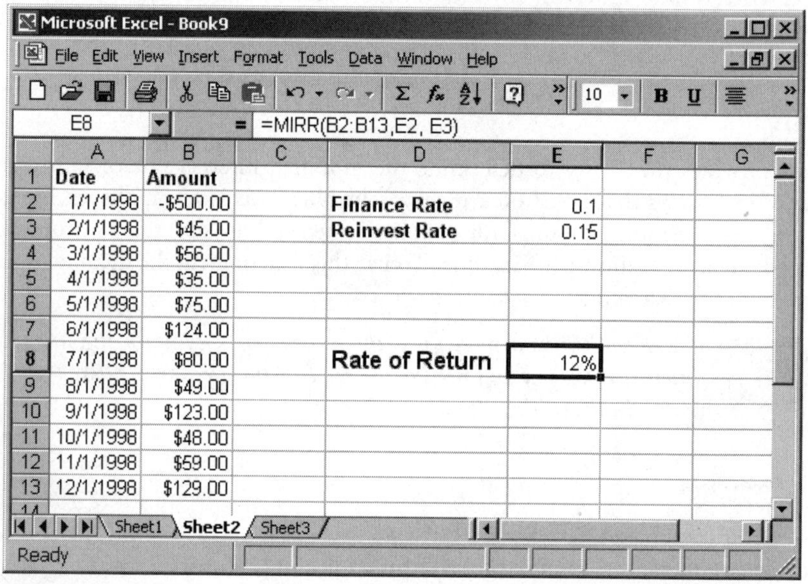

Figure 12-15: If you are reinvesting the amount received from an initial investment you can use MIRR to determine the actual return on the total investment

NOMINAL

You can use NOMINAL (an Analysis Toolpak function) to determine the nominal annual interest rate for an investment. To use this function you need to know the effective annual interest rate and the number of times the interest is compounded per year.

To Calculate

=NOMINAL(*Effect_Rate, Npery*)

Both arguments are required for this function.

Effect_Rate

> A numeric value that indicates the effective interest rate for the investment. For example, if the interest rate is 10.5% the value of this argument would be 0.105.

Npery

> A numeric value that indicates the number of times per year that the interest is compounded.

Example

The EFFECT function covered in this chapter has an example illustrating the results of converting a 12% effective interest rate with interest paid monthly to the equivalent nominal rate. Notice that because the interest is not compounded, it is actually a 11.38% nominal rate.

NPER

You can use NPER to determine how many payments are needed to reach your future value on an investment, or how many payments are needed to pay off a loan. To use this function the loan or any other type of investment must have a constant rate of interest.

To Calculate

```
=NPER(Rate, Pmt, PV, FV, Type)
```

The *FV* and *Type* arguments are optional, but the *FV* argument should only be omitted when calculating the payment for a loan. All other arguments are required for this function.

Rate

> Indicates the interest rate used to calculate the rate for each period. For example, if you make monthly payments and the interest rate is 12% you need to specify an interest rate of 0.01 (0.12/12) for each month.

Pmt

> Indicates payment that is made for each period. This amount is the payment toward principal and interest. For example, if you are making monthly payments of $355, that is the value of the *Pmt* argument. The value of this argument should be negative if the amounts are paid out, such as a loan or deposit in an account. If the payment is received, such as dividend checks, this argument should have a positive value.

Example

NPER determines the number of payments remaining on a loan, as shown in Figure 12-16. The value of the *Rate* argument was determined by taking the annual interest rate of 9.5%, expressed as a decimal value of 0.095, and dividing it by 12, as there are monthly payments made on the loan. Also, the payment amount is negative to reflect that it is a payment. Since the example is showing a loan payoff, we could have omitted the value for the *FV* argument and it would have default to 0.

 If you want to use NPER to determine the number of payments left on a loan, you need to know what the current balance is on the loan. For example, if you purchased a $25,000 car last year you want to know what the current payoff is on the loan in order to figure out how many payments are currently left.

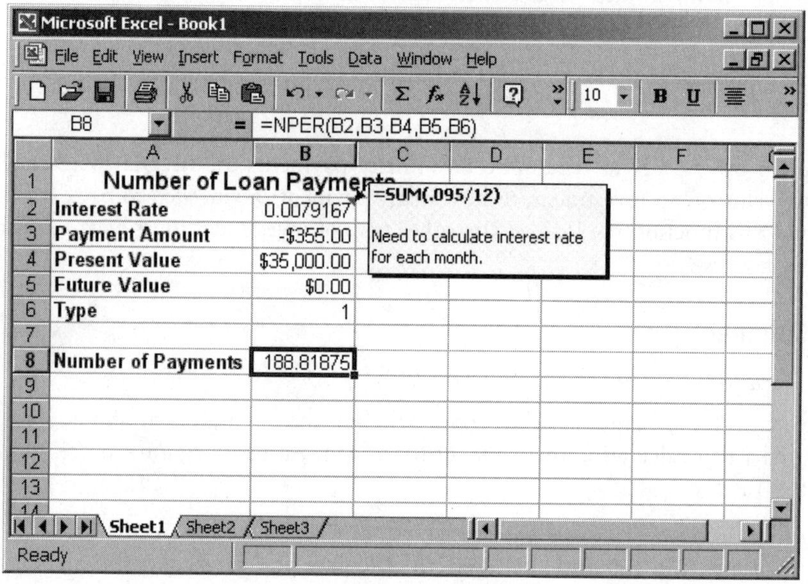

	A	B	C	D	E	F
1	Number of Loan Payments		=SUM(.095/12)			
2	Interest Rate	0.0079167				
3	Payment Amount	-$355.00	Need to calculate interest rate			
4	Present Value	$35,000.00	for each month.			
5	Future Value	$0.00				
6	Type	1				
7						
8	Number of Payments	188.81875				

B8 = =NPER(B2,B3,B4,B5,B6)

Figure 12-16: When using NPER make sure the value of the Rate argument is appropriate for the payment period

NPV

You can use NPV if you want to determine the present value for series of cash flows that are periodic. If you have a series of cash flows that do not occur on a regular schedule, you should use XNPV.

To Calculate

=NPV(*Rate*, *Value1*, *Value2*,...)

You must specify a value for the *Rate* argument and at least one *Value* argument.

Rate

Specifies a decimal value that indicates the discount rate that is applied to cash flows.

Value1, Value2, ...

You can specify up to 29 different cash flow amounts as arguments for the function. Each argument should be negative if the amounts are paid out, such as a deposit in an account. If the payment is received (income), it should have a positive value.

Example

Figure 12-17 shows how NPV can be used to determine the value of a series of cash flows. Unlike other functions, such as IRR, where multiple values are specified for one argument, NPV allows you to specify up to 29 different *Value* arguments.

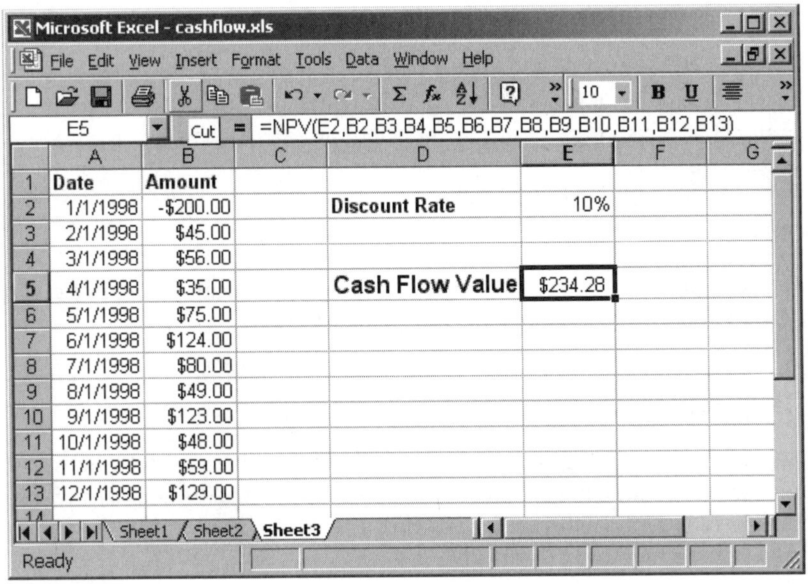

Figure 12-17: NPV should only be used with cash flows that occur periodically, such as monthly or yearly

ODDFPRICE

Use ODDFPRICE (an Analysis ToolPak function) with securities that have an abnormally long or short first period to determine the cost of the security. The cost is based on the amount the security cost for each $100 of the face value.

To Calculate

```
=ODDFPRICE(Settlement, Maturity, Issue, First_Coupon, Rate, Yld, Redemption, Frequency, Basis)
```

The *Basis* argument is the only optional argument. All other arguments must have values.

First_Coupon
> Indicates the date when the first coupon is due. The argument can be an actual date, a cell reference (e.g., A3), or the results of another function.

Rate
> Specifies a numeric value that represents the annual coupon rate for the security. For example, if the security has a coupon rate of 9% the value of this argument is 0.09.

Yld
> Indicates the annual yield (interest paid) of the security. The value of the argument should be a numeric value that represents the yield percentage. For example, if the security pays 5% annually, the value of this argument would be 0.05.

Example

Figure 12-18 illustrates how ODDFPRICE is used to determine the price of a security with an abnormally long or short first coupon period.

ODDFYIELD

You can use ODDFYIELD (an Analysis ToolPak function) to determine the interest earned (yield) on a security with a first period that is abnormally long or short. This function can be used only with a security that pays interest on a set schedule, such as monthly or annually.

 There are four different dates that must be specified for ODDFYIELD: maturity date, first coupon date, settlement date, and issue date. The function will return an error if the dates are not in the proper order. The Issue argument must specify the oldest date, followed by the First_Coupon, then Settlement, and finally Maturity.

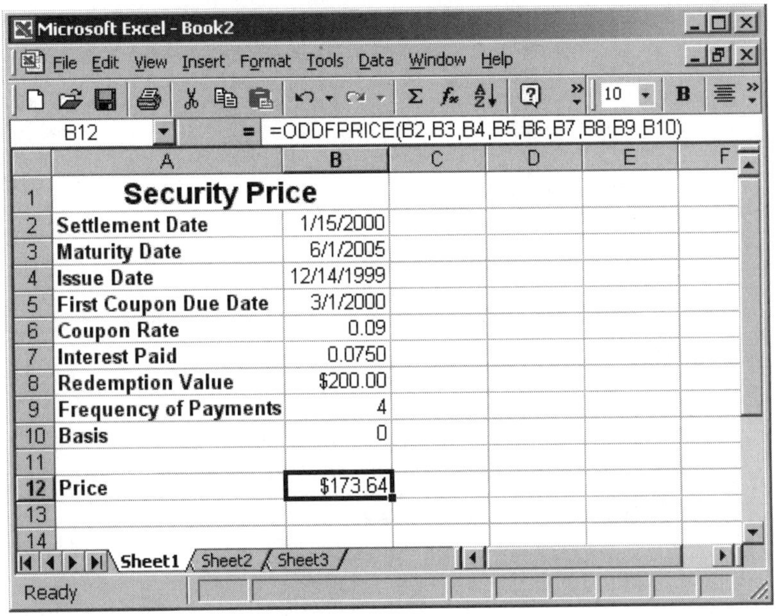

Figure 12-18: Use ODDFPRICE if the first coupon period is not the same length as the other periods

To Calculate

```
=ODDFYIELD(Settlement, Maturity, Issue, First_Coupon, Rate, PR, Redemption, Frequency, Basis)
```

The *Basis* argument is the only optional argument. All other arguments must have values.

First_Coupon
> Indicates the date when the first coupon is due. The argument can be an actual date, a cell reference (e.g., A3), or the results of another function.

Rate
> Specifies a numeric value that represents the annual coupon rate for the security. For example, if the security has a coupon rate of 9%, the value of this argument is 0.09.

Example

Figure 12-19 illustrates how ODDFYIELD is used to determine the yield of a security when the first coupon period is either longer or shorter than normal.

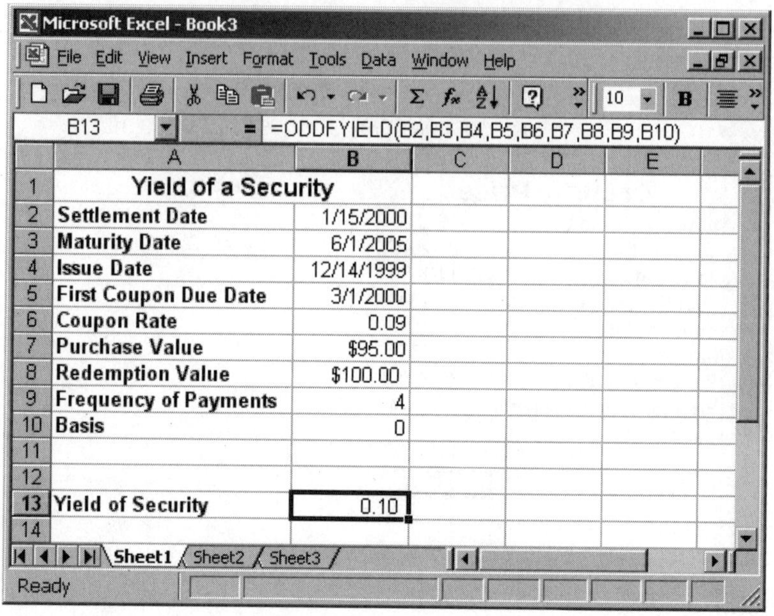

Figure 12-19: Use ODDFYIELD to determine yield for a security with an abnormally long or short first coupon period

ODDLPRICE

Use ODDLPRICE (an Analysis ToolPak function) with securities that have an abnormally long or short last period to determine the cost of the security. The cost is based on the amount the security cost for each $100 of the face value.

To Calculate

=ODDLPRICE(Settlement, Maturity, last_Interest, Rate, Yld, Redemption, Frequency, Basis)

The Basis argument is the only optional argument. All other arguments must have values.

Last_Interest

Indicates the date when the last coupon is due. The argument can be an actual date, a cell reference (e.g., A3), or the results of another function.

Rate

Specifies a numeric value that represents the annual coupon rate for the security. For example, if the security has a coupon rate of 9% the value of this argument is 0.09.

Yld

Indicates the annual yield (interest paid) of the security. The value of the argument should be a numeric value that represents the yield percentage. For example, if the security pays 5% annually, the value of this argument would be 0.05.

Example

Figure 12-20 illustrates how ODDLPRICE can be used to determine the price of a security with an abnormally long or short last coupon period.

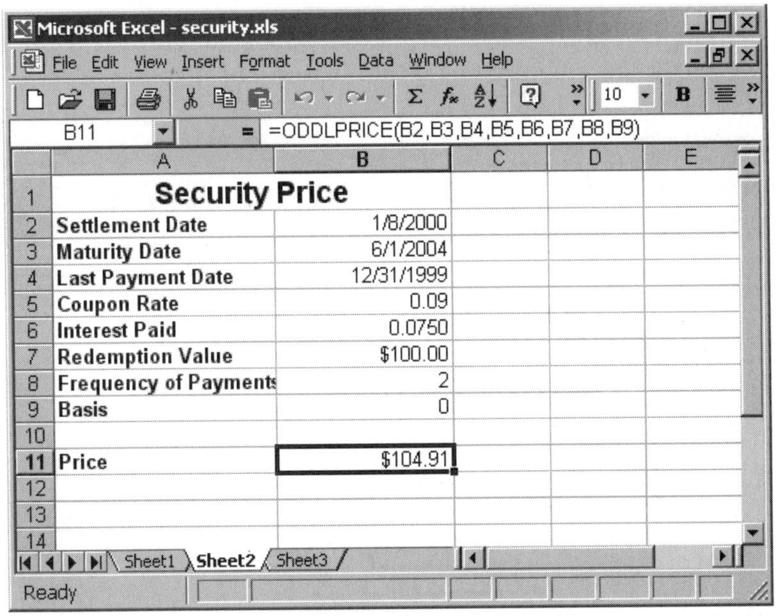

Figure 12-20: Use ODDLPRICE if the last payment period is longer or shorter than the other periods

ODDLYIELD

You can use ODDLYIELD (an Analysis ToolPak function) to determine the interest earned (yield) on a security that has a last period that is abnormally long or short. This function is used only with a security that pays interest on a set schedule, such as monthly or annually.

To Calculate

=ODDFYIELD(*Settlement, Maturity, Last_Interest, Rate, PR, Redemption, Frequency, Basis*)

The *Basis* argument is the only optional one. All other arguments must have values.

Last_Interest

Indicates the date when the last coupon is due. The argument can be an actual date, a cell reference (e.g., A3), or the results of another function.

Rate

Specifies a numeric value that represents the annual coupon rate for the security. For example, if the security has a coupon rate of 9% the value of this argument is 0.09.

Example

Figure 12-21 illustrates how ODDFYIELD can be used to determine the yield of a security when the first coupon period is either longer or shorter than normal.

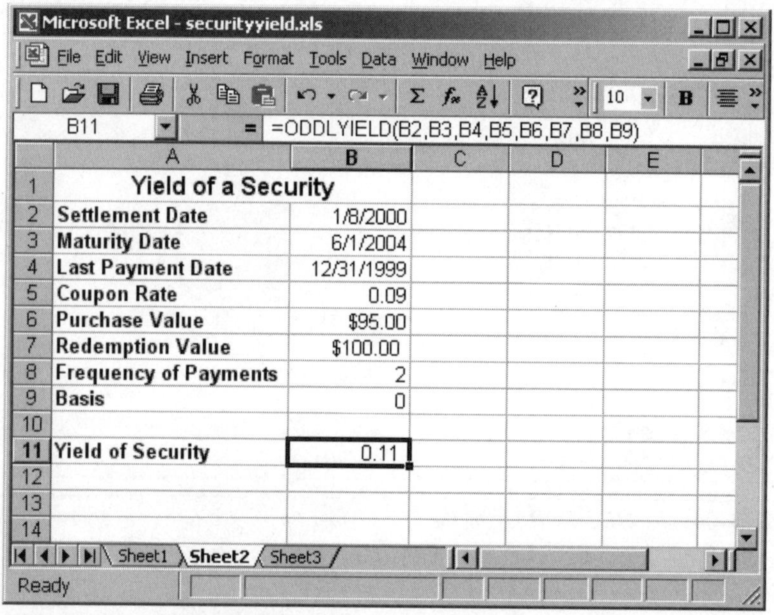

Figure 12-21: Use ODDFYIELD to determine yield for a security with an abnormally long or short first coupon period

PMT

Use PMT to determine what your payments will be on an investment. Use this function to determine payments on a loan when you want to know what amount is required to pay the loan off within the specified timeframe. To use this function, the loan must have a constant rate of interest.

To Calculate

`=PMT(Rate, Nper, PV, FV, Type)`

The *FV* and *Type* arguments are optional, but the *FV* argument should be omitted only when calculating the payment for a loan. All other arguments are required for this function.

TIP # 79

Watch Out for Those Fees and Taxes

Keep in mind that the payment amount returned by PMT does not include any taxes or fees that may also be included in the investment payment. For example, if you are dealing with a mortgage payment, typically there is an escrow payment that is charged to cover property taxes and insurance costs.

Rate
> Indicates the interest rate used to calculate the rate for each period. For example, if you make monthly payments and the interest rate is 12%, you need to specify an interest rate of 0.01 (0.12/12) as the rate for each month.

Type
> Specifies an integer value of 0 or 1 to indicate when the payment is made. If the payment is made at the beginning of the period (beginning of the month) specify a 0, otherwise specify 1 for the end of the period. If you omit this argument, it is assumed to have a value of 0.

Example

Figure 12-13 illustrates how PMT is used to determine the payment on an investment as long as you know the interest rate for each period, number of payment periods, and the present value of the investment.

PPMT

Use PPMT to determine what amount of a payment is applied to principal for any specific period. This function can be used with both loans and investments, such as a savings account. This function can only be used with investments that have both constant payments and a constant interest rate.

To Calculate

`=PPMT(Rate, Per, Nper, PV, FV, Type)`

The *FV* and *Type* arguments are optional; but the *FV* argument should only be omitted when calculating the principal amount for a loan. All other arguments are required for this function.

Rate

> Indicates the interest rate used to calculate the rate for each period. For example, if you make monthly payments and the interest rate is 12%, you need to specify an interest rate of 0.01 (0.12/12) for each month.

Per

> Specifies an integer value between 1 and the value specified for the *Nper* argument indicating the period that you want to calculate the principal payment for. For example, if you want to see the amount of principal paid during the first month of a loan, the value of this argument would be 1.

Example

The IPMT function covered in this chapter has an example illustrating how PPMT determines the amount of the total payment that is applied to the principal for a specific period.

PRICE

PRICE (an Analysis ToolPak function) is designed to allow you to determine the cost of a security per $100 of the face value. In other words, it specifies the amount it will cost for each $100 of the value of a security.

 If the last period of the security is either longer or shorter than the other periods, you need to use ODDLPRICE to calculate the price. If the first period is longer or shorter, use ODDFPRICE.

To Calculate

```
=PRICE(Settlement, Maturity, Rate, Yld, Redemption, Frequency, Basis)
```

The *Basis* argument is the only optional argument. All other arguments must have values.

Rate

> Specifies a numeric value that represents the annual coupon rate for the security. For example, if the security has a coupon rate of 9% the value of this argument is 0.09.

Yld

> Indicates the annual yield (interest paid) of the security. The value of the argument should be a numeric value that represents the yield percentage. For example, if the security pays 5% annually, the value of this argument would be 0.05.

Example

Figure 12-22 illustrates how PRICE is used to determine the cost of a security. This example allows you to compare the results of PRICE to PRICEDISC, used for a discounted security, and PRICEMAT, which provides the price of a security that pays at maturity.

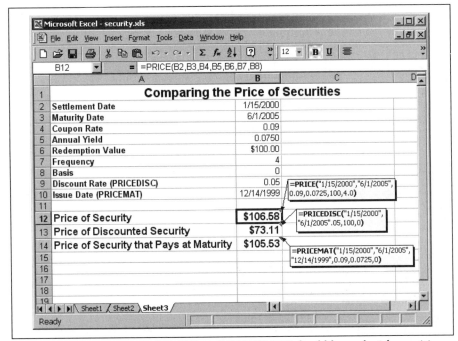

Figure 12-22: PRICE, PRICEDISC, and PRICEMAT should be used with securities that have consistent coupon periods

PRICEDISC

PRICEDISC (an Analysis ToolPak function) is designed to allow you to determine the cost of a discounted security per $100 of the face value. In other words, it specifies the amount it will cost for each $100 of the value of a security.

To Calculate

=PRICEDISC(*Settlement, Maturity, Discount, Redemption, Basis*)

The *Basis* argument is the only optional argument. All other arguments must have values.

Discount

This argument must specify a numeric value that represents the discount rate for the security. For example, if the security has a discount rate of 4.5% the value of this argument is 0.045.

Example

Figure 12-22 illustrates how the PRICEDISC function can be used to determine the cost of a discounted security.

PRICEMAT

PRICEMAT (an Analysis ToolPak function) is designed to allow you to determine the cost of a security that pays interest at maturity. The value returned by the function is based on the cost per $100 of the face value of the security.

To Calculate

=PRICEMAT(*Settlement, Maturity, Issue, Rate, Yld, Basis*)

The *Basis* argument is the only optional argument. All other arguments must have values.

Rate

Specifies a numeric value that represents the annual coupon rate for the security. For example, if the security has a coupon rate of 9% the value of this argument is 0.09.

Yld

Indicates the annual yield (interest paid) of the security. The value of the argument should be a numeric value that represents the yield percentage. For example, if the security pays 5% annually, the value of this argument would be 0.05.

Example

Figure 12-22 illustrates how PRICEMAT is used to determine the cost of a security that pays at maturity.

PV

Use PV (an Analysis ToolPak function) to determine the present value of an investment. This function is used with both loans and investments, such as a savings account. This function is used only with investments that have both constant payments and a constant interest rate.

To Calculate

```
=PV(Rate, Nper, Pmt, FV, Type)
```

You must specify a value for either the *Pmt* or *FV* arguments, but you do not have to specify both. The *Type* argument is optional, but the *Rate* and *Nper* arguments must have values.

Rate

> Indicates the interest rate used to calculate the rate for each period. For example, if you make monthly payments and the interest rate is 12% you need to specify an interest rate of 0.01 (0.12/12) for each month.

Pmt

> Indicates payment that is made for each period. For example, if you are making monthly payments of $355, that is the value of the *Pmt* argument. The value of this argument should be negative if the amounts are paid out, such as a loan or deposit in an account. If the payment is received, such as dividend checks, this argument should have a positive value. If you do not specify a value for the *Pmt* argument you must specify a value for the *FV* argument.

Example

The FV function covered in this chapter has an example illustrating how PV is used to determine the present value of an investment if you know the annual interest rate, number of payments, and the payment amount for each payment period. In the example, the payments were made monthly, so the annual interest rate had to be converted to a monthly rate of 0.008333333 by taking the annual rate of 0.1 (10%) and dividing it by 12.

RATE

Use RATE to determine the interest rate of an annuity for a specific period. RATE uses an iteration method to determine the interest rate for the annuity. If a value is not specified for the *Guess* argument, it starts with a value of 0.1 and performs 20 attempts to determine the correct interest rate.

To Calculate

```
=RATE(Nper, Pmt, PV, FV, Type, Guess)
```

You must specify a value for either the *Pmt* or *FV* arguments, but you do not have to specify both. The *FV*, *Type* and *Guess* arguments are optional, but the *Nper* and *PV* arguments must have values.

Pmt

> Indicates payment that is made for each period. For example, if you are making monthly payments of $355, that is the value of the *Pmt* argument. The *Pmt*

argument normally includes only principal and interest. If you do not specify a value for the *Pmt* argument you must specify a value for the *FV* argument.

PV   Indicates the present value of the annuity. The present value indicates the value of the annuity including the amounts of the future payments.

FV   Indicates the future value of the annuity. If you do not specify a value for the *FV* argument it is assumed to have a value of 0.

Guess

This is an optional argument that can be used to indicate your guess as to the interest rate for the annuity. You need to base your guess on the type of units specified for the *Nper* argument. For example, if you are making monthly payments on the annuity, the Guess argument needs to indicate the amount of interest charged each month. For example, if the interest rate is 12% you would specify a value of 0.01 (1%) as the value for the *Guess* argument.

If this argument is omitted, Excel starts at 0.1 (10%) and tries to calculate the rate to be accurate within 0.00001 percent. If the RATE function cannot find an accurate result within 20 tries, an error value of #NUM! is placed in the cell.

If you get the error value, you will want to specify a value for the *Guess* argument.

Example

Figure 12-23 illustrates how RATE is used to determine the interest rate that would be charged on a five-year, $5,000 loan if you want to have payments of $400.

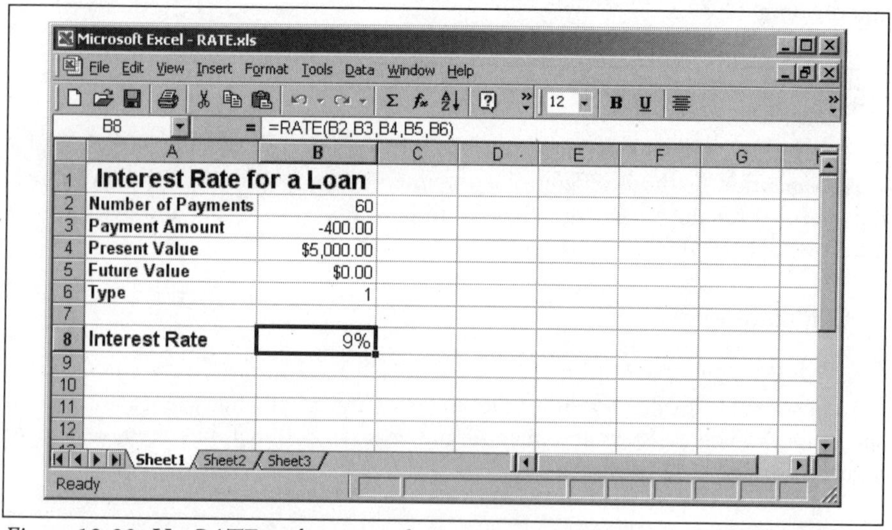

Figure 12-23: Use RATE to determine the interest rate needed to achieve the desired payments and future value

SLN

Use SLN to determine the amount of depreciation for an asset during the specified time frame. The depreciation is calculated using the straight-line depreciation method, which calculates the depreciation of the asset by spreading out the cost of the asset evenly over its useful life.

To Calculate

=SLN(*Cost*, *Salvage*, *Life*)

All arguments of this function must have a value.

Cost
Indicates the total amount paid to acquire the asset.

Life
An integer value that indicates the number of periods that the asset will be depreciated over. For example, if you purchase a computer that will have a useful life of five years you would specify a value of 5 for the *Life* argument.

Example

The DDB function covered in this chapter has an example that allows you to compare the depreciation amount calculated for assets using SLN to the results of DB, DDB, and SYD. Unlike the other depreciation functions, SLN calculates the same amount of depreciation for each depreciation period.

SYD

Use SYD to determine the amount of depreciation for an asset during the specified time frame. The depreciation is calculated using the sum-of-years digits method, which calculates the depreciation of the asset by calculating a different rate for each year.

To Calculate

=SYD(*Cost*, *Salvage*, *Life*, *Per*)

All arguments of this function must have a value.

Cost
Indicates the total amount paid to acquire the asset.

Life
An integer value that indicates the number of periods that the asset will be depreciated over. For example, if you purchase a computer that will have a useful life of five years, you would specify a value of 5 for the *Life* argument.

Per
> An integer value that indicates the period that you want to calculate the depreciation for, such as 2 for the second year's depreciation amount.

Example

Figure 12-5 allows you to compare the depreciation amount calculated for assets using SYD to the results of DB, DDB, and SLN.

TBILLEQ

You can use TBILLEQ (an Analysis ToolPak function) to determine the bond-equivalent interest earned (yield) of a Treasury Bill.

To Calculate

    =TBILLEQ(Settlement, Maturity, Discount)

All arguments must have values for this function.

Discount
> A numeric value that represents the discount rate for the Treasury Bill. For example, if the Treasury Bill has a discount rate of 4.5%, the value of this argument is 0.045.

Example

Figure 12-24 illustrates how you can use TBILLEQ to determine the bond-equivalent interest rate for a Treasury Bill. This example also shows how you can determine the face value of the Treasury Bill using TBILLPRICE and determine the yield of the Treasury Bill with TBILLYIELD.

TBILLPRICE

You can use TBILLPRICE (an Analysis ToolPak function) to determine the value of a Treasury Bill for each $100 of the face value.

To Calculate

    =TBILLPRICE(Settlement, Maturity, Discount)

All arguments must have values for this function.

Discount
> A numeric value that represents the discount rate for the Treasury Bill. For example, if the Treasury Bill has a discount rate of 4.5% the value of this argument is 0.045.

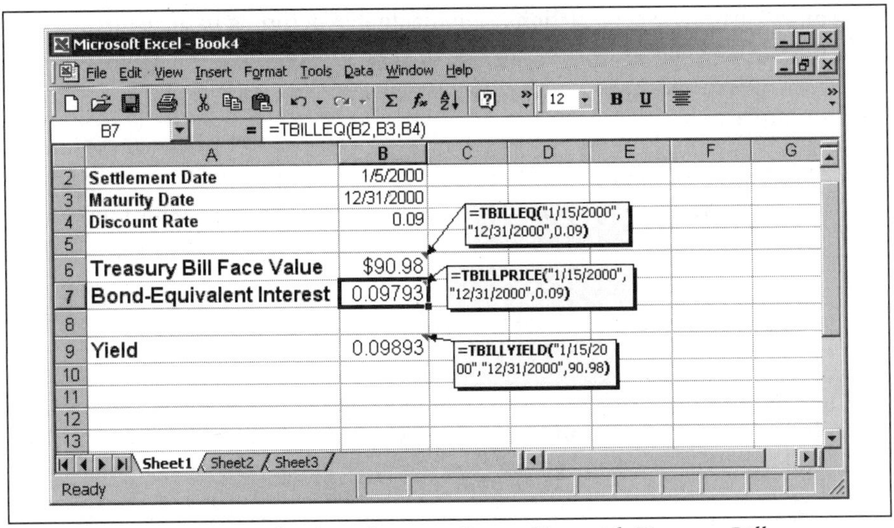

Figure 12-24: Excel provides three functions for working with Treasury Bills:
TBILLEQ, TBILLPRICE, and TBILLYIELD

Example

Figure 12-24 illustrates how you can use TBILLPRICE to determine the face value or cost of a Treasury Bill.

TBILLYIELD

You can use TBILLYIELD (an Analysis ToolPak function) to determine the interest earned (yield) on a Treasury Bill.

To Calculate

    =TBILLYIELD(Settlement, Maturity, PR)

All arguments must have values for this function.

Example

Figure 12-24 illustrates how you can use TBILLYIELD to determine the yield (actual interest earned) for a Treasury Bill. If you notice, the function uses the results of TBILLPRICE as the value for the PR argument.

VDB

You can use VDB to determine the amount of depreciation for an asset across multiple periods of time by specifying a start and end time. As a default, the function calculates the depreciation using the double-declining balance method, but you can use a different method by specifying a value for the *Factor* argument.

To Calculate

=VDB(*Cost*, *Salvage*, *Life*, *Start_Period*, *End_Period*, *Factor*, *No_Switch*)

The *Factor* and *No_Switch* arguments are optional. All other arguments must have a value.

Cost

Indicates the total amount paid to acquire the asset.

Life

An integer value that indicates the number of periods that the asset will be depreciated over. For example, if you purchase a computer that will have a useful life of five years you would specify a value of 5 for the *Life* argument.

Start_Period

An integer value that represents the starting of the period of time that you want to calculate the depreciation amount. If you want to determine the amount of depreciation for the second through the fourth year, the value of the *Start_Period* argument would be 2 and the *End_Period* argument would be 4.

> **NOTE** *If the start period or the end period you want to specify is not a complete period, you can specify a decimal value that represents the expected amount of the period. For example, if the asset was purchased halfway through the first year you would specify 0 as the value for the Start_Period argument and .5 as the value of End_Period to determine the amount of depreciation for the remainder of the year.*

End_Period

An integer value that represents the end of the period of time that you want to calculate the depreciation amount. For example, if you want to determine the amount of depreciation for the first through the fourth year, the value of the *Start_Period* argument would be 1 and the *End_Period* argument would be 4.

Factor

If omitted, VDB uses a *Factor* value of 2 for double declining balance depreciation. If you want to use a different factor to calculate the depreciation for the asset you can specify the factor here. For example, to determine the depreciation based upon 150 percent of the declining balance, you would specify a value of 1.5 for this argument.

No_Switch

If specified, this argument must have a value of either TRUE or FALSE indicating the depreciation method that should be used when the value of the depreciation amount is larger than the declining balance amount.

FALSE

> If you omit a value for the *No_Switch* argument, this is the value that Excel uses. A value of FALSE means that when the depreciation amount for an asset becomes larger than the declining balance of the asset, Excel switches to the Straight-Line depreciation method.

TRUE

> If you specify a value of TRUE, Excel does not modify the depreciation method.

Example

Figure 12-25 illustrates how VDB is used to determine the depreciation for an asset. As shown in the example, VDB provides the ability to determine several different depreciation methods by simply changing the value of the *Factor* argument. If the *Factor* argument is omitted, the function determines the depreciation using the double declining balance method.

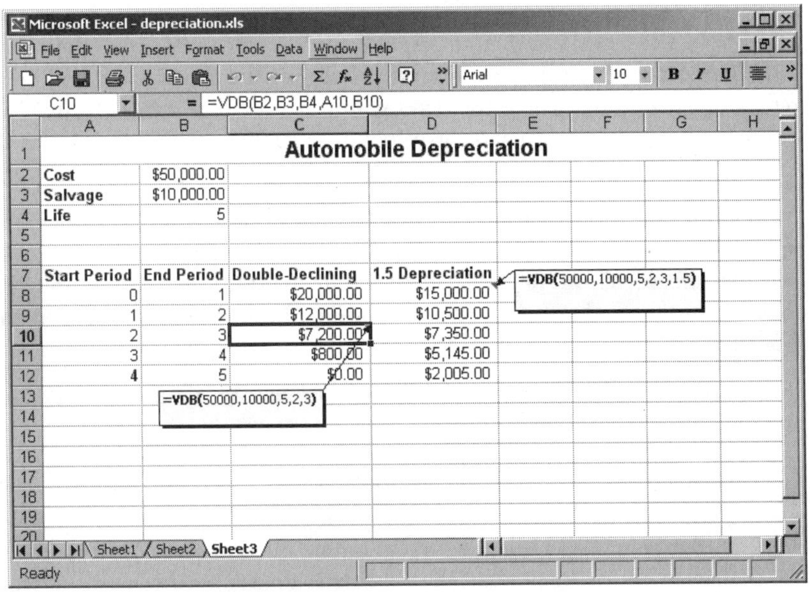

Figure 12-25: VDB provides the flexibility of specifying the factor that you want to use to determine the depreciation

XIRR

Use XIRR (an Analysis ToolPak function) to determine the internal rate of return for a series of cash flows that are not received regularly. The function returns a decimal value that represents the rate of return for a payment and the income for the initial payment. To get the appropriate return value, specify the income amounts and then the corresponding dates of the returns.

To Calculate

=XIRR(Values, Dates, Guess)

The Guess argument is optional.

Values

Contains a series of numbers that you want used to determine the internal rate of return. The series must contain at least one positive and one negative value. For example, to determine the rate of return for a $100 investment over five years your first value in the series would be -100 followed by positive values indicating the amount of interest received during the investment period (i.e., {-100, 10, 20, 15, 20, 30, 55}.

The series of values must be enclosed in brackets ({}) and the values must be separated with commas.

Dates

Contains a series of dates that correspond to the return values specified for the Values argument. Keep in mind that if you specify the actual dates, and not cell references, you must enclose the dates within quotes. The series of values must be enclosed in brackets ({}) and the values must be separated with commas.

Guess

An optional argument that can be used to indicate your guess as to the rate of return. If this argument is omitted, Excel starts at 0.1 (10%) and tries to calculate the rate of return to be accurate within 0.00001 percent. If the XIRR function cannot find an accurate result within 100 tries, an error value of #NUM! is placed in the cell.

If you get the error value, you will want to specify a value for the Guess argument.

Example

Figure 12-26 shows how XIRR is used to determine the rate of return for a series of cash flows that do not occur periodically. The dates do not need to occur at regular intervals with this function.

XNPV

You can use XNPV (an Analysis ToolPak function) to determine the present value for series of cash flows that are not periodic. If you have a series of cash flows that are periodic (occur on a regular schedule, such as monthly) you should use NPV.

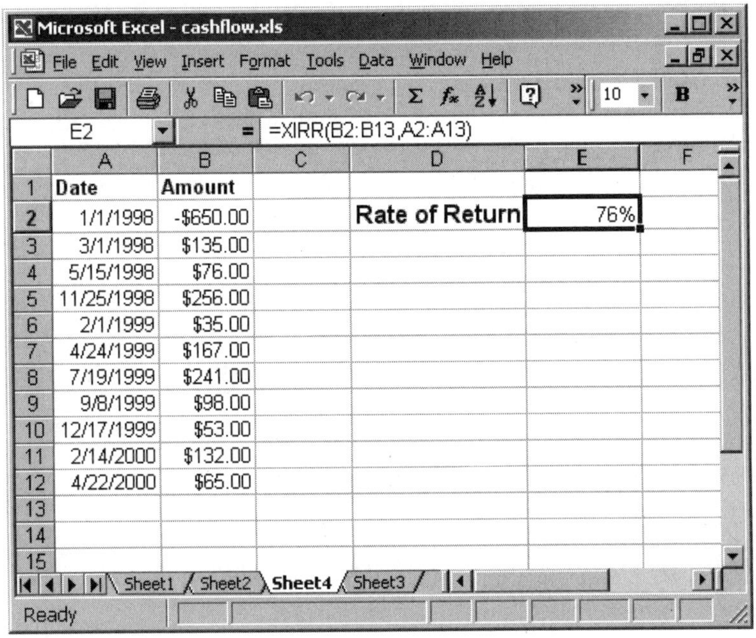

Figure 12-26: XIRR can be used to determine the rate of return for a series of cash flows that do not occur at regular intervals

To Calculate

=XNPV(*Rate*, *Values*, *Dates*)

All of the arguments are required for this function.

Rate
> Specifies a decimal value that indicates the discount rate that is applied to cash flows.

Values
> Contains a series of numbers that specify the cash flows that correspond to the dates specified for the *Dates* argument. If desired, you can specify the first payment, typically the cost of the investment, as the first value in the series. For example, if you invested $4,000 you could specify an initial value of -4000, which represents the initial cost. All remaining cash flow amounts would by positive to show interest earned on the investment.

> The series of values must be enclosed in brackets ({}) and the values must be separated with commas.

Dates
> Contains a series of dates that correspond to the cash flow values specified for the *Values* argument. Keep in mind that if you specify the actual dates, and not

cell references, you must enclose the dates within quotes. The series of values must be enclosed in brackets ({}) and the values must be separated with commas.

Example

Figure 12-27 illustrates how XNPV can be used to determine the value of a series of cash flows that do not occur at regular intervals.

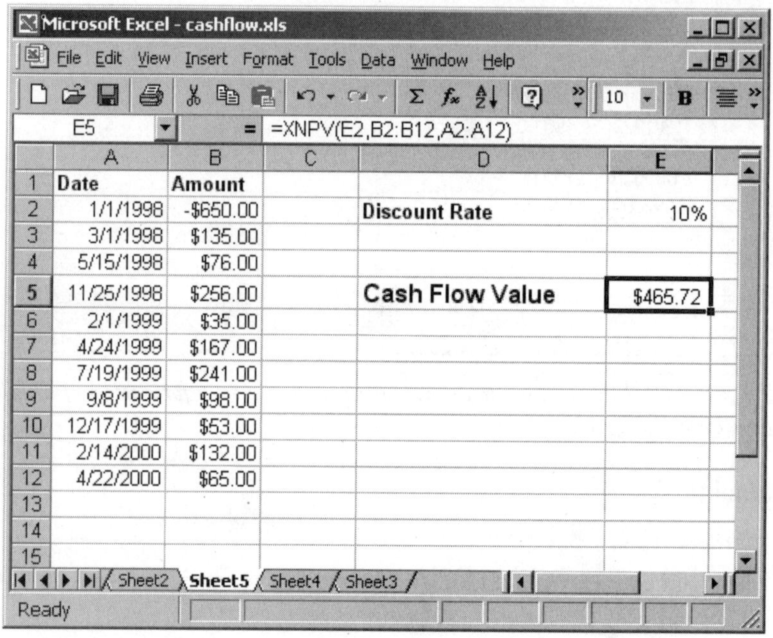

Figure 12-27: Use XNPV with cash flow values that are not periodic

YIELD

You can use YIELD (an Analysis ToolPak function) to determine the interest earned (yield) on a security. This function can only be used with a security that pays interest on a set schedule, such as monthly or annually.

To Calculate

```
=YIELD(Settlement, Maturity, Rate, PR, Redemption, Frequency, Basis)
```

The *Basis* argument is the only optional argument. All other arguments must have values.

NOTE *If the last period of the security is either longer or shorter than the other periods, you need to use the ODDLYIELD function to calculate the yield. If the first period is longer or shorter, use the ODDFYIELD function.*

Rate

Specifies a numeric value that represents the annual coupon rate for the security. For example, if the security has a coupon rate of 9% the value of this argument is 0.09.

Example

Figure 12-28 illustrates how YIELD can be used to determine the yield (interest paid) on a security. This example also compares the results of YIELD with YIELD-DISC and YIELDMAT.

Financial
Functions

	A	B	C	D	E
1	**Comparing the Yield of Securities**				
2	Settlement Date	1/15/2000			
3	Maturity Date	6/1/2005			
4	Coupon Rate	0.09			
5	Purchase Value	$95.00			
6	Redemption Value	$100.00			
7	Frequency of Payments	2			
8	Basis	1			
9	Issue Date (YIELDMAT)	12/14/1999	=YIELD("1/15/2000","6/1/2005", 0.09,95,100,2,1)		
10					
11	**Yield of Security**	0.10	=YIELDDISC("1/15/2000", "6/1/2005",95,100,1)		
12	**Yield of Discounted Security**	0.0098			
13	**Yield of Security that Pays at Maturity**	0.104			
14					
15			=YIELDMAT("1/15/2000","6/1/2005", "12/14/1999",0.09,95,1)		
16					

B11 = =YIELD(B2,B3,B4,B5,B6,B7,B8)

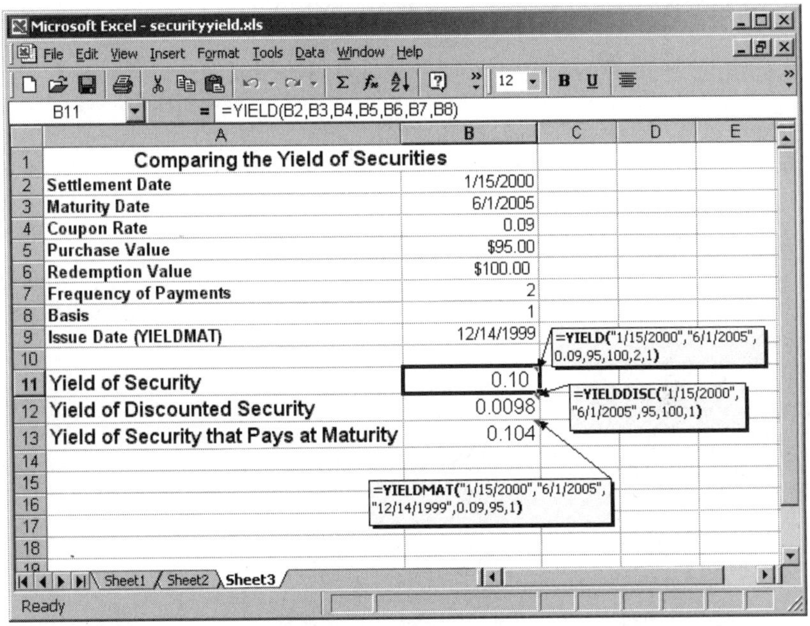

Figure 12-28: YIELD, YIELDDISC, and YIELDMAT should be used with securities that have consistent coupon payments

YIELDDISC

You can use YIELDDISC (an Analysis ToolPak function) to determine the interest earned (yield) on a discounted security. This function can only be used with a security that pays interest on a set schedule, such as monthly or annually.

To Calculate

```
=YIELDDISC(Settlement, Maturity, PR, Redemption, Basis)
```

The *Basis* argument is the only optional argument. All other arguments must have values.

Example

Figure 12-28 illustrates how YIELDDISC can be used to determine the yield of a discounted security.

YIELDMAT

You can use YIELDMAT (an Analysis ToolPak function) to determine the interest earned (yield) on a security that pays interest at maturity.

To Calculate

```
=YIELDMAT(Settlement, Maturity, Issue, Rate, PR, Basis)
```

The *Basis* argument is the only optional argument. All other arguments must have values.

Rate

Specifies a numeric value that represents the annual coupon rate for the security. For example, if the security has a coupon rate of 9% the value of this argument is 0.09.

Example

Figure 12-28 illustrates how YIELDMAT can be used to determine the yield of a security that pays interest at maturity.

Chapter 13

Date and Time Functions

Virtually every worksheet you create uses at least one value relating to a specific time frame. Typically worksheets are used to display information such as the number of sales for the last year or monthly expenses. The time and date functions covered in this chapter allow you to work with these values more effectively. These functions, for instance, let you perform calculations that determine the number of days between payments, or show how many days are between one payday and the next. Since Excel obtains the date and time information from your system, make sure the date and time on your PC are accurate. The following functions are covered in detail later in this chapter. The "AT" represents those functions that exist only by loading the Analysis Toolpak. See Chapter 11, *Working with Functions*, for details.

Date and Time Functions

DATE	MONTH	WEEKDAY
DATEDIF	NETWORKDAYS *AT*	WEEKNUM *AT*
DATEVALUE	NOW	WORKDAY *AT*
DAY	SECOND	YEAR
DAYS360	TIME	YEARFRAC *AT*
HOUR	TIMEVALUE	SECOND
MINUTE	TODAY	

Use these functions to do the following:

- Build a date using values from other cells

- Determine the time interval between two different dates

- Determine the numeric value used by Excel to store a specific date or time value

- Manipulate date and time values to return specific portions such as month or hour value

- Determine the number of days between two dates for accounting purposes

- Determine the day of the week on which a specific date falls

- Use the current date and time in your worksheet; the values are updated each time the worksheet is opened

How Excel Stores Dates and Times

Before delving into the various functions Excel provides for working with date and time values, it is important that you understand how Excel stores the date and time values you place in worksheets.

Excel stores all dates as sequential numbers, also referred to as serial numbers. For example, January 13, 1987 is actually stored as 31790, which also means (if you are using the default Windows calculation) there are 31,790 days between January 1, 1900 and January 13, 1987. By the same token, because all times are actually a portion of a date, they are stored as decimal fractions. For example, 0.5 is 12:00 noon. The decimal number returned by TIME is a value ranging from 0 to 0.99999999, so it represents the times from 0:00:00 (12:00:00) midnight to 23:59:59 (11:59:59 PM). Because dates and times are numeric values instead of strings, they can be added, subtracted, and included in other calculations.

Excel calculates all dates and times based on the Gregorian calendar (or as it is more commonly known, "Western"). By using this calendar, Excel recognizes that the first month of the year (January to the English-speaking world) always has 31 days and that February has 28 days, except for the years that are divisible by 4 (known as leap years), which have 29 days. All remaining months of the year have 30 or 31 days and follow the calendar's normal order. For example, March has 31 days and the next month, April, has 30 days. Keep in mind that for end-of-century years (e.g., 2000) the year must be divisible by 400 in order to be a leap year; so 2000 is a leap year but 2100 is not.

> **NOTE** *Excel for Windows calculates dates based on a 1900 date system. Therefore, 1/1/1900 is interpreted as 1 and the last date, December 31, 9999, is interpreted as 2958465. On the other hand, Excel for Macintosh stores dates based on a 1904 date system, where 1/1/1904 has a value of 1 and the final date of 12/31/9999 has a value of 2957003.*

What About Two-Digit Years?

It may seem as though the only way to ensure the proper translation of a date is to enter all four digits of the year. But in fact, Excel does have built-in measures for handling two-digit dates—you just need to understand what the measures are.

Excel allows two-digit dates to be entered in the format of 12/24/89. When a two-digit year is encountered, it is interpreted as follows:

- All two-digit years between 00 and 29 are interpreted as the years 2000 through 2029.

- All two-digit years between 30 and 99 are interpreted as the years 1930 and 1999.

Excel 2000 can handle two-digit years. However, it is wise to avoid using them because your worksheet is formatted for two-digit years. If you export the data in a text format (*.txt* or *.csv*), only the two-digit portion of the year is exported. For example, a date of 2/23/10 is interpreted as February 23, 2010 in Excel 2000, but it could be interpreted as February 23, 1910 in another application.

> *The DATE function does not follow the two-digit Excel rule when creating dates. If you specify a year value that is less than three digits, Excel adds that year value to 1900 to create the year portion of the date. See the DATE function section later in this chapter for details.*

Date and Time Formatting

Although Excel stores all dates and times internally as numeric values, it attempts to display these values in a format that is easy for the user to interpret. When you use most of the functions in this chapter you will see that by default Excel formats the value returned by the function to correspond to the default date or time format. For example, instead of the Time function returning a value of 0.75 it formats the cell as a time and displays a value of 6:00 PM.

The default time and date formats are actually controlled by the Regional Options dialog of the Windows Control Panel. You can locate this by selecting Start → Settings → Control Panel → Regional Options. You can make modifications to these settings by selecting the Date and Time tabs on the Regional Settings dialog as shown in Figure 13-1. For example, you may want to change the character used to separate months, days, and years from a slash (/) to a dash (-). The default date and time formats are based on your country settings. For example, if you are in the United States, the default date setting is *mm/dd/yyyy*. In the United Kingdom the default setting is *dd/mm/yyyy*.

Also by default, Excel right-justifies all dates and times within a cell. You can change this setting by selecting one of the alignment buttons on the toolbar (Align Left, Center, or Align Right) or by selecting Format → Cells and changing the cell alignment on the Alignment tab of the Format Cell dialog. For more information refer to Chapter 7, *Format*.

If desired, you can specify both a date and a time value within the same cell. If you manually type the values in the cell, the date and time must be separated by a space so that Excel does not mistake the information as text. For example, 12/25/1999 11:45 AM. Although a cell can have a date and time in it, you can format the cell so one value or the other is hidden. The default format for date and time is *mm/dd/yyyy hh:mm*. When you type a date and time value in a cell, the default format is applied. You can change the formatting for the cell by selecting Format → Cell and then selecting from the list under the Date or Time category. You will see that both the Date and Time categories have formatting that can be applied to a cell that contains both a date and a time value. By the same token, you can eliminate the display of the date or time by simply changing the cell formatting.

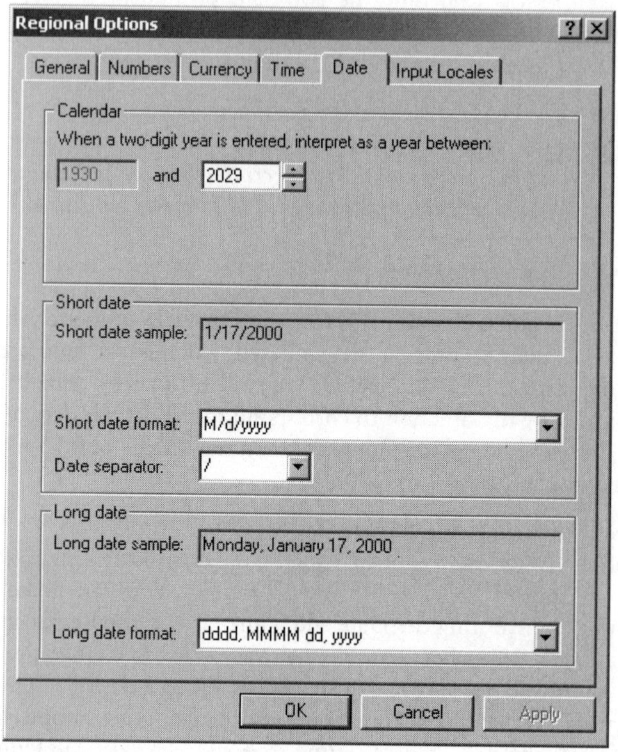

Figure 13-1: Use the Regional Options dialog to modify the default format used to display dates and times within Excel

Make sure you leave a space between the actual time and the time of day. Remember, if you don't specify AM or PM, Excel bases the time you specify on a 24-hour clock.

The Date and Time Functions

Excel provides several different functions for dealing with date values, but only four functions for working with time values (Time, Hour, Minute, and Second). However, because these functions all deal with dates and times, determining which function is appropriate and when is a bit daunting. The functions alphabetically detailed later in this chapter are best categorized as follows.

To create date or time values:

> DATE (Creates a date using the specified year, month, and day values)
> TIME (Creates a time using the specified hour, minute, and second values)

To return portions of the values in the DATE function:

YEAR (determines the year portion of the specified date)
MONTH (determines the month portion of the specified date)
DAY (determines the day portion of the specified date)

To return portions of the values in the TIME function:

HOUR (determines the hour portion of the specified time)
MINUTE (determines the minute portion of the specified time)
SECOND (determines the second portion of the specified time)

To return the current date and time from the system:

NOW (returns the date and time)
TODAY (returns the date only)

To view serial numbers as dates or times:

DATEVALUE (convert serial number to a date)
TIMEVALUE (convert serial number to a time)

To calculate date values using starting and ending dates:

DAYS360 (calculates Days based on 360 days a year)
DATEDIF (calculates DATE values)
NETWORKDAYS (calculates workdays)

To calculate date values without starting and ending dates:

WEEKDAY (returns the day of the week)
WORKDAY (returns the number of workdays)

Specifying a Date or Time Value for a Function

Most of the functions covered in this chapter require you to specify either a date or a time value as at least one of the values for the function. Because Excel is a so flexible, there are actually four different methods that you can use to create the date or time values.

- You can specify an actual date or time, such as 12/14/1999 or 3:45 PM as a value for one of these functions. If you specify the actual date or time, it must be placed inside double quotation marks. For example, =DATEDIF("6/15/1999", "11/14/1999", "d").

- You can reference a value in another cell, such as DATE(A1, A2, A3). The values in the cells need to be in the format required by the function argument. For example, the DATE function requires integer values for the Hour, Month, and Day arguments.

- With most functions you can use another function to return the desired date or time. The NOW and TODAY functions work well for getting the current date and time from the system. For example, you can determine how many days are between the current day (now) and Christmas by combining the NOW function with the DATEDIF function; such as, DATEDIF(NOW(), 12/25/2000, "d").

- A serial number for the date or time value is another method. For example, 35995.75 returns a date and time of 7/19/98 6:00 PM.

Recurring Arguments

The following arguments are available on a recurring basis in many of the functions discussed in this chapter. If differences in the implementation exist in a particular function, they will be explained within the individual function's section.

End_Date

This date must be after the date specified as the Start_Date argument, or again Excel will return an error. You can use a cell reference (e.g., F1) that contains a date or even a calculated date from a function.

Serial_Number

This argument specifies a valid date or time value. The argument can be an actual date, a cell reference (e.g., A3), or the results of another function.

Start_Date

This date must be prior to the date specified as the End_Date argument, or Excel returns an error value of #NUM!. You can use a cell reference (e.g., A3) that contains a date or even a calculated date from a function.

DATE

Use this function to create an actual date by combining year, month, and day values. In order to use this function you must specify all three arguments (Year, Month, and Day); if you omit one, Excel returns an error. When you use this function you can either type in the values for the year, month, and day, such as 12/14/1999 or you can get the values for the Year, Month, and Day arguments from different cells and create a date such as Date(A1, A2, A3). Cell A1 contains the year value, A2 contains the month value, and A3 contains the day value.

 NOTE *The value that you specify for the Month or Day argument of DAY must be an integer between –32,768 and 32,766. If the value is positive, that number of days or months is added to the date. If the value is negative Excel subtracts the specified value from the date.*

To Calculate

=DATE(Year, Month, Day)

The following arguments are required:

Year

Although Excel will accept a year value of one to four digits (between 0 and 9999), I would recommend always specifying a four-digit year to ensure you get the proper date. As outlined in Table 13-1, DATE interprets a two-digit year differently than Excel does when it is typed directly into a worksheet. For example, if you type the date 12/23/01 into a cell of your worksheet, Excel interprets the date as December 23, 2001; if you have the function DATE(01, 12, 23), Excel returns the date December 23, 1901, and formats it based on the cell's current formatting.

Also, be aware of the differences in the values expected if you use the 1904 date system versus the 1900 date system (the Excel standard).

Table 13-1: Excel's Interpretation of Year Values

Year Value	Excel's Interpretation
0 to 1899	Excel adds the year value to 1900 to calculate the year. For example, =DATE(105,4,5) returns the date April 5, 2005.
	Note: With the 1904 date system the values need to be between 4 and 1899.
1900 to 9999	Excel uses the specified value as the year.
	Note: With the 1904 date system the values need to be between 1904 and 9999.
Less than 0 or greater than 10,000	Excel returns the #NUM! error value.
	Note: With the 1904 date system the error value is returned for any value less than 4.

Month

Since each year has exactly 12 months, if you specify a value of 13 for the *Month* argument, Excel adds 1 to the value of the *Year* argument and returns a value of 1 for the *Month* argument.

Day

Excel determines the number of days that should be in the day value based upon the value of the Month argument. For example, if you have specified 5 for the month Excel will base the month on 31 days, since the month of May has 31 days. If the value specified for the *Day* argument is greater than the actual number of days in the specified month, the *Day* argument is calculated by adding one to the month value and subtracting that months' number of days from the day value until the appropriate day value is identified. For example, if the *Month* argument is 2 (February), but the *Day* argument is 45, the new *Month* argument becomes 3 and the *Day* argument becomes 17 (45 - 28). You subtract 28 days since the month of February has 28 days, and return a date of March 17.

Example

DATE is most useful when you need to build a date based on values in other cells of your worksheet. As indicated in the descriptions of the *Month* and *Day* arguments, Excel converts the values of *Month* and *Day* arguments to determine the actual date. Figure 13-2 illustrates how DATE converts 34 days, 15 months, and the year 1984 into April 3, 1985. Cell E3 shows the serial number of 31140 that is used by Excel to store the date based upon the 1900 date system.

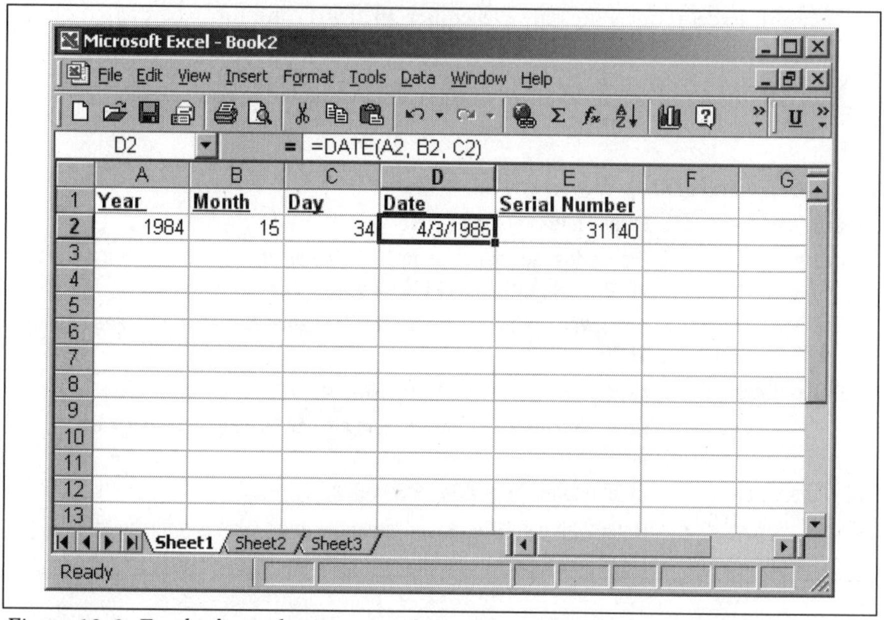

Figure 13-2: Excel adjusts the year, month, and day values to create a valid date

---

TIP # 80

Format Cells to Show Four-Digit Years

Make sure you format cells with dates that show all four digits for the year. It can be confusing for someone looking at your worksheet to determine if 4/13/10 is April 13, 1910 or April 13, 2010. Remember, if you pass a two or three-digit year value to DATE, Excel adds 1900 to that value to create the actual year value. So if you specify =DATE(10,4,13), Excel returns the date April 13, 1910. Whereas, if you type the date 4/13/10 directly into a cell, Excel interprets that date as April 13, 2010.

DATEDIF

If you need to figure out the number of months, days, or years between two different dates, you should consider using DATEDIF. For example, you can quickly determine the number of days that exist between today and the end of the year using this function and NOW by specifying =DATEDIF(NOW(), "12/31/2000", "d").

 Although DATEDIF is supported by Excel, you will not find it listed on the Paste Function dialog that displays when you select Insert → Function. This function was included to provide compatibility with Lotus 1-2-3. To use this function, you need to type the function in the formula bar. For more information on manually typing formulas, refer to Chapter 11.

To Calculate

=DATEDIF(*Start_Date*, *End_Date*, *Unit*)

You must specify values for all three arguments of this function.

Unit

Use one of the six values listed in Table 13-2 to return the number of days, months, or years between the two dates. For example, to return the number of days between the two dates and ignore the year value you should use a value of "yd". Make sure you place the values inside quotes, as indicated in the table.

Table 13-2: Acceptable DATEDIF Unit Values

Value	Description
"m"	Returns the number of complete months between the *Start_Date* and the *End_Date*.
	Remember, if there is not a complete month between the two dates, Excel will return a value of 0.
"d"	Returns the number of complete days between the two dates.
"y"	Returns the number of complete years between the two dates.
	Remember, Excel calculates the year value based on the entire date. If there is not a complete year between the two dates, a value of 0 is returned.
"ym"	Returns the number of months between the two dates, ignoring the day and year values.
	For example, if the first date is 4/3/1999 and the second date is 6/1/2000 Excel returns a value of 2 even though it has really been a year and two months.
"yd"	Returns the number of days between the two dates, ignoring the year value. Excel assumes that both dates occurred within the same year.
	For example, if the first date is 3/1/1998 and the second date is 9/6/1999 Excel returns a value of 189 days.
"md"	Returns the number of days between the two dates, ignoring the month and year values.
	For example, if the first date is 6/14/1999 and the second date is 7/17/1999 Excel returns a value of 3 because there are 3 days between 14 and 17.

Since Excel treats all dates as serial numbers, you do not need to use DATEDIF to find the number of days between two dates. You can simply subtract one date from the other (= "11/24/2000" – 3/31/2000").

Example

Figure 13-3 shows how you can determine the number of days that have elapsed by using DATEDIF to compare the date in a cell to the current date passed by using NOW.

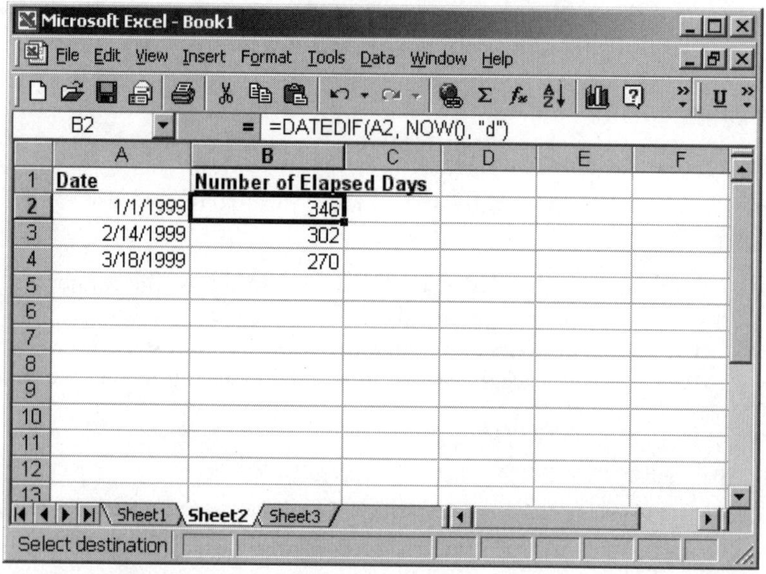

	A	B	C
	Date	**Number of Elapsed Days**	
2	1/1/1999	346	
3	2/14/1999	302	
4	3/18/1999	270	

B2 = =DATEDIF(A2, NOW(), "d")

Figure 13-3: DATEDIF calculates the number of days between the date in the specified cell (A2) and the current date (12/15/1999) returned by NOW

TIP # 81

The DATEDIF Rounding Feature

When you use DATEDIF to determine the number of months between two dates using the "m" value, Excel also looks at the day portion of the date. If there is not a complete month between two dates, such as 11/27/1999 and 12/2/1999, Excel returns a value of 0. The same holds true for comparing years; there must be at least a complete year between the two dates, or a value of 0 will be returned.

DATEVALUE

Unlike the other date functions, DATEVALUE is one that you will rarely use. Probably the only time you will need this function is if you import data from a framesystem. Then DATEVALUE allows you to convert the text dates into the appropriate date value for Excel.

This function allows you to determine the serial number Excel uses to store a date. Since Excel stores all dates as serial numbers, you can easily determine the serial number by formatting the cell as a general number (Format → Cells → Number → General).

To Calculate

=DATEVALUE(Date_Text)

Date_Text
This value can be any date in the range of 1/1/1900 and 12/31/9999. Unlike most other date and time functions, DATEVALUE does *not* accept a cell reference for the date value. You must type in the actual date value.

Example

DATEVALUE is used to determine the numeric value of a date value, as shown in Figure 13-4.

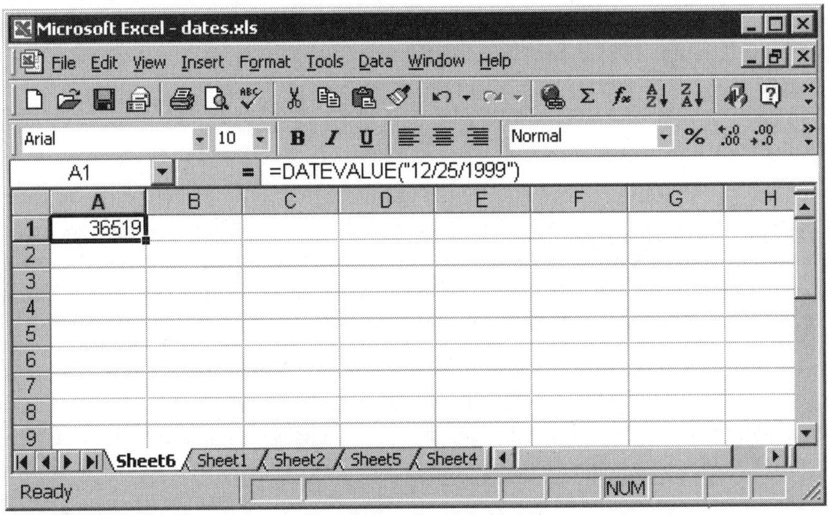

Figure 13-4: The DATEVALUE determines the numeric value of a date value

NOTE *Most functions automatically convert a date to its serial number before performing any calculations. Therefore, it is not necessary to use DATEVALUE before using another function that compares dates. The only appropriate use for this function is when you are working with a function that does not know how to interpret a date value.*

DAY

Use this function to look at a date and determine the numeric value that represents the day portion of the date. For example, if the date is 4/22/92, DAY returns a value of 22.

This function may seem somewhat useless at first glance. But it is typically used when you do not know what the date value will be in the specified cell. For example, you may need to calculate a late fee if a payment was received after the due date. You could use DAY to determine what day it arrived before calculating the appropriate fees.

To Calculate

=DAY(*Serial_Number*)

Example

DAY is typically used to determine the day value of a date in another cell. Figure 13-5 illustrates how it is used to return the day value from a cell and compare it to another day value using IF. For more information about how to use IF, refer to Chapter 19, *Logical Functions*.

DAYS360

If you are performing accounting calculations, DAYS360 provides the ability to quickly determine the number of days between two dates, but it bases its calculations on a 360-day year that equates to twelve 30-day months. Therefore, it assumes that February always has 30 days, (no more leap years) and months like January dates that actually have 31 days, are calculated as 30 days.

In most cases, the best way to determine the number of days between two days is to use DATEDIF. DAYS360 should only be used in different accounting calculations, such as determining the interest that should be charged for a payment. Refer to Chapter 12, *Financial Functions*, for more detailed information about accounting time periods.

To Calculate

=DAYS360(*Start_Date, End_Date, Method*)

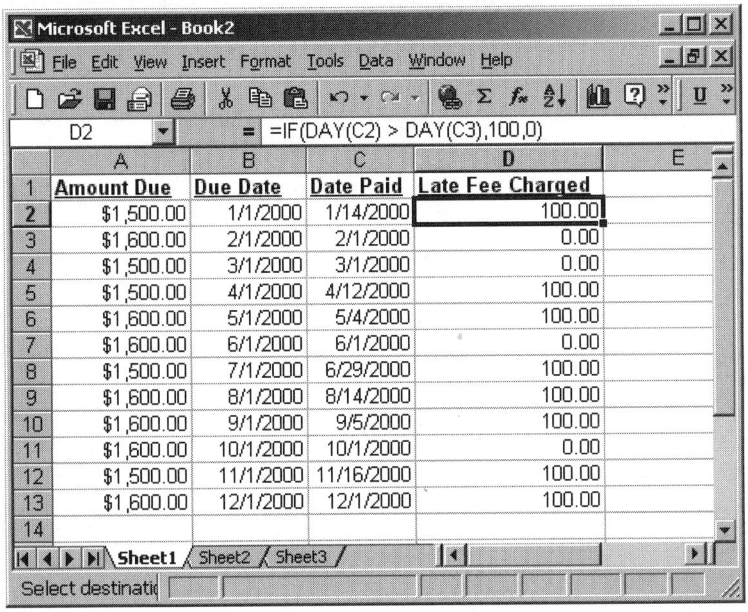

D2 = =IF(DAY(C2) > DAY(C3),100,0)

	A	B	C	D
1	Amount Due	Due Date	Date Paid	Late Fee Charged
2	$1,500.00	1/1/2000	1/14/2000	100.00
3	$1,600.00	2/1/2000	2/1/2000	0.00
4	$1,500.00	3/1/2000	3/1/2000	0.00
5	$1,500.00	4/1/2000	4/12/2000	100.00
6	$1,600.00	5/1/2000	5/4/2000	100.00
7	$1,600.00	6/1/2000	6/1/2000	0.00
8	$1,500.00	7/1/2000	6/29/2000	100.00
9	$1,600.00	8/1/2000	8/14/2000	100.00
10	$1,600.00	9/1/2000	9/5/2000	100.00
11	$1,600.00	10/1/2000	10/1/2000	0.00
12	$1,500.00	11/1/2000	11/16/2000	100.00
13	$1,600.00	12/1/2000	12/1/2000	100.00
14				

Figure 13-5: Use DAY when you do not know what date value will be entered into a cell

You must specify values for the `Start_Date` and `End_Date` arguments. The `Method` argument is optional.

NOTE *If the date specified as the Start_Date is beyond the date specified for the End_Date, a negative value will be returned by the formula. For example, if the Start_Date is 6/12/98 and the End_Date is 5/13/98, a value of -29 is returned by the formula.*

`Method`

The `Method` argument is optional. It contains a logical value of either `TRUE` or `FALSE` that indicates how Excel should round a date that contains a day value of 31. There are two different methods that are used in accounting to deal with this: the U.S. (NASD) and European methods. If you do not specify a `Method` argument Excel assumes a value of `FALSE` and it calculates based on the US method.

`FALSE`

Excel uses the U.S. (NASD) method to deal with the dates that contain a day value of 31. If the value specified for the `Start_Date` argument contains a day value of 31, the date is converted to the thirtieth day of the same month (7/31/99 becomes 7/30/99). If the value specified as the `End_Date` contains a day value of 31 and the value in the `Start_Date` contains a day value of less than 30, Excel converts the date to the first day of the next month (10/31/99 becomes 11/1/99). On the other hand, if the value of the *Start_Date* is 30 or 31, the *End_Date* is converted to the thirtieth of the same month.

Note, this is the default method used if you omit a *Method* value.

TRUE

Excel uses the method commonly referred to as the European method. This means that all dates (specified as either values for *Start_Date* and *End_Date*) that contain 31 as the day value are converted so that the date is the thirtieth day of the same month (3/31/95 becomes 3/30/95).

Example

DAYS360 is typically used to compare the dates in other cells. As indicated earlier in this chapter, the value that is returned can vary based on the method specified. Figure 13-6 shows how you can get different results based on the method selected if cell A2 contains a date value of 7/17/99 and cell A3 contains the value 7/31/99.

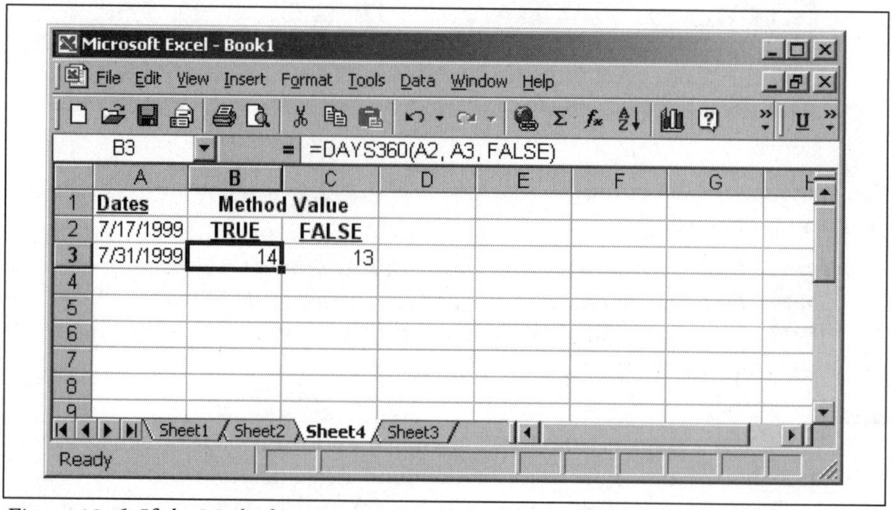

Figure 13-6: If the Method argument is TRUE, DAYS360 returns a value of 13; otherwise, DAYS360 returns a value of 14.

HOUR

Use HOUR to find out the hour portion of a specific time. The function returns a value between 0 (12:00 midnight) and 23 (11:00 PM). For example, if the time is 3:45 PM, the HOUR function will return a value of 15. In other words, since Excel deals with a 24-hour clock, HOUR returns the hour portion of the time value based on a 24-hour clock.

To Calculate

=HOUR(*Serial_Number*)

Example

HOUR is typically used to determine the hour value of a time in another cell. Figure 13-7 illustrates how you can get the hour value from a serial number in another cell.

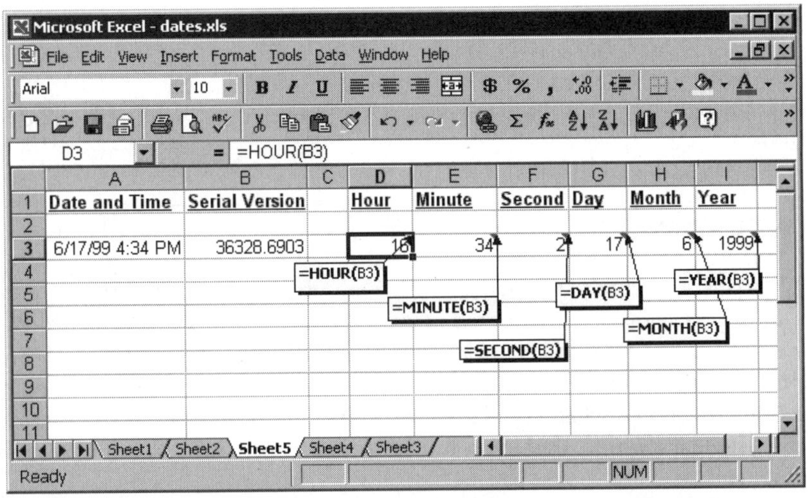

Figure 13-7: You can use the different date and time functions to manipulate any value that can be interpreted as a date or time within your worksheet

MINUTE

Use this function to determine the minute portion of a time. The function returns a value between 0 and 59. For example, if the time is 3:45 PM, MINUTE will return a value of 45.

To Calculate

=MINUTE(*Serial_Number*)

Example

MINUTE is typically used to determine the minute value of a time in another cell. The cell can contain either an actual time value, such as 3:45 PM, or a serial number that can be converted to a time. As illustrated in Figure 13-7, MINUTE is used to determine the minute portion of a serial number.

MONTH

Use this function to return the month portion of a date. For example, if the date is 4/22/92, MONTH will return a value of 4.

To Calculate

    =MONTH(Serial_Number)

Example

This function is typically used to determine the month value of a date in another cell. The value in the cell can either be a typical date value, such as 5/16/1998, or a serial number. Figure 13-7 illustrates how MONTH can get the month value from a serial number.

NETWORKDAYS

This function (an Analysis ToolPak function) provides an effective method for calculating how many workdays exist between two dates (note this is for workdays, not weekdays). For example, you can determine how many days remain before you leave for vacation. Excel assumes there are always two non-workdays each week, so those days are ignored when calculating the number of days. Also, if you know that there are holidays within that time frame, you can specify those dates and Excel ignores them.

To Calculate

    =NETWORKDAYS(Start_Date, End_Date, Holidays)

You must specify values for the *Start_Date* and *End_Date* arguments. The *Holidays* argument is optional.

Holidays

> If desired, you can specify the dates of any holidays that you know exist within the date range. Any dates you indicate will be ignored when calculating the date. You can disregard any holidays that fall on weekends, since this function already ignores two days in each week.

> If you specify multiple holiday dates you must enclose those dates within brackets ({}). For example, if your holidays are Christmas Eve and Christmas Day you would have a function similar to the following:

    =NETWORKDAYS("1/1/2000", "12/31/2000", {"12/24/2000", "12/25/2000"}).

Example

This function returns a numeric value indicating the number of workdays between the two dates, as illustrated in Figure 13-8.

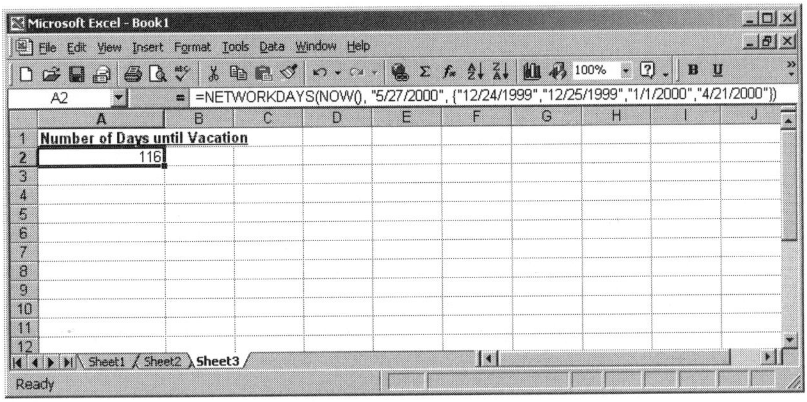

Figure 13-8: The NETWORKDAYS function works great for calculating how many workdays there are between two dates

NOW

NOW provides an easy method for getting the current date and time. Excel gets the date and time value from your system clock, so make sure that clock is accurate. The time value changes only when you open the worksheet, or if you recalculate. This is the only function in this chapter that deals with both a date and a time value.

To Calculate

    =NOW()

Unlike most functions, NOW has no arguments. To use it you simply type =Now().

NOW is typically used with other functions to return the current date and time. Figure 13-7 illustrates how NOW obtains the current date as an argument for NETWORKDAYS.

TIP # 82

Quickly Finding a Date's Serial Number

To view the actual serial number for the date and time value returned by NOW, simply change the cell formatting by selecting Format → Cells and then select the General option on the Number tab.

SECOND

Use this function to return the number of seconds in a time value. The function returns a value between 0 and 59. For example, if the time is 3:45:15 PM, SECOND will return a value of 15.

To Calculate

=SECOND(*Serial_Number*)

Example

This function is typically used to determine the second value of a time in another cell. The cell can contain either an actual time value such as 3:45:15 PM, or a serial number that can be converted to a time. Figure 13-6 illustrates how SECOND is used to determine the second portion of a serial number that is used to represent a time.

TIME

Use this function to create a time by combining values that indicate the hour, minutes, and seconds. You must specify all three values for this function. If you don't want any seconds, for example, you still need to pass a value of 0 to the function. When you use this function you can either reference other cells that contain the values, such as TIME(A1, A2, A3), where cell A1 contains the Hour value, cell A2 contains the Minute value, and cell A3 contains the Second value, or you can type in specific values for the hour, minutes, and seconds.

The value returned by TIME is actually a decimal value that represents the time. For example, Excel stores 6:00 PM as 0.75. Excel automatically formats the cell with the default time format, but you can see the actual numeric value by changing the cell formatting back to General. For more information about how Excel stores time values refer to the section "How Excel Stores Dates and Times" earlier in this chapter.

To Calculate

=TIME(*Hour*, *Minute*, *Second*)

Hour
Excel accepts an hour value of one or two digits (between 0 and 23).

Minute
The value of the *Minute* argument must be an integer representing the minute portion of the time. If the value specified is greater than 59, one hour is added to the *Hour* argument for each value of 60 that can be subtracted from the

Minute argument. For example, if the value of the *Minute* argument is 64, a value of 1 is added to the hour and the minute value is 4.

Second

The value of the *Second* argument must be an integer representing the second portion of the time. If the value specified is greater than 59 one hour is added to the minute value for each value of 60 that can be subtracted from the *Second* argument. For example, if the value of the *Minute* argument is 2, but the *Second* argument has a value of 75, the new value of the *Minute* argument becomes 3 and the *Second* argument becomes 15 (75 – 60).

Example

This function is most useful when you need to build a time based on values in other fields. Figure 13-9 illustrates how Excel builds the time based on the values contained in different cells. The example also shows how you can combine the DATE and TIME output within one cell.

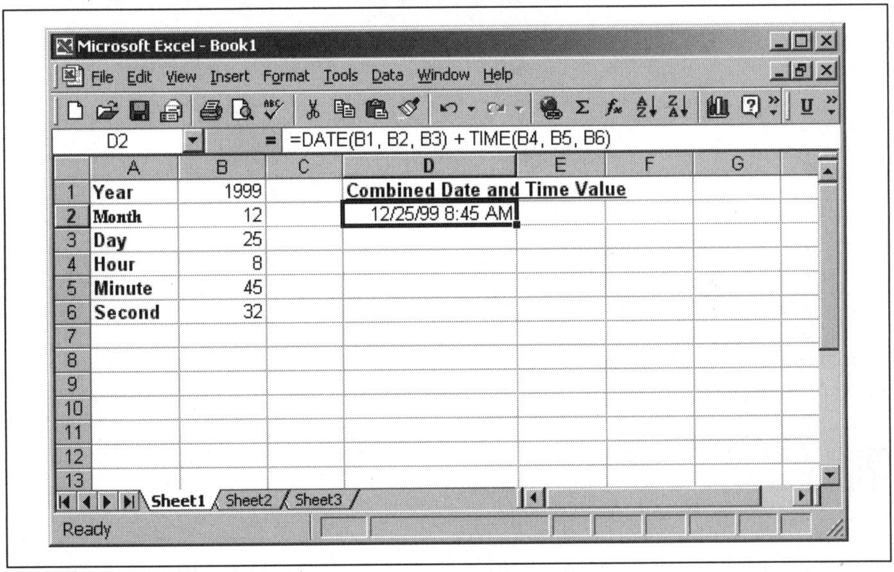

Figure 13-9: You can combine the results of DATE and TIME

TIMEVALUE

This is another function you will rarely use. TIMEVALUE allows you to determine the serial number Excel uses to store a time value, which is a decimal number. In most cases, Excel will automatically convert the time to its numeric value before performing any calculations.

TIMEVALUE does not work with a cell reference, such as =TIME-VALUE(A4). You must specify the actual value you want to convert.

To Calculate

=TIMEVALUE(Time_text)

Time_text

This argument can contain any time in standard time format. The time must be specified directly, such as "3:45 PM"; you cannot reference another cell.

Example

This function allows you to determine the numeric value that Excel uses to store a time, as indicated in Figure 13-10.

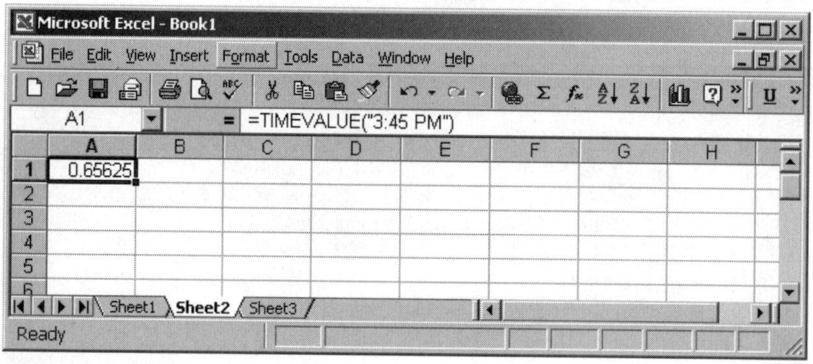

Figure 13-10: Unlike most date and time functions, TIMEVALUE cannot reference a value in another cell

TODAY

Use this function to get the current date. The date value changes only when you open the worksheet, or if you recalculate. Excel gets the date information from your system, so make sure your system clock is accurate.

To Calculate

=TODAY()

Today has no arguments. To use this function you simply need to type =TODAY().

NOTE *TODAY is used as the argument for another function when determining the current date. A good example of this is in Figure 13-7; TODAY is used with NETWORKDAYS to determine the number of workdays between today and a vacation date.*

Example

Although this function actually returns a numeric value (or serial number) Excel automatically formats the value with a date format, as illustrated in Figure 13-11.

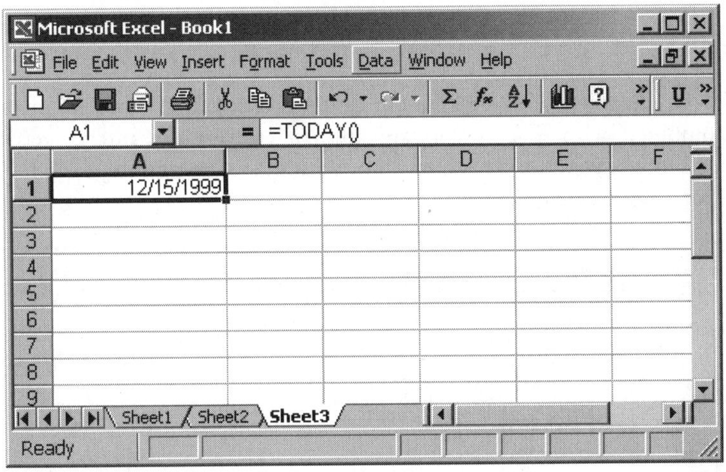

Figure 13-11: TODAY provides a great method for getting the current date from the system

WEEKDAY

Use this function to determine the day of the week that a specific date falls on. Excel returns an integer value between `0` and `7` that represents the day of the week.

To Calculate

```
=WEEKDAY(Serial_Number, Return_Type)
```

Although you must specify a date, the `Return_Type` argument is optional.

`Return_Type`
: This argument indicates what day you choose as the first day of the week. The value of this argument can be an integer value between `1` and `3`, as described in the following list. For example, if you select Sunday as the first day of the week, use `1` as the value. If you do not provide a value for the `Return_Type` argument, the default value is 1.

Date and Time Functions

1   This is the default value for the *Return_Type* argument. If you specify this value, Sunday is considered the first day and has a value of 1, with Saturday the last day of the week with a value of 7. Therefore, if the date is a Wednesday, Excel returns a value of 4.

2   If you specify this value Monday is considered the first day of the week and has a value of 1, with Sunday having a value of 7.

3   If you specify this value Monday is considered the first day of the week, but it is numbered differently than the other methods. The numbering starts at 0 for Monday, with the last day (Sunday) having a value of 6.

Example

Figure 13-11 illustrates how WEEKDAY is used to determine the day of the week. When combined with TEXT you are able to convert the integer returned by WEEKDAY to a text value. For more information about using the TEXT function, see Chapter 18, *Text Functions*.

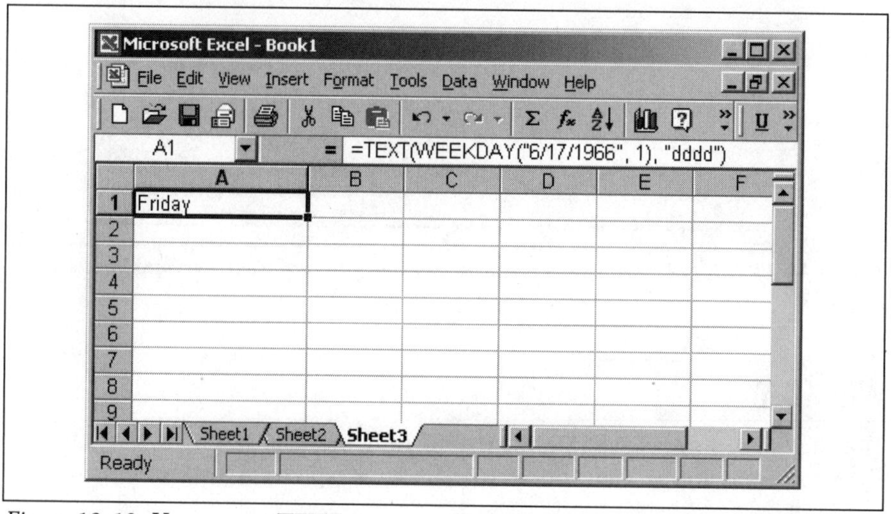

Figure 13-12: You can use TEXT to create a formula that converts the integer returned to a text value

---

WEEKNUM

Use WEEKNUM (an Analysis ToolPak function) to determine the numeric value of the week of the year that corresponds to the specified date.

To Calculate

=WEEKNUM(*Serial_Number*, *Return_Type*)

Return_Type

This argument indicates what day you choose as the first day of the week. The value of this argument can be an integer value of 1 or 2, as described in the following list. For example, if you select Sunday as the first day of the week, use 1 as the value. If you do not provide a value for the *Return_Type* argument, the default value is 1.

1　This is the default value for the *Return_Type* argument. If you specify this value, Sunday is considered the first day of the week.

2　If you specify this value Monday is considered the first day of the week.

Example

Figure 13-12 illustrates how to use WEEKNUM to determine the numeric week value of the specified date. You will notice that the function returns a different week value for the same date when we specify a different value for the *Return_Type* argument. Since the date is on a Sunday when the value of *Return_Type* is 1, it is the first day of the twenty-second week of the year. But, when we indicate that Monday is the first day of the week by specifying a value of 2 for *Return_Type*, the date becomes the last day of the twenty-first week.

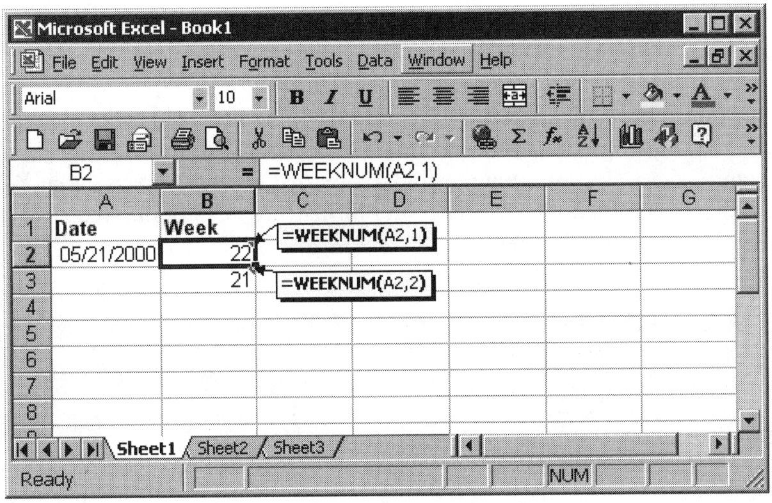

Figure 13-13: Use WEEKNUM to determine the week number of a specific date

WORKDAY

This function (an Analysis ToolPak function) allows you to figure out which date is the specified number of workdays before or after a certain date. Notice I said workdays, not weekdays. Excel assumes there are always two non-workdays each week, so those days are ignored when finding the date. If you know that there are holidays within that time frame, you can specify those dates and Excel will ignore them.

To Calculate

```
=WORKDAY(Start_Date, Days, Holidays)
```

You must specify values for the *Start_Date* and *Days* arguments. The *Holidays* argument is optional.

Days

> This argument indicates the number of workdays to add to find the date. A positive value means that you are looking for a date after the specified date. A negative value gives you a date prior to the specified date. Remember, you are dealing with workdays; you do not want to count weekends or holidays.

Holidays

> If desired, you can specify the dates of any holidays that you know exist within the date range. Any dates you specify will be ignored when calculating the date. If you specify multiple dates, you must enclose the dates within brackets ({}), as illustrated in Figure 13-13.

> You can avoid specifying any holidays that fall on weekends since the function already ignores all weekend dates.

Example

This function returns the date as a serial number. The best method of changing the value to a date string is to simply format the cell as a date by selecting Format → Cell. Figure 13-13 illustrates how to find a date that is 20 workdays away. You can also use the TEXT function to change the formatting of the value returned by the Workday function (see Chapter 18).

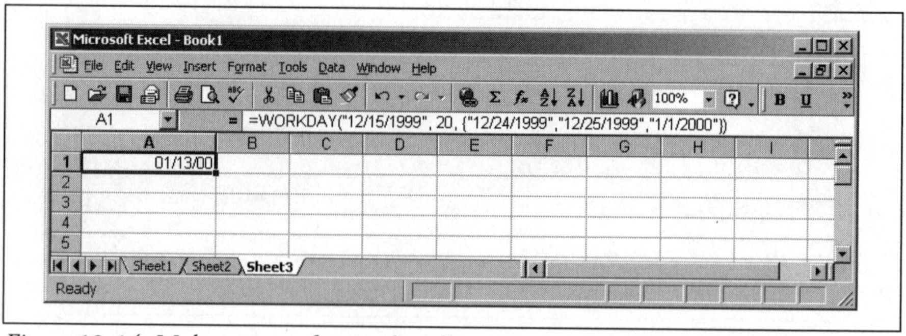

Figure 13-14: Make sure you format the cell as a Date when using WORKDAY

YEAR

Use this function to return the year portion of a date. For example, if the date is 4/22/92, this function will return a value of 1992.

To Calculate

=YEAR(*Serial_Number*)

Example

This function is typically used to determine the year value of a date in another cell. The value in the cell can either be a typical date value, such as 5/16/1998, or a serial number. The HOUR function covered in this chaper has an example illustrating how YEAR can get the year value from a serial number.

YEARFRAC

Use YEARFRAC (an Analysis ToolPak function) to return a decimal value that represents the fraction of a year represented by the number of days between the specified dates. This function is typically used with financial functions to calculate the portion of a year's benefits or obligations to assign.

To Calculate

=YEARFRAC(*Start_Date, End_Date, Basis*)

Basis
> This optional argument indicates how days in a month and days in a year are to be counted when performing calculations. For example, although we all know that all years (with the exception of leap years) have 365 days and each month has either 30 or 31 days (except for February); the 30/360 Day Count Basis assumes that each month has exactly 30 days and that the year has 360 days. By using this type of calculation, the interest paid can be calculated as the same amount each month.
>
> There are five different Day Count Basis methods that can be selected for the Basis argument by specifying a value between 0 and 4, as outlined in Table 13-3. If this argument is omitted a value of 0 is used for the function.

Table 13-3: Basis Values

Basis Value	Description
0	This value selects the US (NASD) 30/360 day count basis that assumes that each month has 30 days and the total number of days in the year is 360 (calculated as 12 months x 30 days per month.) This method makes adjustments for February and months with 31 days. If the date is 2/28 or 2/29 (leap year) it is adjusted to be 2/30. The way it deals with months ending with 31 days, can be a little more confusing. With all of the functions that use the *Basis* argument there are always at least two different dates that are being compared. If the first date has 31 days (such as 1/31/2000) the date is converted to 30 days, such as 1/30/2000. If the second date has 31 days it is changed to 30 days as long as the first date was not 2/28 or 2/29. If the first date was a February date, the second date does not change.
	This day count basis is typically used with mortgages and agency notes.
1	This value uses the day count basis referred to as Actual/Actual. This basis calculates the actual number of days between two dates and assumes the year has either 365 or 366 days depending on whether the year is a leap year. In other words, if the date range for the calculation includes the date February 29 (a leap day), the year is 366; otherwise it is 365.
	This day count basis is typically used with U.S. Treasury Notes.
2	This value uses the day count basis referred to as Actual/360. This basis method calculates the actual number of days between two dates and assumes the year has 360 days. Many money market calculations with less than a year to maturity use this day count basis.
	This day count basis is typically used with Certificates of Deposits (CDs), U.S. Treasury Bills, and Agency Discount Notes.
3	This value uses the day count basis referred to as Actual/365. This calculates the actual number of days between two dates and assumes the year has 365 days. Keep in mind that even leap years will be treated as having 365 days.
4	This value uses the day count basis referred to as 30/360 European. This day count basis is very similar to the US 30/360 basis. The only difference is how it treats months with 31 days. All dates with a day value of 31 are converted to 30 days (i.e., 1/31/2000 is treated as 1/30/2000). February dates of 2/28 or 2/29 are converted to 2/30.

Example

Figure 13-15 illustrates how to use YEARFRAC to determine the fractional portion of a year represented by the specified dates.

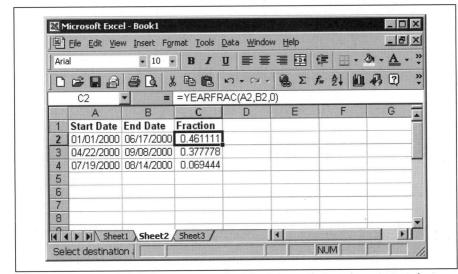

Figure 13-15: Use YEARFRAC to determine the portion of a year between two dates

Chapter 14

Mathematics and Trigonometry Functions

Excel provides a variety of mathematical and trigonometrical functions. These functions let you perform most of those calculations you had to figure out *by hand* in high school trig and calculus classes. And if you are like me, you haven't had to do these types of equations since then. Excel makes it easy for the math-challenged by running these calculations. (Of course, now most students are allowed to execute these calculations on calculators or computers.) The following functions are covered in detail in this chapter. The "AT" represents those functions that exist only by loading the Analysis Toolpak. See Chapter 11, *Working with Functions*, for details.

ABS	LN	ROUNDUP
ACOS	LOG	SERIESSUM *AT*
ACOSH	LOG10	SIGN
ASIN	MDETERM	SIN
ASINH	MINVERSE	SINH
ATAN	MMULT	SQRT
ATAN2	MOD	SQRTPI *AT*
ATANH	MROUND *AT*	SUBTOTAL
CEILING	MULTINOMIAL *AT*	SUM
COMBIN	ODD	SUMIF
COS	PI	SUMPRODUCT
COSH	POWER	SUMSQ
DEGREES	PRODUCT	SUMX2MY2
EVEN	QUOTIENT *AT*	SUMX2PY2
EXP	RADIANS	SUMXMY2
FACT	RAND	TAN
FLOOR	RANDBETWEEN *AT*	TANH
GCD *AT*	Roman	TRUNC
INT	ROUND	
LCM *AT*	ROUNDDOWN	

Use these functions to do the following:

- Make sure a numeric value is positive.

- Round numbers up or down.

- Make sure a numeric value is an even number.

- Truncate a numeric value to the specified number of decimal places.

- Determine the square root of a number.

- Determine if a numeric value is positive or negative.

- Calculate any of the common trigonometrical functions, such as determining the sine, cosine, or tangent.

Understanding Math Lingo

If you haven't attended a high school math class recently, you may run into math terminology in this chapter that sounds Greek to you. These definitions should help you better understand the operations described later in this chapter:

Array
   An array is essentially just a listing of data that is stored in rows and columns. For example, an array could be represented as A1:B5. When a function requires an array as the value for an argument it is looking for a corresponding group of cells.

Exponent
   An exponent indicates the power to which a number should be raised, such as 4^2, which raises the number 4 to the power of 2 (2 is the exponent). The exponent is always indicated on the right side of the number. When a number is raised to an exponential power it basically just means that the number will be multiplied by itself the number of times specified by the exponent (i.e., 4^2 is equivalent to 4×4).

Factorial
   A factorial is the product of multiplying the numbers starting at 1, up to and including the factorial number. For example, the factorial of 5 would be calculated as $1 \times 2 \times 3 \times 4 \times 5$. Keep in mind that a factorial of 0 is equal to 1.

Hyperbolic
   Hyperbolic functions are designed to work with a plane curve that is generated by plotting a series of values. On a hyperbolic curve, the distance between any two points is always consistent for the entire curve.

Matrix
   A matrix is an array of elements that has rows and columns. Matrices are manipulated using various formulas detailed in this chapter. A matrix is typically expressed in the form outlined in Figure 14-1. Although matrices can have

any number of rows and columns, the matrix functions available within Excel only work with matrices that have an equal number of rows and columns (referred to as square matrices).

$$\begin{bmatrix} 17 & 6 & 21 \\ 8 & 3 & 14 \\ 21 & 5 & 19 \end{bmatrix}$$

Figure 14-1: When using Excel matrix functions, a matrix must have an equal number of rows and columns

Pi Pi is a constant used with calculations that relate to circular objects. It is typically represented by the symbol π. It indicates the ratio between the circumference of a circle and its diameter. Pi is approximately equal to 3.1415926536.

Product

This is a mathematical term that refers to the result of multiplying a series of values together. For example, the product of 4×5 is 20.

Radians

Radians are a common method for measuring angles. A radian measurement is based on the fact that a circle can be divided into 360 degrees or 2π (Pi) radians. Thus, one radian is approximately 57.2957 degrees ($360/2\pi$), and one degree is approximately 0.017453 radians ($2\pi/360$). The radian measurement for an angle is based on the portion of a circle that the angle takes. You can convert a degree measurement to radians by multiplying it by $\pi/180$. For example, to convert a 60 degree angle measurement to radians you would multiply 60 by $\pi/180$ to get a value of 1.047.

Square

Determining the square of a number is essentially just taking the number and multiplying it by itself. For example, if you have the number 12^2 it is the same as 12×12, which equals 144.

The Math and Trigonometric Functions

As stated earlier in this chapter, Excel provides several different functions to perform mathematical calculations. These functions are covered later in this chapter in alphabetical order, but they can be categorized as follows:

Determine the value of an angle:

ACOS (determine the arccosine)
ASIN (determine the arcsine)
ATAN (determine the arctangent)
ATAN2 (Determine the arctangent using two coordinates of the angle)

COS (determine the cosine of an angle)
SIN (determine the sine of an angle)
TAN (determine the tangent of an angle)

Determine the hyperbolic values:

ACOSH (determine the inverse hyperbolic cosine)
ASINH (determine the inverse hyperbolic sine)
ATANH (determine the inverse hyperbolic tangent)
COSH (determine the hyperbolic cosine)
SINH (determine the hyperbolic sine)
TANH (determine the hyerbolic tangent)

Convert measurements between radians and degrees:

DEGREES (convert a radian measurement to degrees)
RADIANS (convert a degree measurement to radians)

Round numeric values:

CEILING (round up to a specific multiple)
EVEN (Round to the closest even integer)
FLOOR (round down to a specific multiple)
INT (round down to the nearest integer value)
MROUND (round to a specific integer multiple)
ODD (Round to the closest odd integer)
ROUND (round to a specific number of decimal places)
ROUNDDOWN (round down to the specified number of decimals)
ROUNDUP (round up to the specified number of decimals)
TRUNC (truncate to the specified number of decimals)

Find the logarithm for a numeric value:

LN (find the natural logarithm)
LOG (find the logarithm to any base)
LOG10 (find the base 10 logarithm)

Raise a numeric value to a specific power:

EXP (raise the constant e to a specified power)
POWER (raise a number to any power)

Work with factorials:

FACT (find the factorial for a number)
MULTINOMIAL (divide the sum by the product of factorials)

Work with matrices and arrays:

MDETERM (determinant of a matrix)
MINVERSE (inverse of a square matrix)
MMULT (product of two matrices)
SUMPRODUCT (sum of products of arrays)

Math Functions

SUMX2MY2 (square of one array minus square of another array)
SUMX2PY2 (sum of both arrays squared)
SUMXMY2 (square of the differences between arrays)

Calculate the sum of a convergent series:

SERIESSUM (TK)

Determine the results of dividing two values:

MOD (returns the remainder)
QUOTIENT (returns the integer result of the division)

Work with circle measurements:

PI (TK)

Generate random numbers:

RAND (values between 0 and 1)
RANDBETWEEN (integer values within the specified range)

Work with numeric values:

ABS (find the absolute value)
COMBIN (find number of unique combinations)
GCD (find the greatest common divisor)
LCM (find the least common multiple)
PRODUCT (multiply the values)
Roman (create a Roman numeral)
SIGN (determine if value is positive or negative)
SQRT (determine the square root)
SQRTPI (multiply the numeric value by pi then square root)
SUBTOTAL (perform a specific function on a list of numeric values)
SUM (add the values)
SUMIF (add the values if specified criteria is met)
SUMSQ (add the squares of a range of values)

ABS

Use ABS to determine the absolute value of a number, which is the actual numeric value of the number without the negative or positive sign. For example, both ABS(-34) and ABS(34) equal 34. This function is typically used when you need to get the actual numeric value so you can perform another calculation. I would recommend using it with any function that requires a positive numeric value for the argument.

To Calculate

```
=ABS(Number)
```

Number

> This argument is required, and must have a value that can equal any numeric value.

Example

Figure 14-5 shows how ABS is used to make sure a numeric value is positive before it is passed to another function.

ACOS

Use ACOS to determine the arccosine of a number. The arccosine is the inverse of the cosine. The result of the function is expressed in radians.

To Calculate

    =ACOS(Number)

Number

> This required argument must specify a number between –1 and 1 that indicates the cosine value.

TIP # 83

Converting Between Radians and Degrees

You can convert the result of the function from radians to degrees by multiplying the result by 180/π.

Example

Figure 14-2 illustrates how ACOS is used to determine the arccosine for an angle based on the cosine value. You will notice the arccosine amount is equal to the radian measurement of the angle.

ACOSH

You can use ACOSH to determine the inverse hyperbolic cosine of a number.

To Calculate

    =ACOSH(Number)

Number

> This required argument must specify a numeric value that is larger than 1.

Math Functions

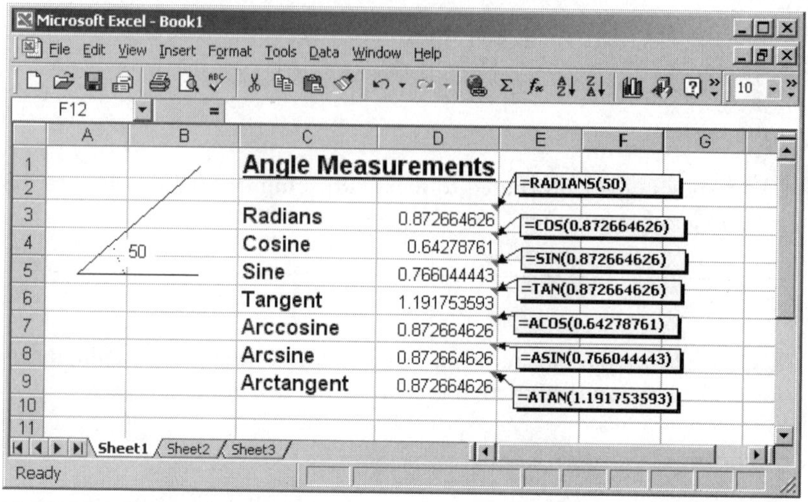

Figure 14-2: Use the various trigonometric functions to work with angle measurements

Example

Figure 14-3 illustrates how you can use the hyperbolic functions. Since ACOSH is the inverse of COSH, you will notice that the value returned by ACOSH is equal to the value that was passed to COSH.

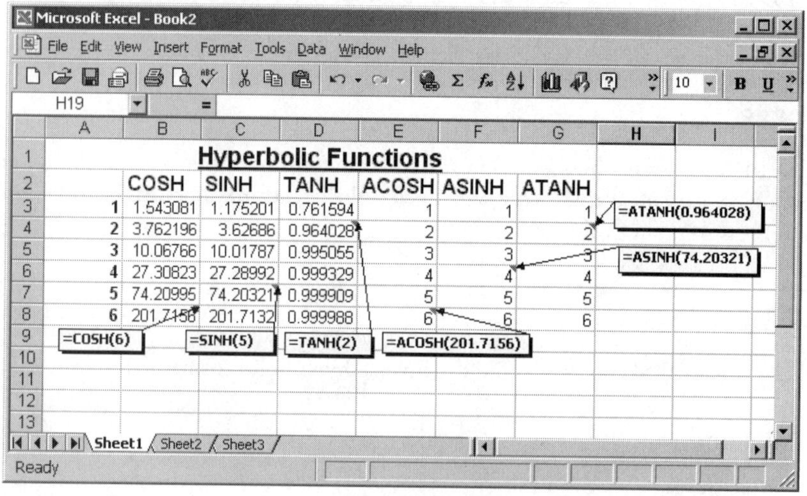

Figure 14-3: You will notice that there is hyperbolic function that corresponds to each trigonometric function

ASIN

Use ASIN to determine the arcsine of a number. The result of the function is expressed in radians.

To Calculate

```
=ASIN(Number)
```

Number

This required argument must specify a number between −1 and 1 that indicates the sine value.

Example

Figure 14-2 illustrates how ASIN is used to determine the arcsine for an angle based on the sine value. You will notice the arcsine amount is equal to the radian measurement of the angle.

ASINH

You can use ASINH to determine the inverse hyperbolic sine of a number.

To Calculate

```
=ACOSH(Number)
```

Number

This required argument must specify a numeric value.

Example

Figure 14-3 illustrates how you can use the hyperbolic functions. Since ASINH is the inverse of SINH, you will notice that the value that is returned by ASINH is equal to the value that was passed to SINH.

ATAN

Use ATAN to determine the arctangent of a number. The result of the function is expressed in radians.

To Calculate

```
=ATAN(Number)
```

Number

This required argument must specify a numeric value that indicates the tangent value.

Example

Figure 14-2 illustrates how ATAN is used to determine the arctangent for an angle based on the sine value. You will notice the arctangent amount is equal to the radian measurement of the angle.

ATAN2

Use ATAN2 to determine the arctangent if you have the x and y coordinates for an angle. The result of the function is expressed in radians.

To Calculate

=ATAN2 (*X_Num, Y_Num*)

The *X_Num* and *Y_Num* arguments are required for this function.

X_Num

Specifies a numeric value that represents the x-coordinate of the point.

Y_Num

Specifies a numeric value that represents the y-coordinate of the point.

Example

Figure 14-4 illustrates how you can take the x and y coordinates for an angle and determine the arctangent. This figure also uses DEGREES to convert the radian measurement that is returned by ATAN2 to a degree value.

ATANH

Use ATANH to determine the inverse hyperbolic tangent of a number.

To Calculate

=ATANH (*Number*)

Number

This required argument must specify a number between −1 and 1.

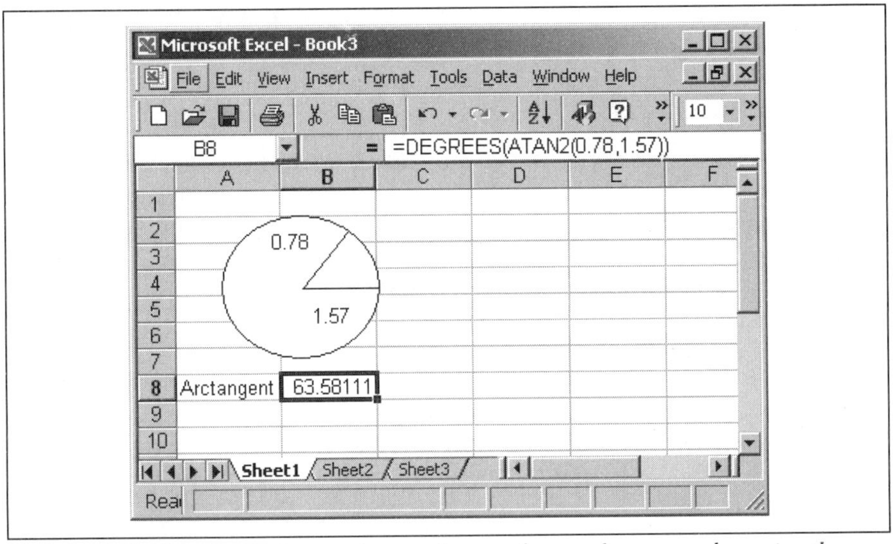

Figure 14-4: If you know the x and y coordinates of an angle you can determine the arctangent

Example

Figure 14-3 illustrates how you can use the hyperbolic functions. Since ATANH is the inverse of TANH, you will notice that the value that is returned by ATANH is equal to the value that was passed to TANH.

CEILING

Use CEILING to round a value up to a specific multiple. In other words, to make sure the price is always a multiple of .25 to eliminate the use of coins smaller than a quarter, you could specify =(CEILING(A2, 0.25) to round whatever value exists in cell A2 up to a value that is a multiple of 0.25. For example, if the cell contained the value of 1.34 it would be rounded to 1.50.

Keep in mind that CEILING is actually rounding up away from zero. For example, if you have =CEILING(1.5, 2) the function returns the value 2.

To Calculate

```
=CEILING(Number, Significance)
```

The *Number* and *Significance* arguments are required and must have a value.

Number
    Indicates a numeric value.

Significance

A numeric value that indicates the value that you want the number to be rounded up to. For example, to round up to an even number (such as 2, 4, 6, etc.) you would specify a value of 2 for the *Significance* argument.

Keep in mind that if you expect the *Number* argument to contain a negative number, such as –2.5, the value specified for the *Significance* argument must be negative. By the same token, specify a positive value for the *Significance* argument if the value of the *Number* argument will be positive. If the *Number* argument is negative and the *Significance* argument is positive, CEILING returns an error value.

Example

Figure 14-5 shows how CEILING is used to round a numeric value up to the next value that is a multiple of by 0.25. Since this function requires a positive value, the ABS function is used to ensure that the numeric value is always positive.

 To round the numbers from zero by rounding values down, use the FLOOR function.

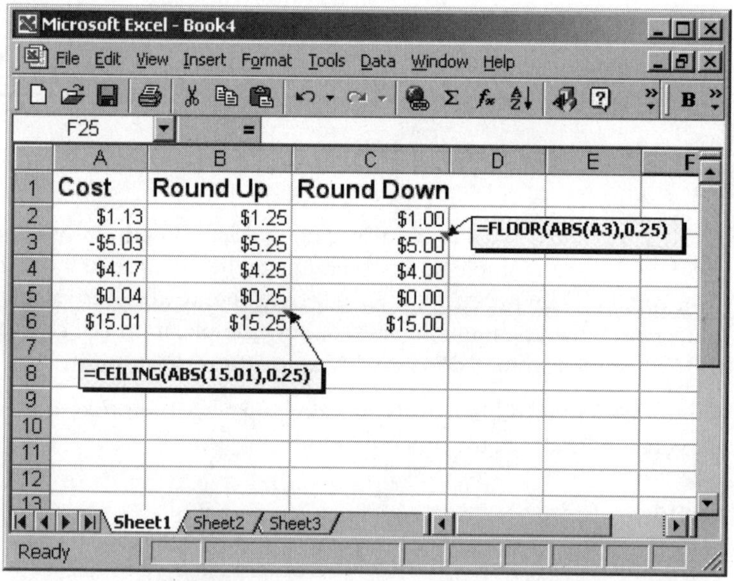

	A	B	C	D	E	F
1	Cost	Round Up	Round Down			
2	$1.13	$1.25	$1.00			
3	-$5.03	$5.25	$5.00	=FLOOR(ABS(A3),0.25)		
4	$4.17	$4.25	$4.00			
5	$0.04	$0.25	$0.00			
6	$15.01	$15.25	$15.00			
7						
8	=CEILING(ABS(15.01),0.25)					

Figure 14-5: Use ABS to ensure that the value passed to CEILING and FLOOR is positive

COMBIN

You can use COMBIN to determine the number of combinations of items of a specified size that are created out of the specified number of items. For COMBIN, the order of arrangement does not matter, so (a,b,c) is the same combination as (b,c,a). If order does matter, you can use PERMUT (refer to Chapter 15, *Statistical Functions*).

To Calculate

=COMBIN(Number, Number_Chosen)

All arguments are required and must have a value.

Number
> An integer value that indicates the number of items that you want to combine.

Number_Chosen
> An integer value that indicates the number of items that you want to place in each group.

Example

Figure 14-6 illustrates how COMBIN is used to determine the number of unique groups of three that are created out of the specified number of items.

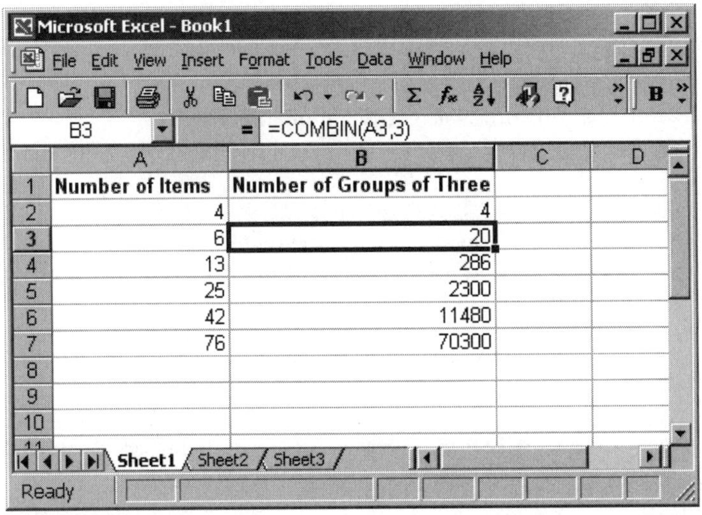

Figure 14-6: COMBIN determines the number of unique combinations that are created from the specified number of items

COS

Use COS to determine the cosine of an angle expressed in radians. In order to use this function the size of the angle must be in radians. You can convert degrees to radians by multiplying by $\pi/180$.

To Calculate

=COS(*Number*)

Number

This required argument must specify the radian measurement of the angle for which you want to determine the cosine.

Example

Figure 14-2 illustrates how COS is used to determine the cosine for an angle as long as you know the radian value. For this example, we used RADIANS to determine the radian measurement for a 50-degree angle.

COSH

Use COSH to determine the hyperbolic cosine of a number.

To Calculate

=COSH(*Number*)

Number

This required argument must specify a numeric value.

Example

Figure 14-3 illustrates how you can use the hyperbolic functions. Since ACOSH is the inverse of COSH, you will notice that the value that is returned by ACOSH is equal to the value that was passed to COSH.

DEGREES

Use DEGREES to convert a radians measurement into a degrees measurement.

To Calculate

=DEGREES(*Angle*)

Angle

This required argument indicates a radians value that you want to convert to degrees.

Example

Figure 14-4 illustrates how DEGREES is used to convert a radian measurement to degrees.

EVEN

Use EVEN to round a numeric value to the closest even integer. This function rounds away from zero, meaning that if the numeric value is greater than zero it rounds up, whereas, if the value is less than zero it rounds down.

To Calculate

=EVEN(*Number*)

Number

This required argument must be a numeric value that you want to round.

Example

Figure 14-7 illustrates the difference in the results returned by the EVEN and ODD functions. Notice that when EVEN receives a negative value it is rounded down (away from zero) to the next even integer. For example, –4.2 is rounded to –6 because the value is less than –4, so the next even integer is –6.

EXP

You can use EXP to determine the value of the constant e raised to the power of the specified numeric value. The value of e is approximately 2.71828182845904. Therefore, if the value of the *Normal* argument is 2, the value of the function is 2.71828182845904^2 (2.71828182845904 × 2.71828182845904), which is 7.389056.

To Calculate

=EXP(*Number*)

Number

This required argument must be a numeric value that indicates the power you want to raise natural logarithm to.

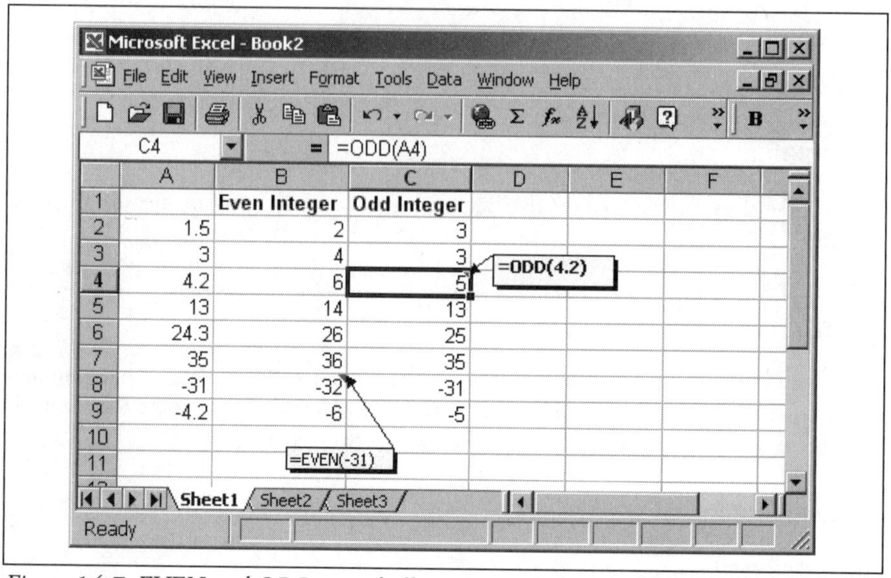

Figure 14-7: EVEN and ODD round all positive values up and negative values down

Example

Figure 14-8 illustrates how you can use EXP to determine the value of raising e to a specific value. The example also shows how LN is used to determine the natural logarithm for any numeric value. The two functions are actually inverses, meaning that =EXP(2) equals 7.389056 and =LN(7.389056) equals 2 (actually 1.99999987).

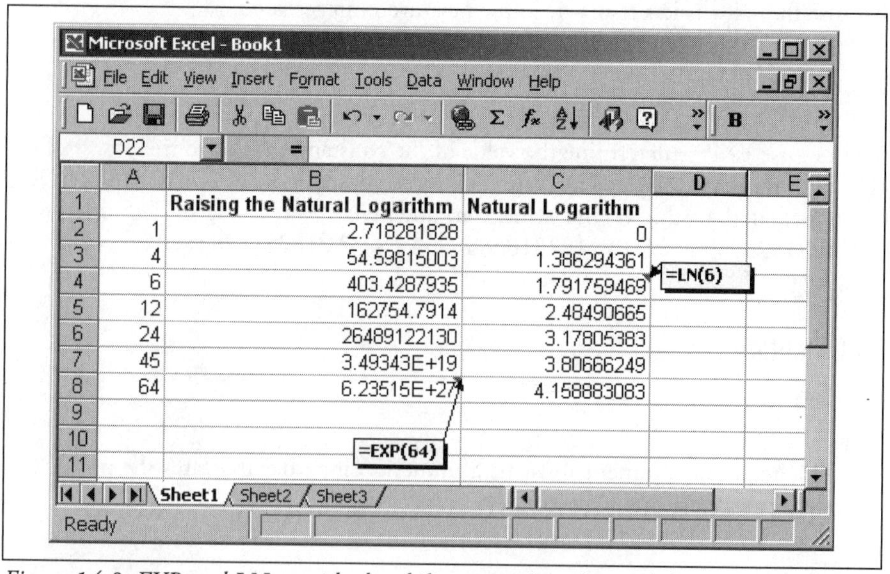

Figure 14-8: EXP and LN provide the ability to work with e and the natural logarithm

FACT

FACT provides the ability to determine the factorial of the specified number. The factorial is equal to $1 \times 2 \times 3 \times 4 \times \ldots \times Number$. For example, if you have =FACT(5) it is equal to $1 \times 2 \times 3 \times 4 \times 5$ or 120. Keep in mind that =FACT(0) equals 1.

To Calculate

=FACT(Number)

Number

This required argument must be a positive numeric value that indicates the factorial you want to calculate. If the value is not an integer, such as 3.45 the value is truncated (3.45 becomes 3).

Example

Figure 14-9 illustrates how FACT is used to determine the factorial of any positive value. Notice that when a decimal value is specified, such as 3.7, the decimal portion of the number is truncated and the result is determined based on the integer value of 3.

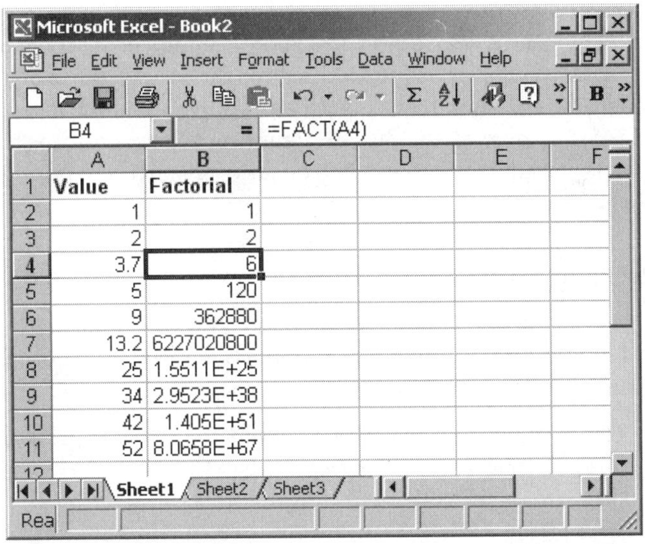

Math Functions

Figure 14-9: FACT truncates any decimal values and only uses the integer portion of the numeric value

FLOOR

Use FLOOR to round a value down to a specific multiple. In other words, to make sure the price is always rounded to a multiple of .5 you could specify =FLOOR(A3, 0.5) to round whatever value exists in cell A2 down to a value that is a multiple of 0.5. For example, if the cell contains the value of 1.84 it would be rounded to 1.50.

Keep in mind that FLOOR is actually rounding positive numeric values down toward zero. For example, if you have =FLOOR(2.5, 2) the function returns 2.

To Calculate

=FLOOR(Number, Significance)

The Number and Significance arguments are required and must have a value.

Number
This argument must be a numeric value.

Significance
This argument must be a numeric value that indicates the multiple value that you want the number to be rounded to. For example, to round down to an even number (such as 2, 4, 6, etc.) you would specify a value of 2 for the Significance argument.

Keep in mind that if you expect the Number argument to contain a negative number, such as –2.5, the value specified for the Significance argument must be negative. By the same token, specify a positive value for the Significance argument if the value of the Number argument will be positive. If the Number argument is negative and the Significance argument is positive, FLOOR returns and error value.

Example

Figure 14-5 shows how FLOOR is used to round a numeric value down to the next value that is a multiple of by 0.25. Since this function requires a positive value, ABS is used to ensure that the numeric value is always positive.

 Use the CEILING function to round the numbers away from zero by rounding positive values down.

GCD

You can use GCD (an Analysis ToolPak function) to determine the largest number that can be evenly divided into the specified values, commonly referred to as the greatest common divisor. For example, the greatest common divisor for 18 and 24 is 6; 6 is the largest number divisible into both 18 and 24 without a remainder.

To Calculate

`=GCD(Number1, Number2, ...)`

Number1, Number2, ...

> You can specify between 1 and 29 different numeric values for which you want to find the greatest common divisor. The values must all be positive. If any of the values are not integers, the fractional portion of the number will be truncated (i.e., 4.5 becomes 4).

Example

Figure 14-10 shows how GCD is used to determine the largest value that is divided into a series of numeric values. You will notice that when a decimal value is specified, such as 24.2 the fractional portion of the number is truncated.

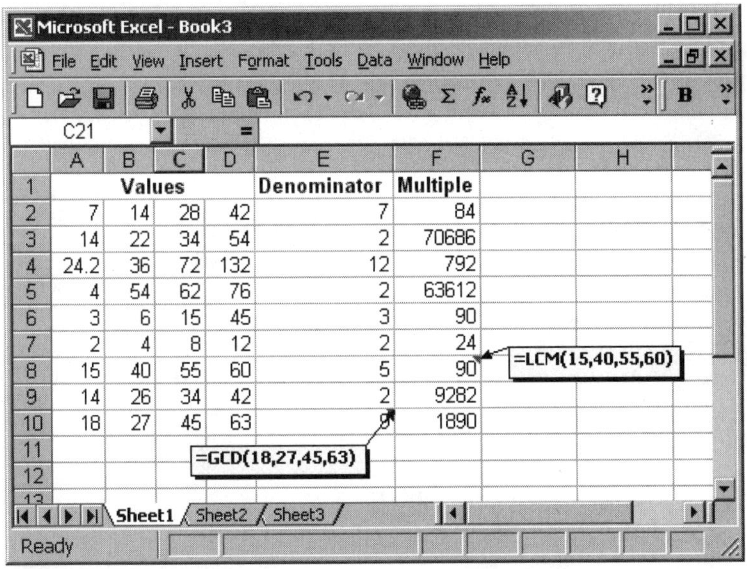

Microsoft Excel - Book3								
	A	B	C	D	E	F	G	H
1		Values			Denominator	Multiple		
2	7	14	28	42	7	84		
3	14	22	34	54	2	70686		
4	24.2	36	72	132	12	792		
5	4	54	62	76	2	63612		
6	3	6	15	45	3	90		
7	2	4	8	12	2	24		
8	15	40	55	60	5	90	=LCM(15,40,55,60)	
9	14	26	34	42	2	9282		
10	18	27	45	63	9	1890		
11			=GCD(18,27,45,63)					

Figure 14-10: GCD and LCM truncate all decimal values

NOTE *Use LCM to determine the smallest number that is a multiple of all of the specified numeric values.*

INT

You can use INT to round a number down to the nearest integer. When you use this function it does not matter what the fractional value of the number is, the function always rounds down. Therefore if you have `=INT(2.65)` the result is 2; whereas, `=INT(-8.23)` has a result of –9.

To Calculate

=INT(*Number*)

Number

This required argument specifies the numeric value that you want to round down to the closest integer value.

Example

As you can see in Figure 14-11, INT works well for ensuring that a numeric value is always an integer. You will notice for all positive numbers it simply truncates the decimal portion, so that 2.789 becomes 2. With negative numbers it rounds the number down to the next integer value (-4.567 becomes –5). This example also shows the results of using TRUNC. If you want to always truncate the decimal portion for both positive and negative numbers, use TRUNC and indicate that you want to display 0 decimal places.

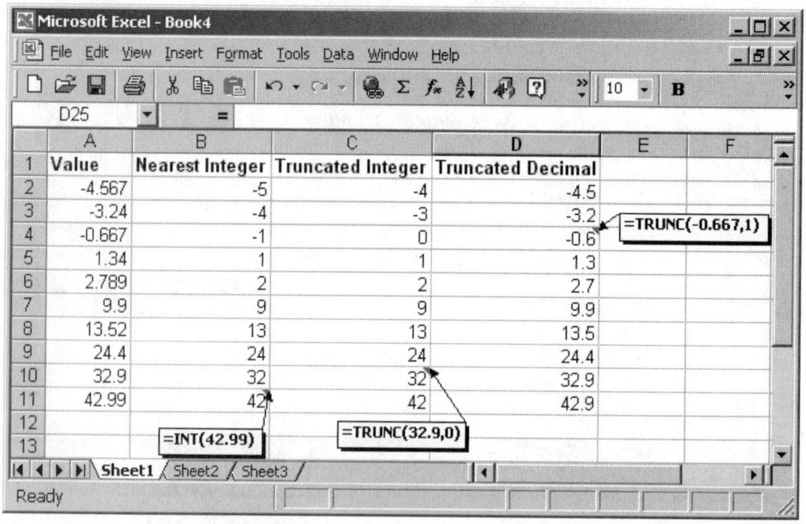

	A	B	C	D	E	F
1	Value	Nearest Integer	Truncated Integer	Truncated Decimal		
2	-4.567	-5	-4	-4.5		
3	-3.24	-4	-3	-3.2	=TRUNC(-0.667,1)	
4	-0.667	-1	0	-0.6		
5	1.34	1	1	1.3		
6	2.789	2	2	2.7		
7	9.9	9	9	9.9		
8	13.52	13	13	13.5		
9	24.4	24	24	24.4		
10	32.9	32	32	32.9		
11	42.99	42	42	42.9		
12		=INT(42.99)	=TRUNC(32.9,0)			
13						

Figure 14-11: INT converts a decimal value to an integer, whereas TRUNC truncates to the specified number of decimal places

 If you want the numeric value to be rounded up or down based on its fractional value, use ROUND.

LCM

You can use LCM (an Analysis ToolPak function) to determine the smallest number that is a multiple of the specified values, commonly referred to as the least common multiple. For example, the least common multiple for 12 and 18 is 36, because 36 is the smallest number that is a multiple of both 12 and 18 (12 × 3 and 18 × 2).

To Calculate

=LCM(Number1, Number2, ...)

Number1, Number2, ...
You can specify between 1 and 29 different numeric values for which you want to find the least common multiple. The values must all be larger than 0. If any of the values are not integers, the fractional portion of the number will be truncated (i.e., 4.5 becomes 4).

Example

Figure 14-10 shows how LCM is used to determine the smallest number that is a multiple of a series of numeric values. You will notice that when a decimal value is specified, such as 24.2, the fractional portion of the number is truncated.

 You can use GCD to find the largest value that is divisible into a series of numbers.

LN

Use LN to determine the natural logarithm of a number. For example, the natural logarithm of 2.7182818245904 is 1 because LN is an inversed function to EXP.

To Calculate

=LN(Number)

Number
This required argument indicates the positive numeric value that you want to find the natural logarithm for.

Example

Figure 14-8 illustrates how you can use LN to determine the natural logarithm for any positive numeric value.

 You can determine the value of raising the constant e to a specific power by using EXP.

LOG

You can use LOG to determine the logarithm of a number to any base. By default, the function assumes you want to determine the base-10 logarithm for the specified numeric value; to use a different base you must specify a value for the *Base* argument.

To Calculate

```
=LOG(Number, Base)
```

The *Number* argument is required and must have a positive value. The *Base* argument is optional.

Number

Indicates the positive numeric value for which you want to determine the logarithm.

Base

This optional argument specifies the base you want to use for the logarithm. The value of this argument must be a positive numeric value. If this value is omitted, the function assumes you want to find a base-10 logarithm of the value specified for the *Number* argument.

Example

Figure 14-12 illustrates the difference between using LOG to find the log to a specific base and using LOG10 to find the base 10 log. The example also shows how POWER is used to determine the value of raising a number to a specific power.

LOG10

Use LOG10 to determine the base-10 logarithm of a positive numeric value.

To Calculate

```
=LOG10(Number)
```

Number

This required argument indicates the positive numeric value for which you want to determine the logarithm.

Example

Figure 14-12 illustrates the difference between using LOG to find the log to a specific base and using LOG10 to find the base 10 log. The example also shows

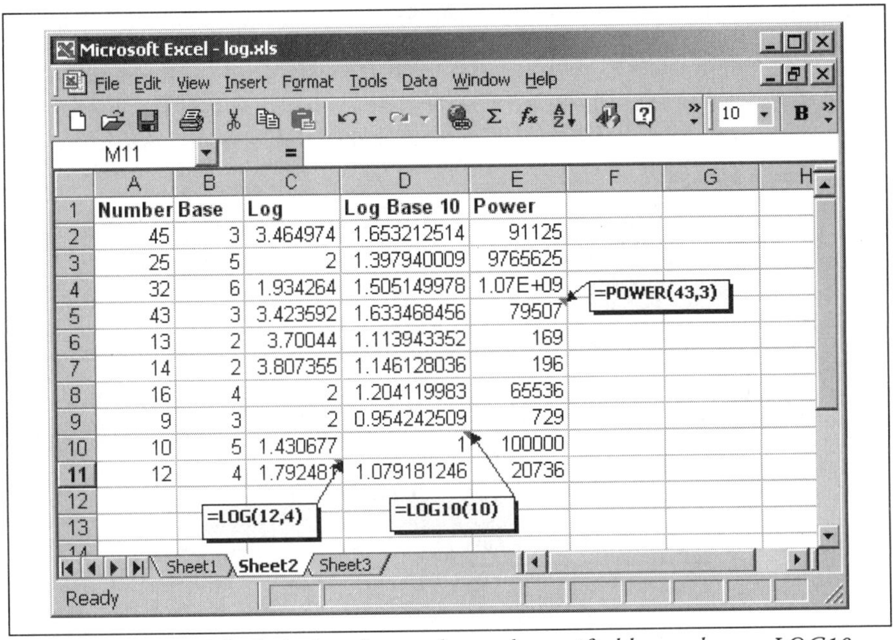

Figure 14-12: LOG finds the log of a number to the specified base; whereas, LOG10 finds the log for a number to the base of 10

how POWER is used to determine the value of raising a number to a specific power.

MDETERM

You can use MDETERM to calculate the matrix determinant for an array. For example, if your matrix array is located in cells A1:B2 the determinant is calculated by taking A1 × B2 – A2 × B1. Of course, the calculation becomes more complex as additional rows and columns are added. Only square matrices have determinants.

To Calculate

    =MDETERM(Array)

Array
    This required argument must specify an array that has an equal number of rows and columns. The values in the array must all be numeric or the function will return an error.

Example

Figure 14-13 illustrates how to use MDETERM to find the determinant of a matrix. The example also shows how MINVERSE is used to find the inverse of a square matrix and MMULT is used to determine the product of two matrices.

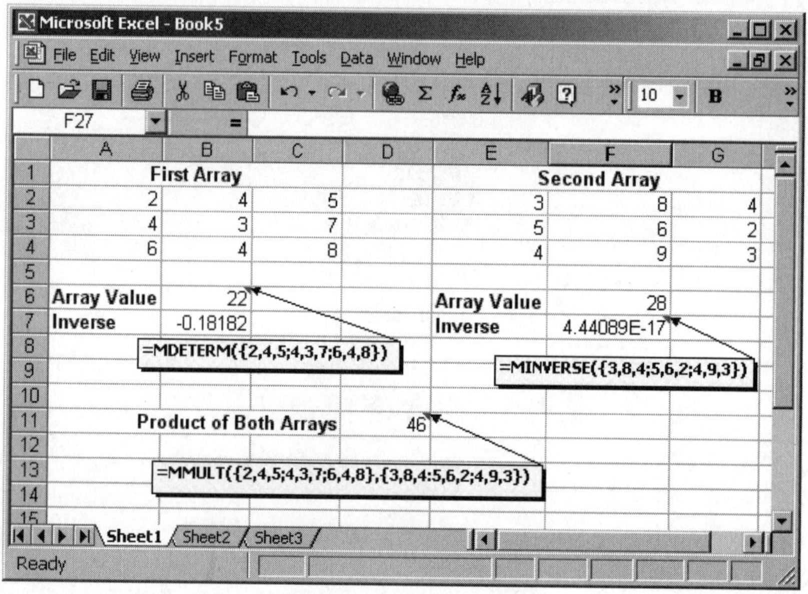

Figure 14-13: When working with matrices they must have an equal number of rows and columns

MINVERSE

You can use MINVERSE to find the inverse of a square matrix. Keep in mind that not all square matrices have inverses.

To Calculate

```
=MINVERSE(Array)
```

Array
    This required argument must specify an array with equal rows and columns. The values in the array must all be numeric or the function returns an error.

Example

Figure 14-13 illustrates how MINVERSE is used to find the inverse of a matrix. The example also shows how to use MDETERM to find the determinant of a matrix and MMULT to determine the product of two matrices.

MMULT

You can use MMULT to find the product of two matrices.

To Calculate

=MMULT(Array1, Array2)

Both of the arguments must be specified for this function. For this function to work, Array1 must have the same number of columns as the number of rows in Array2.

Array1, Array2
Specifies an array that contains only numeric values.

Example

Figure 14-13 illustrates how to use MMULT to find the product of two matrices. The example also shows how MDETERM can find the determinant of each matrix and MINVERSE is used to find the inverse of each square matrix.

MOD

You can use MOD to determine what the remainder is when one number is divided into another number. For example, the number 2 does not divide into the number 5 evenly, so if you were to use MOD it would return a result of 1.

To Calculate

=MOD(Number, Divisor)

The Number and Divisor arguments are required for this function.

Number
Indicates a numeric value. The value specified for the Divisor argument will be divided into this value.

Divisor
Indicates a numeric value that you want to divide into the value of the Number argument.

Example

Figure 14-14 illustrates how MOD and QUOTIENT are related. MOD returns the remainder of the division while QUOTIENT returns the integer portion of the division.

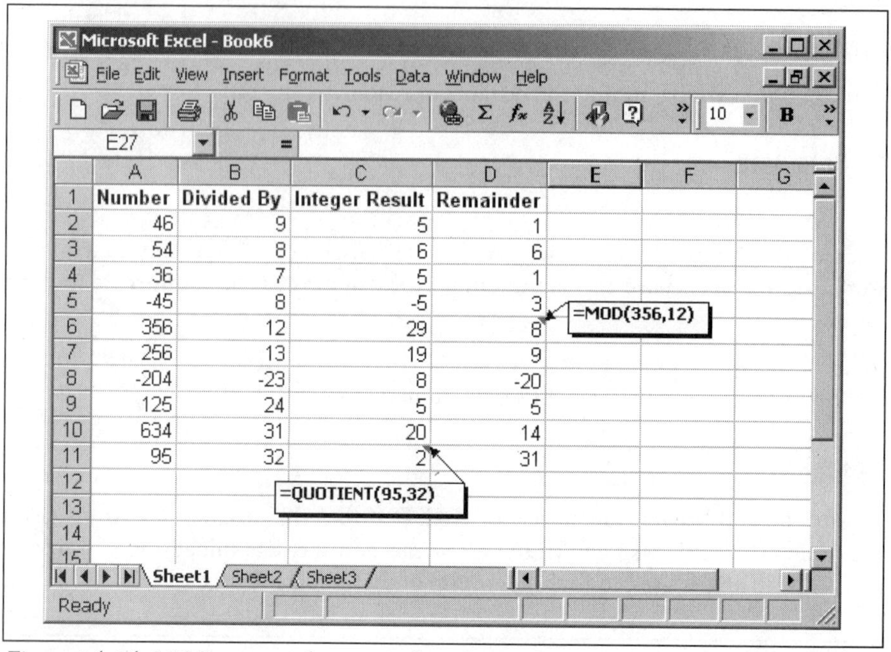

Number	Divided By	Integer Result	Remainder
46	9	5	1
54	8	6	6
36	7	5	1
-45	8	-5	3
356	12	29	8
256	13	19	9
-204	-23	8	-20
125	24	5	5
634	31	20	14
95	32	2	31

Figure 14-14: MOD returns the remainder whereas QUOTIENT returns the integer result of the division

TIP # 84

The Sign of the Remainder

The result of MOD will have the same sign as the value of the Divisor argument. For example, if the Divisor argument is –3 the result of the function will be a negative number.

MROUND

You can use MROUND (an Analysis ToolPak function) to round a numeric value to the closest multiple of the specified value. For example, if you always want the value to be an even number you would specify a `2` for the *`Multiple`* argument and all values will be rounded to even numbers.

To Calculate

```
=MROUND(Number, Multiple)
```

The *`Number`* and *`Multiple`* arguments are required for this function.

`Number`

Specifies the numeric value that you want to round.

Multiple

Specifies a numeric value that represents the multiple you want to round the value of the *Number* argument to.

> *The signs on each value must be the same or the function will return an error. In other words, if the value of the Number argument is positive the value of the Multiple argument must also be positive.*

Example

As you can see in Figure 14-15, Excel provides several functions for rounding a numeric value. The function that you use is based solely on the results that you want to achieve. As shown in the example, use MROUND when you want to round to a specific integer value. To eliminate errors, IF is used to check the sign of the value. If it is negative, a value of –2 is specified for the *Multiple* argument; whereas, if the value is positive, a value of 2 is specified. ROUND, ROUNDUP, and ROUNDDOWN allow you to round a numeric value to a specific number of decimal places.

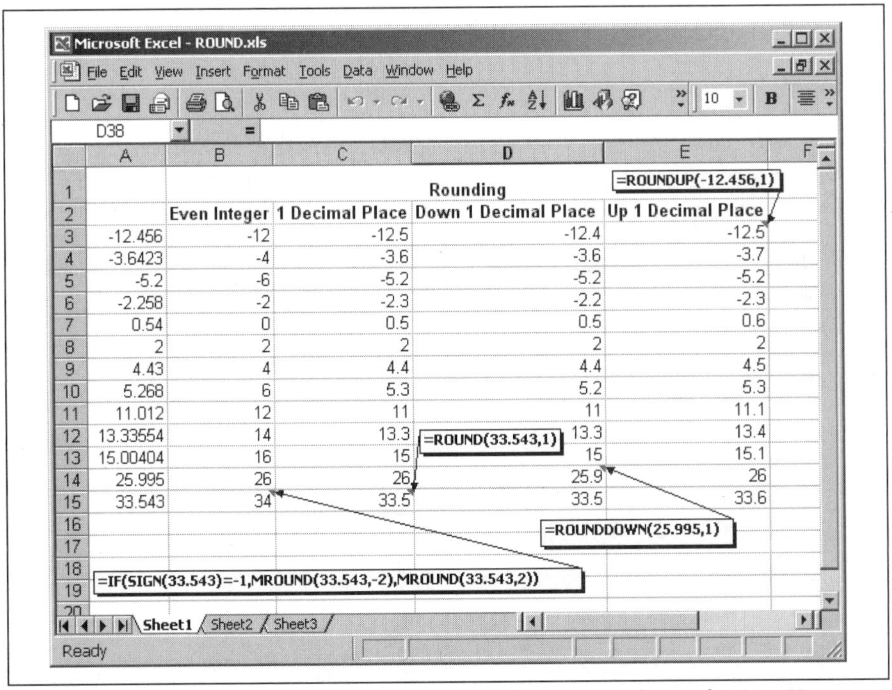

	Microsoft Excel - ROUND.xls				
	File Edit View Insert Format Tools Data Window Help				
	D38 =				
	A	B	C	D	E
1				Rounding	=ROUNDUP(-12.456,1)
2		Even Integer	1 Decimal Place	Down 1 Decimal Place	Up 1 Decimal Place
3	-12.456	-12	-12.5	-12.4	-12.5
4	-3.6423	-4	-3.6	-3.6	-3.7
5	-5.2	-6	-5.2	-5.2	-5.2
6	-2.258	-2	-2.3	-2.2	-2.3
7	0.54	0	0.5	0.5	0.6
8	2	2	2	2	2
9	4.43	4	4.4	4.4	4.5
10	5.268	6	5.3	5.2	5.3
11	11.012	12	11	11	11.1
12	13.33554	14	13.3	=ROUND(33.543,1) 13.3	13.4
13	15.00404	16	15	15	15.1
14	25.995	26	26	25.9	26
15	33.543	34	33.5	33.5	33.6
16				=ROUNDDOWN(25.995,1)	
17					
18					
19	=IF(SIGN(33.543)=-1,MROUND(33.543,-2),MROUND(33.543,2))				
20					

Figure 14-15: Use MROUND to round to a specific integer value and ROUND, ROUNDUP, and ROUNDDOWN to round decimal places

If the fractional remainder when dividing the Multiple into the Number value is larger than half of the multiple, MROUND rounds the value returned up or away from zero. For example, if the value of the Multiple argument is 2 and the remainder is 1.5, the value of MROUND is rounded up to the next even number.

MULTINOMIAL

You can use MULTINOMIAL (an Analysis ToolPak function) to determine the ratio of the sum of the factorials for the specified values divided by the product of the same factorials. In other words, if you have the values 1, 2, 3 the function would calculate it by as follows: `(1+2+3)!/(1!*2!*3!)`.

To Calculate

`=MULTINOMIAL(Number1, Number2, ...)`

`Number1, Number2, ...`

There must be between 1 and 29 different `Number` arguments specified but each one must be a numeric value larger than 0.

Example

Figure 14-16 illustrates how MULTINOMINAL is used to determine the ratio of the sum of three factorials divided by the product of the same three factorials. Since this result is typically rather large, I reformatted the cells to use commas to separate the thousands.

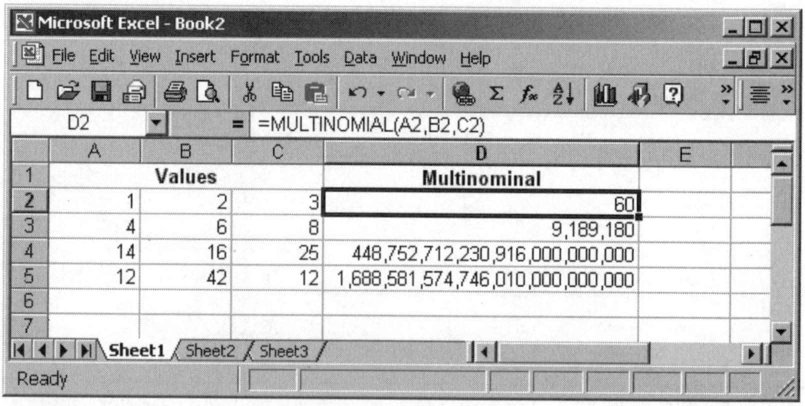

	A	B	C	D	E
1		Values		Multinominal	
2	1	2	3	60	
3	4	6	8	9,189,180	
4	14	16	25	448,752,712,230,916,000,000,000	
5	12	42	12	1,688,581,574,746,010,000,000,000	
6					
7					

D2 = =MULTINOMIAL(A2,B2,C2)

Figure 14-16: Because MULTINOMINAL is working with factorials the result will typically be very large

ODD

Use ODD to round a numeric value to the closest odd integer. This function rounds away from zero, meaning that if the numeric value is greater than zero it rounds up, whereas if the value is less than zero it rounds down.

To Calculate

```
=ODD(Number)
```

Number
This required argument must be a numeric value that you want to round.

Example

Figure 14-7 illustrates the difference in the results returned by EVEN and ODD. Notice that when ODD receives a negative value it is rounded down (away from zero) to the next even integer. For example, –4.2 is rounded to –5.

PI

If you have a formula that requires the use of the mathematical constant pi, you can use PI to return it. Pi is a constant value of approximately 3.14159265358979, typically used when working with circles.

To Calculate

```
=PI()
```

This function has no arguments.

Example

As shown in Figure 14-17, PI works for determining measurements of a circle. The formula for calculating the circumference of a circle is `2*Pi*r` (radius). The example also uses POWER to find the area of the circle.

POWER

You can use POWER to determine the results of raising a numeric value to a specific power. When you raise a number to a value you inidicate that you want to multiply the specified number by itself the number of times specified in the Power argument. For example, 4 raised to the 3 power is same as to $4 \times 4 \times 4$.

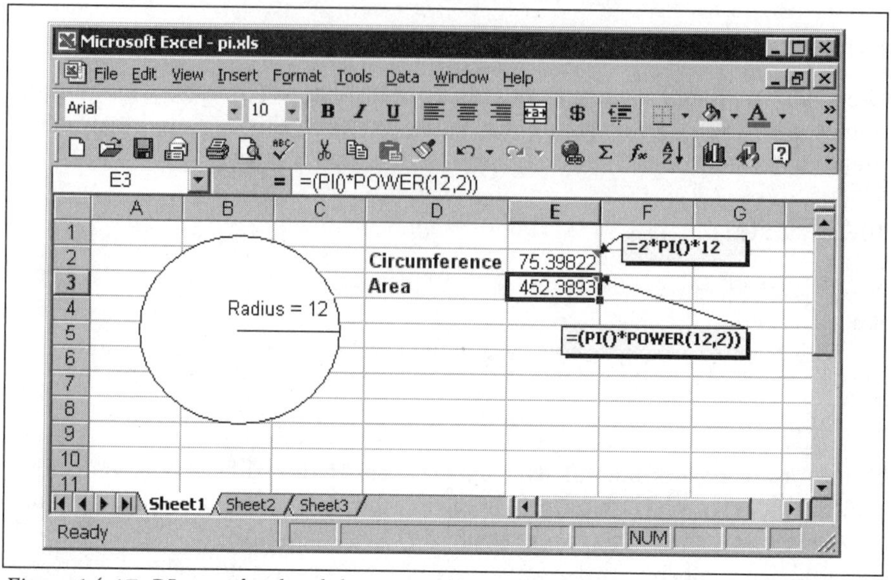

Microsoft Excel - pi.xls

File   Edit   View   Insert   Format   Tools   Data   Window   Help

Arial   ▼ 10 ▼   B *I* U   ≡ ≡ ≡ ▦ $ ᵴ   ▦ ▾ ♦ ▾ A ▾   »

E3   ▼   =   =(PI()*POWER(12,2))

	A	B	C	D	E	F	G
1						=2*PI()*12	
2				Circumference	75.39822		
3				Area	452.3893		
4			Radius = 12				
5					=(PI()*POWER(12,2))		
6							
7							
8							
9							
10							
11							

Sheet1 / Sheet2 / Sheet3 /

Ready   NUM

Figure 14-17: PI provides the ability to quickly perform circle calculations without needing to remember the exact value of Pi

To Calculate

=POWER(Number, Power)

The Number and Power arguments are required for this function.

Number

Specifies a numeric value that you want to raise to the value of the Power argument.

Power

Specifies a numeric value that you want to use as the exponent in the equation.

Example

Figure 14-12 illustrates how to use POWER to determine the value of raising a number to a specific power. It also compares the difference between using LOG and LOG10.

 NOTE   *Instead of using POWER you can use the power operator ^. For example, =POWER(4,3) is the same as 4^3.*

PRODUCT

You can use PRODUCT to multiply a series of numeric values and return the result. For example, if the function received the values 3, 4, 5 they would be multiplied together and return a value of 60.

To Calculate

```
=PRODUCT(Number1, Number2, ...)
```

There must be at least one *Number* argument specified.

Number1, Number2, ...
    You must specify between 1 and 30 numeric values that you want to multiply.

Example

Figure 14-18 illustrates how PRODUCT finds the result of multiplying values. The example compares this function to results of adding the same values using SUM.

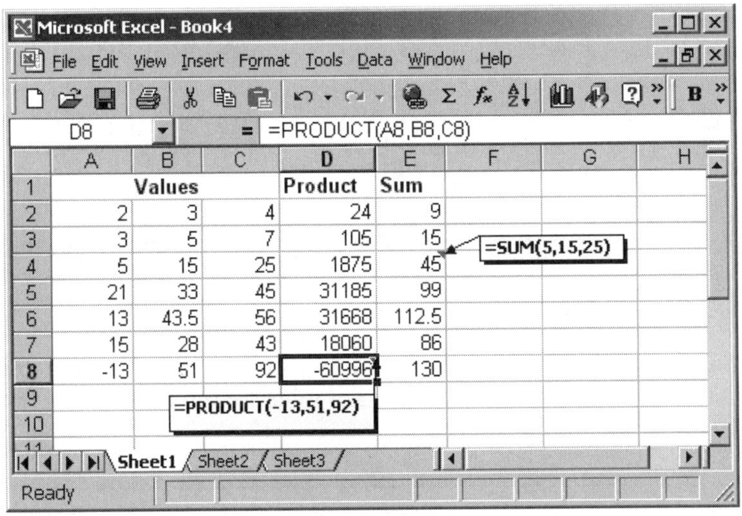

Figure 14-18: You can add or multiply more than one value using SUM and PRODUCT

QUOTIENT

You can use QUOTIENT (an Analysis ToolPak function) to divide one value into another and return only the integer portion of the result. For example, if you were to divide 4 into 9 you would get a value of 2.25 but if you use QUOTIENT the result would be 2.

To Calculate

=QUOTIENT(*Numerator, Denominator*)

The *Numerator* and *Denominator* arguments are both required for this function.

Numerator
This argument must specify a numeric value.

Denominator
This argument must specify the numeric value that should be divided into the value specified for the *Numerator* argument.

Example

Figure 14-14 illustrates how MOD and QUOTIENT are related. MOD returns the remainder of the division while QUOTIENT returns the integer portion of the division.

RADIANS

Use RADIANS to convert angles measured in a degrees measurement into angles measured in radians.

To Calculate

=RADIANS(*Angle*)

Angle
This argument indicates a degrees value that you want to convert to radians.

Example

The ACOSH function covered in this chaper has an example illustrating how RADIANS is used to determine the radians value for an angle if you know the degree measurement.

RAND

You can use RAND to determine a random number between 0 and 1. When you use this function, each time the worksheet is opened or recalculated a new number is generated.

To Calculate

RAND()

There are no arguments required for this function.

Customizing the Range of Random Numbers

You can change the range of random numbers by multiplying the results by a specific value. For example, if you want the random numbers between 0 and 10, multiply the results by 10. Keep in mind you will still get decimal values.

Example

Figure 14-19 illustrates the differences between using RAND and RAND-BETWEEN. Both functions produce random numbers that are regenerated whenever you recalculate the worksheet.

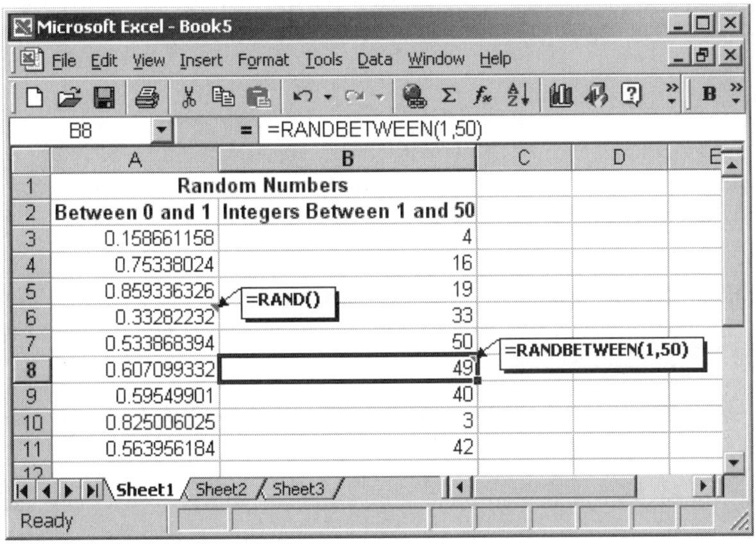

Figure 14-19: RAND returns a decimal value between 0 and 1, whereas RANDBETWEEN returns integer values within the specified range

> **NOTE** *To find random numbers within a certain range, use RANDBETWEEN.*

RANDBETWEEN

You can use RANDBETWEEN (an Analysis ToolPak function) to determine a random integer within the range you specify. When you use this function a new random integer is generated each time you open or recalculate the worksheet. Unlike RAND, this function only returns an integer value.

To Calculate

=RANDBETWEEN(*Bottom*, *Top*)

The *Bottom* and *Top* arguments are required for this function.

Bottom

Indicates the smallest number that you want returned by the function. If you specify a fractional value, the function will not return an integer value smaller than that value. For example, if you specify a value of 0.65 for the *Bottom* argument the smallest value that would be returned by the function is 1.

Top

Indicates the largest number that you want returned by the function. If you specify a fractional value the function will not return an integer value larger than the specified value. For example, if you specified a value of 9.5 for the *Top* argument the largest value that would be returned would be 9.

Example

Figure 14-19 illustrates the differences between using RAND and RANDBETWEEN. Both functions produce random numbers that are regenerated whenever you recalculate the worksheet. RANDBETWEEN always returns an integer value.

 NOTE *To find a random number between 0 and 1, use RAND. RAND also allows you to determine random numbers that contain decimal values.*

Roman

You can use ROMAN to convert a numeric value into a Roman numeral. For example, 1999 is expressed as MCMXCIX in Roman numerals.

To Calculate

=Roman(*Number*, *Form*)

The *Number* argument is required for this function. The *Form* argument is optional.

Number

Indicates the numeric value that you want to convert to a Roman numeral. This number must not be negative and it must be less than 4000, or Roman will return an error.

Form

An optional value that indicates how concise you want to express the numeric value. If this value is omitted it is assumed to have a value of 0, which will return the numeric value in the classic form. When dealing with Roman numerals there are multiple ways to express a value, for example 1999 is expressed as MCMXCIX, which equals one thousand (M) nine hundred (CM) ninety (XC) nine (IX). It could also be greatly simplified and expressed as MIM which equals one thousand (M) and one thousand minus one (IM). Table 14-1 provides a list of the values that are specified for the Form argument and illustrates the results you would receive if specified for the numeric value 1999.

Table 14-1: Roman Numeral Form Values

Value	Description
0	This is the default value that is used if the value is omitted for the Form argument. If you use this value the function returns a classic Roman numeral where 1999 is converted to MCMXCIX.
1	This option makes the Roman numeral more concise by converting 1999 to MLMVLIV.
2	This option makes the Roman numeral more concise than specifying a value of 1. The numeric value 1999 is converted to MXMIX.
3	This option is even more concise; the numeric value 1999 is converted to MVMIV.
4	This option returns a Roman numeral in its most concise or simple form. If you use this option to convert 1999 the function returns a value of MIM.
TRUE	Specifying a value of TRUE for the *Form* argument produces the same results as specifying a 0. The classic method of expressing Roman numerals is used.
FALSE	Specifying a value of FALSE for the *Form* argument produces the same results as specify a 4. The numeric value is converted to its most simplified form.

Example

Figure 14-20 illustrates how Roman is used to convert a number to a Roman numeral. As indicated in the *Form* argument description, you can specify a number between 0 and 4 that indicates how concisely you want the value to be specified.

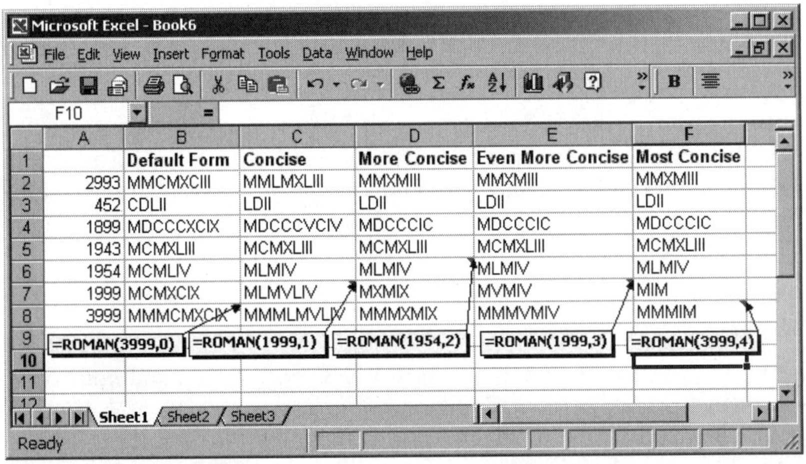

Figure 14-20: There are multiple ways to express a Roman numeral

---

TIP # 86

Roman Numeral Expression

Roman numerals are expressed using the letters C, D, I, L, M, V, and X as outlined in Table 14-2.

Table 14-2: Roman Numerals

Numeral	Description
I	Represents the number 1.
V	Represents the number 5.
X	Represents the number 10.
L	Represents the number 50.
C	Represents the number 100.
D	Represents the number 500.
M	Represents the number 1000.

ROUND

You can use ROUND to round a numeric value so that it has the specified number of decimal digits. For example, if you want to round the value 1.45673 to two digits the function returns a value of 1.46 because the thousandths place contains a value of 6 so the hundredths place is rounded up from 5 to 6.

To Calculate

    =ROUND(Number, Num_Digits)

The *Number* and *Num_Digits* arguments are both required for this function.

Number
> Specifies a numeric value that you want to round.

Num_Digits
> An integer value that specifies the number of decimal places that you want to round the numeric value specified for the *Number* argument to. If this argument is 0 the numeric value is rounded to the closest integer value. If the *Num_Digits* argument is a negative value the value on the left side of the decimal is rounded down. For example, =ROUND(19.45, -2) returns a value of 17.

Example

Figure 14-15 illustrates the results when ROUND is used to round numeric values to one decimal place. The example allows you to compare these results to the ones achieved when you use ROUNDUP and ROUNDDOWN to always round the decimal values up or down, respectively.

Figuring Out How Values Are Rounded

ROUND uses the basic rules of rounding that we studied in school. If the value is less than 5, it is rounded down; if it is 5 or greater, it is rounded up. If you want to always round the value up, use ROUNDUP. To always round down, use ROUNDDOWN.

ROUNDDOWN

You can use ROUNDDOWN to round a numeric value so that it has the specified number of decimal digits by rounding the number down (toward 0). For example, if you want to round the value 1.45673 to two digits, the function returns a value of 1.45; even though the thousandths place contains a value of 6, the hundredths place is rounded down to 5.

To Calculate

=ROUNDDOWN(*Number*, *Num_Digits*)

The *Number* and *Num_Digits* arguments are both required for this function.

Number
    Specifies a numeric value that you want to round.

Num_Digits
    An integer value that specifies the number of decimal places that you want to round the numeric value specified for the *Number* argument to. If this argument is 0 the numeric value is rounded down to the closest integer value. If the *Num_Digits* argument is a negative value the value on the left side of the decimal is rounded down. For example, =ROUND(19.45, -2) returns a value of 17.

Example

Figure 14-15 illustrates the results when ROUNDDOWN is used to round numeric values down to one decimal place. The example allows you to compare these results to the ones achieved when you use ROUNDUP and ROUND.

ROUNDUP

You can use ROUNDUP to round a numeric value so that it has the specified number of decimal digits by always rounding up. For example, if you want to round the value 1.45373 to two digits, the function returns a value of 1.46; even thought the thousandths place contains a value of 3, the hundredths place is still rounded up from 5 to 6.

Math Functions

To Calculate

```
=ROUNDUP(Number, Num_Digits)
```

The *Number* and *Num_Digits* arguments are both required for this function.

Number
> Specifies a numeric value that you want to round.

Num_Digits
> An integer value that specifies the number of decimal places that you want to round the numeric value specified for the *Number* argument to. If this argument is 0 the numeric value is rounded up to the closest integer value. If the *Num_Digits* argument is a negative value the value on the left side of the decimal is rounded up. For example, =ROUNDUP(19.45, -2) returns a value of 21.

Example

Figure 14-15 illustrates the results when ROUNDUP is used to round numeric values up to one decimal place. The example allows you to compare these results to the ones achieved when you use ROUND and ROUNDDOWN.

SERIESSUM

You can use SERIESSUM (an Analysis ToolPak function) to calculate the sum of different kinds of series.

To Calculate

```
=SERIESSUM(X, N, M, A)
```

All of the arguments are required for this function.

X   Specifies a numeric value that indicates the input value for the power series.

N   Specifies a numeric value that indicates the power that you want to raise the value of the *X* argument to for the first term in the equation.

M   Specifies a numeric value that is added to *N* for each successive term in the equation. For example, if *N* is 4 and *M* is 2 for each term, an additional 2 will be added to the power.

A   Specifies an array of values that the *X* argument is multiplied by for each term. The number of arguments in the array determines the number of terms in the equation. For example, if there are three values in the array there will be three terms that are added in the equation.

Example

Figure 14-21 illustrates how SERIESSUM is used to perform a power series. The comment in the example shows how the function calculates the series.

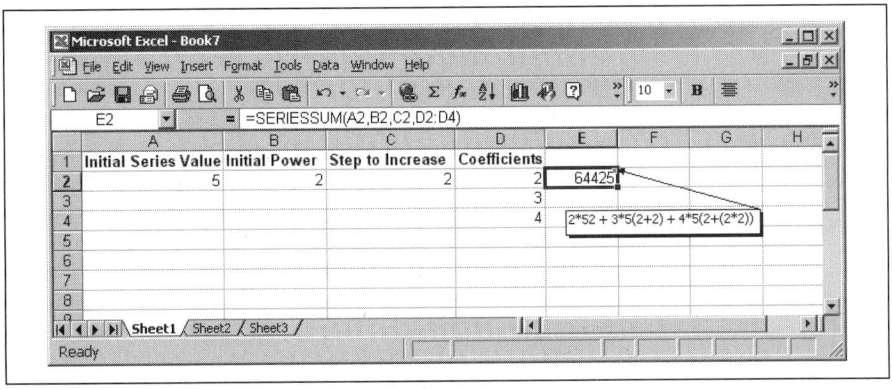

Figure 14-21: Use SERIESSUM to calculate a power series

SIN

If you need to know if a numeric value is negative, positive, or zero, you can use SIGN. This function returns a value of 1 if the numeric value specified is positive, −1 if the value is negative, or 0 if the value is equal to zero.

To Calculate

=SIGN(Number)

Number
This required argument must specify a numeric value.

Example

Figure 14-15 illustrates how SIGN is used to check the sign of a numeric value. In this example, SIGN determines whether the value is negative or positive and then passes the corresponding value as the Multiple argument for MROUND.

SIN

Use SIN to determine the sine of an angle expressed in radians. In order to use this function the size of the angle must be in radians. You can convert degrees to radians by multiplying by $\pi/180$.

To Calculate

=SIN(*Number*)

Number

This required argument specifies the radian measurement of the angle for which you want to determine the sine.

Example

The ACOSH function in this chapter has an example illustrating how SIN is used to determine the sine for an angle as long as you know the radian value. For this example, we used RADIANS to determine the radian measurement for a 50 degree angle.

SINH

Use SINH to determine the hyperbolic sine of a number.

To Calculate

=SINH(*Number*)

Number

This required argument must specify a numeric value.

Example

The ACOSH function covered in this chapter has an example illustrating how you can use the hyperbolic functions. Since ASINH is the inverse of SINH, you will notice that the value that is returned by ASINH is equal to the value that was passed to SINH.

SQRT

You can use SQRT to determine the square root of a positive numeric value.

To Calculate

=SQRT(*Number*)

Number

This required argument specifies a positive number for which you want to find the square root.

Example

Figure 14-22 illustrates the difference between using SQRT and SQRTPI. SQRT determines the square root of the specified numeric value.

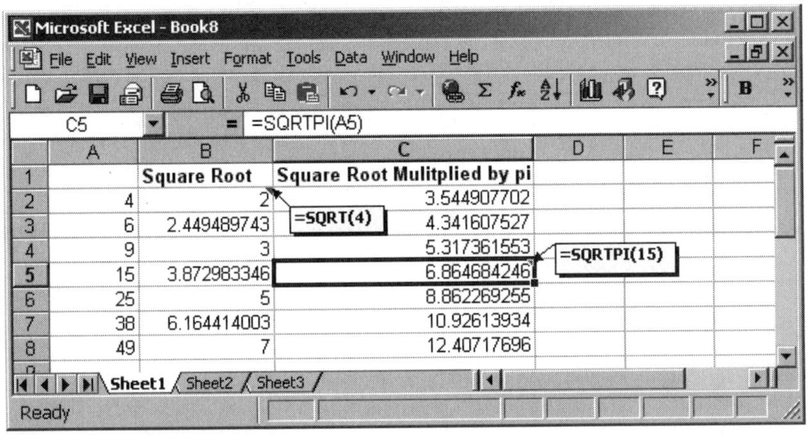

	A	B	C	D	E	F
1		Square Root	Square Root Mulitplied by pi			
2	4	2	3.544907702			
3	6	2.449489743	4.341607527			
4	9	3	5.317361553			
5	15	3.872983346	6.864684246			
6	25	5	8.862269255			
7	38	6.164414003	10.92613934			
8	49	7	12.40717696			

Figure 14-22: SQRT determines the square root of a number, whereas SQRTPI multiplies the value by pi and then determines the square root

> **NOTE** *If the value of the Number argument is negative SQRT returns an error. To ensure you don't receive an error you can combine SQRT with ABS, as in =SQRT(ABS(-36)). By doing this, if the value of the Number argument is negative ABS converts it to a positive value before SQRT sees it eliminating the potential error. Keep in mind, this does not correct the source of the negative number, it only keeps SQRT from returning an error.*

SQRTPI

Use SQRTPI (an Analysis ToolPak function) to determine the square root of a numeric value multiplied by π.

To Calculate

=SQRTPI(Number)

Number
This required argument specifies the numeric value that you want to multiply by π.

Example

Figure 14-22 illustrates the difference between using SQRT and SQRTPI. SQRTPI determines the square root of the specified positive numeric value multiplied by pi.

SUBTOTAL

You can use SUBTOTAL to total a series of values using one of 11 different functions. When you use this function you specify the values that you want to total and then select the function you want to use.

This function works well with the Data → Subtotals option. In fact, it is easier to create the data list using the menu option. When you use the Subtotals option it simply creates a formula using SUBTOTAL.

To Calculate

=SUBTOTAL(*Function_Num*, *Ref1*, *Ref2*,...)

The *Function_Num* argument is required for this function. You must specify at least one *Ref* argument.

Function_Num

    An integer value between 1 and 11 that specifies the function that you want to use to sum the list of values, as specified in Table 14-3.

Table 14-3: Options for Totaling Values

Value	Function Called
1	AVERAGE
2	COUNT
3	COUNTA
4	MAX
5	MIN
6	PRODUCT
7	STDEV
8	STDEVP
9	SUM
10	VAR
11	VARP

Ref1, *Ref2*,...

    There must be between 1 and 29 numeric values specified as arguments for this function.

Example

Figure 14-23 shows how SUBTOTAL is used to perform several different types of calculations on a series of numeric values. The only thing that is different for each use of the function is the value specified for the `Function_Num` argument.

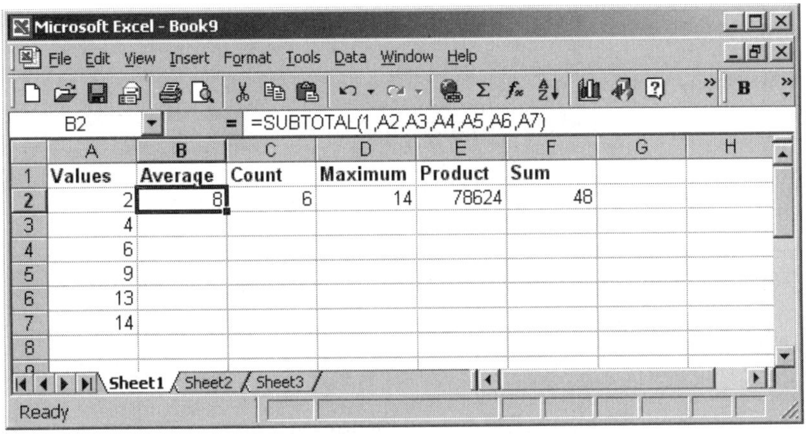

Microsoft Excel - Book9
File Edit View Insert Format Tools Data Window Help
B2
=SUBTOTAL(1,A2,A3,A4,A5,A6,A7)
A B C D E F G H
1 Values Average Count Maximum Product Sum
2 2 8 6 14 78624 48
3 4
4 6
5 9
6 13
7 14
8
Sheet1 Sheet2 Sheet3
Ready

Figure 14-23: SUBTOTAL provides the ability to quickly modify the function used with a series of numbers

SUM

SUM is very handy for summing a series of numeric values.

To Calculate

```
=SUM(Number1, Number2, ...)
```

`Number1, Number2, ...`
: There must be between 1 and 30 different numeric arguments specified for this function.

Example

Figure 14-18 illustrates how SUM is used to find the result of adding multiple values. The example compares this function to results of multiplying the same values using PRODUCT.

NOTE *SUM can also sum logical values; TRUE is translated to 1 and FALSE is translated to 0.*

SUMIF

If you only want to sum a range of cells based on specific criteria, you can use SUMIF. For example, if the number of sales is greater than 0 you may want to total the sales amounts.

To Calculate

=SUMIF(Range, Criteria, Sum_Range)

The *Range* and *Criteria* arguments must have values.

Range
Specifies the cell or range of cells that you want to evaluate.

Criteria
Specifies the criteria that must be met by the cells specified for the *Range* argument. This argument is a numeric value, an expression such as >45, or even text.

Sum_Range
Indicates the cells that should be summed if the criteria specified in the *Range* and *Criteria* arguments are met. This is an optional argument; if you omit it the cells specified in the *Range* argument will be summed.

Example

Figure 14-24 illustrates how SUMIF is used to sum a series of values only when they meet the specified criteria. In this example, the function looks at the sales for the six-month period, and as long as sales occurred the sales amounts are totaled.

SUMPRODUCT

Use SUMPRODUCT to multiply the corresponding elements of the specified arrays and then sum the results.

To Calculate

=SUMPRODUCT(Array1, Array2, ...)

There must be at least two *Array* arguments specified for this function.

Array1, Array2, ...
Each *Array* argument must specify an array with the same dimensions (same number of rows and columns).

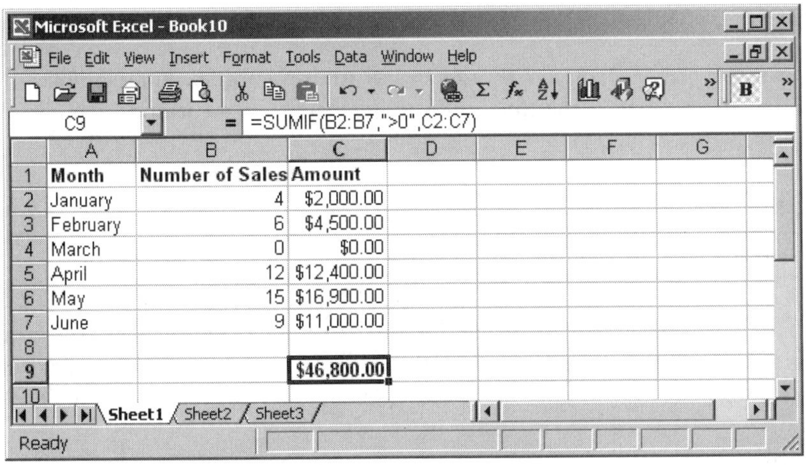

Figure 14-24: Use SUMIF to perform a calculation only when the specified criteria is met

Example

Figure 14-25 illustrates how SUMPRODUCT is used to sum the products of the corresponding elements of two arrays. This example also compares those results to the results produced by SUMX2MY2, SUMX2PY2, and SUMXMY2.

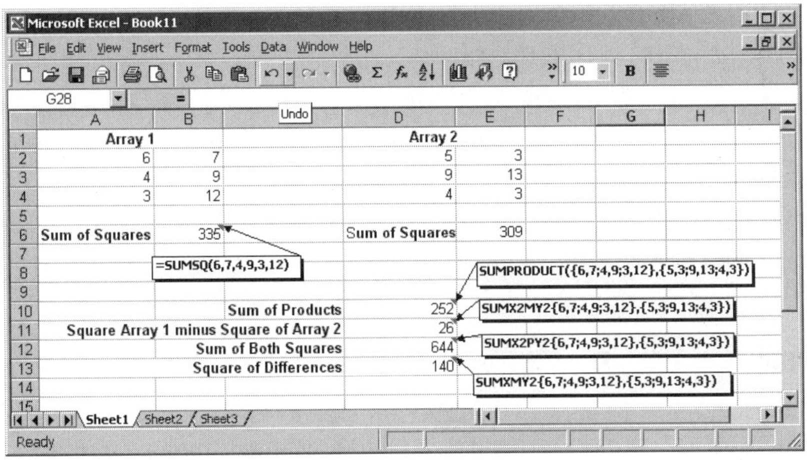

Figure 14-25: Excel provides several functions for summing arrays

> **NOTE** Any elements of the arrays that are not numeric will be treated as zeros.

SUMSQ

You can use SUMSQ to add the squares of multiple values. For example, if you have the values 4 and 5 the function would square each value and then add them together to get a result of 41 (16+25).

To Calculate

```
=SUMSQ(Number1, Number2, ...)
```

Number1, Number2, ...
   You must specify between 1 and 30 different numeric arguments for this function. You can also specify arrays for each argument allowing you to have up to 30 different arrays of numbers, making the number or values basically limitless.

Example

Figure 14-25 shows how SUMSQ finds the sum of the squares for each array. Use the values calculated by the function to compare the results of the other functions in the example. Let's say SUMX2MY2 returns the results of subtracting the square of one array from another array. Compare the value returned by that function to the value you would get by manually subtracting the results of returned by SUMSQ.

SUMX2MY2

Use SUMXWMY2 to take two arrays and add the squares and then subtract the results of the second array from the first.

To Calculate

```
=SUMX2MY2(Array_X, Array_Y)
```

Both arguments must be specified for this function.

Array_X, Array_Y
   Both arguments must specify arrays of numeric values.

Example

Figure 14-25 illustrates how SUMX2MY2 is used to find the result of adding the squares of *array 1* and *array 2* and then subtracting *array 2* from *array 1*.

TIP # 88
Summing Arrays
The arrays specified by the Array_X and Array_Y arguments must be the same size.

SUMX2PY2

Use SUMXPMY2 to take two arrays and add the squares. This is commonly referred to as the sum of the sum of squares.

To Calculate

=SUMX2PY2(Array_X, Array_Y)

Both arguments must be specified for this function.

Array_X, Array_Y
Both arguments must specify arrays of numeric values.

Example

Figure 14-25 shows how SUMX2PY2 is used add the squares of two arrays.

SUMXMY2

Use SUMXMY2 to take two arrays and subtract the corresponding elements and then add the squares of the differences.

To Calculate

=SUMX2MY2(Array_X, Array_Y)

Both arguments must be specified for this function.

Array_X, Array_Y
Both arguments must specify arrays of numeric values.

Example

Figure 14-25 illustrates how SUMXMY2 is used to subtract the corresponding elements in Array 1 and Array 2 and add the squares of the differences.

TAN

Use TAN to determine the tangent of an angle expressed in radians. In order to use this function the size of the angle must be in radians. You can convert degrees to radians by multiplying by PI()/180.

To Calculate

=TAN(Number)

Number
> This required argument must specify the radian measurement of the angle for which you want to determine the tangent.

Example

Figure 14-2 illustrates how TAN is used to determine the tangent for an angle as long as you know the radian value. For this example, we used RADIANS to determine the radian measurement for a 50 degree angle.

TANH

Use TANH to determine the hyperbolic tangent of a number.

To Calculate

    =TANH(*Number*)

Number
> This required argument must specify a numeric value.

Example

The ACOSH function covered in this chater has an example illustrating how you can use the hyperbolic functions. Since ATANH is the inverse of TANH, you will notice that the value that is returned by ATANH is equal to the value that was passed to TANH.

TRUNC

You can use TRUNC to truncate the fractional portion of a numeric value to the specified number of decimal places.

To Calculate

    =TRUNC(*Number*, *Num_Digits*)

Number
> This required argument specifies the numeric value that you want to truncate.

Num_Digits
> This argument is optional. If omitted, the argument has a default value of 0 meaning that all of the decimal portion of the numeric value will be truncated. If a value is specified for the *Num_Digits* argument it must be an integer value.

Example

The INT function coverd in this chapter has an example showing why TRUNC works well for ensuring that you always get the numeric value with the specified number of decimal places. The example compares the results of specified 0 for the *Num_Digits* argument of TRUNC or using INT. You will notice the results are different with negative numbers. TRUNC simply truncates the decimal values where INT rounds the number down to the closest integer.

 Keep in mind that TRUNC simply truncates the fractional portion of the number without rounding. If you want the value to be rounded use ROUND.

Chapter 15

Statistical Functions

Excel offers a wide range of statistical functions. Many of these are highly special-ized, though some are useful for summarizing data and performing basic statistical tasks. There is a continuing debate over the accuracy of some of Excel's statistical calculations, and with all the statistical software tools available, Excel may not be the best tool for professional statisticians.

The following are typical statistical tasks used for analysis:

Summarizing a single dataset
Options available for this are functions for calculating numbers describing the center of a dataset (e.g., mean, median, mode, trimmed mean, etc.) as well as numbers for describing the dispersion of a dataset (e.g., range, standard devia-tion, variance). There are slightly different formulas for the calculation of standard deviations and variances, depending on whether your dataset is a sample from a larger population or the whole population. (Usually, it is the former.) Other descriptive statistics, such as the smallest and largest values in a dataset, as well as percentiles, are also available.

Summarizing relationships between datasets
Options available for this are functions for calculating the strength and direc-tion of linear relationships (the correlation coefficient) and for explaining the shape of a linear or nonlinear relationship (linear regression and logistic regression).

Calculating probabilities
For many statistical techniques, it is necessary to calculate probabilities. There are many different kinds of statistical distributions (Normal, Binomial, Gamma, Beta, Poisson, Chi-squared, t, F, etc.) and you should be pretty sure about which one you need before you use any of Excel's built-in probability functions.

Counting problems
These include problems such as: "How many ways are there to arrange 40 people in groups of three?" Excel provides functions for these calculations (combinations, permutations, factorial, etc.).

Random number generation

Used to generate random numbers between 0 and 1 or between any specified ranges of numbers. Used to generate a sampling scheme.

Statistical inference

Well-known techniques such as confidence interval and hypothesis tests are calculated using Excel functions. You should always check the assumptions underlying these procedures before doing the calculations.

This chapter details the specific instructions for each of the following functions:

AVEDEV	GAMMAINV	PERCENTRANK
AVERAGE	GAMMALIN	PERMUT
AVERAGEA	GEOMEAN	POISSON
BETADIST	GROWTH	PROB
BETAINV	HARMEAN	QUARTILE
BINOMDIST	HYPGEOMDIST	RANK
CHIDIST	INTERCEPT	RSQ
CHIINV	KURT	SKEW
CHITEST	LARGE	SLOPE
CONFIDENCE	LINEST	SMALL
CORREL	LOGEST	STANDARDIZE
COUNT	LOGINV	STDEV
COUNTA	LOGNORMDIST	STDEVA
COUNTBLANK	MAX	STDEVPA
COUNTIF	MAXA	STEYX
COVAR	MEDIAN	TDIST
CRITBINOM	MIN	TINV
DEVSQ	MINA	TREND
EXPONDIST	MODE	TRIMMEAN
FDIST	NEGBINOMDIST	TTEST
FINV	NORMDIST	VAR
FISHER	NORMINV	VARA
FISHERINV	NORMSDIST	VARP
FORECAST	NORMSINV	VARPA
FREQUENCY	PEARSON	WEIBULL
FTEST	PERCENTILE	ZTEST
GAMMADIST		

Use these functions to do the following:

- Find the largest value in an array

- Determine the probability of the specified distribution

- Find the average for a list of values

- Determine the smallest value in a list

- Find the probability of the specified distribution

- Count the number of the specified type of values in a list

- Determine the number of permutations that is created for a group of objects

- Find the standard deviation for a list of values

- Determine the variance in a list of values

Common Statistical Terminology

If you are not an avid statistician you are going to quickly notice that statistical functions use a lot of different terminology. By understanding some of the terms outlined in this section, you should be able to quickly determine which statistical functions you need to use to produce the desired results.

Mean

Indicates the arithmetic average of a set of numbers. This is an attempt to find the center of a distribution.

Median

Indicates a point on a scale of measures where half of the observations are less than or equal to the median, and half are greater.

Population

Specifies a well-defined collection of all the observations in which we are interested, for example, the total number of seniors graduating in Spring 2000.

Range

Indicates the distance between the largest and smallest value.

Sample

Specifies a subset of a population. For example, if a population were the senior class of 2000, a subset would be the seniors who are receiving college scholarships.

Variance

Characterizes the dispersion within a population. The variance is essentially the mean squared deviation of a dataset, where the deviation is the distance between each observation and the mean.

The Statistical Functions

Excel provides several different functions that are used to perform statistical calculations. These functions are covered in the remaining portion of this chapter in alphabetical order, but they are categorized as follows:

Finding an average value:

AVEDEV (average of deviations between values)
AVERAGE (average of numeric values)
AVERAGEA (average of numeric, logical, and text values)

Working with distributions:

BETADIST (cumulative beta probability density function)
BETAINV (inverse of cumulative beta probability density function)
CHIDIST (chi-squared distribution)
CHIINV (inverse of chi-squared distribution)
CHITEST (compare expected range of values to actual range)
CRITBINOM (find the smallest value for the cumulative binomial distribution)
EXPONDIST (exponential distribution)
FDIST (F probability distribution)
FINV (inverse of F probability distribution)
GAMMADIST (gamma distribution)
GAMMAINV (inverse of gamma distribution)
GAMMALN (natural logarithm of a gamma function)
LOGINV (inverse of lognormal cumulative distribution)
LOGNORMDIST (lognormal cumulative distribution)
NORMDIST (cumulative normal distribution with specified mean and standard deviation)
NORMINV (inverse of cumulative normal distribution with specified mean and distribution)
NORMSDIST (cumulative standard distribution with mean of 0 and standard deviation of 1)
NORMSINV (inverse of cumulative standard distribution with mean of 0 and standard deviation of 1)
STANDARDIZE (Standardized value of an observation)
TDIST (Student's T-Distribution)
TINV (Inverse of the Student's T-Distribution)
Weibull (Weibull distribution)
ZTEST (Two-tailed P-value of a Z-test statistic)

Determining the probability:

BINOMDIST (probability of number of successes in a specified number of trials)
HYPGEOMDIST (probability of sample success on the first, second, third, etc. trial)
NEGBINOMDIST (probability of specified number of failures, assuming a negative binomial distribution)
POISSON (probability for the Poisson distribution)
PROB (probability that values are within specified limits)

Finding the variance in a list of values:

VAR (sample of numeric values)
VARA (sample of numeric and logical values)
VARP (entire population of numeric values)
VARPA (entire population of numeric and logical values)

Working with a population mean:

CONFIDENCE (find the confidence interval for a population mean)
TTEST (determine if two arrays are from the same population and mean, assuming both populations are normal)

Determining the standard deviation:

STDEV (sample of numeric values)
STDEVA (sample of numeric and logical values)
STDEVP (entire population of numeric values)
STDEVPA (entire population of numeric and logical values)

Comparing values:

CORREL (determine the correlation coefficient of arrays)
COUNT (count numeric values)
COUNTA (count all cells that contain a value)
COUNTBLANK (count all blank cells)
COUNTIF (count values that meet specified criteria)
COVAR (find covariance of arrays)
DEVSQ (sum squares of deviations between values)
FORECAST (predict a future value)
FREQUENCY (count values within the specified ranges)
FTEST (compare two arrays and determine if variances are equal, assuming populations are normal)
GEOMEAN (geometric mean)
GROWTH (future Y-axis values)
HARMEAN (harmonic mean)
INTERCEPT (find where a line crosses the Y-axis)
LARGE (find values based on how large they are)
LINEST (linear estimation techniques)
LOGEST (values of an exponential curve)
MAX (find the largest numeric value)
MAXA (find the largest value in a list)
MEDIAN (return a median value)
MIN (find the smallest numeric value)
MINA (find the smallest value)
MODE (find the number that occurs most frequently)
PEARSON (find Pearson product moment correlation coefficient)
PERCENTILE (find value specified a percent larger than list)
PERCENTRANK (find percentage rank of specific value in a list)

PERMUT (find number of permutations for objects)
QUARTILE (find value in specified quartile of list)
RANK (find numeric rank of a value in a list)
RSQ (coefficient of determination for linear regression)
SKEW (find the coefficient of skewness of a list of values)
SLOPE (slope of linear regression line through specified points)
SMALL (find values based on how small they are)
STEYX (determine the standard error)
TREND (find future Y-axis values based on current linear trend)
TRIMMEAN (trim high and low values and determine the adjusted mean)

Recurring Arguments

The following arguments are available on a recurring basis in many of the functions discussed in this chapter. If differences in the implementation exist in a particular function, they are explained within that function's section.

Alpha
A positive numeric value that indicates the shape of the distribution.

Array1, Array2
Each array must indicate an equal-sized series of numeric values. If one array is larger than the other an error will be returned. If any of the cells referenced by an array contain a non-numeric value (such as text, logical value, or empty) the cells are ignored.

Beta
A positive numeric value that indicates the shape of the distribution.

Const
Indicates a logical value of TRUE or FALSE that specifies whether there is a constant coefficient in the least squares linear regression equation. If the value is FALSE the line is forced to pass through the origin.

Cumulative
This argument must be a logical value of TRUE of FALSE that indicates actual form of the function. If this argument is TRUE, the function returns the cumulative distribution function. If the value of this argument is FALSE, the function returns the probability mass function.

Degrees_Freedom
Specifies a numeric value between 1 and 1,000,000,000 that indicates the degrees of freedom to allow for the distribution.

Known_Ys
Indicates a series of data point values for the y axis.

Known_Xs
Indicates a series of data point values for the x axis.

Number1, Number2, ...

Each *Number* argument must specify at least one numeric value. There are up to 30 different arguments specified. Each argument can reference one value or an array of numeric values.

Probability

Specifies a decimal value between 0 and 1 that indicates the probability associated with the distribution.

Range

Specifies the cell or range of cells that you want to evaluate.

Value1, Value2, ...

You can specify up to 30 different arguments that you want to check for numeric values. Each argument can reference one value or an array of values.

AVEDEV

Use AVEDEV to take a series of numeric values and find the average of the absolute deviations of the values from the mean. For example, if you have the values −1.1, 3, 5, and 7, the average deviation is 2.4.

To Calculate

```
=AVEDEV(Number1, Number2, ...)
```

There must be at least one *Number* argument specified.

Example

Figure 15-1 illustrates how AVEDEV is used to find the average deviation within a list of numeric values. This function allows you to compare the results of this function to results returned by the AVERAGE and AVERAGEA functions, which return the average of the actual values in the list.

AVERAGE

Use AVERAGE to determine the average between multiple numeric values. This average is commonly referred to as the arithmetic mean. For example, if you have the scores 75, 88, 95, and 89 this function would return an average score of 86.75.

To Calculate

```
=AVEREAGE(Number1, Number2, ...)
```

There must be at least one *Number* argument specified.

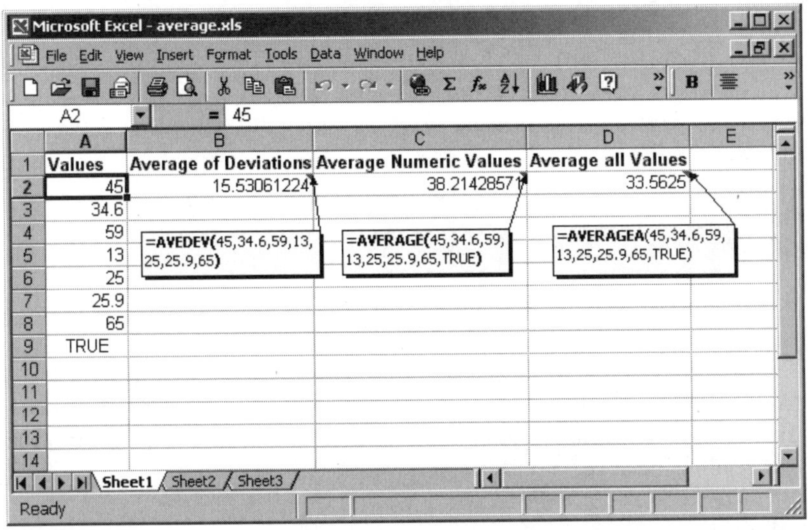

Figure 15-1: Don't get confused when selecting one of the averaging functions—they all produce different results

Example

Figure 15-1 illustrates how AVERAGE is used to find the average of a list of numeric values. You will notice that the logical value in cell A9 is ignored by this function; whereas, AVERAGEA includes the value in the result.

> **NOTE** *The AVERAGE function only calculates the average between numeric values. If you have a range that includes text or logical values you should use the AVERAGEA function.*

AVERAGEA

AVERAGEA allows you to find the average (arithmetic mean) between a list of values. These values are numeric, logical, or text. If you have a logical value of TRUE, the function evaluates it as 1, whereas FALSE is evaluated as 0. All text is evaluated as 0.

To Calculate

    =AVERAGEA(Number1, Number2, ...)

There must be at least one *Number* argument specified.

Example

Figure 15-1 illustrates how AVERAGEA calculates the average of an entire list of values. The logical value TRUE in cell A9 is treated as a 1, causing the average value returned by this function to be lower than the value returned by AVERAGE, which ignores logical values.

 NOTE *If you do not want logical values and text to be included in the calculation, use the AVERAGE function.*

BETADIST

Use BETADIST to find the cumulative beta probability density function for the specified values. This function is commonly used to determine the variation in the percentage of change over various samples.

To Calculate

`=BETADIST(X, Alpha, Beta, A, B)`

The `X`, `Alpha`, and `Beta` arguments are required for this function. The `A` and `B` parameters are optional. The default values of `A` and `B` are 0 and 1, respectively.

`X`   Specifies a numeric value between values of the `A` and `B` arguments that indicates the value that should be used to evaluate the function.

`Alpha, Beta`
    The two positive numeric values describing the Beta distribution.

`A`   An optional numeric value that indicates the lower bound for the value specified for the `X` argument.

`B`   An optional numeric value that indicates the upper bound for the value specified for the `X` argument.

Example

Figure 15-2 illustrates how BETADIST is used to determine the probability value. Notice that the value returned by BETAINV is fairly close to the initial `X` value of BETADIST. The difference in the values is due to the fact that Excel rounds decimal values so that nine digits display on the right side of the decimal point.

BETAINV

Use BETAINV to find the inverse of the cumulative beta probability density function. In other words, if you know the probability value you can determine the value that the function was evaluated on.

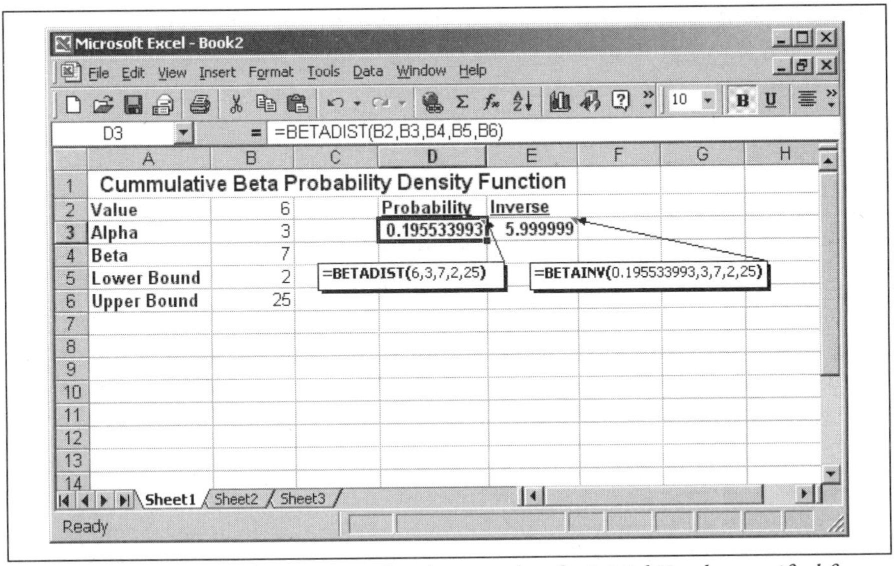

Figure 15-2: BETAINV returns a value that matches the initial X value specified for BETADIST

To Calculate

```
=BETAINV(Probability, Alpha, Beta, A, B)
```

The *Probability*, *Alpha*, and *Beta* arguments are required for this function. The *A* and *B* parameters are optional. The default values of *A* and *B* are 0 and 1, respectively.

A   An optional numeric value that indicates the lower bound for the value specified for the *X* argument.

B   An optional numeric value that indicates the upper bound for the value specified for the *X* argument.

Example

Figure 15-2 illustrates how BETAINV is used to determine the inverse value for the cumulative beta probability density function. Notice that the value returned by BETAINV is fairly close to the initial *x* value of BETADIST. The difference in the values is due to the fact that Excel rounds decimal values so that nine digits display on the right side of the decimal point.

BINOMDIST

You can use BINOMDIST to determine the probability of success for a specific number of trials, assuming certain key things hold. This type of probability is referred to as individual term binomial distribution probability. For example, you can use this function to determine the probability that one half of the 100 cars in the parking lot are red.

To Calculate

=BINOMDIST(Number_s, Trials, Probability_s, Cumulative)

All of the arguments are required for this function.

Number_s

> This argument must be a positive numeric value that indicates the number of successes that you expect to achieve during the trials. If this numeric value is not an integer, it is truncated to an integer by the function. The value of this argument must be smaller than the value of the Trials argument. For example, to see if half the cars are red, the value of the function would be 50.

Trials

> This argument must be a positive numeric value that indicates the number of trials that will be performed. If this numeric value is not an integer, it will be truncated to an integer by the function.

Probability_s

> The Probability_s argument must be a decimal value between 0 and 1 that indicates the probability of success on each trial. In the previously mentioned example, it would be the proportion of the red cars in the population.

Cumulative

> This argument must be a logical value of TRUE or FALSE that indicates actual form of the function. If this argument is TRUE the BINOMDIST function determines the probability that there are up to and including the number of successes specified for the Number_s argument. If the value of this argument is FALSE the function determines the probability that there are exactly the number of successes specified by the Number_s argument.

Example

Figure 15-3 illustrates how BINOMDIST is used to determine the probability of the specified number of successes. You will notice that the values returned by changing the Cumulative argument from TRUE to FALSE add up to approximately 1 or 100%.

CHIDIST

Use CHIDIST to find the probability of a chi-squared variable with the specified degrees of freedom.

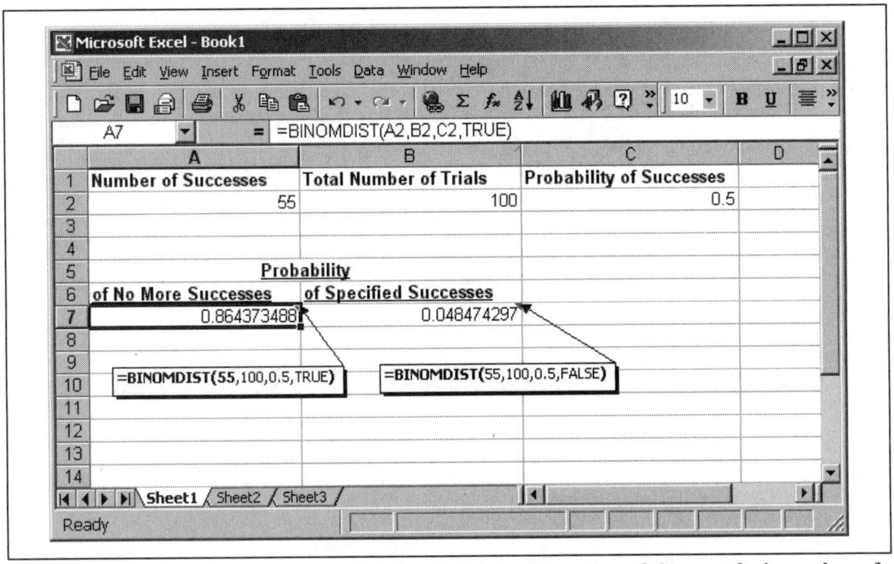

Figure 15-3: BINOMDIST provides the ability to determine if the specified number of successes occurred during the indicated number of attempts

To Calculate

=CHIDIST(*X*, *Degrees_Freedom*)

Both arguments are required for this function.

x   Indicates a positive numeric value that you want to use to evaluate the distribution.

Example

Figure 15-4 illustrates how CHIDIST is used to determine the probability value for a chi-squared variable. You will notice that the value returned by CHIINV is fairly close to the initial *x* value of CHIDIST.

CHIINV

Use CHIINV to find the inverse chi-squared distribution of a value with the specified degrees of freedom. To use this function you must know the probability value for the distribution.

To Calculate

=CHIINV(*Probability*, *Degrees_Freedom*)

Both arguments are required for this function.

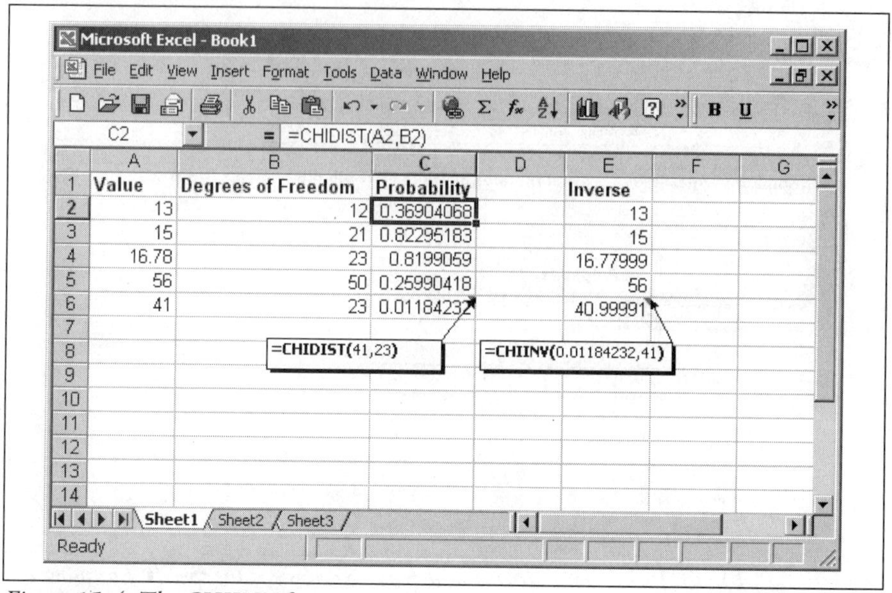

Figure 15-4: The CHIINV function returns a value that matches the X value specified for the CHIDIST function

Example

Figure 15-4 illustrates how CHIINV is used to find the inverse value for a chi-distribution. The value returned by the function is fairly close to the initial x value of CHIDIST.

CHITEST

Use CHITEST to use the chi-squared distribution to determine whether the actual values of the observations match up to the expected values of the observations.

To Calculate

```
=CHITEST(Actual_Range, Expected_Range)
```

Both arguments are required for this function and must contain the same number of values.

Actual_Range

Specifies a range of numeric values that indicates the actual results of the observations.

Expected_Range

Specifies a range of numeric values that indicates the expected results.

Example

Figure 15-5 illustrates how CHITEST is used to determine whether the results are accurate using the chi-squared distribution to compare actual and expected values.

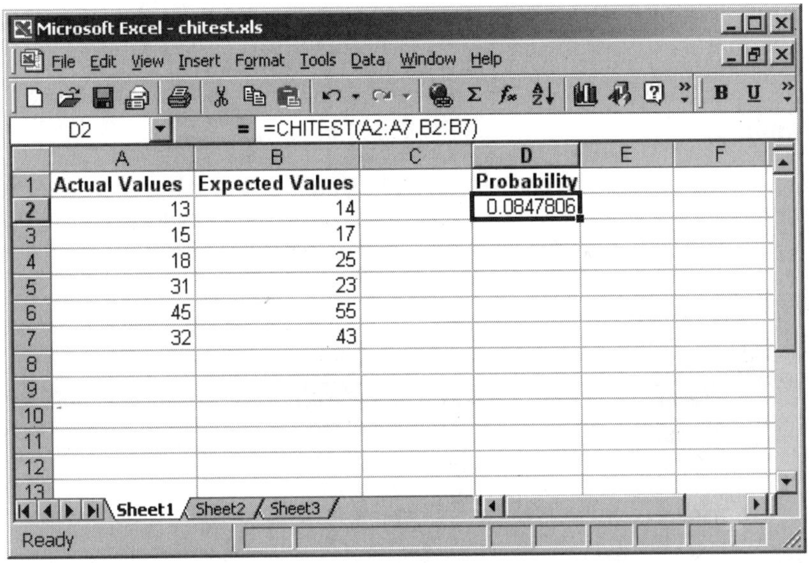

Figure 15-5: CHITEST compares actual results to expected values and returns a decimal value indicating the comparison of the values

CONFIDENCE

Use the CONFIDENCE function to determine the confidence interval for a population mean. In other words, this function determines a margin of error for a sample mean. For example, when you hear that Californians have a mean family income of $40,000, you can use this function to determine the margin of error for the unknown population mean income.

To Calculate

=CONFIDENCE(Alpha, Standard_Dev, Size)

All three of the arguments are required for this function.

Alpha
This argument must be a decimal value between 0 and 1 that indicates the significance level used to determine the confidence level. The confidence level is actually calculated by performing the following calculation: 100 × (1-Alpha)%. If you have a confidence level of 60% the value of Alpha would be .4.

`Standard_Dev`
: This argument must be a positive number that indicates the population standard deviation for the data. If this is not known, you cannot use this interval, but must use a T-interval instead.

`Size`
: This argument is a positive number that indicates the size of the sample. If the value is not an integer, the value is truncated to an integer.

Example

Figure 15-6 illustrates how CONFIDENCE is used to find the confidence interval for different populations. The confidence interval can then be added and subtracted from the sample mean to determine the actual interval. For example, the values in row 2 indicate that the confidence interval is between 33.807 (35–1.1927) and 36. 193 (35 + 1.1927).

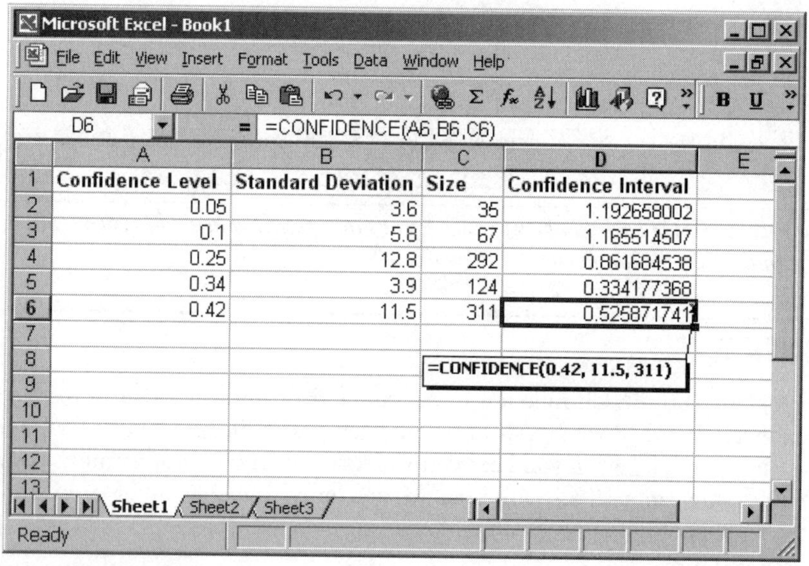

	A	B	C	D
1	Confidence Level	Standard Deviation	Size	Confidence Interval
2	0.05	3.6	35	1.192658002
3	0.1	5.8	67	1.165514507
4	0.25	12.8	292	0.861684538
5	0.34	3.9	124	0.334177368
6	0.42	11.5	311	0.525871741

Figure 15-6: Use CONFIDENCE to find the confidence interval for a population mean

CORREL

Use CORREL to examine two different arrays of values and determine the correlation. For example, you could compare the distance to the office array to the number of bus riders in a second array.

To Calculate

`=CORREL(Array1, Array2)`

Both arguments must be specified for this function.

Example

Figure 15-7 illustrates how CORREL is used to compare two arrays and determine the correlation. The example compares the values in each array and determines the correlation between the changes in values. The example illustrates that there is a strong, positive, linear relationship between the number of bus riders and the distance to work.

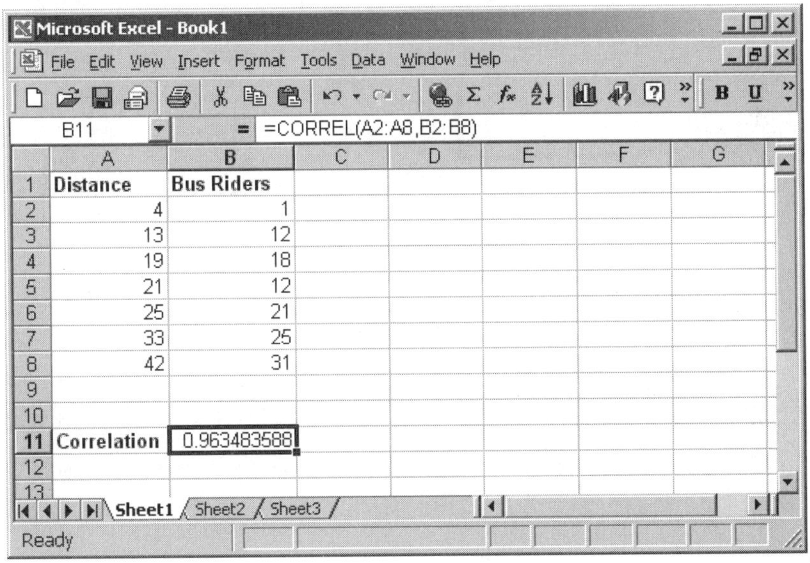

Figure 15-7: Find the correlation between the changes in the values of two arrays with CORREL

COUNT

You can use COUNT to determine the number of numeric values within a range of values. When you use this function, cells containing logical values, error values, or text (except for text that represents a numeric value), or are mpty are not counted.

To Calculate

`=COUNT(Value1, Value2, ...)`

There must be at least one *Value* argument specified for this function.

Example

Figure 15-8 allows you to compare the results returned by the four different COUNT functions available in Excel. Before using one of these functions you need to determine the type of results that you want to return. You will notice that the COUNT function only counts cells that contain actual numeric values. Cell A10 is ignored because, even though it contains numeric elements, they are not expressed as a valid number. The COUNTA function counts all cells that contain a value.

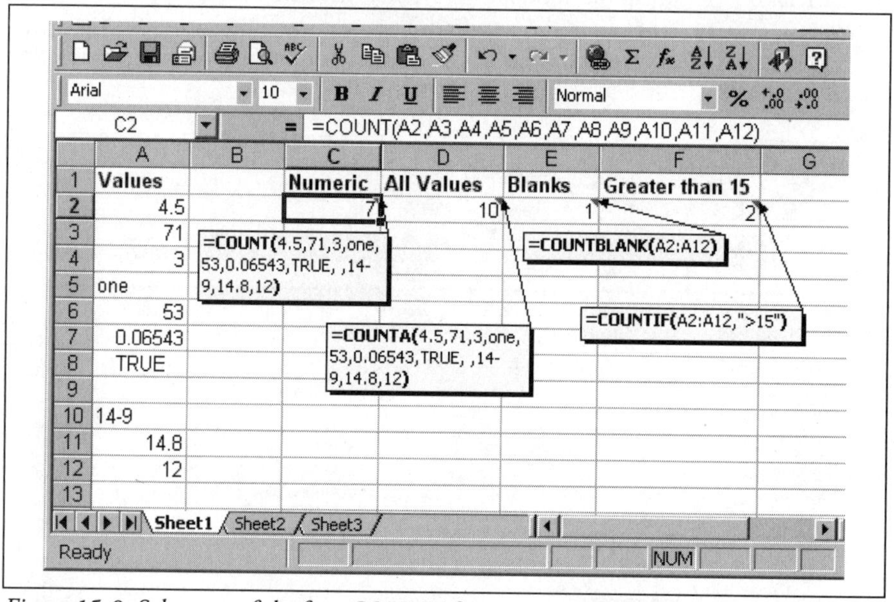

Figure 15-8: Select one of the four COUNT functions to return the desired results

COUNTA

Use COUNTA to determine the number of values within the specified list of arguments. This function counts all arguments that are not empty.

To Calculate

=COUNTA(*Value1*, *Value2*)

There must be at least one *Value* argument specified for this function.

Example

Figure 15-8 illustrates how COUNTA is used to count all cells that contain a value. You will notice that the function counts every cell in the range with the exception of cell A9, which is blank.

COUNTBLANK

Use COUNTBLANK to determine the number of empty cells within the specified cell range. The function also counts cells that contain formulas that return " " (empty text).

To Calculate

=COUNTBLANK(*Range*)

The *Range* argument is required for this function.

Example

Figure 15-8 illustrates how COUNTBLANK is used to determine the number of blank cells within a range.

COUNTIF

Use COUNTIF to count the number of cells within the specified range that meet a certain criteria. For example, you may want to figure out the number of cells that contain sales greater than $1,000 (>$1,000).

To Calculate

=COUNTIF(*Range*, *Criteria*)

Both arguments are required for this function.

Criteria
Specifies the criteria that must be met by the cells specified for the *Range* argument. This argument is a numeric value, an expression such as >45, or even text.

Example

Figure 15-8 illustrates how COUNTIF is used to figure out how many cells contain a value that is larger than 15.

COVAR

Use COVAR to compare the values in two arrays and determine the covariance, the average of the products of the deviations between all possible pairs of elements of the arrays.

To Calculate

```
=COVAR(Array1, Array2)
```

Both arguments must be specified for this function.

Example

Figure 15-9 illustrates how COVAR provides the ability to quickly compare two arrays of values and determine the covariance value.

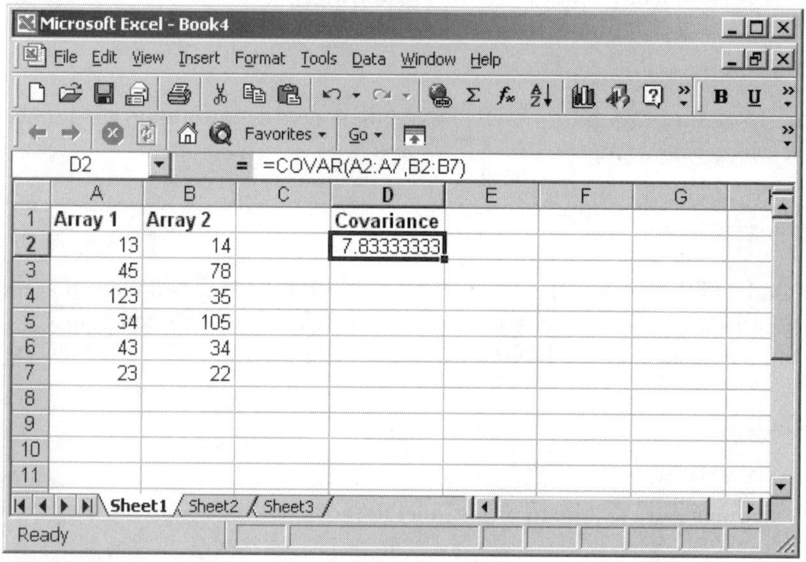

Figure 15-9: Use COVAR to compare two arrays and find the covariance of the arrays

CRITBINOM

Use CRITBINOM to find the smallest value where the cumulative binomial distribution is greater than or equal to the value specified for the *Alpha* argument, which measures the probability of making a type 1 error in hypothesis testing. This function is typically used in quality assurance applications.

To Calculate

```
=CRITBINOM(Trials, Probability_S, Alpha)
```

All arguments are required for this function.

Trials
Specifies a numeric value that indicates the number of Bernoulli trials. If the value specified is not an integer, it is truncated by the function.

Probability_S
Specifies a decimal value between 0 and 1 that indicates the probability of success for each trial.

Alpha
Specifies a decimal value between 0 and 1 that indicates the criterion value.

Example

Figure 15-10 illustrates how CRITBINOM is used to find the minimum number of successes. For example, if these were tests on new products, the result would be the minimum number of successes allowed for each product.

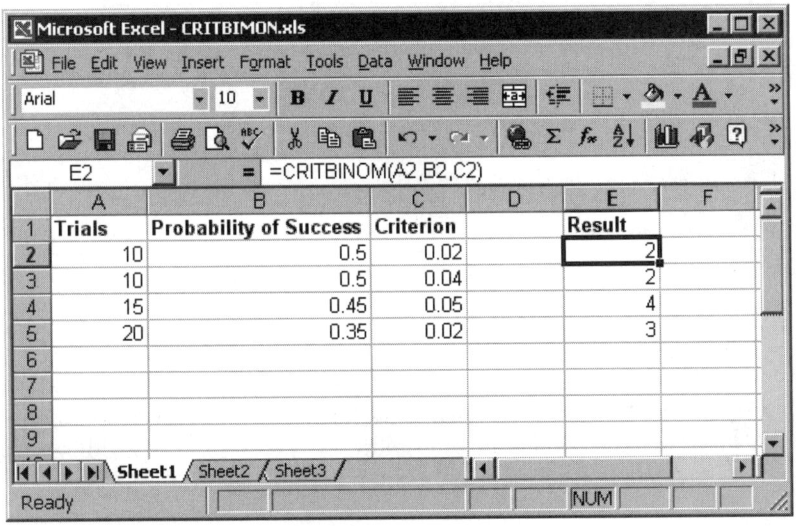

Figure 15-10: Use CRITBINOM to determine the minimum number of successes allowed for the specified number of trials

---

DEVSQ

Use DEVSQ to find the sum of the squares of the deviations of a series of numeric values from the mean of the values.

To Calculate

=DEVSQ(*Number1, Number2, ...*)

There must be at least one *Number* argument specified for the function.

Example

Figure 15-11 shows how DEVSQ takes a list of numeric values and finds the sum of the squares of the deviations between the series of numeric values.

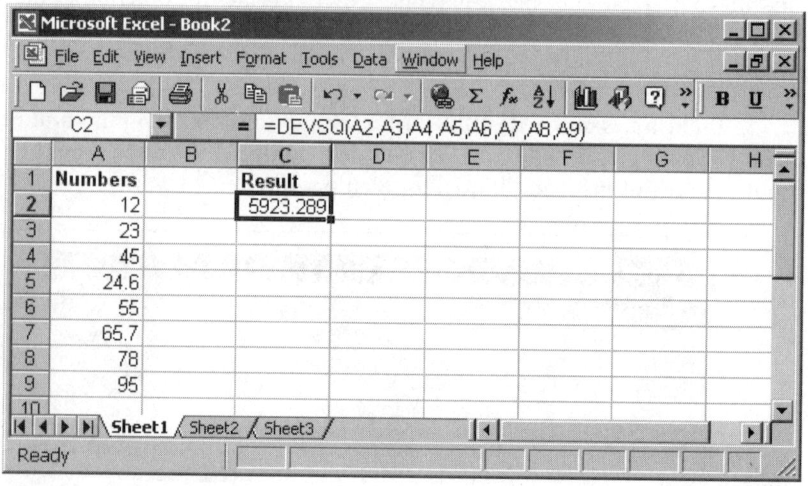

Figure 15-11: DEVSQ finds the sum of squaring the deviations between numeric values

EXPONDIST

Use EXPONDIST to find the probabilities for the exponential distribution. This function works well for finding the probability that events occurred within a specific amount of time under certain restrictive assumptions.

To Calculate

    =EXPONDIST(X, Lambda, Cumulative)

All arguments are required for this function.

X Indicates a positive numeric value that indicates the value of the function.

Lambda
Indicates a positive numeric value that specifies a parameter of the function.

Example

Figure 15-12 illustrates how EXPONDIST is used to determine the exponential distribution. You will notice that the values returned by changing the *Cumulative* argument from TRUE to FALSE add up to approximately a factor of 10.

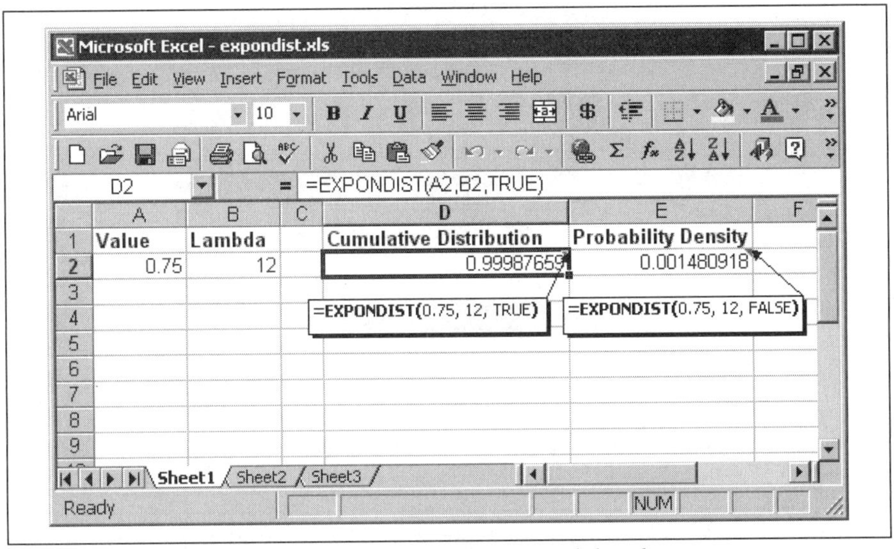

Figure 15-12: Use EXPONDIST to find the exponential distribution

---

FDIST

Use FDIST to find the probabilities associated with the F probability distribution.

To Calculate

    =FDIST(x, Degrees_Freedom1, Degrees_Freedom2)

All arguments are required for this function.

x   Specifies a positive numeric value that should be used to evaluate the function.

Degrees_Freedom1

Specifies a numeric value between 1 and 1,000,000,000 that indicates the degrees of freedom for the first data set. This argument is used as the numerator value.

Degrees_Freedom2

Specifies a numeric value between 1 and 1,000,000,000 that indicates the degrees of freedom for the second data set. This argument is used as the denominator value.

Example

Figure 15-13 illustrates how FDIST is used to determine the probability value. You will notice that the value returned by FINV is fairly close to the initial *x* value of FDIST.

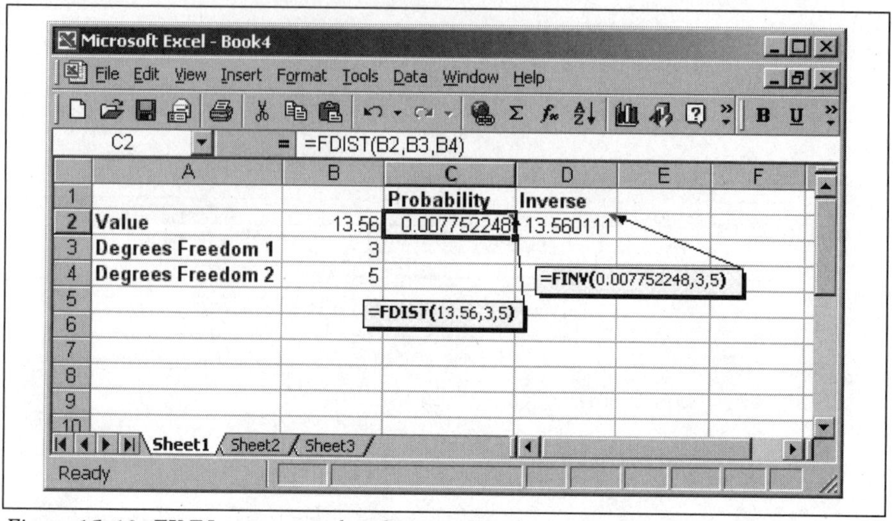

Figure 15-13: FINV returns a value that matches the initial X value specified for FDIST

FINV

Use FINV to find the inverse of the F probability distribution. To use this function you must know the probability value for the distribution.

To Calculate

```
=FINV(Probability, Degrees_Freedom1, Degrees_Freedom2)
```

All arguments are required for this function.

Degrees_Freedom1

Specifies a numeric value between 1 and 1,000,000,000 that indicates the degrees of freedom for the first data set. This argument is used as the numerator value.

Degrees_Freedom2

Specifies a numeric value between 1 and 1,000,000,000 that indicates the degrees of freedom for the second data set. This argument is used as the denominator value.

Example

Figure 15-13 illustrates how FINV is used to determine the inverse value for the F probability function. You will notice that the value returned by FINV is fairly close to the initial x value of FDIST.

FISHER

Use FISHER to determine the Fisher transformation at the specified value. This function is used when you want to perform hypothesis testing of the correlation coefficient.

To Calculate

=FISHER(x)

The x argument is required for this function.

x   Indicates a numeric value between −1 and 1 that you want to use for the transformation. (The value cannot be −1 or 1).

Example

Figure 15-14 illustrates how to use FISHER to find the Fisher transformation for a numeric value between −1 and 1. You will notice that FISHERINV returns the value that was initially used to get the transformation.

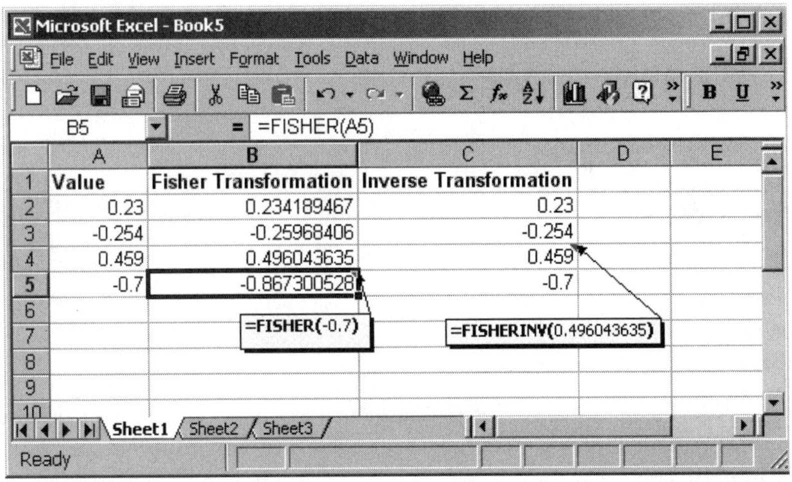

Figure 15-14: Use FISHER and FISHERINV to work with the Fisher transformation for a numeric value

FINSHERINV

You can use the FISHERINV to determine the inverse of a Fisher transformation. This function is used to analyze the correlation between ranges of data.

To Calculate

`=FISHERINV(Y)`

The Y argument is required for this function.

Y   Indicates a numeric value for which you want to find the inverse transformation.

Example

Figure 15-14 illustrates how to use FISHERINV to find the value that was used to get the Fisher transformation.

FORECAST

Use FORECAST to predict a future result for a specified value based upon the known values and corresponding results. For example, you can predict the number of sales this month based upon the inventory and corresponding sales for the previous six months.

 This type of prediction is only valid if there is a linear trend and should be used with caution.

To Calculate

`=FORECAST(X, Known_Y's, Known_X's))`

All three arguments are required for this function.

X   This argument must be a numeric value for which you want to predict the future value.

Example

Figure 15-15 illustrates how FORECAST is use to predict the number of sales for the month of December based upon the sales and inventory for the previous months of the year.

FREQUENCY

Use FREQUENCY to count the number of times values in an array fall within the specified ranges. For example, this function works well for looking at a series of grades and determining how many fall within each specified range. This function returns an array of values that indicates the number within each range and how many do not fall within any ranges. The array returned always contains one more value than the array specified by the *Bins_Array* argument.

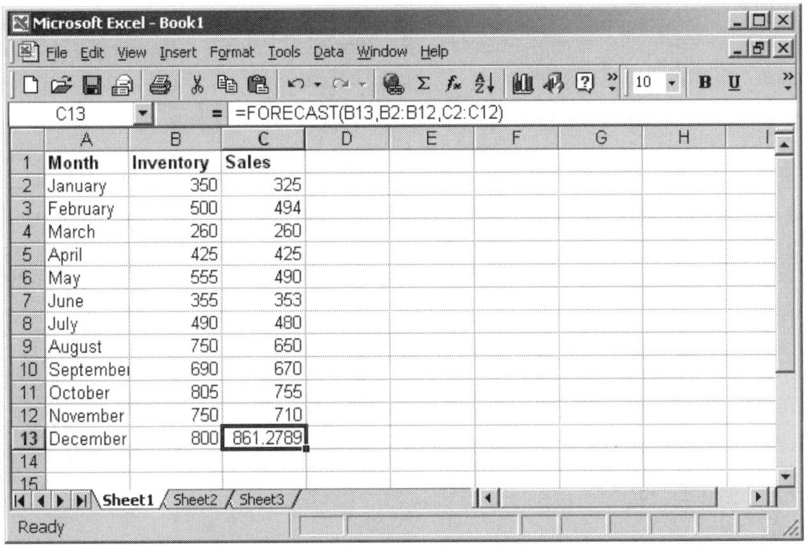

Microsoft Excel - Book1

C13 = =FORECAST(B13,B2:B12,C2:C12)

	A	B	C
1	Month	Inventory	Sales
2	January	350	325
3	February	500	494
4	March	260	260
5	April	425	425
6	May	555	490
7	June	355	353
8	July	490	480
9	August	750	650
10	Septembe	690	670
11	October	805	755
12	November	750	710
13	December	800	861.2789

Figure 15-15: FORECAST uses the correlation between the known X and Y values to predict a future Y value

---

TIP # 89

Getting Results from an Array Function

Some functions return multiple results (an array). If you only apply the function to one cell you will only see the first result of the array. If the array returns multiple results you must first select the number of cells equivalent to the number of values returned in the array, specify the array function, and then press Ctrl+Shift+Enter to apply the function results to all cells in the specified range.

To Calculate

```
=FREQUENCY(Data_Array, Bins_Array)
```

Both arguments are required for this function.

`Data_Array`
: Specifies an array of values that you want to use to determine the frequencies. If this array contains no values the function returns an array of zeros.

`Bins_Array`
: Specifies an array of ranges that you want to group the values specified by the *`Data_Array`* argument into. For example, if you specify values of 60, 80, and 100 the array function counts the values between 0 and 60, 61 and 80, 81 and 100, and the number outside the range.

Example

Figure 15-16 illustrates how FREQUENCY is used to determine the number of grades that fall within each of the specified grade ranges. You will notice that there is a value of 0 in cell D7. This function requires that the array used to display the results have one more value than the *Bins_Array* argument so the function can indicate the number of values that do not fall within the specified ranges. Since all of the grades are under 100, there are no values outside the range for this example. You will also notice that we used the values in column C for the *Bins_Array* argument. The function knows that for each value specified you want the number of values less than the specified value.

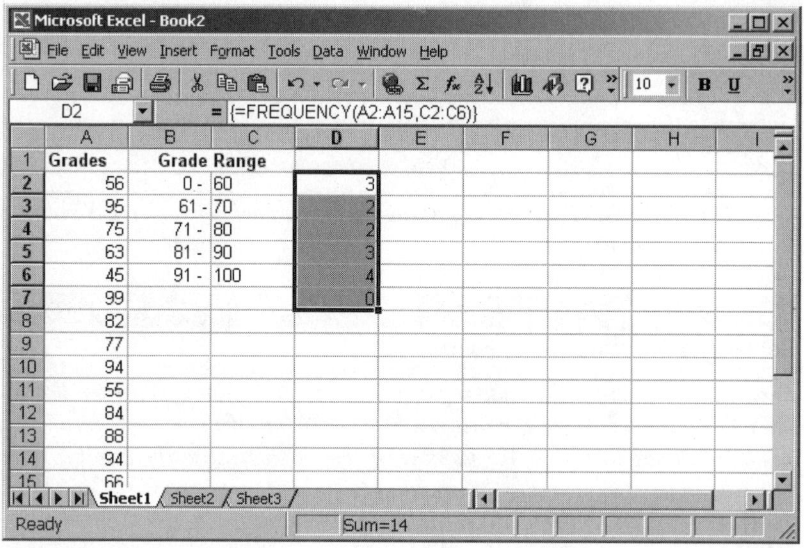

Figure 15-16: Use FREQUENCY to find out how many values are within the specified ranges

---

FTEST

Use FTEST to compare the values in two arrays and return the result of an F-test. The result indicates whether the variances in the two arrays are significant.

To Calculate

=FTEST(*Array1*, *Array2*)

Both arguments are required for this function.

Example

Figure 15-17 uses FTEST to compare two arrays and determine the variance between the arrays if their variances are equal. In this example, there is no reason to suppose that the variances are different, since the P-value of 0.821202 is so large.

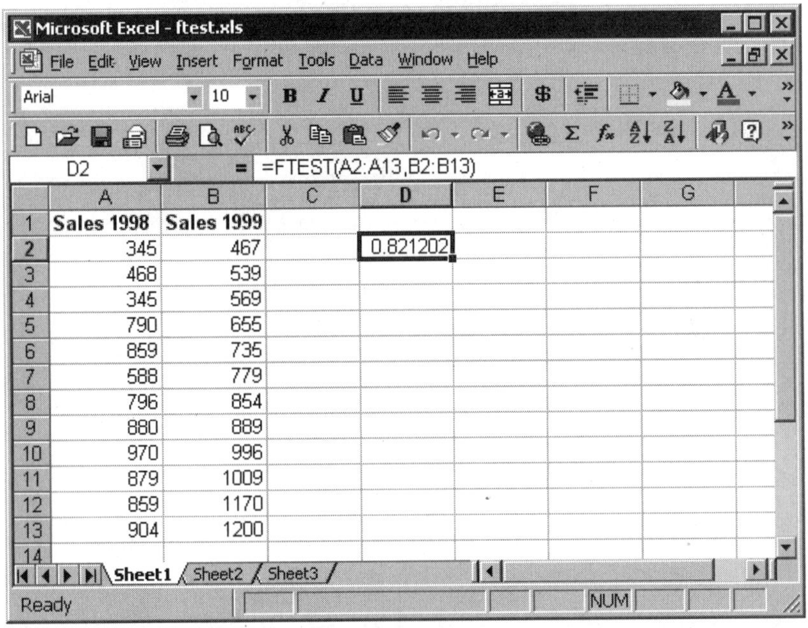

Figure 15-17: FTEST compares arrays and determines if there is a significant difference

Statistical Functions

GAMMADIST

Use GAMMADIST to find probabilities for the gamma distribution. This type of distribution is typically used in queuing analysis to study variables with skewed distributions.

To Calculate

=GAMMADIST(X, Alpha, Beta, Cumulative)

All arguments are required for this function.

X   Specifies a positive numeric value that should be used to evaluate the function.

Example

Figure 15-18 illustrates how GAMMADIST is used to find the gamma distribution. The figure shows how the function returns a different value based upon the logical value specified for the *Cumulative* argument. You will also notice in this example that GAMMAINV returns a value that matches the initial *x* value specified for GAMMADIST. GAMMALN determines the natural logarithm value for the gamma function.

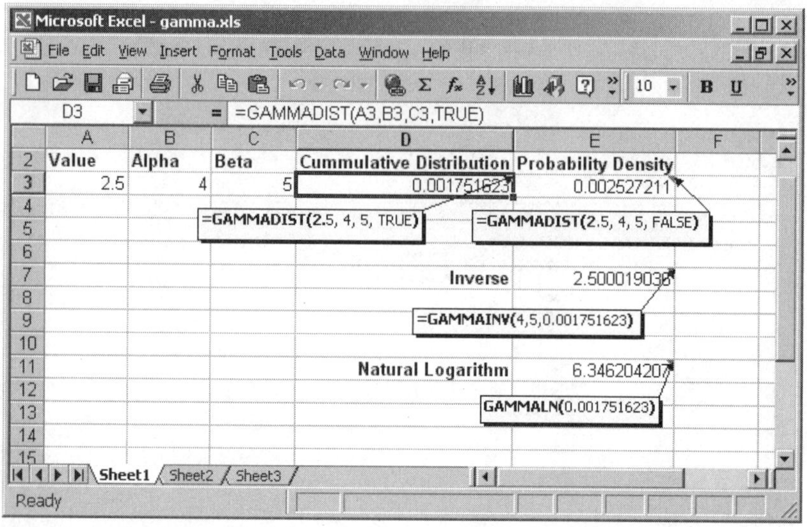

Figure 15-18: Use GAMMADIST and GAMMAINV to determine gamma distributions

GAMMAINV

Use GAMMAINV to find the inverse of the gamma distribution for the specified probability. This type of distribution is typically used with variables that may have skewed distributions.

To Calculate

=GAMMAINV(*Probability*, *Alpha*, *Beta*)

All three arguments are required for this function.

Example

Figure 15-18 illustrates how GAMMAINV is used to find the inverse value of the gamma distribution based upon the specified probability. The function takes the probability value returned by GAMMADIST and uses it to find the original value of the *x* argument.

GAMMALN

Use GAMMALN to find the natural logarithm of the gamma function.

To Calculate

=GAMMALN(x)

The x argument is required for this function.

x Indicates a positive numeric value.

Example

Figure 15-18 illustrates how GAMMALN is used to find the natural logarithm for a gamma function.

GEOMEAN

You can use GEOMEAN to determine the geometric mean for a range of positive numeric values. The geometric mean is typically used when working with rate of returns. For example, you may want to find the average rate of return for an investment that earns a different rate each year. This is different than finding the arithmetic mean because, as each rate is applied, the base amount grows.

To Calculate

=GEOMEAN(*Number1*, *Number2*, ...)

There must be at least one *Number* argument specified and all arguments must be positive.

Example

Figure 15-19 illustrates how GEOMEAN is used to determine the average rate of return over a series of years.

GROWTH

Use GROWTH to predict the exponential growth for the y-axis values based on the known y-axis and x-axis values. This function returns an array of values that indicates the predicted y-axis values, and therefore it must be specified as an array formula. The function determines the values based upon the equation y=b*m^x.

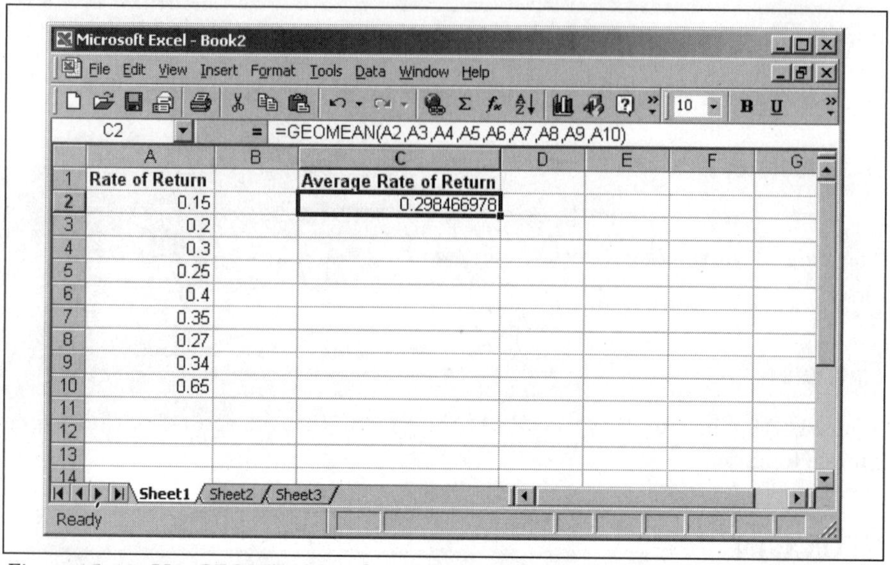

Figure 15-19: Use GEOMEAN to determine the average mean based upon the changes in the base amount

---

TIP # 90

Specifying Values in an Array

When you specify an array of values the values can exist in one column or in multiple columns. If you manually type the values of the array you need to use a comma (,) to separate each value in a column and a semicolon (;) to separate the columns.

To Calculate

=GROWTH(Known_Y's, Known_X's, New_X's, Const)

The Known_Y's argument is required for this function. All other arguments are optional.

Known_Y's

This array must contain a series of positive numbers. If the values in the array are in a single column, then the function interprets the values in each column of the Known_X's as a separate variable. If the values in the array are in a single row then the function interprets the values in each row of the Known_X's array as a separate variable.

Known_X's

If this argument is omitted, it is assumed to be an array of values in the range of {1,2,3,...} that is the same size as the array specified by the Known_Y's argument.

New_X's

Indicates the new x-axis values for which you want to find the corresponding y values. If these values are omitted, they are assumed to be the same as the *Known_X's* argument.

Example

Figure 15-20 illustrates how to use GROWTH to determine the future Y-axis values based upon the existing X-axis and Y-axis values.

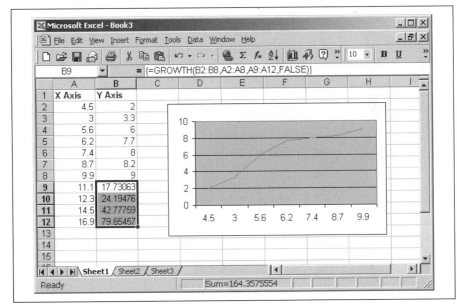

Figure 15-20: Use GROWTH to find the future Y-Axis values

HARMEAN

Use HARMEAN to calculate the harmonic mean of a list of positive numeric values. This function is used to find average rates. For example, if you drive from home to the office at 10 mph and return at 20 mph, you can use HARMEAN to calculate your average speed, which is 13.3333 mph.

To Calculate

```
=HARMEAN(Number1, Number2, ...)
```

There must be at least one *Number* argument specified. All arguments must be positive.

Example

Figure 15-21 illustrates how to use HARMEAN to find the harmonic mean for a list of positive numeric values.

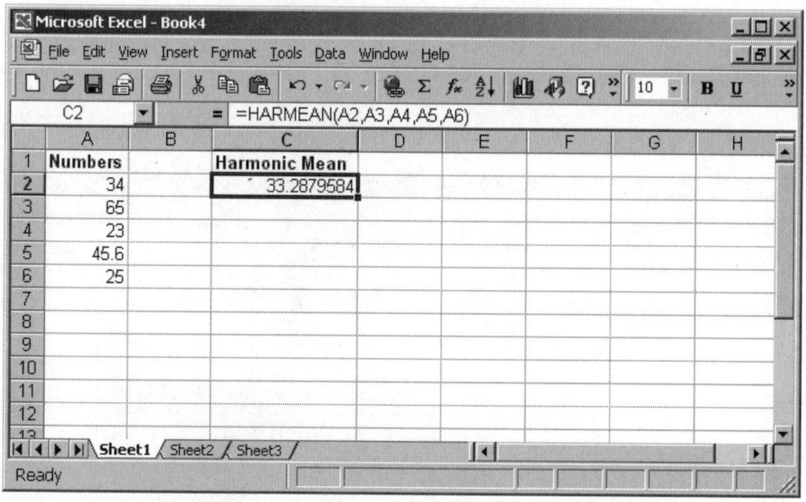

Figure 15-21: Use HARMEAN to find the harmonic mean for a list of numeric values

HYPGEOMDIST

Use HYPGEOMDIST to find the probability of the specified number of successes (hypergeometrical distribution) based upon the specified sample size, population successes, and population size.

To Calculate

=HYPGEOMDIST(Sample_S, Number_Sample, Population_S, Number_Population)

All arguments are required for this function. If the value specified for an argument is not an integer value, it is truncated by the function.

Sample_S
    Indicates the number of successes you expect for the sample.

Number_Sample
    Indicates the number of items in the sample.

Population_S
    Indicates the number of successes within the population.

Number_Population
    Specifies a number that indicates the size of the population.

Example

Figure 15-22 illustrates the probability of a child getting exactly 2 yellow Easter eggs if there are 20 eggs hidden and 15 are pink and the other 5 are yellow. The child is told to find 10 eggs.

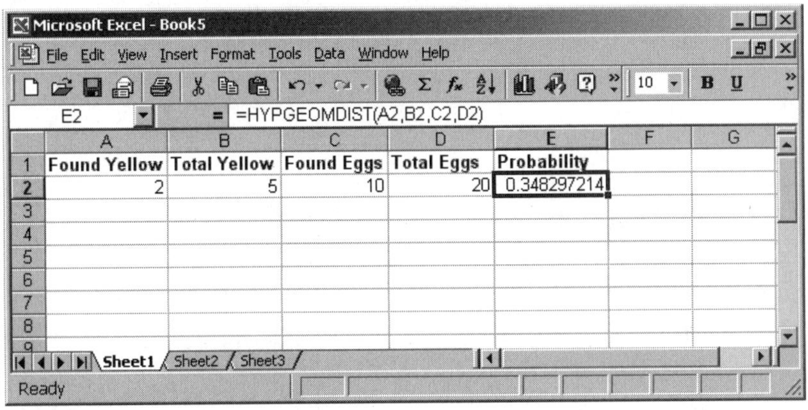

Figure 15-22: Use HYPGEOMDIST to determine the probability of getting the specified sample success

---

INTERCEPT

Use INTERCEPT to examine the x and y values to determine the point where a line will cross the y-axis.

To Calculate

=INTERCEPT(Known_Y's, Known_X's)

Both arguments are required for this function.

Example

Figure 15-23 illustrates how INTERCEPT compares the specified x- and y-axis values to determine the point where the line crosses the y-axis.

KURT

Use KURT to determine the kurtosis for a list of numeric values. The kurtosis of a set of values indicates its "peakedness" in relation to a normal distribution. If the value returned by the function is negative, the numeric value has a flatter distribution. If the returned value is positive, the distribution is fairly peaked.

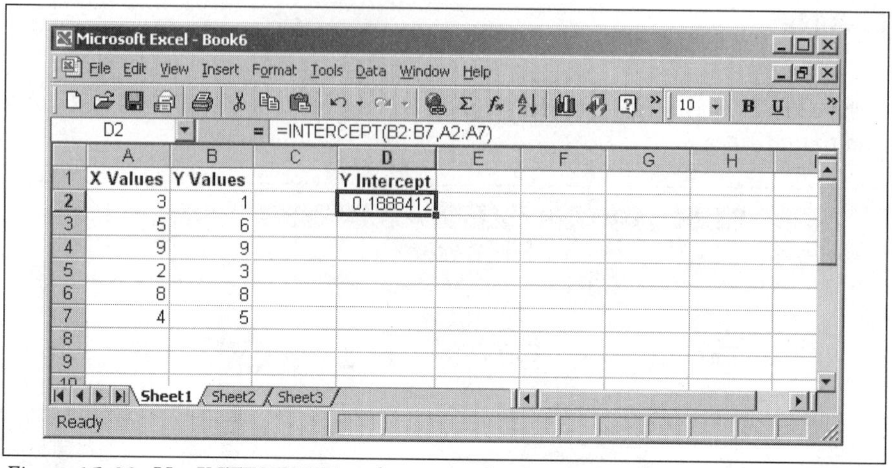

Figure 15-23: Use INTERCEPT to determine the point where the specified line crosses the y axis

To Calculate

=KURT(*Number1*, *Number2*, ...)

There must be at least one *Number* argument specified for this function.

Example

Figure 15-24 illustrates how KURT is used to find the kurtosis for a list of numeric values. You will notice that the example returns a positive value indicating that the distribution of the numeric values is fairly peaked.

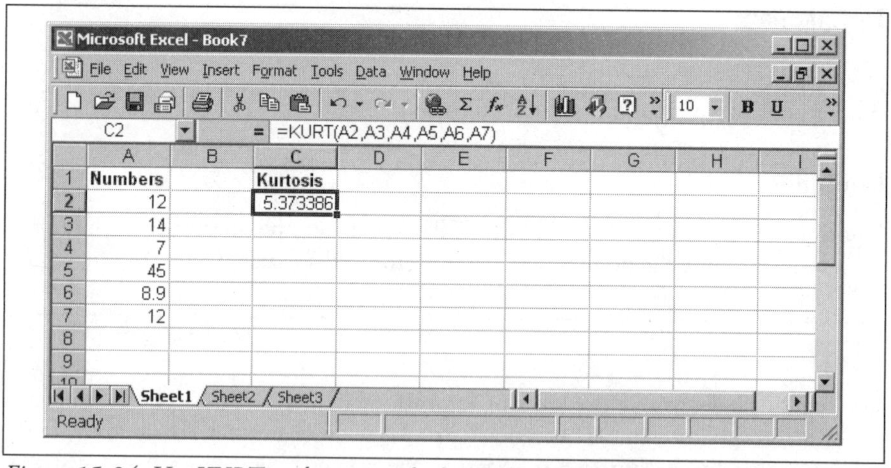

Figure 15-24: Use KURT to determine the kurtosis of a list of numeric values

LARGE

Use LARGE to find a specific value within an array based upon its size. For example, you may want to find the second largest value in the array.

To Calculate

=LARGE(Array, K)

Both arguments are required for this function.

Array
Indicates a range of numeric values.

K Indicates a positive numeric value that specifies the position from largest to smallest that you want to find. To find the largest value in the array you specify a 1 for the *K* argument. If the value specified for the *K* argument is a decimal, it is rounded to the closest integer.

Example

Figure 15-25 illustrates how LARGE finds the largest and second largest values in an array. To find the largest value in the array a value of 1 was specified for the K argument. To find the second largest value, the K argument had a value of 2.

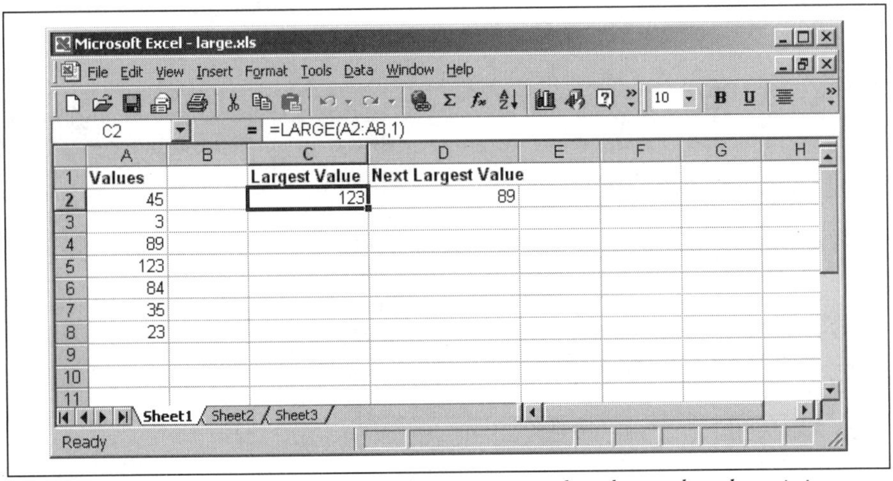

Figure 15-25: Use LARGE to find a value in an array based upon how large it is compared to other values

LINEST

Use LINEST to use the least squares method to find the best-fitting straight line that meets the specified data values. This function returns an array of values that describe the line and, therefore, it must be specified as an array formula. The function uses the equation y=mx + b for a line with one value specified for the Known_X's arguments, or the equation y=m1x1 + m2x2 + ... + b for multiple values.

To Calculate

    =LINEST(Known_Y's, Known_X's, Const, Stats)

The Known_Y's argument is required for this function. All other arguments are optional.

Known_Y's

This array must contain a series of positive numbers. If the values in the array are in a single column, then the function interprets the values in each column of the Known_X's as a separate variable. If the values in the array are in a single row, then the function interprets the values in each row of the Known_X's array as a separate variable.

Known_X's

If this argument is omitted, it is assumed to be an array of values in the range of {1,2,3,...} that is the same size as the array specified by the Known_Y's argument.

Stats

Indicates a logical value of TRUE or FALSE that specifies whether additional regression statistics should be returned with the array. If the value is TRUE, the function returns additional regression statistics.

Example

Figure 15-26 compares the use of the LINEST and LOGEST functions. The LINEST function returns statistics for the specified line whereas, LOGEST returns values for an exponential curve.

LOGEST

Use LOGEST to use the find the exponential curve that meets the specified data values and return an array of values that describe the curve. Since this function returns an array of values that describe the curve, it must be specified as an array formula. The function uses the equation y=b*m^x for a curve with one value specified for the Known_X's arguments or the equation y=(b*(m1^x1) * (m2^x2)* ...) for multiple values.

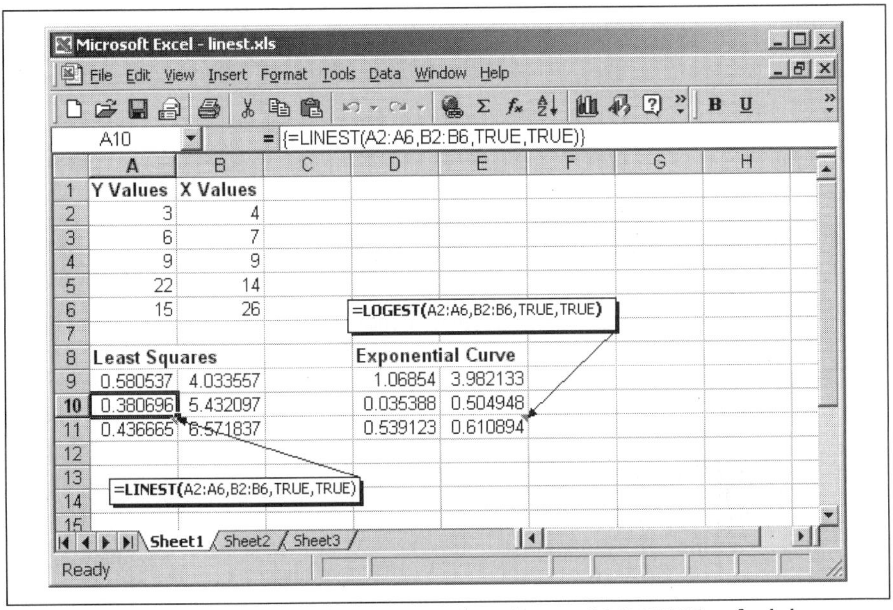

Figure 15-26: Use LINEST to find statistics for a line and LOGEST to find the exponential curve

To Calculate

=LOGEST(*Known_Y's, Known_X's, Const, Stats*)

The *Known_Y's* argument is required for this function. All other arguments are optional.

Known_Y's

> This array must contain a series of positive numbers. If the values in the array are in a single column, then the function interprets the values in each column of the *Known_X's* as a separate variable. If the values in the array are in a single row, then the function interprets the values in each row of the *Known_X's* array as a separate variable.

Known_X's

> If this argument is omitted, it is assumed to be an array of values in the range of {1,2,3,...} that is the same size as the array specified by the *Known_Y's* argument.

Stats

> Indicates a logical value of TRUE or FALSE that specifies whether additional regression statistics should be returned with the array. If the value is TRUE the function returns additional regression statistics.

Example

Figure 15-26 illustrates how to use LOGEST to find the values that describe an exponential curve.

LOGINV

Use LOGINV to find the inverse of the lognormal cumulative distribution when you know the probability. This function is typically used to analyze logarithmically transformed data.

To Calculate

=LOGINV(*Probability*, *Mean*, *Standard_Dev*)

All of the arguments are required for this function.

Mean
    Indicates a numeric value that specifies the mean of the natural logarithm of the distribution.

Standard_Dev
    Indicates a positive numeric value that specifies the standard deviation for the natural logarithm of the distribution.

Example

Figure 15-27 illustrates how to use LOGINV to find the inverse of a lognormal cumulative distribution. The value is found by taking the value returned by the LOGNORMDIST as the value of the *Probability* argument. Notice that the value returned by LOGINV is basically the same value that was initially specified for the *x* argument of LOGNORMDIST.

LOGNORMDIST

Use LOGNORMDIST to find the cumulative probability for the lognormal distribution for the specified numeric value. This function is typically used to analyze logarithmically transformed data.

To Calculate

=LOGNORMDIST(*x*, *Mean*, *Standard_Dev*)

All of the arguments are required for this function.

x   Indicates a positive numeric value.

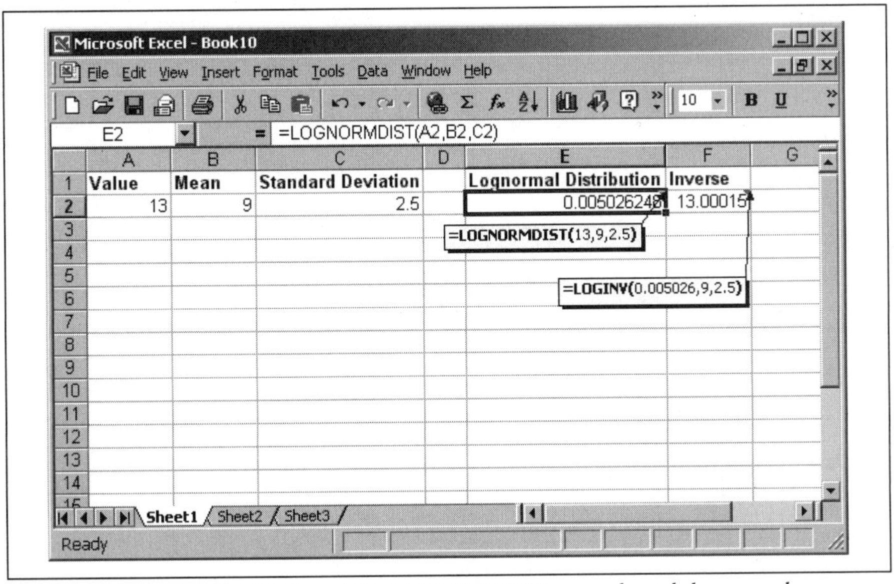

Figure 15-27: Use LOGINV and LOGNORMDIST to work with lognormal cumulative distributions

Mean
   Indicates a numeric value that specifies the mean of the natural logarithm of the distribution.

Standard_Dev
   Indicates a positive numeric value that specifies the standard deviation for the natural logarithm of the distribution.

Example

Figure 15-27 illustrates how to use LOGNORMDIST to find the lognormal cumulative distribution.

MAX

Use MAX to return the largest value in a list of numeric values. When you use this function, cells containing logical values, error values, or text (except for text that represents a numeric value), or cells that are empty are ignored.

To Calculate

```
=MAX(Number1, Number2, ...)
```

There must be at least one Number argument specified for the function.

Example

Figure 15-28 compares the results of MAX and MAXA when used to compare a list of values. Since MAXA converts the logical value of TRUE to 1 it returns that value as the largest value.

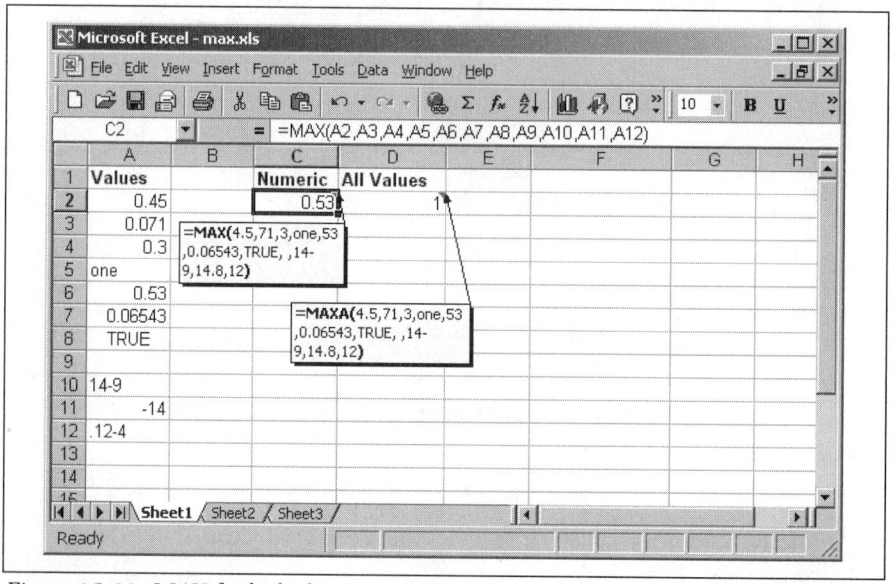

Figure 15-28: MAX finds the largest numeric value and MAXA finds the largest value by comparing numeric and non-numeric values

MAXA

Use MAXA to find the largest value in a list of arguments. This function compares numeric, logical, and text values. The logical value TRUE is evaluated as 1. The logical value FALSE is evaluated as 0.

To Calculate

```
=MAXA(Value1, Value2, ...)
```

There must be at least one *Value* argument specified for this function.

Example

Figure 15-28 compares the results of MAX and MAXA when used to compare a list of values. Since MAXA converts the logical value of TRUE to 1 it returns that value as the largest value.

MEDIAN

Use MEDIAN to examine a list of numbers and find the median value. The function will return a numeric value that is in the middle of all values (half of the values are larger and half are smaller).

To Calculate

=MEDIAN(Number1, Number2, ...)

There must be at least one Number argument specified for this function.

Example

Figure 15-29 illustrates how to use MEDIAN to find a median value for a list of numeric values. You will notice that the non-numeric values in the list are ignored by this function. This example also shows how to use MIN to find the smallest numeric value and MINA to find the smallest value in the list.

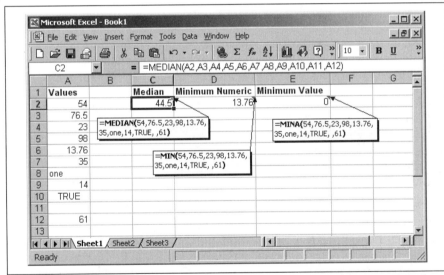

Figure 15-29: MEDIAN, MIN, and MINA provide the ability to examine a list of values and determine the median or smallest value in the list

MIN

Use MIN to return the smallest value in a list of numeric values. When you use this function, cells containing logical values, error values, or text (except for text that represents a numeric value), or cells that are empty are ignored.

To Calculate

=MIN(Number1, Number2, ...)

There must be at least one *Number* argument specified for this function.

Example

Figure 15-29 illustrates how MIN is used to find the minimum numeric value in a list. The function ignores all non-numeric values in the list, whereas MINA looks at all values numeric, text, and logical and returns the smallest value.

MINA

Use MINA to find the smallest value in a list of arguments. This function compares numeric, logical, and text values. The logical value TRUE is evaluated as 1. The logical value FALSE is evaluated as 0.

To Calculate

=MINA(Value1, Value2, ...)

There must be at least one *Value* argument specified for the function.

Example

Figure 15-29 illustrates how to use MINA to find the smallest value in a list. You will notice the function returns a value of 1, because it evaluates the logical value TRUE as a 1.

MODE

Use MODE to examine a list of numbers and find the value that occurs most frequently in the list. If the list does not contain any duplicate numbers an error message of #N/A is returned by the function. If there are multiple numbers that occur with the same frequency in the list, such as (1,2,1,2,1,2), the function returns the number that appears first, which would be 1. The function will ignore any non-numeric values such as logical values and text.

To Calculate

=MODE(Number1, Number2, ...)

There must be at least one *Number* argument specified.

Example

Figure 15-30 illustrates how MODE is used to determine which number appears most frequently in a list.

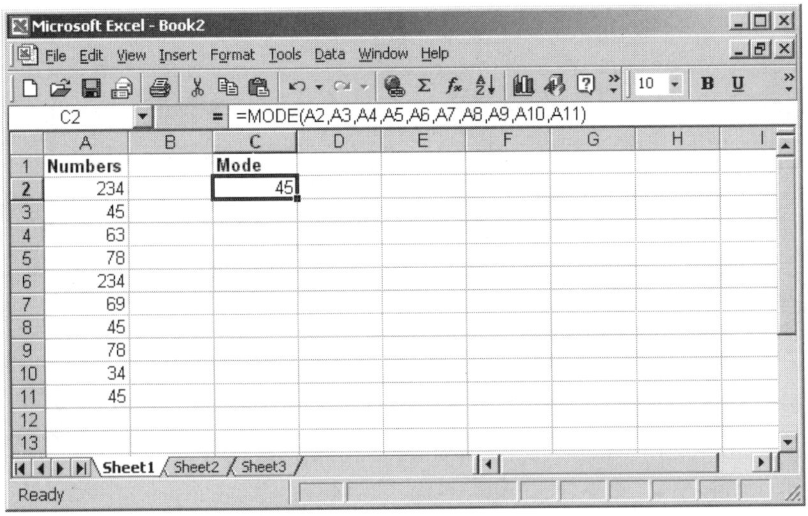

Figure 15-30: Use MODE to find the number that occurs most frequently in a list

NEGBINOMDIST

You can use the NEGBINOMDIST function to determine the probability that a specified number of failures will occur prior to the indicated number of successes, under certain conditions. This type of probability is referred to as negative binomial distribution probability.

To Calculate

=NEGBINOMDIST(Number_f, Number_s, Probability_s)

All arguments are required for this function.

Number_f
> Indicates a positive numeric value; specifies the number of failures you expect to achieve prior to getting the successes specified for the *Number_s* argument.

Number_s
> Indicates a positive numeric value that specifies the number of successes that you expect to achieve during the trials.

Probability_s
> A decimal value between 0 and 1; indicates the success percentage for the trials.

Example

Figure 15-31 illustrates how NEGBINOMDIST is used to determine the probability that the 25 failures will occur before 15 successes happen.

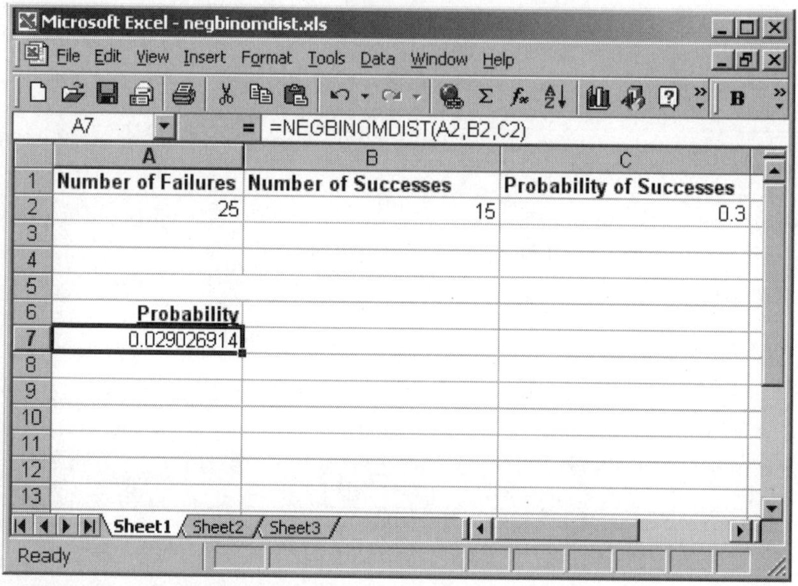

Figure 15-31: Use NEGBINOMDIST to determine if the specified number of failures will occur before getting the desired number of successes

---

NORMDIST

Use NORMDIST to find the normal cumulative probability for a value with the specified mean and standard deviation. This function is frequently used in hypothesis testing.

To Calculate

    =NORMDIST(X, Mean, Standard_Dev, Cummulative)

All arguments are required for this function.

X   Indicates a numeric value for which you want to find the distribution.

Mean
    Indicates a numeric value that specifies the mean of the distribution.

Standard_Dev
    Indicates a positive numeric value that specifies the standard deviation of the distribution.

Example

Figure 15-32 illustrates how NORMDIST is used to find the normal cumulative distribution. The figure shows how the function returns a different value based upon the logical value specified for the *Cumulative* argument. You will also notice in this example that NORMINV returns a value that matches the initial *x* value specified for NORMDIST.

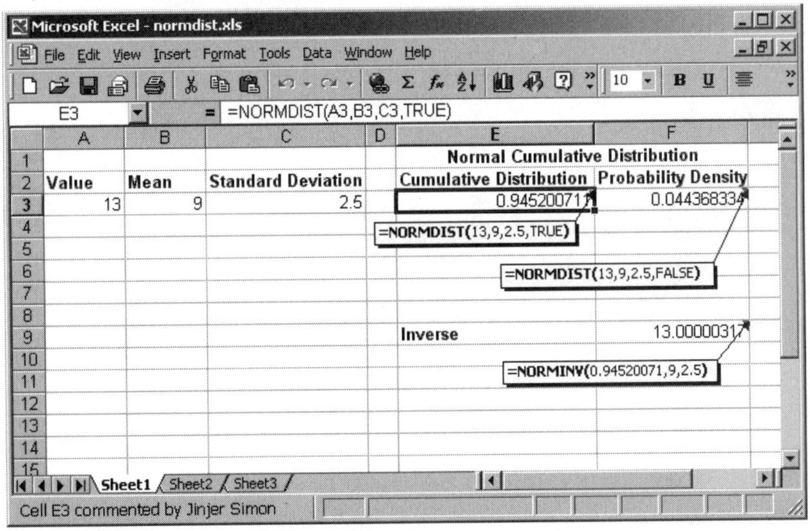

Figure 15-32: Use NORMDIST and NORMINV when working with normal cumulative distribution

Statistical Functions

NORMINV

Use NORMINV to find the inverse of the normal cumulative distribution for the specified mean and standard deviation.

To Calculate

=NORMINV(*Probability*, *Mean*, *Standard_Dev*)

All three arguments must be specified for this function.

Mean
> Indicates a numeric value that specifies the mean of the distribution.

Standard_Dev
> Indicates a positive numeric value that specifies the standard deviation of the distribution.

Example

Figure 15-32 illustrates how to use NORMINV to find the inverse of the normal cumulative distribution. You will notice in this example the value returned by NORMINV is equal to the value specified for the *x* argument of NORMDIST.

NORMSDIST

Use NORMSDIST to find the standard normal cumulative distribution for a value with a mean of 0 and a standard deviation of 1.

To Calculate

```
=NORMSDIST(z)
```

The must be a value specified for the *z* argument.

z   Indicates a numeric value for which you want to find the distribution.

Example

Figure 15-33 illustrates how to use NORMSDIST to find the cumulative normative distribution for a numeric value with a mean of 0 and a standard deviation of 1. The example also shows how to take the probability distribution returned by NORMSDIST and use NORMINV to find the inverse value.

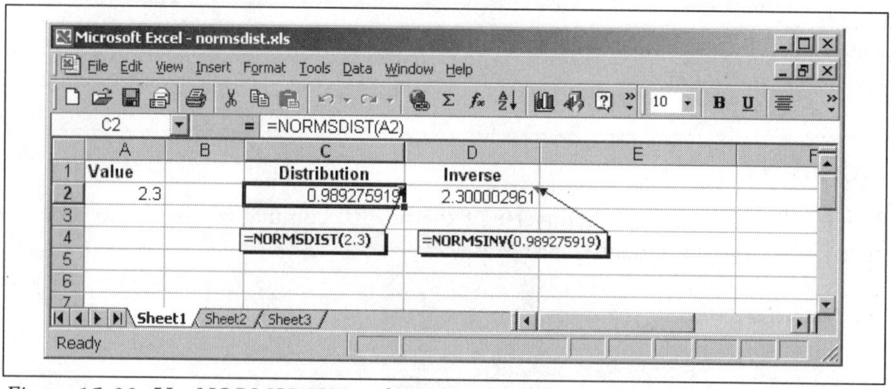

Figure 15-33: Use NORMSDIST and NORMINV for standard normal cumulative distribution with mean of 0 and standard deviation of 1

NORMSINV

Use NORMSINV to find the inverse of the standard normal cumulative distribution for a value with a mean of 0 and a standard deviation of 1.

To Calculate

```
=NORMSINV(Probability)
```

The *Probability* argument is required for this function.

Example

Figure 15-33 illustrates how to use NORMSINV to find the inverse of the standard normal cumulative distribution for a value. The inverse value returned by the function is equal to the value of the *z* argument used by the NORMSDIST function.

PEARSON

Use PEARSON to find the Pearson product moment coefficient *r*. The value returned by the function is between −1.0 and 1.0. The value represents the strength and direction of the linear relationship between the specified lists of data.

To Calculate

```
=PEARSON(Array1, Array2)
```

Both arguments must be specified for this function.

Example

Figure 15-34 illustrates how to use PEARSON to compare two arrays and return a value that indicates the strength and direction of the linear relationship between the values in the two arrays.

PERCENTILE

Use PERCENTILE to find a value that is at the specified percentile of the values in the list. For example, you may want to find the value that is smaller than 25% of the specified values.

To Calculate

```
=PERCENTILE(Array, K)
```

Both arguments are required for this function.

Array
Indicates a range of numeric values.

K Indicates a decimal value between 0 and 1 that indicates the percentile that you want to find.

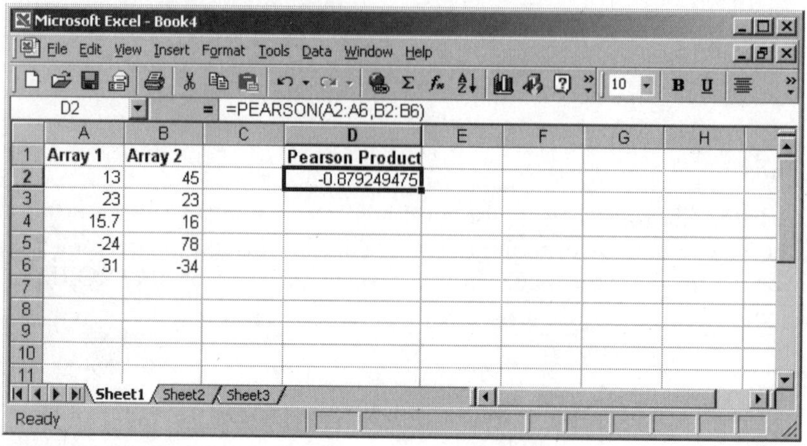

Figure 15-34: Use PEARSON to find r, the Pearson product moment correlation coefficient

Example

Figure 15-35 illustrates how PERCENTILE is used with a list of numeric values to find a value that is 30% of the other numeric values are smaller than. On the other hand, PERCENTRANK indicates the percent ranking of the specified numeric value.

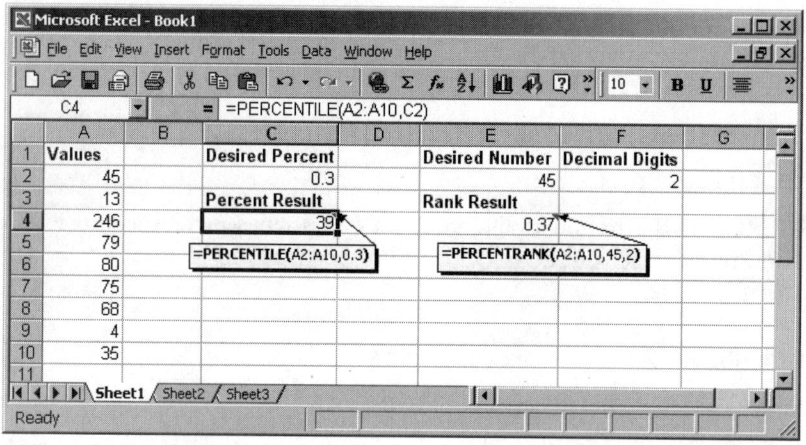

Figure 15-35: Use PERCENTILE to find that value that is larger than the specified percentage of the list and PERCENTRANK to find the ranking of a specific value

PERCENTRANK

Use PERCENTRANK to determine the rank of a specific number within a numeric list. The rank of the number is basically it position in the list if you were to sort the list in ascending order.

To Calculate

=PERCENTRANK(Number, Ref, Significance)

The Number and Ref arguments are required for this function. The Significance argument is optional.

Number
Indicates the number whose rank you want to find.

Ref
Indicates a list of numeric values. Any non-numeric values are ignored by PERCENTRANK.

Significance
Indicates the number of digits that the percentage value should be rounded to. If the value is omitted the default rounds the number to three digits.

Example

Figure 15-35 illustrates how PERCENTRANK is used to determine the rank of the number 45 within the array of values.

PERMUT

Use PERMUT to determine the number of permutations created from the specified number of objects. A permutation is a grouping of items where order is important. If you have three objects that you want to group together, 1,2,3 is a permutation and 2,1,3 is another permutation because the numbers are in a different order.

To Calculate

=PERMUT(Number, Number_Chosen)

Both arguments must be specified for this function.

Number
Indicates a positive integer that specifies the total number of objects.

Number_Chosen
Indicates a positive integer that indicates the number of objects in each grouping (permutation).

Example

Figure 15-36 illustrates how PERMUT is used to find the number of permutations that can occur for several different combinations of total items divided into different sized groups.

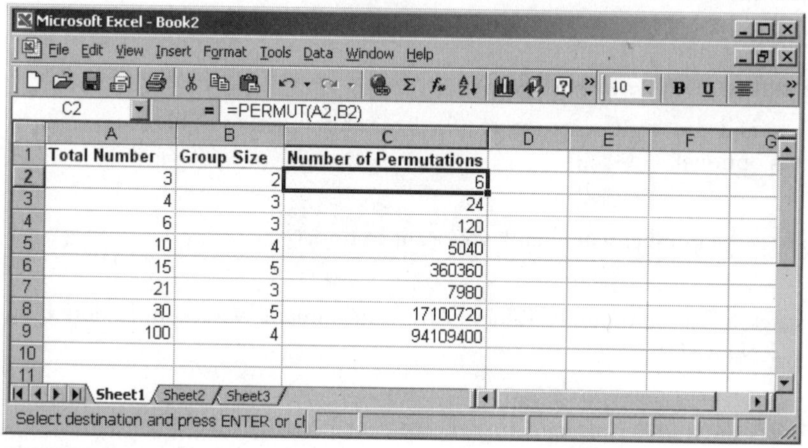

Figure 15-36: The number of possible permutations grows quickly as the total number of items grows

POISSON

Use POISSON to determine the poisson probabilities.

To Calculate

```
=POISSON(X, Mean, Cumulative)
```

All three of the arguments are required for this function.

X   Indicates a positive number that specifies the number of events. If X is not an integer value it is truncated.

Mean
    Indicates a positive number that specifies the expected numeric value.

Cumulative
    This argument must be a logical value of TRUE of FALSE that indicates the actual form of the function. If this argument is TRUE, the function returns the probability that the number of random events will be between 0 and the value specified for the X argument. If the value of this argument is FALSE, the function returns the probability that the number of events will be exactly the value specified for the X argument.

Example

Figure 15-37 illustrates how POISSON is used to determine the probability that the specified number of car accidents occurred yesterday when the average number of daily accidents for the year is 6. The first value indicates the probability that the number of accidents that occurred is between 0 and 10. The second value that is returned indicates the probability that exactly 10 accidents occurred yesterday. There are several important assumptions required before this distribution is used.

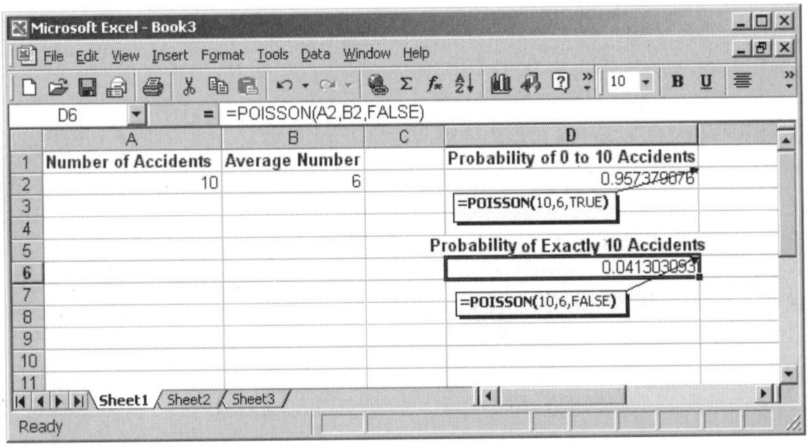

Figure 15-37: Use POISSON to determine the probability that the specified number of events occurred with a set time frame

PROB

Use PROB to determine the probability of a series of numbers being within the specified limits. If the upper limit is not specified, the function returns the probability of the values in the range being equal to the lower limit.

To Calculate

```
=PROB(X_Range, Prob_Range, Lower_Limit, Upper_Limit)
```

The *Upper_Limit* argument is the only optional for this function.

X_Range

Indicates a series of numeric values that are associated with the probabilities specified by the *Prob_Range* argument.

Prob_Range

Indicates a series of decimal numbers between 0 and 1 that indicate the probabilities associated with each value specified for the *X_Range* argument. These decimal numbers must add up to 1.

Lower_Limit

Indicates a numeric value that specifies the lower limit for the range of values.

Upper_Limit

Indicates a numeric value that specifies the upper limit for the range of values. If this argument is omitted, the function returns the probability that the values are equal to the value specified for the *Lower_Limit* argument.

 The X_Range and Prob_Range arguments must contain the same number of values.

Example

Figure 15-38 illustrates how to use PROB to determine if values in the range are within the specified limits.

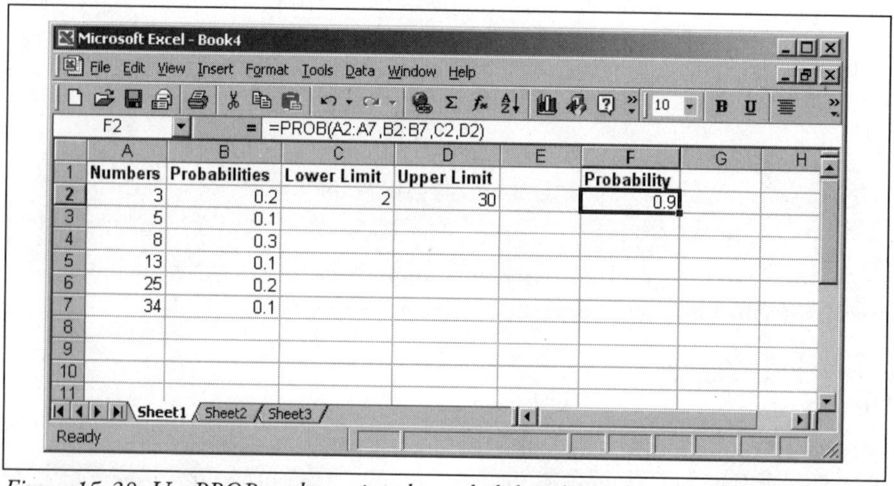

	A	B	C	D	E	F	G	H
1	Numbers	Probabilities	Lower Limit	Upper Limit		Probability		
2	3	0.2	2	30		0.9		
3	5	0.1						
4	8	0.3						
5	13	0.1						
6	25	0.2						
7	34	0.1						
8								
9								
10								
11								

F2 = =PROB(A2:A7,B2:B7,C2,D2)

Figure 15-38: Use PROB to determine the probability that values are within specific limits

QUARTILE

Use QUARTILE to find the value at the specified quartile in a list of values. For example, you may want to determine what the median value (50%) is for the list by specifying a value of 2 for the *Quart* argument.

To Calculate

=QUARTILE(*Array*, *Quart*)

Both arguments are required for this function.

Array

Indicates the list of values for which you want to find the quartile value.

Quart

A value between 0 and 4 that indicates the value that should be returned. If the value is 0 the minimum value in the range is returned; 1 returns the first quartile; 2 returns the median value; 3 returns the third quartile; and 4 returns the maximum value in the list.

Example

Figure 15-39 illustrates how to use QUARTILE to find the value at the specified quartile in a list. In this example, "3" is specified for the *Quart* argument indicating you want the value that is larger than three-fourths of the values in the list. This example also shows how you can use RANK to find the numeric rank of a value in the list if the list was sorted in the specified order.

	A	B	C	D	E	F	G	H
1	Values		Desired Quartile		Desired Number	Order		
2	45		3		45	0		
3	13		Quartile Result		Rank Result			
4	246		79			6		
5	79		=QUARTILE(A2:A10,3)		=RANK(45,A2:A10,0)			
6	80							
7	75							
8	68							
9	4							
10	35							

C4 = =QUARTILE(A2:A10,C2)

Figure 15-39: Use QUARTILE to find value at a specified quartile of the list: Use RANK to determine numeric rank of the value

RANK

Use RANK to find the rank of a specific number within a list of numbers. The rank of the number is an integer that indicates how the size of the number compares to other numbers in the list.

NOTE *Keep in mind that duplicate numbers are assigned the same rank, but the rank of the numbers that follow may not have the anticipated results. For example, if you have the number 1,3,4,3,5 and want to find the rank for the number 3, the number would have the rank of 2, but since there are two of them the number 4 would have the rank of 4.*

To Calculate

=RANK(Number, Ref, Order)

The *Order* argument is optional for this function. The *Number* and *Ref* arguments are required.

Number

Indicates the number whose rank you want to find.

Ref

Identifies a list of values. Any nonnumeric values are ignored by the function.

Order

Indicates a numeric value that specifies the order in which the list of values specified by the *Ref* argument should be sorted. If the *Order* argument is omitted or it has a value of 0, the list is sorted in descending order. If the argument has any other numeric value, the list is sorted in ascending order.

Example

Figure 15-39 illustrates how to use RANK to determine the numeric rank for the value 45 in the list. Since we specified a value of 0 for the *Order* argument the rank is based upon the list being sorted in descending order.

RSQ

Use RSQ to find the square of the Pearson product moment correlation coefficient through the specified x and y data points. This is usually called the coefficient of determination in linear regression situations.

To Calculate

=RSQ(Known_Y's, Known_X's)

Both arguments are required for this function.

Example

Figure 15-40 shows how RSQ is used to find the Pearson product moment correlation coefficient for the specified x and y values. The example also shows the results when the SLOPE function is applied to the same values to find the slope of the linear regression line through the points.

SKEW

Use SKEW to determine the degree of asymmetry for a series of numeric values. If the value returned by the function is positive, it indicates that the distribution of

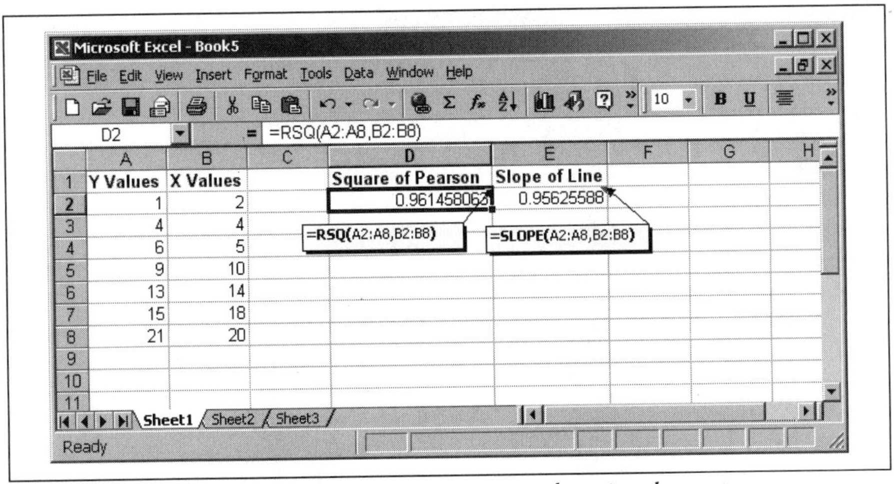

Figure 15-40: Use RSQ and SLOPE to compare x and y axis values

values has an asymmetric tail extending toward more positive values. If the value returned is negative, the distribution has an asymmetric tail extending toward more negative values.

To Calculate

```
=SKEW(Number1, Number2, ...)
```

There must be at least one *Number* argument specified for this function.

Example

Figure 15-41 illustrates how SKEW is used to determine the asymmetry of a list of numeric values.

SLOPE

Use SLOPE to determine the slope of a linear regression line that is closest to the specified data points. The function calculates the slope by dividing the vertical distance by the horizontal distance between two points on the line.

To Calculate

```
=SLOPE(Known_Y's, Known_X's)
```

Both arguments are required for this function.

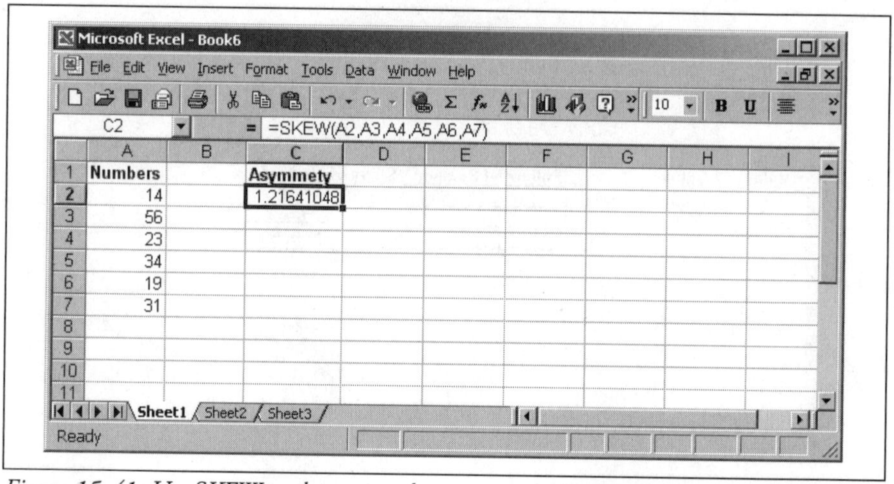

Figure 15-41: Use SKEW to determine the asymmetry of a list of numeric values

Example

Figure 15-40 illustrates how SLOPE is used to find the slope of a linear regression line through the specified data points.

SMALL

Use SMALL to find a specific value within an array based upon its size. For example, you can locate the third smallest number in the list.

To Calculate

`=SMALL(Array, K)`

Both arguments are required for this function.

Array
> Indicates a range of numeric values.

K Indicates a positive numeric value that indicates the position from largest to smallest that you want to find. To find the largest value in the array you specify a 1 for the *K* argument. If the value specified for the *K* argument is a decimal, it is rounded to the closest integer.

Example

Figure 15-42 illustrates how you can use SMALL to find the smallest and the next smallest values in a list of numbers. In order to find the smallest number, a value of 1 was specified for the *K* argument. To find the second smallest number, a value of 2 was specified for *K*.

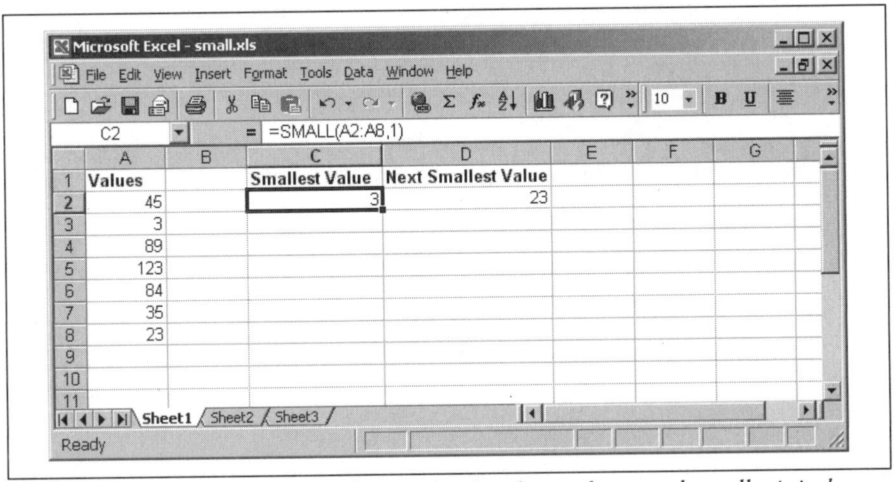

Figure 15-42: Use SMALL to find a number based upon how much smaller it is than the other values

STANDARDIZE

Use STANDARDIZE to find a standardized value for a distribution where you know the mean and standard deviation Z-score.

To Calculate

=STANDARDIZE(*X*, *Mean*, *Standard_Dev*)

All three of the arguments are required for this function.

X Indicates the value that you want to normalize.

Mean
Indicates a numeric value that expresses the arithmetic mean for the distribution.

Standard_Dev
Indicates a number greater than zero that specifies the standard deviation for the distribution.

Example

Figure 15-43 illustrates how to use STANDARDIZE to find the standardized value for a distribution when you know the initial value, mean, and standard deviation for a distribution.

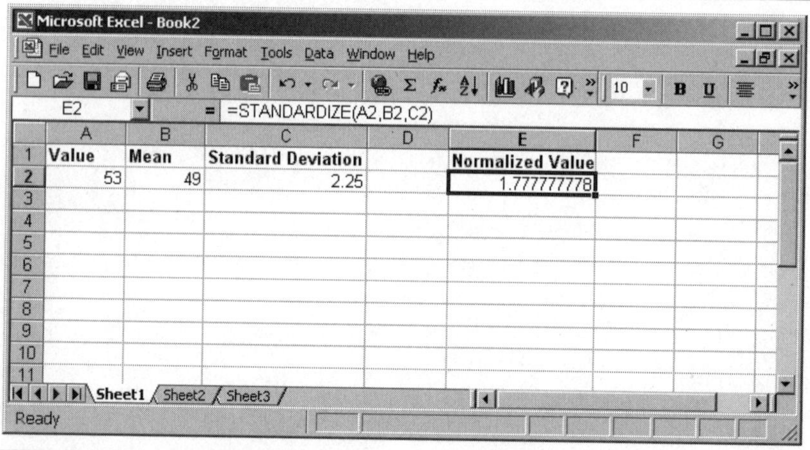

Figure 15-43: Use STANDARDIZE to find the standardized value when you know the mean and standard deviation values

STDEV

Use STDEV to estimate the standard deviation by measuring how far the specified numeric values are dispersed from the mean. All text and logical values are ignored by this function.

To Calculate

=STDEV(Number1, Number2, ...)

There must be at least one *Number* argument specified.

Example

Figure 15-44 illustrates how to use STDEV to find the standard deviation of a list of numbers. You will notice that the list of values that are specified contains two logical values in cells A5 and A7. The function ignores these values because they are not numbers. To include logical values in the standard deviation, use the STDEVA function.

The example also shows how the STDEVP and STDEVPA functions are used to determine the standard deviation for the entire population.

STDEVA

Use STDEVA to estimate the standard deviation by measuring how far the specified numeric values are dispersed from the mean. A logical value of TRUE is evaluated as 1. A logical value of FALSE or a text value is evaluated as 0.

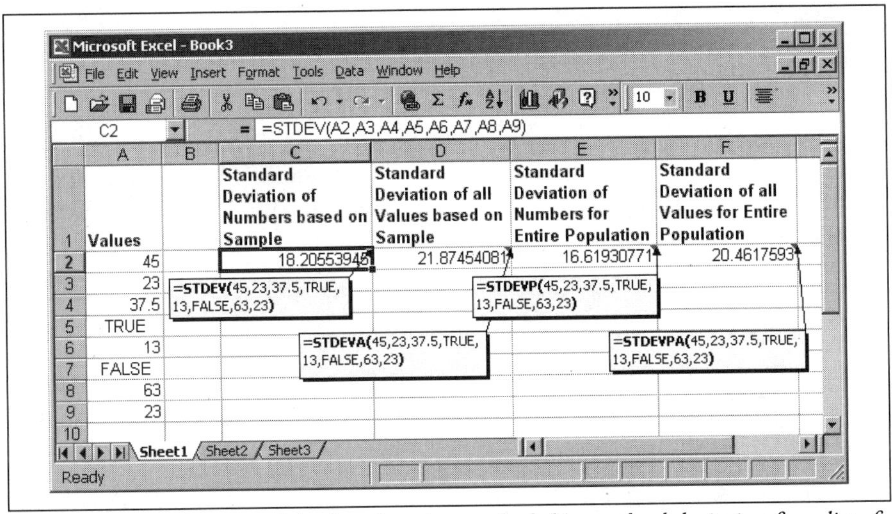

Figure 15-44: Select one of the four functions to find the standard deviation for a list of values

To Calculate

=STDEVA(*Value1*, *Value2*, ...)

There must be at least one *Value* argument specified for this function.

Example

Figure 15-44 illustrates how to use STDEVA to find the standard deviation of a list of values. Since the list includes two logical values, those values are evaluated as part of the standard deviation.

STDEVP

Use STDEVP to estimate the standard deviation, assuming that the numeric values specified constitute the entire population. The standard deviation is determined by measuring how widely the values are dispersed from the mean. All text and logical values are ignored by this function.

To Calculate

=STDEVP(*Number1*, *Number2*, ...)

There must be at least one *Number* argument specified for this function.

Example

Figure 15-44 illustrates how to use STDEVP to find the standard deviation of a list of numbers, assuming that the numeric values specified constitute the entire population. You will notice that the list of values that are specified contains two logical values in cells A5 and A7. The function ignores these values because they are not numbers. To include logical values in the standard deviation, use the STDEVPA function.

STDEVPA

Use STDEVPA to estimate the standard deviation, assuming that the numeric values specified constitute the entire population. The standard deviation is determined by measuring how widely the values are dispersed from the mean. A logical value of TRUE is evaluated as 1. A logical value of FALSE or a text value is evaluated as 0.

To Calculate

=STDEVPA(*Value1, Value2, ...*)

There must be at least one *Value* argument specified for this function.

Example

Figure 15-44 illustrates how to use STDEVPA to find the standard deviation of a list of values for an entire population. Since the list includes two logical values, those values are evaluated as part of the standard deviation.

STEYX

Use STEYX to find the standard error of each y-value for the corresponding x-value in the regression.

To Calculate

=STEYX(*Known_Y's, Known_X's*)

Both arguments are required for this function.

Example

Figure 15-45 illustrates how to use STEYX to find the standard error of the y-values in the regression.

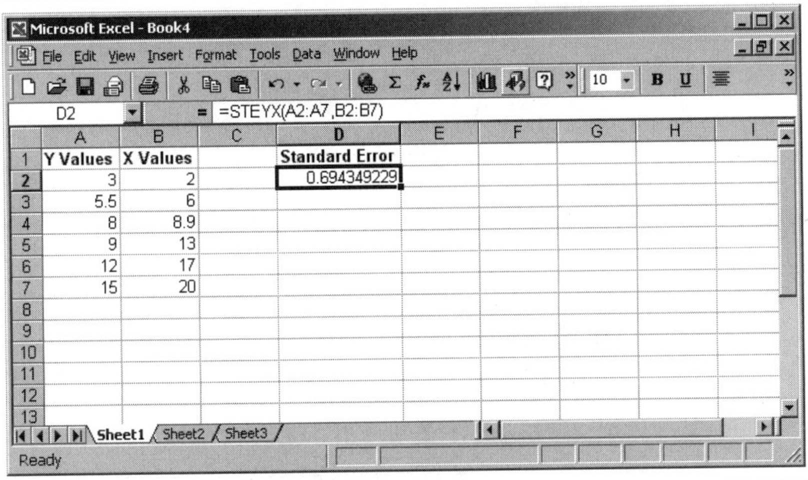

Figure 15-45: Use STEYX to find the standard error for the specified data points

TDIST

Use TDIST to find the Student's T-Distribution (cumulative) probability for the specified numeric value. This function is typically used when hypothesis testing small sample data sets where the population standard deviation is unknown.

To Calculate

```
=TDIST(X, Degrees_Freedom, Tails)
```

The arguments are all required for this function.

X Indicates a numeric value.

Tails
  Indicates an integer value of 1 or 2 that specifies the number of distribution tails to return. A value of 1 returns a one-tailed distribution. A value of 2 returns a two-tailed distribution.

Example

Figure 15-46 illustrates how to use TDIST to find the Student's T-Distribution based upon 45 degrees of freedom and a two-tailed distribution. The example also shows how to take the probability distribution returned by TDIST and use TINV to find the inverse value.

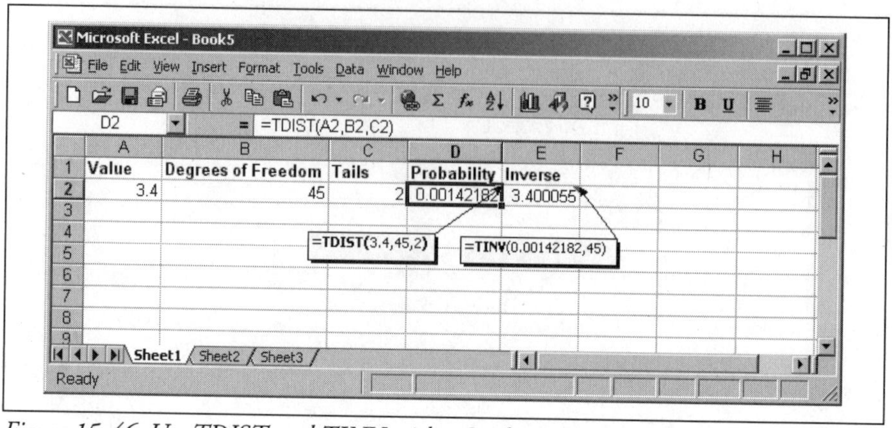

Figure 15-46: Use TDIST and TINV with a Student's T-Distribution

TINV

Use TINV to find the t-value of a Student's T-Distribution if you know the probability and degrees of freedom.

To Calculate

=TINV(Probability, Degrees_Freedom)

The arguments are all required for this function.

Example

Figure 15-46 illustrates how TINV is used to determine the t-value for a student's T-Distribution. You will notice that the value returned by the function matches the value of the *x* argument specified for TDIST.

> **NOTE** *The function assumes you are working with a two-tailed distribution. If the distribution is one-tailed you can find the appropriate result by multiplying the value of the Probability argument by 2.*

TREND

Use TREND to find the values that fit the specified linear trend using the method of least squares. This function returns an array of values that indicate the predicted y-axis values. The function determines the values based upon the equation $y=mx + b$.

To Calculate

=TREND(Known_Y's, Known_X's, New_X's, Const)

The *Known_Y's* argument is required for this function. All other arguments are optional.

Known_Y's

This array must contain a series of positive numbers. If the values in the array are in a single column, then the function interprets the values in each column of the *Known_X's* as a separate variable. If the values in the array are in a single row, then the function interprets the values in each row of the *Known_X's* array as a separate variable.

Known_X's

If this argument is omitted, it is assumed to be an array of values in the range of {1,2,3,…} that is the same size as the array specified by the *Known_Y's* argument.

New_X's

Indicates the new x-axis values for which you want to find the corresponding y values. If these values are omitted, they are assumed to be the same as the *Known_X's* argument.

Example

Figure 15-47 illustrates how to use TREND to determine the future y-axis values based upon the known values for the x-axis, y-axis, and future x-axis values. Remember, this is an array function, so you need to use Ctrl+Shift+Enter to add the function to all cells in the array.

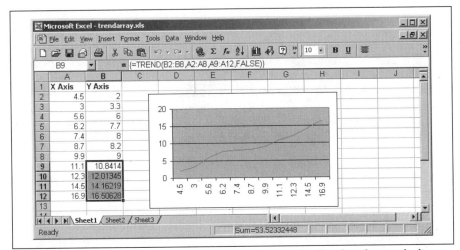

Figure 15-47: Use TREND to determine the future y-axis values based upon the linear trend of the existing values

TRIMMEAN

You can use TRIMMEAN to find the mean of the interior of a list of numeric values. For example, if you have a list of 20 test scores you could eliminate the highest and lowest scores when determining the mean by specifying a *Percent* value of 0.1. By using this function, you would eliminate the high and low scores from skewing the mean value.

To Calculate

=TRIMMEAN(*Array*, *Percent*)

Both arguments are required for this function.

Array

Indicates a list of numeric values for which you want to find the mean.

Percent

Indicates a decimal value between 0 and 1 that represents the percentage that you want to trim from the top and bottom of the list of values.

 The TRIMMEAN function always trims the same number of values from the top and bottom of the list. If the trim value is an odd number the value is rounded down to the closest even integer.

Example

Figure 15-48 illustrates how TRIMMEAN is used to find the mean for a series of grades when the top and bottom 15% of grades are removed.

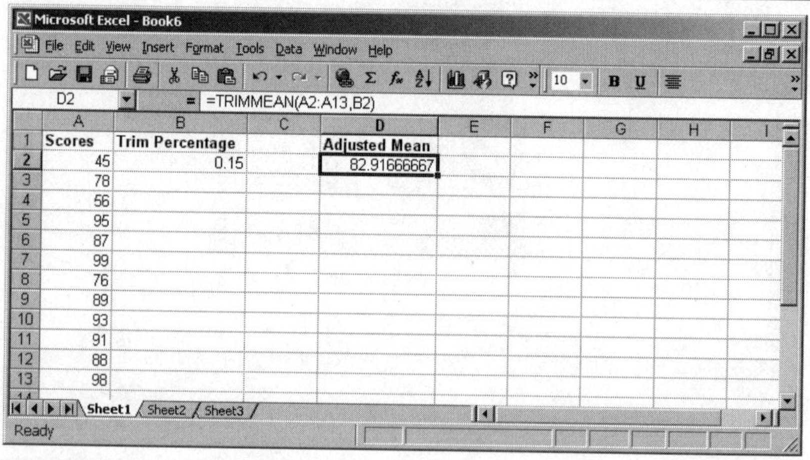

	A	B	C	D
1	Scores	Trim Percentage		Adjusted Mean
2	45	0.15		82.91666667
3	78			
4	56			
5	95			
6	87			
7	99			
8	76			
9	89			
10	93			
11	91			
12	88			
13	98			

D2 = =TRIMMEAN(A2:A13,B2)

Figure 15-48: Use TRIMMEAN to remove excessively high or low values from a list

TTEST

Use TTEST to compare the values from two samples and determine if they are from populations with the same mean or not. This is used only if the two populations are normally distributed.

To Calculate

```
=TTEST(Array1, Array2, Tails, Type)
```

All arguments are required for this function.

Tails

Indicates an integer value of 1 or 2 that specifies the number of distribution tails to return. A value of 1 returns a one-tailed distribution. A value of 2 returns a two-tailed distribution.

Type

Indicates an integer value of 1, 2, or 3 that specifies the kind of T-Test to perform. A value 1 one indicates a paired test, 2 a two-sample equal variance test, and 3 a two-sample unequal variance test.

Example

Figure 15-49 shows how TTEST is used to compare two arrays and determine the probability that the sample means come from populations with the same mean. Here we can see there is no reason to disbelieve the hypothesis that the two population means are the same.

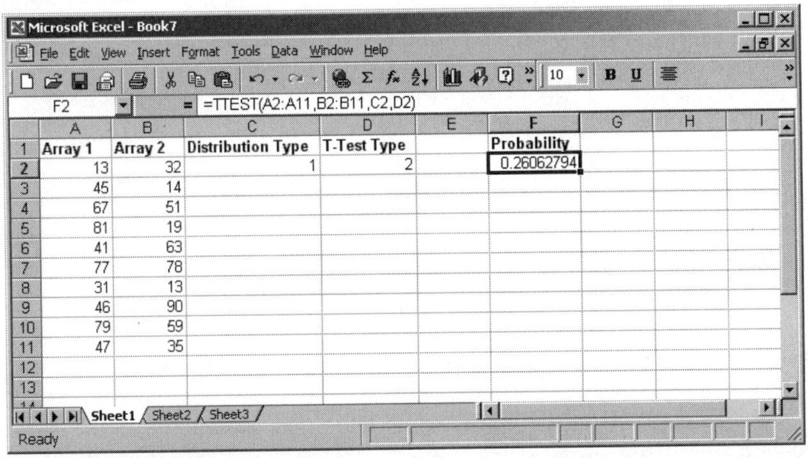

Figure 15-49: Use TTEST to compare two arrays and determine if they are from populations with the same mean

VAR

Use VAR to find the variance in a list of numeric values based on a sample. If any of the values specified contain text or logical values, those values are ignored.

To Calculate

=VAR(*Number1*, *Number2*, ...)

There must be at least one *Number* argument specified for this function.

Example

Figure 15-50 illustrates how to use VAR to find the variance of a list of numbers. You will notice that the list of values that are specified contains two logical values in cells A5 and A7. The function ignores these values because they are not numbers. To include logical values in the variance, you need to use the VARA function.

The example also shows how the VARP and VARPA functions to determine the variance for the entire population.

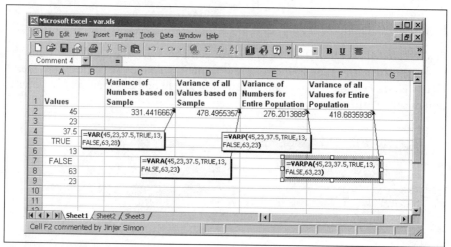

Figure 15-50: Select one of the variance functions to determine the variance value for a list of values

VARA

Use VARA to find the variance in a list of values based upon a sample. If a value specified contains the logical value TRUE it is evaluated as 1. If a value contains text or the logical value FALSE it is evaluated as 0.

To Calculate

=VARA(*Value1*, *Value2*, ...)

There must be at least one *Value* argument specified for this function.

Example

Figure 15-50 illustrates how to use VARA to find the variance of a list of values. Since the list includes two logical values, those values are evaluated as part of the variance.

VARP

Use VARP to find the variance in a list of numeric values based on the entire population. If any of the value specified contain text of logical values, those values are ignored.

To Calculate

=VARP(*Number1*, *Number2*, ...)

There must be at least one *Number* argument specified for this function.

Example

Figure 15-50 illustrates how to use VARP to find the variance of a list of numbers based upon the entire population. You will notice that the list of values that are specified contains two logical values in cells A5 and A7. The function ignores these values because they are not numbers. To include logical values in the variance, you need to use the VARPA function.

VARPA

Use VARPA to find the variance in a list of values based upon the entire population. If a value specified contains the logical value TRUE it is evaluated as 1. If a value contains text or the logical value FALSE it is evaluated as 0.

To Calculate

=VARPA(*Value1*, *Value2*, ...)

There must be at least one *Value* argument specified for this function.

Example

Figure 15-50 illustrates how to use VARPA to find the variance of a list of values for an entire population. Since the list includes two logical values, those values are evaluated as part of the variance.

WEIBULL

Use WEIBULL to find probabilities for the Weibull distribution. This type of distribution is used to perform a reliability analysis.

To Calculate

=WEIBULL(X, Alpha, Beta, Cumulative)

All arguments are required for this function.

X   Indicates a positive numeric value used to evaluate the function.

Example

Figure 15-51 illustrates how to use WEIBULL to perform a Weibull distribution. You will notice that there are two possible values returned by the function depending upon whether you want the Cumulative Distribution or the Probability Mass. These options are selected based upon the logical value specified for the Cumulative argument.

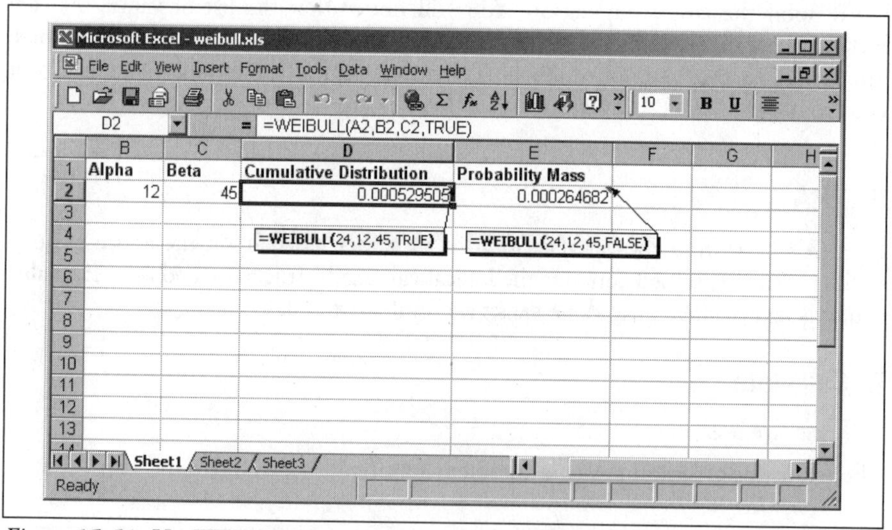

Figure 15-51: Use WEIBULL to perform reliability analysis

ZTEST

Use ZTEST to find the two-tailed P-value of a Z-Test. This function is typically used to determine the likelihood that a particular observation is drawn from a particular population.

To Calculate

```
=ZTEST(Array, X, Sigma)
```

The *Sigma* argument is optional for this function. The other arguments are required.

Array
: Indicates an array of numeric values to test the value of *X* against.

X
: Indicates a numeric value that you want to test against the values in the array specified by the *Array* argument.

Sigma
: Indicates a numeric value that specifies the standard deviation for the population. If this value is omitted, a sample standard deviation is calculated for the values of the *Array* argument.

Example

Figure 15-52 illustrates how ZTEST is used to determine the probability that a specific value is part of the same population as the values specified in the array.

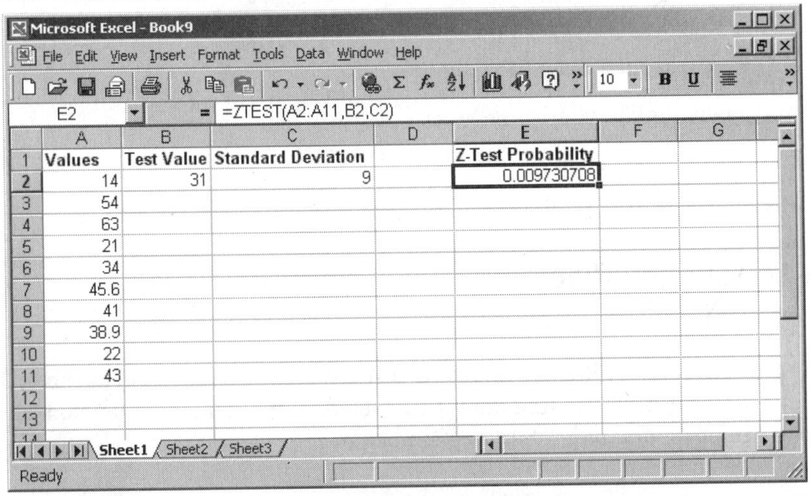

	A	B	C	D	E
1	Values	Test Value	Standard Deviation		Z-Test Probability
2	14	31	9		0.009730708
3	54				
4	63				
5	21				
6	34				
7	45.6				
8	41				
9	38.9				
10	22				
11	43				

Figure 15-52: Use ZTEST to determine the probability that a value is part of the specified array

Chapter 16

Lookup and Reference Functions

Excel offers a group of functions to locate or reference specific values within your workbook. For example, you may want to look up the sales totals for January or the number of books sold in Miami. This chapter provides a detailed description and examples for each of these functions.

The following functions are covered in detail in this chapter:

ADDRESS	HLOOKUP	OFFSET
AREAS	HYPERLINK	ROW
CHOOSE	INDEX	ROWS
COLUMN	INDIRECT	TRANSPOSE
COLUMNS	LOOKUP	VLOOKUP
GETPIVOTDATA	MATCH	

Use these functions to do the following:

- Create a reference to a specific cell

- Select specific values

- Return data from a PivotTable report

- Add a hyperlink to your worksheet

- Create an indirect reference to a cell

- Transpose a range of cells

The Lookup and Reference Functions

Excel provides several different functions that are used to locate or reference values within a worksheet. These functions are covered in the remaining portion of this chapter in alphabetical order, but they can be categorized as follows:

Create references to cells:

ADDRESS (create a reference to a specific cell)
COLUMN (determine the column number)
HYPERLINK (create a shortcut to a document)
OFFSET (find specified number of columns and rows from base)
ROW (determine the row number)
TRANSPOSE (transpose vertical to horizontal range or vice versa

Count elements:

AREAS (determine the number of areas in a reference)
COLUMNS (determine number of columns in an array)
ROWS (determine the number of rows in an array)

Select values:

CHOOSE (select values based upon the specified index value)
GETPIVOTDATA (select values from a PivotTable report)
HLOOKUP (determine the value in the desired row of the matching column)
INDEX (return a value or reference to a value)
INDIRECT (return reference value from another cell)
LOOKUP (find a corresponding value in a vector or an array)
MATCH (find matching value in array)
VLOOKUP (determine the value in the desired column of the matching row)

Recurring Arguments

The following arguments are available on a recurring basis in many of the functions discussed in this chapter. If differences in the implementation exist in a particular function, they will be explained within the individual function's section.

Array
    Indicates a range of cells.

Column_Num
    A positive integer value used to reference a specific column. If the argument specifies a decimal value the decimal portion of the number is truncated.

Range_Lookup
    An optional argument that specifies a logical value of TRUE or FALSE indicating the type of match you want the function to make. If this argument is omitted or contains a value of TRUE an approximate match to the value specified for the *Lookup_Value* argument is specified. That means that if the function cannot find an exact match for *Lookup_Value* it returns the largest value that is less than *Lookup_Value*. If the argument is FALSE the function will find an exact match.

Reference

A reference to a specific cell or a range or cells. You can specify multiple references by placing them in parentheses and separating each range with a comma. For example, (A2:A5,C2:C5).

Row_Num

A positive integer value used to reference a specific row. If the argument specifies a decimal value that decimal portion of the number is truncated.

Table_Array

Specifies the range of the table that contains the data that you want to locate.

ADDRESS

Use ADDRESS to create a reference to a specific cell as text by specifying the desired row and column location as numeric values. For example, to refer to cell B2 you would reference column B as 2 for the *Column_Num* argument and row 2 as 2 for the *Row_Num* argument.

To Calculate

=ADDRESS(*Row_Num*, *Column_Num*, *Abs_Num*, *A1*, *Sheet_Text*)

The *Row_Num* and *Column_Num* arguments are required for this function. All other arguments are optional.

Abs_Num

This optional argument specifies an integer value of 1, 2, 3, or 4 indicating the type of cell reference to return.

1   Absolute reference. If the contents of the cell are cut or copied the address does not change. This is the default value if the argument is omitted.

2   Absolute reference for row but relative reference for column. For example, if the address is B$3 the row would remain 3 if the cell is copied or pasted but the column would change depending upon where the cell is pasted.

3   Absolute reference for column but relative reference for row. For example, if the address is $B3 the column would remain B if the cell is copied or pasted but the row would change depending upon where the cell is pasted.

4   Relative reference to both row and column. For example, if the reference is to cell B3 and the reference is copied and placed in the adjacent cell the pasted reference would be C3.

A1 This optional argument specifies a logical value of TRUE or FALSE that indicates the style used to represent the cell address. If the value is TRUE or it is omitted, the function uses the A1-style reference where a cell is referred to using the letter that represents the column name and a number for the row such as C3. If the value of the argument is FALSE the function returns the address using the R1C1 style where the cell is referenced as R3C3.

Sheet_text

This optional argument is used to specify the name of a sheet that you want to reference. The argument is only needed when referencing an external worksheet. If the argument is omitted the address is assumed to be part of the existing worksheet. For example, to reference the first worksheet in the Accounting workbook you would specify a value of "[Accounting]Sheet1".

Example

Figure 16-1 illustrates how to build a cell range using the column and row numbers gathered from other cells.

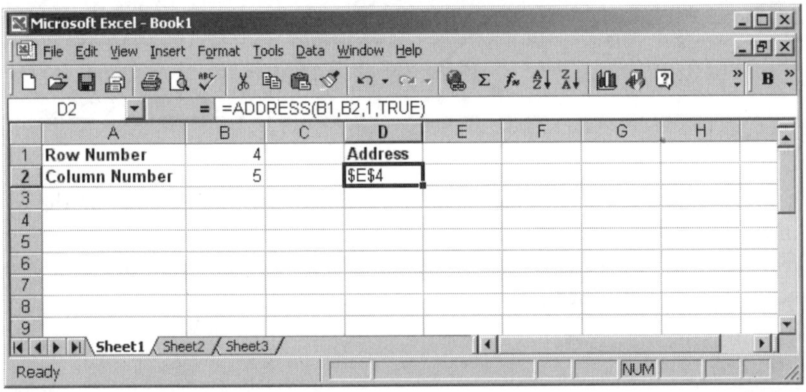

Figure 16-1: Use ADDRESS to create a reference to a specific cell within a worksheet

AREAS

Use AREAS to determine the number of areas within a reference. An area refers to a range of contiguous cells or a single cell.

To Calculate

=AREAS(*Reference*)

The *Reference* argument is required for this function.

Example

Figure 16-2 illustrates how to use AREAS to count the number of sales territories. Make sure you remember to use parentheses to surround multiple ranges.

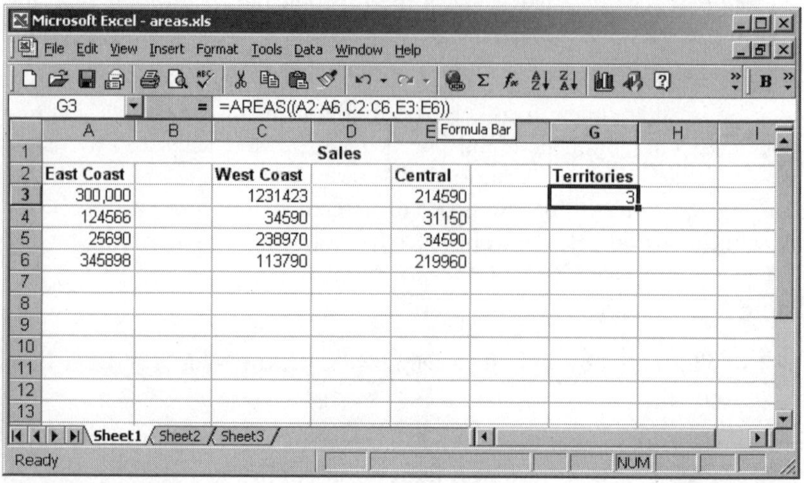

Figure 16-2: Use AREAS to determine the number of ranges within a specific reference

CHOOSE

Use CHOOSE to select a value from a list based upon the order of the values within the list. The value returned by the function is determined by the value specified for the *Index_Num* argument. For example, if you specify a 2 for the argument the second value in the list is returned by the function.

To Calculate

```
=CHOOSE(Index_Num, Value1, Value2,...)
```

The *Index_Num* argument and at least one *Value* argument are required for this function.

Index_Num

An integer value between 1 and 29 that specifies the *Value* argument to select. The value of this argument should not be larger than the number of *Value* arguments specified.

Value1, Value2, ...

You can specify up to 29 different arguments that you want to check that can reference either a single cell or an array of values. If an argument specifies an array the entire range of cells in the array is evaluated by the function.

Example

Figure 16-3 illustrates how to use CHOOSE to select a specific value, in this case, the desired month, from a list based upon its order.

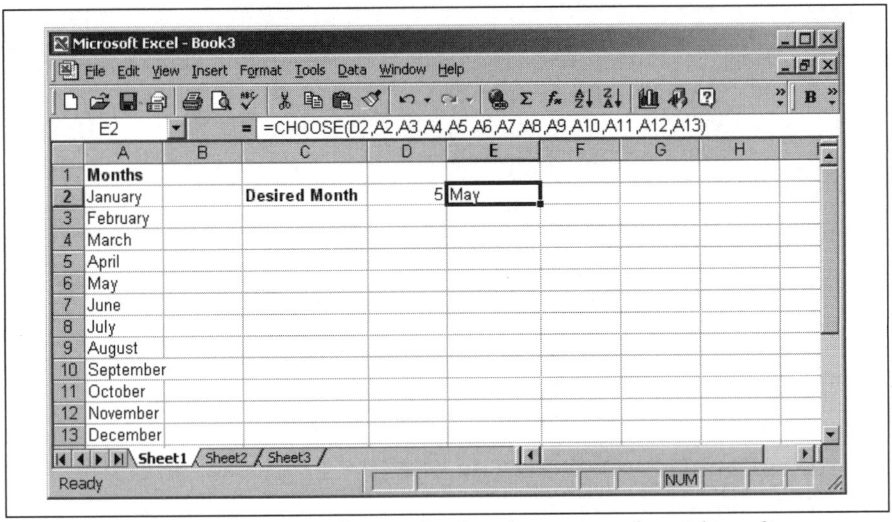

Figure 16-3: Use CHOOSE to select a value based upon its order within a list

COLUMN

Use COLUMN to determine the column number of the specified column. If the function is used without an argument the column number of the cell containing the function is returned.

To Calculate

=COLUMN(Reference)

The Reference argument is optional for this function.

> **NOTE** *If the argument contains a horizontal range of cells and if the function is entered as an array it returns a horizontal array of values.*

Example

Figure 16-4 illustrates how COLUMN is used to determine the column number for a specific range. In this example we are determining the location of the named range West_Coast. The ROW function returns an array that represents the row numbers within the specified range.

COLUMNS

Use COLUMNS to determine the number of columns in the specified array.

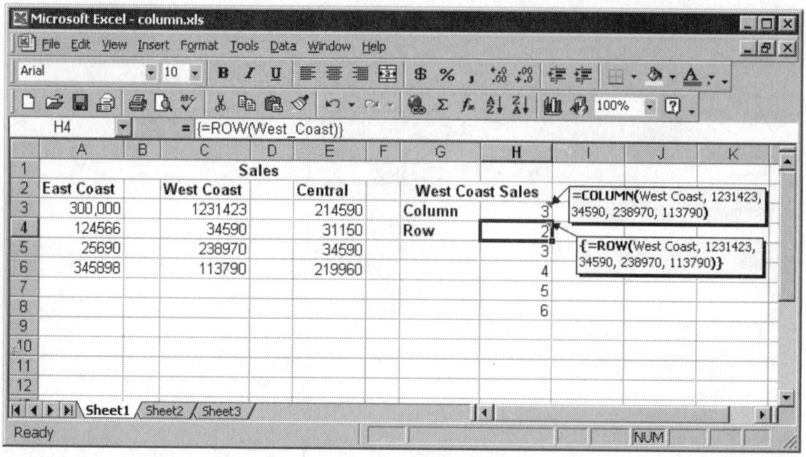

Figure 16-4: Use COLUMN and ROW to find the column and row numbers for the specified reference

To Calculate

=COLUMNS(Array)

The Array argument is required for this function.

Example

Figure 16-5 illustrates how COLUMNS is used to figure out the number of rows in the specified array. In this example the function is used to determine the number of sales locations. The ROWS function indicates the number of sales periods (months) in the array.

GETPIVOTDATA

Use GETPIVOTDATA to get data stored in a PivotTable report.

To Calculate

=GETPIVOTDATA(Pivot_Table, Name)

Both arguments are required for this function.

Pivot_Table

A reference to the pivot table that contains the desired data. The reference can refer to a specific cell, a range of cells, or a label for the table.

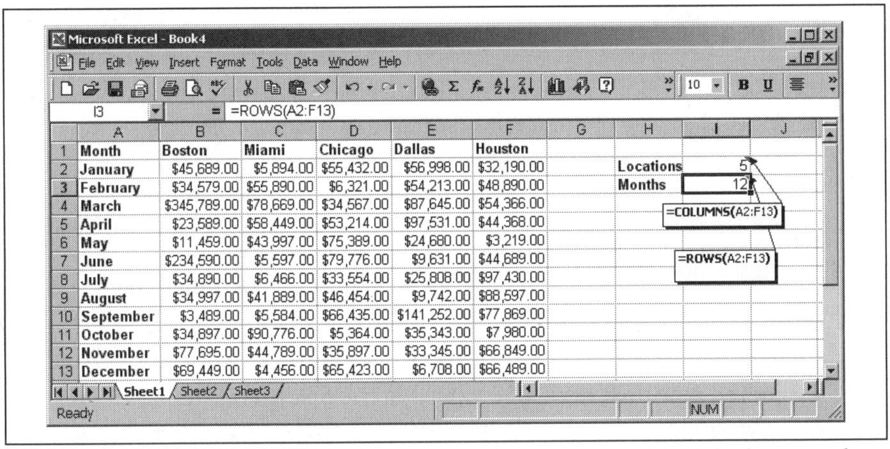

	A	B	C	D	E	F	G	H	I
1	Month	Boston	Miami	Chicago	Dallas	Houston			
2	January	$45,689.00	$5,894.00	$55,432.00	$56,998.00	$32,190.00		Locations	5
3	February	$34,579.00	$55,890.00	$6,321.00	$54,213.00	$48,890.00		Months	12
4	March	$345,789.00	$78,669.00	$34,567.00	$87,645.00	$54,366.00			
5	April	$23,589.00	$58,449.00	$53,214.00	$97,531.00	$44,368.00			
6	May	$11,459.00	$43,997.00	$75,389.00	$24,680.00	$3,219.00			
7	June	$234,590.00	$5,597.00	$79,776.00	$9,631.00	$44,689.00			
8	July	$34,890.00	$6,466.00	$33,554.00	$25,808.00	$97,430.00			
9	August	$34,997.00	$41,889.00	$46,454.00	$9,742.00	$88,597.00			
10	September	$3,489.00	$5,584.00	$66,435.00	$141,252.00	$77,869.00			
11	October	$34,897.00	$90,776.00	$5,364.00	$35,343.00	$7,980.00			
12	November	$77,695.00	$44,789.00	$35,897.00	$33,345.00	$66,849.00			
13	December	$69,449.00	$4,456.00	$65,423.00	$6,708.00	$66,489.00			

Figure 16-5: Use COLUMNS and ROWS to determine the number of columns and rows in the specified array

`Name`

A text string enclosed in double quotes that describes the data that you want to return from the table. The Name argument typically contains the names of rows or columns that refer to the specific data you want to return. For example, it could contain the value "March Sales" to return the total sales for March.

Example

Figure 16-6 illustrates how GETPIVOTDATA is used to determine the sales within Florida for the salesperson with an ID of 12. Notice that you need to use the exact column and row names to retrieve the appropriate data.

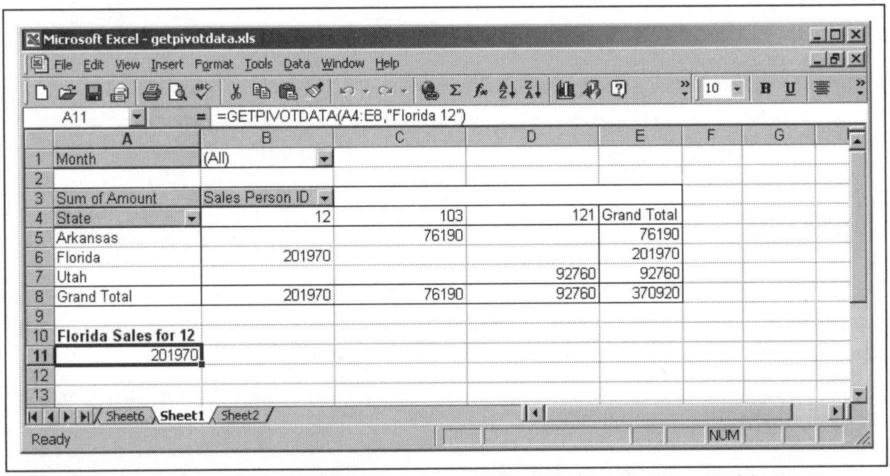

	A	B	C	D	E
1	Month	(All)			
2					
3	Sum of Amount	Sales Person ID			
4	State	12	103	121	Grand Total
5	Arkansas		76190		76190
6	Florida	201970			201970
7	Utah			92760	92760
8	Grand Total	201970	76190	92760	370920
9					
10	Florida Sales for 12				
11	201970				

Figure 16-6: Use GETPIVOTDATA to get specific data from a PivotTable report

HLOOKUP

Use HLOOKUP to locate a column heading in the first row of the specified table and then return the value of the specified cell of that column.

To Calculate

=HLOOKUP(Lookup_Value, Table_Array, Row_Index_Num, Range_Lookup)

The Range_Lookup argument is optional for this function. All other arguments are required.

Lookup_Value

Specifies the value that should be located in the first row of the table. Typically this is the heading for the desired column. This argument can specify a value, reference, or a text string.

Row_Index_Num

An integer value that specifies the specific row in the table that you want to return. The row numbering is based upon the range of the cells specified for the table. For example, if the range of cells is A5:D10 the first row would be 5.

TIP # 91

Sorting the Table

If the value of the Range_Lookup argument is TRUE or omitted, the value in the first row of the table must be sorted into ascending order to make sure the function returns the correct information. Use Data → Sort to sort the items into ascending order.

Example

Figure 16-7 illustrates how HLOOKUP is used to find total sales for the state of Texas. The function compares the value entered in cell B7 to the specified array and then returns the results in row 4 for the corresponding column.

HYPERLINK

Use HYPERLINK to create a shortcut to another document that is stored on your machine, a network, an intranet, or the Internet. Once you create the link the selected document will open each time you click on the link.

To Calculate

=HYPERLINK(Link_Location, Friendly_Name)

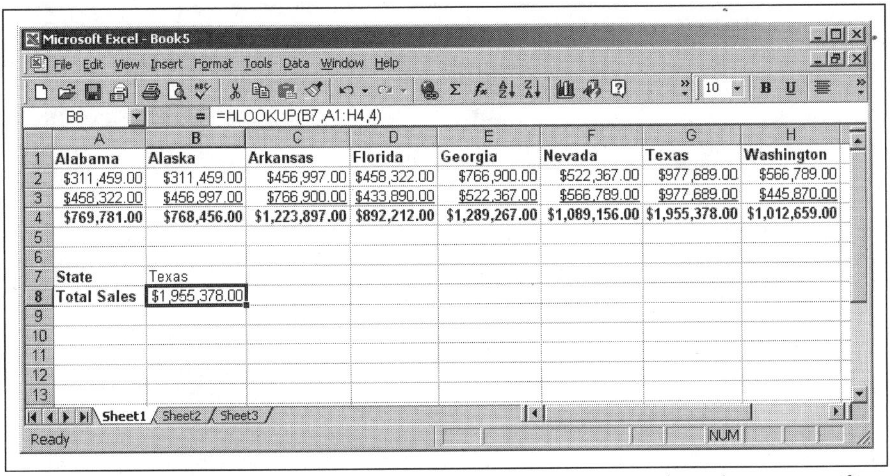

Figure 16-7: Use HLOOKUP to find value in row in an array where the corresponding column head matches the specified value

The `Link_Location` argument is required for this function. The `Friendly_Name` argument is optional.

`Link_Location`

Indicates the path- and filename of a document to which you want to link. If you are linking to an Excel workbook it can refer to a specific range of cells. If you reference a Microsoft Word document it can reference a bookmark in the document. The file is located on any machine you have access, to including the Internet. Make sure the address you specify is enclosed in quotes.

`Friendly_Name`

Indicates the text that you want to have displayed in the cell to represent the link. For example, instead of the link *www.oreilly.com* you may want to use the text "O'Reilly & Associates."

Example

Figure 16-8 illustrates how HYPERLINK is used to create a hyperlink in your worksheet to a specific Internet location.

INDEX

Use INDEX to return a value or reference to a value from within an array or a range of cells. This function has two different forms depending upon whether you are working with an array or a range or cells.

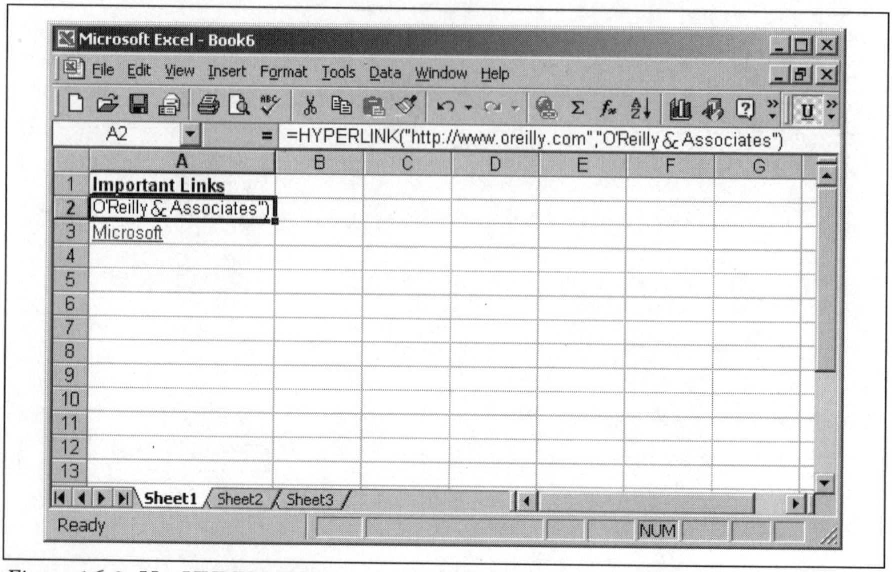

Figure 16-8: Use HYPERLINK to create a link to another workbook, document, or web site within your worksheet

To Calculate (Array)

```
=INDEX(Array, Row_Num, Column_Num)
```

When finding the index for an array the *Array* argument is required. The other arguments are optional.

To Calculate (Range of Cells)

```
=INDEX(Reference, Row_Num, Column_Num, Area_Num)
```

When finding the index for a range of cells the *Reference* argument is required. The other arguments are optional.

Area_Num

An optional argument that indicates an integer value that specifies the range within the *Reference* argument that you want to use to return a value. The first range specified is numbered 1, the second 2, etc.

Example

Figure 16-9 illustrates how to use INDEX to find the value of an array that is in the specified row and column.

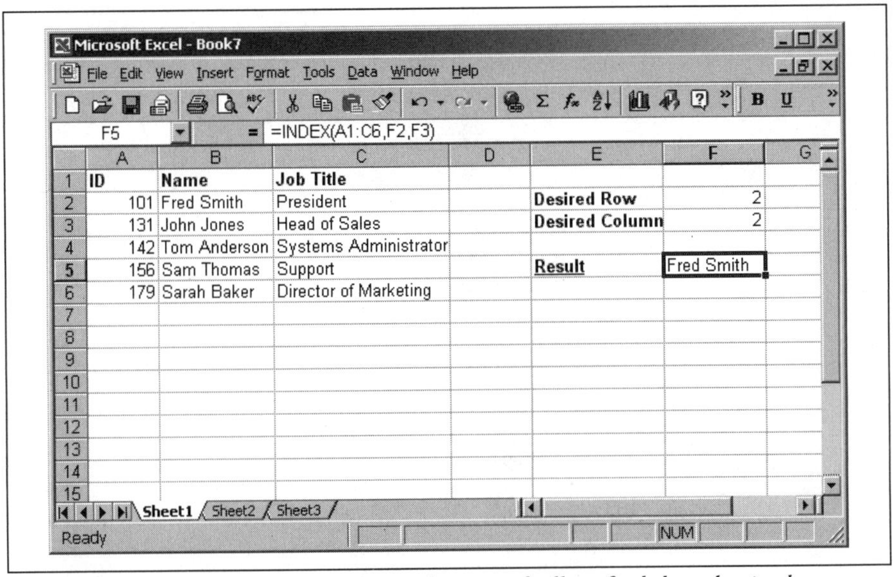

Figure 16-9: Use INDEX with arrays and ranges of cells to find the value in the specified row and column

INDIRECT

Use INDIRECT to return the reference specified by another cell. For example, if cell B2 refers to A2 which contains the value 345 you can use INDIRECT(B2) in cell C2 to return a value of 345.

To Calculate

=INDIRECT(*Ref_Text*, *A1*)

The *Ref_Text* argument is required for this function. The *A1* argument is optional.

Ref_Text
    References another cell or a named range.

A1 A logical value that specifies the type of reference specified by the cell that is referenced by the *Ref_Text* argument. If this argument is omitted or contains a value of TRUE the cell is using A1-style. If the argument has a value of FALSE the cell is using the R1C1-style.

Example

Figure 16-10 illustrates how to use INDIRECT to return the value of the referenced cell. In this example, cell C3 refers to cell B3 which contains the value E13. INDIRECT takes the text reference in cell B3 and returns the value of cell E13, or $29,012.00.

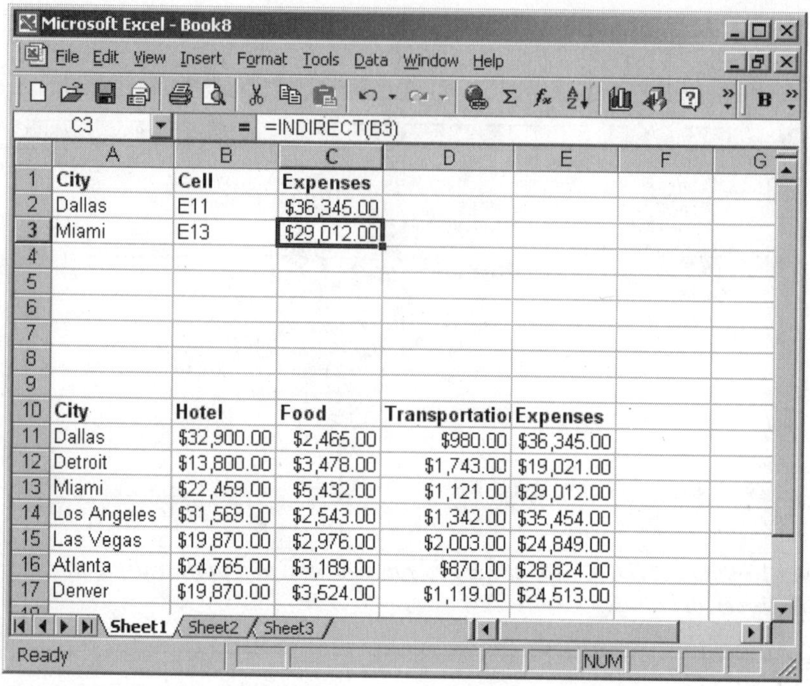

Figure 16-10: Use INDIRECT to determine the value of an indirect reference

LOOKUP

Use LOOKUP to return a value either from a specific row or column or from an array of cells. When you return a value from a single row or column it is referred to as a vector lookup in Excel.

Excel provides two forms of the LOOKUP function, one for vectors and another for arrays. The vector form of the function returns the value in the second row or column of the specified range. The array form of the function finds the specified value in the first row or column of the array and then returns the last value in the corresponding row or column.

To Calculate (Vector)

```
=LOOKUP(Lookup_Value, Lookup_Vector, Result_Vector)
```

Use this form of the function when dealing with vectors. All arguments are required for the function.

Lookup_Value

Indicates the value that you want to locate in a row or column range specified by *Lookup_Vector*. This value can be a number, text, logical value, or a reference.

Lookup_Vector

Indicates the range of cells that you want to search for the value specified for the *Lookup_Value* argument. This argument can only specify a single row or column. If the function does not find a match, it uses the largest value that is smaller than *Lookup_Value*.

 The values in the row or column specified by Lookup_Vector must be sorted into ascending order (i.e., 1,2,3,.., A-Z, FALSE, and TRUE).

Result_Vector

Must indicate a row or column of the same size as the range specified for the *Lookup_Vector* argument that contains the values to be returned.

To Calculate (Array)

=LOOKUP(*Lookup_Value*, *Array*)

Use this form of the function when dealing with arrays. All arguments are required for the function. If the function does not find a match, it uses the largest value that is smaller than *Lookup_Value*.

Lookup_Value

Indicates the value that you want to locate in an array specified by the *Array* argument. This value can be a number, text, logical value, or a reference.

 The values in the first row or column specified by Array must be sorted into ascending order (i.e., 1,2,3,.., A-Z, FALSE, and TRUE).

Example

Figure 16-11 illustrates how to use LOOKUP to return the corresponding vector value. In this example the function takes the desired lookup value of Miami and returns the corresponding expenses. This example used the vector version of the function because the array version would have returned a value from the Hotel column as the expenses. By using the vector version you are able to indicate the specific column you want to select the value from.

MATCH

Use MATCH to find the position of an item in the specified array that matches the value indicated. Depending upon the type of match specified for the *Match_Type*

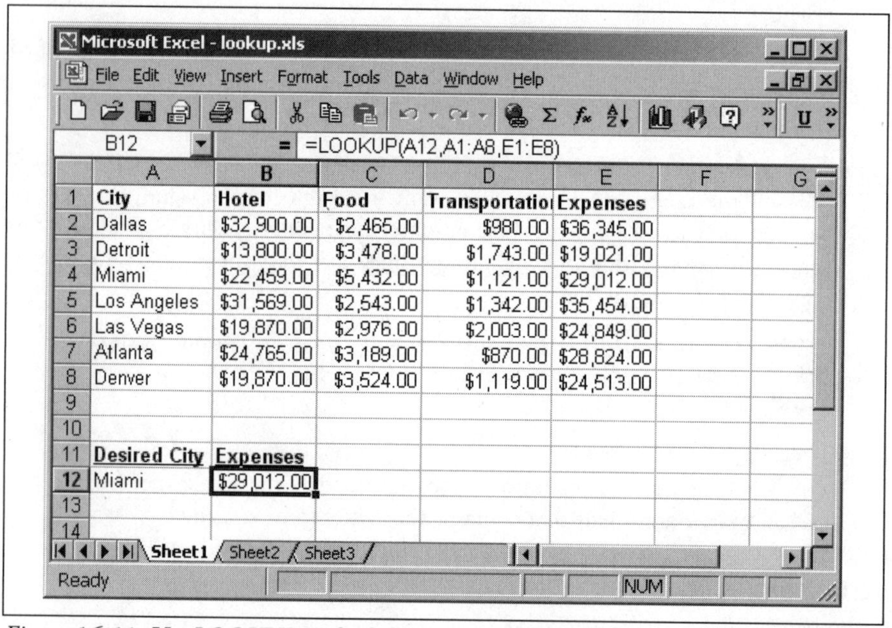

Figure 16-11: Use LOOKUP to find the corresponding value in a vector or an array

argument, the function will return the location of an exact match, the closest value that is larger, or the closest value that is smaller.

To Calculate

=MATCH(Lookup_Value, Lookup_Array, Match_Type)

The Match_Type argument is optional for this function. The other arguments are required.

Lookup_Value

Indicates the value you want to use to find the value in the array. This argument can be any type of value (number, text, logical, or cell reference).

Lookup_Array

Indicates a contiguous range of cells that you want to search for the specified value.

Match_Type

An optional value of –1, 0, or 1 that indicates the type of match that should be made. If the value is omitted or 1 the function finds the largest value that is less than the value specified by Lookup_Value. If the value is 0 the function finds the first exact match. If the value is –1 the function finds the smallest value that is greater than or equal to the value specified by Lookup_Value.

> **NOTE** *If Match_Type equals 1 the values in the array must be sorted in ascending order (i.e., 1,2,3,.., A-Z, FALSE, and TRUE). If Match_Type equals –1 the values in the array must be sorted in descending order (i.e., TRUE, FALSE, Z-A, 3,2,1 …)*

Example

Figure 16-12 illustrates how to use MATCH to determine the position of the specified value within a list. In this example, we use MATCH to determine the numeric value of Tuesday.

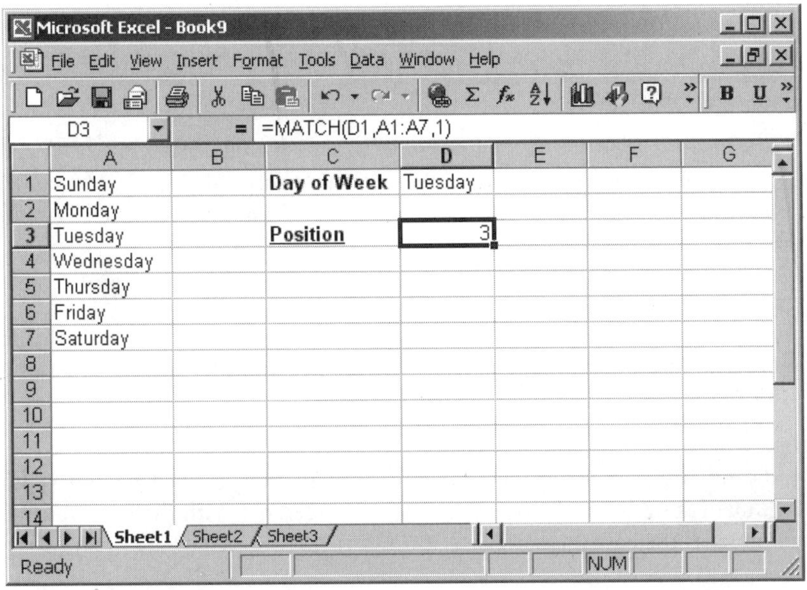

Figure 16-12: Use MATCH to determine the numeric position of the specified value within a list

OFFSET

Use OFFSET to return the reference to a cell or range of cells that is the specified number of rows and columns for the specified cells.

To Calculate

```
=OFFSET(Reference, Rows, Cols, Height, Width)
```

The *Reference*, *Rows*, and *Cols* arguments are required. The other arguments are used optionally to indicate the number of rows or columns to return.

Rows

> An integer value that indicates the number of rows you want to move from the base value specified by the `Reference` argument. If the value is positive the reference is the specified number of rows below the base. If the value is negative, the reference is the specified number of rows above the base.

Cols

> An integer value that indicates the number of columns you want to move from the base value specified by the `Reference` argument. If the value is positive the reference is the specified number of columns to the right of the base. If the value is negative the reference is the specified number columns to the left of the base.

TIP # 92

Specifying Offset Values

The values specified as offsets for the Rows and Cols arguments must specify cells on the worksheet. In other words, the smallest cell reference that is specified is cell A1. If you attempt to reference a cell smaller than that the function will return a #REF! Error.

Height

> Indicates the number of rows you want in the returned reference. If this argument is omitted, the function returns a reference with the same number of rows as the base reference.

Width

> Indicates the number of columns you want in the returned reference. If this argument is omitted, the function returns a reference with the same number of columns as the base reference.

Example

Figure 16-13 illustrates how OFFSET is used to find the value cell that is located the specified number of rows and columns from the starting cell. For this example the starting cell was B3. We moved two rows down and two columns right to cell C5, which has a value of 45.

ROW

Use ROW to determine the row number of the specified row. If the function is used without an argument the row number of the cell containing the function is returned.

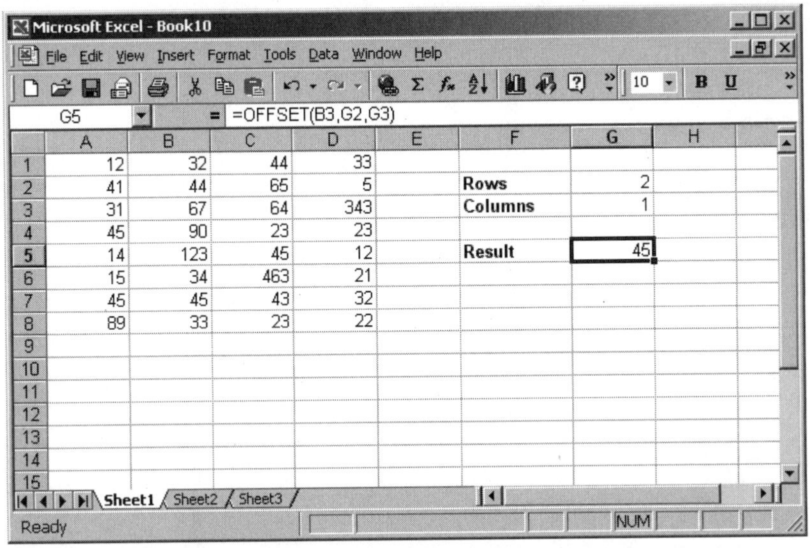

Figure 16-13: Use OFFSET to find the value of a cell or range of cells that is located the specified number or rows and columns from the base cell

To Calculate

=ROW(Reference)

The Reference argument is optional for this function.

> **NOTE** *If the argument contains a vertical range of cells and if the function is entered as an array it returns a vertical array of values.*

Example

Figure 16-4 illustrates how ROW determines the row numbers for a specific range. We are determining the location of the named range West_Coast. It returns an array representing the row numbers within the specified range. If you wanted to determine the row number of the first cell in the range, place the function in one cell. The function returns one row number for each cell selected for the function.

ROWS

Use ROWS to determine the number of rows in the specified array.

To Calculate

=ROWS(Array)

Example

Figure 16-5 illustrates how ROWS is used to figure out the number of columns in the specified array. In this example the function is used to determine the number of sales periods (months) in the array.

TRANSPOSE

Use TRANSPOSE to transpose the values in a vertical range of cells into a horizontal range or vice versa. This function must be used as an array function and the range of cells selected for the function must match the specified array. For example, if the specified array is a column of five cells the function must be placed in a row of five cells.

To Calculate

```
=TRANSPOSE(Array)
```

The *Array* argument is required for this function.

Example

Figure 16-14 illustrates how TRANSPOSE is used to take the values of a column and transpose them into a row of the same length. Keep in mind that you need to make sure you select a row that has the same number of cells as the range of cells in the column you want to transpose. Also, remember you need to use Ctrl+Shift+Enter to paste the function into the selected cells.

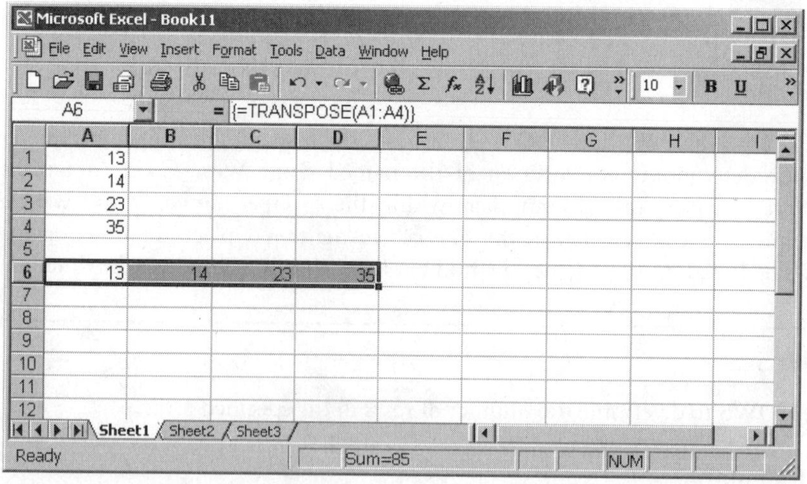

Figure 16-14: Use TRANSPOSE if you need to move values from a row into a column or vice versa

VLOOKUP

Use VLOOKUP to locate a row heading in the first column of the specified table and then return the value of the specified cell of that row.

To Calculate

=VLOOKUP(*Lookup_Value, Table_Array, Col_Index_Num, Range_Lookup*)

The *Range_Lookup* argument is optional for this function. All other arguments are required.

Lookup_Value

Specifies the value that should be located in the first column of the table. Typically this is the heading for the desired row. This argument can specify a value, reference, or a text string.

Col_Index_Num

An integer value that specifies the column in the table that you want to return. The column numbering is based upon the range of the cells specified for the table. For example, if the range of cells is A5:D10 the first column would be A.

Example

Figure 16-15 illustrates how VLOOKUP is used to find the total sales for a specific year. In this example the function finds the specified year, 1998, and returns the value in the sixth column of $2,109,780.00.

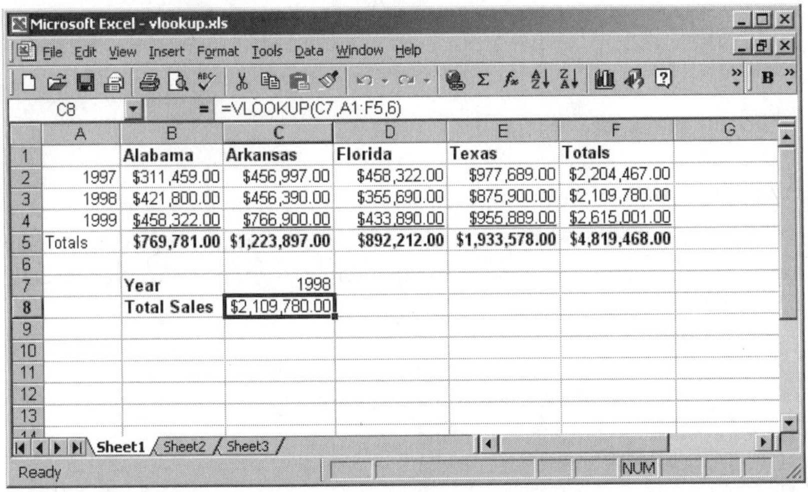

Figure 16-15: Use VLOOKUP to find the value that corresponds to the matching value in the first column

Chapter 17

Database Functions

Excel provides a series of functions designed to work with database tables (commonly referred to as lists). A list is considered a database table if it is rectangular and the top row contains the field names. Notice that all of these functions begin with the letter D and that they closely resemble other functions available in Excel. In fact, each of these functions has a non-database equivalent.

The following functions are covered in detail in this chapter:

DAVERAGE	DMAX	DSTDEVA
DCOUNT	DMIN	DSUM
DCOUNTA	DPRODUCT	DVAR
DGET	DSTDEV	DVARP

Use these functions to do the following:

- Determine the number of values in a specific list

- Find the maximum or minimum value in a list

- Determine the standard deviation for a population based on the numbers in a list

- Find the value that meets the specified criteria

The Database Functions

Excel provides a dozen functions to manipulate the values within a database table in a worksheet. These functions, covered in the remaining portion of this chapter, are categorized as follows:

Compare values:

    DAVERAGE (find the average value in a column)
    DCOUNT (count only numeric fields)
    DCOUNTA (count all non-blank fields)
    DMAX (find the largest value)
    DMIN (find the smallest value)
    DGET (get the matching values)

Perform calculations:

DPRODUCT (find the product of the matching values)
DSUM (sum the matching values)
DSTDEV (standard deviation of a sample)
DSTDEVP (standard deviation of a population)
DVAR (variance of a sample)
DVARP (variance of a population)

Recurring Arguments

The following arguments are available on a recurring basis in many of the functions discussed in this chapter. If differences in the implementation exist in a particular function, they are explained within the individual function's section.

Criteria

Indicates a reference to the range of cells that contains the conditions that need to be met before the function can be applied. Only the cells within the list that match the specified criteria are used by the function. The criteria reference must include at least one cell that contains the column label and one cell below that contains the condition.

Database

Indicates the range of cells that make up the database list. The range of cells is considered a database list when the first row contains the labels for the columns and the columns contain the fields of data. The database table can be referenced as a range of cells or as a named range. Make sure you avoid using the name "Database" for a range name. That name is used internally by Excel.

Field

Indicates the column within the database table that is used by the function. The column reference can either refer to the column name specified in double quotes, for example "January," or indicate a number that specifies the column's position in the table (1, 2, 3, etc).

DAVERAGE

Use DAVERAGE to average the values in the specified database table that match the conditions specified by the *Criteria* argument.

To Calculate

=DAVERAGE(*Database*, *Field*, *Criteria*)

All three arguments are required for this function.

Example

Figure 17-1 illustrates how to use DAVERAGE to determine the average amount of sales in the state of Texas for 1999. The function finds all records that have the value Texas for the State column and averages the sales amounts for those records. The example also illustrates how to use DCOUNT to determine the number of months when demos were done in Texas and DCOUNTA to determine the number of months when there were sales in Texas. Finally, the example shows how to use DGET to find the state with sales over $100,000.00 for one month.

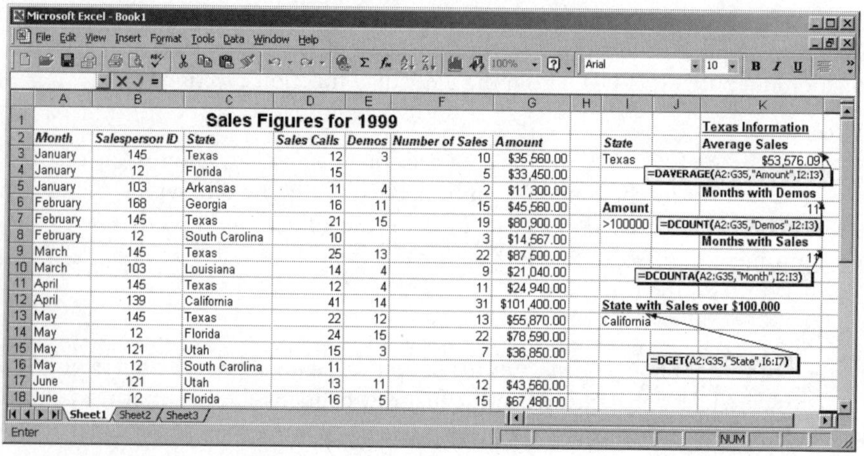

Figure 17-1: Use DAVERAGE to find the average value for records that meet the specified criteria. Use DCOUNT with numeric values and DCOUNTA for all values. Also, DGET finds the values that meet specified criteria

DCOUNT

Use DCOUNT to count the number of cells in the specified column that contain numbers and match the conditions specified by the *Criteria* argument.

To Calculate

    =DCOUNT(Database, Field, Criteria)

The *Field* argument is optional for this function. The *Database* and *Criteria* arguments are required.

Example

Figure 17-1 illustrates how to use DCOUNT to determine the number of months when demos were held in the state of Texas. Remember to use this function when you are counting numeric values only.

DCOUNTA

Use DCOUNTA to count the number of cells in the specified column that contain a value and match the conditions specified by the *Criteria* argument.

To Calculate

=DCOUNTA(*Database*, *Field*, *Criteria*)

The *Field* argument is optional for this function. The *Database* and *Criteria* arguments are required.

Example

Figure 17-1 illustrates how to use DCOUNTA to determine the number of months when there were sales in the state of Texas. We had to use DCOUNTA instead of DCOUNT because we were counting the non-numeric values in the Month column.

DGET

Use DGET to extract the specified value from a database table that matches the conditions specified by the *Criteria* argument.

To Calculate

=DGET(*Database*, *Field*, *Criteria*)

All three arguments are required for this function.

Example

Figure 17-1 illustrates how to use DGET to find the state that had sales totals exceeding $100,000. This function can only return one value, so if there had been multiple states that met the criterion the function would return an error value of #NUM!.

DMAX

Use DMAX to find the largest number in a column of a database table that matches the conditions specified by the *Criteria* argument.

To Calculate

=DMAX(*Database*, *Field*, *Criteria*)

All three arguments are required for this function.

Example

Figure 17-2 illustrates how to DMAX and DMIN to find the highest and lowest sales amounts for the salesperson with an ID of 145. DSUM provides the total years' sales for the salesperson. The example also shows how DPRODUCT is used to multiply the number of demos given by the same salesperson.

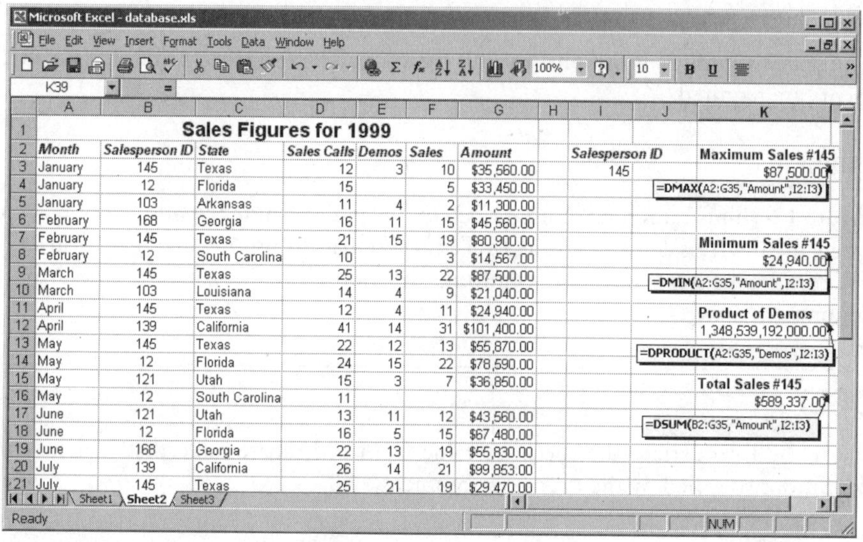

Month	Salesperson ID	State	Sales Calls	Demos	Sales	Amount
January	145	Texas	12	3	10	$35,560.00
January	12	Florida	15		5	$33,450.00
January	103	Arkansas	11	4	2	$11,300.00
February	168	Georgia	16	11	15	$45,560.00
February	145	Texas	21	15	19	$80,900.00
February	12	South Carolina	10		3	$14,567.00
March	145	Texas	25	13	22	$87,500.00
March	103	Louisiana	14	4	9	$21,040.00
April	145	Texas	12	4	11	$24,940.00
April	139	California	41	14	31	$101,400.00
May	145	Texas	22	12	13	$55,870.00
May	12	Florida	24	15	22	$78,590.00
May	121	Utah	15	3	7	$36,850.00
May	12	South Carolina	11			
June	121	Utah	13	11	12	$43,560.00
June	12	Florida	16	5	15	$67,480.00
June	168	Georgia	22	13	19	$55,830.00
July	139	California	26	14	21	$99,853.00
July	145	Texas	25	21	19	$29,470.00

Figure 17-2: Use DMAX and DMIN to find the highest and lowest values within the specified column

DMIN

Use DMIN to find the smallest number in a column of a database table that matches the conditions specified by the `Criteria` argument.

To Calculate

```
=DMIN(Database, Field, Criteria)
```

All three arguments are required for this function.

Example

Figure 17-2 illustrates how to use DMIN to find the least amount of sales dollars generated for a month by salesperson 145.

DPRODUCT

Use DPRODUCT to find the product of the values in a column of a database table that matches the conditions specified by the `Criteria` argument. The product is determined by multiplying the matching values from the specified column.

To Calculate

    =DPRODUCT(Database, Field, Criteria)

All three arguments are required for this function.

Example

Figure 17-2 illustrates how to use DPRODUCT to find the product of the number of demos given by salesperson 145.

DSTDEV

Use DSTDEV to estimate the standard deviation of a sample by using the numbers in the specified column of a database table that match the conditions specified by the `Criteria` argument.

To Calculate

    =DSTDEV(Database, Field, Criteria)

All three arguments are required for this function.

Example

Figure 17-3 illustrates how to use DSTDEV to find the sample standard deviation of the sales amounts for the state of Texas. You can compare this to results of DSTDEVP, which finds the standard deviation for an entire population. DVAR and DVARP determine the sample and population variances for the number of sales within the state.

DSTDEVP

Use DSTDEVP to estimate the standard deviation of the entire population by using the numbers in the specified column of a database table that match the conditions specified by the `Criteria` argument.

To Calculate

    =DSTDEVP(Database, Field, Criteria)

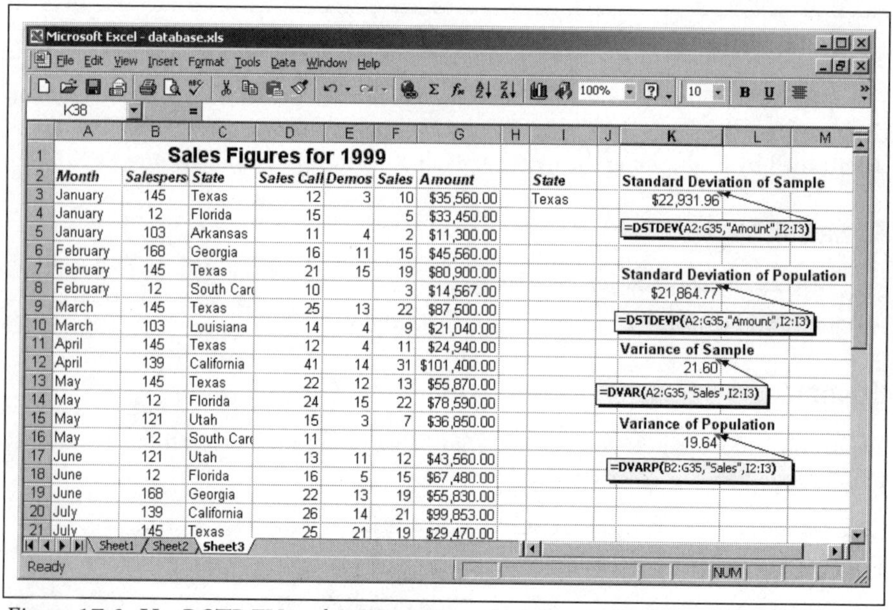

Figure 17-3: Use DSTDEV and DSTDEVP to find the standard deviation within a database table; use DVAR and DVARP to determine the variance

All three arguments are required for this function.

Example

Figure 17-3 illustrates how to use DSTDEVP to find the standard deviation for the sales amounts for the state of Texas, assuming these values are the entire population.

DSUM

Use DSUM to add the numbers in the specified column of a database table that matches the conditions specified by the `Criteria` argument.

To Calculate

    =DSUM(Database, Field, Criteria)

All three arguments are required for this function.

Example

Figure 17-2 illustrates how to use DSUM to determine the total amount of sales produced by the salesperson with an ID of 145 during the year.

DVAR

Use DVAR to estimate the sample variance by using the numbers in the specified column of a database table that match the conditions specified by the Criteria argument.

To Calculate

=DVAR(Database, Field, Criteria)

All three arguments are required for this function.

Example

Figure 17-3 illustrates how to use DVAR to find the variance of the sales numbers within the state of Texas based on the sample.

DVARP

Use DVARP to estimate the population variance by using the numbers in the specified column of a database table that match the conditions specified by the Criteria argument.

To Calculate

=DVARP(Database, Field, Criteria)

All three arguments are required for this function.

Example

Figure 17-3 illustrates how to use DVARP to find the variance of the sales numbers within the state of Texas, assuming these numbers are the entire population.

Chapter 18

Text Functions

Excel provides a series of functions to use to convert and manipulate text values for use in your worksheet. The functions provide the ability to perform tasks such as changing the case of the letters in a text string, or replacing specific characters in the string.

The following functions are covered in detail in this chapter:

CHAR	LEFT	SEARCH
CLEAN	LEN	SUBSTITUTE
CODE	LOWER	T
CONCATENATE	MID	TEXT
DOLLAR	PROPER	TRIM
EXACT	REPLACE	UPPER
FIND	REPT	VALUE
FIXED	RIGHT	SEARCH

Use these functions to do the following:

- Remove unprintable characters from text
- Find the character code for the first character in a string of text
- Join multiple text strings together
- Compare strings to determine if they are the same
- Determine the location of text within a string
- Find the length of a string
- Replace text within a string

The Text Functions

Excel provides several different functions that are used to work with the text values within a worksheet. These functions are covered in the remaining portion of this chapter in alphabetical order, but they can be categorized as follows:

Work with text:

CHAR (get the character value)
CLEAN (remove unprintable characters)
CONCATENATE (join several text strings)
EXACT (determine if two strings are the same)
FIND (locate one string within another)
LEFT (return the specified number of characters from the left side of a string)
LEN (determine the length of a string)
LOWER (convert all letters to lowercase)
MID (return the specified number of characters from the center of a string)
PROPER (capitalize the first letter in each word)
REPLACE (replace text at a specific location within a string)
REPT (repeat text the specified number of times)
RIGHT (return the specified number of characters from the end of a string)
SEARCH (determines location of a text string within another text string)
SUBSTITUTE (replace specific text in a string)
T (return the referenced value)
TRIM (remove excess spaces from text strings)
UPPER (convert all letters to uppercase)

Convert values:

CODE (find a character code for the first value in a text string)
DOLLAR (convert a number to a currency value)
FIXED (round a number to a specified number of decimals)
TEXT (convert a value to a text value in the specified format)
VALUE (convert a text string to a number)

Recurring Arguments

The following arguments are available on a recurring basis in many of the functions discussed in this chapter. If differences in the implementation exist in a particular function, they are explained within that function's section.

Decimals

An integer value that indicates the number of decimal places that you want to round the number to. If this argument is omitted the function rounds the numeric value to two decimal places. If this argument is negative, the number is rounded to the specified number of places on the left side of the decimal place. For example, if the number is 345 and the value of *Decimals* is −1 the number is rounded to $350.

New_Text

Indicates the text string that you want to use to replace the specified characters specified by the *Old_Text* argument.

Text Functions

Number

Indicates a numeric value.

Num_Chars

Specifies an integer value that indicates the number of characters you want to return from the string. If this argument is omitted, the function returns the first character in the string. If the value specified is greater than the number of characters in the string, the function returns the entire string.

Old_Text

Indicates the text string that contains the characters you want to replace.

Start_Num

Specifies an integer value that indicates the first character in the string where you want to start.

Text

This required argument must specify the desired text. This is a reference to specific cells or a string of values.

CHAR

Use CHAR to find the character (letter, symbol, number) represented by the specified numeric value. This function is typically used to translate code pages from other operating systems into the appropriate character values for your computer. For example, the Macintosh operating system uses a different code system than a Microsoft Windows operating system.

To Calculate

=CHAR(*Number*)

Number

This required argument must specify a number between 1 and 255 that specifies the character that you want to display in the cell.

Example

Figure 18-1 illustrates how to use CHAR to find the corresponding character value for the specified numeric value. Keep in mind that the characters returned will vary based upon the font you have specified for the selected cell. The example also shows how to use CLEAN to remove any characters from your text that will not print. Finally, you can use CODE to determine the numeric value of the first character in the specified string.

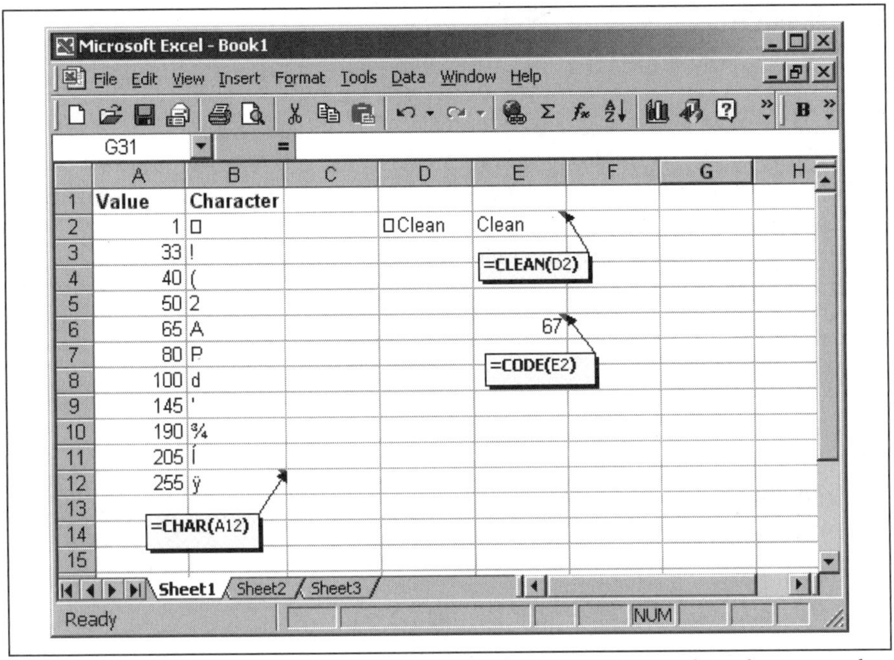

Figure 18-1: Use CHAR to convert a numeric value to its corresponding character value

CLEAN

Use CLEAN to remove all nonprintable characters from the specified text. Unprintable characters can appear in your worksheet when you import text from other applications.

To Calculate

=CLEAN(Text)

Example

Figure 18-1 illustrates how CLEAN is used to remove all unprintable characters from the specified text. In this example, the small box that displays before the text "Clean" is nonprintable so the function removes it.

CODE

Use CODE to determine the numeric code for the first character in a text string. The codes that are returned are based upon the operating system of your computer and the specific font selected for the cell. For example, a Macintosh computer uses a different code set than a computer running Microsoft Windows.

Text Functions

To Calculate

=CODE(*Text*)

Example

Figure 18-1 illustrates how to use CODE to determine the numeric code for the first character in the specified string. In the example, the function looks at the string in cell E2 and returns a value of 67 which is the numeric code for the letter "C" in the currently selected font.

CONCATENATE

Use CONCATENATE to join together multiple strings of text.

To Calculate

=CONCATENATE(*Text1*, *Text2*, ...)

Text1, Text2,...

There must be between 1 and 30 different text strings specified for this function. The strings can be text, numbers, or references to single cells.

Example

Figure 18-2 illustrates how CONCATENATE is used to join text strings from multiple cells. Cell A6 contains the value "multi" and cell A7 contains the value "ple strings." CONCATENATE joins the two strings together to get "multiple strings." To use this function you need to make sure the cells contain the appropriate spacing to separate words, otherwise all the words will be connected.

TIP # 93
Use the CONCATENATE Function with Care
Keep in mind that CONCATENATE joins the text exactly as it appears in the cells.

DOLLAR

Use DOLLAR to convert a number to a currency value with the specified number of decimal places. When you use this function the format of the cell is actually text.

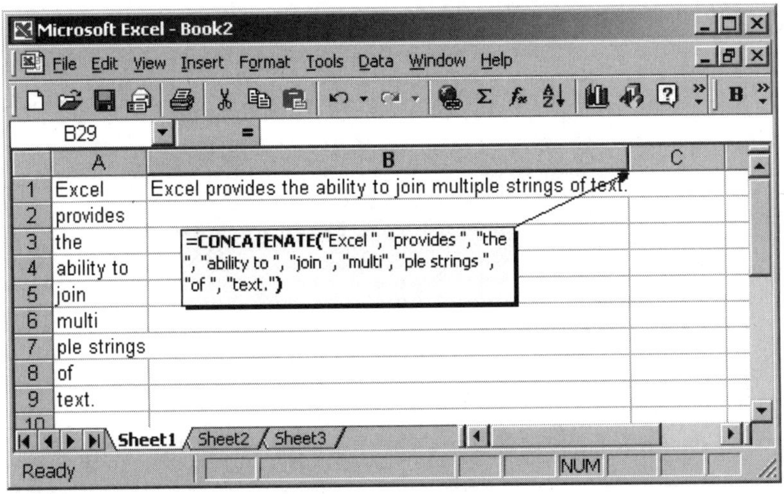

Figure 18-2: Use CONCATENATE to join multiple text strings together

> **NOTE** The only difference between using DOLLAR and the Format → Cells command is that the results of this function have a text format whereas the Format → Cells command returns a numeric value. It doesn't matter which method you use when working with other functions because the function will automatically convert the text value to a number in order to perform calculations.

To Calculate

=DOLLAR(Number, Decimals)

The Number argument is required for this function but the Decimals argument is optional.

Example

Figure 18-3 illustrates how to use DOLLAR to convert a numeric value into a currency value with two decimal places. The example also shows how FIXED is used to round a numeric value to the specified number of decimal places and add commas.

EXACT

Use EXACT to compare two different text strings to determine if they are identical. The function returns a value of TRUE if the strings are the same; otherwise it returns a value of FALSE.

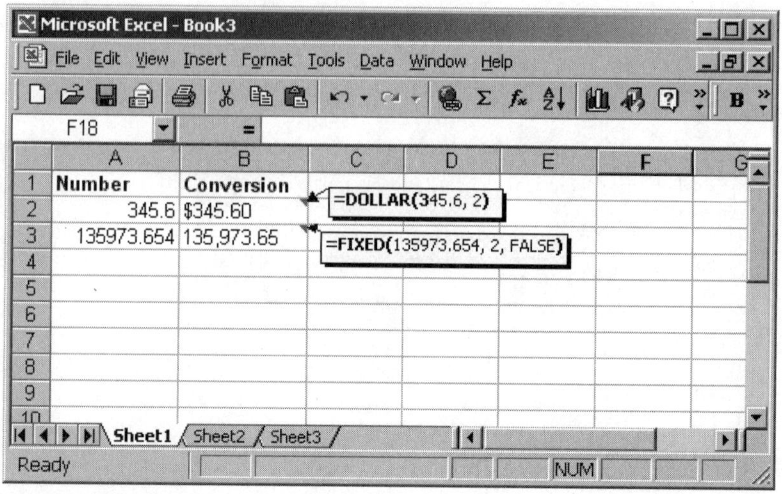

Figure 18-3: Use DOLLAR to convert numbers to currency and FIXED to round to specified decimal places

> **NOTE** *When the function compares the text strings it makes sure they are exactly the same including the case. For example, if one word is all caps and the other is lowercase the function will return a value of FALSE.*

To Calculate

`=Exact(Text1, Text2)`

Both arguments are required for this function.

Text1

Indicates a string of text. The string can be text, numbers, or references to single cells.

Text2

Indicates a string of text. The string can be text, numbers, or references to single cells.

Example

Figure 18-4 illustrates how to use EXACT to compare text strings in two different cells. You will notice that although the cells contain the same words the function returned a value of FALSE because the letters were not the same case (cell A2 is in uppercase). The function also shows how to use FIND to determine the character position of one string within another string.

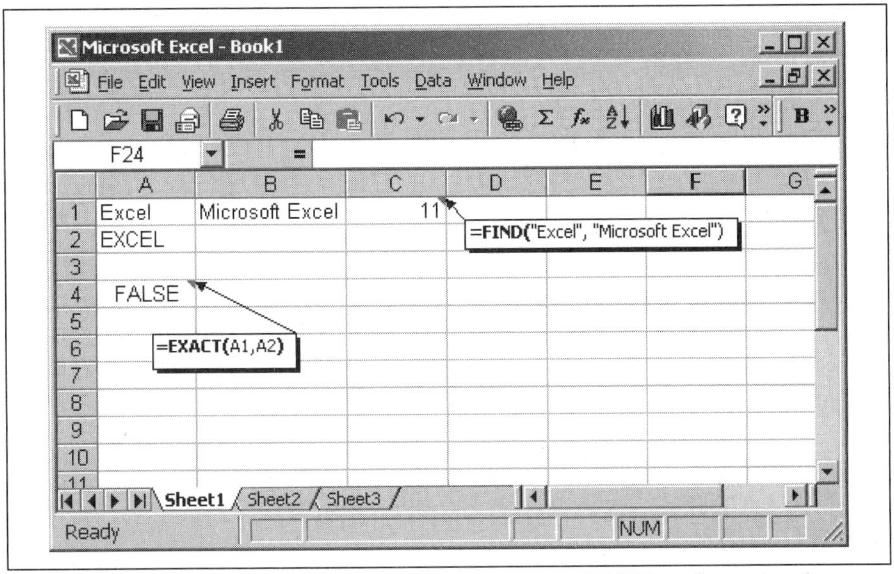

Figure 18-4: Use EXACT to compare two text strings and FIND to determine the location of one string within another

FIND

Use FIND to determine the location of one text string within another string. The function returns a number that indicates the first character location of the specified string. For example, if you used FIND to determine the location of "the" within the word "mother" the function would return the value 3 because the t is in the third place in the word.

To Calculate

=FIND(Find_Text, Within_Text, Start_Num)

The Find_Text and Within_Text arguments are required for this function. The Start_Num argument is optional.

Find_Text
> Indicates the text that you want to find. If this argument references empty text (" ") the function returns the first character specified by the Start_Num argument.

Within_Text
> Indicates the text that you want to search.

Start_Num
> Specifies the first character in the string specified by Within_Text where you want to start looking. If this is omitted the function uses a start value of 1.

Text Functions

Example

Figure 18-4 illustrates how to use FIND to determine the character location of the string "Excel" in the string "Microsoft Excel". Since I wanted to start searching from the beginning of the string, I did not use the *Start_Num* argument.

FIXED

Use FIXED to round a number to the specified number of decimal places and return a text result. If desired, the number will be formatted using commas to make it easier to read.

To Calculate

=FIXED(*Number*, *Decimals*, *No_Commas*)

The *Number* argument is required for this function. The *Decimals* and *No_Commas* arguments are optional.

No_Commas

Specifies a logical value of TRUE or FALSE that indicates whether the numeric value should have commas. If this value is FALSE or omitted, commas are used as needed.

> **NOTE** *The only difference between using FIXED and the Format → Cells command is that results of the function have a text format, whereas the Format → Cells command returns a numeric value. It doesn't matter which method you use when working with other functions because the function will automatically convert the text value to a number in order to perform calculations.*

Example

Figure 18-3 illustrates how FIXED is used to round a numeric value to the specified number of decimal places. In this example, a value of 2 was specified for the *Decimals* argument. Since that is the default value for the argument, if the argument had been omitted the function would have rounded to two decimal places.

LEFT

Use LEFT to return the specified number of characters from the left side of a text string. If you do not specify a value for the *Num_Chars* argument, the function returns the first character in the string.

To Calculate

=LEFT(*Text*, *Num_Chars*)

The *Text* argument is required for this function. The *Num_Chars* argument is optional.

Example

Figure 18-5 illustrates how to use LEFT to get five characters from the left side of a string. MID is used to get five characters starting at position 11 in the string, and RIGHT gets five characters from the end of the string. The example also uses LEN to determine the length of the string, LOWER to convert all letters to lowercase, and PROPER to capitalize the first letter in each word.

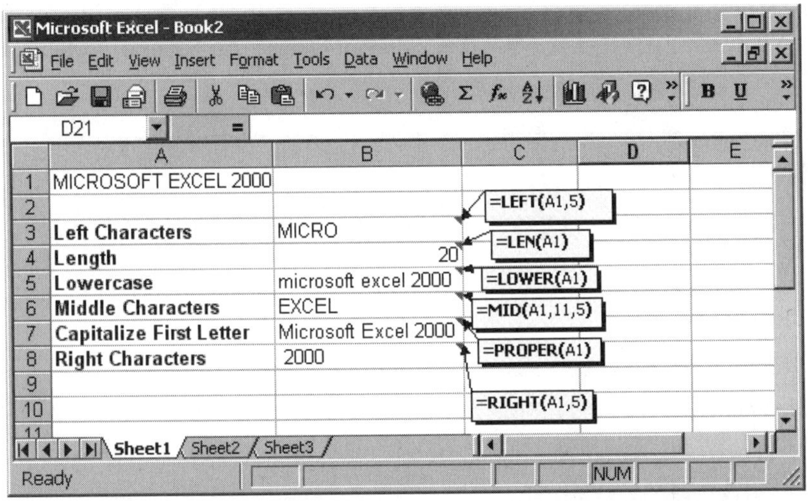

Figure 18-5: Use LEFT, MID, and RIGHT to capture specific portions of a text string

LEN

Use LEN to determine the number of characters in a string of text.

To Calculate

=LEN(*Text*)

Example

Figure 18-5 shows how LEN determines the actual number of characters in a string.

TIP # 94

Character Count

Keep in mind that spaces between words are also counted as characters in the string.

LOWER

Use LOWER to convert all of the characters in the specified text string to lower-case. This function does not affect characters in the string that are not letters.

To Calculate

    =LOWER(Text)

Example

Figure 18-5 illustrates how to use LOWER to convert all letters in a string to lower-case. You will notice that the function does not change the numeric portion of the string.

MID

Use MID to return the desired number of characters starting at the specified location in the string.

To Calculate

    =MID(Text, Start_Num, Num_Chars)

All arguments are required for this function.

Example

Figure 18-5 illustrates how MID is used to get five characters from the center of a string by starting at character 11.

PROPER

Use PROPER to capitalize the first letter in a string and any other letters that are preceded by a non-letter character. All other letters are converted to lowercase. For example, "This is a BOX" is converted to "This Is A Box."

To Calculate

    =PROPER(Text)

Example

Figure 18-5 illustrates how to use PROPER to convert a string so that only the first letter of each word is capitalized.

REPLACE

Use REPLACE to replace the specified number of characters in a text string with a new string.

To Calculate

=REPLACE(Old_Text, Start_Num, Num_Chars, New_Text)

All arguments are required for this function.

Example

Figure 18-6 illustrates how to use REPLACE to replace the characters in a string of text at the specified location. This function only replaces the characters indicated. In this example, we replaced five characters starting at position 11 (the word Excel). On the other hand, SUBSTITUTE finds the specified characters in the string and replaces them with the new string.

This example also shows how to use REPT to repeat a string within a cell, SEARCH to determine the location of characters in a string, and T to return the text reference.

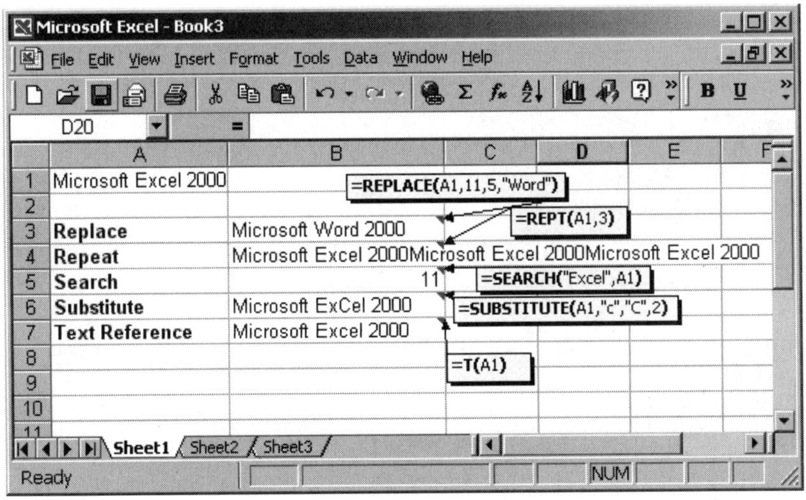

Figure 18-6: Use REPLACE to replace text at a known location; use SUBSTITUTE to replace text that matches specified criteria

REPT

Use REPT to repeat text the indicated number of times within a cell.

To Calculate

=REPT(Text, Number_Times)

Both arguments are required for this function.

Number_Times

Specifies a positive number between 0 and 32,767 that indicates the number of times to repeat the text within the cell. If the value is 0 the function returns an empty cell. If the value is not an integer the value is truncated.

Example

Figure 18-6 illustrates how to use REPT to repeat a string of characters within a cell. You will notice that the string is pasted as is so that the end of the first string is merged with the second string. If you want spacing at the end or beginning, make sure you insert it appropriately.

RIGHT

Use RIGHT to return the specified number of characters from the right side (end) of a text string.

To Calculate

=RIGHT(Text, Num_Chars)

The Text argument is required for this function. If the Num_Chars argument is omitted the last character in the string is returned.

Example

Figure 18-5 illustrates how RIGHT is used to return five characters from the right side of the string. Since there is a space before "2000" the function actually returns " 2000".

SEARCH

Use SEARCH to determine the location of the text string specified by Find_Text within the Within_Text string. The function starts searching at the location specified by Start_Num or at the beginning of the string if this argument is omitted.

To Calculate

=SEARCH(Find_Text, Within_Text, Start_Num)

The Find_Text and Within_Text arguments are required for this function. The Start_Num argument is optional.

Find_Text

Indicates the text that you want to locate. This text string can include wildcard characters (*, ?). To find strings that contain question marks or asterisks, you need to place a tilde (~) before the character.

TIP # 95

Using Wildcards in a Search

You may have heard reference to the use of wildcard characters when performing a search. There are two wildcard characters that are typically used. The asterisk (*) matches any sequence of characters. For example, if you specify the string "mo" it will match "mother," "most," and any other strings that begin with "mo". The question mark (?) matches any one character. For example, you can specify "b?t" to match strings such as "bit" and "bat."*

Within_Text

Specifies the text string that you want to search.

Example

Figure 18-6 illustrates how SEARCH looks at the specified string of text and returns a character position of the indicated characters in the string. In that example, the function returns a value of 11 because that is where the first character in "Excel" is located in the string.

SUBSTITUTE

Use SUBSTITUTE to replace specific text within a text string. When you use this function you can indicate the number of occurrences that you want to replace. For example, you can replace every occurrence of the text, or only the second occurrence by specifying a value of 2 for the Instance_Num argument.

To Calculate

=SUBSTITUTE(Text, Old_Text, New_Text, Instance_Num)

The Instance_Num argument is optional. All other arguments are required for this function.

Instance_Num
>   An integer value that indicates the instance in the text specified by the *Old_Text* argument that you want to replace. If this argument is omitted, the function replaces every occurrence of the specified text.

Example

Figure 18-6 illustrates how SUBSTITUTE is used to replace specific characters within a text string. In the example, we told the function to replace the second instance of "c" with "C." If we had omitted the value for the *Instance_Num* argument the function would have replaced the "c" in both locations.

T

Excel includes this function mainly for compatibility with other spreadsheet programs. If you do not plan to export your worksheet to another program, you probably will never need to use this function. Use T to return the text referenced by the value.

To Calculate

    =T(*Value*)

Value
>   Indicates the value you want to return. If this is a reference to a cell, the function returns the contents of the cell.

Example

Figure 18-6 illustrates how T simply returns the contents of the specified cell.

TEXT

Use TEXT to convert a value to text and display it in the specified format.

To Calculate

    =TEXT(*Value*, *Format_Text*)

Both arguments are required for this function.

Value
>   Indicates a numeric value that you want to convert to text.

Format_Text
>   Specifies a character string that indicates the format you want to convert the numeric value to. For example, to convert a number to a currency value you

would specify a value of "$0.00." Make sure you enclose the specified format within double quotes. You can specify any of the number formats available in the Category box of the Number tab when you select the Format → Cells command with the exception of the General number format.

Example

Figure 18-7 illustrates how TEXT is used to specify how a numeric text value is converted to the desired format. In this example, column A indicates the original value. The function takes the format specified in column B and returns the value indicated in column A in the specified formatting.

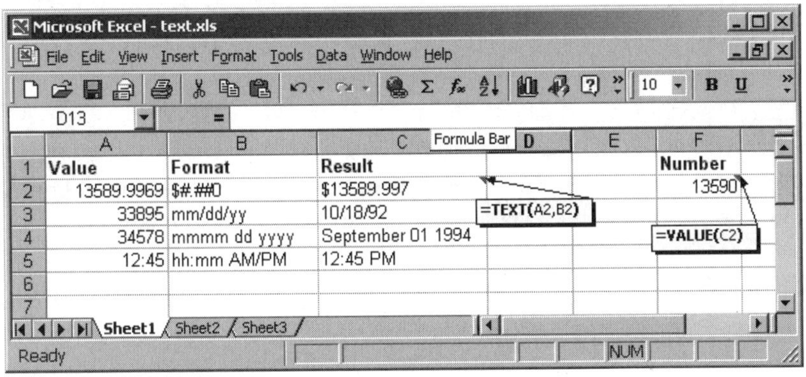

Figure 18-7: Use TEXT to specify the type of formatting you want to use for a cell

TRIM

Use TRIM to remove excess spaces from a text string. The function leaves one space between words in the string and removes all excess spaces.

To Calculate

```
=TRIM(Text)
```

Example

Figure 18-8 illustrates how TRIM is used to remove the extra spaces that may exist within a text string. The example also illustrates how to use UPPER to convert all of the text in the string to uppercase.

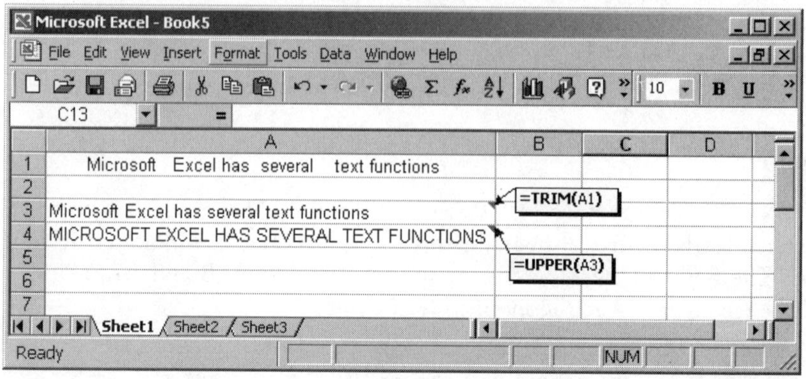

Figure 18-8: Use TRIM to ensure that excess spacing has been removed from a text string

UPPER

Use UPPER to convert all of the characters in the specified text string to uppercase. This function does not affect characters in the string that are not letters.

To Calculate

=UPPER(Text)

Example

Figure 18-8 illustrates how to use UPPER to convert all of the text in a string to uppercase.

VALUE

Use VALUE to convert a text string that resembles a number to a number. Since Excel functions automatically convert text to numbers as needed, this function is only needed for compatibility with other spreadsheet programs.

To Calculate

=VALUE(Text)

Example

Figure 18-7 illustrates how you can use VALUE to convert a numeric text string to a number.

Chapter 19

Logical Functions

Excel provides six functions designed to return a logical value. TRUE and FALSE simply return the specified value. The other functions return a value based on the results of a condition. Typically these functions are going to be combined with other Excel functions.

The following functions are covered in detail in this chapter:

AND	IF	OR
FALSE	NOT	TRUE

Use these functions to do the following:

- Compare two logical expressions
- Always return a value of TRUE or FALSE
- Reverse the value returned by an argument

The Logical Functions

Excel provides six logical functions to use within a worksheet. These functions, which are covered in the remaining portion of this chapter, are categorized as follows:

Compare conditions:

> AND (returns TRUE if all arguments evaluate as TRUE)
> IF (performs conditions based on whether results are TRUE or FALSE)
> OR (returns TRUE if at least one argument evaluates as TRUE)

Return a specific logical value:

> FALSE (always returns a value of FALSE)
> NOT (reverses the value of the argument)
> TRUE (always returns a value of TRUE)

AND

Use AND to look at multiple conditions and return a logical value of TRUE if the conditions are all true. If any of the conditions are false the function returns a value of FALSE.

To Calculate

=AND(*Logical1*, *Logical2*, ...)

Logical1, Logical2, ...

The must be between 1 and 30 logical conditions specified. Each condition must evaluate to a value of either TRUE or FALSE. For example, A>B.

Example

Figure 19-1 illustrates how AND can be used to compare two logical conditions and return a value. The example looks at two logical statements that state the numeric value in column A or B is less than 5. If both statements are true, as in cell C3, the function returns a value of TRUE. You can compare this to the results of OR which returns a value of TRUE as long as at least one of the logical statements is true. Finally, the example illustrates how NOT can be used to reverse the logical value.

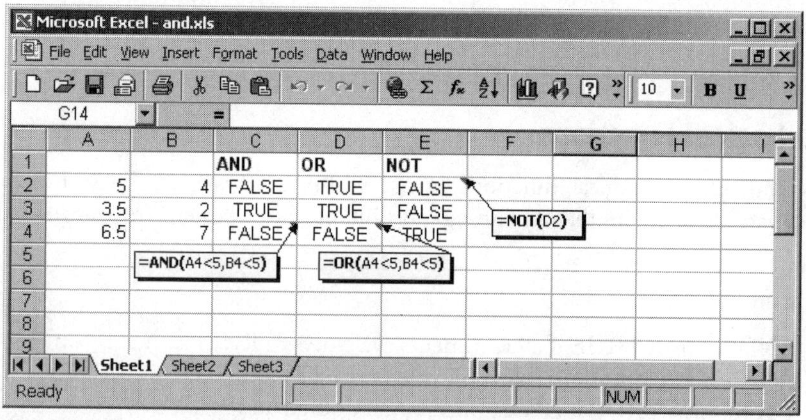

Figure 19-1: Remember with AND all logical conditions must be TRUE to return a value of TRUE; whereas, OR only needs one condition to be TRUE

FALSE

Use FALSE to return a logical value of FALSE. You can also type a value of FALSE directly into a cell of a worksheet and Excel will interpret the value as a logical value of FALSE.

To Calculate

=FALSE()

Example

Figure 19-2 illustrates how you can use FALSE to return a logical value of FALSE in a cell. The example uses IF to compare the logical values in two cells and determine if they are the same or different.

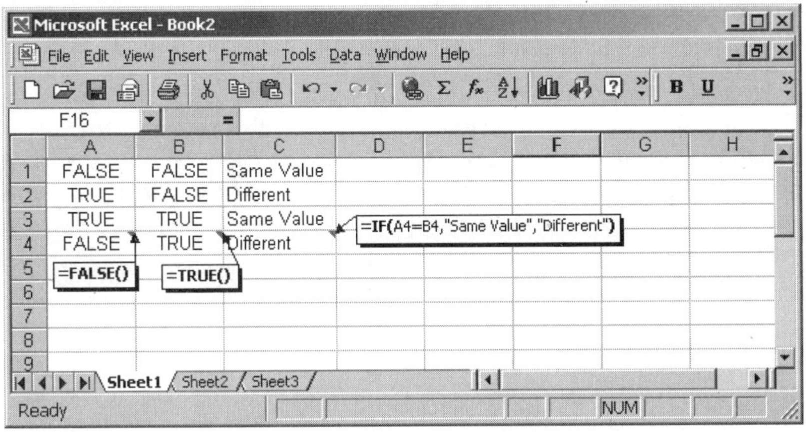

Figure 19-2: You can either use TRUE and FALSE or manually specify a logical value for a cell

IF

Use IF to check a condition and specify the value that is returned based upon whether the result of the condition is TRUE or FALSE.

To Calculate

=IF(*Logical_Test*, *Value_If_True*, *Value_If_False*)

The *Value_If_False* argument is optional. The other arguments are required.

Logical_Test

Indicates a logical expression that can be evaluated to return a value of TRUE or FALSE. This expression can use any operators and functions available within Excel.

Value_If_True

Indicates the value that is returned by the function if the expression specified by *Logical_Test* evaluates to TRUE. If this value is a text string, make sure you enclose it in double quotes.

Value_If_False

Indicates the value that is returned by the function if the expression specified by *Logical_Test* evaluates to FALSE. If this value is a text string, make sure you enclose it in double quotes.

TIP # 96

Creating Nested If Statements

Excel allows you to combine multiple IF statements to create what is commonly referred to as a "nested If statement." This simply means you have an IF statement as part of either the Value_If_True or the Value_If_False argument. For example, you may want to determine if the value is positive and then determine if it is less than 100. Excel allows you to have up to seven different IF statements nested under either the Value_If_True or the Value_If_False argument

---

Example

Figure 19-2 illustrates how to use IF to compare the logical values in two cells and return a value based on whether the logical values are the same or different.

NOT

Use NOT to return the reverse value of a condition. If the condition evaluates to TRUE, the function returns a value of FALSE, or vice versa.

To Calculate

=NOT(*Logical*)

Logical

An expression that evaluates to a value of either TRUE or FALSE. For example, A>B.

Example

Figure 19-1 illustrates how to use NOT to reverse the logical value in a cell. The example shows how the function takes the logical values in column D and returns the reverse value.

OR

Use OR to look at multiple conditions and return a logical value of TRUE if at least one of the conditions is true. If all of the conditions are false the function returns a value of FALSE.

To Calculate

=OR(*Logical1*, *Logical2*, ...)

Logical1, Logical2, ...
> There must be between 1 and 30 logical arguments specified. Each argument must evaluate to a value of either TRUE or FALSE. For example, A>B.

Example

Figure 19-1 illustrates how OR can be used to compare two logical conditions and return a value. The example looks at two logical statements that state the numeric value in column A or B is less than 5. If at least one of the statements is true the function returns a value of TRUE. You can compare this to the results of AND which returns a value of TRUE only if all conditions are true.

TRUE

Use TRUE to return a logical value of TRUE. You can also type a value of TRUE directly into a cell of a worksheet and Excel will interpret the value as a logical value of TRUE.

To Calculate

=TRUE()

Example

Figure 19-1 illustrates how you can use TRUE to return a logical value of TRUE in a cell.

Chapter 20

Information Functions

Excel provides functions that gather specific information about your worksheet and system. Many of these functions check for error values. It is a good idea to make sure the cell contains the appropriate type of value before performing any type of calculation. The following functions are covered in detail in this chapter. The "AT" represents those functions that exist only by loading the Analysis Toolpak. See Chapter 11, *Working with Functions*, for details.

CELL	ISEVEN *AT*	ISREF
ERROR.TYPE	ISLOGICAL	ISTEXT
INFO	ISNA	N
ISBLANK	ISNONTEXT	NA
ISERR	ISNUMBER	TYPE
ISERROR	ISODD *AT*	

Use these functions to do the following:

- Determine the type of value contained within a cell

- Figure out what type of error is contained in a cell

- Convert the value in a cell to a number

- Determine the formatting of a cell

The Information Functions

Excel provides different types of information functions to use within a worksheet. These functions, covered in this chapter, are categorized as follows:

Get specific information about a cell or the operating system:

> CELL (determine formatting, location, or contents of a cell)
> INFO (determine information about operating environment)
> TYPE (determine the type of value contained in a cell)

Convert a value:

> N (convert a value to a number)
> NA (return an error value of #N/A)

Check for specific types of values:

> ERROR.TYPE (determine the type of error in a cell)
> ISBLANK (check for blank cells)
> ISERR (check for any error except #N/A)
> ISERROR (check for any error value)
> ISEVEN (check to see if a number is even)
> ISLOGICAL (check for a logical value)
> ISNA (check for a #N/A value)
> ISNONTEXT (check for any value that is not text)
> ISNUMBER (check for any numeric value)
> ISODD (check to see if a number is odd)
> ISREF (check for a reference)
> ISTEXT (check for text)

Recurring Arguments

The following arguments are available on a recurring basis in many of the functions discussed in this chapter. Differences in the implementation in a particular function are explained within the individual function's section.

Number
> References a numeric value. If the number is not an integer it is truncated by the function.

Value
> References any valid value in Microsoft Excel. For example, it can be a number, text, a logical value, blank, or even an error message.

CELL

Use CELL to get specific information about the formatting, location, or contents of a specific cell.

To Calculate

    =CELL(Info_Type, Reference)

The *Info_Type* argument is required for this function. If the *Reference* argument is omitted, the information is returned for the last modified cell.

Info_Type

Specifies one of the following text values that indicates the type of information that should be returned about the specified cell. Remember to enclose the value in quotes.

address

Returns the cell reference of the first cell in the range of cells specified by *Refererence*.

col

Returns the column number of the reference.

color

Returns a value of 1 if negative values display in color. Otherwise returns a value of 0 (zero).

contents

Returns the contents of the upper-left cell in the range of cells specified by *Refererence*.

filename

If the file containing the reference has been saved, the filename (with the full path) is returned; otherwise, the function returns empty text.

format

Returns a text value that identifies the type of formatting applied to the cell. The text value corresponds to the cell formatting listed on the Number tab of the Format Cells dialog. This dialog displays when you select Format → Cells. For example, the function returns G for a general format and C2 for a currency value with two decimal places. If the cell is formatted to display negative values in color, a - is returned at the end of the text value. If the cell is formatted to display negative value in parentheses, ( ) are returned at the end of the text value.

prefix

Returns a specific character indicating alignment of the text in the cell. A single quotation mark (') indicates the cell contains left-aligned text, double quotation marks (") indicate the cell contains right-aligned text, a caret (^) indicates the cell contains centered text, a backslash (\) indicates the cell contains fill-aligned text; empty text is returned for anything else.

protect

Returns 0 if the cell is not locked, and 1 if the cell is locked.

row

Returns the row number of the reference.

type

Returns a value of b if the cell is blank, 1 if the cell contains a text label, and v if the cell contains anything else.

width

Returns an integer value that specifies the column width of the cell. The width is based on the number of characters that can display in the cell based upon the current font size.

Reference

Indicates a reference to the cell you want to return information for. If this argument is omitted, the function returns the information of the last cell changed.

Example

Figure 20-1 illustrates how to use CELL to return information about a specific cell within a worksheet. The example shows how to use the function to determine the cell format of cell C2. The function returns a value of C2- indicating that the cell is formatted as currency with 2 decimal places and negative values display in color. The example also shows how to use INFO to find out what operating system is currently running on your machine.

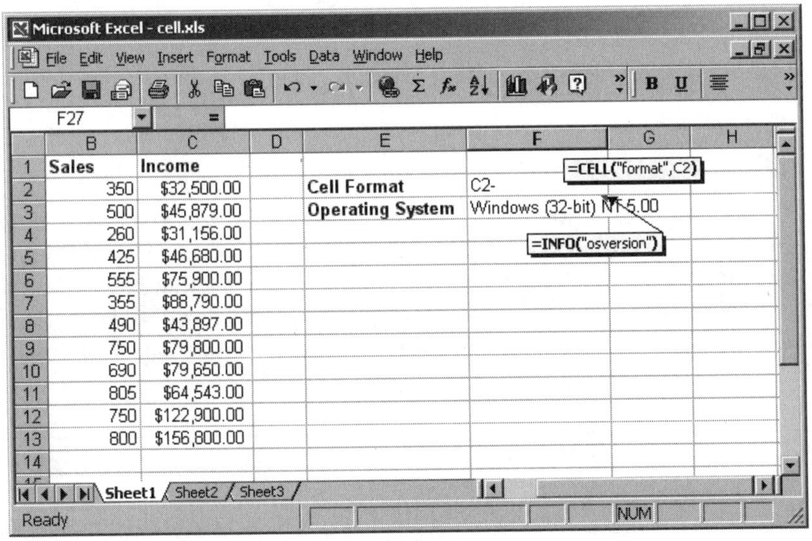

Figure 20-1: Use CELL and INFO to get specific information about your worksheet and system

ERROR.TYPE

Use ERROR.TYPE to return a number that corresponds to one of the error values within Microsoft Excel or #N/A if an error does not exist. This function is typically used in combination with the IF function to check for an error condition and return a specific value instead of the error message.

The function returns either an integer value of 1–7 or #N/A, as outlined in Table 20-1, to indicate the type of error value in the specified reference.

Table 20-1: Excel Error Values

Return Value of ERROR.TYPE	Corresponding Error
1	#NULL!
2	#DIV/0!
3	#VALUE!
4	#REF!
5	#NAME?
6	#NUM!
7	#N/A
#N/A	The cell does not contain an error value

To Calculate

=ERROR.TYPE(*Error_Val*)

Error_Val
This required argument indicates an error value or a reference to a cell you want checked for an error value.

Example

Figure 20-2 illustrates how to use ERROR.TYPE to determine the type of error contained in a cell within a worksheet. The example illustrates how the function returns a different integer value for each of the error values within Excel and a value of #N/A for any non-error values. The example also shows how ISBLANK, ISERR, ISERROR, and ISNA can be used to determine if a cell contains a specific error value.

INFO

Use INFO to get specific information about the operating system you are running.

To Calculate

=INFO(*Type_Text*)

Info_Type
This required argument specifies one of the following text values that indicates the type of information that should be returned about the operating system. Remember to enclose the value in quotes.

directory
Returns the path of the current directory or folder.

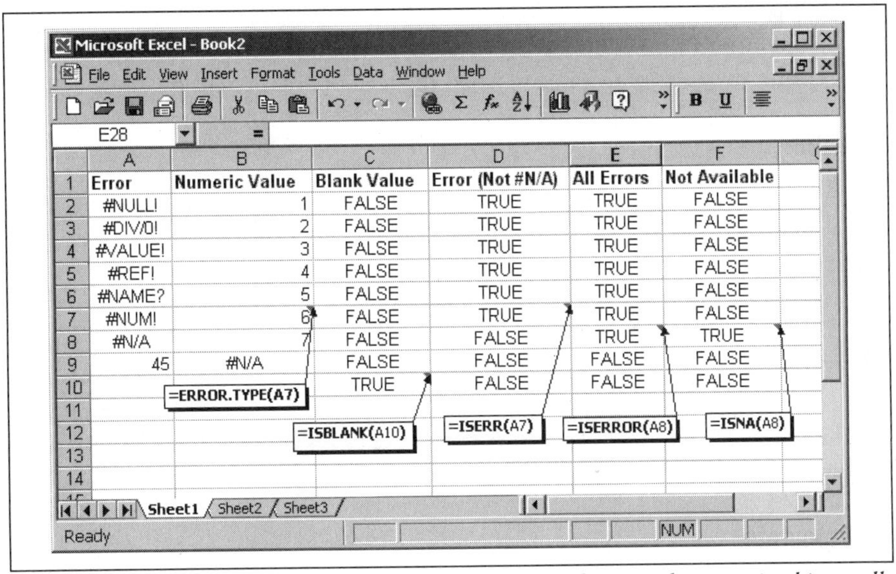

Figure 20-2: Use ERROR.TYPE to determine the type of error value contained in a cell

memavail
> Returns a numeric value that indicates the amount of memory available in bytes.

memused
> Returns a numeric value that indicates the amount of memory currently being used.

numfile
> Returns an integer value that specifies the number of active worksheets.

origin
> Returns a reference to the top-left visible cell based upon the current scrolling position. The reference is returned in the A1 format.

osversion
> Returns a text value that identifies the current operating system version.

recalc
> Returns a value of "Automatic" or "Manual" to indicate the current recalculation mode.

release
> Returns a text value that specifies the current version of Microsoft Excel.

system
> Returns a text value that specifies the current operating environment. If it is a Microsoft Windows environment a value of pcdos is returned. For a Macintosh environment a value of mac is returned.

totmem

    Returns a numeric value in bytes that specifies the total amount of available memory. This value includes the memory that is already in use.

Example

Figure 20-1 illustrates how INFO can be used to determine the current operating system. This is accomplished by specifying a value of "osversion" for the *Info_Type* argument.

ISBLANK

Use ISBLANK to look at the specified reference and determine if it is an empty cell. The function returns a logical value of TRUE if the cell is empty; otherwise, it returns a value of FALSE.

To Calculate

```
=ISBLANK(Value)
```

Example

Figure 20-2 illustrates how ISBLANK can be used to check specific cells to determine if they are blank. You will notice that the function returns a value of FALSE for all cells that contain any type of value.

ISERR

Use ISERR to look at the specified reference and return a logical value of TRUE if it refers to any error value with the exception of #N/A; otherwise, a logical value of FALSE is returned.

To Calculate

```
=ISERR(Value)
```

Example

Figure 20-2 illustrates how ISERR can be used to determine if a cell contains an error value. The function returns a value of TRUE for all error values with the exception of #N/A, for which it returns a value of FALSE.

ISERROR

Use ISERROR to look at the specified reference and return a logical value of TRUE if the cell contains an error value; otherwise, a logical value of FALSE is returned.

To Calculate

```
=ISERROR(Value)
```

Example

Figure 20-2 illustrates how ISERROR can be used to determine if a cell contains any type of error value. The function returns a value of FALSE for all error values in Excel, as shown in the example.

ISEVEN

Use ISEVEN (an Analysis ToolPak function) to look at the specified reference and return a value of TRUE if the number is even, or a value of FALSE if the number is odd. If the value is not numeric, the function returns a #VALUE! error value.

To Calculate

```
=ISEVEN(Number)
```

Example

Figure 20-3 illustrates how to use ISEVEN to make sure the value contained in a cell is an even number. You will notice in this example that ISEVEN and ISODD return #VALUE! errors for the cells that do not contain numeric values. Both of those functions expect a numeric value to be passed to them, otherwise an error is returned. The example also shows how to use ISLOGICAL, ISNONTEXT, ISNUMBER, ISTEXT, and ISREF to check cells for the corresponding values.

ISLOGICAL

Use ISLOGICAL to look at the specified reference and return a logical value of TRUE if it is a logical value; otherwise, the function returns a value of FALSE.

To Calculate

```
=ISLOGICAL(Value)
```

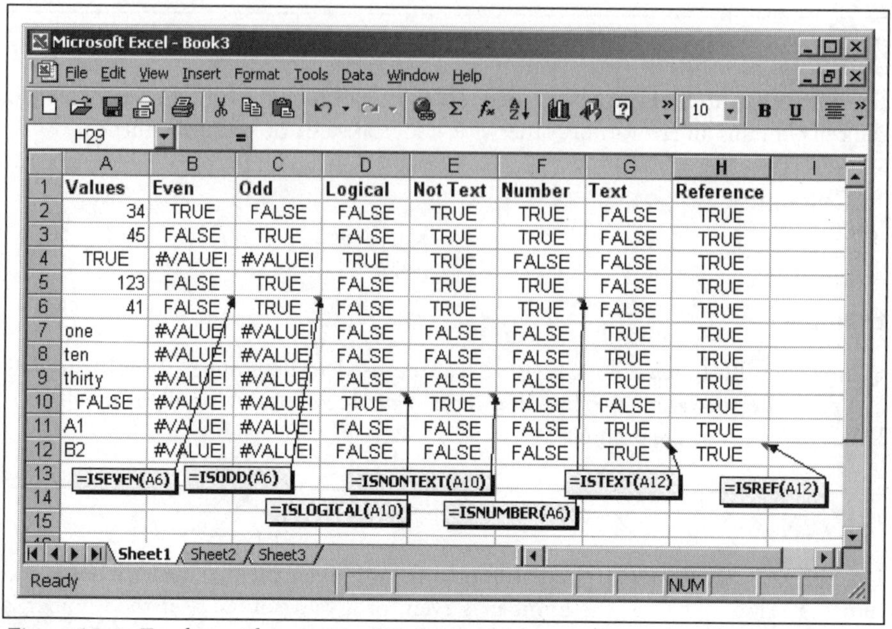

	A	B	C	D	E	F	G	H
1	Values	Even	Odd	Logical	Not Text	Number	Text	Reference
2	34	TRUE	FALSE	FALSE	TRUE	TRUE	FALSE	TRUE
3	45	FALSE	TRUE	FALSE	TRUE	TRUE	FALSE	TRUE
4	TRUE	#VALUE!	#VALUE!	TRUE	TRUE	FALSE	FALSE	TRUE
5	123	FALSE	TRUE	FALSE	TRUE	TRUE	FALSE	TRUE
6	41	FALSE	TRUE	FALSE	TRUE	TRUE	FALSE	TRUE
7	one	#VALUE!	#VALUE!	FALSE	FALSE	FALSE	TRUE	TRUE
8	ten	#VALUE!	#VALUE!	FALSE	FALSE	FALSE	TRUE	TRUE
9	thirty	#VALUE!	#VALUE!	FALSE	FALSE	FALSE	TRUE	TRUE
10	FALSE	#VALUE!	#VALUE!	TRUE	TRUE	FALSE	FALSE	TRUE
11	A1	#VALUE!	#VALUE!	FALSE	FALSE	FALSE	TRUE	TRUE
12	B2	#VALUE!	#VALUE!	FALSE	FALSE	FALSE	TRUE	TRUE

Figure 20-3: Excel provides a series of IS functions that can be used to check a cell to make sure it contains the desired data type

Example

Figure 20-3 illustrates how to use ISLOGICAL to check a cell to see if it contains a logical value of `TRUE` or `FALSE`. You will notice in cell D10 that even though cell A10 contains a value of `FALSE` the function returns a value of `TRUE` because that is a logical value.

ISNA

Use ISNA to look at the specified reference and return a logical value of `TRUE` if it contains the `#N/A` (value not available) error value; otherwise, the function returns a value of `FALSE`.

To Calculate

```
=ISNA(Value)
```

Example

Figure 20-2 illustrates how ISNA can be used to determine if a cell contains a value of `#N/A`. The function returns a value of `TRUE` for the cell that contains an error value of `#N/A` and `FALSE` for all other values.

ISNONTEXT

Use ISNONTEXT to look at the specified reference and return a logical value of TRUE if the cell does not contain text (that includes a blank cell). If the contents of the referenced cell are text, the function returns a value of FALSE.

To Calculate

=ISNONTEXT(Value)

Example

Figure 20-3 illustrates how to use ISNONTEXT to make sure the values in cells are not text.

ISNUMBER

Use ISNUMBER to look at the specified reference and return a logical value of TRUE if the cell refers to a numeric value; otherwise the function returns a value of FALSE.

To Calculate

=ISNUMBER(Value)

Example

Figure 20-3 illustrates how to use ISNUMBER to determine if a cell contains a numeric value. If the value in the cell is not a number the function returns FALSE.

ISODD

Use ISODD (an Analysis ToolPak function) to look at the specified reference and return a value of TRUE if the number is odd, or a value of FALSE if the number is even. If the value is not numeric, the function returns a #VALUE! error value.

To Calculate

=ISODD(Number)

Example

Figure 20-3 illustrates how to use ISODD to determine if the number in a cell is odd. Notice that when the function is used to check cells that do not contain numeric values, it returns an error value of #VALUE!, due to the fact that the function only deals with numbers.

ISREF

Use ISREF to look at the specified reference and return a logical value of TRUE if it is a reference to another cell; otherwise, the function returns a value of FALSE.

To Calculate

```
=ISREF(Value)
```

Example

Figure 20-3 illustrates how to use ISREF. You will notice that the function returned a value of TRUE for all cells in the column. This is due to the fact that the value of the argument Value was a reference to a cell within column A.

ISTEXT

Use ISTEXT to look at the specified reference and return a logical value of TRUE if the cell contains text; otherwise, the function returns a value of FALSE.

To Calculate

```
=ISTEXT(Value)
```

Example

Figure 20-3 illustrates the use of ISTEXT to make sure the value in a cell is text and not a number, error value, or logical value. If the cell contains anything other than text the function returns a value of FALSE.

N

Use N to convert a value to a number. If the specified value is a date, it is converted to the serial number that represents the date. The logical value TRUE is converted to 1 and FALSE is converted to 0. All error values are converted to their corresponding value as outlined in Table 20-1.

To Calculate

```
=N(Value)
```

Example

Figure 20-4 illustrates how to use N to find the corresponding number for a value. The example illustrates how dates and times are converted to the corresponding serial number. The example also uses TYPE to determine the type of value contained in each cell in column A.

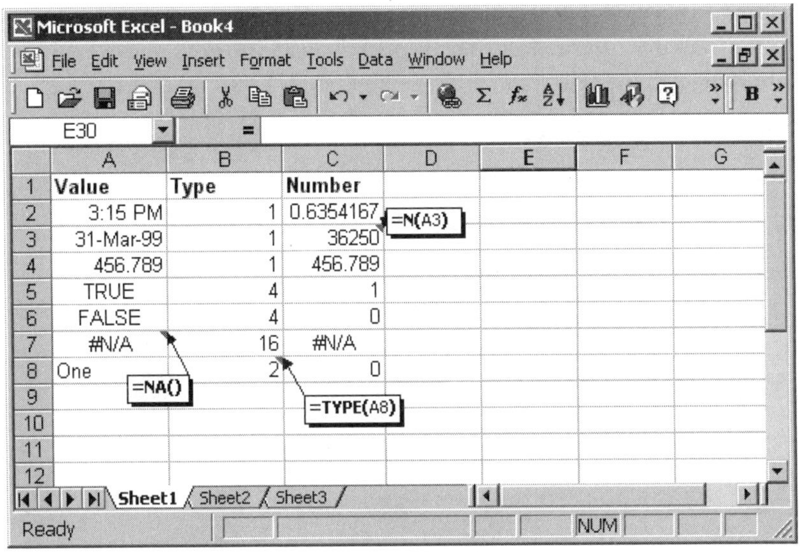

Figure 20-4: Use N to find the numeric form of a value and TYPE to determine what type of value is contained in a cell

NA

Use NA to return an error value of #N/A. Excel interprets this error value as meaning that no value is available. One common use for this function is to mark cells where you may be missing information, rather than leaving the cells blank. If a function tries to perform a calculation on a cell containing this value, the function will return an error value of #N/A.

> **NOTE** *You can also type #N/A directly in the cell and produce the same results. NA is available for compatibility with other spreadsheet programs.*

To Calculate

    =NA()

Example

Figure 20-4 illustrates how NA can be used to place an error value of #N/A in a cell.

TYPE

Use TYPE to determine the type of value contained in a cell. This function is useful for ensuring that a cell contains the desired type of value before performing a calculation. The function returns one of the following integer values identifying the type of contents in the cell:

1   Number

2   Text

4   Logical value

16   Error value

64   Array

To Calculate

=TYPE(*Value*)

Example

Figure 20-4 illustrates how to use TYPE to determine the type of value contained in each cell in column A.

TIP # 97

Cell Type Value

The TYPE function returns an integer value of 1, 2, 4, 16, or 64, all of which correspond to the type of value in the cell.

Part 4

Appendices

Appendix A

Keyboard Shortcuts

Although Excel provides an enormous number of menu and toolbar commands, sometimes it is easier to perform some commands using the keyboard shortcuts that are included with Excel.

 The keyboard shortcuts covered in this appendix do not cover the commands added when you select Tools → Options → Transition → Navigation Keys to emulate Lotus 1-2-3 commands.

The following tables list the keyboard shortcuts available within Excel. To make the commands easier to locate, they are grouped together by functionality; such as navigating the worksheet or formatting selected range.

Table A-1: General Program Shortcuts

Shortcut	Command
Ctrl-N	Create a new workbook.
Ctrl-O or Ctrl-F12	Open a workbook.
Ctrl-S or Shift-F12	Save a workbook (the Save As dialog opens if the workbook has not been previously saved).
F12	Open the Save As dialog to specify the name and location of the workbook.
Ctrl-W or Alt-F4	Close the active workbook. If it is the only workbook open, it also closes Excel.
F1	Open Help or Office Assistant.
Shift-F1	Display the What's This? Question mark.
F7	Run the Spelling checker.
F10	Activate the Menu bar (use arrow keys to move along menu).
Shift-F10	Open a context menu.
F9	Calculate all worksheets in all open workbooks.
Ctrl + F9	Calculate the active worksheet.
Ctrl + F9	Minimize the workbook.
Ctrl + F10	Restore or maximize the workbook.
Ctrl P or Ctrl + Shift + F12	Open the Print dialog.

Table A-2: Worksheet Navigation Shortcuts

Shortcut	Command
Up Arrow	Move the active cell up one row.
Down Arrow	Move the active cell down one row.
Left Arrow	Move the active cell left one column.
Right Arrow	Move the active cell right one column.
Home	Move to the beginning of the current row.
Ctrl + Home	Move to the beginning of the worksheet (typically cell A1).
Ctrl + End	Move to the last cell in the worksheet. This is the cell at the intersection of the last used row and column in the worksheet.
Page Up	Scroll up one screen.
Page Down	Scroll down one screen.
Alt + Page Up	Scroll right one screen.
Alt + Page Down	Scroll left one screen.
Ctrl + Page Up	Move to the previous worksheet in the workbook.
Ctrl + Page Down	Move to the next worksheet in the workbook.
Ctrl-F6	Go to the next open workbook.
Ctrl-Shift-F6	Go to the previously viewed open workbook.
F6	Move between split panes of a workbook.
Shift + F6	Move back to previous pane of split workbook.
F5	Open Go To dialog.
Shift + F5	Open Find dialog.
Shift + F4	Repeat last Find command.
Tab	Move between unlocked cells of a protected worksheet.
Ctrl + .	Move clockwise to the next corner of the selection.
Ctrl + Alt + Right Arrow	Move to the right between nonadjacent selections.
Ctrl + Alt + Left Arrow	Move to the left between nonadjacent selections.

Table A-3: Data Entry Shortcuts

Shortcut	Command
Enter	Complete the cell entry and move down to next cell.
Alt + Enter	Start a new line within the same cell.
Ctrl + Enter	Fill the selected range of cells with the contents of the active cell.
Shift + Enter	Complete the cell entry and move up to the cell above.
Tab	Complete the cell entry and move to next cell on the right.
Shift + Tab	Complete the cell entry and move to the next cell on the left.
Esc	Cancel the cell entry and restore the original contents.
Ctrl + D	Fill Down.
Ctrl + R	Fill to the right.
Ctrl + F3	Define a name for the selected range.

Table A-3: Data Entry Shortcuts (continued)

Shortcut	Command
Ctrl + K	Insert a hyperlink.
F2	Edit the active cell and place the insertion point at the end of the cell.

Table A-4: Data Formatting Shortcuts

Shortcut	Command
Alt + '	Open the Style dialog.
Ctrl + 1	Open the Format Cells dialog.
Ctrl + B	Apply or remove bold formatting.
Ctrl + I	Apply or remove italic formatting.
Ctrl + U	Apply or remove underlining.
Ctrl + S	Apply or remove strikethrough formatting.
Ctrl + Shift + ~	Apply the General number format.
Ctrl + Shift + $	Apply the Currency format with 2 decimal places and negative numbers in parentheses.
Ctrl + Shift + ^	Apply the Exponential formatting with two decimal places.
Ctrl + Shift + #	Apply the Date format with dates formatted as dd-mm-yy.
Ctrl + Shift + @	Apply the Time format with hour, minute and AM or PM.
Ctrl + Shift + !	Apply the Number format with two decimal places, a thousands separator, and a minus sign for negative numbers.
Ctrl + Shift + &	Apply the outline borders.
Ctrl + Shift + _	Remove the outline borders.
Alt + Shift + Right Arrow	Group rows or columns.
Alt + Shift + Left Arrow	Ungroup rows or columns.
Ctrl + 0	Hide columns.
Ctrl + Shift +)	Unhide columns.

Table A-5: Formula Shortcuts

Shortcut	Command
Ctrl + Shift + Enter	Enter a formula as an array.
Ctrl + Shift + A	Insert the argument names in parentheses for the specified function name.
F3	Paste a defined name into a formula.
Shift + F3	Paste a function into a formula.
=	Start a formula.
Alt + =	Insert the AutoSum formula.
Ctrl + ;	Enter the current date.
Ctrl + Shift + :	Enter the current time.

Table A-5: Formula Shortcuts (continued)

Shortcut	Command
Ctrl + Shift + "	Copy the value in the cell above the active cell into the formula bar.
Ctrl + `	Alternate between displaying the value of the cell and the cell formula.

Table A-6: Editing Shortcuts

Shortcut	Command
Ctrl + C	Copy the selection.
Ctrl + X	Cut the selection.
Ctrl +V	Paste the selection.
Backspace	Delete the entire contents of a cell, or the character to the left of the insertion point if you are editing the cell contents.
Delete	Delete the entire contents of a cell, or the character to the right of the insertion point if you are editing the cell contents.
Ctrl + Delete	Delete text from the insertion point to the end of the cell contents.
Ctrl-Z	Undo an action.
Ctrl-Y or F4	Redo or repeat an action.
Ctrl + -	Delete the selection.
Ctrl + Shift + +	Insert blank cells.

Table A-7: Selection Shortcuts

Shortcut	Command
Shift + Right Arrow	Expand the selection one cell right.
Shift + Left Arrow	Expand the selection one cell left.
Shift + Up Arrow	Expand the selection up one cell.
Shift + Down Arrow	Expand the selection down one cell.
Ctrl + Shift + *	Select the current region around the active cell.
Ctrl + Shift + Right Arrow	Expand the selection right to last nonblank cell on row.
Ctrl + Shift + Left Arrow	Expand the selection left to last nonblank cell on row.
Ctrl + Shift + Up Arrow	Expand the selection up to last nonblank cell in column.
Ctrl + Shift + Down Arrow	Expand the selection down to last nonblank cell in colum.
Shift + Home	Extend the selection to beginning of the row.
Ctrl + Shift + Home	Extend the selection to the beginning of the worksheet.
Ctrl + Shift + End	Extend the selection to the end of the worksheet.
Ctrl + Spacebar	Select the entire column.
Shift + Spacebar	Select the entire row.
Ctrl + A	Select the entire worksheet.
Shift + Backspace	Select the active cell only when multiple cells are selected.

Table A-7: Selection Shortcuts (continued)

Shortcut	Command
Shift + Page Down	Extend the selection down one screen.
Shift + Page Up	Extend the selection up one screen.
Ctrl + Shift + Spacebar	If an object is selected, select all objects.
Ctrl + 6	Alternate between hiding objects, displaying objects, and displaying object placeholders.
Ctrl + 7	Show or hide the Standard toolbar.
Shift + F8	Add another range of cells to the selection.

Appendix B

Tip Reference

Tip Reference

Index

cell reference, 270
  absolute vs. relative, 20
cell values
  anticipating needed, 163, 169
    troubleshooting, 169
  changing in multiple cells, 169
  finding at row/column intersect, 185
  Show All option, 193
cells, 19
  alignment, changing, 134
  blank, FVSCHEDULE and, 297
  cell reference, 270
  clearing, 85
  comments
    inserting into, 123
    removing from, 124
  containing error value, ISERROR
    function for, 531
  creating references to with ADDRESS
    function, 476
  deleting contents, 85
  dependents/precedents, 167
  double-underlining contents of, 139
  empty, 184
    ISBLANK function for
      determining, 530
    number of, COUNTBLANK
      function for, 421
  filling with values, 78
  filtering range of, 194
  formatting, 5, 134–146
    conditional, caution when pasting
      data, 144
    data validation, 202
    for four-digit years, 336
    keyboard shortcuts for, 12
    predefined, 143
    task list for, 11
  hidden, styles and, 29
  information about
    CELL function for, 525
    functions for (list), 524
  inserting, 107
  invalid data in, 169
  Last Cell option, 92
  merging, 19, 30, 138
    text justification with, 85
  name of, displaying, 18
  naming, 119

next active, 19
number of
  changed in scenarios, 167
  counting, DCOUNT/DCOUNTA
    functions for, 496
  in range, COUNTIF function
    for, 421
  protecting, 139
  range of
    INDEX function for, 483
    renaming, 120
    selecting for filtering, 194
    totaling with SUMIF function, 398
  red triangle, turning off, 102
  references, changing, 122
  referring to numeric value,
    ISNUMBER function for, 533
  repeating series of at top of
    page, 102
  text in, ISTEXT function for, 534
  values in, TYPE function for, 536
  Visible cells only option, 92
Change Button Image command, 37
change history, 151
  Change History page, 155
  password protection and, 154
  updating, 154
  viewing rejected changes, 156
  (see also tracking changes to
    workbooks)
"Change to" field (spell check
  feature), 148
changes, undoing/redoing, 73
CHAR function, 504
characters
  finding from numeric value, CHAR
    function for, 504
  first in text string, CODE function
    for, 505
  formatting (see text formatting)
  from left side of text string, returning
    with LEFT function, 510
  from right side of text string,
    returning with RIGHT
    function, 514
  in text string, replacing with
    REPLACE function, 513
  lowercase, LOWER function for
    converting to, 512

D

G

gamma distribution, GAMMADIST function for finding probabilities, 431
gamma function, GAMMALN function for finding natural logarithm, 433
GAMMADIST function, 431
GAMMAINV function, 432
GAMMALN function, 433
gathering information, custom template for, 208
GCD function, 372
GCD (greatest common divisor), 372
general number format, 134
General tab (Excel settings), 181, 183
General tab (New dialog), 26
General tab (Properties dialog), 68
generating random numbers (see random numbers, generating)
GEOMEAN function, 433
geometric mean of positive numeric values, GEOMEAN function for, 433
GETPIVOTDATA function, 480
.gif files, 126
  conversion to by Excel, 128
global template book.xlt, 55
go to
  cells, 144
  last row/column, 108
Go To Special dialog, 89
Goal Seek dialog, 164
goal setting, Iterations section, 182
grammar, keyboard shortcut for, 13
grand total row, 199
graphics
  inserting, 125
  linking to, 131
  protecting, 158
  using for background, 139
greater than or equal operator (>=), 170
  used in filtering, 194
greatest common divisor (see entries at GCD)
Gregorian calendar, 330

grid display, turning off, 138
Gridlines tab (charts), 258
Group dialog, 216
Group option (outlines), 215
grouping information, 188, 214
growth fill, 82
GROWTH function, 433

H

HARMEAN function, 435
harmonic mean of positive numeric values, HARMEAN function for, 435
Header dialog, 101
Header row radio button, 189
Header/Footer tab (Page Setup), 59
headers, 99
headings (row/column), vs. print titles, 61
Height option (rows), 139
help, 15, 23
  keyboard shortcut for, 539
  Office Assistant, 23
Help › About Microsoft Excel, 24
Help › Detect and Repair option, 24
Help › Hide the Office Assistant option, 24
Help › Lotus 1-2-3 Help option, 24
Help › Microsoft Excel Help option, 23
Help › Office on the Web option, 24
Help › What's This option, 24
Help button, analysis tools, 186
Help menu, 23
Hide checkboxes (scenarios), 165
Hide Detail option (outlines), 215
Hide option, 142
Hide option (columns), 141
Hide option (rows), 140
hiding
  cells, 139
  columns, 18, 141
  comments, 124
  current workbook, 22
  rows, 18
  worksheets, 142
Highlight Changes dialog, 153

Highlight Changes option
(workbooks), 153
High-Low-Close chart type, 249
history
adaptive menus, 33
of changes made to workbooks (see
change history)
History page, viewing rejected changes
on, 156
HLOOKUP function, 482
horizontal scrollbar, 21
horizontally displayed workbooks, 22
HOUR function, 342
.htm files, opening in browser, 51
HTML files, 44
caution with, 56
worksheets, sending as formatted
messages, 64
(see also web pages)
HTML pages, gathering data from, 226
hyperbolic cosine, COSH function
for, 368
hyperbolic functions, 357
hyperbolic sine of a number, SINH
function for, 394
hyperbolic tangent of numbers, TANH
function for determining, 402
hyperbolic values, functions for
(list), 359
hypergeometrical distribution,
HYPGEOMDIST function for
finding, 436
Hyperlink base field (Summary tab,
Properties dialog), 68
HYPERLINK function, 482
hyperlinks
creating, 78
inserting, 131
tips for, 132
HYPGEOMDIST function, 436
hypothesis testing, FISHER function
for, 427

I

icons, 17
changed according to installation
method, 7
opening Excel, 7

setting to large, 33
IF function, 521
used with ERROR>TYPE
function, 527
IF statements, nested, 522
Ignore button (spell check
feature), 148
"Ignore Relative/Absolute"
checkbox, 123
Image and Text option
(commands), 38
images
of buttons, editing, 37
inserting from scanner/camera, 128
pasting into worksheet
background, 142
protecting, 158
Import Text File dialog, 231
Import Text File option, 231
INDEX function, 483
Index (help search), 23
INDIRECT function, 485
inference, statistical, 405
INFO function, 528
information
grouping and outlines for, 214
about operating system, INFO
function for, 528
information functions, 269, 524–536
list of, 524
Information style only, 201
initial caps, PROPER function for, 512
Input Message tab (data
validation), 201
Insert › Cells command, 107
Insert › Chart command, 5, 111
Insert › Columns command, 109
Insert › Comment command, 123
Insert › Function command, 5, 10, 116,
272
Insert › Hyperlink command, 131
Insert › Name command, 119
Insert › Object command, 130
Insert › Page Break command, 114
Insert › Picture command, 125
Insert › Remove Page Break, 115
Insert › Rows command, 108
Insert › Worksheet command, 4, 48, 110
Insert ClipArt dialog, 125

About the Author

Jinjer Simon has been actively involved in the computer industry as a web site developer, end user trainer, and developer of online documentation for the past 15 years. She has written numerous books, including *Visual Basic Scripting SuperBible* from Waite Group Press, and *Windows CE for Dummies* from IDG Press. Jinjer lives in a suburb of Dallas, Texas, with her husband and two children. In her spare time she likes to play golf and scuba dive.

Colophon

Our look is the result of reader comments, our own experimentation, and feedback from distribution channels. Distinctive covers complement our distinctive approach to technical topics, breathing personality and life into potentially dry subjects.

The animal on the cover of *Excel 2000 in a Nutshell* is a Northern Gannet (*Sula Bassanus*). The Northern Gannet is the largest seabird breeding in North American waters. It feeds primarily on surface-dwelling fish such as herring and makerel, which are taken from diving from heights up to 43 meters and plummeting into the water with great speed and force. The bird enters the water head first and swallows its prey whole. The bird's skull is incredibly strong, and a system of air sacs also helps to absorb the shock of these plunges. Northern Gannets take their winters at sea, from southern Virginia to Florida, and return north the remainder of the year.

The Northern Gannet's nests are found on steep cliffs on Canada's and the United States' east coast. The nests are made of vegetation, seaweed, feathers, and earth, and may be cemented together with guano. The Northern Gannet produces a single egg, which incubates for 44 days. After 90 days, the chick is ready to leave the nest and search for its own food.

Maureen Dempsey was the production editor, and Clairemarie Fisher O'Leary was the copyeditor, for *Excel 2000 in a Nutshell*. Sarah Jane Shangraw provided quality control. Brenda Miller wrote the index.

Hanna Dyer designed the cover of this book, based on a series design by Edie Freedman. The cover image is an original illustration created by Lorrie LeJeune. Emma Colby produced the cover layout with QuarkXPress 4.1 using Adobe's ITC Garamond font.

Alicia Cech and David Futato designed the interior layout based on a series design by Nancy Priest. Mike Sierra implemented the design in FrameMaker 5.5. The text and heading fonts are ITC Garamond Light and Garamond Book. The illustrations that appear in the book were produced by Robert Romano and Rhon Porter using Macromedia FreeHand 8 and Adobe Photoshop 5. This colophon was written by Maureen Dempsey.

Whenever possible, our books use a durable and flexible lay-flat binding. If the page count exceeds that binding's limit, perfect binding is used.

How to stay in touch with O'Reilly

1. Visit Our Award-Winning Site

http://www.oreilly.com/

★ "Top 100 Sites on the Web" —*PC Magazine*
★ "Top 5% Web sites" —*Point Communications*
★ "3-Star site" —*The McKinley Group*

Our web site contains a library of comprehensive product information (including book excerpts and tables of contents), downloadable software, background articles, interviews with technology leaders, links to relevant sites, book cover art, and more. File us in your Bookmarks or Hotlist!

2. Join Our Email Mailing Lists

New Product Releases
To receive automatic email with brief descriptions of all new O'Reilly products as they are released, send email to:
listproc@online.oreilly.com
Put the following information in the first line of your message (*not* in the Subject field):
subscribe oreilly-news

O'Reilly Events
If you'd also like us to send information about trade show events, special promotions, and other O'Reilly events, send email to:
listproc@online.oreilly.com
Put the following information in the first line of your message (*not* in the Subject field):
subscribe oreilly-events

3. Get Examples from Our Books via FTP

There are two ways to access an archive of example files from our books:

Regular FTP
- ftp to:
  ftp.oreilly.com
  (login: anonymous
  password: your email address)
- Point your web browser to:
  ftp://ftp.oreilly.com/

FTPMAIL
- Send an email message to:
  ftpmail@online.oreilly.com
  (Write "help" in the message body)

4. Contact Us via Email

order@oreilly.com
To place a book or software order online. Good for North American and international customers.

subscriptions@oreilly.com
To place an order for any of our newsletters or periodicals.

books@oreilly.com
General questions about any of our books.

software@oreilly.com
For general questions and product information about our software. Check out O'Reilly Software Online at **http://software.oreilly.com/** for software and technical support information. Registered O'Reilly software users send your questions to:
website-support@oreilly.com

cs@oreilly.com
For answers to problems regarding your order or our products.

booktech@oreilly.com
For book content technical questions or corrections.

proposals@oreilly.com
To submit new book or software proposals to our editors and product managers.

international@oreilly.com
For information about our international distributors or translation queries. For a list of our distributors outside of North America check out:
http://www.oreilly.com/www/order/country.html

5. Work with Us

Check out our website for current employment opportunites:
www.jobs@oreilly.com
Click on "Work with Us"

O'Reilly & Associates, Inc.
101 Morris Street, Sebastopol, CA 95472 USA
TEL   707-829-0515 or 800-998-9938
       (6am to 5pm PST)
FAX   707-829-0104

International Distributors

UK, EUROPE, MIDDLE EAST AND AFRICA (EXCEPT FRANCE, GERMANY, AUSTRIA, SWITZERLAND, LUXEMBOURG, LIECHTENSTEIN, AND EASTERN EUROPE)

INQUIRIES
O'Reilly UK Limited
4 Castle Street
Farnham
Surrey, GU9 7HS
United Kingdom
Telephone: 44-1252-711776
Fax: 44-1252-734211
Email: information@oreilly.co.uk

ORDERS
Wiley Distribution Services Ltd.
1 Oldlands Way
Bognor Regis
West Sussex PO22 9SA
United Kingdom
Telephone: 44-1243-779777
Fax: 44-1243-820250
Email: cs-books@wiley.co.uk

FRANCE
INQUIRIES
Éditions O'Reilly
18 rue Séguier
75006 Paris, France
Tel: 33-1-40-51-52-30
Fax: 33-1-40-51-52-31
Email: france@editions-oreilly.fr

ORDERS
GEODIF
61, Bd Saint-Germain
75240 Paris Cedex 05, France
Tel: 33-1-44-41-46-16 (French books)
Tel: 33-1-44-41-11-87 (English books)
Fax: 33-1-44-41-11-44
Email: distribution@eyrolles.com

GERMANY, SWITZERLAND, AUSTRIA, EASTERN EUROPE, LUXEMBOURG, AND LIECHTENSTEIN

INQUIRIES & ORDERS
O'Reilly Verlag
Balthasarstr. 81
D-50670 Köln
Germany
Telephone: 49-221-973160-91
Fax: 49-221-973160-8
Email: anfragen@oreilly.de (inquiries)
Email: order@oreilly.de (orders)

CANADA (FRENCH LANGUAGE BOOKS)
Les Éditions Flammarion ltée
375, Avenue Laurier Ouest
Montréal (Québec) H2V 2K3
Tel: 00-1-514-277-8807
Fax: 00-1-514-278-2085
Email: info@flammarion.qc.ca

HONG KONG
City Discount Subscription Service, Ltd.
Unit D, 3rd Floor, Yan's Tower
27 Wong Chuk Hang Road
Aberdeen, Hong Kong
Tel: 852-2580-3539
Fax: 852-2580-6463
Email: citydis@ppn.com.hk

KOREA
Hanbit Media, Inc.
Chungmu Bldg. 201
Yonnam-dong 568-33
Mapo-gu
Seoul, Korea
Tel: 822-325-0397
Fax: 822-325-9697
Email: hant93@chollian.dacom.co.kr

PHILIPPINES
Global Publishing
G/F Benavides Garden
1186 Benavides St.
Manila, Philippines
Tel: 632-254-8949/637-252-2582
Fax: 632-734-5060/632-252-2733
Email: globalp@pacific.net.ph

TAIWAN
O'Reilly Taiwan
No. 3, Lane 131
Hang-Chow South Road
Section 1, Taipei, Taiwan
Tel: 886-2-23968990
Fax: 886-2-23968916
Email: taiwan@oreilly.com

CHINA
O'Reilly Beijing
Room 2410
160, FuXingMenNeiDaJie
XiCheng District
Beijing
China PR 100031
Tel: 86-10-66412305
Fax: 86-10-86631007
Email: beijing@oreilly.com

INDIA
Computer Bookshop (India) Pvt. Ltd.
190 Dr. D.N. Road, Fort
Bombay 400 001 India
Tel: 91-22-207-0989
Fax: 91-22-262-3551
Email: cbsbom@giasbm01.vsnl.net.in

JAPAN
O'Reilly Japan, Inc.
Yotsuya Y's Building
7 Banch 6, Honshio-cho
Shinjuku-ku
Tokyo 160-0003 Japan
Tel: 81-3-3356-5227
Fax: 81-3-3356-5261
Email: japan@oreilly.com

ALL OTHER ASIAN COUNTRIES
O'Reilly & Associates, Inc.
101 Morris Street
Sebastopol, CA 95472 USA
Tel: 707-829-0515
Fax: 707-829-0104
Email: order@oreilly.com

AUSTRALIA
Woodslane Pty., Ltd.
7/5 Vuko Place
Warriewood NSW 2102
Australia
Tel: 61-2-9970-5111
Fax: 61-2-9970-5002
Email: info@woodslane.com.au

NEW ZEALAND
Woodslane New Zealand, Ltd.
21 Cooks Street (P.O. Box 575)
Waganui, New Zealand
Tel: 64-6-347-6543
Fax: 64-6-345-4840
Email: info@woodslane.com.au

LATIN AMERICA
McGraw-Hill Interamericana
Editores, S.A. de C.V.
Cedro No. 512
Col. Atlampa
06450, Mexico, D.F.
Tel: 52-5-547-6777
Fax: 52-5-547-3336
Email: mcgraw-hill@infosel.net.mx

O'REILLY®